MODERN
POLitiCAL
ECONOMY

Radical And Orthodox Views On Crucial Issues

James H. Weaver

Modern Political Economy

MODERN POLITICAL ECONOMY

radical and orthodox views
on crucial issues

edited by

James H. Weaver

american university

Allyn and Bacon, Inc.
Boston

PHOTOGRAPH ACKNOWLEDGMENTS

Robert T. Averitt / by Gabriel Cooney, p. 406.
Leon H. Keyserling / by Miller, Washington, D.C., p. 349.
Arthur M. Okun / by Chase, Ltd., Washington, D.C., p. 239.
Richard Parker / by Jon Christian, p. 133.
Michael Reich / by School Street Portrait Studio, Boston, Mass., p. 357.
Leonard S. Silk / by Fabian Bachrach, p. 153.
Howard M. Wachtel / by Steve Zweig Studio, Washington, D.C., p. 207.

ACKNOWLEDGMENTS

I am very grateful to those who have contributed the papers for this book. The Student Association of American University provided a grant to pay the speakers' expenses and will receive the royalties from this volume. I am greatly indebted to the students of American University for making the course and the book possible. In particular, I wish to thank the students and discussion leaders in Contemporary Economic Problems (Fall 1970) and the students in Political Economy (Summer 1971) who made many helpful suggestions. The book reflects the great efforts of William Causey and Dennis Miller, president and treasurer of the Student Association, respectively, Elaine Ligelis, who typed the manuscript, and Charles Barone, who assisted in the editing.

To The Students of American University

CONTENTS

Contents

A NOTE TO STUDENTS

This book is designed to stimulate critical thinking about our economic system, the theories used to explain our system, and the economic aspects of problems that we face. You will find sharply conflicting analyses presented here.

The students who heard the discussions on which this book is based were asked the following questions after the discussions. Do the speakers disagree on fundamental issues? If so, what are the major points of disagreement? Why do economists (who have received similar training in graduate school) come up with such widely divergent views of reality? With which paper do you agree? What is the basis of your conclusion? Is it your family background, political biases, the emotional appeal of the presentation, or the correctness of the analysis? Why did a radical political economics develop in the late 1960's–1970's and not earlier? What is the relationship between changes in society and changes in economic theory?

You might find it useful to try to answer these questions as you read the following essays. I hope you enjoy reading the papers as much as I enjoyed hearing them.

J.H.W.

PREFACE

This book is intended for those who might feel vaguely uneasy about presenting students with only one point of view concerning the economic issues that we face. This book is the product of a course that I organized at American University in 1970. I have found it increasingly difficult to present students with only an orthodox approach to economics and at the same time feel that I have adequately analyzed our society. On the other hand, I am reluctant to present to students an avowedly radical approach, such as that outlined by Arthur MacEwan and Richard Edwards (*American Economic Review,* May 1970). In view of this, I decided to present both points of view in a course dealing with contemporary economic problems.

I invited speakers who would present their views in the context of a debate. Thus, the students were exposed to vigorous presentations of radical and orthodox analyses of the economic aspects of such issues as racism, sexism, imperialism, and war, and were then able to choose for themselves the analysis they found most convincing.

If one accepts the basic institutions of American society and wants to improve them, one would find the analyses of the orthodox economists useful. The radical political economists, on the other hand, reject many of the basic institutions of American society and want to transform that society. They hope their analyses will contribute to that transformation.

Although it had been intended that the presentations in this book would be in the nature of debates, sometimes it didn't turn out that way. If the two speakers strongly disagreed on fundamental paradigms, it was difficult for them to debate each other. Their assumptions were so very different that debate became almost impossible.

Radical speakers complained of the bias inherent in short presentations. It was their contention that students have been exposed to the orthodox way of analyzing reality all their lives, and that a radical speaker is therefore at a distinct disadvantage when he or she is given twenty-five minutes to outline his or her views.

The papers in this book are divided into sections that reflect the major themes debated. The Introduction puts the papers in context and outlines the major issues that divide radical and orthodox economists.

Section II contains answers to the question: What is economics? Is economics an objective tool of analysis? Is economics biased to serve the ends of certain classes? Can economics be reformed or do current changes underway in society call for new theories?

In Section III the United States economy is analyzed and three questions are asked. Is the United States an industrial state? Is the United States a middle-class society? What is the role of higher education in American society?

Section IV is concerned with insecurity in contemporary America. Analyses are presented relating to the apparent paradox of poverty amidst affluence, the intractable inflation that has accompanied the Vietnam war, and the issue of crime and its relationship to the economy.

Section V contains analyses of two long-run and deep-seated problems. Is there a relationship between the economy and racism? Can we end racism under capitalism? What classes benefit from racism? Some strikingly similar analyses are presented concerning the economy and economic discrimination against women. Have women been subordinated in all societies? Can and should economic discrimination against women be ended?

Section VI contains analyses of United States foreign policy. The issues of imperialism and war are examined. Is the United States, which started its history with a revolution, a counterrevolutionary force in the world today? Did the war in Vietnam have its origins in the needs of the United States economy?

Section VII is devoted to the future. Is socialism the wave of the future? What problems do socialist economies face? How will American capitalism be changed? Will there be greater reliance placed on markets?

Prior to each paper, you will find a brief biographical sketch of the author or authors, and a summary of some important points treated in the presentation. Some of the questions that were raised by students and discussion leaders follow the papers.

J.H.W.

SECTION I

Introduction

James H. Weaver

Recently some economists have become increasingly disillusioned with orthodox economics as it is currently being taught in American universities. They call themselves radical political economists, and they have come together to launch a concerted attack on the paradigm of orthodox economics and to construct an alternative paradigm.[1]

THE ECONOMIC PARADIGM

They see themselves as making a scientific revolution in economics, just as revolutions occur in all sciences, according to Thomas S. Kuhn's *The Structure of Scientific Revolutions*. Kuhn defines a mature science as one in which there is general agreement upon a paradigm. A scientific paradigm is a way of looking at the world that is being studied. An example of a paradigm is the way scientists prior to Copernicus regarded the earth as the center of the universe. Their view defined reality.

Normal science, according to Kuhn, is puzzle-solving. It involves working out the problems that arise from working within an agreed-upon paradigm. Most scientists spend their lives solving puzzles. Once the paradigm has been enunciated and agreed upon, there are any number of unanswered questions, and the role of the normal scientist is to try to answer these questions.

However, there come times in every science when the old paradigm cannot be used any longer to answer some questions — questions posed by scientists who are quite often young and who quite often have come to the science from another field. After a period of asking questions to which the old paradigm cannot provide answers or of getting answers that contradict the old paradigm, there develops a time of crisis. During the time of crisis, some young scientist puts forth a new paradigm. For a time there are two competing paradigms, but eventually the new one triumphs. This, then, is a scientific revolution. Science settles down again to "normal science" and "everyday puzzle-solving." Again, Copernicus is the example used by Kuhn. He examines the novel idea that the sun is the center of the solar system, and he outlines the revolutionary implications of this paradigm shift for all scientific thought.

Orthodox economics, it is argued, is today a mature science. There is an agree-upon paradigm. Economists working in the United States, the Soviet Union, and in other parts of the world all accept the idea of economic man, i.e., man as a maximizer of pleasure and a minimizer of pain. Economic man derives his primary pleasure or utility from the consumption of material goods and services. Work is assumed to be a disutility. This analysis leads to a society that is organized around the criterion of efficiency of production. If maximum pleasure or maximum utility derives from maximum consumption, then the goal must be to produce as much as possible with the least possible cost, and this is, of course, the definition of efficiency.

Today the radical political economists are arguing that this is a time of crisis in economics. They are asking questions to which the old paradigm does not provide satisfactory answers. Given the orthodox assumptions, neoclassical economics is a useful tool for increasing the output of material goods and services within a system of scarcity. But the questions in which political economists are interested cannot be answered by using orthodox economics.

REVOLUTIONS IN ECONOMIC THOUGHT

In economics, revolutions in thought have come about in times of great social change. The economic doctrine of mercantilism developed out of the need to legitimatize and justify the development of strong nation-states; classical economics developed to support businessmen in their clash with the landed aristocracy; neoclassical economics was developed in response to the need for tools to streamline and rationalize massive bureaucratic and hierarchical firms; Keynesianism was a response to the deep depression of the capitalist economies in the 1930s; and today's orthodox economics has come to embody a synthesis of neoclassical and Keynesian analyses.

Radicals argue that orthodox economics is primarily useful to members of the American elite in pursuit of their goals within the existing institutional framework. The first goal is to increase material abundance and to perpetuate the present distribution of that abundance. A vast corporate establishment has been developed to produce goods and services on an ever-vaster scale. Orthodox economics is particularly useful in this effort. Linear programming models of the firm and mathematical models of the whole economy are necessary tools for today's corporate managers and Councils of Economic Advisers to the President.

The second goal of the elite is to maintain order. A vast bureaucracy has developed within the federal, state, and local governments to achieve this goal. The tools of cost-effectiveness analysis have been contributed to this bureaucracy by the practitioners of orthodox economics.

The third goal of the elite is to prevent the spread of communism and to maintain the present international distribution of income. The national liberation fronts in Third World countries threaten to cut off needed markets and raw materials. The military-industrial complex has been developed to see that this does not happen. Again, orthodox economists have come to the rescue by serving as consultants to the Department of Defense, Rand Corporation, the Agency for International Development, the World Bank, the International Monetary Fund, etc.

Orthodox economics has developed out of the needs of highly industrialized nations and of those who make decisions in them. Although the foregoing examples are taken from the United States, very similar analyses could be made of the Soviet Union, Japan, and the countries of Western Europe.

Radicals argue that social changes underway in the world today call for new theories. The emerging movements among students, minority groups, women, and revolutionaries in the Third World require new theories to legitimize and justify their goals. This is the task before radical political economists.

Orthodox economists would reject this analysis of their doctrine. Mancur Olson, Jr., argues that neoclassical economics is useful in any situation characterized by purposeful behavior and scarcity. It is as widely used in the Soviet Union as it is in the United States. Orthodox economists are not servants of the elite. In fact, the principles of economics can be used to help any group achieve its objectives. Orthodox economics is designed to help people maximize that which they want maximized when resources are limited.

Orthodox economists also reject the notion that the old paradigm is inadequate. They would agree that there are problems in society. All societies have problems. Imperfections are, after all, relative. The fundamental concepts of orthodox economics are still valid, and the economics we have been taught can be patched up and modified. Gerald Peabody[2] has given us a remarkable example of the brilliance with which orthodox economists can use traditional concepts:

There is practically no direct information on whether or not labor is paid its marginal product. Economists take it as an article of faith or else claim that it is the best null hypothesis, and economic theory is based on the assumption that labor is indeed paid its marginal product. Without this assumption, much of economic theory falls apart. The theory of production certainly does. The convenience of the hypothesis for economists, however, does not make it correct.

In the intervening paragraphs the author summarizes the evidence concerning the validity of the marginal productivity theory. He concludes:

What little evidence this technique (production function analysis) provides does not indicate that labor is paid its marginal product . . . There are at least some fundamental doubts about the validity of the productivity theory of distribution. In the rest of this book I shall assume that labor is paid its marginal product unless otherwise stated.[3]

THE NATURE OF MAN

Not only are the goals of radical and orthodox economists different, but so are their basic assumptions. In particular, they make different fundamental assumptions about the nature of man and of a good society.

As has been pointed out earlier, orthodox economists assume that man is economic man. Murray Rothbard argues that everybody wants to improve his standard of living. The nature of man is to want more and better material goods and services, and this is as it should be. People should work individually and collectively to produce and consume as much as possible.

Radicals tend to view man very differently than do orthodox economists. They accept the idea that man is motivated by self-interest and that people act to achieve their own self-interest. But they argue that man's self-interest is served by living in a decent society. And a decent society involves a radical transformation of present society. A good society involves not only having enough material goods and services, but it involves having a good environment; worthwhile, personally fulfilling, and rewarding work in a humane work situation; good relationships with fellow men; the opportunity to have meaningful family relationships; opportunities for aesthetic experiences; and so forth.

Modern industrial society has made many of these aspects of the good life difficult if not impossible. However, we are told that we can attain satisfaction of these basic needs through the consumption of goods. Do you need love? Buy a new car!

Radicals tend to believe that there are institutions in which people could be happy. They do not know what those institutions are, but they tend to believe that such institutions can be designed and implemented if we all think constructively about alternatives instead of merely accepting the status quo as a given.

This debate over materialism runs through all the essays. Gintis and others argue that orthodox economics has a materialist bias, which assumes that welfare is primarily determined by consumption of individually marketable material goods and services. Radicals agree that materialism is a necessary condition for a good life. People do need enough food, adequate housing, sufficient clothing, a good education, and medical care. But radicals argue that in our society materialism has been carried to excess. In fact, many radicals argue that there is no real scarcity in the United States today. It is argued that the fundamental problem of scarcity has been solved. We have reached the point that Keynes described in "Economic Possibilities for Our Grandchildren":

The economic problem may be solved, or be at least within sight of solution, within a hundred years. This means that the economic problem is not — if we look into the future — the permanent problem of the human race . . . Thus for the first time since his creation man will be faced with his real, his permanent problem — how to . . . live wisely and agreeably and well . . . I see us free, therefore, to return to some of the most sure and certain principles of religion and traditional virtue — that avarice is a vice, that the exaction of usury is a misdemeanor, and the love of money is detestable . . . We shall honor . . . the delightful people who are capable of taking direct enjoyment . . . the lilies of the field who toil not, neither do they spin.

Radicals argue that scarcity today is contrived scarcity. There are enough goods and services today in America for everyone to have satisfactory levels of food, clothing, shelter, medical care, and education. Radicals believe that society keeps inculcating values that cause people to desire more and more goods and services. Radicals argue that welfare must be defined in broader terms than those of traditional economists. Welfare does require the consumption of goods and services. But people are more than just consumers. People are also producers, husbands, wives, and neighbors.

NATURE OF A GOOD SOCIETY

Murray N. Rothbard presents the orthodox argument in favor of free and unfettered exchanges as the basis for a good society. Rothbard argues that if you give men freedom, all will work out well. This is a belief perhaps best enunciated by Adam Smith, who argued that men acting to achieve the greatest possible individual gain will be led, as if by an invisible hand, to an end that was no part of their intention, i.e., to the greatest gain for the whole nation. If each person just goes out and tries to maximize his own production and consumption of goods and services, the result will be maximum production for all society. If the state does not interfere in personal exchanges, if each man is free to choose in a market situation, maximum utility will result. *Laissez-faire* capitalism is not seen as the creator of poverty, but it is seen as the system through which the grinding poverty of feudalism was overcome.

Radicals take a very different view. They argue that men are not born with equal ability, and thus equal treatment in the market will simply lead to vastly unequal results. Charles Dickens put it well when he said, " 'It's every man for himself,' cried the elephant, as he danced among the chickens."

Radicals argue that in a free market, men *are* free to choose between lettuce or cabbage. But men who have no capital or land of their own are not free men. They are forced to sell their labor in the market for whatever price they can get. And, although one can argue that the person who cleans toilets for $60 per week has entered into a voluntary and free contract, what is the alternative? The alternative is starvation or a degrading system of welfare. This is not really freedom.

Radicals also dispute the notion that *laissez faire* is a system in which the government does not intervene in the economy. By allowing complete economic freedom, *laissez-faire* government intervened in a most decisive way on behalf of those who were the strongest, the most aggressive, the most acquisitive, the most ambitious, the most powerful, the most cunning, the most clever, and the most intelligent. And it allowed these people to victimize those who were less able. Thus, laissez faire is not a system without government intervention. Rather it is a system in which government, by enforcing private contracts and providing for an army and a police force, intervenes most decisively on behalf of the rich and the powerful.

Another dispute arises over the goal of equality. Lester Thurow argues that equality is impossible. Different people have different preferences for money and leisure, and the best that could be done in moving toward a good society would be to reduce inequality. He gives the traditional liberal argument in favor of increasing inheritance taxes and in favor of pulling the most able poor up through more remunerative work. He argues that work provides many psychic gratifications, that people meet friends and have social intercourse on the job and thus need jobs. He would institute a guaranteed income that would be pegged at half the median family income. Thurow says equality, however desirable in principle, is impossible in practice and he therefore dismisses it.

Radicals affirm the goal of equality. They tend to subscribe to the motto of the French Revolution, "liberty, *equality,* and fraternity." Radicals believe that a just society is one in which equality of result is the goal. Howard Wachtel argues that if you desire the results of economic activity to be equal, unequal people must be treated unequally. For, if you provide equality of opportunity to people with inherently unequal ability, then obviously those with the greatest ability, however that is measured, will wind up with the most goods and services.

In this connection, Paul M. Sweezy cites the case of China and makes reference to an article by John G. Gurley, "Capitalist and Maoist Economic Development."[4] Gurley argues that Maoism is an attempt to build on the worst in great contrast to Western industrial societies, which have "built on the best." For example, as Bowles argues, in the United States, education beyond high school is rationed to those with the greatest income, intellectual ability, and ambition. This practice inevitably means that inequalities will be exacerbated, because those people who are already at the top get the most education, too. This builds further inequalities into the system. By way of contrast, the Maoists are allowing peers to choose those students who will go to universities, and the criteria are not the traditional ones. The Maoists are trying to insure equality of result.

Lester C. Thurow follows the traditional prescription for building on the best when he argues that poverty programs should focus on the most able workers and try to help them improve their incomes. In both the private enterprise capitalism of the West and the state capitalism of the USSR, building on the best has led to fantastic economic productivity. Material incentives, reliance on experts, and equal treatment of unequals have led to a vastly productive economic machine. But Maoists have a fundamentally different vision of a good society. They are deemphasizing material incentives, minimizing the role of experts, attempting to break down bureaucracy and hierarchy, and treating unequals in an unequal fashion in an effort to achieve a society based on equality of results.

Thus, one of the fundamental differences between radical and orthodox economists is the emphasis they place on the goals of freedom and equality. The two goals are in some way antithetical, and this conflict is described explicitly in the papers by Silk and Averitt.

Silk and Averitt put the conflict in historical perspective and argue that the Jeffersonians and the Hamiltonians basically disagreed on the importance of economic freedom, which was necessary for industrialization, as opposed to the goals of democracy and equality. The Jeffersonians put emphasis on equality and democracy. The Hamiltonians emphasized freedom and industrialization. Averitt contends that Jefferson, as President, finally decided on behalf of industrialization and freedom because of military considerations. Thus, the goals of democracy and equality were submerged, not to be revived again until the seventh decade of the twentieth century. They have become the rallying cry of radicals in this country and, to some extent, throughout the world.

Most economists would agree that there is a fundamental conflict between the goals of freedom and equality. Giving freedom to people who are unequal will certainly lead to unequal results. If you want equality of results, then the freedom of the rich, the strong, the powerful, and the ambitious must be limited. Such limitations will almost surely lead to a reduction in incentives and to a reduction in the output of goods and services. Radicals argue that we have enough goods and services to accept some reduction in output in the interest of democracy and equality. Orthodox economists dispute this.

This limitation of freedom also upsets many who are rich, powerful, strong, ambitious, and intelligent, because it is their freedom that would be limited. They are not particularly concerned today about the limited freedom enjoyed by those who are poor, weak, unintelligent, and unambitious. They say that everyone is free today, and they are not particularly worried about those who are left in poverty and hunger. The rich and powerful argue that it is the poor's own fault that they are poor, and nothing can or should be done about it.

Radicals, however, argue that a society that is primarily dedicated to achieving the interests of those who are strong, able, and aggressive is not a good society. They would go much further in trying to provide goods and services for those at the bottom of the scale in terms of abilities and ambition.

ROLE OF GOVERNMENT

An issue closely related to the freedom versus equality argument is the debate over who governs and in whose interest government is conducted. Radicals tend to affirm the goal of democracy at all levels.

They believe people should have the power to decide the issues that concern them: on the job, in the schools, in the community, state, and nation.

Wachtel argues that government in the United States is carried out in the interest of the rich and powerful. He presents evidence on some programs that were ostensibly designed to benefit the poor but have been either ineffective or have wound up benefiting the middle class and the rich.

Orthodox economists view the state in much the same way as it was viewed by Aristotle, i.e., the state is the arbiter of conflicting goals among different groups in society. Men are assumed to be motivated by self-interest. In a society of scarcity, everyone's goals cannot be completely realized. Therefore, conflict results. The state is created to arbitrate the conflicts among the different groups and to work out compromise solutions so that everyone achieves some part of their goal, but no one achieves everything. The state is an arbitrator and compromiser of the conflicts that inevitably arise in all societies.

The issue of the United States government's role finds orthodox economists divided into two camps. The libertarians (in this volume, Rothbard and Tullock) would argue that the role of government should be very minimal. They believe that if the government stopped intervening in the economy and allowed free markets to work, our economic problems would be solved. Liberals such as Thurow, Keyserling, *et al.* agree that we have problems in our society, but they argue that government can be used to solve these problems.

The radical, liberal, and libertarian approaches are in some ways similar to the three states of consciousness described by Charles Reich in *The Greening of America*. Libertarians are in many ways those people whom Reich describes as Consciousness I. They look backward to a day of small firms and small units of government. Liberals (Consciousness II) grew up in the New Deal period and saw American society solving its problems through the massive intervention of the federal government. They think that this kind of transformation can be repeated. Radicals grew up during the 1950s and 1960s, and they see American society from that perspective. They saw President Eisenhower lie to the people about the U–2 incident, President Kennedy support the Bay of Pigs invasion of Cuba, the debacle of the war in Vietnam, etc., etc. This leads to their Consciousness III approach. They argue that neither a retreat to the nineteenth century nor to a New-Deal-type approach will solve our fundamental problems.

Robert T. Averitt argues that a political strategy emphasizing democracy is far more expedient than one emphasizing socialism. Socialism scares people. But democracy has good connotations and is a goal to which Americans are dedicated.

Orthodox economists would argue that not everyone wishes to

participate in government. Oscar Wilde said that the trouble with socialism is that it takes up too many evenings. Anthony Crosland[5] has argued that "the majority prefer to lead a full family life and cultivate their gardens. And a good thing, too."

Do people want to be actively involved in political decision-making? Is man, as Aristotle argued, a political animal? Thomas Jefferson at the end of his life was asked what his vision of a good life would be, and he said, "to be back in the Senate." He saw the good life as one of active participation in deciding the issues of the day. Thucydides in his *History of the Peloponnesian War* puts these words in the funeral oration of Pericles:

. . . An Athenian citizen does not neglect the state because he takes care of his own household; and even those of us who are engaged in business have a very fair idea of politics. We alone regard a man who takes no interest in public affairs, not as a harmless, but as a useless character; and if few of us are originators, we are all sound judges of a policy. The great impediment to action is, in our opinion, not discussion, but the want of that knowledge which is gained by discussion preparatory to action. For we have a peculiar power of thinking before we act and of acting too, whereas other men are courageous from ignorance but hesitate upon reflection. And they are surely to be esteemed the bravest spirits who, having the clearest sense both of the pains and pleasures of life, do not on that account shrink from danger . . .

Most economists argue that workers do not want active participation in the work place. Workers want good pay, short hours, and decent working conditions. They are really quite content to let the boss make the decisions so long as they are given handsome rewards and a good work environment. Radicals would argue that this is the case because American workers have been conditioned to accept material goods as the *sine qua non* of happiness. If they had been given a chance, throughout their schooling, to participate actively, to make decisions, to make meaningful choices, they would wish to make such choices on the job and in their local communities.

ROLE OF AFFLUENCE

One is struck by the great differences in analysis between people who have received identical training in economics. Why is this? Why do economists who have all learned the same tools and techniques look at the system and come up with such diametrically opposite conclusions?

Why has the radical movement developed now? Ever since World War II the United States has experienced what Daniel Bell called an "end of ideology." During the two decades following World War II, intellectuals were engaged in the "American celebration." America had solved its problems. It was the great melting pot. As Richard Parker points out, there was a widespread belief that income had been distributed much more equally. But during the last few years of the 1960s and during the 1970s there has been an outpouring of criticism. There is a feeling among some people that the United States is being destroyed from within by its own self-destructive intellectuals.

Many people have placed great stress on the affluence of American society as a causative factor in the outburst of radicalism. America is an incredibly rich country. Per capita income in 1946 was $1250 and almost $4000 in 1970. During this twenty-five-year period, per-capita income increased more than three-fold. If income could have been divided equally in 1970, the average family of four would have had an annual income of $16,000. Of course we do not know to what level income would have risen or fallen if it had been divided equally. Nevertheless, $4000 per person — $16,000 per family of four is incredible affluence.

This affluence led to two movements of rebellion. One movement was on the part of the poor and the dispossessed, who have been left outside the mainstream of economic life. They saw on television and in other ways how incredibly rich the society was and how poor they were in comparison.

The second movement that has developed began among some of the upper-middle class and upper-class students who have come to question the American Dream. It has always been believed that if you worked hard, saved, and invested, you would get goods and services, and this would bring happiness. Millions of young people have grown up in the post–World War II United States amidst affluence. They are the first generation in American history to have come to adulthood without experiencing a depression. Many of them no longer believe in the American Dream. They know that vast quantities of goods and services do not bring happiness. They have experienced all of these goods and services and find them wanting. Their idea of a good society is vastly different from the idea of their parents.

THE FUTURE OF ECONOMICS

The questions that are raised in this volume — racism, sexism, war, inequality, freedom — are issues that radicals and orthodox economists (many of whom call themselves "liberals") strongly disagree on. Orthodox economists tend to argue that the distribution of income, warfare, etc., are political problems. They argue that economics is primarily concerned with how to maximize the production of goods and services under a system of constraints, where inputs are scarce, as is argued by Olson. Orthodox economics does this very well.

Radicals, on the other hand, unite politics and economics. They call themselves *political economists.* They want to learn how to change the world. They are asking how to bring about a society of equality, democracy, justice, and peace. And it is in asking these questions that they find orthodox economics empty, devoid of answers.

A question that comes out of these controversies is where does it all lead? What will be the impact of the radical political economists? Is economics experiencing a scientific revolution? Will a new paradigm emerge? Or will some of their points be added to economic theory and thus allow it to go on in the same direction in which it has been moving? Economics, as we know it, has grown out of the development of capitalism. Will a new economics emerge as social crises occur? If a new economics does emerge, what will it be?

ENDNOTES

[1] The Union for Radical Political Economics publishes a *Review of Radical Political Economics,* which contains critiques of orthodox economics and presents alternative analyses.

[2] Gerald E. Peabody, "Scientific Paradigms and Economics: An Introduction," *The Review of Radical Political Economics,* Vol. 3, No. 2, July 1971, p. 6.

[3] Lester Thurow, *Investment in Human Capital* (Belmont, California: Wadsworth Publishing Co., 1970), pp. 20–22.

[4] Gurley, *Bulletin of Concerned Asian Scholars,* April–July 1970.

[5] Anthony Crosland, *A Social Democratic Britain* (London: The Fabian Society, 1971).

REFERENCES

Christoffel, Tom, David Finkelhor, and Dan Gilbarg. *Up Against the American Myth.* New York: Holt, Rinehart and Winston, 1970.

Edwards, Richard C. and Arthur MacEwan. "A Radical Approach to Economics." *American Economic Review,* May 1970.

Edwards, Richard C., Michael Reich, and Thomas E. Weisskopf. *The Capitalist System.* Englewood Cliffs, New Jersey: Prentice-Hall, 1972.

Gordon, David M. *Problems in Political Economy: An Urban Perspective.* Boston: D. C. Heath, 1970.

Hunt, E. K., and Howard J. Sherman. *Economics: An Introduction to Traditional and Radical Views.* New York: Harper and Row, 1972.

Kuhn, Thomas S. *The Structure of Scientific Revolutions.* Chicago: University of Chicago Press, 1962.

Lindbeck, Assar. *The Political Economy of the New Left.* New York: Harper and Row, 1971.

Mandel, Ernest. *Marxist Economic Theory* (2 vols.). New York: Monthly Review Press, 1968.

Mermelstein, David. *Economics: Mainstream Readings and Radical Critiques.* New York: Random House, 1970.

Samuelson, Paul. *Economics,* 8th edition. New York: McGraw-Hill, 1970.

"Scientific Paradigms and Economics." *The Review of Radical Political Economics,* Vol. 3, No. 2. July 1971.

Weaver, James H. "Toward a Radical Political Economics." *American Economist.* Spring 1970.

SECTION II

Orthodox Economics and
Radical Political Economy

This section does not deal with the tools of economics as such. You will not find discussions of demand and supply curves, the marginal propensity to consume, the multiplier, and so forth. This discussion centers on the nature of economic science. To what ends are the tools put? Are there inherent biases in the tools of economics that allow economists to answer only certain questions and to answer them in only certain ways? What was the origin of the economic theories in use today? Do economic theories change and develop in response to changes in the social situation? Does current social change call for new theories?

Mancur Olson, Jr., argues that economic theory need not be and indeed is not biased or limited in its usefulness to today's capitalist economies. He contends that microeconomic theory is applicable in most situations, provided two conditions are met. First, behavior must be purposeful — we must act to attain something or to reach some goal. Second, the theory assumes some degree of scarcity. If these two conditions are met, economic theory can be used to deal with the problems of the family, the firm, government spending, and the national economy. The theory is valid in market, collective, and primitive economies. Even though the original framers of economic theory had certain biases and political values, there is no necessary relation between the biases of those who begat an idea and the uses to which an idea may be put.

Gintis and Pochoda argue that our present economic theory has been developed in order to justify, legitimate, and improve the operation of capitalist economies (and the state capitalist system of the Soviet

Union). The theory reveals three biases: a materialist bias that equates increased output of material goods with increased welfare, an efficiency bias that requires that values such as fulfilling work, community, environmental balance, etc., be subordinated to the goal of maximum output at minimum cost, and a government bias that falsely argues that government acts in a beneficent manner to correct the aberrations of the economic system (poverty, pollution, etc.) and carries out its policies so as to be responsive to the wishes of all social classes. Orthodox economists can not adequately deal with such burning issues of the day as war, racism, poverty, and pollution, because of the three biases inherent in the theory.

After this volume had already been turned over to the publisher, a set of papers by Gurley and Solow came to the editor's attention. It was immediately decided to contact the authors for permission to include their papers even though it violated the essential plan of the volume, which was to present only those papers that had been presented in the contemporary Economic Problems course. Gurley and Solow both consented to have their papers reprinted here.

One gets some of the feeling of intellectual excitement and an awareness of the stakes in this controversy from reading their exchange. The papers were presented at the 83rd Annual Meeting of the American Economic Association, which took place in Detroit, Michigan, December 28 through 30, 1970.

Gurley's paper is a review of Nancy D. Ruggles' *Economics*,[1] a book that was the result of an effort on the part of the National Academy of Sciences and The Social Science Research Council to conduct an overall survey of the behavioral and social sciences. The volume was an attempt to present the major contributions and unresolved problems of the various areas of economics.

Gurley's attack on orthodox economics has several aspects. One, he argues that the problems that orthodox economists attack are trivial. Second, orthodox economists accept the goals of the system, that is, the goal of an ever-increasing gross national product. Third, orthodox economists fail to analyze the relationship between the United States and the underdeveloped countries and in particular how the United States profits from its leading role in the hierarchical structure of the international capitalist system. Fourth, orthodox economists refuse to deal with the maintenance of the hierarchical class structure in the United States that produces wealth and poverty, privilege and oppression. All these aspects can be summed up by saying that orthodox economists do not adequately analyze the way wealth and income are distributed on both the domestic and international front.

[1] Nancy D. Ruggles, ed., *Economics* (Englewood Cliffs, New Jersey: Prentice-Hall, 1970).

In part this failure to deal with distribution of income and wealth stems from the ahistorical methodology of orthodox economics. Orthodox economists take the existing social system for granted. They do not realize that this system has a history, that it evolved from earlier societies, and that it is now in the process of further change. Orthodox economists' analyses are weak because they exclude from their analyses the question of power and the conflict and disruptive change that emerges from differential power in society. Gurley argues that political economists deal with the relationships of domination and servitude and approach these power issues so as to put them at the center of political-economic analysis. The political economist generally tends to take the side of the poor and the powerless as opposed to the rich and powerful. The political economist tends to see capitalism as the oppressor of the poor and powerless.

Gurley faults the orthodox economists' approach to the problem of economic development. He argues that their approach ignores the social, political, and economic barriers to development that arise out of class conflicts of interest. They do not ask who gains from economic development and who loses. Nor do they ask which groups have the power to make decisions. Orthodox economists see only harmonies of interest in underdeveloped countries. Everyone is working for development and everyone stands to gain. Gurley argues this is not true, that in many underdeveloped countries the necessary changes will not be in the interest of either those who rule or the foreign corporations that are engaged in exploiting the natural resources found there. Gurley argues that the people living in these countries have two serious roadblocks in their path to development that earlier countries did not face. First, they did not have the opportunity of plunder and slavery and fraud that earlier countries had, and secondly, they are burdened by their place in the international capitalist system, which works for ends that are opposed to their needs for development. Perhaps it is impossible for them to develop because of ecological constraints, i.e., the rich countries are using up the resources of the world in such a way that the poor countries will never be able to raise their standards of living.

Radical economists question the orthodox analysis of income distribution within developed countries such as the United States. Distribution of income is based on the concept of marginal productivity according to orthodox analysis. Workers receive wages, capitalists receive profits, landlords receive rent according to the contribution their factors of production (their capital, labor, or land) make to the final product. Thus there is legitimacy to income shares. Radicals argue that profits are not deserved, that although capital goods are productive this does not justify the assignment of profit to private owners. Radicals argue that there is nothing productive about land and machinery being privately owned. The distribution of incomes between workers and property owners is largely determined by the relative power of the two groups (although Gurley argues that relative supplies of the factors of production set limits within which the power exerts itself). Gurley goes on to argue that the marginal products of workers are conditioned by the working of the economic system. Blacks, Chicanos, and women make less of a contribution to production than they might simply because they have been denied opportunities for education and self-development, which would have allowed them to make a larger contribution.

Finally, Gurley raises questions about the orthodox economists' assumption that welfare is increased when the gross national product is increased. Orthodox welfare theory reflects a lack of concern for ecological considerations and for the consequences of economic growth for individual self-development.

Gurley complains that the review of economics he is discussing has ignored all the questions raised by radical economists. These issues are ignored as are the great number of recent books and articles written from a radical perspective.

Solow rejoins that radical political economics has been neglected because it is negligible. He argues that radical economists have misunderstood and corrupted Thomas Kuhn's notion of the scientific paradigm. Radical economists are not interested in doing normal science, they are mainly interested in role-playing and rhetoric. Solow argues that there are no definitive studies explaining income distribution over time or between countries based on relative power of capitalists and workers. This kind of research would be necessary to make the sort of claims that Gurley has made. Solow argues that the economists were not conducting a survey of the economic system. It was a survey of economic science. Thus, it was perfectly appropriate to dwell on technique and data because acquaintanceship with data and particular technique is what distinguishes economists from other social scientists.

Mancur Olson, Jr., was born in Grand Forks, North Dakota and received his B.A. degree from North Dakota State University, his M.A. from Oxford, and his Ph.D. from Harvard. Perhaps his most well-known work is The Logic of Collective Action. *He has been Assistant Professor of Economics at Princeton University, Deputy Assistant Secretary of the Department of Health, Education and Welfare, and he is presently Professor of Economics at the University of Maryland.*

He was introduced to the class as a representative of the mainstream of economics.

1 What Is Economics?

Mancur Olson, Jr.

I hope that I am in the mainstream of economics, but I'm sure that some people, who would think of themselves as being in the mainstream of economics, would not like to think that I'm there beside them. Perhaps I should react as Rockefeller did when he was running in 1964 for the Republican nomination for President against Goldwater. As I recall, Rockefeller won the Primary in Oregon leaving Goldwater pretty well behind, and then I think he lost in California. And just after he had won in Oregon and lost in California, a reporter asked Rockefeller whether he or Goldwater was in the mainstream of Republicanism. Rockefeller scratched his head and said, "I guess it's a meandering stream." And so I think that economics, too, is a meandering stream, and it is pretty hard to say who is in the middle of it. In any event, I speak not on behalf of any mainstream or any critics of the mainstream, but only on behalf of myself, with some views that I hope would be relevant to you as you begin your studies in economics.

At the onset, it might be useful to present a brief overview of the

Adapted by James H. Weaver from Mancur Olson's talk and from his "Economics, Sociology, and the Best of All Possible Worlds," which was published in *The Public Interest*, 12, Summer 1968. Reprinted by permission of the author and National Affairs, Inc. © Copyright 1968 by National Affairs, Inc.

field of economics. What is the nature of this subject, economics? What is the nature of the economic theory of the mainstream of economics? Is this economic theory an apology or a defense formulated to rationalize the interests of some particular group? Is it, as radical economists claim, a reflection of a particular ideology? If it contains truth, where is that truth applicable? If economic theory is useful, is it useful only in societies of a certain type, or is it useful in all kinds of societies? Is economic theory relevant only to highly developed, capitalistic, Western societies, or is it relevant to societies such as the Soviet Union, and primitive societies such as those an anthropologist might study? Is it relevant only to studying what goes on in the market, or has it relevance as well to the operations of governments and nonbusiness organizations. These are questions, I think, that it is well to keep in mind, because these are questions which are often left implicit in discussions of the nature of economics.

First let's look at the history of economic theory as that term is generally understood in the United States and most of the economically advanced Western countries. How do you form a "body of theory"? While a complete answer to this question would ultimately require numerous volumes, I think one can be fairly accurate in saying that by and large the core of economic theory (in any event the micro-economic foundation) developed mainly in late eighteenth- and nine-teenth-century Europe and most especially in nineteenth-century Great Britain. We find in that time and place early economists who had certain traits which we can readily summarize. Adam Smith, James and John Stuart Mill, David Ricardo, and many others had, in general, rather similar views of the world. They were inspired to intellectual innovation by the immediate practical problems which confronted them, and they often served as passionate ideologues in the political controversies of their time. With some risk of oversimplification, one can say that the early economists were believers in *laissez faire* — that is to say, an economic policy where the role of the government is kept to a minimum. On the whole, one could also characterize them as internationalists who opposed nationalists or parochialists. They advocated free trade; even more, they advocated international cooperation and were very much opposed to war among nations. They tended toward pacifism rather than militarism. They were utilitarians rather than being inclined toward conventional religion, and they were democratic rather than authoritarian in their political views. With few exceptions, they took a much more sympathetic view of the interests of the rising middle-class mercantile and industrial group, and especially in Britain, paid little attention either to the poor or to the class that had the most power: the aristocratic, landed class. Indeed, in nineteenth-century Britain, the word "economist" was often taken to *mean* an advocate of *laissez faire* in general and free trade in particular. The belief that economic theory is applicable only to goods that fetch a price in the markets of "capitalist" economies of the kind the classical economists admired has survived to the present day.

Thus the general applicability of economic theory has not usually been understood by laymen, and indeed many of the older generation of economists also interpret economics too narrowly. Economic theory not only is, but (if it is to avoid arbitrariness and error) *must be* so general that it also applies to "goods" that are *not* traded in markets — and also to traditional and communistic societies. If an economist is studying the housing market, he cannot ignore the fact that some locations have more prestige than others, are in areas occupied by different races or social groups, are in different political jurisdictions, and have different aesthetic attributes. Obviously any of these factors can affect the satisfaction an owner would get from a house, and the market price of that house, as much as its material characteristics.

Indeed, it is in general *not* possible to give an entirely accurate explanation of economic behavior in a situation unless *all* of the perceived advantages of a given alternative, to the actor being studied or advised, are counted as "returns," and all of the disadvantages of that alternative, as perceived by the relevant actor, as "costs." The economist will frequently — but by no means always — predict that the actor being studied will tend to choose the alternative that promises the largest excess of returns over costs, which is by definition most advantageous in terms of the actor's values.

Of course, the actor may lack the intelligence, information, or detachment needed to choose the alternative that is best in terms of his own preferences. He might be a "satisficer" rather than a maximizer, or operate according to an erroneous traditional rule, or let biases distort his perception of the facts. In such a case the economist can take comfort from the fact that the actor being studied may be in the market for a consultant! In any event, economic theory will have relevance, in a normative, if not always positive, way.

In these broader terms, economic theory transcends its interpretation by radicals and some traditional economists as a method of imposing materialistic criteria for solutions to social problems. Given reasonable assumptions about human behavior, economic theory provides a basis for analyzing many facets of any type of society. The motivations of those who conceived these theories is an interesting study in itself. But their motivations should not detract from the value of the economic theory they developed.

Economic theory is relevant whenever actors have determinate wants or objectives and at the same time do not have such an abundance of the means needed to achieve these ends that all of their desires are satiated. The ends in question may be social status or political power, and the means will be anything that is in fact conducive to the attainment of the ends, whether or not these means can bring a price in the market. Economic (more precisely *microeconomic*) theory is in a fundamental sense more nearly a theory of rational behavior than a theory of material goods.

To be sure, economic theory in its most general form can be as vacuous or trivial as it is broad. Many situations are so difficult, or so simple, that no formal method of thinking will be of any practical help. Economics, moreover, has not got very far with the problems of uncertainty, or strategic interaction (in the game theory sense) of acquiring or getting along without information, not to mention other problems we need to understand better before we can have anything like a complete or adequate theory of rational behavior. And where economic theory is not in itself deficient, economists often are: they sometimes lack the fullness of mind, the judgment, and above all, the imagination needed to apply economic theory to problems outside their traditional purview. In any event, the purpose here is not to glorify or belittle economics, but rather to argue that some of the basic theories of social science, including economic theory, are limited not so much in terms of the objects they can be used to study as in other ways.

The generality of economic theory with respect to the objects of study is illustrated by several recent developments. The output of the United States Department of Defense is not sold for money, yet the economic approach inherent in the Planning–Programming–Budgeting System has proved most helpful there. This system has even shown great promise in departments that deal in such obscure intangibles as health, education, and welfare, and that are relatively far removed from the marketplace. In the specialty of international relations, too, one finds that insights of economic theory have sometimes been decidedly relevant, as the work of Kenneth Boulding and Thomas Schelling shows, yet these men have dealt with the political-military rather than the material, wants of nations, and often ignored the market sector in their models. The nations of Eastern Europe have an institutional environment vastly different from that which the classical economists knew or wanted, yet many economists there are beginning to use the same economic theory we know in the West, and sometimes find it helpful in suggesting ways in which their *existing* Marxist-inspired institutions might be made to work more efficiently. (Indeed, economic theory has escaped the original ideological limitations on its generality. I have read some interesting work by economists who, as I later learned, were avowed Communists, but their work was such that if asked, I would have guessed they were typical Western intellectuals, if not *laissez-faire* enthusiasts.) Finally, the developing areas of the world, different and diverse as their cultures and conditions may be, have nonetheless proved to be about as amenable to ordinary economic analysis as the Western democracies.

The fact that economic theory has no unique application to material goods, but deals with any objectives that people value in conditions of scarcity, cannot be adequately documented in any brief discussion. But it may nonetheless be useful to mention one basic idea that has an important — if in many respects overly simple — application to politics. This is the notion of "Pareto-optimality," which is defined as a situation such that no individual in the group at issue can be made better off without someone else being made worse off. This idea is normally used to describe resource allocations that are efficient and ideal, in the sense that they satisfy individual wants to the maximum possible degree, given the available resources, the state of technology, and the distribution of income. If someone could get more without anyone having less, that would mean a way had been found to get more output from the available resources.

The generalization to politics comes from the fact that when we say a Pareto-optimal situation is one in which no one can be made better off without someone else being made worse off, we need not define "better off" or "worse off" in terms of material goods alone. Indeed, if we consider only these so-called "economic" wants of the individuals concerned, the whole analysis could be invalid — for the only relevant measure of value in this context is that of the individuals concerned, and if one of them values a given degree of social status or political power more highly at the margin than some material good, he will be "worse off" if he has to give up that degree of social status or political power in exchange for the material good. An attempt to "sub-optimize" by considering only material objectives could be meaningless, for a step that seemed efficient because it increased the output of material goods might in fact be inefficient because the social or political goods that had to be sacrificed were worth more than the material goods gained. There is thus no way of defining a situation as Pareto-optimal without taking all of the things people value into account.

When "better off" and "worse off" are understood as they must be, it becomes clear that Pareto-optimality is a condition of political equilibrium in democratic societies. (I use the word "equilibrium," which is the object of much controversy in political science and sociology, with the same meaning it has in economics.) If there is some step or combination of steps that will make one or more individuals better off, without making anyone worse off, there is always the possibility some political or administrative entrepreneur will respond to the incentive inherent in the situation and organize a change in policy. This is, to be sure, only one of a vast variety of necessary conditions of political equilibrium, and perhaps a rather weak one. But can we conceive of a complete theory of political change, or of the politics of consensus, that would leave Pareto-optimality out of account?

Some of the other political insights that can be got from the notion of Pareto-optimality have, however, been explored.   The Swedish economist Knut Wicksell pointed out more than a half century ago that optimal measures should be able to command something approaching unanimous support, since by definition there will be some possible distribution of the benefits and costs such that everyone would have an incentive to favor such measures.   (This would not be the case under a *complete* unanimity rule, where an individual might withhold his then indispensable vote in an attempt to extort a larger share of the total gains from the measure.)   More recently, James Buchanan and Gordon Tullock have, in their important book *The Calculus of Consent,* argued that reasoning of this sort shows that the majority rule principle is in certain respects arbitrary and unsatisfactory, and that the bicameralism, two-thirds rules, and general checks and balances of the American system have the admittedly unsuspected virtue of preventing passage of many policies that are not toward Pareto-optimality.

A preoccupation with Pareto-optimality can, admittedly, sometimes support a classical-liberal opposition to the coercive redistribution of income.   Redistribution cannot be expected to attain anything like unanimous support, yet it may be overwhelmingly important.   But there is nothing inherently conservative in the political use of the concept of Pareto-optimality.   I have, for example, argued elsewhere that there may sometimes be a tendency toward what has been called public squalor in the midst of private affluence because of the fact that many Pareto-optimal measures for *local* areas may not be able to get majority support in the *national* government.   Though the gains from a Pareto-optimal measure are by definition greater than the costs, the number of gainers will be smaller than the number of losers when the benefits are local and the taxes are national.   Fortunately, "logrolling" may make it possible for a number of local Pareto-optimal measures to pass as a package.   (Logrolling thus does not necessarily deserve its evil popular reputation.)   But logrolling requires complex and costly bargains and accordingly often will not occur.

Beginning with the notions of purposive behavior, scarcity of necessary resources, and "Pareto-optimality," a concept of the "ideal" society has evolved in economics.   This particular conception differentiates economics from other social sciences which are as generally relevant as economics.   Neither economists nor other social scientists are normally utopians; they do not necessarily believe that their "ideal societies" can be achieved.   The purposes these ideal conceptions serve are entirely different from those of, say, the utopian socialists, or of Plato's vision of an ideally just state run by philosopher-kings.   They serve, not usually as visions of what we can and should obtain, but rather as intellectual models that can clarify and help to indicate whether a given policy leads in a desirable or undesirable direction.   Some misunderstanding may also be caused by the fact that, while the economist's conception of the "ideal society" is at times almost explicit, the analogous concept in other social sciences receives only tacit recognition. But this difference in the degree of explicitness of the ideal conception does not mean that the one ideal is necessarily more influential or important than the other, so we must strip these ideal conceptions of their very different clothing and then set them out in a way that will facilitate explicit comparison.

One part of the economic ideal has already been set out in the literature of welfare economics, which describes the necessary conditions for an "efficient" and "optimal" allocation of resources, so there is not need for a rigorous statement of it here. Roughly speaking, a society with given resources and state of technology can be described as efficient if it is "at the frontier of every production possibility function," which means in plainer English that no more of any good can be obtained without giving up some amount of some other good (including leisure and future consumption as goods, to subsume the possibility that more resources would be devoted to production). *Efficiency* says nothing about whether the goods that are produced are those that would provide the most satisfaction, so it is not a sufficient condition for *optimality*. A necessary condition for an optimal allocation of resources is that no reallocation could be made which would make anyone better off without making someone else worse off. The standard of optimality is then the concept of Pareto-optimality mentioned earlier, and Pareto-optimality is not achieved unless the society is *also* efficient.

The society will not, of course, be economically ideal unless the distribution of income is right, and the "just" distribution of income cannot be scientifically determined. The constructs of welfare economics nonetheless can claim general interest, for they describe necessary conditions that would have to prevail if an economy were to be optimal, *whatever* the ideal distribution of income might be. The necessary conditions for Pareto-optimality in a society are stated principally in terms of a series of marginal conditions. These marginal conditions, and the many shortcomings in this sort of analysis, will not be discussed here, since this paragraph is meant to be only impressionistic, and because the welfare economics texts that set out this analysis more carefully are easily accessible.

Welfare economics is static in that it leaves innovation and the advance of technology out of account. Economists have done a great deal of work lately on innovation and on the economics of education and research, but this has not usually been explicitly tied in with welfare economics. In the rough and ready fashion in which we are operating at the moment, this can perhaps be done. In essence, the economically ideal society would maintain a Pareto-optimal allocation of resources at every moment in time *and* at the same time continually change to the best attainable production functions (or schedules of various combinations of inputs required for production) as knowledge advances.   The rate of accumulation of productive knowledge and other forms of capital would be the maximum consistent with the society's rate of discount of future versus present consumption.   This statement, alas, brushes over a number of unsettled issues (such as the possible Schumpeterian conflict between short-run allocative efficiency and long-run innovation) and many profound complexities (involving particularly what the economists call "optimal growth" theory).   But hopefully the subsequent discussion will reveal that these complications are not so important for the very particular purpose of the moment. That purpose is to suggest that most economists have some fairly clear but incomplete models from welfare economics, and some vaguer notions about the importance of rapid innovation, which can be taken to represent something in the nature of a vision of an economically ideal or optimal society.   This vision derives from the elemental goal of maximum income, which demands an optimal allocation of resources at each moment in time plus a dynamic technology.   This vision is an ideal in the sense that (vexing problems of "second-best" solutions notwithstanding) it serves as a standard which economists use to help them judge practical policies.

Selecting the Parsonian school of sociology as a prototype of a social science, one finds that it does not contain models of "optimality" that parallel the constructs of welfare economics.   But there is probably implicit in it a vision of something like an ideal society, which ideal would serve heuristic purposes and influence judgments about public policy.   This implicit ideal might be more easily evident in the literature on "mass movements" than in Parsons' own writings, but it is also evident to some degree in his works.   The sort of sociological ideal at issue is, moreover, far too complex and comprehensive to be susceptible to brief summary.   It is the result not only of extensive theoretical writing, but also of subtle insights that have emerged from many lifetimes of empirical research.

But perhaps the most basic dimension in that ideal can be mentioned, if not precisely defined.   That dimension is "alienation." However much they differ in other respects, a whole family of sociological studies unite in treating alienation, or some similar psychological estrangement, as the principal sociological pathology.   To say that the minimization of alienation plays a role in many sociological studies not unlike the maximization of satisfaction (or utility) in economics is to enumerate a half-truth — a statement that makes those who believe in the other half angry.   Yet it is a half-truth that, because it refers to a part of the truth that has been neglected, should now be emphasized.

Though the minimization of alienation is in a sense the most fundamental variable in this particular sociological ideal, it is not perhaps the most important, or at any event the most often discussed in the theoretical literature. The degree of "integration" of a society is probably even more central, and the ideal is that this degree of integration should be maximized. The degree of integration, or "institutional integration," as it is more carefully called, is important not only because it affects the amount of alienation, but also because it affects in other ways the chances that the society will cohere.

The degree of integration tends to increase with the extent to which a set of individuals forms a "community," and would be nil in a situation in which a set of individuals had no social structure, common values, or institutions. It would be high in a situation in which everyone in a society was tied into the social order by bonds to a wide variety of associations, in which social structure was elaborate, in which common values, norms, and institutions were cherished, where individual roles were well understood, and where mechanisms of social control were well developed. The number and degree of group associations and affiliations, and the degree to which behavior is institutionalized, or organized, structured, and regularized, tends to be a very high, if not indeed at a maximum level, in this ideal society. It is not only the extent of group association and institutionalization that is emphasized, but also its mutual consistency and stability. If the demands or values of different groups or associations with overlapping memberships or objectives are incompatible, and different people have conflicting expectations about what people with particular roles should do, then the degree of integration is limited and the possibility of societal disintegration increased.

It may be possible to give an impression of this ideal type with some examples. Many of the sociologists whom Parsons has influenced give a great deal of emphasis to "voluntary" associations and other "intermediate" groups (organizations smaller than the state). This is especially true of the literature on the causes of what sociologists call "mass movements," and Professor Parsons has aptly said this literature constitutes a "new pluralism." There are many relevant types of intermediate groups, but perhaps the professional association, the labor union, and the organized pressure group are the leading examples. The professional association is perhaps most important of all. Some of these who share the Parsonian perspective think all types of economic life should be organized the way a profession such as medicine is organized, with a powerful guild organization and a pervasive occupational ethic controlling each industry. To be sure, this idea got most of its strongest support before the Parsonian school began — it was urged by Emile Durkheim, R. H. Tawney, the guild sociologists, some syndicalists, and by some advocates of a corporate or Fascist state. But the systematic conceptions needed to justify a system of economic organization modeled on the professions was developed by Professor Parsons, and he has repeatedly emphasized the functions that professional ethics, institutions, and associations perform.

The labor union and the organized pressure groups have also received special attention. One of the most interesting assertions in this literature is that labor unions, and perhaps even Marxian labor unions, may reduce the chances of a revolution in a modern society, because the labor union, however radical its ideology may initially have been, will provide a source of group participation for many workers, and the sense of belonging or group participation that results may reduce alienation and thereby the desire to overthrow the social order. There is perhaps also a tendency to emphasize the sense of group identity and the feeling of participation fostered by a pressure group rather than its practical impact in the political system. In the sociological conception, it would probably be a necessary condition for an ideal society that there be many groups of the sort we have just discussed.

There will be objections that this ideal is unsatisfactory in its own terms, quite apart from the merits of other types of ideal societies that may be imagined. Many people — probably even some of those who have contributed to the dissemination of this ideal — would say that they personally prefer unstructured and mainly unorganized, if not disorganized, societies. Many of us love ill-defined roles and feel confined by extensive associational networks. A new generation of sociologists, mindful of Marx, emphasizes the inevitability — or even desirability — of social conflict, and thus has only contempt for the Parsonian prediction of consensus. Many people who look at the literature on group participation would agree that more attention ought to be given to the *impact* or share of power that organizational membership can bring, and less to the fact of belonging *per se*. But the disadvantages of the sociological ideal described, and the impressionism and injustice of this brief and selective description of it, are not so important for the special purpose of the moment, which is to show how economic theory and a prevalent type of sociological theory can lead to conflicting conclusions.

IDEALS INTO NIGHTMARES

The point is that *the economic and sociological ideals described are not only different, but polar opposites: if either one were attained, the society would be a nightmare in terms of the other.* There are no doubt many social arrangements so inept that society is inside what the economist would call the production possibility frontier; that is, in a situation where it could get closer to either the economic or the sociological ideal without getting further from the other.   An example of this would be a society with total anarchy, in which a step taken to promote integration, such as the establishment of a government that created law and order, would bring both the economic and the sociological ideals nearer.   But these positions that are inferior by both standards are not very interesting.   The important question is how much of the one ideal to give up in order to get more of the other when you can't get more of both.   This is an important matter, for in terms of the values of most people I know (whatever their disciplinary backgrounds), there is profound merit in both ideals.   The economic and sociological ideals, far from both being destroyed by their contradiction with one another, are in fact expressions of the most fundamental alternatives human societies face.   The fact that most of us want to choose compromise positions between these polar ideals does not negate their value as intellectual constructs that can give us a clearer understanding of the implications of a marginal move in one direction or another.

The fundamental character of the conflict between these two ideals may not, however, be immediately evident, so we must first show how one ideal prevents the achievement of the other.   The economic ideal required that there be an optimal allocation of resources at any moment in time and rapid innovation over time.   An optimal allocation of resources requires that a series of marginal conditions be satisfied throughout the society; the marginal rates of substitution of any two factors of production must be proportional to the ratio of their prices and the same in all employments, and so on.   But if there is rapid growth, the demands for different goods, the methods of production, the location of production, and the marginal products of particular factors of production will change incessantly.   A Pareto-optimal allocation of resources will therefore require *constant reallocations of resources.* This will mean that factors of production, including labor, must frequently move from firm to firm, industry to industry, and place to place.[1]   Since methods of production are rapidly changing, the same *combinations* of labor and other resources won't be needed very long:

---

[1] It is logically possible that reallocations of resources could be constant, but the rate of reallocation might still be so slow that social costs were small.   Only those with a wanderlust, or the young adults who are leaving their parents' homes anyway, would then have to move.   Rates of economic growth that are rapid by modern standards could, however, require much faster reallocations than could be handled in this way if the marginal conditions necessary for complete economic efficiency are to be satisfied at all times.

new *groupings* of workers are needed as the economy changes. This means that individual mobility is normally required, and this in turn means that the rewards of the incentive system must be offered on an individual basis.

Rapid change and growth in an economy means great gains in one area and vast losses in another, for incentives are needed to induce the needed mobility of labor and capital, and the changing pattern of incentives means many *nouveaux riches* and *nouveaux pauvres*. Both social and geographical mobility are at a maximum in the economically "ideal" society, and there can be few if any stable group relationships, apart from those in a nuclear family in which *only one* member is in the labor force. There can be no group loyalties or organizational constraints that limit individual mobility in response to changing incentives. There can be no organizations or other mechanisms that give those whose legitimate expectations are frustrated by the pattern of change the power to defend their interests, for this will (except where normally infeasible "lump sum" transfers can be arranged) pervert the pattern of incentives needed to bring about the resource reallocation which is entailed by the economic ideal. No group with a role in the productive process can restrict mobility by regulating entry, giving privilege for seniority, or "featherbedding."

I have elsewhere discussed some aspects of the relationship between rapid economic growth and social and political stability in more detail,[2] so there should be no need to spell out the argument here. It should in any event already be evident that the society that enjoys the benefits of the economic ideal will, because of the magnitude of social and geographic mobility and the dearth of stable group relationships, for that very reason be one in which individuals are constantly uprooted and in which alienation is probably at a maximum. The rapid change will also work against stable institutions and ethical norms. Moreover, the plurality of intermediate organizations, such as professional associations, labor unions, cartels, and lobbying organizations, which the sociological ideal cherishes, cannot be allowed, for such organizations, by defending the group interests of their clients through the political system, by limiting entry or exit, or by preventing the adoption of new methods of production, would prevent the maximum growth which the economically ideal system will by definition achieve.

It should similarly be obvious that, when the particular sociological ideal at issue has been achieved, the society will tend to become economically stagnant. The guildlike institutional integration and regulation that is inherent in the sociological ideal tends to prevent

2 "Rapid Growth as a Destabilizing Force," *Journal of Economic History*, XXIII (December 1963) , 529–552.

change (just as the medieval guilds did). Without change, there can be no growth, so that the "professionalization" of economic life is one of the surest ways to prevent economic advance. The familiar argument that the Parsonian sociological tradition has a conservative bias turns out to be an heroic understatement when the economic aspect is considered, for the minimization of stress, alienation, and the elaboration and integration of institutions that it involves will tend to prevent economic even more than political change — and opposition even to economic change is indeed conservative! But this ideal must nonetheless not be belittled — its importance is evident whenever we examine the implications of its opposite.

At the most general level, what has been said is that the typical individual's need for some degree of stability in group relationships, and therefore also some institutional stability, can in a wide range of situations work against the maximum attainment of all other individual objectives. To put it another way, the continuous reallocations and rearrangements that are needed to satisfy maximally all of our other individual wants (be they material or not) is not usually consistent with the stable or enduring interpersonal relationships that most people apparently value and need. The ideal situation, interpersonal relationships aside, has been stated, in part explicitly, by economists. A set of ideal arrangements for group interaction, all other things aside, has been described, albeit implicitly, by sociologists. There are many ambiguities and shortcomings in both of these ideals, and even greater failings in my hurried vulgarizations of them, but it surely cannot be denied that it is often important to keep something like both of these polar cases in mind.

All of this argument can be summarized concisely: it is futile to attempt to determine the validity of the methodology of a social science in terms of the objects it is supposed to consider. Economics is distinguished by particular methods and prejudices. Economics is therefore what economists do, or rather what economists do best.

Abstract notions such as "efficiency" and "optimality" are important parts of the methodology of economics. Yet these criteria are not sufficient for either economic or social policy. Social reality as a whole should (and must) be viewed from various perspectives. And when contradictions develop among various "ideal" conceptions of society, economists and other social scientists will search in vain for revealed truths on social policy from within their disciplines. There is no general social welfare criterion in any society that values the preferences and diversity of individuals.

Economics offers a method for analyzing social policy in terms of individual preferences where natural scarcity of means forces choice of efficient patterns of resource allocation. Social sciences with different philosophical bases emphasize different conditions. Makers of social policy should not in general seek advice about one segment of reality from only one discipline. The partial solutions that result from focusing on one aspect of social reality are usually temporary, at least, and often disastrous.

Economics makes important contributions to the study of social policy. Each citizen should be aware of the costs and benefits of alternative social policies in terms of economic criteria. The citizen should equally understand the limits of economic ideals. Both radical and conservative views of economics contribute to an understanding of the best possible economic ideal for society, and the ideal economy is a necessary though not sufficient condition for the best possible social reality.

Herbert Gintis was born in Philadel-phia and received a B.S. in Mathe-matics at the University of Pennsyl-vania. He received his Ph.D. in Economics from Harvard in 1969. His Ph.D. dissertation, Alienation and Power: Towards a Radical Wel-fare Economics, *must be one of the most widely quoted unpublished dissertations in history. Gintis re-wrote his dissertation in free-verse form and the Union for Radical Political Economics published it in that form as an occasional paper in 1970. Gintis is currently doing re-search on the relationship between educational and economic systems at the Graduate School of Education at Harvard University.*

Ralph Pochoda is a graduate student in the Department of Economics at Harvard University.

2 Economics in a Revolutionary Age

Herbert Gintis and Ralph Pochoda

Economics is a human construction. It is the result of the concrete, daily activity of historically concrete men. What men called "econo-mists" choose to consider important, as well as what they choose to disregard, inevitably influences their scientific judgments. Intentions are as important as methods in the development of economic analysis. To answer "what is economics?" we must have a sociology of knowledge.

The intention of economists in any historical period has been to erect encompassing theoretical models to focus their research on the "burning issues" of the day. Only the days are long historical periods. Thus the opening of trade on the Mediterranean and the formation of the nation-state at the close of the Middle Ages led to development of mercantilist economics which promoted commodity exports as a means of increasing national wealth. The eighteenth-century technical revolution in agriculture on the European continent and the burgeoning struggle among monarchists, aristocrats, and urban industrialists in France led to the emergence of Physiocracy. The Physiocrats demonstrated the circular flow of economic activity and tried to relate their economic order to the "natural laws" of social order.

Growth of industrial capital in England and the ensuing struggle between industrialists and owners of agricultural capital gave birth to classical Ricardian economics which provided a rationale for industrial development. Later the growing strength of the industrial proletariat gave rise to Marxian economics.

Crises and depressions in the first decades of the twentieth century sired Keynesianism, and the otherwise stable and continuous development of capitalism over the past century, with its need for rational administration, streamlining, and consolidation, spurred the development of the "Neoclassical Synthesis." The intention of these theories is justification of limited intervention of politics in our present economic system of mixed capitalism. Keynesianism and the Neoclassical Synthesis provide the source for the reassuring homilies which are voiced with catechismic fervor in present-day elementary economics courses.

Now a new historical period is emerging. Advanced economies have entered a period of deep, presumably long-term crisis.

This crisis is manifested in the consciousness of increasing masses of individuals of the inherent irrationalities and forms of repression integral to capitalist and state-socialist economic development. More and more youth are rejecting the bourgeois-materialist vision of personal affluence as the basis of self-realization. Blacks and women increasingly rebel against their subservient and exploited positions in the economy and society. Third-World nations increasingly seek an alternative to both capitalist and state-socialist development and struggle to develop an effective counterforce to the instruments of neocolonialism and the imperialism of advanced industrial countries.

All of this is counter to the traditional theory of economic organization. According to this theory, markets in factors of production and commodities, together with the profit-maximizing capitalist corporation (or its state-socialist counterpart of the rationally directed bureaucratic enterprise) lie at the base of consumer sovereignty and healthy economic development. Where these beneficent core economic institutions fail — as in the case of "social goods" and "market externalities" — traditional theory turns naively to the pluralist-responsive and inherently powerful governmental organization for corrective measures. In this grandly coordinated scheme of private-economy-plus-state-correctives, traditional theory locates the sources of beneficent economic development. Not only the level of commodity consumption and its structure and distribution, but also all other social spheres affected by economic activity — the development of communities, the ecological environment, technology, the educational system, and the structure of work — all increasingly reflect the goals and aspirations of citizens in the course of social development.

Radical economists hold that this traditional view of advanced industrial economics is fundamentally incorrect. We believe — and find increasing theoretical and empirical justification for believing — that capitalist development is an intrinsically *alienated* historical process. Advanced economics grow, but people are not made happier for it. Advanced industrial societies are increasingly formally democratic and egalitarian, but then formal freedom masks increasing totalitarian control of the bureaucratic corporation and the centralized political power of the state.

We hold that the economic growth of advanced industrial societies is alienated in the sense that the historical development of social spheres basic to social well-being — the distribution of income and power, the structure of work and technology, the architectural and social integrity of community life, the vitality of the ecological environment, and the development of the cultural system itself — do not and cannot correspond to even the manifest desires, goals, preferences and aspirations of its citizens. We hold, moreover, that the normal course of day-to-day economic activity in advanced economies leads to forms of social consciousness and individual goals incompatible with true welfare, yet integral to securing the allegiance of citizens and workers to an alienated system.

In capitalist societies this takes the form of subordinating all social spheres, powerless minorities (and the "weaker sex"!) to the logic of profit accumulation and/or the maximization of the material surplus available to an essentially totalitarian central government. Community, environment, technology, work, the distribution of income, and culture itself become instruments toward the maximization of elite power not through the malevolent personalities of those who control economic activity, but through the very logic of the *institutional structures* of advanced economies, structures that inherently deprive individuals of control over their lives, communities, and work.

In this short paper, we shall try to explain how traditional theory arrives at its distorted view of social realities, and also present an alternative approach to the study of economic life. We shall first look briefly at traditional economic theory as it is framed by the intentions of its creators. The current doctrine makes certain implicit assumptions which in practice severely limit the usefulness of traditional economic analysis for solving the crucial problems of our historical age. The current attempt to reconcile economics and ecology will serve as an illustration of the biased nature of traditional economics. Then we can proceed to reconstruct basic definitions in economics so that this important field of study can become meaningful to the creation of a decent, democratic society.

Next we shall attempt to define the intentions of a new economic theory for our revolutionary age. We intend to define what this economics is and how it grows out of this time. It is the historically correct economics that speaks to the present generation and points to the imminent dissolution and recreation of our society's economic institutions.

BIASES IN TRADITIONAL ECONOMIC THEORY

The revealed intentions of traditional economic theory betray several central outmoded, and to radical economists, incorrect biases. First, in presenting the components of individual welfare, ALMOST EXCLUSVE EMPHASIS IS PLACED ON MARKETED GOODS AND SERVICES. This "materialist bias" is most clearly exhibited in the economist's choice of Gross National Product — the total volume of goods and services produced — as the central indicator of social welfare. This emphasis is incorrect for all societies, primitive, developing, or advanced; it is absurd for a highly developed economy. Here priority must be given to other components: individual participation and control over social, political, and economic institutions; equality; the nature and quality of the community and the environment; the quality of work activities and their ability to contribute to individual welfare; and the capacity of the individual to derive welfare from his social and natural environment.

This materialist bias in traditional economics is coupled with a second bias: AN ALMOST TOTAL EMPHASIS ON THE EFFICIENCY OF INDIVIDUAL, COMMODITY PRODUCTION. Alternative economic configurations are analyzed and assessed only on the grounds of such efficiency.

This "efficiency bias" causes orthodox economists to overlook the importance of economic institutions in determining the degree of economic, social, and political equality; the quality and structure of work; the community; and the environment; and especially the character and personality of the people living and working under their sway. Thus traditional economists recommend the use of economic institutions and the implementation of government economic policies consistently on the basis of their relative efficiency in contributing to GNP, irrespective of their general impact on the quality of social life.

The third bias is equally important. By reducing economic analysis to an instrumental adjunct of the economist in his role as government adviser, TRADITIONAL ECONOMICS BETRAY A "GOVERNMENT BIAS."

This bias is the result of two false premises. First, taking the basic economic institutions of capitalism for granted, it is assumed that serious social problems are "pathological abnormalities" in the political process. Second, it is assumed that the state operates impartially in the interests of all, rather than reflecting the differential interests of the various strata in the social structure. The role of the economist *qua* policy adviser flows naturally from these assumptions. The end result is that attention is directed away from any analysis of the basic economic institutions. Indeed, it is ironic that to find a proper discussion of the institutional base of economic systems, we must turn to other disciplines within the social sciences. Thus it is well known from cross-cultural and anthropological research that it is the structure of economic institutions that governs the path of social development and provides the framework within which political intervention takes place (53, 9, 29, 48) .

These three biases in traditional economics render its theoretical tools essentially impotent in shedding light on the complexities of modern society. This impotence is revealed in the discipline's consistent lack of awareness of major social problems *before* they reach the level of provoking severe social dislocation. The discipline's response, moreover, whether the issue is poverty, income distribution, urban decay, or ecological crisis, is to haul out the same old tools and same old biases toward "solving" problems.

AN EXAMPLE: ECONOMY AND ECOLOGY

We may take the recent concern for environmental destruction as a case in point. By overlooking the importance of ecological balance for individual welfare, economic theory[1] betrays its materialist bias. Improving the environment does not contribute to the production of goods and services, and it reduces growth of "economic productivity." According to the efficiency bias, moreover, the *structural* relations between economy and ecology are blithely ignored in both scientific research and the elementary teaching of the subject. That is, the problem of environment is treated as a minor *exception* to the general beneficence of market-exchange relations, and certainly the anomaly of consistent and progressive environmental destruction brings forth no revision in the general formulation of the traditional paradigm. When the social proportions of the problem finally lead to its recognition by the economist, the government bias rears its head: the economist "naively" assumes the basic soundness of economic institutions, the near infinite corrective power of state intervention, and the essential neutrality of the state in mediating between business and consumers and legislating the conflicting interests of different social classes.

The traditional treatment of economy and ecology is little more than intellectual and ideological *soma*. As taught in elementary economics courses, the subject is not introduced until the student has a thorough understanding of the "basic outlines" of the economy (i.e., the production of private goods and services through profit-maximizing market activity). Then it is noted that ecology does not fit the category of "private goods and services." So in true Ptolemaic tradition, epicycles are added in the form of "social goods" and "market externalities" to explain the relation between welfare created by production in idealized competitive markets (private goods and services) and welfare lost by environmental destruction (a negative "social good"). As often happens when it is found that affluent powerful private producers and consumers gain while the general public suffers from ecological waste, the problem becomes the politically vacuous one of "external diseconomics."

Next, the efficiency bias is hauled out, with application of a "marginal rate of transformation" between goods production and environmental preservation along "Pareto-optimal frontiers." That is, the traditional theorist assumes that the basic outlines of the economy are immutable and the utility derived from environment-goods is predetermined, and then he proceeds to devise a means for insuring the "socially acceptable tradeoff" between environmental damage and goods production.

At last the problem of social choice is solved through the use of a "social welfare function," which supposedly derives its value from the sum of all individual tradeoffs between goods and ecology. Once defined, the social choice would be presumed to be implemented by impartial government imposition of taxes, subsidies, and federal projects.

This elegant approach typifies the economist's unique combination of what Robert Heilbroner calls "rigor" and "mortis." It simply fails, through its traditional biases, to deal with the essential issues of ecological imbalance, however gracefully it treats the irrelevant and abstract.

ORTHODOX *VS.* RADICAL THEORY

Traditional economics today grows out of the intent of neoclassical theorists to develop and refine a justification of profits to the capitalist class; materialist, efficiency, and governmental biases permit the traditional economist to construct the proper syllogisms for continued defense of the capitalist system. Basic flaws in the generalized theory are buried in the ongoing process of administering, streamlining, and consolidating the economy.

The frequent admission by economists that the traditional theory still leaves some problems "unresolved" belies yet another bias.[2] The notion of "unresolved problems" carries with it the presumption that these issues can be resolved within the framework of traditional theory. In contrast, radical economists regard the "unresolved problems" as chronic ailments of an outdated theory. And as we believe that the "unresolved problems" are the central problems of advanced economies, we look for new definitions and a new theoretical structure.

Our purpose in redefining economic theory goes far beyond usual interests of abstract theorists. The received doctrine of traditional economics permeates all aspects of capitalist societies. Its biases against economic policy prescriptions that run contrary to capitalist interests, even if these policies are the only means of improving the lot of ordinary citizens, work against the greater number of people in any capitalist social system. A careful examination of the definitions and structure of traditional economics reveals the way in which capitalist property relations condition the ordinary citizen to accept his subservient role.

The traditional economists, as we have seen, begin by equating increased production of goods and services with an increase in social welfare. Thus an increase in gross national product becomes the primary goal of national economies. Economists following this line of reasoning, further assume, explicitly or implicitly, that private production of goods and services offers the best means of increasing social welfare. One implication of this line of reasoning is that individuals will, in their roles as consumers and producers, concurrently serve both their interests and the needs of society. Obvious exceptions to this rule, such as a farmer's choice of using either DDT or a more expensive but more selective means of controlling harmful insects, lead economists to a definition of "social goods."

The distinction between "social goods" and "purely private goods" rests on the assumption that capitalist economies in general contribute to social welfare by matching goods and services with individual preferences. The need for "social goods" then becomes a minor flaw which can be corrected by limited government intervention. This form of analysis carries several problems with it.

First, both traditional economists and government policy-makers begin by subsuming a central problem of social policy in their crude definition of "social goods." When and under what conditions can individuals objectively determine the benefits of "social goods?" This is the problem that must be solved before the usual definition of "social goods" will offer much use in an economic analysis.

The problem is to some extent a simple one in the case of individual commodities. For example, the housewife can decide between peaches and strawberries through experimentation using her "consumer sovereignty" at the local supermarket. But other issues, such as economics and ecology, are quite difficult. Trial and error methods for reaching decisions are often too costly (or deadly). Individuals *qua* individuals cannot experiment with our ecological system and see its impact on their welfare, and then change to another. For experience with one ecological system essentially *conditions* the individual to that system. Only when individuals have direct and community *control* over their environment can they develop the perspective necessary to solving ecological problems. This is part of a more general point in radical economics: individual preferences are more determined by the economic system than the economic system is determined by individual preferences.

The submergence of the environment to the needs of capitalist production is so long-standing, especially in the case of ecologically imbalanced "urban communities," that the poor environment itself represents a basic formative influence on individual preferences themselves. And the natural poverty of this environment, by thwarting the individual's development of capacities to relate to nature, leads him or her especially in a situation where he or she has no control over social outcomes to undervalue the ecological system as a "social good." The ecological example dramatizes the need for a full exploration of the *generation* of needs and preferences through the individual's experience in his social activity, rather than taking them as exogenously given social data [24, 25, 25a, 25b, 26a, 36].

It is often held in opposition to the above formulation that the incomplete provisionment of social needs by the state (e.g., decent communities, environment, etc.) merely reflects the "irrationalities" of individual preferences, unrelated to the structure of the economy or the inflexibility of the state toward the demands of its citizens. An inspection of the operation of the economy shows this to be incorrect. We argue that the common day-to-day observation of individuals in capitalist society leads them to rationally seek increases in personal income as a major source of well-being. By destroying work, community, culture, and environment, it renders consumption the only visible means toward personal welfare. Moreover, although capitalism destroys creative work, the best jobs are still associated with the highest income. Similarly, while capitalism generally fragments both environment and community, the best of both are available to those with highest income. Only in an alternative and more natural *institutional* setting can individuals be expected to act for the social good by pursuing their own interests.

But we must go beyond this. An individual's evaluation of the environment as a social good is more than a product of his personal experience with the ecological system.   It is equally influenced by the pattern of socialization he has been exposed to.   A central axiom of the capitalist belief system is that increase in the volume of individual consumption is the overwhelmingly important axis along which one must travel in increasing individual well-being, and this belief colors the individual's assessment of ecology.   This system of belief (mirrored, of course, in the "materialist bias" of traditional welfare economics) whether correct or not, is of central functional importance in insuring ideological allegiance to an economic system whose institutions are geared almost exclusively to maximizing commodity production.   The relationship between economic belief systems and economic institutions are basic to the individual's understanding of his own economy and its crucial issues, and can best be compared through study of cross-cultural and anthropological research.

The usual analysis of economy and ecology exhibits, as mentioned earlier, a "government bias" through its simple-minded introduction of a "social welfare function" to aggregate individual preferences.   By assuming that various social classes have essentially common interests concerning the environmental problem, and that the government is the impartial arbiter among whatever conflicts arise, it takes for granted what should be one of the central areas of concern for economists. Indeed, the vulnerability of this assumption is evident in the ecological example.   If a decent environment should require basic alteration in economic institutions,[3] how likely is a government dedicated to their preservation to inform the public or take the necessary steps?

Ecological destruction is a result of profit-maximizing by capitalists and their managerial executors, and yet this social class that "gains" from ecological destruction is both the most able to avoid its effects, through access to exclusive "pollution-free" communities and vacations, and the most powerful in influencing government policy.   What then is the nature of the "social welfare function" that results from this political and economic configuration?   This is the real question.   To take "social welfare" as given and exogenous is shocking and absurd.

Government bias is evident again in the traditional view that the political system can alter the outcomes of economic activity at will, virtually independent of the structure of economic institutions.   Hence, there is an absence of concern about the influence of institutionalized, economic decision-making mechanisms on the range of political correctives that the decision-makers (who fill roles defined by existing institutions) deem feasible and admissible.   Yet all evidence indicates that the basic outlines of the economy, when looking at either income equality, technology, the subjective value of work-activities and social community, or environment, are internally conditioned by the existing decision mechanism and embodied in the configuration of economic institutions themselves. When our economic, legal, and social institutions sanction and protect the rights of landowners, capitalists, and other profit-maximizers who control and direct technology and resource use, and thus allow these interests to make economic decisions with important effects on our environment, what chance do workers and revolutionary youth have to alter potentially destructive economic decisions by working within the system? Traditional economics, which has consistently questioned the efficacy of government intervention in setting minimum wage legislation or rent-control against the natural operation of the "market mechanism," seems peculiarly myopic concerning the role of government in establishing social control over environment, income distribution, technology, and other areas of basic social concerns.

Other politicoeconomic issues basic to an understanding of our political economy are also avoided in traditional economic theory. For example, the belief system forging allegiance to capitalist institutions identifies increasing social welfare with raising the volume of goods production. Yet ecological balance, for instance, requires a significant decrease in the rate of growth of personal disposable incomes[4] — indeed, an acceptable solution may require a *negative* rate of growth over a significant period. What would be the effect on social ideology and political affiliation of the widespread realization that the basic economic goal of society — increase in per capita consumption — was no longer available? Americans may have always suspected that their lives, their jobs, and their communities are not "good," but any misgivings have previously been assuaged by the image of progress and the rosy future. Ecological balance requires that advanced economies reject the reliance on future growth as a means of solving present problems. How well our economic institutions stand up to the harsh and nonillusory evaluations of the present is a crucial issue in our present historical age.

What are the implications of enforced ecological balance to business profits and expectations, possible stagnation, and unemployment? When Keynes wrote *The General Theory*, it was taken for granted that the problem to be solved in capitalist economies was that of stagnation, but since the growth of the huge defense-military establishment in the United States, this issue has given way to the more amenable one of business cycle control. Yet the specter of stagnation will rear its head whenever significant restraint is placed on the growth of corporate output, and such restraint is at the heart of environmental cures. Stagnation and the manifold ways in which the capitalist economy has succeeded in artificially avoiding it — through military production, advertising, style change, enforced obsolescence, and attaching social status to conspicuous consumption – have been consistently overlooked by advocates of traditional economic theory, yet it is central to assessing environmental control.

These shortcomings in traditional theory reappear in the treatment of all major economic issues. Efficiency-bias leads traditional economists to discuss income distribution as the outcome of rational decisions in the economic sphere resulting from the efficient allocation of factors of production, rather than the class demarcation of capitalists and state bureaucrats over the social (i.e., hierarchical) relations of the enterprise. The government-bias implies, in a somewhat contradictory manner, that this distribution can be altered at will to conform to the metaphysical "social welfare function." In price theory, economists assume that the existing means of commodity production and work patterning have no influence on individual preference for commodities and work activities, in spite of all the evidence of the interaction between the economy and the structure of individual preferences [20, 23]. Hence, in an age characterized by alienation and anomie, where individual development is more important than the efficient allocation of goods and services, and where the conduciveness of the economic system to promoting individual development is one of the most crucial issues, the economist provides little insight into the relationship between the citizen's own character and the requisites of the economic system.

Similarly, in analyzing the organization of production, traditional economics includes numerous illustrations and analyses of output maximization and cost minimization techniques. But the truly topical issues – hierarchy and bureaucracy in the organization of work and the growth of technological processes serving the dictates of the minimization of accounting costs – are relegated to the realm of idle speculation.

THE INTENTIONS OF RADICAL ECONOMISTS

Our approach is radical in our intent to seek out root causes and deeper issues. We center on the *basic institutions* of capitalism and their general effect on social organization; on the *nature of social and individual welfare* in the most general sense; on the nature of *social class* and its relation to power and to the structure of production; and on the process of *social change* in relation to technology and political consciousness in the course of historical development.

We regard individual well-being as being dependent on the availabilities of social objects. These social objects include not only the private and public goods and services, which are the components of the traditional definition of individual welfare, but also the environment, community, and work activities. The form of the dependency is determined by the individual's personality and preference structure. In fact, if welfare depends on the active capacity to relate to others, the natural world, and oneself, then commodities are merely the *tools* that make possible one's relations with the larger world. Their usefulness depends on the integrity of the social community that imposes the context of his social activity and interpersonal interaction [48, 27], the ecological environment that imposes the content of his relations with the natural and physical world around him, and the work activities that provide (or fail to provide) opportunities for individual creativity and autonomy, substantive relations with fellow workers, and socially useful production [40, 16, 34, 15]. In fact, the individual's personality and preferences are themselves shaped by the characteristics he needs to fill roles in the economic system and are further affected by experiences in performing economic functions. And yet both personality and preferences are prime determinants of the amount of satisfaction and "utility" derived from social objects as mentioned above [15, 24, 20]. Welfare economics must evaluate preference structures, rather than take them as given, and study their genesis as products of economic institutions.

The next step logically involves relating the normal operation of capitalist[5] institutions to the qualities and availabilities of the various components of individual welfare. Beginning with a description of basic economic institutions — free markets in labor, land, and capital; capitalist control of productive activities; incomes derived from the returns of the market-owned factors of production; and the belief-system according to which alternative work-activities are valued according to status, authority, and income, rather than their intrinsic value to the individual's creative self-development [10], we intend to determine whether or not these basic institutions work against the welfare of the majority of citizens.

Economic institutions determine the course of social development. If this development is not conducive to furthering human welfare, alternatives should be considered, and a discussion of their effect on social welfare is in order. The autonomous power of economic institutions to make decisions[6] over commodity production is well known: markets in labor, land, and capital insure that individuals, as well as natural and physical resources, are allocated to their "optimal" use in maximizing output, through the determination of individual incomes by the market returns to privately owned factors of production; capitalist control of productive activities plus profit-maximization implies that the determination of work-activities, the development and use of new technologies, the utilization of resources, as well as the composition and qualities of products, conform to maximally efficient production.

The system of capitalist beliefs about work-activities insures that the staffing of occupational roles will result in a hierarchy fostered by salary differentials without regard for differences in intrinsic value of these roles [17].

The thrust of our new interests, however, is the extension of the analysis of institutions from the usual study of their effect on commodity production to a more meaningful study of their influence on other factors affecting social welfare. First, the present distribution of income (as essentially determined by decisions made within present economic institutions on the basis of allocational efficiency and the maintenance of bureaucratic order in production, and perpetuated by the weakness of the state in altering this initial distribution [35]) must be related to the inherent dislocative effect of income distribution on factor markets — the so-called "dis-incentive effect" applied to the supply of capital and labor. This effect not only delimits the basic decision-making power of economic institutions themselves; it also reveals the relatively weak corrective power of political decision-making units.

The question of income distribution leads naturally to reconsideration of the role of economic institutions in regulating the characteristics of work-activities. The "dis-incentive effect" of political manipulation of the income distribution depends on work's universal subjective disutility in capitalist society. To supply their labor, workers are not motivated by work as a *process* within which a third of their lives are spent, by its contribution to their development as individuals, or by its position as an outlet for creativity and individuality. Nor are they motivated by the *goal* of work-activities — the product as the embodiment of the worker's individuality or his contribution to socially useful production. Rather, worker motivation is secured nearly exclusively by *external reward,* in the form of money, status, power, or security.

Traditional economics takes the disutility of work as a universal fact and certainly not something to be "explained" or "analyzed." In addition, the structure of work-activities are taken as technologically unalterable facts, rather than outcomes of decisions made by a particular set of economic institutions. This aspect of "efficiency-bias" is typified by the treatment of technology itself as an exogenous variable determined by the "physical nature of the universe," a variable of which society can choose "more" or "less," but over whose internal characteristics it has virtually no control. In the same breath, the requisites of technology are taken as a basic limiting condition on the creation of human work-activities in a decent society.

An unbiased examination of work and technology begins with facts rather than metaphysics, and first asks how basic economic institutions affect the structure of work-activities at a point in time, and the course of development of these activities over time. The basic institution affecting this development is profit maximization on the firm level, according to which the criterion for determination of work-roles is profit-maximization. The worker's alienation from his work-activities derives directly from the fact that human development is simply not among the criteria according to which these activities are socially determined [13, 34, 20, 40]. In a similar manner the course of development and utilization of technologies is based not on immutable laws, but on the control of productive resources by capitalists who base their determinations on the goal of profit and the maintenance of hierarchy. Clearly, the development of a human technology, a technology emphasizing worker creativity, decentralization, worker control, and allowing for worker autonomy and cooperation in the determination of aesthetic and utility attributes of goods and services, requires a different set of economic institutions. In this respect, the similarity of work-activities and technologies in the capitalist and state-socialist countries can be explained not by the immutable nature of technology, but by the fact of their common *authoritarian control,* and use of *efficiency criteria* to structure the production process.

But analyses of work-activity must pass from broad generalities to its most defining characteristics in advanced industrial societies — bureaucratic organization and hierarchical control [19, 54, 18, 25]. In the development of productive activity, new technologies will be introduced only if they are *compatible with hierarchical control,* since those who determine the introduction of new technologies are also those who benefit from hierarchy itself. Thus hierarchy and fractionalization of labor come to be seen incorrectly as attributes of "technology" proper, rather than of the institutional forms which govern its development [24, 12], and the alienation of work takes the aura of universal necessity.

The effect of economic institutions on the quantity of goods and services, inequality, and alienation of work-activities must be followed by their effect on the remaining basic welfare ingredients: community and environment. In treating ecology we note that markets in land and natural resources, together with the determination of their use on the basis of profit-maximization, insures that our natural physical world is treated merely as an input into commodity production. This form of analysis implicitly excludes the natural environment from its integral role as the setting of individual and social activity, and as a basic ingredient of welfare in its own right. The maintenance of technology and production in line with ecological needs presupposes a community that is aware, cohesive, and capable of exercising control over purely private interests. In essence, the operation of a market in land and profit-maximization in determining land-use insures that the architectonic unity of the physical community will be sacrificed to maximum output[7] (although here the effects of externalities in reducing efficiency must be given special attention), and the lack of community control of essential economic decisions deprives the community of a central tool in the forging of communal solidarity and synthesizing the bonds that are the basis of positive social interaction among individuals. Again, the operation of our capitalist institutions can be best dramatized by comparison with so-called primitive economies [9, 31], with emphasis on the idea that postindustrial society is not envisioned to be a copy of primitive organization.

The "paradigmatic shift" in this approach is quite evident: we overcome the "materialist-bias" by broadening our analysis of social welfare, and we correct the material and "efficiency-biases" by showing the effects of economic institutions on the nonmaterial components of social welfare. We see that through the normal operation of these institutions, the central ingredients of social welfare — equality, work, community, and environment — are subordinated to individual commodity production and even here, quality is sacrificed to quantity [49, 30, 24].

The final element in our welfare model is the individual preference structure itself, and the next step in our theory is the determination of the relation between individual preferences and economic institutions. Traditional economic theory takes preferences as given, and minimizes the fact that different preference structures — and the personalities and characters that underlie them — offer differential potentialities for deriving welfare from social objects, be they in the form of commodities, work and community relations, or aspects of the natural environment. Yet those of us who are not blinded by the materialist bias recognize that an individual's welfare depends on the level of personal development, as exemplified by his physical, cognitive, affective, aesthetic, and spiritual capacities to undertake human activity, and are codified in the "preference structure" that economists naively take as given and exogenous.

The link between economic institutions and individual personality is discovered in the sociology of role-performance. Given the "slots" that must be filled by individuals in their capacities as workers, consumers, and community members, the patterns of individual development compatible with the staffing of these roles are delineated [51]. Basic differences in personality organization and their relation to different economic systems are illustrated by anthropological and historical writers, but must be examined in detail for each of the separate areas of social life. Thus concerning personality and work-activities, the existence of bureaucracy and hierarchy, the essence of alienated production, makes strong demands on the personalities of workers [19, 40, 59, 15, 34] and the corresponding traits are incorporated in the individual through the socialization instruments of education and media [50, 33, 25]. The essence of this process of socialization is not the development of cognitive traits [22], but the muffling of creativity, initiative, and individuality in favor of the ability to be motivated by external reward in the form of grades and curriculum tracks, in preparation for his future motivation in the form of income and status as a worker [32, 37, 61].

In short, a set of economic institutions must be judged not only on the basis of the amount of commodities produced, or even on the community, work, and physical environments it engenders, but on the types of individuals it produces, the paths of individual development to which it is conducive, and the degree and extent to which its associated roles permit true human and personal liberation.

To this point, we have treated the economic system as functioning, and potentially capable of functioning, without intervention from the political system. This assumption is of course false, and a major contribution of radical economics to an understanding of basic issues takes the form of a description and analysis of state activities. Descriptions of the usual technical operation of fiscal control and stabilization, generation of certain "social goods," and correction of income makes a good starting point. Following this, our new analysis must be capable of assessing the *power* of state intervention in producing "socially ·desirable" outcomes in the economic sphere. Our previous close scrutiny of the operation of economic institutions and their determination of major economic variables — whether in the area of income distribution, development of work-activities and technologies, use of environmental resources, or what have you — facilitate what we consider the correct conclusion: save in the area of Keynesian fiscal and monetary policy, the power of the state apparatus to significantly affect outcomes is severely delimited by the degree of control the state exercises over economic institutions. Since extensive state intervention tends to undermine the effective functional operation of these institutions, the state is reduced to the ineffective manipulation of the *manifestations* of their normal operation (or misoperation), giving a false and temporary feeling of security to those adversely affected.

Analyses of the areas of state intervention and its power to produce desirable outcomes must be followed by analysis of the criteria which in fact govern the direction of its intervention in the economic sphere. We noted earlier the usual assumption in traditional economics exhibits an extreme "government-bias" in its implicit, naive premise that the state operates neutrally in the service of all social groups, and the adjudication of conflicts among social groups.

We begin our consideration of the political system with an analysis of class structure. Social stratification begins with the hierarchical stratification of authority in bureaucratic productive organizations. By conditioning individuals for roles on particular levels of productive processes and reinforcing this pattern of socialization through experience in day-by-day work [59, 6], bureaucracies create distinct class cultures [60] whose members view their social interests as being different and hence conflicting [3, 5, 42, 45]. Moreover, different social classes have differential power in influencing the direction of government activity [11, 1, 57, 18], with highest-level groups possessing essential control in the political sphere, through lobby groups, financing political elections, and through the power of the corporate enterprises they control (e.g., the operation of the military-industrial complex). While the nature of the conflict of interests among social classes is exceedingly complex, the basic division places capitalists and those who obtain their social position by supporting their economic interests (corporate managers, politicians, and some professionals), on the one hand, and workers, consumers, and general citizens on the other [12].

In analyzing the theory of state operation in economic affairs, the radical theorist must be careful to avoid a crude "ruling-class" theory. First, the political arena is often a battleground for conflicting interests among capitalists themselves, and in certain areas, members of the white and blue-collar working class find their interests coinciding with sections among the economically powerful. Second, the basic function of the state vis-à-vis the economic system is simply the preservation of the economic institutions that, through their normal operation, confer differential benefit upon the upper levels in the occupational hierarchy. These interests exercise their power basically by stopping any state intervention which interferes with these institutions (e.g., through veto-power over wage-legislation, ecological preservation measures, progressive taxation, community control over economic resources). The use of state power to direct additional benefits toward these social classes (e.g., through defense expenditure, the use of the military to protect corporate profits abroad, the state financing of educational institutions with differential access to members of different social classes, and the control of regulatory agencies by the industries they are supposed to regulate), while important, play a secondary role.

The supreme issue for the future of America, as for all advanced industrial societies, is the creation of economic institutions treating fruitfully and positively, and with proper emphasis, the ingredients of social welfare: equality, community, unalienated work-activities and technologies, and ecological balance. While our approach furnishes critical tools for evaluating our present institutions and the goals for the future, it falls short on several points.

First, it fails at present to present a viable set of *alternative* institutions. This shortcoming is in part due to our understanding of what such institutions are and should be,[8] although many of us agree that they involve decentralization of production and community life, of community and worker control over the structure of our economic life, and the development of technologies that allow for the replacement of hierarchy and bureaucracy by democracy and creative work outlets where possible, and through equal sharing of undesirable work where it is not. Some treatnent of this issue is possible through an analysis of alternative economic systems (primitive, archaic, feudal, modern socialist, Chinese, Cuban, the Israeli Kibbutz, etc.), but a great deal remains for future research.

Second, it fails to analyze the process of social change itself. The analysis of *social evolution* has of course been outlined in the description of the normal operation of economic institutions [52, 39, 25]. But social change also has a significant *disequilibrium component* [25, 42, 12, 41] wherein changes in class consciousness result in the appearance of important strains and contradictions in the working-out of technological and social development. The source and nature of these contradictions in American society should be the basis of future analysis and theoretical inquiry.

CONCLUSION

Early in his career Karl Marx passed judgment on the dismal science of economics as it appeared through the filter of youthful exuberance and infinite expectation for social progress. His words: "The fact that the growth of needs and of the means of satisfying them results in a lack of needs and of means is demonstrated in several ways by the economist . . . Political economy, the science of wealth, is therefore, at the same time the science of renunciation, of privation and of saving, which actually succeeds in depriving man of fresh air and of physical activity. This science of marvelous industry is at the same time the science of asceticism. Its true ideal is the ascetic but productive slave, and the ascetic but usurious miser . . . Thus, despite its worldly and pleasure-seeking appearance, it is a truly moral science, the most moral of all sciences. Its principle thesis is the renunciation of life and of human needs . . . the less you think, love, theorize, sing, paint, fence, etc., the more you will be able to save and the greater will become your treasure which neither moth nor rust will corrupt — your capital. The less you are, the less you express your life, the more you have, the greater is your alienated being. Everything which the economist takes from you in the way of life and humanity, he restores to you in the form of money and wealth, and everything you are unable to do your money can do for you . . . It can acquire learning, art, historical treasures, political power . . . It can appropriate all these things for you, can purchase everything; it is the true *opulence*. But although it can do all these things, it desires only to create itself, and to buy itself, for everything else is subservient to it . . . Thus all passions and activities must be submerged in avarice." Let us hope that our children and the intellectual scions of the coming generation do not find cause to pass similar judgement upon our imminent political choices.

ENDNOTES

[1] Here we are talking about welfare theory. The theory of the firm will correctly ignore the impact of the decision of any actor on the environment since it is not part of the profit maximizing function. The function of welfare economics, however, is to determine the impact of any decision on individual and social welfare and for this an ecological criterion must be included.

[2] "Thus, I shall hardly be surprised if we conclude that some problems of the 70s are nothing other than a continuation of problems already with us. To include those in our research interests it is really only necessary to decide that they are not likely to be solved quickly. . . . one hardly need much insight to suspect that all of these problems will be of concern to us for at least one more decade or so!" John R. Meyer, in President's introduction to the fiftieth annual report, September 1970, of the National Bureau of Economic Research, Inc.

[3] Many noted environmentalists have asserted that a basic alteration of values is the only solution to the ecological problem. But these values are those generated by economic institutions and are necessary for their survival. The requisite "value reorientation" therefore implies a drastic change in our economic institutions.

[4] This assumes again, as many environmentalists have stated, that anti-pollution techniques cannot solve the problem, but rather change in our acquisitive values is needed.

[5] To the many critics of the left who feel that the evidence from Eastern Europe and the Soviet Union destroys the radical argument for socialism, we reply that we apply the same criteria to judge any system. Eastern Europe and the Soviet Union fare little better than American capitalism. However, rather than evidence of the failure of socialism, this is a consequence of the inability of those nations to confront and eliminate their materialist and efficiency biases. Rather than "communist" they should be called *"state capitalist."* This is not true of Cuba and China where confrontation with these biases has continued and progressed further than in other countries.

[6] Economic institutions don't make decisions: economic actors do. This means that the choices open to actors are so constrained by the institutional framework that the decisions must lead to the noted results.

[7] Editor's Note: For example, Jim Montgomery reports in the May 4, 1971, issue of the *Wall Street Journal* ("The Peasant Traditions of Puerto Rico Become Issue for Copper Shareholders") that the plans of Kennecott and American

Metal Climax, both large multinational firms, for development of the interior hill country of Puerto Rico threatens the traditional culture of 80,000 (impoverished!) peasants. Montgomery quotes Episcopal Bishop Reus's characterization of the hill people: "Very simple, very moral . . . very old-fashioned, very trusting — and very vulnerable."

"They are the ones who end up in the slums of San Juan and New York. It takes them a long time to adjust to a new way of life." Montgomery's analysis continues: "Bishop Reus proposed a resolution for the Kennecott and American Metal Climax annual meetings designed to stall the project or block it completely. The companies barred the resolution from the proxy statements and meeting agendas, and the (United States) Securities and Exchange Commission upheld their decision."

According to Montgomery, the companies did agree to hold votes on proposals forwarded by Rt. Rev. John E. Hines, Presiding Bishop of the United States Protestant Episcopal Church, which would call for measures to guard against "ecological damage." And "shareholders at the meetings will vote on these proposals."

[8] The dearth of research on alternate economic institutions even in the abstract is another result of the government bias. The failure to connect most social problems to the economic institutions and, where made, the belief in the corrective apparatus of the state, lead to a failure to consider systemic change as even a possible solution. We, of course, say it is the only solution. Research needed is not only on the form of the new system but on the costs of transformation which most economists implicitly assume are too high to allow consideration of radical change as a serious alternative.

REFERENCES

[1] Bachrach, Peter, *The Theory of Democratic Elitism.* Little, Brown, 1967.

[2] Baran, Paul, and Paul Sweezy. *Monopoly Capital.* Monthly Review Press, 1966.

[3] Bendix, Reinhard, and Seymour Martin Lipset. *Class, Status, and Power.* Free Press, 1966.

[4] Bloch, Marc. *Feudal Society.* Routledge, 1961.

[5] Bottomore, T. B. *Classes in Modern Society.* Vintage, 1966.

[6] Breer, Paul, and Edwin Locke. *Task Experience as a Source of Attitudes.* Dorsey Press, 1965.

[7] Dahl, Robert. *Who Governs?* Free Press, 1961.

[8] Dahl, Robert, and Charles Lindblom. *Politics, Economics, and Welfare.* Harper & Row, 1963.

[9] Dalton, George, ed. *Primitive, Archaic, and Modern Economies: Essays of Karl Polanyi.* Doubleday, 1968.

[10] Dobb, Maurice. *Studies in the Development of Capitalism.* International Publishers, 1963.

[11] Domhoff, G. William. *Who Rules America?* Prentice-Hall, 1967.

[12] Edwards, Richard, Arthur MacEwan, and the staff of Social Sciences 125 "A Radical Approach to Economics: Basis for a New Curriculum." *American Economic Review,* May 1970.

[13] Ellul, Jacques. *The Technological Society.* Vintage, 1967.

[14] Engels, Friedrich. *Condition of the Working Class in England in 1844.* Merit Press, 1968.

[15] Fromm, Erich. "Individual and Social Origins of Neuroses." *American Sociological Review,* June 1944.

[16] ―――. *Marx's Concept of Man.* Ungar, 1966.

[17] Fullerton, Kemper. "Calvinism and Capitalism: An Explanation of the Weber Thesis," in Robert W. Green, ed., *Protestantism and Capitalism.* Heath & Co., 1959.

[18] Galbraith, John Kenneth. *The New Industrial State.* Signet, 1967.

[19] Gerth, Hans, and C. W. Mills. *Max Weber: Essays in Sociology.* Free Press, 1958.

[20] Gintis, Herbert. *Alienation and Power: Towards a Radical Welfare Economics.* Unpublished Ph.D. dissertation, Harvard University, 1969.

[21] ―――. "American Keynesianism and the War Machine," in David Mermelstein, ed., *Economics: Mainstream Readings and Radical Critiques.* Random House, 1970.

[22] ―――. "Education and the Characteristics of Worker Productivity." *American Economic Review,* May 1971.

[23] ―――. "Commodity Fetishism and Irrational Production." *Union for Radical Political Economics Proceedings,* 1970.

[24] ―――. "Neo-Classical Welfare Economics and Individual Development." Union for Radical Political Economics occasional paper, 1970.

[25] ―――. "New Working Class and Revolutionary Youth." Harvard Institute for Economic Research occasional paper, 1970.

[25a] ―――. "Welfare Theory and the Economics of Education," forthcoming.

[25b] ―――. "Towards a Theory of Economic Sovereignty." *American Economic Review,* May 1972.

[26] Goodman, Paul. *Growing up Absurd.* Vintage, 1960.

[26a] Andre Gorz. *Strategy for Labor.* Beacon Press, 1966.

[27] de Grazia, Sebastian. *The Political Community: A Study in Anomie.* University of Chicago Press, 1948.

[28] Harrington, Michael. *The Other America.* Penguin, 1963.

[29] Heilbroner, Robert L. *The Making of Economic Society.* Prentice-Hall, 1962.

[30] Henry, Jules. *Culture Against Man.* Random House, 1963.

[31] Herskovitz, Melville. *Economic Anthropology.* Norton & Co., 1965.

[32] Holt, John. *How Children Fail.* Pitman, 1964.

[33] Inkeles, Alex. "The Socialization of Competence." *Harvard Educational Review,* June 1966.

[34] Keniston, Kenneth. *The Uncommitted.* Dell, 1960.

[35] Kolko, Gabriel. *Wealth and Power in America.* Praeger, 1962.

[36] Lichtman, Richard. "Capitalism and Consumption." *Socialist Revolution,* May–June 1970.

[37] Leonard, George. *Education and Ecstasy.* Delacorte Press, 1969.

[38] MacEwan, Arthur and Thomas Weisskopf. *Perspectives on the Economic Problem*. Prentice-Hall, 1970.

[39] Marx, Karl. *Contribution to a Critique of Political Economy*, Kerr, 1911.

[40] ———. *Economic and Philosophical Manuscripts of 1844*, International Publishers, 1964.

[41] ———. "The So-Called Primitive Accumulation of Capital," in *Capital*, Vol. 1, Part 8, International Publishers, 1967.

[42] Marx, Karl, and Friedrich Engels. *The Communist Manifesto*. International Publishers, 1948.

[43] Mermelstein, David, ed. *Economics: Mainstream Readings and Radical Critiques*. Random House, 1970.

[44] Miller, Herman. *Rich Man, Poor Man*. Signet, 1964.

[45] Mills, C. Wright. *The Power Elite*. Oxford University Press, 1966.

[46] Mitchell Juliet. "Women: The Longest Revolution." New England Free Press pamphlet, 1968.

[47] Myint, Hla. *The Economics of Underdeveloped Countries*. Praeger, 1965.

[48] Nisbet, Robert. *Community and Power*. Oxford University Press, 1953.

[49] Packard, Vance. *The Waste Makers*. MacKay, 1960.

[50] Parsons, Talcott. "The School Class as a Social System: Some of its Functions in American Society." *Harvard Educational Review*, Fall 1959.

[51] ———. *The Social System*. Free Press, 1951.

[52] ———. *Societies in Evolutionary and Comparative Perspective*. Prentice-Hall, 1966.

[53] Polanyi, Karl. . *The Great Transformation*. Beacon Press, 1957.

[54] Presthus, Robert. *The Organizational Society*. Vintage, 1966.

[55] Rose, Arnold M. *The Power Structure*. Oxford University Press, 1967.

[56] Ross, A. M., and Herbert Hill, eds. *Employment, Race, and Poverty*. Harcourt Brace & World, 1967.

[57] Sweezy, Paul M. *The Theory of Capitalist Development*. Monthly Review Press, 1968.

[58] Union for Radical Political Economics, 2503 Student Activities Building, University of Michigan, Ann Arbor, Michigan 48104.

[59] Venable, Vernon. *Human Nature: The Marxist View*. World, 1966.

[60] Warner, W. Lloyd, and Paul S. Lunt. *The Social Life of a Modern Community*. Yale University Press, 1950.

[61] Weaver, James H. "Student as Worker," in James H. Weaver and Gary R. Weaver, eds., *University and Revolution*. Prentice-Hall, 1969.

[62] Zeitlin, Maurice. *American Society, Inc.* Markham, 1970.

John G. Gurley was born in Alameda, California and received his B.A. and Ph.D. degrees from Stanford University. He is best known for Money in a Theory of Finance *(with E. S. Shaw). He served as editor of the* American Economic Review *during the 1960s and is currently Professor of Economics at Stanford University. He is doing research on Maoist economic development.*

3 The State of Political Economics

John G. Gurley

This book is intended as a survey of the present state of economics. Accordingly, it contains chapters on the methods and theories of economics, including basic micro and macro theory, and on many of its applied fields, such as public finance, international trade, and agricultural economics. If one accepts the authors' own conceptions of what economics is all about, there are few grounds for serious complaint — although I can imagine a loud one from Milton Friedman to Gardner Ackley for his discussion of inflation without one — not one! — mention of the money supply. Even allowing for such grievances, the survey, for what it set out to do, is still admirable, as one would expect from such a distinguished group of theorists.

But what is and what is not surveyed is something else again. The volume appears at a time when the assumptions and methods of economics are being challenged, almost as never before, by a growing

A review of Nancy D. Ruggles, editor, *Economics*, Englewood Cliffs, N.J., 1970. For helping me to improve this paper, I am indebted to Samuel Bowles and Tibor Scitovsky.

number of our younger economists, and indeed by many older ones, too. Some of the attacks have reflected dissatisfaction with the many trivial problems that economists seem to spend so much of their time on. Still others have questioned the economic goals so widely-accepted by economists, especially that of ever-increasing GNP, and a few have examined this issue within the wider framework of ecological systems. Many of the attacks on present-day economics have taken the form of radical analyses of U.S. imperialism — of how the United States profits from its leading role in the hierarchical structure of rich and poor countries that make up the international capitalist system. Other radical analyses have examined how certain groups in the United States itself profit from the maintenance of a hierarchical class structure which produces both wealth and poverty, both privilege and oppression. These analyses, which generally conclude that capitalism is largely responsible for such social and economic disparities, accordingly deny that capitalist society is able (i.e., willing) to solve these problems. All of these studies may be said to deal with various aspects of wealth and poverty — that is with the broad social, economic, and political determinants of income and wealth distribution — both domestically and internationally. All of them strike at the very heart of conventional economics, and many of them come from young economists associated with the Union for Radical Political Economics.

The authors of this survey have disregarded all of this literature of dissent and of challenge to the basic tenets of present-day economics. As a result, an innocent reader of this survey would never know of the deep rethinking that is now going on by many members of our profession. In fact, he would gain quite the opposite impression from his reading — namely, that all is well with economics; that there is almost unanimous agreement on the fundamentals of the discipline; that economists are superbly prepared to solve what these authors call — incredible as it may seem — "newly-emerging problems" like poverty and "hot subjects" like urban decay. The dominant tone of the survey is one of great self-satisfaction and self-confidence.

I write this review to say that such a tone is unwarranted.

I.

The conventional economics surveyed in this volume is rich in many ways, as one author after another so ably demonstrates. But conventional economics does have serious deficiencies, the most important being its distorted conception of the world we live in. This point has recently been developed by Paul Sweezy in the following way:

Orthodox economics takes the existing social system for granted, much as though it were part of the natural order of things. Within this framework it searches for harmonies of interest among individuals, groups, classes, and nations; it investigates tendencies toward equilibrium; and it assumes that change is gradual and nondisruptive. . . . [But] the world we live in is not one of harmonies of interest, tendencies to equilibrium, and gradual change. Rather, it is a world dominated by conflicts of interest, tendencies to disequilibrium, and recurring breaks in the continuity of development. A would-be science which starts with a false or irrelevant conception of reality cannot yield very significant results, no matter how refined and sophisticated its methods may be. The answers a scientist gets depend, first and foremost, not on the methods he uses, but on the questions he asks. . . . [Orthodox economics] has concerned itself with smaller and decreasingly significant questions, even judging magnitude and significance by its own standards. To compensate for this trivialization of content, it has paid increasing attention to elaborating and refining its techniques. The consequence is that today we often find a truly stupefying gap between the questions posed and the techniques employed to answer them.[1]

This statement describes, with a high degree of accuracy, what is and what is not in this book. The existing social system is taken for granted by every author of the survey. There is barely a mention of socialism, for example, as an alternative system. Indeed, Harberger is so oblivious to its presence that he can write of "a virtually worldwide capital market" which, in fact, excludes at least a third of the people of the world living in socialist systems. And one would never know from this book that society has a history — that industrial capitalism, its institutions, and its values have evolved from earlier societies and are now in the process of further change — for this book is about as unhistorical as it is possible to be. Furthermore, the book is long on techniques — on micro- and macrotechniques, econometrics, simulation, survey research, operations research, linear programming; and there is obsessive attention throughout to problems of data availability. Moreover, the book is short on social relevance, precisely because its ruling paradigm — its conception of the world — excludes power, conflict, and disruptive change within a historical setting — this is, because it excludes a large part of reality.

Political economics, as distinguished from this book's conventional economics, studies economic problems by systematically taking into account, in a historical context, the pervasiveness of ruler-subject relations in society. "The realm of the political," as political scientist Robert Tucker has written, "[is] the realm of power and authority relations among people. Such relations between man as ruler and man as subject occur not alone through the medium of the state — they occur in virtually every other form of society as well, starting with the family. All established human groups and institutions," Tucker goes on to say, "have their inner structure of authority, their pattern of ruler-subject relations. If they stand outside the institutional structure of the state, they are not on that account nongovernmental. Rather, they belong to the sphere of private, as distinguished from public government. Government itself, in the elementary sense of rulership of man over man, is pervasive in human society."[2]

I will add that it is these pervasive relations of domination and servitude, these relations of power and authority that lead to conflict, disharmony, and disruptive change. A political economist sees these power structures and puts them at the forefront of his analysis; a conventional economist — who sees only a society of free, self-interested economic men interacting as equals in the marketplace — does not.

To extend the discussion of these differences, the conventional economist, because he sees harmonies of interest almost everywhere, can visualize himself as a neutral technician, applying his techniques as objectively as possible. If class or group conflicts do not exist, one can, of course, work for the "general interest." The political economist turned radical, on the other hand, not only studies economic problems within the historical context of ruler-subject relations, but he actively takes the side of the poor and the powerless, and he generally sees the system of capitalism as their oppressor.[3] He believes, therefore, that the conventional economist not only fails to take account of relations of power and authority, and so fails to grasp the most socially relevant aspects of the problem, but, by being so blind to class interests and so caught up in his data and his techniques, he in effect supports a system that maltreats large numbers of people.[4]

II.

These observations apply with full force, I believe, to Hollis Chenery's chapter on economic development. In these pages, there are no power relations of domination and servitude, no basic conflicts between countries or within countries, no social disharmonies — only some technical difficulties. The heavy emphasis, therefore, is on research techniques to overcome the technical difficulties — on input-output analysis, cost-benefit studies, linear programming models with shadow prices — and on the availability of data to feed these techniques. In Chenery's world, and Harberger's too, international society consists of free, self-interested nations, some rich and some poor, each with a more or less socially homogeneous population, interacting as equals on international markets.

Now Chenery's paradigm omits enough of reality to make it likely that he would overlook some important questions about economic development. What his model permits him to see are narrow economic barriers to the development of poor countries — inadequate savings, inappropriate relative prices, shortages of entrepreneurs, imbalances between this and that, and so on. These are, without question, important. But what he cannot see are factors of at least equal importance — the social, political, and broader economic barriers to development that arise out of class conflicts of interest. Thus, he does not discuss whether economic development is even possible, given the social and political requirements of the domestic oligarchies and the financial interests of the foreign investors (indeed, foreign investors are not discussed at all). Who gains from economic development, and who loses? And which groups have the power to make the decisions? These are questions of political economics, questions of power, class conflicts, and resistances to change. Chenery does not ask them because he sees only harmonies of interest; everyone is working for development, the rich and the poor together, and everyone stands to gain.

But this is often not true. A thoroughgoing development program that reaches deeply into all the stagnant backwaters of society is clearly in the interest of the poor in underdeveloped countries, but it is not necessarily the top priority of those who rule them, nor of the foreign corporations engaged in exploiting their resources. The overriding goal of the ruling oligarchies is usually to maintain, and if possible to enhance, their privileged positions of wealth and power in the economic, political, and social life of the country. The principal requirement of the foreign corporations is for a stable and highly favorable environment for their investment and trading activities.

A broadly based and deeply penetrating development effort is a serious threat to both of these priorities, for such an effort often demands nothing less than a social revolution. Landlords may lose power and with it the ability not only to exploit peasants economically but to oppress them politically and socially. Peasants and workers may have to be educated, awakened, and organized to fulfill the tasks of a serious development effort, and this awakening may prove subversive in the end to the ruling class's privileged positions. In many of these countries there is already organized armed resistance by the poor to their governments, which could be greatly strengthened by the newly released energy of a general shakeup of the society. Consequently, it is not surprising that there are often strong alliances between the domestic oligarchies and the foreign corporations for the promotion of stable environments, for this serves the priorities of both groups. If economic development is encouraged at all, it is advanced within the safe framework of the existing power structure, and this calls for moderate policies of marginal improvements in agriculture and light industry, roadbuilding, family planning agencies, and the like — policies that will not rock the boat. Such development efforts are more likely to serve the financial interests of the wealthy than the basic needs of the poor.

Furthermore, it is not correct to assume that a major goal of successive United States governments has been the economic development of poor countries. It has not. The principal drive has been, as Harry Magdoff has put it, "to keep as much as possible of the world open for trade and investment by the giant multinational corporations."[5] And this aim is often vigorously supported by the international financial institutions. Sometimes the pursuit of this goal requires economic aid from the United States to poor countries; but sometimes it does not. Economic aid is most likely to be forthcoming when it serves the above goal by providing much needed overhead capital for the foreign investors and by helping to quiet general unrest and to defuse potential insurrections. However, economic aid is not always necessary to quell unrest, for potential threats to the ruling classes can also be met by military aid to them, counterinsurgency operations against dissident forces, and, if worst comes to worst, military intervention itself — which has been used by the United States around forty times since the 1890s. Militarism in the United States is integrally related to United States imperialism.[6] These are alternative means to a given end, and economic aid, as only one of the means, may or may not play a large role, depending on the circumstances in each case. There is thus a powerful alliance within the international capitalist system working for ends that are often opposed to the basic needs of the poor.[7]

Since Chenery fails to discuss these obstructions to the welfare of the poor, his chapter excludes a rapidly growing body of literature which, in fact, addresses itself to just such problems and which contains some of the most promising work now being done in the development field. Among others, I have in mind A. G. Frank's studies of Latin American development; Michael Tanzer's book on the political economy of international oil; Harry Magdoff's empirical researches on United States imperialism; Paul Baran's pathbreaking historical analysis of world economic development; Paul Sweezy's many contributions to the same topic; Robert Heilbroner's and Gunnar Myrdal's works, which delve into the social and political aspects of development; and the expanding literature on imperialism and development contributed by some of the younger economists.[8] In a book which purports to survey the state of economics, any chapter that slights such a large and challenging body of work cannot be considered entirely representative of what economists are doing, nor can it be considered to have posed the most significant questions about its subject.

III.

As I noted previously, radical economists have also been interested in the political economics of wealth and poverty right here in the United States — and that means, to repeat, that they have analyzed their topics within a historical context of ruler-subject relations. These topics include how the capitalist system produces simultaneously both wealth and poverty; the economic, political, and social power bases of the rich; the political economics of poverty, of slavery, and of black ghettos; and, in general, the broad social determinants of income and wealth distributions in our contemporary society. It goes without saying that conventional economists too, over the years, have contributed much to our knowledge of income and wealth disparities.[9]

But this survey is strangely silent on such matters. Not only does it disregard radical economists' work in this area, but it does not deal in any serious way with the plain old topic of income distribution. In fact, the topic is so chopped up in the volume that it is impossible for any author, even if he wanted to, to come to grips with the heart of the issue. Caves considers why some corporations get higher profit rates than others. Ruttan wonders briefly about income distribution in agriculture, and Rothenberg refers to inequities in urban areas. Reder asks why some workers earn more wages than others. After all this, there is nobody left to ask questions about the overall distribution of income; and, of course, the assumption that capitalists deserve the profits they get and the wealth they have is never challenged at any point in this survey. Solow, for example, can write about the competitive model in this way — "There is a given set of households owning specified assets (including the ability to supply certain types of labor and *the right* to a share of the profits of each firm) . . ."[10] — presumably without batting an eye, for in that formulation everyone sounds pretty much equal. Solow takes the existing economic system so much for granted that it limits his imagination — ". . . one would guess that the elimination of substantial unemployment — let alone mass unemployment — does as many good things to the income distribution as any direct measure one can imagine."[11] Well, any radical economist can imagine a direct measure that would do even better things — expropriation of the capitalist class and the turning over of ownership of capital goods and land to all the people. That, of course, sounds wild — unimaginable — to anyone who does not question the existing social system.

But if one is concerned with gross inequalities of income and wealth, as radical economists are, it is best to begin with property incomes, and especially with the profits going to private owners of capital goods. Are these profits deserved? Radical economists analyze this problem, as they do most problems, from the standpoint of power and conflict within a historical setting. To begin with, as Joan Robinson has pointed out, capital goods *are* productive but that does not justify the assignment of their productivity to private owners. There is nothing productive about land and machinery being privately owned, and it is certainly no sacrifice or burden to own such wealth. In fact, the present ownership of capital has a historical background that is scandalous, as our Indian, chicano, and black contemporaries have been trying to explain to us in recent years.

Furthermore, the sacrifice associated with current saving by the wealthy is more truly a burden of the poor whose very poverty — whose forced abstinence from consumption, to put it politely — allows such wealth, from which most of the saving comes, to continue to exist. It is not the abstinence and waiting of the rich that should be rewarded but rather the general deprivation of the poor. Also, the long established economic argument against private acquisition of returns on land has not been forgotten by radical economists, even though its political implications are seldom discussed any more in mainstream economics. In short, radical economists reject the attempts by conventional economists "to raise profits [and other property incomes] to the same level of respectability as wages."[12]

As radical economists see it, the shares of national income going to workers and to property owners are largely determined by the relative power of the two groups, although relative factor supplies set limits within which the power exerts itself. But that is hardly the whole story, for even if, in some sense, workers got something close to their marginal products, the marginal products themselves are considerably influenced by the very fabric of the society in which people work.

Adam Smith was acutely aware of this when he suggested that labor specialization, while increasing productivity in some narrow sense, is often at the expense of the worker's general intelligence and understanding. It was his view that "the man whose whole life is spent in performing a few simple operations . . . generally becomes as stupid and ignorant as it is possible for a human creature to become." The difference between the most dissimilar of human beings, according to Smith, is not so much the cause of the division of labor as it is the effect of it. Consequently, while an economy might gain from the division of labor in some small sense, it could lose in the larger sense of creating men who are little more than passive and unreasoning robots.[13]

In general, the marginal products of workers are not independent of the opportunities the society affords to all its citizens to become fully participating members of that society — to become fully awakened and myth-free individuals.   In particular, in our own society, these marginal products are not independent of the inferior status accorded to women, the racism that is so widespread, the class-oriented education system, or the officially sponsored efforts to divert the energies of millions of people into imaginary worlds.[14]

These are all subjects which are not only worthy of discussion by economists, but which have, in fact, been discussed, and never more than in recent years, but none of them finds a place in this survey.[15]

IV.

What does find a place in every nook and cranny of the survey is the assumption that the source of human welfare is commodities, i.e., GNP. In these terms, greater welfare requires more "productive" workers — workers molded by capitalist institutions to the narrow pursuit of pro- ducing ever more to consume ever more.   Nowhere in this survey does any author discuss the implications of these limited goals of capitalism for the human development of the people involved.[16]

Instead, we learn from the survey that *the* economic goal is growth — and that's that.   It is really unbelievable that no author questions this.   For years there have been discussions on the high costs of growth[17] (hasn't Boulding proposed to change GNP to Gross National Cost, and others to Gross National Pollution?) and even a great deal of speculation about whether growth, even if wanted, is, in fact, possible for very much longer.   This topic, which is a serious challenge to both conventional and radical economists, deserves some place in a survey of what's going on in economics and where economics is going.

In its most comprehensive form the argument is based on the burgeoning growth of population relative to resources and food; on the limited waste-absorbing capacity of the soil, water, and atmosphere; and on the special environment-destroying potential of newly developed technologies, like nuclear radiation.[18]   Among economists, the argu- ment in this form was stated most cogently several years ago by Kenneth Boulding, but it has recently been put into even more dramatic form by Robert Heilbroner, in this way:

[In] our Spaceship Earth . . . sustained life requires that a meticu- lous balance be maintained between the life-support capability of the vehicle and the demands made by the inhabitants of the craft.   Until quite recently, those demands have been well within the capability of the ship, both in terms of its ability to supply the physical and chemical requirements for continued existence and to absorb the waste products of the voyagers. . . . It is only in our time that we are reaching the ceiling of earthly carrying capacity, not on a local but on a global basis. Indeed . . . we are well past that capacity, provided that the level of resource intake and waste output represented by the average American or European is taken as a standard to be achieved by all humanity. To put it bluntly, if we take as the price of a first-class ticket the resource requirements of those passengers who travel in the Northern Hemisphere of the Spaceship, we have now reached a point at which the steerage is condemned to live forever — or at least within the horizon of the technology presently visible — at a second-class level; or at which a considerable change in living habits must be imposed on first class if the ship is ever to be converted to a one-class cruise.[19]

This analysis has many implications for both the rich and the poor, but I have space to mention only one of them. In attempting to achieve economic development, today's poor around the world have a few advantages over their predecessors of a few hundred years ago — the advantages of increased knowledge and of better technologies. But they are at a disadvantage in several crucial ways. First, they do not have the opportunities which the early Europeans and Americans had of gaining huge flows of economic resources through plunder, slavery, and fraud. Second, I have argued that they are burdened by a powerful alliance within the world capitalist system which works for ends that are often opposed to their basic needs. And, finally, to the extent that the above "ecological argument" is correct, the present poor are further condemned by the fact that the rich states are hell-bent on a growth path of demanding and producing ever more GNP, and in the process using up exhaustible resources that the poor must have if they are ever going to raise their own living standards to halfway decent levels.

So the poor of the world have problems on their hands, and one of them is the rich and their pecuniary ways. The rich might reform. Or the poor, in their hundreds-of-millions, might one of these days become an organized revolutionary force against the rich — and so, incidentally, disprove my first point that they have no opportunity these days for plunder.

V.

At the beginning of this paper, I argued that conventional economists unduly emphasize, at the expense of more important things, methods and techniques and the data to feed them. I repeat this because I want it as immediate background to what I now wish to read to you: the final six recommendations of this panel of economists who have surveyed the entire field of economics. Here they are:

1. The panel recommends that the federal government direct immediate attention to the development of a data base for economics and social research by the establishment of a National Data System . . .
2. The panel recommends that private foundations and government agencies aid in the establishment and support of large scale social science research centers which can provide continuing facilities for economic and social research . . .
3. The panel recommends that universities and research centers co-operatively with the federal government assume the responsibility for providing computer facilities for economic research . . .
4. The panel recommends that private foundations and government agencies together with universities and research centers provide for the funding and organization of long-term economic research efforts . . .
5. The panel recommends that departments of economics reorient graduate training towards providing more competence in research methods and more research experience . . .
6. The panel recommends that professional societies and research organizations accept greater responsibility for and give explicit consideration to improving the channels of communication in the profession . . .[20]

I would like to counter with a single recommendation of my own — that the economics profession, instead of worrying so much about national data systems, research money from foundations and the government, computer facilities, and research techniques, pay more attention to the economic implications of the fact that the United States is heavily involved as the dominant power in a hierarchical international capitalist system. Once this fact is recognized, economists are bound to have interesting and important things to say about United States objectives within this system, the various means employed by successive United States governments to achieve these objectives, the sources of power in the United States which promote such ends, the impact of all this on militarism and on stabilization policies in this country, and the economic implications for poor countries of being subordinate members of such a system. One doesn't need fancier computer facilities or national data systems to make important contributions in these areas, and one doesn't need more research money to gain a better understanding of the awful problems that the poor and oppressed people of the world are up against.

ENDNOTES

[1] Paul M. Sweezy, "Toward a Critique of Economics," *Review of Radical Political Economics,* Spring 1970.

It is necessary to add that the questions posed by conventional economists do, of course, include "important" and "socially relevant" problems. No one can deny that some of these economists work on poverty, pollution, racism, or whatever is considered important by the most radical members of our profession. But what is also true is that the heavy emphasis that conventional economists put on techniques tends to draw them, not to the most important social problems, which are usually terribly complex, but to those most amenable to the employment of the techniques on hand, and these are usually rather trivial problems. Furthermore, when conventional economists do address themselves to important problems, they do so through a paradigm that is such a distortion of reality that their answers are at best highly misleading ones.

[2] Robert C. Tucker, *The Marxian Revolutionary Idea* (W. W. Norton & Company, 1969), p. 80.

[3] One can be a political economist without being a radical political economist, though there are probably few economists who fall into such a category — say, of right-wing political economist. These two types of political economist, though opposed to each other on political grounds, nevertheless have much in common in that they share essentially the same paradigm. The relation of either type of political economist to a conventional economist, whether the latter is of conservative or liberal persuasion, is necessarily less close because their paradigms are so very different.

[4] Consider a concrete problem. In looking at the tradeoff between inflation and unemployment, a conventional economist would consider this to be a technical problem of quantifying a functional relationship, which might be solved with good data and appropriate econometric techniques. He would, therefore, spend most of his time in trying to get the data into the best form for rigorous testing of some hypothesis about this tradeoff, and in the interpretation of his results.

A radical political economist, looking at the same problem, would also be interested in its quantitative and theoretical aspects, but in addition he would ask why it is that the institutional arrangements of advanced capitalism require that we have either inflation or unemployment. He would further ask who gains and who loses by the various tradeoffs between inflation and unemployment, and he would assume conflicts of interest among groups in the society and a highly unequal distribution of power among these groups to influence decision making in this area. These thoughts might lead him to investigate whether the Nixon administration's strong emphasis on stoppng the inflation, at the cost of more unemployment, might not serve a powerful group of bankers and industrialists whose financial interest heavily depend on the continuing dominance of the United States in the world capitalist system and hence on the enduring strength of the dollar. He would, of course, at the same time reflect that unemployed blacks and chicanos have very little power over such decisions compared to, say, David Rockefeller.

[5] Harry Magdoff, *The Age of Imperialism* (Monthly Review Press, 1969), p. 14.

[6] Harry Magdoff, "Militarism and Imperialism," *American Economic Review,* Papers and Proceedings, May 1970.

[7] Conventional economists, of course, deny this, because they believe that the rich are helping the poor. Radical economists, on the other hand, find enough evidence to assume that the rich are helping themselves; in the process the poor may be helped to some extent, or they may not.

[8] I shall list only a few of these writings. A. G. Frank, *Capitalism and Under-development in Latin America* (Monthly Review Press, 1967) ; Michael Tanzer, *The Political Economy of International Oil and the Underdeveloped Countries* (Beacon Press, 1969) ; Harry Magdoff, *op. cit.;* Paul Baran, *The Political Econ-omy of Growth* (Monthly Review Press, 1957) ; Paul Sweezy, *The Theory of Capitalist Development* (Oxford University Press, 1942) ; Robert Heilbroner, *The Great Ascent* (Harper Torchbooks, 1963) ; Paul Baran and Paul Sweezy, *Monopoly Capital* (Monthly Review Press, 1966) ; Edward Boorstein, *The Economic Transformation of Cuba* (Monthly Review Press, 1968) ; Eric Wil-liams, *Capitalism and Slavery* (University of North Carolina Press, 1944) ; James O'Connor, "International Corporations and Economic Development," *Science and Society,* Fall 1969; Dudley Seers, "Big Companies and Small Coun-tries," *Kyklos,* XVI, No. 4, 1963; Thomas Balogh, "The Mechanism of Neo-Imperialism," *Oxford University Institute of Statistics Bulletin,* August 1962; Tom Weisskopf, "Capitalism, Underdevelopment, and the Future of the Poor Countries," Unpublished, 1970; Richard D. Wolff, "Modern Imperialism: The View from the Metropolis," *AER,* May 1970; Theotonio Dos Santos, "The Structure of Dependence," *AER,* May 1970. I have attempted to summarize some of the ideas in these studies in "Economic Development and Economic Imperialism," *Plain Wrapper,* April–May 1969, and in "Economic Conversion and Beyond," *Industrial Management Review,* Spring 1970.

[9] The following is a selection of these writings, mostly on the radical side. Eugene Genovese, *The Political Economy of Slavery* (Vintage Books, 1965) ; Gabriel Kolko, *Wealth and Power in America* (Praeger, 1962) ; William K. Tabb, *The Political Economy of the Black Ghetto* (Norton, 1970) ; James C. Knowles, *The Rockefeller Financial Group* (mimeo., 1970) ; F. Lundberg, *The Rich and the Super-Rich* (Lyle Stuart, Inc., 1968) ; Victor Perlo, *The Em-pire of High Finance* (International Publishers, 1957) ; Robert J. Lampman, *The Share of Top Wealth-Holders in National Wealth,* 1922–1956 (Princeton University Press, 1962) ; Charles E. Silberman, *Crisis in Black and White* (Vin-tage, 1964) ; Paul Sweezy, "Interest Group in the American Economy," *The Present as History* (Monthly Review Press, 1953) ; J. G. Gurley, "Federal Tax Policy," *National Tax Journal,* September 1967; Daniel Fusfeld, "The Basic Economics of the Urban and Racial Crisis," *Conference Papers of the Union for Radical Political Economics,* December 1968; Stephan Michelson, "On Income Differentials by Race: An Analysis and a Suggestion," *ibid.;* Barry Bluestone, "Black Capitalism: The Path to Black Liberation?", *Review of Radical Political Economics,* May 1969; Raymond Franklin, "The Political Economy of Black Power," *Social Problems,* Vol. 16, No. 3; Victor Perlo, "People's Capitalism and Stock Ownership," *American Economic Review,* June 1958; Margaret Benston, "The Political Economy of Women's Liberation," *Monthly Review,* September 1969; Donald Light, "Income Distribution: The First Stage in the Considera-tion of Poverty," *Occasional Papers of the Union for Radical Political Eco-nomics,* December 1969; Stephen Michelson, "The Economics of Real Income Distribution," *The Review of Radical Political Economics,* Spring 1970.

[10] Robert Solow, "Microeconomic Theory," p. 4 in mimeographed version. My emphasis.

[11] *ibid.,* p. 15 in mimeographed version.

[12] Joan Robinson, *Economic Philosophy* (Anchor Books, 1964). See also, by the same author, *An Essay on Marxian Economics* (St. Martin's, 2nd ed., 1966); *Economics: An Awkward Corner* (Pantheon, 1967); and *The Accumulation of Capital* (St. Martin's, 1965).

[13] Adam Smith, *The Wealth of Nations* (Irwin, 1963), Vol. II, pp. 284–85. I have pursued these and associated ideas in "Maoist Economic Development," *The Center Magazine,* May 1970. See also Nathan Rosenberg, "Adam Smith on the Division of Labour: Two Views or One?" *Economica,* May 1965.

[14] This general theme has been developed by several radical economists. For example, as Eugene Genovese has shown, in the ante-bellum South, the maintenance of slavery as an entire social system required the slaveowners to keep their slaves stupid. This in turn meant that the level of technology had to be kept down to the low quality of the labor force. Thus, slaves used the cruder "nigger hoe" instead of the better but more easily breakable "yankee hoe," and they were forced to work with mules and oxen instead of faster horses because the former "could more easily withstand rough and perhaps vengeful handling." Further, the more complicated tools and machinery could not be used because the social system militated against encouraging slaves as specialists to service the equipment. Thus, the entire social system required stupid slaves, and stupid slaves required crude tools. Educated, technically trained, and wide-awake slaves, although they would have been far more productive in the fields, would have threatened the slave society as a whole. So slaves got low pay, it could be said, because their marginal product was low, but it was low because it was imposed on them by the social requirements of the ruling class. See Eugene D. Genovese, *The Political Economy of Slavery* (Vintage Books, 1965), especially pp. 3–10, 43–69, 244.

If today's conventional labor economist had lived in that society, judging from Reder's survey of the field, he would not have discussed any of these fundamental forces determining the income-share of slaves — including the basic fact that slaves did not own the means of production — but would have concentrated instead on slave X receiving more than slave Y because he invested capital in himself and learned the alphabet; or slave X receiving more because slaveowners had a "preference" or "taste" for his lighter colored skin. And if a Caves had been on the scene in those days, he would have carefully examined whether slaveowners were trying to maximize profits, why slaveowner A got a higher profit rate than slaveowner B, and the implications of this for differences in market conduct and performance between the two slaveowners. And Morgan presumably would have conducted consumer surveys to see what makes slaves tick. If the conventional economists ran true to form, the emphasis of these analyses would have been on harmony of interests and possibilities for reforming the worst abuses; the analyses would not have penetrated into the heart of the slave society itself.

[15] However, as I have already explained, this is not unexpected because the paradigm of conventional economists, which takes the existing social system for granted, greatly reduces their chances of seeing power structures, social conflict, and strong resistances to change — all of which form the very core of the problems of wealth and poverty, as radicals see them.

[16] See Herbert Gintis, "Neo-Classical Welfare Economics and Individual Development," *Occasional Papers of the URPE,* July 1970.

[17] I will note only two of the many studies that question our singleminded dedication to high growth rates: E. J. Mishan, *The Costs of Economic Growth* (Praeger, 1967) and J. K. Galbraith, *The New Industrial State* (Houghton Mifflin, 1967).

[18] This formulation is based on that of Robert Heilbroner, "Ecological Armageddon," *The New York Review of Books,* April 23, 1970.

[19] Heilbroner, *op. cit.* This article also appears in *Between Capitalism and Socialism* (Vintage, 1970). It was a review of a book by Paul and Anne Ehrlich, *Population, Resources, Environment* (W. H. Freeman & Co., 1970). The above passage of Heilbroner is a paraphrase of the Ehrlichs' argument.

See also Kenneth Boulding, "The Economics of the Coming Spaceship Earth," in Henry Jarrett (ed.), *Environmental Quality in a Growing Economy* (Johns Hopkins Press, 1966). Boulding's article may also be found in Garrett de Bell (ed.), *The Environmental Handbook* (Ballantine Books, 1970). For much the same argument, see Herman E. Daly, "The Canary Has Fallen Silent," *N.Y. Times,* October 14, 1970, p. 43.

[20] Chapter 17, in mimeographed version.

Robert M. Solow was born in Brooklyn, New York, and received his B.A. and Ph.D. degrees from Harvard University. His major publications are in the fields of capital theory, production functions, and economic growth. He is currently Professor of Economics at the Massachusetts Institute of Technology.

4 Discussion of the State of Political Economics

Robert M. Solow

I have no substantial disagreement with Charles Schultze. He is, perhaps, what you might call a little justifiably unfair to the *Report*. It was, after all, supposed to describe the present state of economics — with outsiders as the main audience — not to blaze new paths. I'm afraid it *is* an unexciting document. (It was written by a Committee!) It suggests no double helix or miracle rise, probably because none of us could see such a thing on the horizon in economics. (Those are Famous Last Words, I realize.)

Some of the things Schultze talks about were indeed mentioned in the *Report*. I had a paragraph in my chapter on "Microeconomic Theory" suggesting that the study of commodity taxes and user charges to accomplish allocational purposes would be an important research topic for the future. I mentioned urban economics as a major source of

Reprinted from the *American Economic Review*, Vol. LXI, No. 2, May 1971, by permission of the author and the American Economic Association. © Copyright 1971 by the American Economic Association.

such problems. I had traffic congestion rather than pollution in mind. I might as well confess that I discovered the interesting and important work of Kneese and his associates only after I had written my chapter; otherwise I would certainly have mentioned it prominently. It carries an important message that economists have to transmit to others.

Schultze may be a little less than fair when he says that economists have tended to regard the design of public programs as a problem of specifying objectives and regulations rather than as one of providing correct incentive schemes for decentralized decisions. There may be some truth in that — he is in a better position to know than I am — but it is at best a partial truth about a profession that has invented and spread the whole idea of shadowprices in the last twenty years.

Generally, I see the immediately promising directions of theoretical and applied research where Schultze sees them. Despite the flurry over monetarism-and-fiscalism and natural-rate-of-unemployment vs. permanent-trade-off, I think these are essentially minor issues in which good sense will eventually win out. As Schultze argues, microeconomics is due for a revival as problems of regulation and decentralized management of the economy come to the fore. The Averch-Johnson literature is another example of the analysis of the subtle distortions caused when the regulatory process provides improper incentives.

For some reason, economists often meet radical blasts like Professor Gurley's with a kind of embarrassed silence. Perhaps that is because one tends to swallow the notion that doing conventional economic analysis somehow identifies you with the System and its inequities, not to mention its foreign policy. I think that notion is false. If you want to work for reform of the System, or even for revolution, that is no excuse for abandoning the usual standards of scientific work. To do so is to add ignorance to injury. I have known Professor Gurley for a long time. I have always taken him seriously and I propose to do so now. But I'm going to take a tough line, just as he did.

The *Report* under review is a survey of the present state of economics, and clearly not an exhaustive survey. Gurley's review is much more an attack on the present state of economics than an attack on the *Report*. The *Report* itself is faulted only if the body of radical political economics is so large and so important that it demands mention. But I don't believe that is the case. Radical economics may conceivably be the wave of the future, but I do not think it is the wave of the present. In fact, to face the issue head on, I think that radical economics as it is practiced contains more cant, not less cant; more role-playing, not less role-playing; less facing of the facts, not more facing of the facts, than conventional economics. In short, we neglected radical economics because it is negligible.

First I want to say that I think radical economists have corrupted

Thomas Kuhn's notion of a scientific paradigm, which they treat as a mere license for loose thinking. If you look at Kuhn's examples — all from natural science, of course — you will see that they represent well developed models or frameworks for thought. Some of his examples are Newtonian dynamics, Copernican astronomy, Ptolemaic astronomy for that matter, wave optics, etc. In this sense, neoclassical economics is pretty clearly a scientific paradigm. It may be a bad one, or a worn-out one, or it may have served to advance the interests of the capitalist class, but it is the sort of thing Kuhn means. As far as I can see, radical political economics is no such thing. It is more a matter of posture and rhetoric than of scientific framework at all. (Classical Marxian economics is a different matter, of course, though there is a problem about its relation to the classical paradigm. Anyhow that is another story. "It is no accident," as they say, that modern radicals are not much interested in the old man who wrote *Capital*. They are much more interested in the Hegelian Marx, and the author of the Paris Manuscripts of 1844.) Maybe I can put my point in Kuhn's language. The function of a scientific paradigm is to provide a framework for "normal science." But there is little evidence that radical political economics is capable of generating a line of normal science, or even that it wants to.

Here are some examples of what I mean. Professor Gurley says: "As radical economists see it, the shares of national income going to workers and to property owners are largely determined by the relative power of the two groups, although relative factor supplies set limits within which the power exerts itself." Am I to presume from this that there are studies of time series that show that short-run fluctuations in distributive shares reflect short-run fluctuations in the distribution of power in society? This would mean that workers are more powerful when there is a lot of unemployment than they are when there is very little, because the share of wages is highest when the economy is most depressed. Or has it been found in many countries that the direction of long-run change in distributive shares corresponds to the long-run trend in the independently measured distribution of power in society? Or are there perhaps cross-section studies among industries showing that the share of wages in value added is highest in industries where the power of the workers is highest, and lowest where the social power of capitalists is highest? Or is it demonstrable that international differences in functional income distribution correspond more or less closely to international differences in the relative power of workers and property owners?

According to Gurley, contemporary underdeveloped countries "are at a disadvantage in several crucial ways. First, they do not have the opportunities which the early Europeans and Americans had of gaining huge flows of economic resources through plunder, slavery and fraud."

I presume this means that it is well understood why Spain and Portugal, which must have had more than a fair share of plunder, slavery, and fraud, are today little more than underdeveloped countries themselves, while Sweden and Australia (and, because they were late on the scene, perhaps also Germany and France), which did not, are well-developed high-income economies. I presume that there are estimates of the extent to which Japan's success comes from its earlier adventures in China and how much from other sources. I presume that radical economists have a way of finding out how much England profited from India, from central Africa, and from the Atlantic colonies. And I hope it is understood that I can doubt that answers to these questions exist without in any way favoring plunder, slavery, or fraud.

Professor Gurley says, meaningly, that a radical economist might "investigate whether the Nixon administration's strong emphasis on stopping the inflation at the cost of unemployment might not serve a powerful group of industrialists whose financial interests heavily depend on the continuing dominance of the U.S. in the world capitalist system." Apart from his current pressing need to explain why the Nixon administration appears to have changed its mind early in November, the radical economist has presumably calculated whether the strength of the dollar is worth enough to those bankers and industrialists to offset the large drop in profits they experience whenever there is strong emphasis on stopping inflation at the cost of unemployment.

As you all know, none of these calculations has been done by radical economists. And when and if any of them is done, you know who will do it — some poor damned graduate student in some conventional department, supervised by some conventional professor of conventional economics. That's why I don't think a survey of the current state of economics needs to pay a lot of attention to radical political economics.

May I saw a word in my own defense? Professor Gurley charges me with having, without batting an eye, described a model in which each household has a given capacity to supply specified kinds of labor, and a right to a specified share of the profits of each firm. He says this in a tone of hushed shock, for all the world as if he were a Victorian literary critic announcing that in Chapter 12 of my novel I actually say, without batting an eye, that Cedric put his hand on Gwendolen's breast! In the first place, I was describing the competitive model, which does just as I said. Secondly, the competitive model was intended as a description of capitalism. Third, the right in question is patently a legal right, not a moral right. And fourth, with trivial modification, the same model could be adapted to describe many alternative social-economic systems because the surplus generated in firms has to be distributed somehow.

Moreover, when I remarked that ending unemployment did as much good to the income distribution as any imaginable direct measure, I was plainly referring to any direct measure that one could imagine actually happening between 1960 and 1965. Talking about expropriating the capitalist class in that context is what I mean by role-playing. By the way, does Gurley think that the phrase "turning over of ownership of capital goods and land to all the people" says anything precise? Does he think the distributional consequences are implicit in the phrase? Does he have any clear idea what the income-distributional consequences would be, or have been in the various socialist countries who have done this in a wide variety of institutional ways? And why, in this connection, does he stop talking about "power and servitude" and ruler-subject relations, which I thought were more or less ubiquitous, and are certainly not noticeably absent in places where the capitalists have been expropriated?

Finally, I must say I don't think it's wrong for a survey of economics to talk mostly about technique and the availability of data. There is a difference between a survey of medicine and a survey of health, or between a survey of meteorology and a survey of the weather. So why not between a survey of economics and a survey of economic life? I presume that knowledge of technique and acquaintance with data *are* what distinguish an economist from somebody else. I'd even have thought that it is the command over certain techniques and the familiarity with certain bodies of data that distinguish the radical economist from the radical journalist, or the radical sociologist, or the radical clarinetist. What else?

QUESTIONS

Economics

1. Can radical economics deal with economic problems of a technical nature, e.g., inflation, unemployment, balance of payments, etc?
2. Is orthodox economic theory relevant to today's problems?
3. Does an intellectual have any responsibility for the results of the implementation of ideas he has promulgated?
4. Can orthodox economic theory present an adequate explanation for the distribution of income and wealth in the United States and in the world?
5. Do radical economists present an adequate explanation for the distribution of income and wealth?
6. Does orthodox or radical theory better explain the plight of underdeveloped countries today?

SECTION III

The Nature Of American Capitalism Today

A. Is the United States an Industrial State?
B. The Costs and Benefits of Economic Growth
C. Is the United States a Middle-Class Society?
D. What is the Role of Higher Education?

In 1967 John Kenneth Galbraith published *The New Industrial State,* in which the author argued that the United States economy has become an industrial state. Perhaps no modern book has stirred as much controversy among economists. Other writers, including Charles Reich, have used the same analysis, but have called it a corporate state. The outline of the theory follows.

Galbraith is openly a technological determinist. He believes that the imperatives of technology and organization determine the shape of the economy and of the society.

Modern technology requires enormous capital outlays. These capital outlays are costly — fantastically costly. But large industrial firms cannot invest millions of dollars simply on the hope that consumers will buy the product. They must be able to control consumer purchases. Therefore, modern technology requires economic planning. And this has been accomplished in all industrial economies. In the Soviet Union the economic system is much like that in the United States. Industry is organized into large hierarchical and bureaucratic firms managed by a technostructure. The goals of the organization are the same, i.e., success of the organization, autonomy from outside control, technological progress, and the greatest possible rate of growth. In the United States we have achieved a symbiosis between large industrial firms and the government. The government is responsible for providing for a high level of national income and smoothing out fluctuations in that level of income.

All this planning requires that prices and costs be relatively stable. This responsibility is allocated to government. Thus, despite the Nixon administration's devotion to free markets, wage and price controls were imposed when the system required them.

Corporations stimulate demand for goods through advertising. Advertising performs the service of bringing demand under control, but it also propagandizes on behalf of goods in general, so that even though goods are more abundant, we still feel they are just as important as ever. The system requires a reliable pattern of consumption. It requires that people will work without limit to procure more and more goods. If people quit working after acquiring a certain quantity of goods, there would be limits on the expansion of the system. Growth could no longer be the goal.

Thus Galbraith's book heralded the end of the market as the dominant force in American economic society. Business and government were virtually one. They complement each other and work together.

Many economists have reacted very negatively to Galbraith's analysis. Some orthodox economists have damned him for his downplaying of market forces in the economy. Radicals, on the other hand, have criticized him for his assertion that the present organization of society is inevitable. They argue that he is justifying the present distribution of wealth and power; that he is accepting the fact that the rich, the technostructure, the scientific and technical elite have positions of control in our society. The analyses contained here reflect these concerns of orthodox and radical economists.

Scott Gordon presents an orthodox critique of Galbraith's contention that the United States economy is an industrial state. He agrees in large part with Galbraith's analysis of the internal operation of the firm. He says, "The modern large corporation is largely free of stockholder control; it does supply from within a very large part of its capital requirements; it is run by its managers; and the managerial bureaucracy is a coherent social-psychological system with motives and preferences of its own."

It is Galbraith's analysis of the external relations of the modern corporation to which Gordon objects. The main defect of Galbraith's analysis is that he fails to explain the organization of the economy. How do the five or six hundred largest industrial firms interact with each other? Galbraith has rejected the market mechanism as no longer applicable but has presented us no alternative.

Gordon denies that the modern American consumer is manipulated by advertising. He agrees that human wants are cultural phenomena. But he finds it of little validity to claim that modern man is in some sense forced to want the things that industry produces. Instead, Gordon argues that material welfare and humanism are complementary. The "civilized sensibilities flourish where there is economic plenty; and the more the better, even when it is devoted in part to automobiles and television sets. The common man is not a noble primitive who has been spiritually pauperized and morally enslaved by material progress; he has in fact been freed and elevated by it."

Finally, Gordon argues that Galbraith leaves us with no alternatives. Galbraith believes that technology determines social organization and that this is inevitable. Gordon argues that there is "no practical (and perhaps no philosophical) difference between asserting that something is inevitable and considering it to be desirable." Thus Galbraith downgrades antitrust policy and says that it is obsolete. He tells us that the old market analysis of economics is obsolete. What then would Galbraith have us do? Gordon says, "There is no coherent analytical system that meets the test of relevance, realism and usefulness in Galbraith's work."

Douglas Dowd argues that the major failure in Galbraith's *New Industrial State* is Galbraith's inability or unwillingness to deal adequately with the question of power. Galbraith sees the hope for restructuring the industrial state in the technical and scientific estate. Dowd, on the other hand, argues that this group is paid and controlled by those at the top in today's society. The technical and scientific estate accept the values of those at the top; thus, they will do the bidding of the elite. They will act to conserve rather than to change the system.

Dowd argues that beneficial changes will come from the bottom. The role of intellectuals should be to use their knowledge to help those at the bottom achieve their goals.

Galbraith has pointed out that the industrial state is primarily devoted to the goal of economic growth. And, indeed, the United States government (along with the governments of all industrialized nations) has pursued a steady and devoted policy since World War II of attempting to maximize the rate of growth of the gross national product. Economists in all countries have worked steadily and enthusiastically toward this goal. It was really not until the last part of the 1960s that questions were raised about the benefits of economic growth. Galbraith raised questions somewhat parenthetically, but in 1967 E. J. Mishan published *The Costs of Economic Growth,* an explicit attack on the "growth gospel." At first, the argument was pretty well ignored. But as the result, perhaps, of the environmental crisis and our awareness of the deterioration of the environment, and concurrent with the development of the student movement, the denunciation of growth became a widespread phenomenon.

It is widely asserted that this is a middle- and upper-middle-class concern. The poor and the working class, it is argued, are still primarily concerned with material goods. But isn't this a great slur on workers? Don't workers need clean air and pure water and a quiet place to live? To argue that environmental concerns are middle-class concerns is to say that working-class people are really indifferent to the environment in which they live, that somehow their lungs have adapted to breathing smog, their bodies to eating contaminated food and drinking impure water. Many analysts of the problem argue that environmental pollution affects the poor most of all. The very rich can opt out of the bad environment. They don't ride on subways or on crowded buses. They don't live in the center cities, or if they do have residences there, they are in luxury highrise apartments in which artificial air, light, and cooling are provided. But these are only temporary residences for the rich. They have weekend homes in the country and summer places at the beach or in the mountains, where they can escape the worst effects of industrial pollution. (It is interesting to note that during the 1960s when the number of people living in slums was increasing each year and when we were alleged to have a desperate housing shortage the number of housing vacancies actually rose. This was because of the number of newly constructed vacation homes. More and more families built second homes, which were left vacant, of course, during most of the year. This is the way society chose to allocate its resources, i.e., second homes for the upper class rather than decent homes for those at the bottom.)

Another criticism leveled against the antigrowth argument is that we don't know how to provide for zero economic growth. But most economists questioning growth have not called for zero economic growth. How does one bring about a situation in which the economy grows at 4 per cent or 2 per cent or 0 per cent or minus 2 per cent? We don't really know the answers to these questions. What the critics of growth are saying is that the society whose primary goal is increasing the rate of economic growth produces enormous social and environmental costs. In a society in which nothing matters so much as money, there are going to be incredible problems.

Weaver writes of the need for community. But some critics argue that there is an inherent contradiction between autonomy and community. It is possible to have community in small towns across the United States of America. And yet persons are fleeing those towns every day in droves. Doesn't the individual give up a good bit of freedom when he exists in a close community? Are people really willing to sacrifice the autonomy one has in a large city with its impermanence and anonymity?

Wouldn't an end to economic growth imply a stifling of creativity? There are people who would argue that economic growth is a result of man's innate curiosity. Others would argue that one can be as curious and as creative as one wishes, but one does not have to implement the new technology. For instance, the Greeks were extraordinarily curious people and came up with some rather amazing inventions, e.g., the steam engine. They did not, however, produce these and use them in their society.

Do people really think all that much about whether they are absolutely happier than they were before they acquired more goods? Perhaps it is almost an unconscious or automatic process to which we have been socialized. Tanzi argues that an individual would not continue to work for more goods after finding that he was not any happier than he was before. This may be true in the long run and is perhaps what we may be seeing today among many young people. In the short run, however, there is no reason to suppose that an individual reasons to such an extent about this process. Everyone is doing it, society is organized to reinforce the tendency, and the behavior is probably carried out at an unconscious level of motivation within the individual. It is a reflex action.

That people do not want to give up what they have is not proof that people are happier at higher levels of income than lower levels. This tells us nothing. Nor does the fact that foreigners want to come to affluent America. We have created a society and a world in which goods have become the goals around which modern societies are organized. In a world such as this, the individual may delude himself into a false sense of happiness with his bundle of goods, or the source of his unhappiness may not be identifiable to him.

Why should there be any correlation between per capita income of cities and pollution? Do antigrowth economists claim such? Pollution in cities is the result of economic growth. Development created vast cities and crammed people into them. Whether or not growth is in fact taking place is not really the issue, for in the underdeveloped countries the process of production is still going on — even though the people in that country may not get the benefits. The pollution in the underdeveloped countries may in some sense be the result of the growth of the rich countries.

What is the nature of the class structure in the United States? Are there social classes, and if so, why? Are social classes disappearing? Isn't one of the results of economic growth the development of a large and affluent middle class? America is really a middle-class society, isn't it? These are the main issues in the papers by Parker and Silk.

Richard Parker writes from a radical perspective and argues that the myth of the middle class is just that — a myth. He presents data on the distribution of income and argues that many Americans are either poor or deprived, that the distribution of income has not changed appreciably during this century, and that most wealth is controlled by the very rich. The myth that everyone belongs to the middle class is useful because it implies the abolition of both great wealth and great poverty in the United States.

Leonard S. Silk writes sympathetically of the problems of the lower-middle class. He sees their problems as inherent in the American system. He traces the problem all the way back to the struggle between Jeffersonian egalitarianism and Hamiltonian libertarianism. As the result of liberty, inequality results. This means that those who are at the bottom feel resentful of those at the top. Franklin D. Roosevelt and the New Deal masked these conflicts and united blue-collar workers, ethnic groups, Southerners, and intellectuals in one party. Today that coalition may be coming apart. New pressures are leading to the alienation of the lower-middle class. The resentment of this group has two aspects today — economic and social. The economic problem stems from inflation, unemployment, and heavy indebtedness. The social problem comes about because the lower-middle class feels looked down upon by richer and better-educated whites above them and also feels pressed by blacks and other minority groups coming up from below them.

Both authors concede that America has social classes and that the middle class has some important social and economic problems. The nature of those problems is seen differently by the two authors, and Parker casts doubt on the whole notion that America is a middle-class society.

The fourth aspect of the domestic economy that is investigated here is the role of higher education. During the 1960s, higher education came to the forefront of American consciousness. In part this was a numerical phenomenon. The number of students in colleges and universities increased by more than a hundredfold from 1960 to 1970, so that in 1971 there were more than 8,000,000 students enrolled. Riots, demonstrations, and sit-ins became the order of the day. Many people saw the universities and colleges as staging grounds for a frontal assault on the institutions of American capitalism. What was the relationship between changes taking place in the economy and the frustration and despair that was felt among many students in universities? Was there an economic explanation for the disaffection of students?

Radical economists expect this alienation and disaffection among students to continue and to lead to revolutionary changes in the society. Orthodox economists expect the student protest movement to fade away. Many economists argue that the student protest movement was in large part a quantitative phenomenon. The very large number of students enrolled in many universities such as Berkeley, Michigan, and Wisconsin led to feelings of alienation and despair and gave the small minority of radicals a mass base from which to operate. As the percentage of young people in the population peaks in the 1970s and as the percentage of the population enrolled in universities declines, this student movement is expected to disappear. The recession and slow growth rate of the 1970s is expected to lead students to become interested in getting jobs. Later they will be interested in getting houses, assuming mortgages, making payments, buying furniture, and the other normal concerns of middle-class people in America.

What is the role of education in the United States economy? Orthodox economists tend to view education as essentially a device for creating human capital. The educational system increases skills, which enable people to produce more. Thus people come to embody capital as well as labor. Orthodox economists view education as comparable to any other industry. It should be organized along the most efficient lines. This involves hierarchical, bureaucratic organization and specialization of labor.

Sam Bowles argues that the traditional functions of education in the United States were socialization of young people into adult roles and legitimation of existing inequality. The schools educated young people to come on time, to do boring and repetitive tasks, to take orders from someone they had no voice in selecting, to have no control over what one produced, and to value rewards external to oneself — grades, gold stars, teacher's approval — as incentives. In order to socialize children from different social classes into differentiated patterns, a hierarchy of schools was established. Colleges and universities were established to socialize the elite. They encouraged independence and creativity because such attributes were useful for elites.

The necessity to legitimate inequality arose because of the democratic and egalitarian ethos of the society. Great economic inequality obviously contradicted this ethos. Thus, some way had to be devised to get those at the bottom to acquiesce to this contradiction because political stability required this. Schooling was a perfect device. Schooling and income are correlated. Therefore, if people are rich, it is based on their education! And if people are poor, their poverty is based on their lack of education! This myth is contradicted by Bowles's evidence that one's level of schooling is a function of the social class background of one's parents.

Expansion of the educational system also contributed to the myth of social mobility. If the level of education is rising, children's educational level will be higher than their parents. This appearance of upward mobility is, however, an optical illusion. The whole educational level is rising; thus, one's relative position has not changed even if one does have more education than one's parents.

The performance of the second role — legitimating inequality — requires the growth of the educational system. This was compatible with the growth of the economy in the past. But today there are contradictions in this system. Social stratification by educational level is no longer so easy when 40 per cent of high school graduates go to college. Also, the growth of the economy has produced a level of affluence that has led young people to reject materialism and occupational success as their primary goals. Economic growth has also led to more and more specialization of labor and the disappearance of independent "no-boss-jobs."

Robert W. Hartman of the Brookings Institution debated Sam Bowles on the subject of higher education but was not able to prepare a manuscript for inclusion in this volume. Some of the major points Hartman made are summarized in the following paragraphs:

Hartman criticizes Bowles's assumption that higher education is a form of investment. He thinks that a great deal of higher education is consumption spending. This leads him to argue that we are taking higher education far too seriously.

He argues that Bowles's analysis of state government support of higher education is oversimplified. Studies do show that some poor and some rich kids do benefit considerably from state tax support. These benefits are paid for by many families who do not use the system — both the less affluent (who are rejected on academic standards grounds) and the affluent (whose children choose to go to private institutions). The data suggest that a) families with income below the median are, as a whole, better off with the present systems of state support than if there were no support, but, b) there are alternative systems of state support that would be more redistributive than the present one, and c) the principles by which some young people are included and some excluded from public support are difficult to justify on any rational basis.

Hartman finds Bowles's argument concerning the relationship between the economic system and higher education unpersuasive. Why does New York support students in private colleges, whereas California has a hierarchical system of support, Florida emphasizes junior colleges for everyone, and Massachusetts does next to nothing for higher education, if the same basic political and economic forces are driving the system throughout the country?

One can question Bowles's consistency. On the one hand, he

argues that the needs of the economic system have led to the development of our present system of higher education. On the other hand, he argues in favor of radical reform of education today. If the present educational system is an outgrowth of the economic conditions in the country, why won't the educational system of the future be an outgrowth of the economic needs of the future? Doesn't Bowles's methodological framework require him to argue that the dictates of the economic system will be met?

Hartman raised serious questions about Bowles's emphasis upon radical students as a transforming segment of the American society. Hartman finds that only about 10 per cent of the American student body is really nonvocationally oriented. He argued that as the economic growth rate slows and as it gets harder for college graduates to find jobs that this emphasis on nonvocational objectives will diminish.

*Scott Gordon was born in Halifax,
Nova Scotia, received his B.A. de-
gree from Dalhousie, his M.A. from
Columbia, and his Ph.D. from Mc-
Gill. He is currently Professor and
Chairman of the Department of
Economics and Associate Member
of the Department of History and
Philosophy of Science at Indiana
University.*

5 The Close of the Galbraithian System

Scott Gordon

I. THE PROBLEM OF EVALUATION

J. K. Galbraith's new book, *The New Industrial State,* can be regarded
as the further elaboration of ideas which first caught wide public attention sixteen years ago with the publication of his *American Capitalism*
and subsequently with *The Affluent Society.* Some significant differences can be seen between the first and last of these, but it is apparent
to anyone who reads them together that the three are to a considerable
extent companion volumes, amplifying themes which run through all.
The title of this review article may be premature in the sense that one
should not assume that further books on these great themes will not
flow from Galbraith's prolific pen, but with *The New Industrial State,*
his view of the nature of the modern economy and his identification of
its major problems are now clear and can be considered as a potential

Adapted from Scott Gordon, "The Close of the Galbraithian System," which was
published in the *Journal of Political Economy.* Reprinted by permission of the author and the *Journal of Political Economy.* © Copyright 1968 by the *Journal of Political Economy* and The University of Chicago Press.

system of ideas. Ten years ago, in *The Affluent Society*, Galbraith noted that his mind was turning toward matters which now find expression in his new book and, despite the fact that he has been writing other books and doing many other important things these past ten years. *The New Industrial State* may be considered as a work of mature reflection by America's most widely known economist. It is perhaps time, then, to make a general evaluation of Galbraith's economic thought, to try to locate its place in the history of the science, and to appraise the contribution it may make to our understanding of the modern world.

One must begin with a candid recognition that the academic reader of Galbraith's books is under a strong temptation to react negatively to the author's style and method of discourse. He waives the scholarly conventions in favor of a rhetoric which is designed to appeal to the lay reader. But the stylistic techniques he employs to this end increase the difficulty of grasping the substance and structure of his thought and work against a fair and objective appraisal of it by an orthodox, scholarly mind. Galbraith is satiric, scornful, and flippant. There is often a sneer at his pen point. He makes use of much verbal fretwork and delights in the sudden reversal. He loves paradoxes and aphoristic generalizations so much that he often allows a witty sentence to stand when it really requires retooling in order to carry accurately the content of his thinking. An even greater barrier, especially to the economist, is that Galbraith is *simpliste*. There are innumerable passages in his books which make one ache with vexation at his overgeneralization, exaggeration, and stereotyping. His treatment of the "conventional wisdom" of the older economists, one of his favorite pegs on which to pin a donkey's tail, reflects an occluded memory of some old lectures in the history of economic thought that would have been better if completely forgotten. His treatment of what modern economists think is derived largely from the Arcadian world of the elementary textbook. When he himself deigns to be analytical along the lines of conventional economic theory, he is often sloppy. In addition to all this, he carries on a continuous vendetta against the economists of the academic establishment; his barbs sting and some go close to the vitals, which makes it difficult either to be objective in evaluating his work or to avoid bending over backward in the effort to be so.

Nevertheless, these difficulties must be overcome. Galbraith's ideas have become important elements in the contemporary popular culture of American social thought. If we are to assess their validity, we must not be put off by his disregard for the scholarly conventions or by our own wounded pride. We must go to the substance of his main themes.

II. THE NEW INDUSTRIAL STATE AS A PLANNED ECONOMY

The pivotal point of Galbraith's economic thought is the theme of *American Capitalism* — that the American economy is characterized by a high degree of concentration and that the analysis of economic processes by means of the traditional models of economic theory is therefore meaningless. In *The New Industrial State* he carries this argument further, not in the direction of the "theory of countervailing power," which was the constructive analysis of the earlier book, but toward the conclusion that the American economy is not only no longer a competitive economy but that it is not even a market economy. The independence of consumer preferences and factor offers, the profit incentives of the producing units, and the price mechanism which, in traditional theory, knits the system together, are all swept away, and the "heartland of the economy" (the industrial sector) is represented as "managed" by the giant corporations which dominate its various industries. "The firm controls the prices at which it buys materials, components and talent, and takes steps to insure the necessary supply at these prices. And it controls the prices at which it sells and takes steps to insure that the public, other producers or the state take the planned quantities at these prices. So far from being controlled by the market, the firm, to the best of its ability, has made the market subordinate to the goals of its planning" (1967, p. 110). The qualification in the last sentence quoted would suggest an examination of the constraints that act as exogenous controls over the firm, but Galbraith does not proceed in this direction. The qualification disappears utterly, and the picture that emerges of the modern large corporation is that it has unlimited power to reach forward and control its product demands and to reach backward and control its factor supplies. The demand and supply functions of the Galbraithian world all have price elasticities that are either infinite or zero, and often they degenerate to single points. Under such assumptions, it is not surprising that traditional market theory is regarded as yielding little insight into the mechanism of economic organization. In *American Capitalism* the business firm was considered to be constrained by the other major institutions of the economy, labor unions, and government, but in *The New Industrial State* these are viewed not as competing repositories of power but as complementary organisms which have joined with the great corporation to assist it in its "planning."

These developments, in Galbraith's view, have not resulted from fortuitous circumstances; they are inherent in the logic of modern technology. The day of the "entrepreneurial firm" is over. The modern industrial firm is operated by a "technostructure" of talents that manages the various processes of the firm down through its hierarchical levels and whose goals are primarily to maintain the autonomy of the organization itself and to promote its growth. What makes the modern giant corporation effective in the pursuit of its aims is organization. If there is genius at work, it is not to be found in any human frame; the "technostructure" consists of quite ordinary men who are welded into a managerial team. The English language does not contain a voice that is passive enough to express the essential idea. The corporation is simply "doing its thing," as the hippies would say, and its managerial members are doing theirs, governed by the imperatives of modern technology. Moreover, Galbraith asserts, these imperatives are not confined to capitalistic economics. Technological determinism is a law of industry which transcends political ideologies and social systems. He sees, accordingly, a convergence of the economic systems of all mature industrial states not, as some have claimed, because the Soviet-type economies are introducing some markets and capitalistic economies are introducing some macromanagerial elements, but because in both cases the "heartland" of the economy consists, as it *must,* of planning systems.

The Galbraithian view of the modern economy has innumerable antecedents in the sense that the death of the market has often been announced and with it, usually, the impotence of traditional economic analysis. But one need not linger over this. In specific terms, Galbraith's picture most distinctly evokes memories of Thorstein Veblen, who foresaw a kind of revolution by the technocrats who would take over the operation of the economy. Galbraith tells us that this revolution is already complete. Veblen's "Soviet of Engineers" is essentially the same as Galbraith's "technostructure." In both views, these developments are considered to evolve from the inherent nature of modern production technology. There are normative similarities too. Veblen looked forward to the replacement of the price system by "engineers" as an advance in logic, order, and efficiency: yet he could not keep from speaking of it with a tinge of irony and even bitterness. The same is true of Galbraith. When he writes on these matters, his adjectives and adverbs carry reproaches and misgivings, but the substance of the argument is that the new world that is managed by the technostructures of the large corporations is far more efficient, both in the static sense and in the promotion of innovation, than a world of market organization. In the last chapters of *The New Industrial State,* Galbraith pleads for intellectuals to bestir themselves over the problems of political and economic power that these developments have created and asks, rather vaguely, for the use of government as a controlling and directing force. His main difficulty is, however, the same as Veblen's in the end: there is no practical (and perhaps no philosophical) difference between asserting that something is inevitable and considering it to be desirable.

Galbraith's analysis of the American economy is constructed upon his conception of the legal and organizational nature of the modern industrial firm. The essentials of this conception derive from Berle and Means' classic of thirty years ago, *The Modern Corporation and Private Property*. The delineation of the modern firm offered in *The New Industrial State* is, in such terms, largely conventional, but it is expressed vividly and effectively. There are some people left, including some economists, who persist in regarding the corporation as a purely instrumental device, an association of individual venturers of capital, and there are some areas of economic policy where anachronistic conceptions of this sort have been seriously misleading. Because it is so widely read, *The New Industrial State* may render good service in bringing, once again, to the attention of a wide audience one of the most momentous facts of the modern age, the emergence of the corporation as a primary social institution.

Galbraith's concept of the "technostructure," however, overstresses the monolithic nature of the corporate managerial system, and it is more likely to become a cliché than a useful tool of analysis. The decentralization of modern managerial organization indicated by Peter Drucker's *The Concept of the Corporation* has no reflection in *The New Industrial State,* though this development is, one would think, of the utmost importance in appraising the corporation's role as an economic and social institution. Galbraith also has little to say about other important modern developments, such as the growth of the conglomerate-type corporation and the phenomenal rise of pension funds as actual and potential owners of corporate stocks. In short, *The New Industrial State* does not enter upon an examination of the important recent and current developments in corporate evolution, some of which would seem to this reviewer to be very germane to the central thesis there presented. That the picture of the corporation contained in the book is consequently somewhat old hat and commonplace should not, however, obscure the fact that it is essentially true, and very important. The modern large corporation *is* largely free of stockholder control; it *does* supply internally a large part of its capital requirements; it *is* run by its managers; and the managerial bureaucracy *is* a coherent social-psychological system with motives and preferences of its own.

When we turn from Galbraith's picture of the internal organization of the modern corporation to his view of the external environment in which the corporation operates, however, the picture becomes much less satisfactory. The corporation here appears as a very strange organism indeed. It controls completely all the important elements of its environment. It has no need to accommodate itself to any exogenous circumstances; it is able to mold these to suit itself. Such a corporation would be like no organism, biological or social, that ever was, for it would encounter no constraints upon what it wishes (or is impelled) to do, which is to grow. Theoretically, we should observe all major industrial firms growing infinitely large, each of them — moreover, instantaneously! This is a caricature, but it serves to focus attention on the important question, which is: What are the factors that prevent this from occurring and how do they operate? It is not sufficient simply to say that "of course" rabbits or ants or humans or General Motors cannot overrun the earth, eliminating all other organisms. One must discover the mechanism that prevents this from happening. Scientific explanation is an essay on the constrained maximum: no less so when we examine the growth of firms. But the Galbraithian firm knows no constraints. "The size of General Motors is in the service not of monopoly or the economies of scale but of planning. And for this planning — control of supply, control of demand, provision of capital, minimization of risk — there is no clear upper limit to the desirable size. It could be that the bigger the better" (1967, p. 76) .

But it can't be the bigger the better (relative to the total economy) for General Motors, United States Steel, and General Dynamics all at once. The Galbraithian picture is only plausible at all if one considers one firm at a time. It may be plausible to say that there is no market, as economists understand it, for automobiles or for steel, but what happens in the case of automotive steel where two "technostructures" confront one another? It is hardly sufficient to say, as Galbraith does, that they make contracts with one another (1967, p. 30) without describing what governs the terms they arrive at. The "countervailing power" thesis of *American Capitalism* might be invoked here, but Galbraith does not employ it in the analysis of *The New Industrial State,* and nothing else is introduced that might play a similar explanatory role. We are left with a microeconomics *sans* Walras — a particular equilibrium analysis in which the equilibrium is nonsensical.

This points to the main defect of Galbraith's conception. He deals with the organization of the individual firm, but he says nothing about the organization of the *economy*. How is the economy organized into a coherent system? By means of what mechanism or procedure are the activities of the "five or six hundred firms" that constitute "the heartland of the modern [U.S.] economy" (1967, p. 9) made to mesh? Galbraith rejects the market mechanism of traditional economics, but he offers no answer of his own to these fundamental questions. *The New Industrial State* fails to present a coherent picture of what it sets out to describe, the organization of the American economy. It seems to me that Galbraith slips from the proposition that the firm plans to the proposition that the economy is planned, without realizing that such statements possess only a verbal similarity. His view of the forces making for a convergence of Soviet-type and capitalistic economies is marked by similar elisions.

Nevertheless, this does not mean that the traditional conception of American capitalism is a satisfactory one. There is no central planning agency which commands the economy, but there has been an immense proliferation of government policies at federal, state, and local levels over the past fifty years, and it is conceivable that the United States today is, in this way, more of a planned economy than is, say, Yugoslavia. On another plane, we have to recognize that fundamental changes have taken place in the control of American industry and that the traditional concept of private property is now inapplicable to this sphere of American life. Perhaps "private enterprise" as a concept for the analysis of the American economy and "socialist enterprise" for the Soviet Union are of little use, and we should regard both economies as essentially bureaucratic systems. Perhaps the "iron law of oligarchy" is necessary to make the "imperatives of modern technology" into a fruitful analytical conception. Galbraith, however, does not explore any of these avenues of investigation, nor does he develop any others to amplify his analysis. The main lines he draws are correct (though not as novel as he consistently implies), but though he writes at length, he puts very little upon his canvas that does more than ink over ever more heavily the first broad intuitive strokes.

III. REALISM OR ROMANTICISM

The consumer enters the Galbraithian picture of the American economy as a puppet of the production system; his function is to purchase whatever the technostructure has decided to produce in the quantities and at the prices set by the technostructure's plans. It is tempting to discuss this view as an exaggeration or to try to dispose of it by demonstrating its analytical or empirical invalidity. It would be easy enough to argue, for example, that if the management of demand costs anything, an efficient technostructure would try to accommodate whatever independent preferences consumers possess rather than try to mold them into exotic shapes. Or, it would be easy to challenge Galbraith to show empirical support for his view that the techniques of demand management he speaks of are effective in altering the allocation of income between savings and aggregate consumption or among broad consumption categories.[1] But this would be a profitless contention.

---

[1] Note this astonishing statement: "If advertising affects the distribution of demand between sellers of a particular product *it must be supposed that* it affects the distribution as between products" (1967, p. 205; emphasis added).

Galbraith himself has noted that "although the truth rarely overtakes falsehood, it has winged feet as compared with a qualification in pursuit of a bold proposition" (1958, p. 30).

The big issue that is really involved here is that human wants are cultural phenomena. Galbraith is not to be faulted on this fundamental point or on his view that great consequences for economic theory spring therefrom. In a society where the production system forms a large part of the culture, and thus helps mold the wants it is created to satisfy, how do we establish any solid footing for the analysis of the economic process and the determination of its efficiency? But here again, the main criticism that must be leveled against Galbraith is that he does not explore the important issues raised by his own viewpoint. On the question of the determinants of consumer wants, he is in fact astoundingly naïve. He seems to believe that it is the affluence of America that has made wants susceptible to manipulation and that in poor societies wants are natural or, as he puts it, "original" with the individual. Every gothic spire in Europe, every temple in India, certifies the power of dominant social institutions in achieving major manipulations of income allocation, even in very poor societies. Any anthropologist could tell him how far removed from the "original" are the consumption patterns of even the most primitive peoples who live on the edge of existence.

The opposition Galbraith draws, in both *The Affluent Society* and *The New Industrial State,* between the natural wants of the poor and the culturally attenuated wants of the rich cannot be sustained. As a basis for a philosophy of distributional equity, it is the weakest of foundations: as an explanation of "social imbalance" — why we live in a society of clean houses and dirty streets — it is not penetrating. But that does not mean that the underlying issue — the culural determination of wants — is unimportant. Eighty years ago, Alfred Marshall, who created so much of the modern economics which Galbraith deplores, noted that as civilization advances, wants are more and more the *results* of economic activity rather than the causes of them. The point is fundamental. It is hard enough to view economic theory as an exploration of the logic of allocating given resources to the satisfaction of given wants in a world where neither wants nor resources will stand still. In a world in which the wants change *as a result of* our economic efforts to satisfy them, economic theory is faced with subtle and difficult problems and, moreover, problems which will not remain within the boundaries of "positive" economics.

A great deal of Galbraith's writing may be viewed as hinging on this question. In a sense, there is an economic sociology or, as Marshall would have put it, an "economic biology" contained in his theory of technological determinism. But it does not seem to me that the issue is examined in Galbraith's books with the profundity of thought or scholarship it deserves and requires. In his specifics, Galbraith sticks to the most hackneyed theme of modern social literature — the power of advertising. His general stance is also an old and dusty one — the degradation of man by the economic system. His writing recalls the bitter plaints of the Victorian romantics — Carlyle, Dickens, Ruskin, and others — who looked upon the youthful face of industrialism and found it a monstrous evil. Galbraith looks upon it in its "maturity," and though his reaction is more urbane, it is essentially the same cry. The machine has been installed in the garden; the human birthright is being sold for a mess of GNP; the economic mechanism does not feed man but feeds upon him, and calmly spits out the bones. A century ago Ruskin admonished, "There is no wealth but life," and Galbraith echoes, "What counts is not the quantity of goods, but the quality of life" (1967, p. 8) .

It is a great and lyrical theme, one of the most emotive in romantic literature, and it has always enjoyed a good market among the kind of public that, as Harry Johnson once observed, read (or, at least, buy) only one book a month. Who is there philistine enough to care not if he seems to deny the superiority of aesthetic and humane values over mere "goods"? But the argument is essentially wrongheaded. If there is anything that deserves to be called "conventional wisdom" with all the derision that Galbraith has so firmly attached to that phrase, it is the idea that there is an inherent conflict between the satisfaction of material wants and the needs of the cultivated spirit. Material welfare and the "higher" humanism are complementary, not competing things. The civilized sensibilities flourish where there is economic plenty; and the more the better, even when it is devoted in part to automobiles and television sets. The common man is not a noble primitive who has been spiritually pauperized and morally enslaved by material progress; he has in fact been freed and elevated by it. There is much more distance to go along this road, even in the "affluent society" of the United States.

Not to mince words, there is an unavoidable tinge of dissimulation in the claim that we should not concern ourselves any longer with raising the levels of national output and material welfare. It simply comes too easily to anyone who resides some two or two and a half sigmas to the right of the nation's average income. My ophthalmologist tells me (at thirty dollars an hour) that he has property in New Mexico and that things were fine until the Braceros began to go into the factories and their wages rose. "But," I demur, "their incomes were very low before." "Ah," he informs me firmly, "but they were happy — happier than you and I." Such a one as that will nod comfortably over numerous passages in *The Affluent Society* and *The New Industrial*

State, enjoying a little costless mental anchoritism and a mild flirtation with "progressive" ideas. He might even convince himself that he appreciates and sympathizes with the superior values of those youthful aesthetic ascetics who flock to the asphalt Waldens of Haight-Ashbury and Washington Square.

Even if we regard Galbraith solely as a popular social philosopher whose main aim is to question the values of contemporary American society, there is much in his writing that is, in my opinion, misguided. But an economist must recognize that his argument goes beyond this. To Galbraith, the modern economists are Pharisees and Talmudists — they are to be driven from the Temple altogether and their methods of analysis and investigation banished from the discussion of public affairs. But, one must ask, what is to take their place? If the analysis of the economy as a system of markets is not relevant to the study of current American trends and problems, then what is? On this point Galbraith leaves us with a void. He offers no alternative system of economic analysis or even the sketch lines of one that might be built. (There was a suggested approach in *American Capitalism,* the first and best of Galbraith's major works, but it has not been developed in the subsequent books.)

If we are persuaded, for example, that a gross imbalance exists between social and private consumption, does Galbraith offer us anything as promising for dealing effectively with it as the modern analysis of "public goods" which has been constructed upon the foundations of orthodox economics? If we take the view that corporate giantism is a consequence of industrial technology and the development of planning systems in management, does it help at all to conclude, as Galbraith does, that antitrust policy is obsolete and let it go at that? He offers no system of economic or political analysis that would enable us to construct an alternative line of policy. How would we tackle, by means of Galbraithian economics, such serious current problems as racial discrimination in our systems of production and consumption, the decay of the central cities, the further promotion of equity and security, the maintenance of an open and viable international economy? If we read *The Affluent Society* and *The New Industrial State* with such questions in mind, we emerge emptyhanded. We may, I think, claim that orthodox economics has contributed a modest bit to the examination of such questions, and there are certain lines of current investigation that promise a great deal more. Galbraith berates and ridicules contemporary economic theory, but if realism, relevance, and usefulness are to be the criteria, he cannot make his criticisms from the standpoint of an advocate of a superior system. There is no coherent analytical system that meets such tests in his own work of the past decade.

Galbraith's books have not been well received by economists. He has by now grown to expect that and cunningly suggests, with the aid of *ad hominem* argument, that the merit of his views is thereby certified. He writes with wit on the "conventional wisdom" of economists, but there is a sour taste in many of these passages — as of grapes, perhaps. Yet, by any test except the rigorous one of scholarship, he is a highly successful author. His books and articles enjoy a very large audience and have opened to him the doors of prestige, power, and wealth. He has chosen to write *sub specie temporis,* and has done so with consummate skill, but it is clear that he hopes his books will prove to be *sub specie aeternitatis* also. How do they seem to rank in that great contest?

It is always hazardous to declare what the Muses will in time decree; the history of economic and social thought is filled with many surprises. But it seems quite certain to this reviewer that Galbraith's work will not be the foundation of a new school of economics and that its impact on social thought in general is unlikely to outlast the immediate consciousness of the author's contemporaries. But immortality has many circles, and Galbraith's name is now firmly fixed on the high middle ranges where dwell the spirits of the effective gadflies of an age. His books will be of scholarly interest to the library moles of the future who will use them in their attempts to understand the complex intellectual agitation of a society that is powerful beyond measure and yet is cataleptic with doubt and fear.

REFERENCES

Galbraith, John Kenneth. *American Capitalism, the Concept of Countervailing Powers.* Boston: Houghton Mifflin Co., 1952.

———. *The Affluent Society.* Boston: Houghton Mifflin Co., 1958.

———. *The New Industrial State.* Boston: Houghton Mifflin Co., 1967.

Douglas F. Dowd received his undergraduate and graduate degrees at the University of California at Berkeley and has been Professor of Economics at Cornell. His books include Thorstein Veblen *and* Modern Economic Problems in Historical Perspective. *He has been extremely active in the antiwar movement.*

6   Idol with Feet of Clay: Galbraith's Political Economy

Douglas F. Dowd

I.

Galbraith's major failing has to do with his conception of power; and it is that to which I shall confine myself in what follows. In doing so, I wish neither to set aside as unimportant other weaknesses in his many books, nor seem to lack appreciation for what I think are the considerable virtues in all his writings. In my view, Galbraith is the very best of the nonradical economists, and it may be that his most valuable contribution will be that he has shown us just how sharply limited such a stance is for the problems of our day.

The book that occupies us most here is *The New Industrial State* (1967). However, what Galbraith attempts there he earlier moved toward in the most important of his other books: namely, *American Capitalism* (1952), and *The Affluent Society* (1958). In all these books there are two themes that provide both their strength and their weakness.

The first theme is the recurring attempt by Galbraith to come to grips descriptively and analytically with a contemporary and most troubling development. In 1952, it was the decline or disappearance of market competition. By 1958, the problem was to explain the coexistence of great wealth and spreading squalor. In 1967 the problem had become one that, symbolized in the term "military-industrial complex," was how to come to grips with an extraordinary concentration of combined economic and noneconomic power. Thus, one of Galbraith's two themes in all three books was an analytical response to troubling tendencies and structures in the functioning of American society. The second theme had to do with how we should feel about the problem and what, if anything, should or could be done about it.

II.

In *American Capitalism,* the solution was suggested by the subtitle: *The Concept of Countervailing Power.* There, Galbraith argued that the failure of market competition was more apparent than real; that, in fact, although giants were walking the earth, they were doing so in ways that neutralized their great power. In place of Adam Smith's "invisible hand" of market competition, the U.S.A. had developed the ugly but benign hand of countervailing power. The only remaining problem of significance, as seen in 1952, was how to prevent the great powers (in business and labor) from acting in such a way as to promote chronic inflation.

It is to Galbraith's credit that he is flexible enough to change his mind, probably because he is secure in his own person. *The Affluent Society* constituted such a change of mind, a change somewhat obscured by the concomitant change in focus. In that book, Galbraith was concerned with the failure of even a well-working private sector to come to grips with the public, nonmarket needs of the society — in education, housing, transportation, the conditions of our cities, and, *inter alia,* with what he then saw as "pockets of poverty" that were intransigent even to rapid economic growth.

The Affluent Society was an important book, for it immediately opened the eyes (in and out of the profession) of many directly and, through innumerable discussions, the eyes of many more. It altered the focus of argument in the nation (and even outside of it), and in doing so stimulated many of the books that followed it — such as Harrington's *Other America* — and that, quite naturally, tended both to modify and to expand its conclusions. Galbraith's "solutions" to the problems he enumerated were almost comically inadequate, or even potentially harmful — such as a board representing labor, corporations, and consumers that would affect the course of prices and wages; a scheme of "cyclically graduated compensation" that aimed simultaneously at making unemployment bearable (but not comfortable) for the individual, but that was neither disabling for the unemployed nor a cause of inflation for the economy; and having taken care of inflation and unemployment, the problem of imbalance between private and public sectors was then dealt with by his proposal that a specified share of increasing national income be taken up by taxes earmarked specifically for filling in the gap between social reality and need. The automaticity of the two latter schemes would remove their year-to-year meaning from the realm of controversial politics. These three proposals — for inflation, unemployment, and redress of the social imbalance — have one feature in common: they do not specify how those involved in existing power relationships (which have created and intensified the problems under examination) could be prevailed upon to step aside in favor of schemes that would involve their acquiescence — but in directions they oppose. As is always true with Galbraith, when faced with a problem of power, he skirts it by proposing schemes that assume it away (or that implicitly assume that because power is used irrationally it is also used thoughtlessly) .

This is most clearly so in *The New Industrial State*. There, after putting forth his most ominous analysis, Galbraith emerges with his most reassuring prospect. It also requires his most acrobatic performance concerning the nature and meaning of power. After all, in *American Capitalism* Galbraith was dealing only with market power, as held by corporations and unions; and in *The Affluent Society* he was concerned with areas neglected by the private sector. But in *The New Industrial State* he sees concentrated market power as having grown substantially since 1952, and he perceives its connections with state — military and nonmilitary — power. For Galbraith to be more optimistic in his latest than in his earlier book can occur only by his ignoring the thrust of his own presentation.

It is worth noting that the kind of concentrated power Galbraith noted in *American Capitalism* was less compelling in its origins and in its functioning than that in *The New Industrial State*. The latter book has as one of its prime virtues the manner in which it shows the reader — layman or economist — how the imperatives of contemporary industrial capitalism translate themselves into the imperatives of the contemporary *corporate state*. (Galbraith calls it the "industrial" not the "corporate" state, and that is a telling difference of terminology, not least when we recognize that Galbraith is among the most literate of economists, and, as a writer, one who chooses his words with exacting care.)

Wherein lies his source of optimism? It is in the "scientific and technical estate." It is these highly trained personnel who not only will, but can, inject considerations of — what else can we call it? — *humanity* into the functioning of corporations, and, I suppose, the military, the government. And even in the universities?

That seemingly whimsical question is not all that whimsical. We can learn much about what is wrong with contemporary America, and what the prospects are for its beneficial change, by looking at the behavior of faculty in the universities. The faculty are the "scientific and technical estate" par excellence; and, if anyone were to take significant steps to alter the ominous social trends and structures Galbraith notes in his book, presumably faculty would have begun to do so on their campuses. In fact, of course, faculties have not only been among the prime beneficiaries of university (and extra-university) trends in the past generation; they have also been among the staunchest defenders of those trends and of the resulting structures. To put it vulgarly, it is difficult to find a university today in which the overwhelming majority of the faculty is not a polysyllabic advocate of law and order. As is true off campus, law and order is a euphemism for the use of coercive repression to prevent any change other than that willed by those presently in power — and that includes faculties, on all but the seediest campuses.

Faculties in the past few years have found themselves increasingly defending the indefensible — e.g., the existence of military training and paramilitary research on campuses — and doing so in the name of academic freedom or, what's worse, in the name of keeping political questions from intruding on campuses. (To keep military training, in this view, is not to be political; to try to get rid of it is.)   There is no need to go on with more instances of the conservative function of faculties; what may be useful is to ask what this close-to-home example teaches us about power.

What we must know about power is not only who has it, and how they get it, and how it is used. All those things we must know. But we must also know who acquiesces in particular uses of power, and why; and for present purposes, we must know whether acquiescence is likely to be greater or lesser as one is closer to or farther away from the seats of power. My own reading teaches me that the closer one is to those seats the more likely he is, first, to benefit from the existing uses of power and, second, to find those uses by and large reasonable.

The structure and functions of power, like its origins, are complex, not simple. But power is used in the terms of those who hold it, and those terms are almost always developed in the process of seeking and gaining power — and that is another way of saying, in the process of adapting to the main thrusts of an ongoing system. The "scientific and technical estate" is composed of those who, from their earliest school days and on through their most advanced training, have learned to accept certain criteria as valid — those that enhance profit and power and glory. They have learned to serve certain masters, and to serve without consciousness of strain or coercion. The standards of the "scientific and technical estate" are the standards of those who write their checks. Of course there is dissent, but it is tolerated only so long as it is ineffectual, which is to say, idiosyncratic. There are few campuses without a house radical or two, and there are few corporations without "independent thinkers." But such cranks are kept on only insofar as they are seen as serving the ongoing purposes of their corporation, or their bureau, or their corps.

It is, of course, true that as the society becomes conscious of the crisis in which it turns, there will be increasing numbers of people on the second and third levels of power who will become restive about the present, and wish a different future. They will mean nothing unless they are responding to the growth of power on the bottom. The power that is organized from the bottom will turn on the needs of the people who get the least benefit and the most harm from the status quo, and who consequently reject not only the results but the standards of their society. They will be able to use the technical services of those near the top; but the criteria will be set by those on the bottom — as it is true that the criteria of the scientific and technical estate at present are set by the men at the top.

In closing, let me point out that in his most recent writings, concerned with the viability of the Democratic party, Galbraith has pointed to the need and desirability of that party beginning to speak in the tones of socialism, which he confines to the public sector. In doing so he once more confirms his penchant for avoiding the question of power. Galbraith needs no instruction on the relationship between economic and political power; and, even though that relationship is far from being one-to-one, it is a relationship that cannot be ignored when we speak of what lines the Democratic party should (or can) take. I think it downright mystifying that Galbraith finds it possible to ignore something that is so important and that he, more than most economists, knows about.

Galbraith is himself part of the scientific and technical estate. His own performance as an analyst, and the ineffectiveness of his own political efforts to keep the ADA honest, let alone to change this country's foreign and domestic policies, are strong testimony as to why his hopes for quiet change in America, guided from near the top, are vain. And if they are appealing as well as vain; if, that is, they set up false hopes, they weaken rather than strengthen the prospects of ridding this country of its present murderous characteristics.

QUESTIONS

Galbraithian System
Gordon / Dowd

1. Is orthodox economics applicable and relevant in explaining the operation of the United States economy today?
2. Are the major industrial firms truly subject to market forces as Gordon argues?
3. Are large firms able to determine consumer demand as Galbraith has argued?
4. How can power be shifted from one group to another?
5. Is the technical and scientific elite as subject to the control of the owners of American industry as Dowd maintains?
6. Who should have power in our society?
7. Is it really those in power who have rendered agents for change ineffective in the United States? Or is it really technology that has rendered our institutions resistant to change? Are our institutions really resistant to change? Some people would argue that more change is taking place in the United States today than in any other society in the world.
8. Will the youth rebellion play a role in shifting power? If so, will it work through the masses of people in society? Or will it work through the technical-scientific elite?
9. Conservative economists see Galbraith as a dangerous radical because he argues that the market is dead and that corporations control demand for their products and the supplies of their factors of production. Radical economists see Galbraith as an apologist for the status quo because he says nothing much can be done about the situation in the United States or the Soviet Union. Why is he seen in such a different light by these different groups?

James H. Weaver was born in Prairie Grove, Arkansas, and received a B.S. in Business Administration from the University of Arkansas and a Ph.D. in Economics from the University of Oklahoma. He has been at the American University since 1963 and served as Chairman of the Department of Economics from 1967 to 1969. He has published several articles and books and co-edited (with Gary Weaver) The University and Revolution.

7 The Social and Environmental Consequences of Economic Growth

James H. Weaver

Economics has been referred to as the dismal science. Although I have some doubts as to whether it is a science, my treatment of the topic of economic growth will be appropriately dismal. The topic is the social and environmental consequences of a commitment to economic growth and I have subtitled the essay "The Worst is Yet to Come."

The analysis is limited to the industrialized countries and is based on the experience of the United States, although the analysis seems equally applicable to the countries of Western Europe, Australasia, the USSR, and Japan. No attempt is made to deal with the consequences of growth in Africa, Asia, and Latin America.

Many of the ideas expressed here have grown out of discussions with Sam Bowles, Herbert Gintis, E. J. Mishan, and Charles Wilber. I would like to gratefully acknowledge their contributions to my thinking on this subject. I have been particularly impressed by a lecture by E. J. Mishan at American University in May 1970, which was later published as "Futurism: And the Worse That is Yet to Come," *Encounter* March 1971.

The recentness of economists' concern over the consequences of growth must be emphasized. My colleague at the American University, Professor E. J. Mishan, really started this discussion with his book *The Costs of Economic Growth,* which was published in 1967. Thus this whole discussion is only four years old. In another tradition, however, the criticism of economic growth is much older and can be encountered readily in the works of some writers of the nineteenth century; Ruskin, Dickens, and Carlyle come to mind immediately. But, among economists, the overwhelming sentiment has been to view economic growth as a singularly beneficent process. Growth Centres flourish in many universities around the world. Anti-Growth Centres are a new concept.

Many of us today no longer feel that economic growth is an unmixed blessing. Of course, an economist is naturally a materialist and a person who believes that people who are well fed, adequately housed, comfortably clothed, well educated, and medically cared for are better off than those who are hungry, naked, homeless, ignorant, and sick. There is no doubt that economic growth has brought us enormous benefits. The goods and services we take for granted would have boggled the minds of earlier generations — television, trips to the moon, electricity, computers, automobiles, telephones, atomic energy, airplanes, penicillin, etc. Mose Allison has a song that goes, "things are getting better than ever, it's people I'm worried about." The things we have produced are, no doubt, great boons to mankind and have allowed more people to live better and longer than in any previous age — and that is progress. One cannot take very seriously those young critics of our society who damn all economic growth and modern technology and then plug their guitars into the electric outlet for accompaniment to a song.

In addition to goods and services, economic growth has given us far greater geographic and social mobility than previous societies have had. Affluence and jets have enabled millions of people to travel to the beauty spots of this earth. Economic growth has contributed to the emancipation of women. Washing machines, driers, dishwashers, frozen foods, etc., mean that women are freed from household duties that consumed their entire day in earlier societies.

Economic growth has allowed us choice in family arrangements. We no longer have to live and work exclusively with our relatives as was true in earlier societies. We are far better informed. We can vicariously experience events all over the world: sports, art, music, drama, politics, even war. We are no longer so dependent upon the whims of nature. We are not faced with starvation if we do not have sufficient rainfall for the crops in our area this season.

These benefits have been so great and so obvious that traditional welfare economics has posited one single premise — that individual

welfare is increased when an individual gets more goods. Simply put —
more is better. This premise is based on two assumptions concerning
man and nature which underlie all economic analysis. The first
premise is that man's wants are insatiable and second, that resources are
limited. This leads to the fundamental economic problem: scarcity.
Given these assumptions, the logical policy prescription is: produce the
most goods and services possible at the least possible cost. The criterion
of efficiency becomes the most important criterion.

My task here is to try to demonstrate that the fundamental premise
of welfare economics is false, that more is NOT better.

Traditional economics has argued that economic welfare is increased when an individual moves from goods bundle A to goods
bundle B, B being the preferred goods. This premise is false on two
grounds; it ignores what happens to the individual as he moves from
goods bundle A to goods bundle B, and it also ignores what happens to
society and the environment in order to produce the additional goods.[1]

To demonstrate the falsity on the personal level first, an example
might be made of the man who wears cotton shirts but would prefer silk
shirts. They look better, feel nicer, etc. He gets silk shirts. Is his
welfare increased? Not necessarily. Why not? Because, in the process
of obtaining the silk shirts, his preference structure has been transformed. He is no longer the same individual he was when he had
cotton shirts. His preferences have been altered. He now thinks in
terms of cashmere.

An alternative way of looking at this is to measure welfare as the
ratio between realizations and expectations. When you expect a car for
a Christmas present and receive a car, welfare is high. But when you
expect a car and receive a bicycle, welfare is low.

The process of economic growth does increase realizations. But,
expectations constantly go up as well; in fact, expectations may rise
faster than realizations. This is a necessary process, if growth is to
continue. New goods are created, and demands for the goods must also
be created. Expectations must continually rise.

This fact is immediately obvious to anyone who considers it for a
moment and is, of course, the basis upon which all industrial economies
operate. If all of us suddenly decided that our homes were adequate,
our cars satisfactory, our clothing sufficient, etc., our economies would
collapse tomorrow. The industrial economy is based on people wanting more and more material goods. People buy things; they go into
debt; and then they have to work to pay off the debt. So we are all on a
treadmill of goods-debt-work, goods-debt-work.

In industrialized countries, advertising plays some part in this
process. In India, by contrast, one does not see big billboards on the
highways saying, "Eat food!" The people know what they need; they
are hungry. But in the United States, we spend $15 billion a year on

advertising. One and a half per cent of the Gross National Product is spent to convince us that we want all the goods the economy is producing, and some of these goods are truly bizarre. Americans have, for example, been introduced to retractable automobile headlights. The headlights retract, disappear when not in use. Now, does anyone believe that car owners really need retractable headlights? And yet how many millions of dollars have been spent designing, engineering, and producing them? Soon, no doubt, all of us will feel positively indecent driving down the highway with our headlights exposed in broad daylight.

People who get more goods, beyond some minimal level needed for subsistence, are not necessarily happier than they were before. Many of us, no doubt, have twice as many goods as our fathers had; but, would anyone argue that we are twice as happy? Economists are fond of saying that economic growth delivers the goods. We are learning that this is simply not so, for in the process of delivering the goods, more wants are created than are satisfied. Thus, we reject the fundamental premise of welfare economics because it can be demonstrated to be false on the personal level.

A second reason for rejecting the fundamental premise of welfare economics is that the premise ignores the social and environmental consequences of a commitment to produce more and more goods in the most efficient manner possible. Those consequences shall now be considered.

One seemingly necessary consequence, at least it appears in all industrialized countries, is undemocratic, bureaucratic, and hierarchical organization. Now obviously hierarchical organizations are not new and are not limited to industrialized countries. But massive bureaucratic and hierarchical organizations are consequences of the Industrial Revolution. In order to produce efficiently, people are organized from the top down, with officers, captains, foremen, supervisors, etc. Orders flow in one direction, compliance flows in the other. Virtually all work is done in anonymous, undemocratic, faceless, impersonal, smoothly functioning institutions.

A second institution that growth requires is a labor market. People work in whatever place and at whatever task will pay the most money. Labor becomes a commodity to be bought and sold on the market like sacks of flour or bales of hay. This is necessary if goods and services are to be produced efficiently.

We must remind ourselves that this is a recent development. Prior to the Industrial Revolution, labor markets did not exist.[2] People did that task to which tradition consigned them. This is not said to glamorize traditional economies. Obviously life for peasant farmers leaves something to be desired. All this goes to point out is that labor markets are new and are consequences of economic growth, and they are efficient. Most labor moves from place to place, to that place where one can get the highest price for one's labor. Economists get awfully angry with those pockets of people who refuse to move — the people of Appalachia or Southern Italy — because it is not efficient to remain in the area you grew up in, merely for sentimental reasons, if there are greater economic rewards available elsewhere. The impact of labor mobility on any sense of community is obvious.

What is not as obvious, but no less necessary, is inequality of income. Labor markets require differentiated incomes in order to operate. If everyone received even approximately equal wages, there would be no incentives with which to manipulate people into various jobs. If equal incomes were available to all, who would carry out the garbage or clean our houses and hotel rooms?

Now, economic growth did reduce income inequality. Income is more equally distributed in the United States than it is in India. But beyond some point — reached in the States in the 1940s — no further movement toward income equality has occurred. Thus it can be said that economic growth requires labor markets, and labor markets require income inequality. Therefore, that country which opts for economic growth opts for a permanent state of inequality and this is true whatever the ideology: capitalist, communist, fascist, or whatever. The Soviet Union has just as great differentials in wages and salaries as the most avowedly capitalistic countries.

A third institution that must be created in the interest of efficiency is specialization of labor. Most work must be divided into minute parts with each employee doing only one small task. But, how do you get workers to do these mindless tasks? You create alienated labor. You develop workers who will deny all their creative instincts, their desire for autonomy, fresh air, exercise, etc. — and will do so gladly in exchange for material goods and services. A materially productive society requires people who value goods and services. And a materially productive society creates that kind of people.

All societies can produce something, and each society produces people who will value whatever the society is capable of producing. A society that can produce spirituality will produce people who value spirituality. We can produce goods and services, so we create people who place high values on those goods.

Each society has certain roles which must be filled, and people are conditioned to fit those roles. Man is what he is because he does what he does. We need workers to do alienated, mind-numbing, boring work, so we create alienated labor. In exchange for loads of goodies, men spend their lives in utterly dehumanizing occupations.

But how do we create such people? All of the institutions of industrial society contribute, but perhaps the most important single institution is the school. In the nineteenth century, society required workers who could work long hours and do hard physical labor. So, they put the children in the factories to be trained for their roles. Today, we no longer need such people. Instead, we need people who can read, write, and do simple arithmetic, but, more importantly, who can do what they are told. So, we put the children in schools. Today's schools fulfill some of the functions of the nineteenth-century factory. Children are taught to work for externally imposed rewards — to compete for grades, gold stars, teacher's approval — rather than for the inherent worth of the work itself. This is the beginning of alienated labor. Just as a youngster learns geography for a gold star, so will he as an adult turn the wrench for a gold dollar. Never in his working life will he learn or do what he wants simply because he wants to do it.

There is a very high correlation between educational level and income in the United States. But there is virtually no correlation between income and cognitive skills — the ability to read, do math, etc. What then do our schools teach? They teach competitiveness, docility, and obedience. We prattle about being democratic societies and put our children in schools that are among the most undemocratic and authoritarian institutions in our society. There they spend their most impressionable years.

What do our schools really teach? They teach that society has the right to require you to spend six hours a day, five days a week, thirty-six weeks a year, for twelve years doing tasks you would not choose to do, under the direction of someone you had no voice in choosing. Or, as my children put it, "to sit down, turn around, and shut up." Without the alienated labor produced by such an educational system, our modern efficient economy could not operate. It is a necessary consequence of economic growth.

Along with a willingness to do alienated labor, people in a growing economy must have a psychological need for more and more goods. One's status, one's sense of self-respect, one's self-worth comes to depend on the quantity and quality of goods consumed. This is perhaps the most devastating cost of economic growth — the psychological cost. Modern society is in many ways a good society. People live longer and eat better; they are healthier, better clothed, better housed, etc., than in any previous age. It is also, however, a psychological nightmare. Everyone is always and forever frustrated. The constant drive is for more and better. Everyone feels in some sense a failure and feels under enormous pressure. Produce more. Consume more. The harried leisure class rushes about consuming, maintaining their possessions, using their possessions. Real leisure disappears. Modern men have far fewer feast days and holidays than primitive men. We have far less real leisure time.[3] Many aspects of the good life tend to disappear. We have no time. Cooking becomes a process of thawing and heating. In order to be able to use our possessions, and save time, we eat and watch television at the same time.

Just as we argued earlier that economic growth required that labor become a commodity to be bought and sold in the market, so also does growth require that land, and we use land to refer to all of nature's resources, become a commodity to be bought and sold on the market.[4] This is also a relatively new phenomenon in human society, dating only from the Industrial Revolution. Prior to this time land was usually owned socially — whether in feudal manors or in tribal villages — and it was used for traditional purposes from year to year.

With growth, land — all of nature — becomes a commodity to be used for those purposes that will return the greatest profit. If these profitable activities involve depleting the soil, cutting down the forests, polluting the rivers, and fouling the air — so be it. The goal of society is to produce the most individually marketable goods and services possible. John Muir referred to this type of system as a "gobble, gobble economy," and that is a most descriptive term.

A logical consequence of a "gobble, gobble economy" is environmental pollution — what economists call externalities and then forget. Society is devoted to producing the most goods and services at the lowest possible cost. This means constant efforts to find new, cost-saving methods of production. Each firm is under pressure to reduce costs and if possible to convert private costs into social costs. Those firms that do not engage in such activity will fall by the wayside. Those things which are "free goods," such as air, water, quiet, and natural beauty, will be used to the utmost. It makes perfectly good sense for each firm to "gobble" as much as possible.

Now, of course, there are other causes of environmental pollution than economic growth. Water pollution in Calcutta immediately comes to mind. What is also obvious, however, is that the kind of economic growth we have had in industrialized countries produces special kinds and quantities of environmental pollution. Everyone is aware of the results.[5]

Pollution is an international problem. Except for certain worms and a mutant species of carp that lives on poison, Lake Erie, one of the world's truly great lakes, is dead. Lake Michigan is dying, its Coho salmon gone. In the United States, the milk of some human mothers contains three to ten times as much pesticide as is permitted in the milk of dairy cows. Even the American bald eagle, the very symbol of America's fierce might and independence, seems destined for extinction. An article in a recent *New York Times* told us that the air in parts of Sydney contains forty parts per million of carbon monoxide, a higher ratio than that found in any city in the United States. The penguins of

Antarctica show high concentrations of DDT in their tissues. Industries in Britain lengthened their smokestacks to carry off the factory fumes. As a result, Sweden has acquired polluted air and smog.

Perhaps T. S. Eliot's most famous lines were

> *This is the way the world ends*
> *This is the way the world ends*
> *This is the way the world ends*
> *Not with a bang but a whimper.**

Eliot died some years ago in London, after having been struck down by one of London's "killer fogs." These phenomena should not surprise us. George Orwell pointed out a long time ago that in a money economy, good things only happen by accident. Good things happen if they coincide with making money, that is, by accident.

Once growth is introduced as the primary goal, environmental pollution is inevitable. Each firm must pollute in order to compete with other firms, and each nation must pollute in order to compete with other nations. The Soviet Union is just as busy despoiling its natural environment as is the United States. Perhaps we should congratulate ourselves on the fact that such a destructive system has left us with the natural environment in as good a condition as it is.

There has been much concern expressed that the future of the human race is uncertain because of the differences between the Soviet Union and the United States. The clash of ideologies, the different social, economic, and political institutions in capitalist and communist countries are thought to be leading us into a suicidal conflict. It is not, however, the differences between the Soviet Union and the United States that threaten man's future — but their similarities. Our fate is so uncertain because both countries are committed to policies of economic growth which can only lead to Ecological Armageddon.

Everyone remembers Aesop's fable of the grasshopper who played and sang all summer without thought of the bitter winter ahead. We have been a planet of grasshoppers. But, it is time to stop. In the nineteenth century, miners used to take a canary down into the mine with them. When the dust and gases had so fouled the mine that the canary had trouble staying alive, then the miners knew it was time to stop. All of our senses tell us that the canary has fallen silent in our world today.[6] It is time to stop.

Geographic mobility was mentioned above as one of the obvious benefits of economic growth. But this has become a curse as well as a blessing.   Millions of people have been able to travel to our spots of great natural beauty.   But their presence there in such numbers is destroying the natural beauty.   On a recent Fourth of July, some 57,000 people camped in Yosemite National Park.   They came in automobiles and trailers belching exhaust and on motorcyles that roared up and down the highway.   The smoke of 10,000 campfires poured into the air until it almost blotted out the sky.   The blaring of radios added to the din.   The highway was choked with traffic, the river with garbage.   The 57,000 people came to Yosemite to enjoy the beauties of nature.   They managed to convert the valley into a slum.[7]

The same story is being repeated all over the world, although perhaps less dramatically.   We are lucky to be living now.   Many of us have been able to see the natural beauty of this magnificent planet we call home.   We have seen the Riviera, Hawaii, Tahiti, Yosemite National Park.   We have been able to swim in unpolluted rivers, to fish in clear mountain streams, to climb mountain trails alone.   Our children and our children's children will never be able to do any of these things.   The Riviera is one vast dump; Hawaii has become a gaudy and artificial tourist trap; Tahiti is being transformed into a busy, bustling thoroughfare.   As affluence increases and transportation becomes even faster with the coming of the supersonic transport plane, this process of destroying our natural beauty will accelerate.

A further consequence of economic growth is the destruction of our great cities.   Professor Mishan has pointed out that the pleasures of strolling along the streets of a city are more a memory than a current pastime.   Buses, motorcycles, and cars belching fumes, filth, and stench; snarling engines; screeching brakes; and defective mufflers have combined to make movement through the city an ordeal for the pedestrian while the mutual strangulation of the traffic makes it a purgatory for motorists.

The transportation mess is only one small aspect of life in cities.   In addition we have the phenomenon of deteriorating housing.   The growth of slums in the United States has been one of our most rapidly burgeoning problems.   The appalling increase in crime which has accompanied our economic growth has left the downtown section of many American cities virtual ghost towns at night.   The residents of certain parts of Washington, D.C., lock themselves in their apartments at the end of the day and are for all practical purposes like animals in the zoo, unable to move about and take advantage of the benefits the city might offer.

The uglification of cities has also accompanied economic growth.   Massive skyscrapers create dreary concrete canyons.   One has to travel to Venice or Florence to see cities that are beautiful, artistic creations in and of themselves.   Few of us travel to modern cities to see them as artistic creations.

And the noise. Dear God, the noise. In the United States, the noise level in our cities is twice what it was in 1955; and, in busy sections of our cities, the level is doubling every ten years. We are just now becoming aware of the severe physiological and psychological results of exposure to these noise levels.

All of these phenomena — traffic, crime, ugliness, noise — have combined to make many cities almost unlivable. They are economically efficient, but the human spirit does not thrive there.

Another consequence of a commitment to economic growth is a loss of community. I have mentioned above the requirement for mobility of labor in an efficient economy and the reduction of community which follows. But there are other forces at work which make community difficult. Highways and freeways are built where they can be built most efficiently. Houses are torn down, neighborhoods destroyed. How many adult Americans could return to the neighborhood of their childhood and find it as it was when they were children? To ask the question is to answer it.

Modern technology is biased toward labor-saving, people-eliminating, impersonal devices. Television is an impersonal invention. The family may sit together to watch it, but they do not interact. We know what's going on halfway round the world, but have not the vaguest idea of what is happening to our neighbors next door. The automobile is an impersonal force, as is the supermarket; no human contact is involved. Family farms are eliminated to be replaced by agricultural factories. One room schools are closed, and children are sent to consolidated schools. Teaching machines, computers, and television sets replace teachers. Young people leave home to go to ever larger cities hoping to find better employment opportunities. The entire population of the nation becomes mobile — a society of transients, with no ties to church, school, or family — with no roots, no feeling of belonging.

These consequences of growth hit the young very hard as exemplified by their rootlessness and lack of community ties. The films *Alice's Restaurant* and *Easy Rider* make this point. But the rootlessness and the cult of efficiency also cause great suffering to the middle aged and especially to the old. Mishan has described the nursing homes and retirement villages where the old are isolated from the rest of society, "Where they are entertained from time to time by social workers and, somehow, jollied along to the grave"; and this is undoubtedly an "efficient" way of disposing of the old.

The unit of concern has been narrowing throughout the last 200 years of rapid economic growth. One's unit of concern was, at one time, the extended family. One thought of one's self-interest as being synonymous with the interests of the extended family. With industrialization, survival was no longer dependent upon extended families. The nuclear family emerged as the basic unit of concern. One's immediate family, wife or husband and children, became the only people whose interests merged with one's own. Today, families are no longer necessary for economic survival. Whereas one used to need the family to provide food, clothing, nursing, and child care, all of these are now available on the market. The individual can provide for all of his physical needs without being a part of any social unit larger than himself. Thus, the individual is becoming the unit of concern, replacing the nuclear family that has long since displaced the extended family. I. Me. Mine. My interest is my only concern as the nuclear family recedes into memory, and the children grow up in day care centers run by the state.

A final consequence of growth is the constant widening of the income gap between the industrialized and the nonindustrialized nations. Those who start early on the growth path can monopolize technology and resources. They can and do impose international order on terms favorable to themselves. The poor countries' share of world income constantly falls. Sixty per cent of the world's people got 13 per cent of world income in 1950 and only 11 per cent in 1964. Gunnar Myrdal has suggested that Saint Matthew was the first development economist, describing the phenomenon most incisively when he wrote, "For unto everyone that hath shall be given, and he shall have abundance; but from him that hath not shall be taken away even that which he hath" (Matthew 25:29). In the Ozark Mountains of Arkansas, where I grew up, they have a folksier way of saying the same thing, "them as has, gits."

These social and environmental consequences of economic growth must lead one to reject the fundamental premise of welfare economics. When we take account of the true costs of the additional goods and services provided us each year we must conclude that "more is not better," and that we may be producing more bads than goods each year the Gross National Product increases.

A question comes to mind. Why have we done all these things to ourselves? Obviously we thought the benefits were greater than the costs. On a deeper level, however, the answer lies in our blindness to the long-run consequences of technological change.

We can look at society as made up of five interacting parts — social institutions, including marriage and the family; political institutions — representative government, autocracy, etc.; economic institutions, private property, corporations, etc.; value systems — beliefs, attitudes principles shared by the people; and lastly — technology — the way o doing things. All these five institutions must be compatible. A rough equilibrium must exist between them. Now it is pretty well agreed tha changing any of the first four institutions is extraordinarily difficult Take any of them and recall the frontal assaults on them — the Sovie Union's attempts to alter the family, Mexico's attempt to alter the church, Turkey's attempt to alter the role of women. All of these have been met by monumental resistance. People are everywhere conservative. They refuse to give up institutions into which they have been socialized and to which they have become accustomed.

But what about technology? How do people react to a change in technology? An informative example is to be found in the introduction of textile machinery in eighteenth- and nineteenth-century England. The people who owned the new machinery saw it as a way of making more profits, which it was. The common man saw the machinery as a way of getting cheaper clothes, which it was. Only those workers who were disemployed by the machinery could see any harmful consequences. They protested but were met by a massive move for law and order. So the limited opposition to technological change was quieted, the new technology was introduced, and it led to revolutionary changes in all the other institutions of society. Massive cities developed to provide labor for factories; city housing arrangements and factory jobs made it unnecessary and, in fact, impossible to continue the extended family; businessmen gained political power to challenge the landed aristocracy. Virtually no institution was left unchanged — not the social, political, economic institutions, nor the values.

No one could have predicted any of this. We are not interested in the long-run effects of new technology on our lives. We see the brass ring on the merry-go-round and we want it. Now! There is little likelihood that this process will be stopped or even altered. We will continue introducing every new profitable technology that comes along, and the Devil take the hindmost.

The analysis just outlined must be understood as one that is evolving. It is not worked out in as complete detail as it might be. There are rough places still. I do not claim that this analysis is either new or original. All that I claim is that it is true. However, it is a different truth than that to which we have been accustomed. In this short space, an attempt has been made to prove that what we have all been taught is no longer valid. A brief analysis of two centuries of economic growth is no simple task to set oneself, and it has required a series of assertions, without the proper qualifications or clarifications and often without examples or supporting data. Given these limitations, an effort will now be made to answer the nagging questions that come to mind: What is left? Where does it all lead? What will society be like if present trends continue?

The future is nowhere more accurately described than in Aldous Huxley's *Brave New World*. It is a world controlled by a technical and scientific elite, an elite dedicated to consumption, to order, to pleasure, to efficiency, and to growth. The young are created in test tubes and raised in state-run day-care centers. When they become adults, they enter that occupation in which they will be most productive. When they are frustrated or in the slightest degree unhappy, they take drugs. Television and the feelies keep them constantly entertained. Sexual promiscuity is encouraged, and instant gratification of all sexual urges is the rule. One has no concern for a family; one lives only for oneself. The unit of concern is clearly and unalterably the individual. The old are kept vigorous by drugs until they are finally carried off to the nursing homes that are run by the state.

We need not be reminded of how accurate a picture this is of present trends in industrialized countries, particularly the United States. Everything Huxley described thirty-five years ago is either in existence or just around the corner. It has been pointed out that this future society can be characterized as orderly, scientific, and efficient. In such a society, men may experience pleasure; but that which makes them human has disappeared.

There are obvious things that we could do to reverse the present trends that are bringing us ever closer to Huxley's envisioned future:

1. We could try to convince people of the falsity of the fundamental premise upon which the commitment to economic growth rests.
2. We could use less rather than more technology, although this is an inherently ambiguous area. We obviously do need nonpolluting factories, recycling plants, etc., and yet one must be quite suspicious of our practice of adopting every new technological gadget put before us. If we do adopt new technologies, at least they must be severely tested over long periods of time to determine all possible harmful side effects. No more DDTs!
3. We could use public transportation systems in our central cities rather than relying on automobiles for transportation. If the motorists of Washington, D.C., had to compensate all pedestrians for the noise, the air pollution, the accidents — for the loss of joy in walking in cities — if automobile owners had to pay the true social costs of operating their cars — there would be no cars in downtown Washington. They could not afford to drive cars if they paid the true social costs.

   The introduction of private cars into a society increases unhappiness, rather than happiness. Those without cars are made worse off by the introduction of cars for those who can drive. And those who can drive cars will always be a minority of the population, in any society, because a transportation system based on cars immobilizes the old, the young, the poor, and the disabled, not to mention the wife whose husband takes the family's one car to work.

   With fewer resources than we are presently devoting to producing cars, building highways, etc., we could have marvelously efficient and cheap public transportation, a system that would benefit everyone, not just the minority who drive cars. Thus, it seems that both economic efficiency and social justice dictate that we substitute public transportation systems in our cities for transportation systems based on cars.

4. We could recover some of the freedom of choice that has been lost in the race for economic growth. We could build pollution-free cities for those who might prefer to do without air, water, and noise pollution and are willing to do without cars, airplanes, motorcycles, gasoline-powered lawn mowers, etc.

5. We could ban commercial advertising and replace it by factual reports much like those published by the Consumers' Union in the United States.

6. We could tax polluters an amount equal to the cost of cleaning up the pollution. This would raise the costs of products to the point where their cost to the purchaser would be equal to the true costs to the society. The result would clearly be that fewer pollution-creating goods would be produced and sold.

7. We could institute comprehensive national land use planning, as has been outlined by Ian McHarg[8] and others. It should be recognized, however, that to turn anything else over to the federal government is to ignore the horrors of the last ten years in the United States. The federal government is too big; it is too insensitive to human needs, etc., and yet one is forced into the realization that if we do not plan land use on a national scale, chaos will surely result. It seems we are damned if we do, and damned if we don't.

8. We could reach international agreements to stop funding every activity every scientist wants to undertake. In particular, we should ban research designed to create test-tube babies.

9. We could limit population growth in many different ways.

10. We could institute some type of workers' control over their jobs — perhaps along the lines of the Workers Management System in Yugoslavia, or the industrial kibbutz, or various Scandinavian experiments. These steps are necessary in order to reduce worker alienation, but they are not sufficient. A man who makes retractable headlights for cars is going to be alienated even if he makes the whole headlight and even if he gets to elect his supervisor.

11. This leads to the next suggestion, which is for some sort of community control over what is produced. Many people excoriate the auto manufacturers of Detroit. But Mr. Henry Ford II is a very intelligent, humane man. He is doing the only thing the head of Ford Motor Company can do, and that is to produce more cars. He is certainly aware of the need to redirect our resources from auto production to mass transit, environmental clean-up, and so on. But the system we have does not permit such a redirection. A different kind of system has to be devised.

2. We need a great decentralization of government and industry and a return to neighborhood control of schools, police, and so on, if a sense of community is to emerge.

3. We could alter the way income is distributed. So long as income is tied to jobs, the number of jobs available must increase at a rate commensurate with population growth. In order for the number of jobs to grow, the economy must continue to expand. Alternatives to this system are possible. We could distribute income on a

basis other than jobs. Robert Theobald and others have been advocating this for years. We are about to adopt a guaranteed annual income in the United States, which is a move in this direction. Another alternative is to restructure work and reduce the work week. One possibility with which the Swedes are experimenting is a drastic reduction in the normal work week and a restructuring of jobs. The goal is to allow both husband and wife to work half-time and carry out family responsibilities on an equally shared basis. Restructuring jobs to make them more fulfilling, less pressurized, and capable of being pursued on a half-time basis would absorb the increasing population in the labor force without requiring economic growth.

14. We could introduce considerations of aesthetics and livability into our planning and designing of cities. We could bring residents back into downtown, which would be a pleasant place again if we substituted public transportation systems for cars and reduced the noise level. Having people living in cities, having housing mixed up with shops, offices, hotels, parks, and so on, would help to reduce crime. Economists and engineers can tell us whether a city is efficient, whether it makes sense from an economic point of view. But we are discovering that economically efficient cities may be unlivable. As Winston Churchill pointed out, "We shape our buildings, and afterward our buildings shape us."

15. We could stop destroying our scarcest natural resource, the beauty of this earth. We could limit admission to our parks and other natural beauty spots in an effort to keep them in their natural state. We could hold lotteries to allocate nontransferable tickets for people to visit Yosemite, Hawaii, Tahiti, the Riviera, etc.

16. We could share the earth's output in an equitable fashion, since it is obviously impossible, from an ecological point of view, for today's poor countries to industrialize, use resources, and pollute the environment like Americans, Europeans, and Australians. If everyone in the world behaved as we do, life on the planet would come to an end.

The average per capita income of the world is approximately $600, or $2400 for a family of four. With certain changes, this level of affluence could probably be increased somewhat without ecological disaster. What is needed is an international negative income tax — just like a national negative income tax — but extended to the whole world. Such a proposal has been outlined elsewhere,[9] and it is economically feasible.

Some economists call for a zero rate of economic growth or for a plus 2 per cent rate or a minus 2 per cent rate, but this is meaningless. What is included and what is excluded in the Gross National Product is purely a matter of arbitrary definition. For example, the work done by wives in the home is not included in the Gross National Product.

indicating that the definition of GNP was obviously worked out by a group of male chauvinists. We could change the rate of growth tomorrow by changing the definition. The subject of consideration here is a fundamentally different kind of society.

The difficulties and costs involved in implementing any of these suggestions must be conceded. The question of coercion immediately comes to mind when many of these ideas are mentioned. There are real questions as to whether we can have an affluent world in which men are also free. But the point is that there are alternatives before us.

It is not likely these alternatives will be adopted, however, and the reasons are twofold. The first is greed, apparently an ubiquitous human phenomenon; everyone wants to improve his standard of living. However, when greed is allowed to become the dominant motive in society — as it has in industrialized countries — it becomes cancerous and ultimately destructive. We have unloosed this genie from the bottle in order to achieve unprecedented economic growth. Now it is futile to hope that the genie can be contained.

The second reason is fear. No industrialized nation will dare to control and limit its technology for fear that other nations will develop some new technological device which would make world domination possible. The American Indians and the Australian Aborigines stand as constant reminders of what happens to a technologically backward society when it is confronted by a technologically sophisticated society. They got zapped. Thus, all nations live in constant fear of what will happen to them if they do not adopt the latest technology and continually seek new techniques.

When we combine unfettered greed and deep-seated fear with our utter inability to foresee the long-run consequences of technological change, the future of man is indeed bleak. There is, however, some basis for another conclusion than the one just reached.

Many of the people in the world today need more goods and services than they have. But some parts of the world are incredibly rich. Per capita income in the United States in 1970 was $4000, which means that if income were divided equally the average family of four would have had an income of $16,000. The children of this affluence may come to realize that economic growth is a false god. They may realize that with all of our vaunted growth, this century has produced more wars, more mass murders, more systematic genocide, and more ecological catastrophes than any previous age.

The example of Germany always comes to mind. A nation that had experienced enormous economic growth, one of the most industrialized, most educated, most prosperous countries in the world, put six million people in gas ovens. The atrocity of the war in Vietnam must also be mentioned here. On December 7, 1971, we marked the fact that the United States had been at war continually for the last thirty years. Sometimes hot war, sometimes cold — but continuous warfare, nevertheless.

The young are questioning, in their often inept way, many of the institutions that have created these results. One would have thought that all of our material possessions would have made us happy. But our system seems to be fatally flawed. The young today are asking the same question asked of old, "For what doth it profit a man to gain the whole world, if he loses his own soul?" This questioning of our institutions and the directions they are taking us may be healthy. When our analysis fails, we can always hope, hope that men who have learned to swim under the water like fish, who have learned to fly in the air like birds, can learn to walk upright and unafraid like men.

ENDNOTES

[1] See Herbert Gintis, *Alienation and Power* (Ph.D. dissertation, Harvard 1969).

[2] See Karl Polanyi, *The Great Transformation* (Boston: Beacon, 1944).

[3] Staffan B. Linder, *The Harried Leisure Class* (New York: Columbia University Press, 1970).

[4] See Polanyi, *op. cit.*

[5] The following examples have been suggested by Loring Chase, "The Land Cries Out" (Mimeograph, 1970).

[6] Herman E. Daly, "The Canary Has Fallen Silent," *New York Times*, October 14, 1970, p. 47.

[7] *Forbes* magazine ad in the *New York Times* of May 3, 1967.

[8] Ian McHarg, *Design with Nature* (Garden City, New York: The Natural History Press, 1969).

[9] James H. Weaver, Leroy Jones, Nancy Wolf, "An International Negative Income Tax" in *The International Grants Economy*, Kenneth Boulding, Jane Horrath, and Martin Pfaff, eds.

REFERENCES

Allan, J. D. and A. J. Hanson, eds. *Ecology, Society, and Man.* Wadsworth 1971.

Ayres, Robert, and Allen Kneese. "Production, Consumption, and Externalities." *American Economic Review.* June 1969.

Boulding, Kenneth. "The Economics of the Coming Spaceship Earth." *Beyond Economics: Essays on Society, Religion, and Ethics.* Ann Arbor: University of Michigan Press, 1970.

Buber, Martin. *Paths in Utopia*. New York: Macmillan Co., 1949.

Dales, J. H. *Pollution, Property, and Prices*. Toronto: University of Toronto, 1968.

Daly, Herman. "The Canary Has Fallen Silent." *The New York Times*. October 14, 1970.

————. "Towards a Stationary-State Economy." in J. Harte and R. Socolow, eds., *The Patient Earth*. New York: Holt, Rinehart and Winston, 1971.

Ehrilich, Paul and Anne. *Population, Resources, Environment*. San Francisco, Calif.: W. H. Freeman & Co., 1970.

England, Richard, and Barry Bluestone. "Ecology and Class Conflict." *The Review of Radical Political Economics*. Vol. 3, No. 4 (Fall–Winter 1971).

Goldman, Marshall I. *Controlling Pollution: The Economics of a Cleaner Air*. Englewood Cliffs, New Jersey: Prentice-Hall, Inc., 1967.

————. "The Convergence of Environmental Disruption." *Science*. October 2, 1970.

Hardesty, John, Norris C. Clement, and Clinton E. Jencks. "Political Economy and Environmental Destruction." *The Review of Radical Political Economics*. Vol. 3, No. 4 (Fall–Winter 1971).

Heilbroner, Robert. "Ecological Armageddon." *The New York Review*. Vol. 14, No. 8. April 23, 1970.

Hicks, J. R. "Growth and Anti-Growth." *Oxford Economic Papers*. No. 3. November 1966.

Hoffman, Michael. "Development Finance and the Environment." *Finance and Development*. September 1970.

Johnson, Warren A. and John Hardesty. *Economic Growth vs. The Environment*. Belmont, Calif.: Wadsworth, 1971.

Kennan, George. "To Prevent a World Wasteland: A Proposal." *Foreign Affairs*. April 1970.

Keynes, J. M. "Economic Possibilities for our Grandchildren." *Essays in Persuasion*. London: MacMillan, 1931.

Lee, Dorothy. *Freedom and Culture*. Englewood Cliffs, New Jersey: Prentice-Hall, 1959.

Leopold, Aldo. *A Sand County Almanac*. New York: Oxford University Press, 1966.

Leontief, Wassily. "Environmental Repercussions and the Economic Structure: An Input-Output Approach." *Review of Economics and Statistics*. August 1970.

Lewis, Arthur W. "Is Economic Growth Desirable?" in *The Theory of Economic Growth*. Homewood, Ill.: Irwin, 1955.

Linder, Staffan B. *The Harried Leisure Class*. New York: Columbia University Press, 1970.

Marx, Karl. *Early Writings*. Translated and edited by T. B. Bottomore. New York: McGraw-Hill, 1964.

Marx, Leo. *Machine in the Garden: Technology and the Pastoral Ideal in America*. New York: Oxford University Press, 1964.

McHarg, Ian. *Design with Nature*. Garden City, New York: The Natural History Press, 1969.

Mills, Edwin. "Economic Incentives in Air Pollution Control." in Harold Wolzin, ed., *The Economics of Air Pollution*. New York: Norton, 1966.

Mishan, E. J. *Technology and Growth*. New York: Praeger, 1970.

Orleans, Leo, and Richard Suttmeier. "The Mao Ethic and Environmental Quality." *Science*. December 11, 1970.

Pecora, W. T. "Science and the Quality of Our Environment." (Commencement Address, George Washington University, June 7, 1970, Washington, D.C.).

Phelps, Edmund S. *The Goal of Economic Growth*. Revised Edition. New York: Norton, 1969.

Polanyi, Karl. *The Great Transformation*. Boston, Mass.: Beacon Press, 1957.

Report of the Study of Critical Environmental Problems, *Man's Impact on the Global Environment*. Cambridge, Mass.: M.I.T. Press, 1970.

Roszak, Theodore. *The Making of a Counter Culture*. Garden City, N.Y.: Doubleday, 1969.

Reich, Wilhelm. *The Mass Psychology of Fascism*. New York: Farrar, Straus & Giroux, 1970.

Ruff, Larry. "The Economic Common Sense of Pollution." *The Public Interest*. Spring 1970.

Russell, Clifford, and Hans Landsberg. "International Environmental Problems — A Taxonomy." *Science*. June 25, 1971.

Solow, Robert M. "The Economist's Approach to Pollution and Its Control." *Science*. Vol. 173. August 6, 1971.

Turnbull, Colin. *The Forest People*. New York: Simon and Schuster, 1961.

Vito Tanzi was born in Mola di Bari, Italy, received his B.A. from the University of Bari, his M.A. from George Washington University, and his Ph.D. from Harvard. He was on the faculty of George Washington University from 1963 to 1965, and was a Senior Economist at the Organization of American States from 1965 to 1967. In 1967 he came to the American University, where he is now Professor of Economics and currently serving as Chairman of the Department of Economics. He has published The Individual Income Tax and Economic Growth, *as well as numerous articles.*

8 Should We Stop Economic Growth?

Vito Tanzi

I. INTRODUCTION

The current controversy about economic growth reminds one of an exchange that took place some time ago between Maurice Chevalier, the world-famous French entertainer, and an interviewer. Chevalier was asked, on his eightieth birthday, how it felt to have reached that ripe age. His answer was brief and to the point: "Very well" he said, "considering the alternative." That answer summarizes the main thesis of this essay: Economic growth *has* its serious and substantial costs that have much too often been ignored by both economists and governments; an increase in the GNP index *is not* tantamount to an equivalent improvement in the people's welfare; governments *have been* wrong in developing an attitude of "growthmanship." Yet, when all

would like to thank Professors Ezra J. Mishan and James H. Weaver for their comments on this paper. It is obvious that I cannot make them share the responsibility for it since they disagree with many of the things said in it.

this is said and the merits as well as the demerits of growth are taken into account, a strong case can still be made than even the United States, with its very high level of income, is likely to be better off with growth than without growth.

A discussion of economic growth must necessarily go beyond the mere listing of its many costs and benefits in an *ex post* sense. It must consider the costs of future growth against the costs which would be associated with a zero-growth situation. The now-fashionable anti-growth literature has simply paid precious little attention either to the benefits of economic growth or to the consequences of a no-growth policy. It is thus guilty of the same sin as the more traditional point of view; it has biased the benefit/cost calculus of growth in a direction which makes its point of view sound more convincing than it really is.

The best-known piece of antigrowth literature — Mishan's *The Costs of Economic Growth* — after 170 pages of closely reasoned, at times entertaining, and always incisive criticism of what he calls "growth-mania," states that "The general conclusion of this volume is that the continued pursuit of economic growth by Western Societies is more likely *on balance* to reduce rather than increase social welfare."[1] What is remarkable about this statement is that very little mention is made throughout the book of the positive side of continued growth. Thus one cannot decide, by reading this book, if *on balance* future growth would be desirable or undesirable.[2] It is possible, as it will be argued in this essay, that although the costs of economic growth are certainly very high, those of economic stagnation are likely to be even higher so that *on balance* one might wish a continuation of growth.

It is always difficult to classify ideas since classification implies that there is a particular place for every thought and that the categories available exhaust all the possibilities. Yet, for convenience, a taxonomic approach will be followed for a brief discussion of the major views encountered in the antigrowth literature or movement.

II. A SURVEY OF ANTIGROWTH VIEWS

First of all one encounters what could be called the *bucolic* or *romantic* criticism of growth. This view, which most likely can be traced back to Rousseau, laments the disappearance of pure springs, of beautiful forests, of primitive agricultural pursuits — where man grew his own food or perhaps just hunted or fished for it — of the pastoral life with its idyllic simplicity and nobility. This view equates what is normally called civilization with an inevitable corruption of the natural goodness of man. Thus, it prescribes a return to nature as the only escape from the chaotic and corrupting modern world. The establishment of rural communes which has recently attracted much attention in the United States is a logical outgrowth of this view.

There is not much that one can say about this back-to-nature movement. It is obviously not a viable alternative except for a relatively small number of people. It represents a nostalgic view of a world that never was and never will or could be. It is unlikely to recruit people who were brought up on a farm. It is more likely to recruit them from Scarsdale or Cook County or Montgomery County and for relatively short periods.

The second type of criticism, which could be called the *sociological one,* is far more significant. It emphasizes the negative impact that a highly developed economy is supposed to have on man and on society and concludes that if a $4000 per capita income economy is bad for man and society, $5000 must be worse, and $6000 even more so. Thus growth is bad and generates more "bads" than "goods."[3]

There are several ramifications to this argument as typified by the works of several writers including James H. Weaver, Herbert Gintis, and others. The substance, however, is basically the same: economic scarcity no longer exists. Only a high expenditure for advertising prolongs the fiction that there are unsatisfied wants in a macrosense. The sale of useless commodities such as the "nothing box" or retractable headlights for cars is the best and most incontrovertible proof that we have really reached such a level of affluence that all our wants are satisfied.[4] In a microsense, of course, some genuine wants might still go unsatisfied but this is supposed to be a problem of distribution, not production. Remove Madison Avenue, rearrange the distribution of income and you can stop growth; you can then sit back, relax and enjoy life. If you don't do that, you will be caught in the growth trap: you will think that position B (a higher level of income) is preferable to A, but in the process of moving from A to B you will be changed so that you will end up being worse off at B than at A. The solution that is often suggested is elementary: just change the nature of the economic system and the nature of man; that is all that is needed.

Several objections could be raised to this line of thought. In the first place one could point out that advertising in one form or another is really not a new phenomenon. The big fairs of the Middle Ages were nothing else but an extravagant form of advertising; and so were the huge outdoor markets in most European cities. One could point to the fact that *paid* advertising on a large scale is really limited to a few groups of products (soaps, cars, cigarettes, liquors, etc.) that may not account for an overwhelming portion of our income.

With respect to the usefulness or uselessness of what we buy it is obvious that there is no way to decide which commodities are useful and which are not.   Who is to decide?   Is the "nothing box"[5] more useless than the pyramids or the very large number of churches in previous cultures or the Mao portraits in China?   Was the purchase of the "nothing box" the result of advertising pressures or simply the belief on the part of an individual that he could derive enjoyment from it?   It is obvious that the real issue here is the inevitable conflict between an individualistic view of society and a more collectivistic approach.   If we stick to the first, and barring paternalistic attitudes, we have no right to judge how an individual is to satisfy his wants.   If we shift to a more collectivistic view, we will inevitably come to grips with the question of who is to make the decisions for the masses.

To say that all wants can be satisfied with today's resources is to fail to realize that we, really, desire specific goods as means toward the maximum satisfaction of certain categories of wants; within each category there must often be infinite combinations of specific goods that can provide the same level of satisfaction.   We do not necessarily want bread, what we want is the abatement of our hunger in the most pleasant way possible; we can do this with bread or rice or we can do this with caviar and filet mignon.

The same for shelter or for transportation or for entertainment or for clothing.   We must remember that the Louvre and Versailles were at one time private residences; so was Villa d'Este in Rome.   We must recall that the function of the Colosseum was entertainment.   The same is true for transportation.   The desire for air and sea travel is not a fabrication of Madison Avenue.   After all, Icarus lost his wings and his life, according to the legend, much before Madison Avenue came into existence and so did Ulysses.   They lost their lives because of a natural desire on the part of man to fly or navigate the high seas.   The experiments of Leonardo and many others with flying machines is certainly a further proof of that desire.   Equally true, television did not create the desire for entertainment, or the refrigerator the desire for cold storage

The Gintis argument[6] — that man may prefer, *ex ante,* position B to A but when he reaches B his nature changes in such a way that he is no better off or may even be worse off is also not convincing.   One can agree that by error such a situation could develop; in other words, one could choose position B to A but once he reached B he might not be better off than he was at A.   This is obviously possible.   What seem unlikely, however, is the almost Pavlovian consistency of man in making the wrong decision.   Growth is not just a movement from A to B but a series of continuous movements from A to B, then from B to C, from C to D, and so on.   Granted that one could make the mistake of going from A to B, wouldn't he then realize that he made an error and thus should not move to C?   If he erred again, wouldn't he finally learn and not move to D?

This is an almost pathetic view of man blundering his way through life. One does not have to believe that man is the all-rational and the all-calculating creature of orthodox economic theory to reject the Gintis argument. Furthermore, at least many millions of foreign-born Americans would have the option, at some point, of stepping out of the movable escalator on which they find themselves by going back to their countries and the same would be true of the Americans who were born on farms but moved to the cities. There is still no sign of any such exodus. In fact, all the evidence seems to indicate that many foreigners, if given the chance, would prefer to suffer a higher level of income in the United States than enjoy a lower one in their own countries. A recent Gallup Poll asked the residents of many foreign cities if 1. they wanted to leave their countries and 2. which country would rank first in their preference if they did leave. The answer to question 2. was almost uniformly the United States, and many wanted to leave.

The third type of criticism of economic growth is the *technological* one. It follows two major aspects: one emphasizes the effect of growth on the environment; the second, which is very much related to the *sociological* type of criticism, links growth to science and science to many disturbing trends in modern life.

The first of these aspects is simple. A high level of income puts a tremendous pressure on the environment by creating a large amount of effluence. This disturbs the fragile ecological balance and endangers the very existence of many species; eventually, it may endanger human life itself. The capitalistic form of production is supposed to contribute to this problem by not making the polluters pay for the social cost that they are imposing on society. There is a lot of validity in this line of reasoning. Our air is much dirtier today than it was in the past and so are our streams. We are told that some lakes are dead — whatever that means — and that our seas may be in serious danger of dying. Our beaches are in continuous danger of being spoiled by oil and some cities are threatened by health catastrophes caused by air pollution. Few would disagree with this assessment. However, what is not clear is how stopping growth would help in this direction.

Let us, for a moment, close our eyes and imagine that we could "stop growth." What would be the environmental consequence of this? This is a question that deserves much more attention than it has received up to now. But this is really the basic question. As orthodox economics teaches us, fixed costs are not relevant for future decisions. Equally, the costs and benefits of *past* growth are not to be taken into consideration. What one needs to consider are the costs and benefits of *future* growth. One can be against past growth and in favor of future growth.

It is reasonable to assume that the stopping of growth would be reflected in a decrease in capital accumulation. But this slowdown of capital accumulation would most likely be accompanied by an aging of the stock of capital. Take the stock of automobiles, for example. Stopping growth would inevitably lead to an increase in the average age of this stock. The same would happen with ships, or planes, or steel mills, etc. This aging of the stock of capital could very well make worse, at least for quite some time, the environmental problem. If we want to bring technology to bear in this area, it will have to be mostly through new capital, new machines, new automobiles, etc. By stopping growth, we may preclude this possibility.

The importance of the age of capital in the environmental problem is obvious when one tries to relate air pollution to the per capita income of various cities. Any well-traveled person should be aware of the fact that there is really no positive correlation between a city's per capita income and its degree of air pollution. Any traveler to the developing world would easily realize that the cities in this part of the world are as polluted as the American cities and that this is due to a large extent to the much older age of the average car in those cities than in United States cities. But if cities with $200 or $500 per capita income are as polluted as the American cities, what can we say about the relationship between growth and pollution? Probably very little. It is more likely that the size of the city is more important than its per capita income. But in this too, growth seems to play a rather passive role: three out of the four largest cities in the Americas are outside of the United States (i.e., Buenos Aires, São Paulo, and Mexico City).

This brings us to the consideration of what it means to stop growth. Does it mean stopping it in per capita terms or in terms of total output? If it means the former, we would still have growth in total terms. If it means the latter then we would either have a declining per capita income or we would have to stop population from growing. But forcing a stop in population growth would have serious welfare implications. For the Catholics those considerations are rather obvious. But they exist for others too: if I have the will and the means to decide on the number of children that I want, and I decide on three, my welfare will decrease if I am forced to have only two. Thus, for the individual population control does have real welfare costs.

A further problem with this control of population, at least in the United States, originates from the fact that such control would conceivably come through the removal of incentives to have children. It would come through the elimination of the personal exemption in income tax legislation, through the elimination of welfare payments to dependent children and through the elimination of various other programs that assist children. In other words, it would come mainly from the elimination of whatever welfare measures we have. At least in the short run the implications of these changes for income distribution are quite disturbing.

There is certainly much evidence that industrialization contributes to pollution, but the relation between pollution and growth is not as simple as it is made to be. The Ganges is at least as dirty as the Potomac and we are told that Calcutta, with less than $100 per capita income, may very well be the most polluted city in the world. Also the concept of pollution ought to be more embracing than dirty rivers and dirty air. With all the pollution derived from being the richest country on earth, the United States provides, from a health point of view, still a far more sterile environment than most other countries. Growth may have polluted the rivers but it has also given Americans the means for providing water that is drinkable. In how many places on earth is this true?

The second aspect of this technological type of criticism emphasizes the effect of growth on science and science is seen as a kind of Pandora's box containing a monster that cannot be contained and that sooner or later will destroy all of us. Here again one can take his pick. He can either underline the *potential* danger of science, or he can point to the actual and *potential* benefits. Science could develop the method for duplicating individuals and exterminating nations. Or it could develop a cure for cancer and many other diseases as well as the means to free man from the prison called Earth. But in which direction scientific development will move depends on conscious policy and not on the rate of growth. The change in attitude toward certain aspects of scientific development caused by the Vietnam war is already reported to be having an impact on research.

What is more important, however, for the discussion at hand is whether it is really correct to say that growth affects scientific knowledge, which in turn affects society. It seems that at least in our type of society the relationship is more in the opposite direction. It is more likely that science is the one that affects growth, rather than the other way around. The Age of Genius preceded rather than followed the Industrial Revolution.

The fourth type of criticism of economic growth could be called the *political* one. This approach emphasizes the effect of growth on the political and economic relations among countries. A discussion of this literature would take us too far afield. Here I shall limit myself to a mention of three aspects of this politico-economic criticism. The first is, of course, the political economy of imperialism. This theory that is generally based on Marxian thinking argues that growth creates an economic surplus that forces countries to look for ways to dispose of this surplus. In the process of finding new markets, as well as new sources of raw materials, the "imperialistic" countries will come to dominate the less-developed countries. Implicitly, the faster is the rate of growth in the developed countries, the greater will be the need for these markets, and the stronger will be the colonizing effort which in particular cases will lead to war. War may itself be a way of disposing of this economic surplus.

The second of these aspects is the so-called Prebisch thesis.[8] Differential past rates of growth led to very different economic structures for the industrialized and the developing countries. These different structures eventually came to have an influence on the terms of trade between the two groups of countries. The terms of trade tended to deteriorate for the developing countries. Consequently, such a deterioration facilitated a faster rate of growth for the industrialized countries, which in turn affected again the terms of trade and so forth. Conceivably, if the industrialized countries could be prevented from growing at faster rates than the developing ones, this situation would eventually correct itself.

The third of these aspects is the so-called international demonstration effect, which is obviously Nurkse's adaptation to countries of Duesenberry's relative income hypothesis of consumption.[9] Here one finds an international externality of the negative kind. A fast rate of growth in the Western countries and especially in the United States will increase the disparity in living standards between these countries and the developing world. This will lead to an increase in the dissatisfaction that the residents of developing countries feel with their own consumption standards and will lead them to save less and consume more. This curtailment of saving will reduce their potentiality for growth and will thus maintain or even widen the gap between poor and rich countries.

There is little that one can say about this politicoeconomic literature. As to its imperialistic branch, one can either accept it or reject it. It all depends on one's political views. The other two branches, however, i.e., the Prebisch, and the Nurkse's arguments, are less dependent on political considerations. How important these arguments are depends on more objective considerations. The literature dealing with them is somewhat controversial especially with respect to the Prebisch thesis.

III. THE COSTS OF ECONOMIC STAGNATION

Reference has been made several times, above, to a zero-growth economy. The implication was that it would be in our power to stop growth if we just wanted to do so. Now we must ask if this is a realistic assumption. Suppose that the American voters, faced with a special referendum, decided to add a no-growth amendment to the United States constitution: it is one of the inalienable rights of the American citizens as a group to live in a zero-growth economy. Consequently, a Council of Economic Stagnation (C.E.S.) is organized to suggest policies for stopping growth. We should inquire what kind of policies would such a Council recommend. Just what policies would a zero-growth economy imply? Would such policies be politically palatable to the majority of the United States population? Let us briefly consider these two questions in turn.

There is no clear answer to the first of these questions. The Council on Economic Stagnation would be at a loss to decide which policies to recommend. The truth of the matter is that our knowledge of the causes of economic growth is too limited to be very helpful in indicating to us how to achieve a zero-growth rate. Something we do know. We know, for example, that investment helps growth. But its contribution to *per capita* growth may be very small — in the order of 15 per cent of the *per capita* growth rate, if we believe some writers. In other words, a full 85 per cent of the *per capita* growth rate may be the result of factors other than investment. Which are these other factors? The list would have to include education, technology, economies of scale, health of the labor force, composition of the labor force, and many others. Thus, for example, public expenditures for education and R and D could be reduced. But what reduction would be needed to provide a zero-growth rate? Our state of knowledge does not permit an answer to that question. Besides, there would be substantial and unknown lags between the time when the policy action would be taken and the time when the impact on the rate of growth would be felt.

Under present circumstances growth can only be stopped in the short run by use of monetary and fiscal policies. In other words, it can be stopped by generating a recession. But these policies would not stop the growth of potential output but only of actual output. The gap between potential and actual output would lead to a growing level of unemployment.

But let us suppose that somehow our knowledge of the working of the economy becomes so precise and detailed that we can predict with complete certainty the effects on the growth rate of certain policy actions. We could then legislate how much people ought to save; how much they ought to invest; which type of investment they could carry out since a change in the composition of investment may imply different growth rates even when the total is not changed; how much schooling people ought to have and what kind; how many inventions people ought to make; how many hours a day they ought to work, how many children they ought to have, etc. In summary, only a fairly complete regimentation of society would assure a zero-growth rate.

This raises an obvious question: if people are willing to subject themselves to such policies, wouldn't they be even more willing to accept those policies that would allow them to have their cake and eat it too? In other words, would they not prefer to continue having growth but making sure that many of the serious consequences of growth are taken care of? For example, as the Russian experience has shown, a country can grow at a very fast pace even without the automobile. Thus, if the automobile is such a serious challenge to the real welfare of man, why don't we tax it out of existence? The standard answer — that this is not possible politically — is not acceptable since, if that is true, the policies to stop growth would also not be possible politically. In other words, if we are willing to give the government the power to stop growth, we must also have given it the power to eliminate the evils of growth.

There could be circumstances in which growth might not be desirable any longer. This would occur when:

1. everybody is happy with the country's income distribution and with his own level of consumption;
2. everybody is happy with the quality of the public services;
3. there is no developing world;
4. there is no population growth;
5. there is no wish to conquer space, etc.

As long as these conditions are not met, growth will continue to be a desirable goal even though an increasing share of output must be used to protect the environment and to eliminate the more serious consequences of growth.

Let us consider, briefly, these conditions. We all know that income distribution in the United States is far from what it should be. In fact, there may be large sections of the population that are living in squalor in the midst of a so-called affluent society. A correction of this situation in a no-growth economy would mean that some sectors would have to reduce sharply their incomes and their consumption so that their share of the unchanging pie could be reduced. Economic theory teaches us that there is such a thing as a ratchet effect in consumption behavior: a reduction in consumption is very painful regardless of the initial level. Thus, the elimination of growth with income redistribution would imply very severe welfare costs on part of the population.[10]

Since J. K. Galbraith wrote *The Affluent Society,* it has become an article of faith in the United States that the quality of public services is very poor. It is argued that the country is simply not allocating a large enough share of its GNP to public services. This is confirmed by the relatively low average tax ratio in the United States as compared with the European countries.[11] The anticipated costs of certain programs

— such as income maintenance, general health care, etc. — that the government is supposed to assume in the future give a dramatic demonstration of the impossibility of stopping growth. In fact, the financing of these programs in a zero-growth rate economy would impose such a tremendous sacrifice on the population that it is very unlikely that these programs would ever be considered in a stationary economy.

The same reason is valid with respect to the developing world. There is now something almost obscene in the industrialized countries' unwillingness to raise the level of their assistance to the developing countries. However, as long as the former keep growing, there is at least the hope that some day the flow of resources from rich to poor countries will increase. But if growth came to an end, even that hope would fade since an increase in the flow of resources in a situation of economic stagnation would again mean an actual decrease in the standard of living in the United States and in the other developed countries.

IV. CONCLUDING COMMENTS

In a very stimulating paper written in 1964, Tibor and Anne Scitovsky speculated on some of the costs of economic growth.[12] Their general conclusion, supported in part by statistical evidence, was that much of those costs were borne by the middle and higher classes. The professional people in particular seem to have been victimized by the trends which accompanied the development of the American economy: the prices of many of the things that weighed heavily in their budget — services, entertainment, leisure, etc. — rose much faster than the general price level; their earnings, on the other hand, declined in relative terms.

This conclusion may go a long way to explain why this antigrowth movement has been pretty much limited to professionals and to people with upper-middle and higher-class background. Workers and lower-class people in general do not seem too concerned with the costs of economic growth and their demand for higher and higher incomes is in fact one of the major reasons for the continuation of the "growth-mania" decried by Professor Mishan.

As a final note to this essay, it must be repeated that growth, in spite of the many costs that it generates, does enlarge the size of the pie, which, if *properly* used, should improve the welfare of the population. Unfortunately, the failure of the governments to introduce the policies that are required often leads to the aggravation of many problems which are then seen as a direct consequence of growth. Growth, however, should not be considered such an important objective as to make us pursue it at all costs at all times. The antigrowth literature has served a very useful role in opening our eyes to some of the dangers associated with the blind pursuit of this objective.   But we should not accept uncritically its implied recommendation about *stopping* growth since this might create more problems than it would solve.   In the next several years, let us go after the polluters, let us restrict the role of the automobile, let us increase our allocation to public services, let us try to allocate our yearly increase in income to all those functions that can increase general welfare.   If in spite of these changes the quality of our life and our environment does not improve, then we might want to follow the recommendation of the antigrowth literature.   In the meantime it would be good for that literature to do some homework on the basic question of how we could implement their general recommendation.

ENDNOTES

[1] Ezra J. Mishan, *The Costs of Economic Growth* (New York: Frederick A. Praeger, 1967), p. 171.   Italics added.   The interested reader should also read Mishan's article, "Making the Future Safe for Mankind," *The Public Interest*, No. 24, Summer 1971.

[2] To be fair to Professor Mishan, he did state in the foreword to the book that he was not going to discuss the benefits which derive from growth.   Still, reading the book one cannot say whether *on balance* growth is good or bad.

[3] See for this view Mishan's paper in *The Public Interest*.

[4] See James Weaver, "Toward a Radical Political Economics," *The American Economist*, Spring 1970.

[5] *Ibid.,* p. 59.

[6] As reported by Weaver, *loc. cit.,* p. 58, and as outlined at a conference at the American University.

[7] Another problem: should blacks as a group have the same birth rate as whites? But then, since they have a higher death rate, they would experience a fall in their absolute number.

[8] See United Nations Economic Commission for Latin America, *The Economic Development of Latin America,* 1950.

[9] Ragnar Nurkse, *Problems of Capital Formation in Under-Developed Countries* (Oxford: 1953).

[10] Professor Mishan, in commenting on this paper, has argued that the reduction in consumption is painful only in the short run.   In other words, it is a transitional effect.   He may or may not be right.   In any case, even if just for a transitional period, a reduction in income and consumption *will be* painful.

[11] See Vito Tanzi, "Comparing International Tax Burdens: A Suggested Method," *Journal of Political Economy,* October 1968.

[12] Tibor and Anne Scitovsky, "What Price Economic Growth?" in E. S. Phelps ed. *The Goal of Economic Growth* (New York: W. W. Norton, Revised Edition), pp. 31–46.

Richard Parker was born in California, was graduated from Dartmouth, and is reading politics and economics at Magdalen College, Oxford. He has been a Junior Fellow at the Center for the Study of Democratic Institutions, and an intern in economics at the United Nations Development Programme. He was a member of Phi Beta Kappa and Students for a Democratic Society, but resigned from both. He is completing a book on wealth and income distribution.

9 The Myth of Middle America

Richard Parker

Middle America has become an amazingly popular subject in the past few years. President Nixon appeals to it for support. Vice-President Agnew harangues it about its "radical-liberal" enemies. Journalists and editorial writers worry about the depths of its alienation. One recent writer has even attributed to it a "consciousness," distinct from both the young and the dedicated advocate of public interest.

Yet for all the talk, the anxiety, the attempts to probe the psyche of this social monolith, surprisingly little seems to be known about it. Occasionally Middle America has been classified in terms of hard hats, the "little man," and the "average guy in the street." Given the complexity of modern American society, however, nobody seems even to know who that man in the street is anymore. That fact is not surprising, however, because it indicates to what an extent our social categories have been jumbled in the past few decades, so thoroughly in fact that we have lost the ability to describe our society coherently.

For the orthodox economist, the inability to describe our society should not be much problem; macroeconomics has never depended much on social structures anyway, and microeconomics disclaims any interest in larger social relations to begin with. For the radical economist, however, the confusion we seem to be undergoing at present offers

133

a real challenge; presuming that our social realities reflect (how accurately depends on one's radicality) economic realities, by careful examination of changes in our economic structure, it may be possible to recognize some of the reasons for our state of confusion.

The question seems to be, as far as we're concerned here, what are people talking about when they talk about Middle America? And given who is speaking respectfully and who is speaking disrespectfully, what can we deduce about the state of American society?

Not so long ago to be a Middle American simply meant to belong to the middle class. By that, people usually meant that you were part of a vast majority, living in the most affluent society on earth, where poverty had been virtually abolished and opportunity existed for all. If you were growing up in the fifties, you probably thought of yourself as part of the Atomic Age, the Post-Industrial Age, the Technological Age when mankind (or at least America — it was never quite clear) was preparing to begin a fundamentally new phase in its history, in which scarcity, that common plight of all societies heretofore, would be abolished, and the chief problem, once automation was completed, would be what to do with all the leisure time. Even growing up in the early sixties (remember when we only had "advisers" in Vietnam?), you still might have had an optimistic outlook on life. After all, though the poverty we once thought had been abolished was back again, it was being cared for by sincere men and a War on Poverty; and life was getting better all the time, wasn't it?

All that benign optimism seems terribly far away now, after the experiences of the war in Vietnam, the uncountable assassinations, and the murder of students at Kent State. Yet the myth of a great middle class, homogeneous, well off, and secure, still persists. Why? After admitting that at least 20 per cent of the nation is poor, why the persistent confidence in the affluence of all the rest? That 20 per cent figure relies on an income of $3000 for a family of four, an income that allows seventy-five cents per person per day for food. If it is possible that many people live below the line, how many more live only a short distance above it? And with unemployment high again, after the artificial decline induced by the war, how can we be so certain that the working class is not pressured also, feeling the squeeze, and moving further and further away from the commonly held notion of the middle class? But if we count up all the people affected by such conditions, they represent at least a third, and possibly a half, of the nation. How is it that we can call ourselves an Affluent Society faced with such realities?

Historically the answer is both complex and straightforward at once: the myth of a middle class has lain at the heart of America since the time of de Tocqueville, and the myth of a near-universal affluence since the end of the Second World War. The second is in some sense the logical outgrowth of the first, but the reasons for its importance after World War Two should become more apparent after a few moments' reflection.

It was a tenet of both liberal and conservative dogmas following World War II that, economically, life in America was getting better all the time. Aside from the political flurry of McCarthyism in the early 1950s, the economy was everyone's favorite topic of discussion. After economists had predicted a major postwar recession, the American economy fooled them and began what seemed like a skyrocket burst. Between 1945 and 1965, the Gross National Product quadrupled, and disposable personal income increased two-and-a-half fold. Postulating a "trickle-down" theory of income distribution, economists assumed that it was only a question of time before poverty was eliminated in America.

Suckled on the Horatio Alger myth, and teethed on depression and war, the American public was glad to hear the news. Madison Avenue blared the New Affluence across front pages and invited all of us to join the feast of consumption. The new myth of America was the suburb, the grass-lined, tree-shaded Eden of responsible Americans. There a family was safe and happy with its two cars, two children, dog, and barbecue pit. Social science, and the academy in general, took over the affluence myth virtually in toto, declaring the end of scarcity, and with it the end of ideology, and the dawn of a new technocratic age where abundance, rather than scarcity, would be our bane. A Gallup Poll would most likely have found wide acceptance of David Lilienthal's views that "one finds the physical benefits of our society distributed widely, to almost everyone, with scant regard to status, class, or origin of the individual."[1]

But the myth of the New Affluence was a cruel distortion of reality. Composed of half-truths, it closed our eyes, cut us off from a recognition of America, and closed off political and social alternatives. Today, poverty in the midst of prosperity seems almost characteristic of mature capitalism. Moreover, deprivation also seems characteristic, and together with poverty describes the living conditions of nearly half the American people. What once appeared to be a New Affluence, I contend, is in fact an expansion of the economy that has disproportionately benefited the upper and upper-middle classes, while it has left the poor and the deprived to gather what crumbs fall from the table.

Marx contended in *Das Kapital* and elsewhere that poverty was a normal condition of capitalism even in the best of times.[2] He argued that even if workers' actual wages rose, the differential between their wages and the income of the rich would continue to increase. The issue was settled to the satisfaction of most American economists by the performance of their own economy after the Second World War. A number of them had their faith in capitalism shaken by the Depression, but the postwar boom quickly allayed most of their doubts. The original

Marxian criticism that wages might rise but differentials between classes grow larger was lost sight of in the general euphoria of the 1950s.

The euphoria, moreover, was not limited to the traditional, or *laissez-faire,* economists. Liberal interventionists and Keynesians alike joined with conservatives to announce the death of poverty in mature capitalism. John Kenneth Galbraith, for example, claimed that by the late fifties American poverty was limited to "the insular poor" and "the case poor."[3] The former were the inhabitants of areas like Appalachia and the rural South, where shifting employment patterns were causing "painful, but temporary hardship." The "case poor" were the alcoholics, invalids, and elderly who could not, or would not, get ahead. Keynes himself (like Marx) had, of course, foreseen no such amelioration, even in Keynesian capitalism. "Keynesian interventions in the economy necessarily adjust production and consumption in favor of investments. Such adjustments cannot end the paradox of poverty in the midst of plenty, and are not designed to do so."[4]

The problem of economists was to explain *why* poverty was disappearing at such a rapid rate. Census statistics indicated that families with incomes below three thousand dollars had declined from 28 to 14 per cent between 1947 and 1966.[5] But why? Obviously prosperity in general, and unionization in particular, had improved the lot of the working man. But raw data, as well as a few highly sophisticated studies, indicated not only that the economic pie was getting bigger but that a significant reallocation was taking place. It appeared that because of some poorly understood reasons a real change was taking place in the economy. Arthur Burns, then an Eisenhower adviser, rejoiced: "The transformation in the distribution of our national income . . . may already be counted as one of the great social revolutions of history." Paul Samuelson spoke for the liberals when he said, "The American income pyramid is becoming less unequal."[6]

Though still lacking an explanation, the economists' statistical foundations seemed eminently solid. Simon Kuznets' massive study, *Shares of Upper Income Groups in Income and Savings,* indicated a major decline in the percentage of personal income controlled by the upper strata of the society, a decline that "would continue." The late Selma Goldsmith and her associates showed that the share of personal income received by the top 5 per cent declined from 30 per cent in 1929 to 26.5 per cent in 1936–37, and to 20.7 per cent by 1944. Similarly, she showed that the share of the top 20 per cent declined from 54.4 to 51.7 to 45.8 per cent in the same periods.[7] At the other end of the spectrum, the bottom 20 per cent began to show some, if sizably smaller, gains.

Using this data, plus rawer data collected by the Bureau of the Census and other governmental agencies, economists postulated a theory for income distribution. According to the theory, income was slowly but irreversibly "trickling down" the income scale from the rich to the poor, to result finally in Samuelson's "flattened pyramid." It was presumed to be only a question of time before the last vestiges of poverty would disappear entirely; by the late fifties, Galbraith declared calmly, poverty in America would no longer be "a massive affliction but more nearly an afterthought."[8]

As a consequence, the study of income distribution as an economic discipline rapidly declined throughout the fifties. The university, like the nation at large, mesmerized by the new Affluent Society, was content to rest its discussions of poverty on clichés and rudimentary data. In economics, the new interest was in "value-free" econometrics; in the popular consciousness, it was in *The Organization Man* and *The Man in the Gray Flannel Suit.* Affluence was the presumed condition of almost all, and discussion centered on suburbia, martinis, and psycho-analysis. Maladies were the result of too much rather than too little.

The "rediscovery" of poverty in America, then, came as a rude awakening to most. Michael Harrington's *The Other America,* which got widespread attention in the early sixties, provided graphic por-trayals of the personal impact as well as the extent of poverty. It inspired a major reexamination of the country's goals. Harrington's estimation that one quarter of the American people lived in poverty shattered not only national pride but also the sublime self-confidence of the economic establishment. To them, his words were heresy.

But even after Harrington pricked the popular balloon, air leaked out with surprising slowness. Those running the federal government's War on Poverty (and many social scientists) agreed to define as poor only those families with annual incomes below three thousand dollars. This swift bit of statistical legerdemain immediately shrank Harring-ton's one-quarter to a less frightening one-fifth. The effect was not only to isolate and minimize the poverty in America but to ignore the basic contradictions in the myth of prosperity.

A reëvaluation of postwar prosperity leads to major second thoughts about "trickle down" theories of income distribution. As early as 1957, Robert Lampman, of the University of Michigan, noted that initial gains by the poor to increase their share of the wealth had not only stopped but were reversing.[9] By the early sixties, the rich were again increasing their control of the lion's share of personal income.

The premature optimism of economists like Burns lay in statistics that took no official notice of their unusual circumstances. During the war and shortly thereafter, the income of laborers and service workers increased almost twice as fast as that of professionals and managerial workers. But this was due chiefly to war-related factors that would be unlikely in a peacetime economy, such as full employment mixed with a shortage of nonskilled labor. By the late fifties, the lower categories no longer showed high-rate gains: laborers' and service workers' income increased only 48 per cent while managerial income increased 75 per cent.[10]   Joseph Pechman concluded in 1969 that "the distribution of income in the nineteen-fifties period may not have been very different from what it was in the early nineteen-twenties."[11]

These gross figures, some would argue, are misleading because of shifts in the labor market. Thus the small gains for laborers might be offset by the diminishing number of common laborers, or the high incidence of poverty among farmers offset by decreasing numbers of farmers. But Herman Miller, an economist with the Census Bureau, disagreed. Writing in a Bureau monograph, *Income Distribution in the United States,* he concluded that shifts in job distribution did not substantially affect patterns of income distribution. "Of course it could still be argued that the over-all stability of income distribution for the urban population masks important changes which have taken place for various subgroups within the population. But this hypothesis . . . does not appear to be supported by the facts. Income distribution within the urban population has not shifted even when that population is further classified by labor force status of wife, age of head, or size of family."[12]

Miller, however, does underline one important trend: the increasing number of families in which both husband and wife work. "It should be noted that incomes are much more equally distributed among families where the wife is working than where she is not working; the sizable increase in the proportion of families with working wives has therefore tended to decrease income inequality during the past decade."[13]   Moreover, census projections show that the proportion of women in the labor force will continue to grow over the next two decades.

Yet even the increased family income provided by a second earner was unable to offset the gains by upper and upper-middle classes in control of personal income. Using census data as well as studies by various economic agencies, Joseph Pechman acknowledged that the rich, but not the poor, had prospered in the postwar era. He pointed out that the simplest census tables, those most often cited, exclude capital gains and therefore grossly misrepresent income trends in the upper fifth of the economy. For example, the following table shows the

Year	Top five per cent of families	Top twenty per cent of families
1952	18%	42%
1957	16	40
1962	16	42
1967	15	41

standard before-tax income shares of the rich, according to census data: What this table indicates obviously is confirmation of Burns' "great revolution." But are the figures accurate?

Tax data are needed to push the analysis further. These data are more useful, because they show the realized capital gains of these families and net income after federal taxes. The salient observation here is that, contrary to another popular myth now also on the wane, the federal income tax is *not* progressive. Computing total disposable (i.e., after-tax) income, we find the following:

Year	Tax Units Top five per cent	Tax Units Top fifteen per cent
1952	16%	30%
1963	17	33
1967	17	34

However, this table itself can only be considered an estimate that falls to the low side. Since the Second World War, innumerable tax benefits and payment forms have grown up which benefit only the rich. Pechman names tax-exempt interest and depletion allowances as sources of income, then adds: "During World War II, methods of compensation were devised to funnel income to non-taxable forms. The devices used are well known: deferred compensation and pension plans, stock option arrangements, and direct payment of personal consumption expenditures through expense accounts."[14] Having listed these varieties of unreported income, he prefers caution, and concludes, "Little is known about the impact on the distribution of income."

Gabriel Kolko is not so timorous. In *Wealth and Power in America,* Kolko announced that "the impact of the federal income tax on the actual distribution of income has been minimal, if not negligible."[15] Drawing on a number of sources for his data, he deduced that adding the uncomputed income of the upper classes would raise their total disposable income 2 or 3 percentage points above Pechman's own figures. (Thus the top 5 per cent received about 20 per cent of the personal income, and the top 1 per cent about 10 per cent of that income.) Since 1952, the effective federal tax rate on the upper one per cent of the population has dropped from 33 to 26 per cent.[16]

What may be said of the federal tax structure can be repeated *ad nauseam* for state and local tax structures. The impact of property and sales taxes is clearly regressive, and as one economist put it, this is "disturbing because the state-local tax system is the growing element of the national system."[17] Federal tax revenues have remained fairly constant as a proportion of Gross National Product, hovering around twenty per cent since 1951. State and local taxes, by contrast, have risen from 7.1 per cent of the Gross National Product in 1951 to 11.9 per cent in 1968. "Assuming that state-local taxes respond more or less proportionately to the rise in national product . . . the states and local governments must have increased rates of sixty-eight per cent in these seventeen years to push up their tax yields to the present level."[18]   The motivation is obviously not simple greed, but a reflection of increased demand on public services and increasing population concentration in metropolitan areas.   Nonetheless, the burden of these social changes falls most heavily on those least able to pay.

   The Economic Report of the President, 1969 shows the following:

Income Classes	State and Local Taxes (percentage of income)
Under $2000	25%
$ 2000– 4000	11
4000– 6000	10
6000– 8000	9
8000–10,000	9
10,000–15,000	9
15,000–and over	7

   Analysis of income alone, in the case of the rich, obviously also misrepresents the actual concentration of economic well-being in the country.   Affluence for the rich, unlike income for the middle and lower classes, is rarely limited to wages and salaries.   Rent, dividends, interest, all go into the total wealth of the upper class.   James D. Smith, of the Office of Economic Opportunity, in analyzing data of persons with gross assets in excess of sixty thousand dollars, found a highly concentrated wealth structure.[19]   This group, representing the top 1.5 per cent of the wealthholders in the country received the following amounts of income:

Type	Billions	Per cent of Total
Wages and salaries	$25.9	10.8%
Dividends	8.0	74.8
Interest	3.1	27.9
Rent	6.4	52.5
Capital gains	57.6	71.4

Furthermore, this table is an understatement of concentration.   It excludes $1.7 billion in dividends paid to trust funds and nonprofit foundations; it assumes only average yields on assets, rather than optimum figures to be obtained through the advice of investment counselors, etc.; its data are for 1958, and all subsequent information shows increasing pyramiding of the wealth structure.

Gabriel Kolko also contributes significant figures on the concentration of total wealth in the upper brackets which supplement Smith's own research. For example, in 1960 the top 10 per cent controlled two thirds of all assets, while 51 per cent of the spending units headed by unskilled or service workers had no assets.[20] Other, more shocking data suggest that between .2 and .3 of 1 per cent of the population control 22 per cent of the personal wealth and 60 to 70 per cent of all privately held corporate wealth.[21]

What in fact was the condition of the poor through the fifties and into the sixties? First of all, we must have a definition of poverty. The federal government has chosen the income-line method, with all families falling below three thousand dollars (now thirty-seven hundred, because of inflation) defined as poor, and therefore eligible for charitable assistance. Before 1962, little was known about this group; since then, an antipoverty industry has dredged up quantities of information about these people, from their illiteracy rates to their reproduction out of wedlock.

Given all this information, what have we learned? First of all, the income-line method is misleading. It fails to account for assets, temporary impoverishment, and several other factors. Second, and more importantly, the three thousand dollars has been recognized as ridiculously, if not criminally, low.

How in fact was the government's poverty budget originally arrived at? Politically, several factors interacted; methodologically, the explanation is simple. An annual food budget was prepared, and then that figure was tripled. The budget followed Department of Agriculture guidelines that included the notion that food occupies about one third of normal family expenditures. But simple methodology belied the gross underestimation of need. Kolko summarized the government's projection of "an adequate minimum" budget for a family of four:

"Three members of the family see a movie once every three weeks, and one member sees a movie once every two weeks. There is no telephone in the house, but the family makes three pay calls a week. They buy one book a year and write one letter a week. The father buys one heavy wool suit every two years and a light wool suit every three years; the wife, one suit every ten years or one skirt every five years. Every three or four years, depending on the distance and time involved, the family takes a vacation outside their own city. . . . The family spent a total of eighty to ninety dollars on all types of home furnishings, electrical appliances, and laundry equipment. . . . The family eats cheaper cuts of meat several times a week, but has more expensive cuts on holidays. The entire family consumes a total of two five-cent ice-cream cones, one five-cent candy bar, two bottles of soda, and one bottle of beer a week. The family owes no money, but has no savings except for a small insurance policy. . . . The family buys a new car every twelve to eighteen years."[22]

The government's budget is unrealistic on other scores. It fails to take account of the overpricing and shoddy quality of food in poor areas, as documented in books like David Caplovitz's *The Poor Pay More*. It ignores the high cost of other items such as housing and furniture, etc. (usually 10 to 25 per cent overpriced, according to one Bureau of the Census economist) that drive up maintenance costs in the other two

Percentage of National Personal Income, Before Taxes, Received by Each Income-Tenth*

	Highest Tenth	2nd	3rd	4th	5th	6th	7th	8th	9th	Lowest Tenth
1910	33.9	12.3	10.2	8.8	8.0	7.0	6.0	5.5	4.9	3.4
1918	34.5	12.9	9.6	8.7	7.7	7.2	6.9	5.7	4.4	2.4
1921	38.2	12.8	10.5	8.9	7.4	6.5	5.9	4.6	3.2	2.0
1929	39.0	12.3	9.8	9.0	7.9	6.5	5.5	4.6	3.6	1.8
1934	33.6	13.1	11.0	9.4	8.2	7.3	6.2	5.3	3.8	2.1
1937	34.4	14.1	11.7	10.1	8.5	7.2	6.0	4.4	2.6	1.0
1941	34.0	16.0	12.0	10.0	9.0	7.0	5.0	4.0	2.0	1.0
1945	29.0	16.0	13.0	11.0	9.0	7.0	6.0	5.0	3.0	1.0
1946	32.0	15.0	12.0	10.0	9.0	7.0	6.0	5.0	3.0	1.0
1947	33.5	14.8	11.7	9.9	8.5	7.1	5.8	4.4	3.1	1.2
1948	30.9	14.7	11.9	10.1	8.8	7.5	6.3	5.0	3.3	1.4
1949	29.8	15.5	12.5	10.6	9.1	7.7	6.2	4.7	3.1	0.8
1950	28.7	15.4	12.7	10.8	9.3	7.8	6.3	4.9	3.2	0.9
1951	30.9	15.0	12.3	10.6	8.9	7.6	6.3	4.7	2.9	0.8
1952	29.5	15.3	12.4	10.6	9.1	7.7	6.4	4.9	3.1	1.0
1953	31.4	14.8	11.9	10.3	8.9	7.6	6.2	4.7	3.0	1.2
1954	29.3	15.3	12.4	10.7	9.1	7.7	6.4	4.8	3.1	1.2
1955	29.7	15.7	12.7	10.8	9.1	7.7	6.1	4.5	2.7	1.0
1956	30.6	15.3	12.3	10.5	9.0	7.6	6.1	4.5	2.8	1.3
1957	29.4	15.5	12.7	10.8	9.2	7.7	6.1	4.5	2.9	1.3
1958	27.1	16.3	13.2	11.0	9.4	7.8	6.2	4.6	3.1	1.3
1959	28.9	15.8	12.7	10.7	9.2	7.8	6.3	4.6	2.9	1.1

* In terms of "recipients" for 1910–37 and "spending units" for 1941–59.

Source: Data for 1910–37 are from National Industrial Conference Board, *Studies in Enterprise and Social Progress* (New York: National Industrial Conference Board, 1939), p. 125. Data for 1941–59 were calculated by the Survey Research Center. Figures for 1941–46 are available in rounded form only. Previously unpublished data for 1947–58 are reproduced by permission of the Board of Governors of the Federal Reserve System, and data for 1959 by permission of the Survey Research Center.

thirds of its budget. In farm areas, it still relies heavily on the presumption that the rural families produce much of their own food, although as a percentage of the total food consumed, home-grown items have fallen from 70 to 36 per cent in the past twenty years. It makes no allowances for the higher education of the children, unless one presumes they will receive full scholarship aid, which is highly unlikely. Finally it assumes no major medical expenses in the family, although over half of the poor are not covered by medical insurance.

The actual meals upon which the entire budget is based inspire greater disbelief. The words of the census that "assuming the homemaker is a good manager and has the time and skill to shop wisely, she may prepare nutritious, palatable meals . . . for herself, a husband, and two young children" on a budget of seventy cents per day per person inspired one pundit to comment that "Betty Crocker herself would starve." A statistician for H.E.W. describes how a housewife must spend her money:

"For a meal all four of them ate together, she could spend on the average only ninety-five cents, and to stay within her budget she must allow no more a day than a pound of meat, poultry, or fish all together, barely enough for one small serving for each family member at one of the three meals. Eggs could fill out her family fare only to a limited degree because the plan allows less than two dozen a week for all uses in cooking and at the table, not even one to a person a day. And any food extras, such as milk at school for the children or the coffee her husband might buy to supplement the lunch he carries to work, have to come out of the same food money or compete with the limited funds available for rent, clothing, medical care, and all other expenses. Studies indicate that, on the average, family members eating a meal away from home spend twice as much as the homemaker would spend for preparing one for them at home. The twenty to twenty-five cents allowed for a meal at home in the economy plan would not buy much even in the way of supplementation."[23]

Despite the obvious subminimal character of this "minimum budget," some optimism has been generated by the War on Poverty and a booming economy, inducing people to believe that the poor are "disappearing." But this optimism needs closer scrutiny. First of all, a three-thousand-dollar limit is a ridiculously low level separating the poor from the nonpoor. Second, the government has continued to play games with its own figures ever since the War on Poverty began. For example, the cut-off limit of poverty is measured by pretax income figures, although the poverty budget was constructed on an after-tax basis. Third, politics has taken a heavy toll on the poor. According to the McGovern Committee: "In 1968, government statisticians estimated there were between twenty-two and twenty-seven million Americans

143

living in poverty." But at the beginning of 1969 "the higher of these two figures was dropped without explanation"[24] and the twenty-two million used as the official estimate. Finally, government economists have consistently underestimated the effect of taxes and inflation on the poor, or so say a group of nongovernment economists (writing in *Life*, August 15, 1969). Since fixture of the three-thousand-dollar figure in 1960–61 dollars, inflation and taxes have required a gain of 41 per cent in actual income to maintain a real income equivalent. This would require a present definition of the poverty level at $4240 or $540 more than the government now allows. Such an adjustment would add several million more families to the rolls of the poor.

For the extremely poor, times are now even harder. As the Southern Rural Research Project reported: "The poor and the hungry had their brief moment in the sun: America may lionize its victims, but the vogue of compassion passes quickly on; the hungry have now become somewhat passé. Americans seem to take it for granted that once such alarming conditions are publicly known, the appropriate authorities will automatically step in and clear the matter up."[25] Dr. Arnold Schaefer, who headed the Public Health Service's National Nutrition Survey, had been among the first to document malnutrition in sample counties in Texas and Louisiana; now the survey has been discontinued, and Dr. Schaefer has passed quietly from the scene. One wonders if the fifteen million malnourished have passed as quietly.[26]

President Nixon's contributions to the crisis of poverty remain to be seen, since his proposed revamping of the welfare system has yet to pass Congress. The central feature, a minimum income, is an advance over existing programs, since it recognizes working as well as nonworking poor, but its own ceilings of aid are so low as to offset the extension in coverage. His proposal to tie Social Security to cost-of-living indices also seemed designed to benefit one segment of the poor, but this was rejected by Congress in favor of a one-shot 15 per cent bonus.

The central fallacy, or perhaps the central design, in the government's designation of the poor is its narrowness. Given the present definition of the poor, we avoid the larger contours of our social reality. Compared with the wealthy or near-wealthy, the gains of the poor have been almost immaterial. In 1946, the bottom 20 per cent of all families (the government estimate of the "poor" hovers around 16 per cent) received 5 per cent of the income; by 1967, the same fifth — now forty million people — received 5.4 per cent.[27] In other words, the intonations of "trickle down" by economists of the fifties now sound hollow indeed.

Crucial to the isolation of the poor is not only government's action, but the basic American myth. We are people of the *middle* class, bourgeois, home folks, people who still like Norman Rockwell and live decent, unextravagant lives.   De Tocqueville did not instigate the myth, but *Democracy in America* certainly strengthened it.   His comments on the "tendencies toward the equalization of the conditions of life" set the pattern for all later social scientists and historians who sought to capture the fundamental character of the country.   Louis Hartz, as recently as the middle fifties, still wrote of "irrational Lockeanism" as the controlling factor in American political life, and saw this as a reflection of the dominant "middle class."

The belief in progress has always caused Americans to see their past in an ambivalent light.   They have viewed the past romantically, choosing to see our problems as smaller and our victories larger than life. What is imperialism to some has been Manifest Destiny in America. What for some was genocide directed toward the Indian was only "resettlement" of the natives.   Even when we made mistakes, there was seldom an accusation of guile or willfulness on our part.   The Spanish-American War was "misguided," but it was fought with the best of intentions.

By this kind of logic, our poor today are still better off than 90 per cent of the world, and certainly in a better state than they were fifty years ago.   The discomfort that greeted disclosures by the muckrakers and writers of the naturalist school at the turn of the century has been replaced today by a comfortable agreement that things were bad then, but just look at them now.   After all, the middle class has always been America's strength and salvation.   If we do have poor, well, either they are lazy and inefficient (the conservative view) or they are victimized minorities — blacks, the old, unwed welfare mothers (the liberal view). In any case, nobody opposes welfare anymore — Nixon is pushing the guaranteed income.

The fundamental misdirection of all this is away from analysis of the "middle class" to a blind invocation of the myth itself.   As recently as October 1969, *Newsweek,* for example, ran an otherwise perceptive article entitled simplistically *The Troubled American — A Special Report on the White Majority.*   Studded with references to "America's vast white middle-class majority," it intoned the familiar lauds: "America has always been the most middle class of nations, the most generous and the most optimistic."   But what in fact the article showed most clearly is that for an enormous proportion of the "middle class," embourgeoisement has been a half-filled dream, a set of unsatisfied hopes.   These are the people Leon Keyserling has called, not the poor, but "the deprived Americans" — "above poverty but short of the minimum requirements for a modestly comfortable level of living."   In 1964, Keyserling estimated their number at seventy-seven million men, women, and children.[28]

Keyserling's distinction between a family income of thirty-five hundred dollars ("poverty") and forty-five hundred ("deprivation") should be clear to an economist: the "deprived" all work. Unlike the poor, whose ranks are swelled by the elderly, the infirm, and the blacks, the "deprived" are functioning, productive members of our economic system: the manual laborers, the clerks, the launderers, the hospital workers of our society. They may have their own home, but it is heavily mortgaged; they may have a late-model car, but it has been financed at steep rates. Their savings, which form a family's cushion against disaster, are marginal: 40 per cent are either in debt or have savings of less than one hundred dollars. Liquid assets show even less room for error: 20 per cent of all families own no assets, and 48 per cent own less than five hundred dollars worth.[29] Yet, as Kolko rightly points out, "Liquid assets — such as checking and savings accounts, shares in savings-and-loans associations and credit unions, and government savings bonds — are of decisive importance to low and even middle-income families exposed to layoffs, unemployment, or medical and other emergencies. Often they represent the entire margin between security and the relief rolls."[30]

The myth of the middle class works as a permanent bond on the deprived. Lacking the income, they are still expected to provide their families with the amenities that advertising, television, and the academic mythmakers have told them the "middle class" enjoy. Constantly under pressure, they retain all of the old American virtues as a desperate bulwark against the encroachment of the "shiftless poor." They, like the poor, bear a heavy burden of the taxation because of regressive tax structures. They aspire for better education for their children, their own home, and more leisure. Yet, in a great many cases, both father and mother must work simply to maintain their present condition.

The disparities within the "middle class" and the number of the "deprived" are brought out most clearly when one examines the data of income growth over the past half-century. The table on page 142 shows control of the income shares by population tenths since 1910. Omitting the top tenth as "upper class" and the bottom two-tenths as "poor," analysis of the remaining "middle class" yields striking results.

The most interesting observation is that there are two distinct strata in the "middle class," the upper of the two having gained markedly greater control of income. Between 1910 and 1959, the second, third, and fourth deciles increased their percentage of the total income almost one-third, while the fifth, sixth, seventh and eighth deciles were able to advance only from 26.5 per cent to 27.9 per cent in the same period.[31]

This information sheds light on much of the writing over the past two decades on the Affluent Society. The "middle class," as a homogenous group, has done well, but closer examination reveals that that success becomes smaller and smaller as one moves down the income scale within that class. The astigmatic concern of the social scientists for suburbia, executive anomie, and the crisis of "the abundant society" has proceeded from myths that now seem badly worn — from the myth of the New Affluence, from the myth of "trickle-down" income and wealth, redistribution and the omnipotence of Keynes, and from the capstone myth of them all — the myth of the American middle class.

As a matter of fact, the "middle class" may have escaped the grasp of more than the poor and the deprived. If by "middle class" one means a decent, modest standard of living, it seems that perhaps 60 to 70 per cent of the country has difficulty in reaching it. In 1966, the Bureau of Labor Statistics announced that the average urban family required $9191 per year to live comfortably, yet the median income that same year was fourteen hundred dollars less than that figure. At this point, it seems wise to stop and make two observations: the first an estimation of some present and possibly future realities; the second, an historical speculation.

The first observation is about the "unmentioned middle class," the professional, technical elite and its immediate support structure. These people are the true beneficiaries of the Affluent Society, and are the class which has sought to reshape the American myths in its image. College-educated, employed as lawyers, engineers, advertisers, and real-estate dealers, these people are the upper strata of the middle class that experienced the greatest gains in postwar years. The suburban crises of the fifties were *their* crises, the suburban malaise was drowned in *their* martini glasses. If one were to seek a paradigm for their group, one would find it during the Kennedy era, in the bright young men around the seat of power, but one could also find it in the older and younger men in corporations and universities. They are those whom Daniel Bell described as the "technocratic elite."[32]

An attack on this group here is not immediately relevant. The Vietnam war has already prompted a number of incisive critiques of them, particularly on the university level. However, critique and solution are not synonymous. It seems likely that the import of young people's radicalism will be diffused and compromised back into electoral party politics, and the thrust of radical restructuring lost, as it was in the New Deal. Already the "beautiful people" seem to be emerging as the new archetype of this social caste — human beings who span Establishment and anti-Establishment factionalism, who work for corporations by day, yet smoke dope by night. The horrible prospect is not so much of their immorality as of their lack of moral concern.

The difficulty is that their amorality is hard to detect because it so often hides behind a veil of rhetorical concern. Unlike the industrial captains of the last century, their contemporary lieutenants feign not indifference but impotence. After all, they *are* concerned, God knows, but they are only vice-presidents or mere managers. They may give occasionally to the political *outré* or talk of "repressive tolerance" at cocktail parties, but those mark the boundaries of their social concern.

One index of that social indifference emerges in an ironic place: Michael Harrington recently had an article in *The Atlantic* entitled "The Betrayal of the Poor." The irony is that *The Atlantic,* for all its enlightenment, is still an organ of that upper-middle class who have not so much resisted, as they have ignored, social change.

The article begins: "For all the rhetoric of recent years about the war on poverty, the poor in America are almost as numerous as ever. . . . Unless the government makes immensely greater commitments of resources and planning, the country is doomed to a social explosion in the seventies that will make the turbulent sixties seem tranquil by comparison."[33] The article, like articles on the malnourished, on execrable housing conditions, on the quality of education in the ghetto, will be read and then lost in the comfortable notion that once federal programs are established, everything will be taken care of. Enter the New Deal, Phase II.

The error in this remains the presumption of the liberal upper-middle class since the first decade of this century: that social legislation by the federal government will cure what ails us. Jane Addams suggested it; Ralph Hunter, one of the nation's first social welfare workers, endorsed it; the New Deal itself put the seal of approval on it; and now, on the verge of the twenty-first century, even Republicans have begun to see merit in the idea. Unfortunately, the theory has never worked. The critical assumption behind liberal optimism about coalition between the federal government and corporate capitalism has been that things keep getting better all the time. There are more cars, more homes, better schools, etc., than ever before, and in the midst of this prosperity, the distribution of all this largess has been getting better as well.

Taking the first half of this claim — that the total quantity of goods has increased — there is no dispute. But one *can* make some comparisons between the United States and other industrialized nations. Other nations have higher literacy rates. Other nations have lower infant mortality rates. To my knowledge, the United States is the only industrialized nation that does not offer comprehensive medical insurance for all its people. It offers perhaps the worst unemployment protection, and the worst welfare system among the developed countries. It has fifteen million malnourished. It has thirty million poor. It has seventy-seven million deprived. Few other nations can claim such tawdry conditions amid such phenomenal growth.

On the second half of the comfortable liberal optimism — that distribution has been getting better and better — there is a fundamental error in the assumption. Since the Second World War, the only significant redistribution of income in the United States, has been between the upper and upper-middle classes. Furthermore, distribution has remained essentially stable not only over the past twenty years but over the entire twentieth century.

There are three sources for this statement. The first is the chart on income distribution (see page 142) that shows the limits of change. The second is from Joseph Pechman, a conventionally liberal economist, writing in *The Public Interest,* who states: "The year 1929 must have been the high point of inequality during the nineteen-twenties, so that distribution of income in the more recent period may not have been very different from what it was in the early twenties if account is taken of undistributed profits."[34] The third is a much earlier source. Published in 1904, Robert Hunter's *Poverty* is probably the first attempt made to estimate the number of poor in America. Highly sympathetic to the poor, it uses the data of state and private welfare agencies (since federal data were nonexistent). While emphasizing the wretched conditions of the poor, Hunter limits their number to only 12 per cent of the population. Today economic historians agree that Hunter's estimate was low, but not by more than half, thus leaving at the turn of the century a minority poor of 18 per cent.[35] Yet 18 per cent was the government's estimate of the poor sixty years later!

None of these three estimates is perfect (none can ever be, because crucial data are lacking), but they can give a newer and perhaps more accurate contour of poverty and affluence in America. We are, as de Tocqueville said, and as American social scientists have reaffirmed ever since, "a people of the middle class." But to be middle class is both a social-psychological and economic problem. Among those who call themselves "middle class," perhaps a majority have always lacked the money to be in fact what they believe they are. Not only are the poor still with us, but they have been there for years. Michael Harrington's announcement that our poor are the "first minority poor in history" is wrong; the poor have always been a minority in America, but a stubborn minority that refuses to decrease and disappear. The rich in America just keeping getting richer. All the talk of income distribution, of flattening pyramids, and of peaceful economic revolutions has been nonsense, fabricated in part out of optimism, in part out of a myopia in the professional classes who themselves gained so rapidly after the Second World War.

We began this article with a discussion of Middle America and what it means. What should be apparent by now is that "Middle America," if it exists at all, is a far different group, with far different worries and problems, than the one we had expected. As used by journalists and politicians, Middle America seems to mean not the middle of America at all, but the lower middle of an economic and social system in which to be lower middle means to be deprived of what once was piously, and myopically, referred to as an Affluent Society. Far from being the well-off racist, beer-guzzling, flag-waving man who sits comfortably in his expensive home watching color TV and driving his late model car to the factory, the lower-middle-class American and his poor brethren seem the victims of a cruel hoax designed to deprive them of both the means and desire to enjoy what, in a just society, would be theirs.

The confusion about Middle America stems from a more ubiquitous confusion we seem to be suffering about America as a whole. Until we recognize that our country is not at all what it dreams of being, will the fulfillment of that dream come true.

ENDNOTES

1 David Lilienthal, quoted in Kolko, p. 6.

2 Cf. J. K. Galbraith, *The Affluent Society* (New York, 1958), pp. 252 ff.

3 Karl Marx, in Herman Miller, "So What's Happening to Our Social Revolution?," *Poverty In Affluence,* ed., Will and Vatter (New York, 1965), p. 34.

4 Paul Mattick, *Marx and Keynes* (Boston, 1969), p. 132.

5 *The U.S. Book of Facts, Statistics, and Information* (New York, 1969), p. 324. (This is the privately printed version of the *Statistical Abstract*.)

6 Quoted in Herman Miller, *ibid.,* p. 33.

7 Quoted in Joseph Pechman, "The Rich, the Poor, and the Taxes They Pay,' *The Public Interest,* Fall 1969, p. 22.

8 Galbraith, in Ferman and Kornblauh.

9 Robert Lampman, "One-Fifth of a Nation," from *Challenge: The Magazine of Economic Affairs,* Vol. 12, No. 7 (April 1964), p. 11.

10 Herman Miller, *ibid.,* p. 36.

11 Joseph Pechman, *ibid.,* p. 22.

12 Herman Miller, *Income Distribution in the United States* (Bureau of th Census, 1966), p. 22.

13 Herman Miller, *ibid.,* p. 22.

14 Pechman, *ibid.,* p. 28.

15 Gabriel Kolko, *Wealth and Power in America* (New York, 1962), p. 45.

16 Pechman, *ibid.,* Table 3, p. 27.

17 Pechman, *ibid.,* p. 31.

18 *Economic Report of the President* (Washington: U.S. Government Printin Office, 1969).

[19] James D. Smith, "An Estimate of the Income of the Very Rich," Papers in Quantitative Economics (Lawrence, Kansas, 1968).

[20] Gabriel Kolko, *ibid.,* p. 49.

[21] William Domhoff, "How the Power Elite Makes Public Policy," *The Center Magazine,* Vol. III, No. 2 (March 1970).

[22] Gabriel Kolko, *ibid.,* p. 98.

[23] Mollie Orshansky, "Counting The Poor: Another Look at the Poverty Profile," *Social Security Bulletin,* January 1965.

[24] *I. F. Stone's Weekly,* Vol. XVII, No. 16 (September 9, 1969), p. 1.

[25] Linda Hunt *et al.,* "Nixon's Guaranteed Annual Poverty," *Ramparts,* December 1969, p. 64.

[26] The fifteen million figure is the one used by Dr. Jean Mayer, President Nixon's specialist on hunger and malnutrition.

[27] *The U.S. Book of Facts, Statistics and Information,* p. 324.

[28] Leon Keyserling, *Progress or Poverty* (Washington, D.C.: Council on Economic Priorities, 1964).

[29] *U.S. Book of Facts,* p. 335.

[30] Gabriel Kolko, *ibid.,* p. 47.

[31] Quoted in Kolko, p. 14.

[32] Daniel Bell, *The End of Ideology,* 2nd rev. ed. (New York: Collier Books, 1962).

[33] Michael Harrington, "The Betrayal of the Poor," *The Atlantic,* January 1970.

[34] Joseph Pechman, "The Rich, the Poor, and the Taxes They Pay," *The Public Interest* (Fall 1969).

[35] Ralph Hunter, *Poverty: Social Conscience in the Progressive Era* (New York, 1965). See especially Peter Jones's introduction. See also Kolko, p. 99.

REFERENCES

Bureau of Labor Statistics. "Three Budgets for an Urban Family of Four Persons." Washington, D.C.: U.S. Department of Labor, 1970.

Federal Reserve Board. *Survey of Consumer Finances.* Washington, D.C., 1966.

Galbraith, John Kenneth. *The Affluent Society.* Boston: Houghton Mifflin Co., 1958.

Heriot, Roger A., and Herman P. Miller. "Who Paid the Taxes in 1968?" Mimeograph. Washington, D.C.: U.S. Bureau of the Census, 1971.

Hunter, Robert. *Poverty: Social Conscience in the Progressive Era,* ed., Peter D. Jones. New York: Harper Torchbooks, 1965.

Keyserling, Leon. *Progress or Poverty: The U.S. at the Crossroads.* Washington, D.C.: Council on Economic Priorities, 1964.

Kolko, Gabriel. *Wealth and Power in America.* New York: Praeger, 1962.

Kuznets, Simon. *Shares of Upper Income Groups in Income and Savings.* New York: National Bureau of Economic Research, 1950.

Lampman, Robert J. *The Share of the Top Wealth-Holders in National Wealth 1922–56.* Princeton, 1962.

Lundberg, Ferdinand. *The Rich and the Super-Rich.* New York: Lyle Stuart, 1968.

Mattick, Paul. *Marx and Keynes.* Boston: Porter Sargent, 1969.

Miller, Herman. *Income Distribution in the United States.* Washington, D.C.: U.S. Census, 1966.

Pechman, Joseph. *Federal Tax Policy.* Washington, D.C., 1970.

————. "The Rich, the Poor, and the Taxes They Pay," *The Public Interest,* Fall 1969.

Riesman, David, *et al.* *The Lonely Crowd.* New Haven: Yale University Press, 1961.

Smith, James D. "An Estimate of the Income of the Very Rich." *Papers in Quantitative Economics.* Lawrence, Kansas: University of Kansas, 1968.

Statistical Abstract of the United States, 1970. Washington, D.C., 1970.

"The Troubled American — A Special Report on the White Majority." *Newsweek,* October 6, 1969.

Leonard S. Silk was born in Phila-delphia and studied at the Uni-versity of Wisconsin (A.B., 1940) and Duke University (Ph.D., 1947). He has served as Chairman of the Editorial Board of Business Week and is currently a member of the Editorial Board of the New York Times. He is the author of several books and articles.

10 Is There A Lower-Middle-Class Problem?

Leonard S. Silk

THE CONTINUITY OF CLASS CONFLICT

"They have been loud in their praise of legally constituted rights; but they have shown an instinctive and implacable distrust of intellectual and moral independence, and have always sought to suppress it in favor of intellectual and moral conformity."[1]

The man who wrote that was referring neither to the law-and-order issue of 1970 nor to the attitude of "hard hats" toward students, professors, hippies, and blacks. He was Herbert Croly, one of the founders of *The New Republic,* and he was writing in 1909 about Thomas Jefferson and his followers, who were largely drawn from the class of workers and farmers. Croly was contrasting the populism of Jefferson with the elitism or establishmentarianism of Alexander Hamilton, whose political philosophy, he said "was much more clearly thought out than that of Jefferson." Hamilton, Croly wrote,

[1] Herbert Croly, *The Promise of American Life* (New York: E. P. Dutton, 1909, reprinted 1963) , p. 44.

has been accused by his opponents of being the enemy of liberty; whereas in point of fact, he wished like the Englishman he was, to protect and encourage liberty, just as far as such encouragement was compatible with good order, because he realized that *genuine liberty would inevitably issue in fruitful social and economic inequalities.* But he also realized that genuine liberty was not merely a matter of a constitutional declaration of rights. It could be protected only by an energetic and clear-sighted central government, and it could be fertilized only by the efficient national organization of American activities. For national organization demands in relation to individuals a certain amount of selection, and *a certain classification of these individuals according to their abilities and deserts. It is just this kind or effect of liberty which Jefferson and his followers have always disliked and discouraged.*[2]

To show how unchanging these clashes of philosophy have been since the earliest days of the Republic, one need only quote from a letter published in *The New York Times* on October 23, 1970. The letter was written by Martin Duffy of Susquehanna, Pennsylvania, in response to an article by Professor Edward C. Banfield of Harvard University on "the lower class." Duffy stated:

Professor Edward C. Banfield's opinions do indeed cause one to doubt the value of higher education. Not that I wish to lump together all professors — as he lumps together the "lower class" — but how can one hold his temper when he reads such nonsense?

Professor Banfield is writing about people, not insects. "The violet smells to him as it doth to me; all his senses have but human conditions." Is he so removed from humanity that he cannot feel his way into another's pain and pride? Is this what cultivating the mind produces?

Banfield, in the letter writer's view, was blithely accepting social and economic inequalities, as the Hamiltonians had always done.

The conflict of Hamiltonianism and Jeffersonianism is a deep and recurrent theme in American political history. One can trace it through the debates over the First and Second Banks of the United States and in the contests over protective tariffs; in the conflicts between the agrarian West and the industrial East, and between the agrarian South and the industrial North; in disputes between farmers and railroads, between small business and big business, and even between labor and management. The genius of Franklin D. Roosevelt in the 1930s was to mask the conflict, at least temporarily, by bringing together "the forgotten man" — the unemployed workers and all those others who feared unemployment, the intellectual, and the Southerner. Roosevelt's master stroke made the Democratic party the majority force in American politics for almost four decades. Today, in a time of social

[2] *Ibid.* (Italics added)

upheaval, Richard M. Nixon is seeking to bring forth a new majority coalition, including the Southerner, the businessman, and what he calls "the forgotten American" — who is basically the same person as F.D.R.'s "forgotten man." Nixon also calls him a member of the "silent majority."

George Meany, president of the American Federation of Labor-Congress of Industrial Organizations (AFL–CIO), raised the hopes of Republican leaders that blue-collar workers could indeed be brought into this new coalition. In the early fall of 1970, Meany declared that trade unionists were "looking less to the Democrats" because, in his view, "the Democratic party has disintegrated — it is not the so-called liberal party that it was a few years ago. It almost has got to be the party of the extremists insofar as these so-called liberals or new lefts, or whatever you want to call them, have taken over the Democratic Party."

Meany thus appeared to be confirming the thesis of Kevin P. Phillips, the conservative political strategist, that Nixon's "southern strategy" is actually national in scope, with a strong appeal to "the hitherto Democratic blue-collar workers, hard hats and ethnic (mostly Roman Catholic) conservatives from New York to California."

This shift to the right by blue-collar workers, according to Phillips, is "not simply a question of hostility towards blacks." It also reflects, in his view, "unhappiness with permissiveness and erosion of traditional values, opposition to the principle of federal welfarism and social engineering, and resentment of the anti-Middle American bigotry practiced by the liberal metropolitan intellectual elite."

But the movement of organized labor from the Democratic party to the Republican party is still far from an accomplished fact, especially because of the concern of workers and their leaders over economic issues. Meany himself stopped well short of saying that the AFL–CIO should support the Republicans. Instead, his principle appeared to be a reversion to the traditional policy first developed by Samuel Gompers, the founder of the AFL, that organized labor should reward its friends and punish its enemies. In the fall of 1970, Meany also stated that it would certainly not be outside the labor movement's tradition if AFL–CIO members supported Republicans, and he praised President Nixon for favoring collective bargaining for government employees at every level. Meany's position illustrated what the late Professor Selig Perlman of the University of Wisconsin called the "job consciousness" of American labor — its dominant concern with such issues as job security, pay and fringe benefits, and working conditions. It should be noted that President Roosevelt drew organized labor to the Democratic party mainly by encouraging union organization and collective bargaining, by increasing job security as well as Social Security, by boosting rates of pay, and by the New Deal's assault on unemployment. With all his discontents about the Democratic party, Meany still was highly critical of the Republicans for increasing the level of unemployment (from 3.5 per cent of the labor force when the Nixon administration took office to 5.6 per cent in October 1970) in order to check the inflation but still failing to bring inflation under control — consumer prices moved up at an annual rate of about 6 per cent during the first year and three quarters of the Nixon administration.

Thus, organized labor in the United States is being pulled in different directions by the crucial issues of the time — the Vietnam war, the upheaval and protests of students on college campuses and many high schools as well, the demands of Negroes for equal rights and access to better paying jobs formerly reserved for whites only, urban crime and violence, economic stagnation, unemployment, and inflation.   Generally speaking, the Vietnam war, student protests, the black drive for social and economic equality, and "crime in the streets" have tended to drive blue-collar workers toward the right politically.   In some instances, as in the attack of hard hat construction workers on students demonstrating in Wall Street during the summer of 1970, the blue-collar workers have themselves turned to violence.   But the economic issues of stagnation, unemployment, and inflation seem likely to drive the blue-collar workers leftward, or at least to hold them in the Democratic party.

President Nixon has been sensitive to the political cost to his party of rising unemployment and inflation.   He had hoped to check inflation without more than a slight rise in unemployment; that was the purpose of his policy of economic "gradualism."   But inflation and unemployment proved to be less soluble than the Nixon administration had anticipated and undoubtedly presented the most serious obstacle to the Republican party in capturing greater support from working men and women.   But President Nixon sought to offset these economic issues by calling for patriotic support of his Vietnam policy and by stressing his opposition to crime, drugs, pornography, social permissiveness, and student protests.   These were all issues on which the President felt that he would have the support of the conservative "silent majority," including much of the lower-middle class.

The worsening economic picture during 1970 appears to have been decisive in strengthening the Democratic party in most industrial states during the mid-term congressional and gubernatorial elections.   With joblessness rising and real take-home pay shrinking, the "economic issue" apparently outweighed the so-called "social issue" among blue-collar workers.   In these circumstances, the love feast between George Meany and the Nixon administration proved to be short-lived.   But it may yet prove to be a movable feast, especially under improved economic conditions permitting blue-collar workers to resume their movement up the economic and social scale.

THE HEMMED-IN WORKERS

The rising income of blue-collar workers during the postwar years has made them more conservative — and anxious.   During a Labor Day interview in 1970, George Meany asserted that trade unionists were disturbed about the Democratic party because, he said, it is too far to the left and "our members basically believe in the American system, and maybe they have a greater stake in the system now than they had 15 or 20 years ago, because under the system and our trade union policy they have become middle class."

Workers making thirty cents an hour could be quite radical, said Meany, "but you have people who are making $8000 or $9000 a year, paying off mortgages with kids going to college."   In fact, the data show that in 1969 the median income of white families headed by blue-collar workers had reached $10,700 — a 30 per cent increase in constant dollars from 1960.[3]

The change in the financial status of blue-collar workers, said Meany, makes for a very different situation when it comes to calling workers, with heavy fixed obligations, out on strike; he suggested that this might even cause the strike to atrophy as a means of bringing pressure on employers for higher pay and better working conditions.

To be sure, the AFL–CIO President does not speak for all trade unionists — and obviously not for all American workers, more than two thirds of whom are not union members.   Some trade unionists are more militant than Meany, and many workers — both organized and unorganized — are still closer to the poverty line than the middle class. Nevertheless, the emergence of a working class that is to such a large degree middle class is posing a new set of political, economic, and social problems with which the nation is just starting to grapple.

Moving up in the world seems to have intensified rather than calmed certain discontents of the blue-collar workers. A generation ago, during the great organizing drive of the American labor movement, blue-collar workers could say, with G. K. Chesterton, "And we were angry and poor and happy, and proud of seeing our names in print."   Today, after three decades of economic growth, the workers' plaint should go, "Still we are angry but now we are middle class and unhappy, and longing to see our names in print."   For the workers feel that they have again become, as Nixon says, "forgotten Americans," and they want more attention paid to their grievances.

But what are the real grievances of the blue-collar workers?

[3] U.S. Bureau of the Census, *Occupation and Earnings of Family Heads in 1969, 1965, and 1959* (Washington, D.C.: Government Printing Office, 1970) .

Even though many of them have moved up the income ladder, the "gut issue," as Meany said, still is the pocketbook issue. Many workers (like other Americans) feel that inflation is making them poorer despite higher dollar earnings. But is this really so? Overall data indicating that real per capita income has declined slightly since 1965 are misleading, because they lump part-time and female labor with full-time male workers, thereby understating the rate at which the average income of blue-collar family heads has been rising. In fact, since 1965, the average white married man employed in a blue-collar job has had a 15 per cent increase in his annual income, measured in constant dollars. During the entire decade of the 1960s, white men in blue-collar jobs had real gains of 25 per cent — about the same as did whites in other occupations. With more wives working and more men moonlighting, family incomes of white workers rose still more dramatically during the 1960s.

But that gain in average family income, which lifted so many into the middle class, may have come at the cost of heightened personal and social strains. Moonlighting is certainly a source of tension for many, and so is the far greater participation of wives in the labor force. Particularly for women with children living at home, the double responsibility of a job away from home and of rearing a family and taking care of cooking, cleaning, and other household chores can be a source of serious tension. A further source of tension or concern among white blue-collar workers may have been the even faster progress of Negroes in income and employment. Not only did Negroes narrow the income gap during the 1960s, but they also succeeded in increasing their share of blue-collar jobs, especially in manufacturing.

Both the greater competition for jobs and the narrowing of the income gap between whites and blacks undoubtedly offended some whites; expressions of resentment were widespread. These attitudes doubtless had much to do with the support of many blue-collar workers for George Wallace of Alabama during the presidential campaign of 1968 and helps to explain why proponents of the "southern strategy" for the Republican party feel that it is a Northern and working class strategy as well.

Relative income may be more important to the ego and self-esteem than absolute income. The social reformer's dream of greater equality of incomes may intensify social bitterness and bigotry as the gap between white and black income is narrowed, even though the absolute real income of both groups rises.

It is even possible that many white workers feel less secure with higher incomes — and middle-class values — than they did before. As Meany stressed, they have taken on large debts: they have acquired homes and real estate that represent the largest share of their assets, and they fear that they will sustain huge losses in property values if there is "block busting" in the neighborhoods and Negroes move in. Thus, worries about debts and financial equity feed into the anxieties of lower-middle-class whites about open housing and integrated neighborhoods — and these anxieties are further aggravated by fears of crime, drugs, sexual license, and violence. Many white workers who feel that they have finally succeeded in moving up a bit in the world are fearful of community changes that will wipe out the middle-class economic values that they have struggled so hard to achieve — by working overtime, by moonlighting, by having their wives go to work, and by going heavily into debt.

Similar threats to their social values turn many blue-collar workers bitterly against demonstrating students, hippies, and opponents of the Vietnam war — all of whom they tend to lump together. For them the "greening of America," in Professor Charles A. Reich's arresting phrase, seems like social degeneration and subversion. During the election of 1970, leaders of the Republican party sought to turn these social anxieties into political assets.

The grievances of the blue-collar workers thus appear to be of two basic types, economic and social. The *economic* pressures result from both inflation and unemployment or threats of unemployment and reduced hours of work. For the many blue-collar workers who are middle-aged, these economic pressures are intensified by the fact that, while their capacity to earn reaches a plateau in their forties, family expenses keep rising as they acquire debts, as their children grow and seek to get college educations, and as their parents age. The *social* pressures are intensified as they feel that they are looked down upon by richer and better educated whites above them, and pressed by blacks and other minority groups coming up from below them. Many white workers feel frustrated, hemmed in, neglected, and despised in a generally affluent society by their inability to make it. For many their feelings of social inferiority are intensified by a sense that they are the *victims* of bigotry — directed at them because they are Italian, Polish, or of some other nationality that they believe the upper classes regard as low, vulgar, ignorant, or stupid. Their resentments are intensified by their feeling that the manual work they do, which is often exhausting, backbreaking, and frustrating, receives so little social esteem. Many feel dissatisfied with the rewards — psychological and social as well as economic — of their jobs. Some observers maintain that a lack of pride and satisfaction in blue-collar work is producing shortages of skilled hands, with inflationary consequences both because the supply of labor to many difficult and demanding manual occupations is reduced and because workers in such jobs translate their deep resentments into exorbitant wage demands.

WHAT IS TO BE DONE?

What can be done about the economic and social grievances of the blue-collar workers or the lower-middle class generally?

It is not difficult to think of long lists of measures that government might take to improve the lot of this group in the population. A task force of the Nixon administration studying the problems of the blue-collar worker concluded that the four main areas for concern are: *upgrading,* that is, helping workers to get better jobs; *income,* getting more money to lower-middle-class families not just by upgrading the jobs of the husbands but also by making it easier for wives to work, or possibly in other ways; *expenses,* finding ways to relieve the working-man's budget through subsidized housing, transportation, recreation, education, and various kinds of tax relief; and *social issues,* including efforts to raise the low status of blue-collar work, improve the urban environment, and correct inadequate health and medical facilities. More specifically, the task force proposed job training programs for workers and their wives and children; child care services for working wives, not just for welfare mothers; more adult education in high schools and community colleges; government assistance to make it easier for children of blue-collar workers to go to college; more tax breaks for those in the $5000 to $10,000 income class; public relations programs, such as awards to skilled workers and special postage stamps, to give more status to blue-collar jobs; improved recreational facilities, more parks, improved local transportation, better disability protection, better housing, and other social benefits.

A study group of the American Jewish Committee similarly suggests that the federal government should try to meet the needs of lower-middle-class white Americans in two major directions: first, "fulfilling our government's obligations to a large population of taxpayers no longer capable of adequately meeting economic, social, child-rearing, communal and intergroup relations needs because of urban decay and metropolitan disorder"; and, second, "offering, interpreting and delivering programs in such a way as to depolarize racial and other intergroup tensions in our metropolitan centers." Again, this is translated into a long list of specific measures to raise real income by reducing taxes on the lower-middle class, providing tax benefits for parents who send their children to private schools and colleges, encouraging discount buying through government support for cooperatives, and subsidizing interest rates for home buyers or the rents of tenants. At the same time that taxes are reduced, the study group would increase social services and health services, improve public education, expand job and manpower programs, provide more financial support for housing, guarantee homes in racially changing neighborhoods against loss of value, expand the Model Cities program, sponsor "urban fairs," provide "impacted aid" to support local services, and encourage private entrepreneurs, public agencies, and voluntary organizations to build "new towns." The group also called for more effective law enforcement, programs to improve community and intergroup relations, and more research on social policy in order to find better ways to reduce group tensions and hostility.

But all such proposals for increasing the after-tax incomes and social benefits of the lower middle class run up against one basic obstacle: forty per cent of all American families — including 70 million family members — have incomes between $5000 and $10,000 a year. It is simply not possible to provide a significant increase in social benefits for these 70 million people without increasing taxes, including the taxes they themselves must pay. If their taxes are to be cut, then the taxes of others must be raised all the more.

Certain specific programs could and should be targeted at the low end of the lower-middle class. The Family Assistance Plan (FAP) of the Nixon administration, which ran up against such heavy resistance in Congress, would help those just above the poverty line — the so-called working poor. But, without huge increases in funds, running into many billions of dollars, FAP cannot do much for the vast majority of the lower middle class.

The problems of this third of the nation cannot be solved in isolation from those of the rest of the nation, including unemployment, underemployment, inflation, a strained federal budget, the level and distribution of income and taxes, urban congestion and decay, air and water pollution, crime, choked transportation, the inadequacies of public education and the heavy costs of college education, strained race relations, problems of mental and physical health, as well as war and threats to national security. At bottom, the blues of the blue-collar workers (and the lower-middle class generally) are the blues of America, and the solutions to their problems must be national.

In fact, there is nothing uniquely American about these problems; they are found in varying degrees in all advanced industrial societies. In Great Britain, for example, Anthony C. Crosland has set forth what he regards as the primary goals for the Labour party during the 1970s. It includes:

First, an exceptionally high priority, when considering the claims on our resources, for the relief of poverty, distress and social squalor . . . Second, a more equal distribution of wealth, not because redistribution will make all the workers rich, but to help create a more just and humane society; third, a wider ideal of social equality, involving not only educational reform, but generally an improvement in our social capital so that the less well-off have access to housing, health and education of a standard comparable, at least in the basic decencies, to that which the better-off can buy for themselves out of their private means; and fourth, strict social control over the environment to enable us to cope with the exploding problems of urban life, to protect our countryside from the threat posed by more industry, more people and more cars, and to lessen the growing divergence between private and social costs in such fields as noise, fumes, water pollution and the rest.

Crosland adds that these environmental goals are another aspect of social equality, "since the rich can largely buy privacy and protection from these intrusions; only social action can give the less well-off the same protection."

But a quite different sort of approach can be made in responding to the problems and anxieties of the lower middle class — for instance, the racist approach of a George Wallace in the United States or that of an Enoch Powell in Great Britain. Still more frightening must be the realization that Adolf Hitler found the mass base of support for his Nazi party in the lower-middle class.

Concerns about improving the quality of life are not limited to any one political party in Britain, the United States, or other Western democracies. The heart of the political issue in our time, indeed in all times, is determining the priorities within which social and economic problems shall be placed on the national agenda, and deciding on the allocation of resources and the mixture of public and private means for solving those national problems.

BRINGING OURSELVES TOGETHER

We cannot say, however, that there is no such thing as a "blue-collar problem" or "lower-middle-class problem." Its essence seems to be a drawing apart of the people at the bottom of the society and those who have moved up into the lower reaches of the middle class. Although this split is made more dramatic and obvious in the United States because of the sharp cleavage between blacks and whites, it can be found in other advanced industrial societies. In Sweden, for instance, after the setback of the Social Democratic party in the September 1970 election, Prime Minister Olof Palme said that he was greatly concerned about the dangers of a split in his own country between "hard hat workers" and the poor, similar to that taking place in the United States. Referring to Vice-President Agnew's contention that there is a shift to the right in the world, Palme admitted:

There are complaints about people living on welfare. There are complaints about law and order, a general vague sense of discontent. There are complaints against demonstrations and anarchists and people with long hair, people with beards, and all that . . .

But he appealed for unity among the various social groups:

It is a terribly dangerous situation because the split widens. One recurring point of my speeches during the elections was that we must never come to a situation where we talk about *we and they*, but only *we*. That is a basic philosophy of solidarity this movement has. We should never allow this type of gap to arise, and I tried to say to my people that people receiving social benefits are not special people — they are usual people who have come into a special situation as leftovers or drop-outs of a highly technocratic society.

Palme added that conservatism about modern art or life-styles is not so important, "but if it becomes a conservatism that turns against the poorer section of the community, you are in great danger for the future."

In the American scene, there are signs that this lower-middle-class group may be turning against not only the poor and the blacks, but also against liberals and intellectuals. However, it is extremely difficult to make any sure statements about the attitudes of this group and its state of discontent, indeed, it is difficult even to define the group. A Conference on Blue-Collar Alienation sponsored by the Ford Foundation on January 22, 1970, agreed that "disaffection *does* exist within a large segment of the white working class, a segment that has been alternately ignored and attacked, and in whose name very little in the way of positive action has been forthcoming." The conferees noted that "this segment, while not easily definable, crosses ethnic, cultural, economic, and social lines. The disaffection, while not reducible to a 'common thread,' is more than superficial and involves social and psychological as well as economic variables."

However great the difficulties of definition may be, there is reason to fear that the hostility of large numbers of white workers toward the poor and the black and toward intellectuals, may pose a serious danger for this democratic society. Alienation may lead white workers to raise walls against others and turn our cities and suburbs into bitter and militant enclaves. And the danger exists that the lower middle class may seek an escape from its tensions and fears and frustrations by supporting reactionary and repressive political movements.

If this nation is to move ahead socially, it urgently needs the kind of political and trade union and community leadership that will lessen the alienation and hostility of groups within our society. Americans need to know one another better and to draw closer as a people, while respecting each other's individuality and cultural identity.

The tension between Jeffersonianism and Hamiltonianism seems unending in American life. We are at our best as a people when these philosophies achieve a kind of dynamic equilibrium within our political parties and within our nation as a whole. The so-called blue-collar problem seems to me to present us with a very old issue in a new guise.

QUESTIONS

Middle Class
Parker / Silk

1. What are the ways in which Parker and Silk complement each other?
2. Is there a difference in what workers see to be their problems and what in reality are their true problems? If so, why?
3. Is the myth that everyone is affluent accepted by people because they want to believe it even when they may not be affluent themselves?
4. Does the myth that everyone is affluent keep people from awareness of poverty and that their affluence may be at the expense of others?
5. Are freedom and equality compatible goals?
6. Were economic factors important in causing people to support George Wallace for President?
7. What are the policy implications of Parker's analysis? What are his solutions to the problems of Middle America?
8. What relationship is there between technology and the alienation of workers in an advanced economy?

Sam Bowles received his B.A. from Yale and his Ph.D. from Harvard. He is an Assistant Professor of Economics at Harvard. He submitted the following statement of his position within the economics profession:

"My current work is based on the explicit recognition of the political nature of all intellectual work. I try to evaluate my research and teaching against the likely long-run consequences for the larger community. While this involves a certain amount of pretentiousness, it does avoid the copout which has allowed so many economists to spend their lives working on intriguing and elegant little puzzles. While puzzle-solving has offered a comfortable life for the bulk of our profession, as it did for me for most of my graduate work and a good part of my early teaching, the social consequences of this approach to intellectual work now appears to me, at best, as a waste of intellectual resources and more likely, as a perpetuation of ideologies and concepts that are a barrier to the types of social change that would be required to insure a decent society.

"The political perspective on which my work is based flows from the belief that human beings have the capacity for a type of individual and social life far more humane and far more exciting than would be conceivable if one took seriously the implicit assumptions concerning human nature which are embodied in the conventional economic analysis. My economic and political analysis leads me to believe that these human potentials cannot be realized under the capitalist system, and its overthrow is a necessary (certainly not a sufficient) condition for our movement towards that objective."

11 Contradictions in United States Higher Education

Samuel Bowles

1. INTRODUCTION

The appearance of a radical student movement and the organization of radical professional and other white-collar workers in the late sixties and early seventies raise an important question: will this radicalism among

This paper grew out of discussions with Herbert Gintis and owes much to his "The New Working Class and Revolutionary Youth" (*Review of Radical Political Eco-*

the well educated play an important role in bringing about revolution-ary changes in United States society? Will the movement be assimi-lated, bought off, isolated, or destroyed; or will it grow and spread into other sectors of the society?

Answers to these questions will be sought in an analysis of the economic and social forces underlying the movement. I will argue that the student movement and radicalism among young professionals is the manifestation of structural weaknesses endemic to the advanced capi-talist system, that the continuing evolution of the capitalist system will exacerbate these weaknesses and thus help to create the opportunity for radical change in the United States.

The argument is an extension and an application of a set of general principles concerning social class, schooling, and social change in capitalist societies. Because these principles (which have been elaborated at some length elsewhere) provide the conceptual framework for my analysis of U.S. higher education, I will summarize them at the outset.

1. The social relations of production in capitalist societies — the relations of authority among those engaged in production and the system of control over production processes — are characterized by a hierarchical ordering of work roles. The work hierarchy ascends in fine gradations from those with virtually no control over production, through workers with control over a very limited sphere, to those who exercise effective control over entire firms, government departments, educational systems, and other large economic organizations.[1] The class structure is a reflection of this hierarchical division of labor.

2. The social relations of education — the relations between stu-dents and teachers, students and students, and students and their work — replicate the social relations of production.[2] The conditions of office or factory work are seen reflected in the student's lack of control over his or her education, the irrelevance of school work to the student's own interests, the motivation of work by a system of grades and other external rewards rather than by the student's interest in either the process of production — learning — or its product — knowledge, the persistent and ostensibly objective ranking and evaluation of students, the emphasis on discipline and acceptance of authority, and the su-premacy of strict and unvaried routine. By attuning young people to a set of social relations similar to those of the work place, schooling teaches future workers not so much how to work as how to behave.

nomics, Vol. II, No. 2, Summer 1970) . I have benefited from the comments of many friends, particularly from the members of the Union of Radical Political Economics seminar at Harvard. © Copyright Samuel Bowles, 1971. Printed by permission of the author.

3. The two main functions of schooling in a capitalist society are the expansion of the forces of production and the reproduction of the social relations of production.   The forces of production — the technological, organizational, and laboring capacities of the population and the stock of productive equipment that make up society's overall production potential — are expanded by the reduction of workers to instruments of production, by their assignment to highly specialized tasks, and by the application of science to production.   Education serves both aspects of this process by producing low- and middle-level workers psychologically equipped to do boring and alienating work under someone else's command, and by producing a smaller number of technical and administrative workers possessing the intellectual capacities and particular personality characteristics required to calculate, innovate, decide, organize, and rule.

The amount and kind of education received by each child is closely correlated with the level of his parents in the hierarchy of work relations.   Those whose parents occupy subordinate positions in the production hierarchy are ordinarily enrolled in schools that lay heavy stress on the types of behavior required in those work roles: obedience and the ability to follow instructions.   The sons and daughters of people holding positions of authority in the work hierarchy are usually educated in more "progressive" institutions — suburban high schools and liberal arts colleges, for example — which lay greater stress upon developing the student's own abilities to use information and to make independent decisions.[3]   Thus the educational system plays an important part in the intergenerational reproduction of the social relations of production.[4]

4. A contradiction arises in the process of growth when the further extension of the forces of production conflicts with the reproduction of the social relations of production.   This may occur, for example, where the existing social relations of production preclude taking advantage of available advances in production,[5] or where the existing social relations of production are increasingly difficult to reproduce as the forces of production expand.[6]

In my application of these principles to the case of higher education in the United States, I will show that the two roles of higher education — expansion of the forces of production and reproduction of the social relations of production — have come into conflict.   Further, I will argue that the continuing radicalization of students and young professionals is a political manifestation of this underlying contradiction.   Section two is a discussion of the ways in which higher education operates to reproduce the class structure of the United States.   In Section three I will survey the recent evolution of higher education and demonstrate that increasing enrollments have produced serious strains in the system.   I will argue in Section four that these strains are manifestations of fundamental contradictions that have their origin in the structure of the United States economy.   Section five is a recapitulation of the argument.   Some political implications of the analysis are suggested in the concluding section.

2. THE SOCIAL FUNCTIONS OF HIGHER EDUCATION

The fact that colleges and universities have often been centers of radical discontent should not obscure the more fundamental functions of these institutions, namely, the expansion of the productive capacities of the nation, the reproduciton of the social class system from generation to generation, and the legitimation of the resulting inequalities.   The argument of this section may be summarized at the outset.   The reproduction of class relations is facilitated by social inequalities in higher education.   Acquiescence to class stratification is encouraged by maintaining the illusion that social mobility and personal betterment are possible through open access to higher education.   Higher education further contributes to political stability through its contribution to the forces of production and thereby to a rapid rate of economic growth.   It will be seen that rapid growth in both the levels of college enrollment and in the output of goods and services in the economy has been necessary for the performance of these functions.

Political stability has been maintained in the United States in very large measure through the achievement of a moderately high rate of increase in per capita income.   The maintenance of stability is no simple task, for we live in an open and formally democratic society which has leaned heavily on an equalitarian ideology and yet failed to make good its promises.   The distribution of income has shown no trend towards equality for over twenty years, and the amount of intergenerational social mobility is apparently no greater now than it was as much as half a century ago.[7]   Yet economic growth has made it possible for almost all groups in the population to share in an ever-increasing intake of consumer goods.   Whatever capitalism has failed to do, it has purchased acquiescence — if not loyalty — by delivering the goods.[8]

Recent economic development has depended heavily upon organizational and technical change, in short, upon the ability to devise new things to be produced and new ways to produce old things.   Rapid technical and organizational change and the associated increase in output per capita have led to major shifts in the occupational structure.   Workers have shifted out of agriculture; the service occupations and the professions have grown rapidly.   Concomitantly, the size and struc ture of firms have changed — large hierarchical bureaucratic organizations have replaced smaller firms and independent producers. A hierarchy in the social relations of production has been more clearly demarcated, with a relatively small number of capitalists and managers directing the work of others. At the same time, the number of technical workers — highly skilled and well educated, but excluded from the central decision-making powers — has risen much faster than the labor force as a whole.

Higher education in the United States has made a major contribution to stability, both as a stimulus to economic growth and as a means to adapting to the needs generated by a growing economy. First, higher education has had a hand in the development of new technologies, both through the research sponsored at major universities and through the training of research personnel to work for private firms or for the government.

Equally important, higher education has been a major producer of labor — labor with the skills and attitudes appropriate to the new methods of production and the changed occupational structure. Higher education is the last stage of the long process of socialization and training for those who will move into positions of authority in the occupational hierarchy of our society. It has been called the most complicated initiation rite ever devised by man, but it is not simply a labeling ceremony. A college education contributes to a person's future earnings or productivity in part through the knowledge gained in college, but of equal or greater importance are the patterns of behavior and the attitudes toward work, toward fellow workers, and toward authority that are inculcated in college. It is these attitudes and behavior patterns, more than the cognitive skills acquired in college, which facilitate the entrance of college graduates into the upper levels of the hierarchy of work relations.[9]

The fact that until recently students in higher education were destined for relatively similar positions at the top of the occupational hierarchy, allowed colleges and universities to perform this socializing function through the imposition of a set of rules of procedures that would effectively prepare their students for positions of power in the worlds of business, the professions, and government. The social relations of the colleges reflected the social relations of production into which the students would enter in their adult life. There were few rules, and most of them could be gotten around; a wide choice of courses and majors was offered; the student was trained to exercise a considerable amount of independent discretion, as well as authority over much of his own affairs.

Thus the social relations of college education have helped to produce graduates capable of the effective exercise of authority in large organizations.   At the same time, the content of the curriculum has been geared to the production of graduates with the specialized knowledge and skills needed in the performance of the high-level bureaucratic and technical roles into which college graduates move.   The molding of a productive high level labor force by higher education has required that students' choices of specialization be dictated by the needs and scarcities generated in the economy.   Although federal and state governments have directly intervened in higher education to ensure adequate supplies of labor with particular skills, the main mechanism for ensuring that colleges and universities produce the right outputs has been less conscious.   Professions or skills in short supply tend to receive higher salaries, and students tend to choose their majors and postgraduate specializations with at least some attention to the expected economic payoff.[10]

The prospect of monetary and hierarchical status rewards has served to discipline university students in a larger sense.   Success, it was thought, hinged on making it through college and doing well there.   The student who behaved himself and asked little more of his education than that it pay off in economic terms was virtually certain to be rewarded.   On the other hand, the prospects for the dropout, the failure, or, worse still, those expelled from college, were dismal.

Thus the mechanisms of the market — supply and demand — have imposed an economic discipline upon college and university studies, establishing a built-in responsiveness of higher education to the needs of a growing economy.   But it is not merely through its contribution to the forces of production that higher education has served to maintain existing social institutions.   It has at the same time played a direct role in the reproduction of the class stratification system from generation to generation.

Whatever determined the occupational success of the older generation of the upper class — inherited wealth, nepotism, theft, political power, or ambition — it is clear that in order to reproduce this success, the next generation was virtually required to obtain a college degree. This reproduction of class roles has been facilitated to a remarkable extent through unequal access to higher education.   Table 1 shows that even among those who had graduated from high school, children of families earning less than $3000 per year were over six times as likely *not* to attend college as were the children of families earning over $15,000.[11]   Children from poorer families were also much less likely to graduate from high school, and for those who did attend college, much more likely to enroll at the inexpensive, less prestigious colleges, particularly two-year rather than four-year institutions.[12-14]

Access to higher education by a limited number of children of poorer families has served a number of important functions, for it has lent credence to the myth of equal opportunity while at the same time recruiting talented new blood into the upper class and draining off potential leadership from the lower class.

TABLE 1.   College Attendance in 1967 among High School Graduates, by Family Income[a]

Family income[b]	Per cent who did not attend college
Total	53.1
under $3000	80.2
$3000 to $3999	67.7
$4000 to $5999	63.7
$6000 to $7499	58.9
$7500 to $9999	49.0
$10,000 to $14,999	38.7
$15,000 and over	13.3

[a] Refers to individuals who were high school seniors in October 1965 and who subsequently graduated from high school.
[b] Family income for 12 months preceding October 1965.
Source: U.S. Department of Commerce, Bureau of the Census, *Current Population Report,* Series P-20, No. 185, July 11, 1969, p. 6. College attendance refers to both two- and four-year institutions.

Higher education in the United States has served not only to reproduce the class structure, but to justify it. The fact that inequalities in educational credentials "fairly" gained have been added on to inequalities of class background has served to hide the importance of class itself in getting ahead. And because higher education has ostensibly been open to all, and promotion within the educational system has appeared to depend solely on one's own achievements, those who are successful tend to be seen as deserving. Partly for this reason, the bitterness arising from one's job or one's income or status is directed against oneself rather than against the social system or those whose "success" was facilitated — if not predetermined — by that system. Radical thrusts against the dominant groups in society are blunted by the sentiment that "it's only fair; they have the education to do the job." By this same line of reasoning, poverty is often "blamed" on the poor: they are referred to as the "economically weak," not as the exploited.[15]

Successful completion of higher education has thus come to confer a modern form of "right to rule" at least as persuasive and politically invulnerable as any of its divine, aristocratic, or plutocratic predecessors.

The belief in the fairness of the game has not been undermined by the fact that one class is always the winner. The conviction that all groups receive roughly equal opportunities in education has survived because the inequality of the process was disguised, first by adherence to a set of "rules of the game" that only appeared to contain no class biases, and second through the rapid expansion of the educational system itself.

I have outlined elsewhere the harmless appearance and inegalitarian consequences of such "rules of the game" as the principle of rewarding academic excellence as measured by "objective" tests, and the heavy reliance on local revenues in school finance.[16] In what follows it is particularly important to note that inequalities in education — in finance, curriculum, or anything else — are less easily detected and less easily combatted politically when they exist *between* levels of schooling or *between localities* than when they appear within levels and within local areas. Thus as long as higher education was the preserve of the upper class, massive subsidies to the children of the rich could be achieved under the guise of fostering intellectual achievement in the national interest. Until recently, segregation of residential communities by social class and the decentralization of school finances allowed a similar and largely undetected and unopposed unequal allocation of resources to rich children in their elementary and secondary schooling.[17]

It is not these institutional arrangements alone which buttress the illusion of fair competition in schooling. The growth of higher education itself has offered apparent verification of the myth in people's daily experiences. Because of the rapid growth of education at all levels, children are almost certain to attend school for a significantly longer period than their mothers and fathers did, and so are likely to achieve a level of schooling that in their parents' day would have ensured high status and a good job. Thus the educational system appears to be open, and to sponsor a significant amount of mobility.

Quite apart from its role in verifying the myth of equal opportunity, university expansion, like the growth of per capita income, has helped to legitimize the capitalist system by demonstrating its capacity continually to produce more of everything. The rapid growth of higher education has provided for at least some parents who themselves did not make it, the satisfaction of having been able to provide well for their children.

Thus the growth of enrollments in higher education and the growth of the economy were highly complementary developments, contributing both to each other and to the capacity of the educational system at the same time to reproduce and legitimize the system of class stratification. Rapid growth of university enrollments, however, might have posed two difficult problems. First, increasing admissions to higher education would seem to necessitate greater equality of access. That this has not been the case is amply demonstrated in Table 2, which shows that as the fraction of each age cohort attending college has increased, the trend, if any is discernible at all, has been *away* from social class equality in graduation from higher education.[18]

A second possible problem posed by rapidly increasing enrollments and the resulting flooding of the labor market with college graduates is the necessity to maintain the monetary payoff to higher education without depressing the earnings of less educated workers. Educational growth without economic growth would have required a lowering of the earnings of at least one category of workers.[19] If increasing enrollments had implied a falling monetary payoff to higher education, discontent among students and their families would have been difficult to avoid, and the illusion of intergenerational betterment through increased schooling would have lost credibility. The political ramifications of imposing the necessary income losses on less educated workers would have been equally unsettling.

As Table 3 clearly demonstrates, the monetary payoff to higher education has not suffered, nor have the earnings of other groups been lowered.[20]

3. COPING WITH GROWTH: TECHNOCRACY AND THE JUNIOR COLLEGE BOOM

Though the expansion of enrollments has neither lowered the monetary payoff to a four-year college degree nor equalized access to college, it has brought about two important changes in the social position of higher education. First is the increasing scientific, cultural, and social role of the college community. Second is the frank recognition that colleges

TABLE 2. Among Sons who had Reached High School, Percentage who Graduated from College, by Son's Age and Father's Level of Education

Son's age in 1962	Likely dates of college graduation[a]		Father's education					
			Some high school		High school graduate		Some college or more	
		<8 years	Per cent graduating	Ratio to <8	Per cent graduating	Ratio to <8	Per cent graduating	Ratio to <8
25–34	1950–1959	07.6	17.4	2.29	25.6	3.37	51.9	6.83
35–44	1940–1949	08.6	11.9	1.38	25.3	2.94	53.9	6.27
45–54	1930–1939	07.7	09.8	1.27	15.1	1.96	36.9	4.79
55–64	1920–1929	08.9	09.8	1.10	19.2	2.16	29.8	3.35

[a] Assuming college graduation at age 22.

Source: Based on U.S. Census data as reported in William G. Spady, "Educational Mobility and Access: Growth and Paradoxes," American Journal of Sociology, Vol. 73, No. 3 (November 1967).

TABLE 3.   Present Value of Expected Lifetime Real Income[a] for All Male Workers 18–64 Years Old with Various Levels of Educational Attainment, 1956–1968

| | Level of Schooling Completed | | | Per cent difference, college over high school | |
	High School (1)	College 4 years (2)	4 years or more (3)	((2) / (1)) (4)	((3) / (1)) (5)
1956	95	b	129	—	36
1958	89	124	132	39	48
1961	95	138	141	45	48
1963	101	138	142	37	41
1964	103	143	147	39	43
1966	111	156	161	41	45
1967	110	152	157	38	43
1968	112	159	164	42	46
Per cent increase					
1956–1968	18	b	27		
1958–1968	26	28	24		

[a] In thousands of 1968 dollars, discounted at 5%.
b Data not available.

Source: Bureau of the Census, *Current Population Report,* Series P-60, No. 74, October 30, 1970, Tables 9, 11, 12–18.

have become the training ground for much more than the economic elite; junior colleges and many four-year institutions have taken up the task of training the middle level bureaucrats and technicians of the future.   While the adaptation to both of these consequences of growth has for the most part preserved the fundamental functions of higher education, the adjustments are far from perfect, and have revealed some of the underlying weaknesses of the advanced capitalist system.   In this section I will first argue that the culture of the university community is anachronistic and dysfunctional, given its now greatly enlarged clientele, and second that the junior college movement may be seen as an only partly successful attempt to deal with some of the unsettling consequences of the increasing diversity of socialization functions that have been imposed on higher education by the increasing enrollments.   Last, I will suggest that teaching methods capable of socializing college students for their future roles in the hierarchy of production are becoming increasingly inconsistent with effective teaching and learning.

The recent growth in student numbers has been associated with a spectacular increase in the size of the total college community.   Because the expansion of faculties and student bodies was in part a response to the technological and organizational needs of the economy, the growth in university size has been accompanied by the growth in prestige of the teachers and researchers associated with the university.   Universities have become more than the production centers for high level labor and the focal point for basic research; they are more than ever before major sources of policy advice, opinion, and ideology.   To a limited extent the political attitudes and life styles of college teachers serve as models for the students.   More importantly, the culture of the college community as a whole, with its long hair, communes, marijuana, and peace signs, has become a model for young people throughout the country.

Many aspects of the culture of the college community will be easily assimilated; others may prove to be indigestible.   The persistence of an antimaterialistic and humanistic university ideology — perhaps a hang-over from the days when universities trained aristocrats rather than the leaders, managers, and technicians of a capitalist society — may cause especially severe problems.

Quite apart from the cultural milieu of the colleges, the process of college study itself undermines much of the legitimacy of the capitalist system, for it is simply impossible for higher education to transmit useful high level skills to students without at the same time developing some of the students' critical capacities, and without transmitting some of the truth about how the society operates.   Uncritical acceptance of the legitimizing myths of the capitalist system by the economic and political elites does not provide the intellectual basis for the extension and preservation of its main institutions.   As long as the vast propor-tion of college students were destined for positions of leadership, the tradition of scholarship and unfettered inquiry was probably an appro-priate context for college training.   Yet with over half of each age cohort going to college, it is clear that both leaders and followers are being trained.   The educational processes best suited to training an elite may be less successful in fostering quiescence among followers Incompatibility of functions seems certain to arise as higher education is forced to combine the teaching of intellectual skills with an increased role in the perpetuation of a conservative social mythology and the socialization of docility among middle level workers.

The political ramifications of a failure to adapt the culture and objectives of the university community to its new diversity of social functions are fairly obvious.   The economic consequences are no less important, for they seem to undermine the very functioning of a funda-mental institution of capitalist society: the market in labor.   The im-portance of this point can best be seen in historical perspective.

The achievement of high levels of material output and rapid growth in capitalist economies historically has required the develop-ment of markets in the main productive resources.   Early in the devel-opment of capitalist societies, communal rights in land and other restraints on the most "profitable" use of our natural surroundings were extinguished. Technology and legislation combined with new forms of economic organizations — notably, the factory — to sever human beings from community and family, thus setting labor free-floating on the market, to be allocated for its most profitable use. Newly created banks, limited liability companies, and world empires insured the free movement of capital.[21] But land, labor, and capital as traditionally defined no longer provide an exhaustive list of the forces of production. High-level skills and the capacity to introduce or adjust to new technologies may be thought of as crucial elements in the production process. And the conditions of production of these new "human resources" strongly militate against the creation of markets to facilitate their most profitable use.

Skilled and professional labor power, like all labor power, is embodied in people. The process of embodiment — training and education — is time-consuming and is for good economic reasons undertaken at a young age, in large measure in specialized institutions — schools, colleges, and other training institutions. Yet for the reasons outlined above, the culture of many of these institutions and the nature of many of the skills themselves do not allow the simple augmentation of competence in a vacuum — the educational process seems increasingly to provide the means but not the motivation to be a useful cog in the capitalist system. Moreover, the fact that high-paid skills and competence are embodied in workers — and unlike capital cannot be severed from them — provides an insurance against dire poverty and economic hardship, and thus relieves the economic pressures which force less well educated labor into the labor market at the mercy of employers.

As a result, there have been strong barriers to the development of a market in skills and ideas in which services flow readily to the highest bidder. Teachers, researchers, and other college graduates may increasingly impose ethical as well as monetary conditions upon the rental of their services to business and the government. These conditions are not likely to be fulfilled by those organizations most in need of university research and university-trained labor.

Recent tendencies in high-level teaching and research may be seen as an only partially successful attempt to deal with this problem. With the specialization of jobs in the economy has come a fragmentation of studies and research. Increasingly, no student, no researcher, is encouraged to deal with a whole problem, any more than a worker is allowed to produce a whole product. The artificial compartmentalization of intellectual pursuits allows the development of advanced technique within each area and simultaneously militates against the application of comprehensive moral standards or the consideration of the larger social consequences of one's work. The narrowing effect of academic specialization is furthered by the modern conception of professionalism, in which the intellectual is seen as a technician, whose success may be adequately judged by his skill in devising technical solutions to technical problems.[22]

In addition, the research functions of the intellectual community are increasingly severed from their university base, to be carried out in large private or government laboratories and institutes where the cultural climate is more favorable.

But these strategies are met with resistance from all sides. Researchers ordinarily prefer to be associated with a university, partly for reasons of status emanating from the peculiar culture of intellectuals, and partly to maintain easy access to graduate students and the broader scientific community. Far more important, students at both the graduate and undergraduate levels increasingly reject specialization and "professionalism," demanding multidisciplinary approaches to whole problems.

The increasingly "technocratic" view of intellectual pursuits fostered by today's colleges is but one outgrowth of the conflict between the traditional elite-training function of the university and the greatly expanded numbers of students enrolled. The growth of two-year colleges and postsecondary technical institutes is another manifestation of the same underlying problem, namely, the impossibility of accommodating one half of each age cohort in "elite" institutions. In what follows I will argue that the junior colleges have served to create a class stratification *within* higher education, thus allowing an expansion of the number of students in higher education without undermining the elite status and function of the established institutions.

With a small fraction of each age group attending college, most could be accommodated at four-year institutions from which graduation assured a high chance of economic and social success. Of course there were always institutions which could not confer automatic status, but these were confined largely to a few fields (such as education and divinity) and to the South (particularly black colleges).

The idea that those who had made it into college had made it to the top could not survive the tremendous increase in enrollments. But it was not merely the expectation of success that had to change; the entire structure of higher education had become inadequate. A relatively uniform system of higher education enrolling such a large fraction of each age group would fail in a number of ways. The right to rule and the expectation of power would be extended to social groups who in their jobs and their political activities had previously exercised very little influence over their own lives or those of others. Unrealistic status and occupational expectations would be encouraged in lower and lower-middle-class children; disappointment would undoubtedly result in discontent. Equally important, the social relations of the educational process itself — based on the notion that the colleges and universities were socializing an elite — would prove to be inappropriate when these institutions began training middle level workers. Thus a uniform system of higher education would foster discontent and competition for power, for it would legitimize the power aspirations of much more than the old elite, and fail to inspire the expectations and submissiveness appropriate to the future work roles of most of the newcomers to postsecondary schooling.

Structural change in educational processes has been necessitated by a shift in the occupational destinies of the students. Higher education in the sixties and seventies thus presents many parallels to secondary education around the turn of the present century, as working-class and immigrant children began to attend high school. They could not be kept out, for the economy apparently demanded a more thorough inculcation of skills and attitudes than was being provided in the elementary schools, and in any case, the ideology of the American system — including the mobility myth — had to be taught to these new participants in the political process. Yet if they were to sit in the same classrooms with the children of the privileged groups, education would cease to confer the badge of status, and moreover, the newcomers might begin to expect to take up white-collar occupations for which the academic curriculum of the high school was ostensibly a preparation. These problems were perceived and debated during the first decades of this century.[23] The outcome, purportedly based on the best interests of all, was to accept the fact that working-class children would take up working-class jobs, and to provide them with an education appropriate to their future work. This was the era that saw the beginnings of the industrial education movement, vocational tracks in high schools, and the development of class stratification within high school education.

The repetition of this process in higher education has been under way for some time, and for similar reasons. Concerns about poverty and racial discrimination and the desire to placate previously excluded middle- and lower-income families have given increased impetus to the movement. Enrollments in junior colleges are over three times what they were ten years ago and are now by far the most rapidly growing body of college students. Higher education has developed a multitiered system dominated at the top by the ivy league institutions and the great state universities, followed by the state colleges, and ending with the burgeoning junior colleges. This system reflects both the social class structure of the families of the students and the hierarchy of work relations into which each type of student will move after graduation.

The results of a recent study of one of the more equalitarian systems — California's — illustrates this stratified system. As Table 4 indicates, over 18 per cent of the students at the University of California in 1964 came from families earning $20,000 or more, while less than 7 per cent of the students in junior colleges came from such families. (Less than 4 per cent of the children not attending higher education came from such families.) Similarly, while only 12.5 per cent of the students attending the University of California came from families earning less than $6000, 24 per cent of the students attending junior colleges and 32 per cent of the children not enrolled in higher education came from such families.[24]

The segregation of students not destined for the top has allowed the development of procedures and curricula more appropriate to their future needs and actual life chances.[25] The vast majority of students in junior colleges are programmed for failure, and great efforts are made — through testing and counseling — to convince students that their lack of success is objectively attributable to their own inadequacies.[26] The magnitude of the task of lowering student expectations can hardly be exaggerated, as something like seven times as many entering junior college students plan to complete four or more years of college as actually succeed in doing so.[27]

Studies at junior colleges are, much more often than in four-year colleges, explicitly vocational, emphasizing such middle-level training as nursing, computer work, and office skills. The student is allowed less discretion in selecting courses or pursuing a liberal education. Systems of discipline and student management resemble those of secondary education more than those of the elite universities; some have called junior colleges "high schools with ashtrays." The teaching staff is recruited heavily from the corps of high school teachers. Pressures from state legislatures seek to increase teaching loads and class sizes, and in some cases even to standardize curriculum and teaching methods.[28] Whatever the original educational intent may have been, the social relations of the junior college classroom increasingly resemble the formal hierarchical impersonality of the office or the uniform processing of the production line.[29]

All of this, of course, must not be seen as a failure of the junior college movement, but rather as a successful adaptation to the tasks that they were set up to perform: processing large numbers of students to competently and happily fill the skilled but powerless upper-middle positions in the occupational hierarchy of the advanced capitalist economy

But as the channeling of junior college graduates into these middle level jobs becomes increasingly evident, these institutions lose the capacity to legitimize the class system that they so obviously reproduce. Increased access to junior colleges cannot reinforce the myth of mobility and personal betterment through education unless a junior colleg

TABLE 4. Distribution of Families by Income Level and Type of College or University, California, 1964

Income class	All families	Families without children in California public higher education	Families with children in California public higher education			
			Total	Junior college	State college	University of California
$ 0– 3,999	16.1%	17.0%	6.6%	8.1%	4.1%	5.0%
4,000– 5,999	14.8	14.9	13.0	15.9	10.2	7.5
6,000– 7,999	18.9	19.0	17.6	19.6	17.0	11.1
8,000– 9,999	18.1	18.3	16.4	16.9	17.2	13.1
10,000–11,999	12.4	12.1	15.8	14.4	19.9	13.3
12,000–13,999	7.4	7.3	8.8	7.2	10.8	11.3
14,000–19,999	7.9	7.5	13.0	11.1	13.0	20.3
20,000–24,999	1.8	1.6	3.4	2.6	3.3	6.6
25,000 and over	2.6	2.3	5.4	4.2	4.5	11.8
Total	100.0%	100.0%	100.0%	100.0%	100.0%	100.0%
Median income	$8,000	$7,900	$9,560	$8,800	$10,000	$12,000

Source: W. Lee Hansen and Burton A. Weisbrod, *Benefits, Costs, and Finance of Public Higher Education* (Chicago, 1969), p. 69. The figure 7.2 in the junior college column is a correction of a printing error which appears in the source.

education actually holds some promise of paying off in access to the high-paying, high-status jobs ordinarily held by college graduates. And this it does not do. First, it is clear from Tables 5 and 6 that the occupational opportunities and likely incomes of workers with less than four years of college fall far short of the opportunities open to four-year college graduates.[30]   Second, Table 6 suggests that the monetary payoff to less than four years of college education is falling, particularly when compared to the monetary rewards of a four-year college degree.

The new role of colleges in training workers for middle-level jobs in the bureaucratic hierarchy poses problems of greater long run significance than the possibility of a continued fall in the monetary payoff to a

TABLE 5.   Occupational Distribution by Educational Level, March 1970

	Schooling Completed		
	High School	1–3 years of college	4 years of college
Percentage distribution of workers aged 25–64			
1. Professional, technical and kindred workers	7.2	20.2	45.1
2. Farmers & farm managers	3.1	2.0	0.8
3. Managers, offs., & propr's. exc. farm	17.9	27.1	31.9
Per cent in first 3 categories	28.2	49.3	77.8
4. Clerical & kindred workers	9.5	11.2	5.0
5. Sales workers	5.9	10.8	10.5
Per cent in clerical and sales	15.4	22.0	15.5
6. Craftsmen, foremen & kindred workers	26.9	14.9	3.5
7. Operatives & kindred workers	19.3	8.2	1.8
8. Service workers	6.0	3.8	0.9
9. Farm laborers and foremen	0.5	0.3	0.1
10. Laborers, except farm and mine	3.8	1.5	0.4
	100.00%	100.00%	100.00%

Source: "Population Characteristics," *Current Population Reports*, Series p-20, No 207, Nov. 30, 1970, Table 6, p. 27.

TABLE 6.   Present Value of Expected Lifetime Income for Various Levels of Schooling, 1958–1968ᵃ (in thousands of 1968 dollars)

Schooling completed	1958	1961	1964	1966	1968
High school	89	95	103	111	112
1–3 years college	98	104	111	119	119
Excess of 1–3 years college over high school	9	9	8	8	7
4 years college	124	138	143	156	159
Excess of 4 years college over high school	35	43	40	44	47

ᵃ Refers to males calculated for a working life of ages 18–64, using a discount rate of 5 per cent.

Source: Bureau of the Census, *Current Population Report,* Series P-60, No. 74, October 30, 1970, Tables 9, 13, 14, 16, and 17.

two-year college education. This is the growing inconsistency between the socialization functions of education and the opportunities for more effective learning. The problem may be sketched as follows.

Stability of the capitalist system requires that the process of growth not conflict with the preservation of the social relations of production — namely, the hierarchical division of labor. Growth is achieved through the generation of a surplus which is then used in the production of productive equipment. Because educated labor is a major productive resource, growth requires that some of the surplus be devoted to the production of schooling. In the production of productive equipment, a fair degree of efficiency is consistent with hierarchical social relations of production. But in the production of education a discrepancy arises: the most efficient techniques for teaching and learning some kinds of skills appear not to be consistent with the hierarchical social relations typical of the capitalist firm. In the first place, despite all the effort expended on educational testing, there is no satisfactory system of accountability for one's work, a crucial element in bureaucratic hierarchy. How many times do teachers complain that "you can't really test for what I'm trying to teach," a statement as true for teachers attempting to instill obedience as for those more interested in the personal liberation of their students. The movement against grading and particularly against exams in colleges is partly a reflection of the patent irrelevance of the content of the exams to the students' and teachers' educational objectives.

Second, though some hierarchy is unavoidable when education is seen as a simple information-dispensing process, the most effective teaching methods are ordinarily inconsistent with rigid hierarchy. Teachers and students generally agree that the more informal tutorial and seminar methods are superior to lectures.

Much of the history of United States education may be seen as a playing out of tensions between the dictates of a set of social relations based on the discipline and hierarchy of the workplace, and the often inconsistent requirements of an efficient pedagogy. In the early nineteenth century Horace Mann and other educational reformers rejected the authoritarian, discipline-oriented Lancasterian pedagogy in favor of a more "child-centered" education aimed at self-discovery by the students.[31] They did this not out of any abhorrence of the social relations of the Lancasterian system *per se,* but because they perceived that extreme hierarchy and authority in education do not work well and, in any case, were probably not the best preparation for the child's later productive roles. Similar reasons, disguised by a child-centered sentimentality, underlay the so-called progressive education movement in the early part of this century. Much of the current criticism of United States education identifies the hierarchy and repressiveness of schools as a barrier to learning.[32]

Two recent developments have served to exacerbate the tension between the dictates of effective learning in higher education and the requirements for socialization appropriate to adult work roles: changes in the clientele of colleges and changes in educational technology. Because the main economic contribution of schooling at the elementary and secondary level lies more in the development of the child's personality than in his or her knowledge, conflicts between effective learning and appropriate personality development could be resolved at very little economic cost in favor of the latter. Yet cognitive development *is* an important part of the economic function of higher education. Until recently, however, educational procedures and policies, dictated by the personality requirements of the likely high-level work roles of college graduates, coincided with the more informal "student-centered" structures thought to be most effective for cognitive development. The new role of colleges as training centers for middle-level technocrats and bureaucrats has produced a serious conflict between educational policies adequate to the inculcation of obedience, respect for authority, and other personality traits required of workers in the middle reaches of the production hierarchy, and policies aimed at the development of the quite substantial technical and other intellectual capacities required in many of these positions.

At the same time, developments in educational technology have made formal schooling increasingly unnecessary to the educational process. We now have the technological capacity for effective and exciting learning through mass media or through educational resource centers — places where audio-visual facilities, books, and other learning aids would be available to the student on his own terms. Computerized learning exchanges could easily bring learners with similar interests and teachers with requisite skills into contact with each other.[33]   Even in its now primitive stage of development, computer-aided instruction offers the student the opportunity for individual "attention" in a learning experience that does not require punctual attendance in a class under the direct supervision of a teacher.   The social relations of schooling as we know it have become a fetter on the educational process.

There is some evidence that efficient production techniques in other sectors of the economy are also inconsistent with hierarchy and bureaucratic authority.[34]   Such inconsistencies are serious enough in commodity-producing sectors, for they give rise to a direct contradiction between the social relations of production and the forces of production. But in education the problem is doubly serious, for this sector produces people, and influences their expectations, normal behavior, and personality.   An educational process that is not only a barrier to the development of one's own creative, aesthetic, and interpersonal capacities but also patently inefficient given the alternative methods of learning, invites discontent and attack.   Thus as education becomes increasingly important in the United States economy, and as the tension between the possibilities for an effective pedagogy and the requirements of socialization of workers for hierarchical production intensifies, the political as well as the economic manifestations of the contradiction are likely to become increasingly severe.

4. THE POVERTY OF EDUCATION: AN EMBARRASSMENT OF RICHES

The consequences of rapid growth in enrollments — the now anachronistic culture of the university community, the admission of an increasing portion of college students into institutions which effectively channel their graduates into the middle-level jobs in the occupational structure, and the growing tension between effective learning situations and the need to socialize workers for hierarchical production — have produced serious strains in the structure of higher education.   These strains are not simply the growing pains of a healthy organism, but are instead evidence of fundamental contradictions.

The nature of the contradiction may be briefly summarized: the growth of both enrollments and the economy continues to be essential in legitimizing the class structure and allowing its reproduction from generation to generation.   Yet economic growth has produced an incongruence between the job expectations of college students on the one hand, and the manpower requirements of the economy on the other. The increasing discrepancy between jobs and expectations is no passing phenomenon, for both the change in student consciousness and the declining opportunities for rewarding work are firmly rooted in three aspects of the United States economy; namely, in the level of affluence, in the alienating social technology of production that is the price of affluence under capitalism, and in the pervasiveness of waste and irrational production necessitated by the difficulty in absorbing the surplus productive capacity of the economy.

The success of the economic growth process has itself undermined much of the rationale for higher education, for it has changed the way in which students value the economic payoff to their studies. The increased affluence of the families from which the students come, and the increased affluence that the students may expect in their adult life, tend to make the calculation of monetary gain secondary to other aspects of education. It is no longer enough that education pay off; college study must be interesting and enjoyable and must contribute to the individual's personal development in terms of more than just his productive capacities or likely future earnings. Thus while economic growth has led to an increasing dependence of the economy on the production of both a high-level labor force and new techniques in the universities, it has at the same time undermined the traditional bases of discipline and "rational" choice of "economically productive" specializations in the universities.

While the very success of the economy seems to lie at the heart of the problem, it might be thought that an advanced economy would generate tasks requiring a creativity and perspective that would justify a wholesale transformation of our schooling system toward a more liberating education. Yet the economy has little use for the products of a truly liberating education. The resort to production on a large scale and to efficient bureaucratic organization in which both materials and personnel are molded into specialized parts is a major source of our recent increase in output of marketable goods and services. Work tasks are fragmented, the mental processes associated with them are more specialized, and the social relations defined by work roles are more limiting. Increasingly, the rewarding work in the economy is eliminated in the interests of efficiency and hierarchical control of production.[35] Even in those occupations for which hierarchical production relations are not the most efficient form of organization, the natural instinct of management not to commit economic suicide by allowing its role to become redundant has set severe limits on the destruction of hierarchy in work.

In part, the increasing fragmentation of work has been brought on by the elimination of hundreds of thousands of independent positions held in the past by small proprietors, self-employed professionals, and independent skills craftsmen.   Equally important, many previously rewarding jobs, while not eliminated, are transformed by the pervasive specialization and fragmentation of tasks.

The case of teaching provides a good example.   Among all of the jobs available to college graduates, teaching is probably one of the more rewarding and least restrictive.   The teacher is in direct contact with her material and has at least a modicum of control over her work; given a sufficiently vivid imagination, she may even entertain illusions of social usefulness.   However, the teacher's job has undergone subtle change, and it is probably true that work in education is less rewarding today than it was in the not-too-distant past.   The educational efficiency binge of the 1920s led to the application of business management methods to the high schools.[36]   The concentration of decision-making power in the hands of administrators, and the quest for "economic rationalization" had the same disastrous consequences for teachers that bureaucracy and "rationalization" of production had on most other workers.   In the interests of scientific management, teachers lost control of curriculum, selection of texts, and even to a major extent, methods of teaching.   A host of specialists arose to deal with minute fragments of the teaching job.   The tasks of thinking, making decisions, and understanding the goals of education were placed in the hands of educational experts and bureaucrats.   Teachers, apparently, were not expected to be particularly intelligent.   To facilitate administration and reap economies of large scale production, schools became larger and more impersonal.   The possibility of intimate or complicated classroom relationships gave way to the social relations of the production line.[37]

The fragmentation of tasks and the demise of intimate personal contact has not been limited to teaching, but rather has pervaded all of the "service" professions.   In medicine, for example, the pursuit of efficiency has spelled the rise of large impersonal medical bureaucracies, the ascendancy of specialists, and the demise of the general practitioner who once ministered to the health of the whole body and the whole family.

But the nature of the work task is not the only source of alienation. The product of work may be as alienating as the process.   The waste and irrationality of what is produced in the United States is becoming increasingly evident; having a hand in producing it has little appeal to more and more young people.   The growing number of such people, who feel that too many commodities for private consumption are produced already, balk at most work prospects available in a capitalist economy.   Others, sensitive to concerns such as environmental issues, can feel nothing better than ambivalence about their work.   And while employment in military and war-related work was not long ago seen as a social contribution, it is now more often taken on with only a sense of humiliation, embarrassment, or even contempt. Even work in the production of education itself has lost much of its appeal. The smug ideology that once celebrated the enlightening and equalizing mission of the teaching profession has given way under the pressure of radical political movements and recent scholarship to a more persuasive though less inspiring view of education, stressing its inegalitarian and repressive function.

As the elimination of rewarding work proceeds, the difficulty of finding a "good" job is exacerbated by the fact that the numbers of college graduates are growing much faster than the total labor force. Even if the number of "good" jobs were proportionally unchanged, there would not be enough rewarding work to go around.

The contradiction thus created is a largely unrecognized facet of the problem of the absorption of the social surplus in an advanced capitalist economy.[38] The imperative of educational expansion — like capital accumulation — has an internal dynamic of its own. Yet as I have argued above, increases in the stock of college graduates — like increases in capital stock — are absorbed into the economy with increasing difficulty, and in ways that tend to undermine the motive for further accumulation. Paradoxically, further educational expansion itself — like continued investment — provides a short-run solution to the problem by generating demand for the products of the previous expansions: the most obvious vent for the surplus of highly educated workers is to plow them back into the educational system itself. At the present time, education is by far the largest field of study, constituting almost one fifth of total enrollments at all colleges and a considerably larger number at four-year colleges. Another vent for the surplus is the graduate and professional schools, which now absorb a substantial portion of the graduating classes of four-year colleges. But it can be seen at once that absorbing the surplus educated labor in the educational system, while alleviating the problem in the short run, exacerbates it in the long run, as it builds up the pressures for producing yet more higher education in later years.[39]

For the above variety of reasons, the absorption of the surplus of educated labor through the schooling system itself is increasingly difficult. Expanded employment in other jobs of potential social usefulness does not seem to hold much more promise. The practice of medicine at all levels, because of its direct and obvious usefulness, would seem to be a likely outlet. But here we are confronted with the monopolistic power of the medical lobbies, particularly the American Medical Association, which, by restricting the supply of medical personnel, severely limits the capacity of the medical sector to absorb a greatly increased number of high level workers.[40]

Of course some of the surplus can be absorbed outside the area labeled "social service." The growing role of the United States in the world economy allows the "export" of some of the surplus educated labor. Direct United States foreign investment overseas and the operations of multinational corporations have resulted in an intensification of the international division of labor, with directing, coordinating, and innovating functions retained in the United States, and functions requiring unskilled labor being shifted abroad.[41] Though considerable, the opportunities thus afforded for absorption of both high-level labor and capital are limited, as much by nationalism and increasingly effective competition in the advanced countries as by the anti-imperialist movement in the poor nations.

At home, the legal profession has devised a set of procedures and conventions which manage to use up the services of millions of dollars more of lawyers than would be necessary in a more rational system. Some write tax laws and others become adept at tax evasion. In the spirit of Newton's third law, every new legal activity begets at least one opposing activity. But while contrived need may be a remunerative strategy, it must be transparently wasteful to many of those who participate in it, and hardly appears as a rewarding way of life for many young people. Large legal firms of course recognize this, and to recruit today's top law students effectively, have allowed some young lawyers to work a day a week on company time serving ghetto organizations and other good causes. In other professions and industries, similar concessions are being made.

But there are limits to these concessions. Given what young people now want in a job, concessions may be the most profitable solution for firms, but nonetheless they are expensive. The day off per week and the productivity foregone through radical despecialization have to come out of somebody's pockets. With the present technological alternatives and social priorities, it seems doubtful that the demands for creative and rewarding work can be met by business without seriously impairing its ability to meet the political necessity of a rapid increase in output. Even major concessions in job content cannot obscure the pervasive waste and irrationality of *what* is being produced and *for whom*.

While the hope of generating a sufficient amount of rewarding work in private employment seems dim, it might be thought that government programs to rectify the social ills of the nation would open up a virtually limitless number of creative and socially useful jobs. Similarly, it was once believed that the full utilization of the economy's capital stock and other productive resources could be insured by a federal commitment to decent housing, urban community development, and the like. Of course one can conceive of government social improvement programs that would at once absorb the surplus productive capacities of the nation and attract the enthusiasm and commitment of young people in pursuit of rewarding work. But while such programs are technically feasible, they seem to lack political viability.[42] The experience of VISTA, the community organizing aspects of the poverty program, and the Peace Corps illustrate how difficult it is to devise programs which sustain the commitment of idealistic young people and at the same time survive congressional scrutiny.[43]

The difficulty of finding rewarding work has sent shock waves from the labor market back into the schools. The urge to develop competence is undermined by the limiting and wasteful ways in which competence is used in the present economic system and by the very definition of competence which arises out of the alienating organization of work. Thus young people in increasing numbers reject "useful" studies in favor of less economically "productive" but more personally rewarding pursuits. Many of the more affluent leave college or choose not to go. Many more stay, but reject much of the curriculum or turn away from intellectual activity altogether.

5. RECAPITULATION

Before considering the political consequences of contradictory development in higher education, I will attempt to pull together the strands of the above argument.

For at least a century, the growth of higher education in the United States has contributed to economic expansion and promoted stable political evolution within the context of a capitalist system. Until recently, colleges and universities have successfully produced the high-level labor and much of the advanced technology needed for economic growth. In addition, these institutions have given collective consciousness and legitimacy to groups occupying the peaks of the occupational and political hierarchy, while at the same time forestalling social discontent by maintaining the illusion of upward mobility through open access to education. The expansion of higher education has served at once to enhance the forces of production and to reproduce the social relations of production.

Yet a hundred years of economic growth and continued expansion of higher education have revealed some basic weaknesses. The role of higher education in the further extension of the forces of production has come into conflict with its role in the reproduction of the social relations of production. The compatibility of the reproductive functions of higher education in the past was not rooted in any inherent versatility of our educational institutions. Rather, it was a consequence of the particular level of development of both the economy and the educational system. With continuing economic growth and college expansion, the reproductive functions and policies which were once complementary are rapidly becoming contradictory.

The imperatives of continued expansion of the forces of production and the need both to obfuscate and to justify a system of social stratification based on hierarchy in the social relations of production have required an increasingly large enrollment of students and employment of faculty at colleges and universities. Yet the level of economic growth itself, and the process by which it has been achieved, have had contradictory consequences. As high-level organizational skills and the capacity to handle new technologies have become increasingly important elements in economic growth, the culture of the college community has become anachronistic, dysfunctional, and particularly unsuited to the new role of colleges in training technicians and bureaucrats for the middle levels of the production hierarchy. The socialization required for the new clientele of higher education has come into conflict with the potential for good teaching and effective learning.

The expansion of enrollments has necessitated the replication *within* higher education of class distinctions reflecting the hierarchical nature of production relations in the economy. As the internal structure of higher education has come to mirror the social relations of production, it has begun to expose the myth of mobility and at the same time (as I will suggest below), to create a new, potentially radical political force in the society.

It seems likely that further expansion of the system will not ameliorate but intensify these problems. Radical movements have in the past been bought off through a redistribution of the increases in output achieved through the expansion of the forces of production. Yet the crisis in higher education differs from most past challenges to stability: further expansion of the forces of production does not provide the means for the solution of the problem. It is part of the problem.

And a slower or negative rate of economic growth would hardly solve the problem, for there are numerous groups in the society whose continued acquiescence to the capitalist system is purchased by the expectation of an economic payoff which can be provided only through the continued expansion of the forces of production. Moreover, even the most optimistic economists doubt that it would be possible to achieve full employment and high business profits, were the rate of economic growth significantly reduced.

The contradictions in United States higher education are deeply rooted, and will not easily be circumvented.

6. POLITICAL CONSEQUENCES OF CONTRADICTORY DEVELOPMENT

The immediate political consequences of the contradictions in United States higher education have been widely felt, particularly on the more elite campuses. Since the Berkeley uprising of the early 1960s, students have revolted against mechanized, mass-produced, and ineffective education. Attempts to hitch up the intellectual community in more direct service to the state and the business community are met with ever more direct resistance. Attacks on ROTC and other campus war-related establishments have been widespread. Scientists at MIT initiate a symbolic strike. Young city planners and lawyers forego prestigious employment and dedicate their skills to radical community movements. Dozens of radical professional organizations have sprung up in medicine, sociology, the physical sciences, economics, engineering, law, city planning, and Asian, African, and Latin American studies, to mention just a few. These groups give tangible political expression to a growing commitment among students, young teachers, and other professionals, that their function is not to administer society but to change it drastically. Dr. Edward Teller's recent assessment of the strength of the movement is clearly extravagant, but heartening nonetheless. He told a presidential commission that events in universities in 1969 and 1970 had "practically cut the connection between universities and defense related industries. . . . In twenty years," he warned, "the U.S. will be disarmed."[44]

Campus recruiters for big business and the government are finding an increasingly cool reception and a narrower selection to choose from. Direct political action which was originally focused against companies in the war business is now aimed at a much broader range of targets — General Motors, General Electric, Polaroid, and the Peace Corps, for example. Student attacks on campus recruitment by the United States Information Service, Department of State, and companies with substantial international operations are indications of the repugnance felt by many students at being trained to administer the United States world empire. These political actions are but surface manifestations of a far more general problem. Business and government are being struck — more, it is true, by a wave of indifference to their pursuits than by open hostility — but struck nonetheless at a crucial point in their network of production and distribution: the source of supply of their skilled and professional labor.

While some of the roots of student radicalism lie within the system of higher education itself, others have grown out of broader contradictions in the society as a whole. Attacks on campus racism arise less from the peculiarities of college life than from the nationwide movement for racial self-determination. The fight against ROTC and campus military recruiters is just a small part of the worldwide anti-imperialist struggle. Likewise, the radicalism of many young teachers, technicians, social workers, and other professionals is a response to the continuing failure to place the nation's productive capacities and fiscal resources in the service of the people.[45]

Similarly, the fact that the political manifestations of the movement are confined largely to the campuses and the professional societies should not obscure their broader social importance. The breakdown of the reproductive role of higher education represents an opportunity for radical change, not only on the campuses, where the contradictions are now most acutely felt, but also in other sectors of the society, where the crisis in higher education will help to destroy the mythology of opportunity and progress and thus reveal the shortcomings of the social institutions that regulate our lives.

Dramatic campus political struggles — the Berkeleys and Columbias that have captured the headlines for the past decade — should not obscure two political consequences of the contradictory development of higher education and the economy which, though of seemingly minor importance at the present are likely to manifest themselves in strength over the next decade. First, by escalating serious class and racial inequalities from secondary to higher education, the expansion of enrollments has done much more than increase the awareness of the degree of inequity in our school system. It has created in the mass of nonelite college students a group of people who have had at least a taste of inequality and hardship, who are old enough to be politically active and yet young enough to have dreams and take chances, and who are brought together on a day-to-day basis through common experiences and in some cases common residence. No such potential political force could be found when the main work of social class selection was being done at the high school level. For until recently, at least, the high school students themselves were barely aware of what was being done to them, and perhaps too dependent on their elders to act. The parents, in turn, were both too busy providing for themselves and their children, and too diffuse and unknown to each other, to be a potent political force. Not surprisingly, only rarely did working-class and minority-group parents of high school students develop cohesive political movements with the staying power to engage in more than episodic struggles.

Recent campus political discontent outside the elite colleges may signal the beginning of a broad struggle for greater equality in higher education. Certainly events such as the strike at San Francisco State College in 1968 have brought into the open the shortsighted and narrow limits within which the dominant groups are willing to make concessions to third world and less affluent students.   The conflicts have thus helped to clarify the fundamental role of the junior colleges and some state colleges in the class hierarchy of higher education, thereby undermining one of the central legitimizing beliefs of our social system.

A second source of potential radicalization arises from parallel contradictions in United States higher education and in the evolution of the class structure.   Until recently, professional workers and white collar labor have smugly accepted the comforting view that they constituted a privileged group — a modern aristocracy of labor.   They had greater job security, greater control over their work, and of course, more money.   They had little reason to be critical of the hierarchical social division of labor characteristic of capitalist production.   Along with the substantially overlapping group of property owners, they were the main beneficiaries of the capitalist system and constituted the foundation of its political defense.

While the earnings of professional and other white-collar workers continue to exceed those of blue-collar workers by a good margin,[46] the resulting consumption privileges accruing to this labor elite have become increasingly unimportant for many.   At the same time, highly valued privileges in production are rapidly being withdrawn.   The working conditions of office and "brain" labor are increasingly coming to resemble those of the production line.   The widespread unemployment and job insecurity of engineers, teachers, and technicians is symptomatic of these changes.[47]   Since the late 1950s the difference between white- and blue-collar unemployment rates has steadily diminished.[48]

Though the labor force remains highly segmented by occupational level as well as by race and sex, the continuing "rationalization of production" has greatly reduced the number of workers with a direct personal interest in maintaining the hierarchical division of labor.   Just as the concentration of capital and the demise of the small property-owning producer have narrowed the base of support for private ownership of the means of production, the concomitant decreasing number of workers exercising independence and control in their work weakens the political defenses of hierarchy in production.[49]   Continued growth in the advanced capitalist economy may belatedly create a common condition of work among all segments of the labor force, and thus give rise to a comprehensive working class consciousness.

Much will depend on the immediate objectives pursued by students and by organizations of young white-collar and professional workers.   If they seek to restore their lost privileges in the hierarchy of production — as independent decision makers and the directors of the labor of others — they will isolate themselves from other workers.   Similarly, if they seek compensation for their lost independence in higher earnings, allies will be hard to come by.   But if these backward-looking goals are rejected in favor of demands for wider participation in control over production, the movement will find roots in a broad segment of the population.   For it seems likely that over the next decades, workers in all occupational categories as well as students will increasingly trace their frustrations to a common set of obstacles barring their pursuit of rewarding work and a better life.   The capitalist economy — with its bias towards hierarchy, waste, and alienation in production and its mandate for a school system attuned to the reproduction and legitimation of the associated social division of labor — may then be seen as the source of the problem.

As the individual salvation once seemingly offered through access to higher education is shown to be an empty promise, the appeal of political solutions will increase.   With much of the legitimizing ideology of the capitalist system destroyed by everyday experience, the ground would be laid for a broad-based movement demanding participatory control of our productive and educational institutions and the development of a liberating education and its complement — a humane and efficient social technology of production.

ENDNOTES

[1] This proposition is developed at some length by Andre Gorz in *Strategy for Labor: a Radical Proposal,* Chapter 5 (Boston, 1967), and by Herbert Gintis in "The New Working Class and Revolutionary Youth."   A similar hierarchy characterizes the social relations of production in most of today's communist nations as well.

[2] Herbert Gintis, "Education, Technology, and Worker Productivity," *American Economic Association Proceedings,* May 1971, pp. 266–279.

[3] Samuel Bowles, "Unequal Education and the Reproduction of the Social Division of Labor," *Review of Radical Political Economics,* Vol. 3, No. 3, Fall 1971; and Andre Gorz, "Capitalist Relations of Production and the Socially Necessary Labor Force," *International Socialist Journal,* Year 2, No. 10, August 1965.

[4] Samuel Bowles, "Schooling and Inequality from Generation to Generation," *Journal of Political Economy,* forthcoming.

[5] For example, Eugene Genovese, in *The Political Economy of Slavery* (New York, 1965), argues that the social relations of production characteristic of the Southern slave economy prohibited the use of the most productive agricultural techniques and were a main source of that society's economic backwardness and eventual demise.

[3] Karl Marx and Friedrich Engels in *The Communist Manifesto* (1848) identify the main contradiction in capitalist society as the conflict between the system

of private ownership and control in production and the increasingly social nature of the production process brought about by the integration of the national and even international economy associated with the continuing expansion of the forces of production.

[7] Data on the distribution of income can be found in Herman Miller, *Income Distribution in the U.S.* (U.S. Dept. of Commerce, 1966), and U.S. Bureau of the Census, *Trends in the Income of Families and Persons in the United States: 1947–1964,* Technical Paper No. 17 (Washington, D.C., 1967). Data on occupational mobility is available in P. Blau and O. D. Duncan, *The American Occupational Structure* (New York, 1967), Chapter 5.

[8] This argument is best expounded in Herbert Gintis, "The New Working Class and Revolutionary Youth."

[9] For a more complete statement of this interpretation of the economic contribution of schooling, applied to education in general, see Herbert Gintis, "Education, Technology, and Worker Productivity," *AEA Proceedings,* May 1971, pp. 266–279; and Robert Dreeben, *On What Is Learned in School* (Reading, Mass., 1968). James Weaver, "The Student as Worker" (*URPE Newsletter,* Vol. II, No. 1; also in Gary and James Weaver, *The University and Revolution,* New York, 1969) is an application to higher education.

[10] The engineering profession provides a good example, as it has been shown that the choice among the various subcategories of engineering is highly responsive to the relative salaries of each type of engineer. See Richard Freeman, *The Market for College Trained Manpower: A Study on the Economics of Career Choice* (Cambridge, Mass.: 1971).

[11] For recent evidence on these points, see U.S. Bureau of the Census, *Current Population Reports,* Series P-20, Numbers 185 and 183.

[12-14] Thus the figures in Table 1 greatly understate the degree of class inequalities in schooling. If we define social class standing by the income, occupation, and educational level of the parents, a child from the 90th percentile in the class distribution may expect on the average to achieve six more years of schooling than a child from the 10th percentile. The data for this calculation refer to white males who in 1962 were aged 25–34. See S. Bowles, "Schooling and Inequality from Generation to Generation," paper presented at the Far Eastern Meetings of the Econometric Society, Tokyo, 1970.

[15] See G. Kolko, "Blaming the Poor for Poverty," *New Politics,* Vol. III, No. 2, pp. 30–33, for an elaboration of this view.

[16] S. Bowles, "Unequal Education and the Reproduction of the Social Division of Labor."

[17] For an analysis of school resource inequalities at the elementary level, see J. Owen, "An Empirical Analysis of Economic and Racial Bias in the Distribution of Educational Resources in Nine Large American Cities" (Center for the Study of Social Organization of Schools, Johns Hopkins University, 1969), and "Towards a Public Employment Wage Theory: Some Econometric Evidence on Teacher Quality," *Industrial Labor Relations Review,* forthcoming 1972.

[18] More recent data do not contradict the evidence of no trend towards equality. A 1967 census survey, the most recent available, shows that among high school graduates in 1965, the probability of college attendance for those whose parents had attended college has continued to rise relative to the probability of

college attendance for those whose parents had attended less than eight years of school.   See U.S. Bureau of the Census, *Current Population Reports,* Series P-20, No. 185, July 11, 1969.

[19] A simple example will illustrate the point.   Consider an economy with only two categories of workers.   If college educated workers are paid twice what elementary educated workers receive, and if the labor force is composed equally of the two groups, then a shift to 60 per cent college educated and 40 per cent elementary school educated requires a growth in per capita income of at least 6 per cent in order that neither the college educated nor the elementary school educated workers suffer a fall in earnings: 6 per cent $= (.60 \times 2 + .40 \times 1)/ (.50 \times 2 + .50 \times 1) -1$.   At recent rates of U.S. educational growth, national income must grow at least 2 per cent per annum merely to accommodate the increased numbers of workers in the well-educated (well-paying) categories without imposing income losses on any group of workers.

[20] Data pertaining to an earlier period — 1939 to 1961 — confirm the absence of any downward trend in the economic payoff to a college education.   See Herman Miller, *Income Distribution in the United States* (Washington: Department of Commerce, Bureau of the Census, 1966), p. 163.

[21] See Karl Polanyi, *The Great Transformation* (Boston, 1957) and Maurice Dobb, *Studies in the Development of Capitalism* (New York, 1963).

[22] For an exposition of the role of intellectual as technician in capitalist societies, see Paul Baran, "The Commitment of the Intellectual," *Monthly Review,* Vol. 16, No. 11, March 1965, and Richard Lichtman, "Ideological Functions of the University," *Upstart,* No. 1, January 1971, pp. 22–40.

[23] See Sol Cohen, "The Industrial Education Movement, 1906–17," *American Quarterly,* Vol. 20, Spring 1968, and Lawrence Cremin, *The Transformation of the School* (New York, 1964), Chapter 2.

[24] Similar studies of Florida confirm this pattern (D. Windham, *Education, Equality, and Income Redistribution: A Study of Public Higher Education* (Lexington, Mass., 1970)), as does a nationwide Census survey showing that college students from families earning less than $5000 a year are over twice as likely to be enrolled in two-year (as opposed to four-year) colleges, compared to students from families earning $15,000 and over.   See Bureau of the Census, *Current Population Reports,* Series P-20, No. 183, May 22, 1969.   See also American Council on Education, *National Norms for Entering College Freshmen, Fall 1970* (Washington, D.C., 1970).

[25] I have benefited greatly from Jean Binstock's comparative study of the internal social relations of seven different types of United States institutions of higher learning, from junior colleges to private secular elite colleges.   See her *Survival in the American College Industry* (unpublished manuscript).

[26] Burton R. Clark, "The 'Cooling Out' Function in Higher Education," *The American Journal of Sociology,* Vol. LXV, No. 6, May 1960, pp. 569–577.

[27] Though the proponents of junior colleges make much of the opportunity for students to transfer at the end of two years and receive a bachelor's degree from a four-year college, less than 10 per cent of the entering freshmen in California's junior colleges actually do this.   See W. Lee Hansen and Burton Weisbrod, "The Distribution of Costs and Direct Benefits of Public Higher Education: The Case of California," *Journal of Human Resources,* Vol. IV, No. 2,

Spring 1969, p. 180.   Over three quarters of a large nationwide sample of entering junior college freshmen in 1970 stated that they intended to receive a B.A., B.S., or higher degree.   (American Council on Education, *National Norms for Entering College Freshmen: Fall, 1970*.)

[28] We may expect to see resistance to these pressures from junior college faculties.   Their professional status depends on their membership in the community of university and college teachers.   Acquiescence to these pressures would not only make their work more difficult and less rewarding, it would signal their descent into the mass of white-collar proletarians, following the route of the high school teachers some decades ago.   See R. Callahan, *Education and the Cult of Efficiency* (Chicago, 1962), for a description of the high schools' capitulation to similar pressures in the early part of this century.

[29] This statement does not apply to the small number of exceptional liberal arts junior colleges.   See Z. Gamson, J. Gusfield, and D. Riesman, *Academic Values and Mass Education* (New York: 1970).

[30] Compared to workers with only a high school education, workers with one to three years of college tend to have come from wealthier families and to have had better grades in high school.   Thus it is reasonable to expect that these workers would have had occupational opportunities and earned incomes superior to other high school graduates, even had they not attended college.   Thus Table 4 exaggerates, perhaps by a factor of two, the economic returns to one to three years of college.   The same upward bias applies to those who completed four years of college.   See S. Bowles, "Schooling and Inequality from Generation to Generation," paper presented at the Far Eastern Meetings of the Econometric Society, Tokyo, 1970.

[31] See Michael B. Katz, "From Voluntarism to Bureaucracy in U.S. Education." Mimeograph, 1970.

[32] See for example H. Kohl, *Thirty-Six Children* (New York: New American Library, 1967), J. Holt, *How Children Fail* (New York: Dell, 1964), and C. Silberman, *Crisis in the Classroom* (New York: Random House, 1970).

[33] Ivan Illich, "Why We Must Abolish Schooling," *New York Review of Books,* Vol. 15, No. 1, July 2, 1970, pp. 9–15.   Educational technology by itself is not likely to achieve a liberating education.   An early educational innovation — the textbook — might have freed the student from strict dependence upon teachers.   The fact that this did not happen may suggest the extent to which the social relations of production have historically limited the evolution of the educational system.   See S. Bowles, "Unequal Education and the Reproduction of the Social Division of Labor."

[34] See Andre Gorz, *Strategy for Labor,* Chapter 5, and Victor Vroom, "Industrial Social Psychology," in Gardner Lindzey and Elliot Aronsen, eds., *The Handbook of Social Psychology,* Vol. V, second edition (Reading, Mass.: Addison-Wesley, 1969).   Some of Vroom's piece is summarized in Herbert Gintis, "Economics in a Revolutionary Age," in this book.

[35] See K. Keniston, *The Uncommitted: Alienated Youth in American Society* (New York, 1960), Ch. 9, and H. Gintis, "Alienation in Capitalist Society: A Structural Approach," in R. Edwards, M. Reich, and T. Weisskopf, eds., *The Capitalist System* (Englewood Cliffs, N.J.: Prentice-Hall, Inc., 1971).

[36] See Raymond Callahan, *Education and the Cult of Efficiency* (Chicago, 1962), for an account of the educational efficiency movement.

[37] It seems more than accidental that these changes in the social relations of high school education coincided with the influx of minority group and poor

children to the high schools. Note the similarity to the current changes in the social relations of higher education — standardization of curriculum and methods and centralization of the evaluation function, for example — associated with the rapid expansion of junior colleges.

[38] See P. Baran and P. Sweezy, *Monopoly Capital* (New York, 1966). They and most Marxist and other economists have stressed the problem of profitably utilizing the resources available for investment.

[39] Unlike capital accumulation, there *is* a technical limit to educational expansion set by the downward pressure exerted on the monetary returns to education as the length of schooling is extended and the length of the working life of the graduates correspondingly reduced. Unlike the case of capital, the durability of the educational "asset" is reduced by the process of investment.

[40] Other medical lobbies follow similar practices. The American Nurses Association recently sought to limit the supply of nurses by phasing out the current three-year nurse's training programs in favor of a four-year degree, despite the greatly increased expense to the student of the four-year program and some evidence that four-year nurses are in no way professionally superior.

[41] S. Hymer, "The Multinational Corporation and the International Division of Labor." Mimeograph, 1971.

[42] Paul Baran and Paul Sweezy outline the political obstacles to such programs in *Monopoly Capital*, Chapter 6.

[43] Since 1967 an organization of ex-Peace Corps volunteers has called for its abolition.

[44] *New York Times*, July 25, 1970, p. 1.

[45] See James O'Connor, "The Fiscal Crisis of the State," *Socialist Revolution*, Vol. I, Nos. 1 and 2, January–February and March–April 1970.

[46] Evidence for the period 1959–1969 is contained in Bureau of the Census, *Current Population Report*, Series P-60, No. 73, September 30, 1970. For the half century prior to the 1950s the earnings of white-collar workers fell in relation to those of skilled blue-collar workers. See V. Bonnel and M. Reich, *Workers in the American Economy* (Boston: New England Free Press, 1969), Table 25.

[47] Pressures for unionization among white-collar workers in part reflect an attempt to achieve at least the degree of job security held by unionized blue-collar workers.

[48] For recent data, see *Manpower Report of the President, 1971* (Washington, D.C.: 1971) and Bureau of Labor Statistics, unpublished data made available to the author.

[49] The argument concerning property ownership is from J. A. Schumpeter, *Capitalism, Socialism, and Democracy* (New York, 1942).

QUESTIONS

Education

1. Sam Bowles has discussed the function of education in a capitalist society. What is the function of education in a socialist society?

2. Doesn't Bowles's analysis ignore the 60 per cent of the people who don't go on to college?

3. As college students take jobs and move out into the world, will this bring changes in the society?   Or will these people simply adapt to society's roles?

SECTION IV

The Nature of Insecurity in Contemporary America

A. Can We Eliminate Poverty?
B. What Is the Relationship Between Unemployment and Inflation?
C. What Are the Relationships Between the Economy and Crime?

The first area of insecurity to be examined is that of poverty. A concern over poverty in America arose during the mid-1960s and was in some part a response to Michael Harrington's *The Other America*. However, the theme of the literature of the period was clearly that of Henry George in *Progress and Poverty,* which was written in the middle of the nineteenth century. George pointed out that where the greatest economic progress had occurred in the United States, there was the greatest poverty also. New York City had the most spectacular mansions, the most fantastic wealth, and also the most despicable slums.

This contrast between the great wealth and great poverty that we find in the United States today has never been rivaled in all history. In pre-industrial societies, there were certainly inequalities. The gap between the richest persons and the poorest persons in eighteenth-century England was enormous, but nothing like that obtaining in the United States today. For example, if we assume that American billionaires have invested at all wisely, they must obtain a return of 10 per cent. H. L. Hunt and J. Paul Getty have much of their wealth invested in petroleum and by use of oil depletion allowances, are able to avoid significant federal income taxes. Thus, it is quite likely that these billionaires have *annual* incomes on the order of fifty to a hundred million dollars. This occurs at the same time that whole families in Mississippi are living on less than $1000 per year. This means that the ratio between the top and the bottom incomes is on the order of 100,000 to 1. Never before in history has there been such a gap as this! And it is increasing!

If we define exploitation as a system in which persons are denied the opportunity to achieve their maximum potential, then it is certainly clear that exploitation is on the increase in the United States of America. In earlier periods, hunger, poverty — all kinds of human distress — were lamentable but explainable. There was real economic scarcity. The economic system was not productive enough to provide everyone with adequate food, clothing, shelter, medical care, and education. But that day has long since passed. We have the resources today. Only the will is lacking. Thus, exploitation is increasing. We are, by our organization of society, condemning people to live far below their human potential. And the situation worsens from year to year.

Can we alter this? Can we change directions? These are the questions asked by Thurow and Wachtel.

Thurow believes change is possible and argues that political and economic power do not go hand in hand. It is possible to bring about economic change in America. Wachtel argues that poverty is a necessary prerequisite for the effective functioning of labor markets, that poverty is a continuing aspect of our economy and as long as we have the institutions we have, people will always be condemned to live in poverty.

Wachtel makes six points: 1) Poverty is not randomly distributed among the population, 2) there are discrepancies between the way income derived from labor as opposed to income derived from capital is taxed, 3) there are important social stratifications within classes, 4) a large percentage of the poor are in fact working poor, 5) government programs do not move in the direction of greater income equality, but tend to exacerbate present inequalities, and 6) the state serves the interest of those who own capital.

Wachtel criticizes the social security system for its class bias, agricultural programs for their subsidies to rich farmers, and current manpower training programs for their inhuman approach. He claims that it is not the poor who create their own problems, but that it is easy for society to blame the poor for their poverty.

Wachtel stresses the necessary interrelationship between political and economic power. Thurow says this relationship has been exaggerated, greatly exaggerated. More importantly however, Thurow feels that if one studies all the efforts made on the part of the government,

one will conclude that governmental efforts have led to a more equitable distribution of income. Thurow argues that the gap between the
rich and the poor has been slowly but steadily decreasing. He presents
evidence that when one considers taxes and benefits of governmental
programs, the total impact of government is progressive. People at the
bottom get more benefits relative to their taxes than those at the top.
Wachtel disagrees and suggests that the gap between the rich and the
poor has been constant or is perhaps growing. He finds that government programs ostensibly designed to benefit the poor wind up either
being ineffective or subsidizing the middle class and the rich.

The question with which we are left is, how much can be done
within the existing structural framework? Thurow claims there is room
for significant change within the existing political system; Wachtel
implies that any improvement that can be made will at best be
marginal.

Toward the end of the 1960s, Americans became less concerned
about the issue of poverty as inflation became the economic topic of the
day. President Nixon took office in January 1969 with an announcement that he was going to follow a hands-off policy toward big business
and big unions. There were to be no more guidelines for prices and
wages as there had been in the Kennedy administration, no Johnsonian
jawboning against excessive price or wage increases, and certainly no
wage and price controls. Nixon was devoted to the classical economic
remedies for inflation, i.e., recession and unemployment. Nixon
analyzed the inflation in orthodox economic terms.

As a result of too much demand for goods and services, prices rose.
The solution was to reduce demand by cutting government spending,
raising interest rates to slow down investment (especially homebuilding), and a continuation of the 10 per cent surtax on consumers
and business. Nixon did all of these things and brought on a recession
and unemployment just as he had planned.

His decision could be seen as politically motivated in that inflation
affects everyone. Although it benefits some people and harms others,
everyone is aware of higher prices for food, housing, clothing, automobiles, college tuitions, etc. However, unemployment does not affect
everyone. During the Nixon recession unemployment rose from 3.4 per
cent of the labor force in January 1969 to 6.2 per cent in the summer of
1971. In January 1969 there were 2,700,000 people unemployed. In
the summer of 1971 there were more than 5,000,000 unemployed.
More than 2,000,000 were disemployed as a result of deliberate planning on the part of the federal government. Many of these 2,000,000
were members of minority groups and many were unskilled workers.
Probably very few of them were Republican voters. Thus, little was

lost politically by causing widespread unemployment and if it had stopped inflation, it would probably have paid off handsomely at the polls.

However, it didn't work. The recession and unemployment continued and so did inflation. Thus, in the summer of 1971, the Nixon administration abandoned the hands-off policy and adopted wage and price controls.

Original plans for *Modern Political Economy* included a discussion of inflation featuring Nat Goldfinger, Director of Research of the AFL–CIO, and Carl Madden, Chief Economist for the Chamber of Commerce of the United States. Goldfinger called for selective controls on big business. Madden, speaking in December, 1970, praised President Nixon's adamant stand against devaluation of the United States dollar, economic expansion and wage-price freezes (he called the latter issue "a difference in approach between Mr. Nixon and the Democrats").

History, especially since August, 1971, has not been kind to either view. Labor now opposes the current form of wage-price controls, and business interests applaud the bold moves of the Nixon administration.

The views of Arthur M. Okun, and John G. Gurley offer an interesting perspective on the issue of unemployment, inflation, and incomes policy. Each selection appears in the *Papers & Proceedings of the 84th Annual Meeting* of the American Economic Association (*American Economic Review*, May 1972, Vol. LXII, No. 2; see also a more empirical study in the same volume, Milton Friedman, "Have Monetary Policies Failed?" pp: 11–18). Primary questions inclule "The Role of Market Forces in Market Economies," "The Role of Economic Class Interest in Political Measures for Manipulating a National Economy," and "Should We Evaluate the Composition as Well as the Level of Aggregate Economic Output."

Aristotle said that poverty was the parent of crime and revolution and it has been an article of faith since Aristotle that poverty and crime are somehow related. However, in the United States as real per capita incomes more than doubled in the period after World War II, the crime rate went up even faster. Why?

David Gordon would probably accept the connection between poverty and crime. However, he would define poverty in a relative rather than an absolute sense. Part of the reason for the increased crime rate is because people at the bottom of our society are so much relatively worse off as the rich have achieved their unprecedented wealth — and through the media of television, the poor are aware of their poverty as compared to the ever-increasing opulence of the rich.

Gordon believes that crime is a rational act for a person with little likelihood to make a high income in the "straight" society, e.g., blacks,

Puerto Ricans, slumdwellers, etc., and he argues that this same desire for a high income and the status that comes with having vast quantities of material goods leads to white collar and business crime as well.

Gordon Tullock writes about the economics of crime from a traditional economist's point of view, assuming that criminals are not sick but act on the basis of rational calculation. Crimes are committed because crime is more rewarding than taking regular jobs. However, Tullock argues, if we raised the cost of crime — fewer people would engage in criminal activity. The thesis is remarkably simple. Crime is subject to the law of demand. If you raise the price of crime, less crime will be demanded. Raising the cost of crime involves higher penalties and a higher probability of being caught.

Howard Wachtel was born in Philadelphia. He received his B.A. from Temple University, his M.A. from the University of Connecticut, and his Ph.D. from the University of Michigan. His past research has focused on workers' management in Yugoslavia and will be published as Workers' Management and Workers' Wages in Yugoslavia: On the Theory and Practice of Decentralized Socialism (*Cornell University Press*). *He is currently engaged in research on the working poor in the United States. He is a member of the Union for Radical Economics, Editor of the* Review of Radical Political Economics *and an Assistant Professor at American University.*

12 Looking at Poverty from a Radical Perspective

Howard M. Wachtel

> If the Word was the Beginning,
> Then a new beginning must need another Word.
> Carl Oglesby, from "Lemon Light"

Poverty is a condition of society, not a consequence of individual characteristics. If poverty is a condition of society, then we must look to societal institutions to discover the cause of poverty rather than to the particular individual characteristics of the poor. The societal institutions that have been of particular importance for Western industrialized countries are the institutions of capitalism — markets in labor and capital, social stratification and class, and the state.

The interaction of these institutions of capitalism manifest themselves in a set of attributes and problems that we normally associate

For their help in preparing this paper, I thank: David Gordon, James Weaver, Jim Campen, Stephan Michelson, Frank Ackerman, and Dawn Wachtel. Many of the ideas in this paper have grown out of conversations with Mary Stevenson and Barry Bluestone.

with the condition of poverty in society.   These *attributes* of poverty, however, are incorrectly viewed as the causes of poverty.   For example, income distribution, the living conditions of the poor, education, health, and the personal characteristics of the poor are merely surface manifestations (the superstructure) of a systemically caused problem. It is important to differentiate between these manifestations of poverty — normally called "the poverty problem" — and their underlying causes. We return to this theme later, but first let us contrast this formulation with the orthodox view of poverty and its causes.

Since the industrial revolution commenced in Great Britain and spread to other Western nations, the poor have been blamed for their own poverty.   The causes of poverty have been assigned to the characteristics of the individual rather than to societal institutions.   In nineteenth-century America this was given a crude formulation within the industrializing ideology of individualism.   The New Deal provided a temporary break from this tradition.   However, this ideology has reappeared in the more sophisticated midtwentieth-century liberalism in which we now reside.   Public policy has mirrored these trends in social ideology, starting with the Elizabethan Poor Laws and their American counterparts down to the Great Society's poor laws.

Social science research has mirrored our social ideology.   Virtually all of the past and contemporary social science research has concentrated on the characteristics of individuals who are defined as poor by the federal government.   Being poor is associated with a set of individual characteristics: age, sex, race, education, marital status, etc.   But these are not *causes* of poverty.   There have been dozens of studies of the so-called "causes of poverty"; not surprisingly, these studies merely associate the "cause" of poverty with a particular set of individual characteristics.   For example, if you are poor and have low levels of education, it does not *necessarily* follow that low levels of education are a cause of poverty since education itself is endogenous to the system. The causes of inequality in education and their impact on incomes must be analyzed by examining social class, the role of the state, and the way in which educational markets function.[1]

There has been essentially no social science research in the last ten years on the question of poverty that has gone beyond a mere cataloging of the characteristics of the poor.[2]   A proper formulation of the problem would start with poverty as a result of the normal functioning of societal institutions in a capitalist economy.   Given the existence of poverty as a result of the functioning of societal institutions, the next question is: who is poor?   Is poverty randomly distributed across the population with respect to various individual characteristics or is i nonrandomly distributed?   Poverty research has demonstrated that the incidence of poverty is *nonrandomly* distributed in America.   Blacks

Mexican-Americans, Indians, women, the old, etc., have a higher probability of becoming poor than do individuals without these characteristics. The so-called studies of the "causes" of poverty have simply estimated the differential importance of the individual characteristics associated with the poor. The research has only demonstrated which groups of people are affected most adversely by capitalist institutions.

The orientation of this poverty research has not been accidental, and it reveals some interesting insights into the sociology of knowledge. Since the industrial revolution, the poor have been blamed for their own condition. They have been charged with causing squalor rather than the reverse. Hence, the research of the 1960s has been rendered compatible with the prevailing ideology of capitalist countries with only a few minor modifications of the crude formulations of earlier centuries to make the ideology more palatable to a supposedly more enlightened populace. In this context, the research has performed an important stabilizing and obfuscating function; it has received wide acceptance precisely because it has been conveniently supportive of existing social arrangements and our prevailing social ideology.

THEORIES OF POVERTY

Examined from a perspective of radical political economics, poverty is the result of the normal functioning of the principal institutions of capitalism — specifically, markets for labor, social class, and the state. (For purposes of this paper, let us consider "poverty" to mean any household unit with income of less than 50 per cent of the median income.)

An individual's class status — his or her relationship to the means of production — provides the point of departure for an analysis of income inequalities and low incomes in an absolute sense. If an individual possesses both labor and capital, his chances of being poor or in a low-income percentile are substantially less than if only labor is possessed. For individuals earning incomes under $10,000, nearly all income comes from labor. However, for individuals earning between $20,000 and $50,000 (in 1966), only slightly more than half comes from labor; while for individuals with incomes between $50,000 and $100,000 only a third comes from labor. And if you are rich — earning in excess of $100,000 — only 15 per cent comes from wage and salary earnings while two-thirds comes from capital returns (the balance is composed of "small business" income) .[3]

More important than the magnitude of capital income is its unequal distribution in our economy. Were we to redistribute this income, we could alleviate the purely financial aspects of low incomes. A direct transfer of income that would bring every family up to the Bureau of Labor Statistics' "Moderate but Adequate" living standard in 1966 (roughly $9,100) would have required $119 billion.[4] This comes to about 20 per cent of total personal income, slightly *less* than the proportion of personal income derived from ownership of capital.

Consequently, any meaningful discussion of the causes of income inequalities or low incomes must start with a discussion of Marx's class categories. The plain fact is that the probabilities of being both a capitalist and poor are slim compared with the opportunities for poverty if labor forms the principal means of acquiring income. And under capitalism, there is no mechanism for sharing the returns from capital — it all goes to the private owners of capital.

The individual's relationship to the means of production is only the starting point in the analysis. The labor market is the next institution of capitalism that must be analyzed to understand the causes of poverty. Given the fact that one is only a worker, the chances of becoming poor are increased. However, not all workers are poor in any sense of that ambiguous term. This leads us to our next concept in the analysis — *social stratification*. Social stratification refers to the divisions *within* a social class as distinct from the class itself. In this context, the divisions among workers in the labor market lead to social stratification among the class of workers that has had important implications for the cyclical and secular movements in class consciousness.

The functioning of labor markets, interacting with individual characteristics of workers, determines the wage status of any particular individual in stratified labor markets. The labor market causes poverty in several important ways. Contrary to conventional wisdom, nearly every poor person is or has been connected with the labor market in some way. Poor individuals sift into several categories. First, there are enormous numbers of *working poor* — individuals who work full-time and full-year, yet earn less than even the government's parsimonious poverty income. These people earn their poverty. Of all poor families attached to the labor force in 1968, about *one-third* (1.4 million) were fully employed workers. Of the more than 11 million families with incomes under $5000 in 1968, nearly *30 per cent* were headed by a full-time wage earner. The incidence of the working poor is greater among Black poor families and families with female heads. About *22 per cent* of all Black poor families were headed by an individual working full-time in 1968. And a *third* of all Black families with incomes under $5000 worked full-time. The Department of Labor reports that 10 million workers in 1968 (nearly 20 per cent of the private nonsupervisory employees) were earning less than $1.60 per hour — the wage rate that yields a poverty income if fully employed.[5]

A second significant proportion of the poor are attached to the labor force but are not employed full time. Some of these individuals suffer intermittent periods of employment and unemployment, while others work for substantial periods of time and then suffer severe periods of long-term unemployment.

A third significant portion of the poor are handicapped in the labor market as a result of an occupational disability or poor health. However, these occupational disabilities are themselves related to a person's earlier status in the labor force. There are greater occupational hazards and opportunities for poor health in low-wage jobs. Low incomes can contribute significantly to poor health, especially in the American markets for health care where enormous incomes or proper health insurance are an absolutely essential precondition for the receipt of medical care. Disabilities are widespread throughout the economy. In 1966, nearly *one sixth* of the labor force was disabled for a period longer than *six months*. Only 48 per cent of the disabled worked at all in 1966, while 12 per cent of the employed disabled workers were employed only part-time. As a consequence of disability, many households with disabled heads are poor — about 50 per cent.[6]

Thus we see that nearly all of these poverty phenomena are endogenous to the system — they are a consequence of the functioning of labor markets in the economy. This argument can be extended to birth defects as well. There is a growing body of evidence that suggests that many forms of birth defects are related to the nutrition of the mother that, in turn, is related to family income (itself dependent upon the class status of the family and the labor market status of the family wage earners). Even with the evidence as tentative as it is, we can say that the probability of birth defects is greater in families with low incomes and the resultant poor nutritional opportunities.[7]

Another category of the poor is not presently attached to the labor market — the aged, the prison population, members of the military, the fully handicapped, and those on other forms of public assistance (principally women with dependent children). Though these individuals are not presently attached to the labor force, in many instances their low income is determined by past participation in the labor force.

For example, the ability of aged persons to cope with their non-employed status depends upon their wealth, private pension income, savings, and public pension income (social security). Each of these, in turn, is related to the individual's status in the labor force during his working years. The one partial exception is social security, which is typically cited as an income-equalizing program where payments are only partially related to contributions. But even in this case, the redistributive effects of social security are not as great as they have been advertised, as we shall see later in this paper. This point aside, the payments for social security are so small that retired people, dependent solely on this source of income, end up in the government's poverty statistics.

The important elements of income for retirees are all associated with past labor force status and with the class status of the individual. High paid professional and blue-collar jobs typically provide private pension supplements to social security, while low-paid jobs do not. Individuals with income from capital can continue to earn income from capital beyond the years they are attached to the labor force, while wage earners cannot. High income workers and owners of capital have vehicles for ensuring their security in old age, while medium- and low-wage earners have only social and financial insecurity to contemplate in their old age.

To a somewhat lesser extent other poor nonparticipants in the labor force attain their poverty as a result of their (or their spouse's) past association with the labor force. Even for the handicapped, the prisoner, or the welfare mother, the labor market is not a trivial determinant of their poverty status.

If labor force status provides such an important and inclusive explanation of poverty among individuals, the next question is: what determines an individual's status in the labor force? For simplicity, we will take occupation as an imperfect proxy for labor force status, bearing in mind that there is substantial variation in wage status within occupational categories as well as among occupational categories.

In broad terms, an individual's wage is dependent upon four types of variables:

1. Individual characteristics over which the individual exercises no control — age, race, sex, family class status, and region of socialization.
2. Individual characteristics over which the individual exercises some degree of control — education, skill level, health, region of employment, and personal motivation.
3. Characteristics of the industry in which the individual is employed — profit rates, technology, product market concentration, relation of the industry to the government, and unionization.
4. Characteristics of the local labor market — structure of labor demand, unemployment rate, and rate of growth.[8]

One observation is immediately apparent: there are very few variables that lie within the individual's control that affect his labor market status. Even the individual characteristics placed in category two are not completely within the control of the individual. For example, as Coleman, Bowles, and others have shown, education is heavily dependent upon the socioeconomic status of the family, an attribute which lies outside of individual control.[9] Health is partially endogenous to the system as discussed above.   Geographic mobility depends upon income and wealth.

This classification scheme is a useful starting point, but a more formal analysis is needed to understand the way in which these several categories of variables interact in the labor market to yield low incomes.

The occupation an individual enters is *associated with* individual characteristics: educational quantity and quality, training, skills, and health.   These attributes are normally defined as the *human capital* embodied in an individual.   The differences in these variables among individuals, which influence their entry into occupations, are dependent upon race, sex, age, and class status of the family.   Although hunan capital is *defined* by the set of characteristics associated with the individual, the *determinants* of the differing levels of human capital among individuals are found in the set of individual characteristics that lie outside of the individual's control.[10]

The story does not end here; the wage is not solely dependent upon the occupation of an individual.   The fact that one person is a janitor, another a skilled blue-collar worker tells us something about the wage that each will receive but not everything.   There is a substantial variation in wages within each of those occupations that is dependent upon the industry and the local labor market in which an individual works. There are a variety of industrial and local labor market characteristics which yield different wages for essentially the same occupation and level of human capital.   The wage will be higher for a given occupation in an industry with high profit rates, a strong union, highly productive technologies, a high degree of product market concentration, and a favorable status with the government.[11]   A similar type of analysis holds for the impact of local market conditions.

In sum, the individual has very little control over his or her labor force status.   If you are Black, female, have parents with low socioeconomic status, and are dependent upon labor income, there is a high probability that you will have relatively low levels of human capital which will slot you into low-paying jobs, in low-wage industries, in low-wage labor markets.   With this initial placement, the individual is placed in a high risk category, destined to end up poor sometime during her working and nonworking years.   She may earn her poverty by working full-time.   Or she may suffer either sporadic or long periods of unemployment.   Or she may become disabled, thereby reducing her earning power even further.   Or when she retires, social security payments will place her in poverty even if she escaped this fate throughout her working years.   With little savings, wealth, or a private pension income, the retiree will be poor.

In contrast with this radical political-economic theory of the causes of poverty, both conservative and liberal political-economic theories look for the cause of poverty in terms of some individual characteristic over which the individual is presumed to exercise control. The conservative theory of poverty relies upon markets in labor and capital to provide sufficient mobility either within a generation or between generations to alleviate poverty. If one does not avail himself of the opportunities for social and economic mobility through the market, the individual is to blame. The poor cause their own poverty and its continuation. The individual is presumed to be master of his own destiny, and individualism will lead any deserving person out of poverty. (Of course, the people who posit these notions are the nonpoor.) For the undeserving poor, only institutionalization of one form or another will do.[12] These people are trapped by their lower-class life styles that prevent them from escaping poverty. If the poor would only work, there would be no poverty. The Elizabethan Poor Laws and their American counterpart considered unemployment a crime for which the penalty was work. Gilbert and Sullivan were appropriate when they said "let the penalty fit the crime."

The liberal (and dominant) theory of poverty grants some recognition to institutions as partial causes of poverty as well as social class as an intergenerational transmitter of poverty. But rather than seeking remedies by altering these social institutions or searching for ways to break class rigidities, liberals concentrate their energies on trying to find ways to use government either to ease the burden of poverty or assist the individual in adapting to prevailing institutions. The liberals reject exclusive reliance upon the market to foster social mobility and attempt to use government to equalize opportunities within the market or assist individuals in coping with their poverty status by direct income transfers. Nonetheless, their commitment to "alleviating" poverty without systemic changes is as deep as any conservative's. Manifestations of this orientation abound. The entire social work profession, born out of liberal social reform, exists principally to help people cope with a rotten personal or family situation. Hungry people are given nutritional advice rather than access to food, which would involve structural changes in agricultural markets.

The objective of liberal social policy is equal opportunity — a random distribution of poverty — though we are far from that goal today. The radical challenge goes as follows: if you start from a position of inequality and treat everyone equally, you end up with continued inequality. Thus the need to create equality in fact rather than in opportunities.

Manpower programs, educational assistance, and the like are the principal policy results of the contemporary liberal human capital approach to social mobility. All of these programs are based on an essentially *untested* view of the labor market: namely, that persona characteristics over which the individual has control are the major causes of unequal and low incomes. These programs are quite similar in their ideological premise to virtually all the poor laws of capitalist society, starting with the Elizabethan Poor Laws. Poverty is associated with the absence of work for which work is the cure. The poor are incapable of managing their own affairs so they must be "social worked" to adapt to the rigor and needs of an industrialized and urbanized society.

This view of poverty is wrong in theory, in fact, and in social values. The causes of poverty lie outside the individual's control in markets for labor and capital and class backgrounds. Equally important, something happens both to the people seeking to help the poor and to the poor themselves when we take as our starting point the premise that people are poor because of some manipulable attribute associated with the person.

THEORIES OF THE STATE AND THE POOR

Corresponding to the several political-economic theories of poverty are *theories of the state* — i.e., theories which discuss the origins and the role of government in eliminating poverty.

The *conservative* theory of the state views the origins of government as emerging from the consent of the governed. The proper economic role of the state is to leave things alone — *laissez faire*. The state exists solely to protect the basic institutions of capitalism — private property, markets in labor and capital, and markets in goods and services. It does this by providing both a domestic and a foreign military and by providing a system of courts to protect property and adjudicate disputes arising out of private property conflicts. The deserving poor will attain social mobility in this generation or the next via the normal functioning of markets. Any efforts by the state to interfere in this process will only distort these opportunities for mobility. Hence, the role of the state is simple: do nothing about the poor but protect their means to social mobility — free markets and capitalism.[13]

Liberals view the state as a mediator between conflicting interest groups in a pluralistic society. Since market institutions work imperfectly at best, the role of the state vis-a-vis the poor is to compensate for these shortcomings of the market by providing the opportunities denied to individuals by markets. "Where *opportunities* are free, the poor will disappear" might be a good liberal slogan. While the conservative would retort: "where markets are free, the poor will disappear." Liberals also recognize the existence of a residual population for whom no amount of indirect compensation will prevent their poverty. For these people, public welfare — direct payments — are the only solution.[14]

Radicals view the origin of the state in terms of a class of people who exercise dominant decision-making power in state institutions and who transmit their class power intergenerationally.[15]   One's relationship to the means of production is an essential, but not exclusive, determinant of power, and the education system is an intergenerational transmitter and legitimator of this power.   This is not the place to probe deeply into this complicated subject, but ask yourself this question: who is powerful in your local community?   Are these people workers or owners (and managers) of capital?

Given this view of power in the state, as distinct from the liberal pluralist view or the conservative consent-of-the-governed view, the role of the state is to ensure the continued survival and perpetuation of its class of decision-makers.   If this analysis is valid, then the state becomes part of the problem rather than part of the solution.   This does not mean that the same individuals or their inheritors have power in perpetuity, though this occurs — merely ponder the name Lodge, Harriman, or Rockefeller for a while.   That is why the term class is used, analytically distinct from a ruling elite or conspiracy theory of the state. In fact, liberals rather than radicals are the major proponents of conspiracy theories — witness the interest among liberals in a "military-industrial complex" conspiracy rather than a class analysis of the power of the military and its camp followers.

Several hypotheses flow from the radical theory of the state.   First, government as a totality will reinforce the disequalizing tendencies of the market through its support of basic capitalist institutions even though liberals for the past forty years have been attempting to do precisely the opposite.   Second, programs to assist the poor will perhaps have some impact in the short run, but in the long run will either atrophy, become anemic in their impact, or become distorted in their purpose.   Third, only those public programs that are compatible with the basic institutions of monopoly capitalism will see the light of day in the first instance and will survive to suffer the fate outlined above in the second hypothesis.

In contrast, liberals assume that the state intervenes on behalf of the underclass to redistribute wealth, opportunity, and privilege.   In fact, the term used to characterize collective decision-making in economics is the *social welfare function*.   By pointing to some doubtful consequences of state intervention, I hope to show that the possibility of illfare as the outcome of state intervention cannot be dismissed.

Since 1789 there have been many
administrations but only one regime.
Edward Lutvack, "A Scenario for
a Military Coup d'Etat in the United States,"
Esquire (July 1970), p. 60.

THE STATE AND THE POOR

The basic problem is: Who benefits from state intervention? What is the distribution of the benefits of state intervention by socioeconomic class? Unfortunately, the question is easier to pose than it is to answer.

One point is clear, however. When analyzing the role of government, one must look at the *totality* of government activity, not just its antipoverty activities. Subsidies to rich farmers, to the airlines, railroads, and maritime industry, to suburbanites via housing and highway programs, to rich defense contractors, etc., must be considered against so-called poverty programs.[16] Even if poverty programs, broadly construed, benefited the poor, the analysis of the impact of state intervention should not end there. These *welfare* effects must be tallied along with the *illfare* effects of other government programs to determine whether the net effect of state intervention is to enhance the welfare or illfare of the people. It is inappropriate to simply analyze the *progressive* redistributional aspects of transfer payments without analyzing the *regressive* redistributional aspects of other government programs as well.[17]

When analyzing the purpose of any public program, one must probe beneath the rhetoric of the program to analyze its actual operations. Public programs have what the sociologist Robert Merton describes as *manifest* and *latent* functions.[18] Manifest functions are normally contained in stated legislative objectives and announced administrative missions. Invariably, these manifest functions are stated in ideologically and socially acceptable terms. On the other hand, programs also have hidden or latent functions. At times the latent functions reflect the true objectives of public programs; in other instances, the latent effects of public policy may be unintended, though no less important. In the present discussion, this means that many programs with a *manifest function of poverty reduction* also have latent functions which at times lead to *unintended consequences*. A radical analysis must deal with both of these functions.

With this framework in mind, let us examine three major antipoverty programs — the social security system for the aged poor, the various New Deal farm programs for the rural poor, and contemporary manpower and antipoverty programs.

POVERTY AND OLD AGE — THE SOCIAL SECURITY SYSTEM:

Today, the aged constitute one of the largest segments of the poor even though the New Deal Social Security program was supposed to deal with this problem. Many reformers consider the Social Security System our greatest welfare achievement. But in 1968, 24 per cent of all the poor (classified by the government's definition) were over 65; about one-third of all persons in that age group are poor.[19]

The radical theory provides us with an interesting group of variables to isolate for investigation — especially, the question of class as it relates to the Social Security program. The Social Security System is class-biased. It is supported by a regressive tax system, while its benefits are graduated somewhat with higher wage earners receiving higher benefits. An individual earning between $4000 and $5000 (in 1967) paid an effective tax rate of *9.3 per cent* while an individual earning over $25,000 paid only *1.5 per cent* because only the first $7800 of wage and salary income was taxable in that year.[20] The system is class-biased against labor since only wages are taxed, leaving income from property (rent, interest, dividends, capital gains) untaxed.

Individuals receiving Social Security payments are restricted as to the amount of money they can earn in wages (up to age seventy-two) or they lose their payments. Presently, an individual may earn only $1680 before she begins to lose her Social Security payments. However, this restriction only applies to earnings from employment or self-employment, not income from capital. An individual can acquire unlimited amounts of income from rent, interest, dividends, private pensions, personal trusts, or capital gains with no reduction in Social Security payments. These two aspects of the program reveal its class bias. In both instances the program discriminates *against the working class* and in favor of the *owners and managers of capital.* Moreover, the shorter life expectancies of poor people (especially Blacks) reduce the benefits received by that group.

An important, but neglected, unintended consequence of the Social Security System is the latent function of the Social Security Trust Fund as a *war chest*. The Social Security Trust Fund (OASDI) is one of the three trust funds associated with social welfare programs. The size of these trust funds between 1959 and 1969 is contained in Table I. Between 1965 and 1969 — the period of the Vietnam build-up — the public debt increased by $50.3 billion. Essentially, all of this was for the Indochina war since the debt had increased by much less between 1960 and 1964. During the 1965–1969 period, the investments of social welfare trust funds increased by $16.1 billion. In short, the *increase* in

TABLE I.   Investments in U.S. Government Securities of Social Welfare Trust Funds, Selected Years 1959–1969
(Millions of Dollars)

Fiscal Year	OASDI Trust Fund	Hospital Insurance Trust Fund	Unemployment Insurance Trust Fund	Total
1959–60	21,849.6	a	6,668.5	28,518.1
1964–65	20.641.3	a	7,819.3	28,640.6
1965–66	19,371.2	785.7	9,278.2	29,435.1
1966–67	23,596.7	1,776.9	10,601.0	35,974.6
1967–68	25,584.0	1,651.6	11,602.6	38,838.2
1968–69	29,710.9	2,359.3	12,624.1	44,694.3

a. Program did not exist

Source: Social Security Bulletin, Vol. 32, No. 12 (December, 1969) , p. 52, Table M-5; p. 53, Table M-6; p. 54, Table M-7; and p. 88, Table Q-18.

social welfare trust funds accounted for nearly one third (32 per cent) of the net increase in the national debt incurred to finance the Indochina war.   The increase in social welfare trust funds was due to the initiation of new programs, increases in taxes, and increases in payrolls. I am not suggesting that the manifest function of the increase in social welfare trust funds was for war financing.   However, at a time when the government was desperately trying to find ways to camouflage the financing of the war, the increase in trust funds provided a convenient means for the long-run financing of the war.

The failure to provide adequate benefit levels in the Social Security system has led to the growth of a vast exploitative private insurance industry, feeding on individual and group pension plans.   These vast sums of money are a major prop to the stock market.   Additionally, these vast concentrations of money have led to enormous concentrations of economic and political power.[21]   In 1968, there were over 9 million individuals covered by private pension plans and close to $35 billion in reserves were held by private insurance companies.[22]

The question is not whether the aged are "better off" with the present Social Security System.   That is a trivial formulation; obviously they are.   But this is similar to the argument that Blacks are better off as freemen after the Civil War, and therefore we should not criticize our society for being racist.   These are not the only alternatives — as other less rich societies have demonstrated.   Compared with any vision of a decent system for the aged, American's Social Security System must be judged a failure.   America has made old age synonymous with insecurity and poverty.   This insecurity, in turn, is one of the levers used to discipline us in the workplace — make us seekers after individual protection from old age — so that we can avoid the social *in*security created by the state's failures to deal with the basic economic problems of capitalism.

RURAL POVERTY — THE FARM PROGRAM:

The New Deal placed great hopes on farm programs to eliminate rural poverty. Radicals like Henry Wallace helped design the farm program. But today, the rural poor live at starvation levels while large corporate farmers dig into the government trough to line their pockets. The farm program, like the social security system, is class biased. The state pays the *owners* of farm property not to produce, but pays virtually nothing to *farm workers* who become unemployed as a result of this dole to property owners. Even the payments to farm owners are not equitably distributed. The larger farmers get higher subsidies. Of the ten major crops under price supports, the top 10 per cent of farm owners (in terms of income) received from 36 per cent (tobacco) to 72 per cent (sugar cane) of all price support payments. The lowest decile received from 0.1 per cent (rice) to 1.9 per cent (sugar beet).[23] But the story does not end there. Agriculture extension services have fostered technological change that has led to the displacement of farm workers and the concentration of farm ownership. The government's agricultural program, originally designed to alleviate rural poverty, has led to subsidized concentrations of wealth and power for *property owners* at the expense of *farm* workers.

CONTEMPORARY ANTI-POVERTY PROGRAMS — MANPOWER PROGRAMS AND THE WAR AGAINST POVERTY:

But the farm program is an effort at poverty reduction from another decade. What about more contemporary efforts? An important component of the government's total poverty program is contained in the various manpower programs initiated in the 1960s. The program has grown from an expenditure of *$245 million* in 1961 to *$2.2 billion* in 1968.[24] Although this program has undoubtedly benefited some of those trained, other groups in the economy have not let this opportunity pass without dipping into the public trough. The government's efforts at training have certainly reduced private expenditures on training, thereby transferring a private cost onto the public. In effect, these programs constitute training subsidies to business.[25]

Evidence in support of this contention is found in the composition of training programs in the 1960s. In the midsixties the Department of Labor shifted its training programs away from *institutional* training — where the worker is given general skill training that enables him to achieve some flexibility and mobility in the labor force — to *on-the-job training*. The latter is more beneficial to employers since it trains the worker for a specific job associated with a particular firm.[26] On-the-job training as a per cent of MDTA programs increased from 5 per cent in 1964, to 20 per cent in 1966, to 41 per cent in 1968.[27] However, the General Accounting Office found, even in the case of on-the-job training, that monies were essentially being used to subsidize training that would have otherwise taken place. In their words:

OJT Contracts had served primarily to reimburse employers for OJT which they would have conducted even without the Government's financial assistance. These contracts were awarded even though the intent of the program was to induce *new or additional training efforts* beyond those usually carried out.   (emphasis in original) [28]

In addition, special programs developed in "cooperation" with private industry were supported by public funds. The JOBS program was given $60 million in 1968 to work with the National Alliance of Businessmen to hire and train the hard-core unemployed.[29] What is wrong with this, one may ask? The government did not provide job training for the development of collective enterprises or for neighborhood control of economic development in the inner cities. Instead, the training monies were direct subsidies to the very corporate interest whose power has thwarted the abolition of poverty in America.

No doubt, the programs of the War on Poverty *per se* assisted some of the poor. However, the evolving purpose of the programs became one of integrating the poor into the American mainstream to avoid extreme social disorder. For those who resisted in the early years of the war, more intense socialization programs were developed. For example, the Job Corps was created to prepare the disaffected young, in the legislation's words, "for the responsibility of citizenship."[30] Two eminently authoritative sources close to the poverty program frankly admit that "The assumption underlying this mission was that many youths from impoverished homes should be removed from their home environment before they could be rehabilitated through training and education."[31] One of the most persuasive arguments used to achieve enactment of the legislation was the high rejection rate of the poor among potential draftees for the military revealed in a Defense Department funded study called *One-Third of a Nation.*

Large contracts were given at high profit markups to defense contractors seeking to diversify their operations in anticipation of a deteriorating defense budget.   (This activity began before the war in Vietnam rectified the situation in the defense industry.)   Unused military bases became Jobs Corps Centers — apparently these installations had the needed environment for rehabilitation.[32]   Job Corps members were subjected to military type environments — even down to the wearing of uniforms.   John H. Rubel, Vice-President of Litton Industries (one of the contractors), viewed his function accurately:

I think of the Job Corps as a complex transforming machine with many internal parts.   The input — the raw material — that is fed into this machine is people.   The output is people.   It is the function of this machine to transform these people.[33]

Other poverty programs, though not as explicitly designed for social control had, as part of their latent function, behavioral engineering — e.g., the attempt to create better work discipline through manpower training.   Headstart programs for preschoolers, the Job Corps for teen-agers, and a variety of community programs for adults were all designed to make the poor adapt to the society to prevent large social disaffection with its attendant potential for insurrection.

But somewhere the effort failed — witness the extensive urban insurrections of 1966 and 1967.   The Kerner Commission concluded that the urban insurrections were the consequence of unrealized expectations and blocked opportunities attributable to the racist nature of American society.[34]

They pointed to the failure of civil rights legislation.   It was an easy step for Nixon to blame these unrealized expectations, in part, on the War on Poverty.   At this juncture public policy shifted toward police repression — an antipoor program that cannot be neglected.   Agnew-type attacks on fuzzy-thinking social scientists sounded the end of the pernicious, but more subtle, experiments at social control and signaled a new period of public policy that may lead to an attempt to eliminate the *poor* instead of *poverty*.

There is some evidence for this.   For example, the surprisingly insightful analysis of racism and poverty of the Kerner Commission produced several dozen policy proposals.   But only one has been implemented — vast sums of money and armaments for riot police and riot-trained National Guard.   We have witnessed the work of these people in the last several years.   The manifest function of these police programs — originally proposed by liberals — was to fight street crime.   This is ideologically and socially acceptable.   However, the *actual allocations* of these vast sums have not been against street crime but against political opposition and radical anti-poverty groups (National Welfare Rights Organization, Black Panthers, Young Lords, etc.) as well as other antiracist and anti-imperialist movements.   The police do not need helicopters, M–16 rifles, armored personnel carriers, riot-equipped civil disorder squads and the like to stop street muggings! The Urban Coalition reports that 58 per cent of all federal grants to police were for equipment that bore little relation to street crime.[35]

In the last two years, the fastest growing area of government research and instructional grants to universities has been for this effort at "Vietnamizing" the United States. Expenditures for "academic assistance" by the Justice Department's Law Enforcement Assistance Administration (LEAA) was planned at $18 million in fiscal 1970 and $21 million in 1971, a threefold increase over the $6.5 million spent in 1969.[36] In 1968, close to fifty colleges and universities were given grants by the Justice Department for research and instruction.[37]

The newest antipoverty scheme, not yet enacted into law, is represented by the various income maintenance programs under consideration. Nixon has proposed giving every urban family of four a generous $1600 a year, less than one half of the subsistence government poverty level and less than all but a handful of states presently pay in public welfare. The National Welfare Rights Organization (NWRO) has proposed $6500. The BLS "Moderate But Adequate" standard would call for $9,100. All of these programs would involve redistribution of income — especially the NWRO and BLS standard.

Critics of the Nixon Family Assistance Plan have raised a fundamental question that bears on our earlier discussion. Who will perform the many low-wage jobs if roughly equivalent sums of money can be obtained by not working? My prediction is that no income maintenance system will be introduced unless it can be made compatible with the structure of the labor market and its large number of low wage jobs. This is the explanation for the administration linking the receipt of social welfare and social services to work, a social ideology deeply ingrained in Western societies since the Industrial Revolution. Nixon wants to turn the federal government into a national company store!

In sum, there is supportive evidence for the several hypotheses which flow from a radical theory of the state and the poor. Government expenditures, as a totality, are not as progressive as liberals have presumed, and, indeed, they may be regressive. Even poverty programs, *per se*, benefit groups beside the poor. Programs have been distorted in their implementation — witness the farm program. Programs have been introduced only when rendered compatible with the structure of the economy and the prevailing ideology.

More important, none of these public programs has been based on a serious analysis of the causes of poverty. Nearly all are in the tradition of the Elizabethan Poor Laws, which assume that poverty is the result of some manipulable personal attribute. This explains why more money is spent each year on poverty programs (broadly defined) than is required to close the poverty income gap! Poverty persists because it derives from a low-wage labor market, which benefits the nonpoor by providing essential goods and services at lower prices than would prevail if we eliminated this low-wage labor market.   But this is the essence of capitalism, and therein lies the contradiction.

The failure to construct public programs based on an analysis of the causes of poverty is the reason for the ambiguous accomplishments of public policy in the 1960s.   Completers of manpower training programs have become members of the working poor.   The median wage for all trainees between 1962 and 1967 was $1.74 per hour — $1.60 for Blacks.   Job Corps trainees received only about $1.45 per hour.[38]

Our earlier analysis suggests that poverty flows from the structure of the economy, but policy does not recognize this reality.   George Shultz, former Secretary of Labor, candidly admitted this in his testimony on the Nixon Family Assistance Plan:

I hasten to add that the labor market itself must be recognized as a constraint . . .   It is a fact that our economy has a lot of jobs that pay low wages.   We are not going to be remaking the economy in this program.   (Family Assistance Plan).   We can only put people in the jobs that exist . . . we will have to thread our way between our goals of providing good jobs— . . . and the qualities of the kinds of jobs that are available.[39]

RECAPITULATION

The argument of this paper is that poverty is endogenous to our society and a logical consequence of the basic institutions of capitalism — class, labor markets, and the state.   The interaction of these institutions is both a breeding ground and a perpetuator of poverty.   Public policy to combat poverty has failed precisely, because, under present arrangements, it is incapable of challenging the supremacy of these "institutions."

Problems of a fundamental nature require an equivalent response.   Nonradical social scientists and nonradical policy have failed to comprehend this.   The result has been the persistence of poverty amid affluence.

ENDNOTES

[1] The contribution of Sam Bowles in this volume deals with this question.

[2] Even some of the more "sophisticated" statistical work has merely *measured* the differential importance of various personal characteristics while providing minimal insights into the *causes* of poverty.   For example, see Lester C.

Thurow, *Poverty and Discrimination* (Washington, D.C.: The Brookings Institution, 1969), chap. 3.

3 Frank Ackerman, Howard Birnbaum, James Wetzler, and Andrew Zimbalist, "Income Distribution in the United States." Mimeograph, 1970, pp. 14–16.

4 Donald Light, "Income Distribution: The First Stage in the Consideration of Poverty," *Occasional Papers of the Union for Radical Political Economics* (December 1969), p. 5.

5 A few lone researchers have been trying to alert us to the plight of the working poor. The most comprehensive studies are: Barry Bluestone, "The Tripartite Economy: Labor Markets and the Working Class" *Poverty and Human Resources* (July–August, 1970), pp. 15–35, and Barry Bluestone, "Lower-Income Workers and Marginal Industries," in Louis A. Ferman, Joyce L. Kornbluh, and Alan Haber, eds., *Poverty in America* (Ann Arbor: University of Michigan Press, 1968), revised edition, pp. 273–302.

6 The President's Commission on Income Maintenance Programs, *Background Papers* (Washington, D.C.: Government Printing Office, 1970), pp. 139–142.

7 See Leon Eisenberg, "Racism, the Family, and Society: A Crisis in Values," *Mental Hygiene* (October 1968), p. 512; and R. L. Naeye, M. M. Diener, W. S. Dellinger, "Urban Poverty Effects on Prenatal Nutrition," *Science* (November 21, 1969), p. 1026.

8 This classification of variables is used to analyze low-wage employment in Howard M. Wachtel and Charles Betsey, "Employment at Low Wages." Mimeograph, 1970.

9 See Bowles's essay in this volume and James S. Coleman, *et al., Equality of Educational Opportunity* (Washington, D.C.: Government Printing Office, 1968).

10 This model is borrowed from the work in progress of Barry Bluestone and Mary Stevenson.

11 Barry Bluestone, "Lower Income Workers and Marginal Industries," pp. 286–301.

12 Edward C. Banfield, *The Unheavenly City* (Boston: Little, Brown and Co., 1968).

13 A recent statement of this view is in Milton Friedman, *Capitalism and Freedom* (Chicago: University of Chicago Press, 1962), especially Chap. 2.

14 For an exposition and critique of the pluralist theory, see Jack L. Walker, "A Critique of the Elitist Theory of Democracy," *The American Political Science Review,* Vol. LX, No. 2 (June 1966), pp. 285–295, and the reply in the same issue of the APSR by Robert A. Dahl, "Further Reflections on the 'Elitist Theory of Democracy'," pp. 296–305. Democratic pluralism has been integrated into economic literature by John Kenneth Galbraith, *American Capitalism: The Concept of Countervailing Power* (Boston: Houghton Mifflin Co., 1952).

15 For a recent exposition of this theory, see Ralph Milliband, *The State in Capitalist Society* (New York: Basic Books, 1969).

16 This novel approach is taken by Stephan Michelson, "The Economics of Real Income Distribution," *Review of Radical Political Economics,* Vol. 11, No. 1 (Spring 1970), pp. 75–86.

17 The redistributive effects of transfer payments are substantially less than most social scientists have assumed. See Irene Lurie, "The Distribution of

Transfer Payments Among Households," in The President's Commission on Income Maintenance Programs, *Technical Studies* (Washington, D.C.: Government Printing Office, 1970), pp. 143–158.

[18] See Robert K. Merton, "Manifest and Latent Functions," in N. J. Demerath III and Richard A. Peterson, eds., *System, Change, and Conflict* (New York: The Free Press, 1967), pp. 10–76.

[19] U.S. Department of Commerce, Bureau of the Census, *Poverty in the United States, 1959–1968* (Washington, D.C.: U.S. Government Printing Office, 1969), p. 4.

[20] Joseph A. Pechman, Henry J. Aaron, and Michael K. Taussig, *Social Security: Perspectives for Reform* (Washington: The Brookings Institution, 1968), p. 307. These calculations are based on the assumption that employer taxes are shifted "backward" to the employee.

[21] These questions are discussed in the fascinating, but little-known work of Robert Tilove, *Pension Funds and Economic Freedom* (New York: The Fund for the Republic, 1959); and Joint Economic Committee, *Investment Policies of Pension Funds* (April 1970).

[22] Institute of Life Insurance, *Life Insurance Fact Book*, 1969 (New York: Institute of Life Insurance, 1969), p. 39.

[23] The President's Commission on Income Maintenance Programs, *Background Papers*, p. 290; and John A. Schnittner, "The Distribution of Benefits from Existing and Prospective Farm Programs." Mimeograph, 1969.

[24] Sar A. Levitan and Garth L. Mangum, *Federal Training and Work Programs in the Sixties* (Ann Arbor: Institute of Labor and Industrial Relations, 1969), p. 11.

[25] There is a growing body of evidence in support of this contention, for example: U.S. General Accounting Office, *Improvements Needed in Contracting for On-The-Job Training Under The Manpower Development and Training Act of 1962* (Washington, D.C.: General Accounting Office, 1968); and U.S. General Accounting Office, *Need to Enhance the Effectiveness of On-The-Job Training in Appalachian Tennessee* (Washington, D.C.: General Accounting Office, 1970).

[26] The differential utility to a firm of general and specific training is analyzed in Gary Becker, *Human Capital* (New York: Columbia University Press, 1964), pp. 11–29; and Michael J. Piore, "Public and Private Responsibilities in On-The-Job Training of Disadvantaged Workers." Mimeograph, 1968, p. 1.

[27] U.S. Department of Labor, *Manpower Report of the President, 1969* (Washington, D.C.: U.S. Government Printing Office, 1969), p. 238.

[28] U.S. General Accounting Office, *Improvements Needed in Contracting . . .*, p. i.

[29] Corporate abuses of the Jobs program are discussed in United States Senate, Committee on Labor and Public Welfare, *The Jobs Program* (Washington, D.C.: Government Printing Office, 1970).

[30] Quoted in Levitan and Mangum, p. 163.

[31] *Ibid.*

[32] This discussion is based on the analysis of two economists close to the program. See *ibid.*, pp. 163–210.

[33] Quoted in *ibid.*, p. 173.

[34] *Report of the National Advisory Commission on Civil Disorders* (New York: Bantam Books, 1968), p. 204.

[35] National Urban Coalition, *Law and Disorder II* (Washington, D.C.: U.S. National Urban Coalition, 1970), p. 5.

[36] *Ibid.,* p. 3.

[37] Office of Law Enforcement Assistance, U.S. Department of Justice, *LEAA Grants and Contracts, Fiscal 1966–1968* (Washington, D.C.: U.S. Government Printing Office, 1968), pp. 61–86.

[38] Levitan and Mangum, pp. 51 and 206.

[39] George Shultz, "The Family Assistance Act of 1969" (Statement before the Committee on Ways and Means, House of Representatives, October 16, 1969).

Lester C. Thurow is Professor of Economics and Management at Massachusetts Institute of Technology. He grew up in Montana, attended Williams College, was a Rhodes Scholar at Oxford, and received his Ph.D. from Harvard in 1964. He is the author of several books, including The Economics of Poverty and Discrimination, *and numerous articles.*

13 The Elimination of Poverty

Lester C. Thurow

The question of whether poverty can or cannot be eliminated should be split into two questions. First, can the economic environment be altered to eliminate poverty? Second, are the necessary economic changes politically feasible? Since I am an economist, I will primarily comment on the economic changes necessary to eliminate poverty, but I will return to the political problems. I recognize the interconnections that exist between economic power and political power, but the two are not rigidly linked together.

In Southeast Asia ethnic Chinese dominate economically but have almost no political power. In the economic arena they are the discriminators and in the political arena they are the discriminatees. In this sense I am a non-Marxist. To know a group's economic power is not to know its political power. To know a group's economic position is not to know its attitudes about the economic positions of other groups. Basically I will be arguing that an economic revolution does not necessarily require a political revolution as a precondition.

THE DEFINITION OF POVERTY

Before it is possible to define the conditions for eliminating poverty it is necessary to define precisely what is going to be eliminated. If poverty is defined as the lowest quarter of the income distribution, then poverty can only be eliminated by making every family's income precisely equal. The difficulties of organizing a society where each family receives precisely the same income in spite of real differences in abilities (or interest in monetary incomes) is probably insurmountable. This is not to say that more equality would not be good, but it is to say that complete equality would probably not be worth the enormous effort that it would require.

If poverty is defined as the government currently defines it, poverty is a trivial problem and easily eliminated. In 1969 the poverty line for a family of four was $3721. Given such poverty lines and economic growth, poverty falls rapidly in the absence of any specific programs for eliminating poverty. Between 1962 and 1969 the percentage of persons in poverty fell from 21 per cent to 12 per cent. None of these declines can be attributed to government programs. Because approximately half of the families now in poverty have no member who can work and take advantage of economic growth, economic growth cannot eliminate poverty but it can cut the current poverty percentages in half. At that point less than $5 billion in transfer payments would be necessary to completely eliminate poverty. I believe that such transfer will be made simply because politicians will be unable to resist the thought of going down in history as the man (or Congress) who eliminated poverty in America. Thus if we are talking about eliminating poverty as it is officially defined, the problem is a relatively trivial problem. It will be done and is merely a crime that it has not yet been done.

To move to a more meaningful definition of poverty, it is necessary to recognize that basically we do not have poverty problems if the word poverty is used in its conventional sense. In America we are talking about relative incomes; not absolute survival. We thus have an income distribution problem not a poverty problem. The word "poverty" has been applied to this problem because it was supposed to have more political sex appeal than income redistribution. In fact the word "poverty" has led us into Byzantine discussion as to whether families were or were not in poverty.

As a result, I suggest that we start talking about income redistribution and state that we want an income distribution where no family has an income less than 50 per cent of the median income. With a 1969 median family income of $9433, this would mean an average income redistribution line of $4717. There is nothing magic about 50 per cent. I merely suggest it since this is approximately where the poverty line was originally set back in 1962. With growth it has now fallen to 39 per cent. Thus in the rest of this discussion I will comment on how this objective might be brought about.

The relative income problem is much harder to correct since economic growth does not provide a solution. In America the top 20 per cent of the population receives 40 per cent of total income while the bottom 20 per cent of the population receives 5 per cent of total income. Thus the average income of the top quintile is eight times as large as the average income of the bottom quintile. Looking even more closely at the extremes of the income distribution, the average income of the top 5 per cent of the population is thirty times as large as the average income of the bottom 5 per cent of the population. (Remember that constant relative differences imply increasing absolute differences as incomes grow.) These relationships have not changed during the post–World War II period. There was some narrowing of the gaps during both the depression and World War II, but none since. The question is how to bring about such a narrowing. The problem is made more acute by the distribution of wealth. In the United States the top 2½ per cent of all families own 44 per cent of all privately held assets. Such differences are intolerable in my frame of reference.

A STRATEGY

Focusing on redistributing income or wealth widens our perspectives of the problem. In some sense middle Americans (the hard hats) are quite right in their resistance to the war on poverty and income redistribution. The satisfaction that any individual derives from his income depends on his absolute income, but it also depends on the income gaps between himself and others, both up and down the scale. Just focusing on the bottom of the income distribution places an unfair burden on the man just above the income redistribution line. The gap between himself and those below him is to be severely reduced yet nothing is being done about closing the gaps between himself and those richer. As a consequence his real welfare is to be much more severely reduced than those with higher incomes.

I submit that an effective income-redistribution program must focus on making the income distribution more equal at both the top and the bottom. Otherwise there is no conceivable method for obtaining a political majority for income redistribution. In essence this means that half of our effort must be directed to constructing effective income, wealth, and consumption taxes on the rich. By rich I mean that 3.2 per cent of our population that has household incomes in excess of $25,000.

This is not the new radicalism, but the old radicalism of egalitarian America. As an abstract principle, Americans have always believed in stiff inheritance taxes. Perhaps individuals should be allowed to keep what they earn, but they should not be allowed to simply inherit great wealth. Yet this is exactly what happens in America. We have nominal inheritance taxes, yet the loopholes are so extensive that for all practical purposes inheritance taxes are nonexistent. Loopholes in the income tax are better known, but no less noxious for their greater visibility.

It is interesting that democratic societies only seem capable of constructing effective income redistribution tax systems during times of war. The desire to share burdens equitably and pull together for a united war effort leads to progressive, effective taxes. The cynic could argue that this is merely a plot to get the suckers to be willing to die to protect the rich. And the constant erosion of the tax system during peace time would certainly back him up. Thus the political challenge is to see whether the American society can construct a good tax system in other than times of war. The answer is by no means obvious, but I regard this part of the problem just as important as constructing programs to raise the lower tail of the income distribution.

While altering the top portion of the income distribution can be viewed as a return to traditional values, one of the necessary ingredients in altering the bottom of the income distribution runs contrary to traditional American values. Between one quarter to one third of the families who are more than 50 per cent below the median income are there because there is no one in the family that can participate in the labor force on a full-time basis. The lame, the halt, the blind, the sick, and the aged can only be raised to satisfactory income levels through effective income transfer mechanisms. This means breaking the traditional link between work and income and throwing away our puritan beliefs about "no work, no income" at least for these individuals.

For some of these individuals sheltered employment provides a halfway house. Useful public jobs are provided to match individual capabilities, but the wages in these jobs are not matched to individual productivity but to individual needs. The jobs must be public since wages will exceed productivity. Losses, rather than profits, are to be expected. An argument can be made for sheltered public employment jobs on the grounds that individuals are performing useful public services. This argument is true, but not the compelling reason for public employment. On a simple efficiency basis there are probably better methods of producing desired public services. Public employment is desirable because there are individuals who would rather feel that they were earning their own living rather than living on the public dole.

Their self esteem with a $100-per-week job is simply much higher than with a $100-per-week check. In addition, work generates certain consumption benefits (psychic income) that cannot be duplicated with a simple check. Friends are made; the individual is forced to look beyond his own problems.

Income transfer mechanisms must have two key characteristics to be satisfactory. First, income should be transferred in such a manner that individuals who receive transfer payments are not individually identifiable by their neighbors. Second, income should be transferred in such a manner as to maintain incentives for improving one's own position. Together these two requirements point toward some variant of the negative income tax (the Nixon Family Assistance Plan is one such variant).

By combining positive and negative taxes, it is impossible for neighbors to know whether an individual is or is not on welfare (receiving negative taxes). They simply will not know whether he is writing checks to the government or receiving checks from the government; just as they do not know the exact amount of the checks he is now writing. No welfare workers come to determine need. Inspections may be made but they are simply tax audits that may be inflicted on either rich or poor.

Negative income taxes also guarantee that an individual will always be increasing his income whenever he is willing and able to work. Effective tax payments can never equal or exceed 100 per cent. Such is not the case at present. When an individual on welfare goes to work the combination of federal income taxes, state, or local income taxes, and reductions in welfare payments or food stamps can easily equal or exceed the individual's earnings. Negative income taxes, however, cannot be instituted at the local level. They must be national or one area would end up being responsible for the entire burden of national welfare payments. Conversely this means abolishing local welfare systems and shifting control to the federal government.

It should also be recognized that preserving work incentives involves costs. While the 1969 income deficiency between what people have and what they would need to meet official poverty lines is $10 billion, a negative income tax with a 50 per cent tax rate would cost $20 to $25 billion to bring every family up to their poverty line. This occurs since some of the payments must go to people who are above the poverty line if no individual is to have less than the poverty line. The *only* method for being "efficient" — not spending more than $10 billion to eliminate official poverty — is to levy a 100 per cent tax on individuals who are receiving welfare payments.

In any comprehensive program to narrow the distribution of income, programs to increase working skills and to improve work opportunities have an important role, but their role needs to be carefully analyzed. In many senses formal work credentials (education and formal training) are relative. If labor markets work according to the queue hypothesis, employers work down the labor queue starting from the worker with the best work credentials and working toward the worker with the worst work credentials. To improve the work credentials of the worst worker is fine, but if the credential of better workers rises even faster, it does little good. His relative position does not increase and may deteriorate. Thus it is not possible to work on improving the human capital of low-income workers without at the same time looking at the human capital of high-income workers. Relative improvements can only occur by raising the human capital at the bottom of the income distribution faster than at the top or by lowering the human capital of those at the top.

Since formal education is easy to measure (and was popular) it has been overemphasized as a determinant of incomes. Instead of serving as a direct determinant of incomes it is much more of a cheap screening device that lets individuals into different on-the-job training programs or into different occupations. While education may be a cheap screening device for employers (they merely note education levels on a piece of paper), it is an extremely costly screening device for governments and for private individuals. They pay the necessary costs. Thus serious attention needs to be given to alternative methods of screening. They may be expensive compared to what private employers now spend on screening, but they will be cheap in comparison with what society is now spending on education.

In some sense discrimination based on education is like discrimination based on race or color. Individuals should be treated as individuals based on individual characteristics that are pertinent to job requirements rather than being classified based on group characteristics that may not be pertinent to job requirements.

It should be almost axiomatic that eliminating low-income families means eliminating racial discrimination, but again this is one of the implications of eliminating poverty that has not been directly faced. The instigators of the War on Poverty knew this but thought that no one else would know if they did not mention it. Middle America did know and the attempt to avoid the connection probably proved to be worse than a frank discussion of this implication. In any case income redistributions (as defined above) cannot be accomplished without eliminating discrimination.

This involves some use of both the stick and the carrot, but it primarily involves the use of the stick. Private firms and public agencies must be forced to hire racial minorities. To be realistic, "force" means quotas that must be met. No amount of investment in the individual skills of racial minorities will solve the problem.

Substantial amounts of money are currently being spent on on-the-job training programs without great success. Their lack of success is partly due to a faulty diagnosis of the problem and partly due to a faulty set of priorities. Programs have been set up as if the main problem is getting a job. In periods of high employment (unemployment less than 4.0 per cent) there are few individuals who cannot find some kind of a job. In 1969 only 10 per cent of poverty-stricken families had unemployed family heads and almost none of these were unemployed for the entire year. The real problem is finding a "good" job with advancement possibilities. Even on the official definition of poverty 47 per cent of the working heads of poverty-sticken households worked full-time (fifty to fifty-two weeks per year and thirty-five or more hours per week). For those families more than 50 per cent below the median income, the percentage rises to 54 per cent. These family heads do not have entry job problems, they have upgrading problems. Since most of our incentives payments have been designed to bribe firms to hire different workers into entry jobs, it is not surprising that these payments have not led to job upgrading.

There is no reason, however, why incentive systems cannot be changed. Instead of paying for hiring disadvantaged workers, incentives systems should make payments depending upon how much the employer is able to raise the income of his disadvantaged employees over some specified period of time. Since income increases are what society wants, income increases are what society should reward.

The focus on unemployment led to a faulty diagnosis of the problem, but it also led to a faulty set of priorities. Under the Johnson administration it became popular to be against "creaming." The good manpower training program was the program that found the most disadvantaged man and attempted to minister to his needs. Ghetto hard-core were often singled out for special attention. While this might have been a noble aim from the point of view of social welfare (minister first to the man most in need), it was a practical blunder.

Since no one knew how to administer to the needs of the most disadvantaged man, programs failed. Instead of leading to the formulation of new and better programs, these failures merely led to the dismemberment of the poverty program. They provided convenient cannon fodder for the attackers. What the program needed to get off the ground was not failures but successes.

Essentially the failures occurred because the hard-core did not have "industrial discipline" and no one knew how to create it. Technical job skills did not prove to be a major problem. While it is certainly possible to argue that many forms of commonly accepted "industrial discipline" are unnecessary for efficient production, some forms of "industrial discipline" are necessary. Assembly lines cannot start until everyone is in place. No organization can work with wholesale theft

Just as monkeys randomly pecking at the typewriter will not write Shakespeare, workers randomly walking around a factory will not produce steel. Some system of organization must be imposed.

To some extent the problem can be reduced with more sympathetic management interest in reducing it. Proper use of queueing theories and other statistical techniques could substantially reduce the need to have workers show up every day or at some precise instant. To some extent the problem can be reduced by public realization that changing adult attitudes is expensive and difficult. To demand a cheap program for changing adult attitudes is to demand the nonexistent. The remainder of the problem must be eliminated with the realization that transfer payment support systems may have to carry the burden of some individuals who could work physically but cannot work sociologically.

This problem could have been avoided initially by focusing programs on the full-time workers who were simply making low wages. They have demonstrated "industrial discipline." They just need the easily taught technical job skills plus opportunities. Based on successes and experience with this group, the poverty-training programs could then have moved on to workers who are more difficult to aid.

In addition, the hard-core strategy implied that it was politically feasible to take individuals from the bottom of the income distribution and raise them above millions of other hardworking individuals who were also in poverty. While there is nothing sacrosanct about rank-order equity, tax systems and most other government programs work on the presumption that the government may increase or reduce income differences but it should not affect rank order incomes.

For all of these reasons the order of priorities in manpower training programs should be inverted. Instead of starting with the hardest to help, they should start with the easiest to help. Instead of focusing on the unemployed, they should focus on the employed and upgrading. Most manpower programs have failed, but there was and is no need for this failure. Manpower training programs can be made to work.

THE POLITICS

While it is fashionable to charge that American government is a self-interest group in the service of the rich and while examples of this phenomenon can certainly be found (the farm programs widen the gap between rich and poor farmers rather than narrowing it), such is not the case when all government programs are systematically examined. As Table 1 indicates, when all levels of government are combined and when all taxes and expenditures are considered, the budgetary inci-

TABLE 1. Budgetary Incidence as a Percentage of Total Income for All Families by Income Class, 1965

	under $2000	$2000 to 2999	$3000 to 3999	$4000 to 4999	$5000 to 5999	$6000 to 7499	$7500 to 9999	$10000 to 14999	$15000 and over	Total
Taxes										
Personal	2.9	3.8	5.2	6.9	7.2	7.9	9.1	10.7	28.2	9.6
Corporate	1.2	2.1	4.3	1.7	2.3	1.7	2.0	5.4	15.5	3.8
Social Insurance	4.1	4.2	4.5	4.8	4.6	4.4	4.2	3.9	2.1	4.2
Consumption	9.8	8.5	8.6	7.9	7.5	7.0	6.4	5.9	4.4	6.9
Property	7.1	5.3	4.5	3.7	3.4	3.1	3.1	3.4	6.3	3.8
Total Taxes	25.1	23.9	27.1	25.0	25.0	24.1	24.8	29.3	56.5	28.3
Expenditures										
General Benefit	46.2	26.7	21.2	17.9	16.0	14.3	12.8	11.3	9.3	15.6
Defense and International	26.2	15.1	12.0	10.1	9.0	8.1	7.2	6.4	5.3	8.8
Other	20.0	11.6	9.2	7.8	7.0	6.2	5.6	4.9	4.0	6.9
Non-General Benefits	62.3	38.3	24.8	15.8	13.4	11.1	9.3	8.7	6.9	14.3
Total Expenditures	109.0	65.0	46.0	33.7	−29.5	25.4	22.1	20.0	16.3	29.9
Total	83.9	41.1	18.9	8.7	4.5	1.3	− 2.7	− 9.3	−40.2	1.6

Lester C. Thurow, *The Impact of Taxes on the American Economy*, Praeger, 1971. Reprinted by permission of the publisher.

dence of government rises from net benefits of 84 per cent for families with incomes under $2000 per year to net costs of 40 per cent for families with incomes over $15,000 per year. The government budget should provide for more redistribution, but it does provide for some. Budgets are progressive, not regressive.[1] The American political system has demonstrated a capacity for income redistribution. The problem is enlarging that capacity; not creating a new system that will have such a capacity.

Perhaps I am being naive and a program of effective taxes, adequate transfer payments, the eliminating of discrimination (racial and educational), and manpower programs that focus on the easiest to help is unsalable. There may be evidence to this effect, but I remain unaware of it.

QUESTIONS

Poverty
Wachtel / Thurow

1. Aren't the real differences between Thurow and Wachtel over whether or not income redistribution can or cannot take place within the existing institutional framework?

2. Does Thurow use the money budgeted to government programs or the actual amount received by low-income families to show the redistributional effect of government budgets? How is the benefit from national defense allocated to families in Thurow's table?

3. Has either author provided adequate proof that poverty can or cannot be eliminated within the existing system?

4. Is it really government policy to eliminate the poor through repression? Is it to eliminate the threat some of the poor pose to society?

5. Are the upper classes or ruling classes really flexible enough to support income redistribution?

6. Is unequal distribution of income a problem or a symptom?

7. How can we account for the fact that Thurow finds government spending to be redistributional overall, while Wachtel examined three programs aimed at helping the poor and found they were not, in fact, helping the poor?

8. Can we eliminate poverty in a capitalist society?

9. If we eliminated poverty, who would do the low status work?

10. What is the relationship between education and income?

See Table 1.

11. Why is it that countries that have 50 per cent of our per capita gross national product have less of a poverty problem than we have?

12. Thurow defines poverty as half the median income. If the median income is constantly increasing, aren't the people who are at half the median going to feel deprived? Won't keeping up with the Joneses mean that they will still feel themselves to be poor?

13. Is work a good thing?

14. Do people need jobs in order to be happy?

15. What is Thurow's explanation for poverty?

16. What are the causes of poverty?

17. Wachtel criticizes the operation of the Social Security, agricultural, and manpower programs of the United States government. Is he implying that our society would be better off without these programs? What programs would Wachtel propose to deal with these problems? What are the policy implications of Wachtel's analysis?

18. Lester Thurow defines poverty in relative terms. He argues that those people are poor whose income falls below half the median family income. What is Wachtel's definition of poverty?

Arthur M. Okun was born in Jersey City, New Jersey, and received his A.B. and Ph.D. degrees from Columbia University. He was a Professor of Economics at Yale University until he joined the Council of Economic Advisers to the President. He served as Chairman of the Council during the last years of the Johnson administration, and is presently doing research at the Brookings Institution.

14 Have Fiscal and/or Monetary Policies Failed?

Arthur M. Okun

The provocative, loaded question addressed to this panel asks for an evaluation of the capabilities of fiscal and monetary tools and the performance of the policymakers. Any evaluation of anything is, of course, a relative matter. Successes or failures emerge only by comparison to some set of standards or by virtue of some competition.

In the case at hand, many possible standards of comparison emerge; and they point toward different verdicts:

. Measured against the standards that prevailed at the time of passage of the Employment Act in 1946, fiscal-monetary policy has been a resounding success throughout the postwar period.

enior fellow, The Brookings Institution. The views expressed are my own and are ot necessarily those of the officers, trustees, or other staff members of the Brookings nstitution.

This article is reprinted from *The American Economic Review*, LXII, 2, May 972, by permission of the author and the American Economic Association. © Copyright 1972 by the American Economic Association.

2. Judged by its contribution to generating social welfare or to solving the big social problems, fiscal-monetary policy can be regarded as trivial and perhaps somewhat obsolete.
3. By the standard of the hopes and aspirations that prevailed in the mid-sixties, the performance of recent fiscal and monetary policies must be deemed a great disappointment.
4. Measured against what can and should be accomplished in the future, the past record of fiscal-monetary policy is a promising start.

THE PERSPECTIVE OF A GENERATION

It is against the perspective of the attitudes and expectations of a generation ago that fiscal-monetary policy looks best. At that time, even ardent Keynesians accepted the business cycle as a fact of economic life. They hoped that countercyclical stabilization policy would reduce the sharpness of business cycle peaks and fill in the abysses, but even their promised land was marked by a terrain of hills and valleys. Paul Douglas spelled out his prescription: urging stimulative fiscal policy whenever the unemployment rate exceeded 8 per cent, but warning against the use of deficit financing in order to drive unemployment down below 6 per cent. In retrospect, the emphasis in the early postwar years was on the avoidance of catastrophe — like the Great Depression — rather than the attainment of perfection.

By that yardstick, the profession and the policymakers have clearly delivered more than was expected. The median annual unemployment rate for the last twenty-five years has been 4.5 per cent. The worst yearly unemployment record of the postwar era was 6¾ per cent in both 1958 and 1961; 1949 and 1971 follow with about 6 per cent. Annual real *GNP* has declined only three times — 1954, 1958, and 1970. Recessions have been milder, shorter, and less frequent than in the prewar annals. And their inevitability has been subjected to question with the record of 105 months of economic expansion during the sixties — a phenomenon that would have qualified as a 400 to 1 longshot on the basis of the business cycle chronology prior to 1960. In a generation, we have moved, conservatively estimated, half the distance from our previous performance to perfection.

THE CONTRIBUTION TO SOCIAL WELFARE

The easiest way to deprecate the accomplishments of stabilization policy in the postwar era is to judge its contribution in terms of the ultimate goals and the big problems of our society. That kind of appraisal, o course, ignores the purposes and the limited scope of these policies; it would condemn polio vaccine as a failure because it hasn't cured cancer. Fiscal and monetary policies can contribute to social welfare only by regulating the level and growth of aggregate demand. In the 1930s, the inadequacy of aggregate demand was the cancer of our society, destroying social tissue at a rate previously experienced only during the Civil War. Since a depressed economy created such an unhappy society, prosperity was, naively though understandably, expected to produce a happy society. Precisely because prosperity has typically prevailed during the postwar era, it has been demonstrated that the nation does not live by economic growth alone. The achievement of "maximum employment" does not necessarily provide jobs that are rewarding in ways that go beyond the pay check. The achievement of "maximum purchasing power" cannot guarantee that consumers get satisfaction from the goods available in the private market place or that they get a sufficient quantity and quality of public services that are not offered in the market. And no amount of prosperity closes the enormous gap between our lofty principles of equality of opportunity and our lowly performance in tolerating huge inequities that persist over generations.

Although prosperity is a small component of any broad social appraisal, it is an essential vitamin for the body politic, and is sorely missed in its absence. The deficiency of prosperity of the past two years shows up everywhere: productivity is depressed; the number of people in poverty has risen for the first time in a decade; advances of the disadvantaged up the job ladder have been set into slow motion; state and local budgets are squeezed; the contrast of urgent needs with idle resources taints the whole picture of the efficiency of our institutions. The scarcity of jobs produces a search for scapegoats: some blame those cheap foreign goods, while observers on the left and the right, in a curious agreement, identify military cutbacks as the key source of joblessness. Despite these misconceptions, there is enough recognition of the truth to make prosperity the number one political issue when we don't have it.

There is another important limitation to the significance of fiscal-monetary policy, reflecting the fact that effective regulation of aggregate demand cannot eliminate the problem of the unemployment-inflation tradeoff. At best, fiscal-monetary policy can pick the desired point on the tradeoff.

The nature of the tradeoff is a matter of extreme social concern today. In my judgment, there is much greater hope and greater need for a breakthrough in professional understanding of the nature of the tradeoff and of policy measures to improve it than in our knowledge of fiscal-monetary tools. Macroeconomists are responding and will increasingly respond to that challenge by investigating the nature of the inflationary biases in our society, the characteristics of the process of wage and price determination, the key elements of job turnover and job search, and the way these are and could be influenced by a variety of techniques of public policy, ranging from manpower programs to incomes policies. This effort is bound to push research on fiscal and monetary policies off the center of the professional stage. But that trend is emerging, not because demand-management has failed, but because it has had a measure of success. When the economy fluctuated violently, it did not stay close to full employment long enough to pose serious worries about the conflict of price stability and high employment. The tradeoff problem is a noxious weed in the garden of a prosperous economy. But the weeds bother us only because we can grow flowers in the garden.

THE PERSPECTIVE OF THE RECENT RECORD

A third relevant standard for the appraisal of fiscal-monetary policy is the disappointing record of the last half dozen years. Indeed, the loaded question we are being asked today undoubtedly reflects that record.

Herbert Stein has dated the high point of prestige of macroeconomic policymaking to the moment early in 1966 when *Time Magazine* put John Maynard Keynes on its cover. The prescription Walter Heller and his "new economist" colleagues had written for the economy had finally been administered and the patient had recovered brilliantly. The enthusiasm of the press was unrestrained; with friends like that, the "new economists" needed no enemies. And they knew it. At these professional meetings just six years ago, Gardner Ackley presented a model of temperance in a moment of triumph. He warned that the success scored in achieving high level employment could not be extrapolated into the future:

> We would all like the economy to tread the narrow path of a balanced, parallel growth of demand and capacity — at as high a level of capacity utilization as is consistent with reasonable price stability. . . But the macroeconomics of a high employment economy is insufficiently known to allow us to map that path with a high degree of reliability . . . It is easy to prescribe expansionary policies in a period of slack Managing high level prosperity is a vastly more difficult business and requires vastly superior knowledge. [pp. 174 and 176]

But the record of the past dozen years has been disappointing even to a temperate man. Only someone cursed with neurotic pessimism — or blessed with omniscience — could have believed at that time that the next six years would witness an average growth of real output of barely 3 per cent and an average inflation rate over 4 per cent. We can profit from the lessons of that period if we read them properly. Viewed in light of some unique events like the Vietnam war and some typical phenomena like the imperfect capability of economic forecasting and the persistent gap between economic analysis and political feasibility, the record of 1966–71 provides no basis for revising significantly downward — or upward — the estimates of the capability of stabilization policies that a temperate man should have held a half dozen years ago.

THE ROLE OF VIETNAM

The Vietnam buildup was a unique destabilizing force that fortunately should not be and need not be extrapolated into any peacetime experience. Of course, the stimulus of an anticipated upsurge in military outlays can be neutralized *in principle* by any of various stabilizing devices: an increase in taxes, reduction in civilian public expenditures, or a tightening of monetary policy. And this principle applies equally to crusading wars and senseless ones; to victorious wars, stalemates, and defeats. In practice, however, the unpredictability of military outlays adds to economic instability in every period of hostilities.

In the particular event of Vietnam, the national unwillingness to face up to the issue of guns versus butter — to recognize the resource costs of the war — vastly complicated the problem of stabilization. In the Korean war, when our military posture won the support of a reasonably broad social consensus, the political feasibility of restrictive tax and monetary policy was far greater. Because it did not command that kind of broad public support, Vietnam created a major problem of economic instability, as well as many other — and, in perspective, far more important — social and political problems.

No one can produce a valid hypothetical history of the last six years on the assumption that the Vietnam war had never happened. But history provides some clues, both favorable and unfavorable, on the performance of economists in diagnosing and prescribing. The unfavorable clues confirm Ackley's concern that economists don't yet know enough to offer policy makers very good prescriptions for managing high-level prosperity. Indeed, events that had taken place prior to his talk make that clear in retrospect. The amount of fiscal-monetary stimulus supplied to the economy had probably gone a little too far by the middle of 1965. However, fiscal policy was scheduled to move toward restraint after the third quarter of 1965 and would have worked to slow down the pace of aggregate demand if the war had not intervened. Some gradual turn toward restraint in monetary policy would also have been required. These turns would not have been made on an ideal schedule and the economy would have strayed into inflationary territory. But it strayed as far as it did only because fiscal policy became paralyzed by the uncertainties and the politics of war.

THE SIDE EFFECTS OF TIGHT MONEY

When the fiscal paralysis became evident, monetary policy was used in 1966 to apply a massive dose of restraint that offset the huge fiscal stimulus. Judged by its success in halting the boom and curbing inflation, the Federal Reserve strategy must be scored a remarkable success. The cost of living, which had been rising at a 4 per cent rate during much of 1966, slowed down to an annual rate of 2½ per cent in the first half of 1967. And unemployment never rose significantly above 4 per cent; the pause of 1967 was as different from the five postwar recessions — including 1969–70 — as a cold is different from pneumonia. That experience demonstrated that aggregate demand can be restrained (or stimulated) as much as required by the use of monetary policy (or fiscal policy) alone. But it also demonstrated the multiplicity of objectives of macroeconomic performance, which can be pursued jointly only through a carefully coordinated use of fiscal and monetary tools. For the same good reasons that the public dislikes losses in income and instability in the prices of goods and services, it also dislikes losses in wealth and instability in the price of credit. The adverse side effects of tight money in 1966 were enormous — a huge jump in interest rates, distortions of asset values, consternation in financial markets, and a depression in homebuilding.

In light of that experience, the Federal Reserve made a conscious and deliberate decision early in 1967 *not* to make a further effort to offset fiscal stimulus with monetary restraint. At that time, both the Fed and the Administration saw a new boom coming, as is evident from their remarkably accurate forecast of the year. They also knew that monetary policy could be used to stop that boom, just as it had been in 1966, but they decided — rightly or wrongly — that the disease of inflation was a lesser evil than the cure offered by tight money. The consequent decision to provide a reemerging boom with the liquidity it demanded may or may not have been a wrong decision, but it was not based on a wrong forecast or a wrong assessment of the potency of monetary policy.

THE 1968–69 DISAPPOINTMENT

When the Revenue and Expenditure Control Act of 1968 was finally enacted at midyear, fiscal policy came back into line with the recommendations of government economic officials for the first time in nearly three years. It was a particularly distressing experience that, when we were able to call the policy tune once again, the economy did not dance to it. The economic forecast used within the government at that time was the most inaccurate short-term prediction for which I have ever shared responsibility. Because I and my colleagues did not recognize how feverish the economy was, we wrote some inappropriate prescriptions, particularly for an unduly easy monetary policy in the second half of 1968. I cannot explain why my forecast was particularly unsuccessful at that time any better than I can explain why it was unusually accurate at the start of 1967 and 1971.

"You can't win them all" is not a satisfactory explanation of anything, but it is a more accurate and less harmful lesson of the 1968 experience than others that have been advanced. One particularly wrong and harmful alleged lesson is the claim that temporary changes in personal income taxes don't work. Several cross-section studies of consumer behavior, conducted and published prior to the surcharge experience, provide compelling empirical evidence that households do not treat small windfalls (positive or negative) differently from permanent income in their consumption-saving decisions.[1] Nor does the time-series evidence following the imposition of the surcharge suggest that consumer outlays on services and non-durable goods were higher than would have been predicted by econometric consumption models that treated the drain of income resulting from the tax surcharge as equivalent to any other loss of disposable income.[2] Although the permanent income hypothesis illuminates many aspects of consumer behavior, it sheds no light on the strength of the economy from mid-1968 to mid-1969. The myth about the ineffectiveness of small temporary changes in income taxes threatens to rob fiscal policy of its most legislatively feasible and socially acceptable tool for combatting economic fluctuations. The U.S. Senate came within one vote this autumn of adopting a $50 credit per family on personal income taxes as a temporary measure for 1972; "expert opinion" may have helped to swing this regrettable adverse verdict.

The surprises of late 1968 and early 1969 occurred in the strength

---

[1] See references on pp. 177–8 of my article in *Brookings Papers on Economic Activity*. In particular, Michael Landsberger's contribution deserves attention.

[2] *Ibid.*

of demands for automobiles, for business plant and equipment, and for new homes. As information from that episode is incorporated into statistical studies of the determinants of investment, it strengthens the estimated link between investment outlays and various financial factors. In that sense, it marks up the estimated potency of monetary policy to influence aggregate demand. But it reaffirms the conclusion that money is only one of the major determinants of aggregate demand and that a monetary growth rate of 7 per cent or higher would be constructive under some economic conditions.

In general, the 1968–69 experience reminds us that forecasts that turn out to be wrong lead to errors in policy. But it also demonstrates that, when policies are flexible, errors are not irretrievable. Monetary policy deviated from an appropriate track for six or perhaps eight months; more adversity has been blamed by some observers on that deviation than on any other event in human history since Eve's encounter with the serpent.

THE 1969–71 GAME PLAN

Perhaps the most serious consequence of the 1968–69 disappointment is that it made many macroeconomists lose their nerve. They became receptive to formulas for economic instruments and formulations of economic theory that claimed to offer salvation from the perils of assessing and forecasting the economic outlook and appraising the impact of policy actions.

Concluding that the fiscal and monetary policy errors of 1965–68 had reflected excessive tampering and excessive dependence on economic forecasting, the Nixon Administration committed itself to a "game-plan" economic policy featuring a steady course: a maintained posture of the full-employment budget, stable growth of the money supply, and consistent nonintervention in the wage-price process. The strategy was followed with remarkable consistency: the full-employment surplus was barely nudged downward despite the recession and inadequate subsequent recovery; although it fluctuated over short periods of time, the money supply was kept at a growth rate that averaged close to the game-plan rate of 6 per cent for any substantial period; price-wage jawboning was not practiced.

With the nation's unemployment rate still at 6 per cent and the deceleration of inflation visible only in a microscope, the President of the United States pronounced the practical verdict on this test of "steady-course" economic policy on August 15. It is no coincidence that the administration most committed to a steady course made the biggest reversal in the course of economic policy in forty years. Because it had made such a virtue of unvarying instrument settings and had therefore waited so long before making any adjustments, the administration felt obliged to make a 180-degree turn when it did decide to change course. The enormous shift from the old game plan to the "new economic policy" should be particularly instructive to those economists who are most concerned about disruptive changes in economic policy. It is far more disruptive than the small, flexible, and frequent adjustments made under a discretionary policy that keeps trying to stay close to a track of sustainable balanced economic growth. This lesson is like the one economists have been trying to teach international bankers: small continuous fluctuations in exchange rates are less disruptive than the major, though infrequent, crises and revaluations that marked the traditional fixed-rate system. Like the fixed-rate system for currencies, steady-course economics obtains stability in the small by courting instability in the large.

In light of recent experience, the profession can no longer shirk its responsibility to make the best possible diagnoses and the best possible forecasts, in full recognition that they can be wrong, and to recommend economic policy measures that seem likely to promote the nation's economic goals, recognizing that they may impede them. Fortunately, the record of 1971 may help economists to screw up their courage and restore their nerve. This has been a good year for most macroeconomists, although not for the economy. Private economists who forecast *GNP* on an eclectic Keynesian basis were generally accurate a year ago in predicting that real economic growth in 1971 would be only 3 per cent. They saw correctly that the economy was stuck in the mud and unlikely to get rolling without a fiscal-monetary push. And they correctly judged at midyear that the rapid growth of money during the first half of 1971 was not the harbinger of an imminent boom. To be sure, the future will bring disappointments like 1968, as well as successes like 1967 and 1971. Still we are likely to be right more than half the time in recommending prompt and flexible adjustments of fiscal-monetary policy. And we can fairly conclude that the only realistic alternative to such a strategy of sensible-steering economics is an oscillation between game-plan economics and crisis economics.

More effective regulation of aggregate demand remains one of the important tasks of the profession and the policymakers; that task can be pursued through better analysis, more timely diagnosis, more appropriate prescription, and more effective conversion of prescription into public policy. The mistakes of the last six years can serve us well to improve the record over the next generation. In 1996, the fiftieth anniversary of the Employment Act, perhaps the American Economic

Association can schedule a session entitled "Have Fiscal and Monetary Policies Triumphed?"

REFERENCES

G. Ackley, "The Contribution of Economists to Policy Formation," *Journal of Finance,* 21, May 1966.

P. H. Douglas, *Economy in the National Government.* Chicago 1952, 253–54.

R. Eisner, "Fiscal and Monetary Policy Reconsidered," *American Economic Review,* 59, December, 1969, 897–905.

A. M. Okun, "The Personal Tax Surcharge and Consumer Demand, 1968–70," *Brookings Papers on Economic Activity,* January, 1971.

H. Stein, *The Fiscal Revolution in America.* Chicago: The University of Chicago Press, 1969, 131.

*John G. Gurley was born in Ala-
meda, California and received his
B.A. and Ph.D. degrees from Stanford University. He is best known
for* Money in a Theory of Finance
*(with E. S. Shaw). He served as
editor of the* American Economic
Review *during the 1960s and is
currently Professor of Economics at
Stanford University. He is doing
research on Maoist economic development.*

15 Have Fiscal and Monetary Policies Failed?

John G. Gurley

Monetary and fiscal policies are commonly judged by how successful
they are in attaining the national goals of full employment, stable
equilibrium prices, high output growth rates, and balance-of-payments
equilibrium. Inasmuch as we presently have none of these things,
recent monetary and fiscal policies have received rather low marks from
many economists, even after they have considered the claims that these
policies, consisting of only a limited number of tools, cannot do everything, that what they can do takes time, and that they have not always
been utilized perfectly, to say the least.

The low marks have come mainly from those economists who
believe that the market power of business corporations and labor unions
is largely responsible for rising prices, that this market power grows or is
more fully utilized as employment rates rise, and that full employment

This article is reprinted from *The American Economic Review*, LXII, 2, May 1972,
by permission of the author and the American Economic Association. © Copyright
1972 by the American Economic Association.

is good and inflation is bad. For many of these economists, monetary and fiscal policies can and should be used to attain high levels of employment, but in their view they cannot do the whole job and so must be accompanied by an incomes policy to retard the inevitable inflationary developments. Other economists in this group agree with this analysis, except that they would, in various ways, minimize the adverse effects of an open inflation, instead of using an incomes policy to suppress it.

Those more critical of monetary and fiscal policies have claimed that the present inadequate state of our theory precludes the wise use of these policies, even for the limited purpose of attaining high employment levels. The impact of fiscal policy, it is said, cannot be judged by the simple relation of expenditures to receipts, even if calculated at high employment levels, because of balanced-budget multiplier effects and, more importantly, because the impact of fiscal policy on output, employment, and prices depends heavily on the types of expenditures made by the government and on the types of taxes it imposes. Similarly, monetary policy's impact cannot be accurately determined without a more thorough investigation into the problem of expectations, and without considering a wider range of financial assets and financial institutions. With respect to both monetary and fiscal policies, it is alleged, our theory does not begin to measure up to the tasks at hand.

On the other side of the argument, monetary and fiscal policies have received high marks from those economists who do not accept the thesis of increasing market power and who believe that, if these policies are properly utilized and if allowance is made for the inevitable lags between their implementation and the economy's response to them, such policies are quite capable of achieving their limited goals. Within this group are the monetarists, who argue this case mainly for monetary policy, and primarily for its impact on the price level. The group also contains those Keynesians who present the case mainly for fiscal policy and for its impact on both real and nominal variables.

I

That, as I understand it, is the framework within which these issues are usually debated. The framework has many strong features, but, in one vital respect, it clouds and distorts reality, for it is based on the assumption that postwar Administrations, in their monetary, fiscal, and other policies, have been ultimately concerned with the broad public-interest goals of full employment, high growth rates, and so on. Thus, it is felt, the government's economic actions can be explained in terms of these goals, and any failure to attain the goals cannot be because Administrations have not desired them, but because of deficient tools of implementation, the unfortunate intrusion of exogenous factors, conflicts between the goals, and other complications. This way of looking at the problem is obviously useful, but I believe that it diverts attention several degrees away from what is really happening.

The ultimate and overriding objective of all capitalist governments is the preservation and strengthening of capitalism — that is, of the private enterprise system. In our own economy, this means that successive Administrations, above all else, have looked out for the welfare of business corporations; and in the final reckoning, they have been principally engaged in promoting the welfare of the few hundred industrial, commercial, and financial giants that define and shape the United States economy. Since the welfare of these huge corporations is best measured by their profits, the basic concern of United States Administrations has been the protection and promotion of these corporate profits.

This viewpoint does not imply that other claims have been systematically ignored or rejected, for the health of capitalism demands much more than a simple diet of rising profits. But it does imply that other claims, such as full employment, welfare programs, and price stability, are, in the final analysis, judged by the extent to which they are compatible with private profit making. If a goal, such as 3½ per cent unemployment, is clearly incompatible with the continued rise of corporate profits, it stands little chance of serious consideration, though its rejection will always be expressed in public-interest, rather than class-interest, terms.[1] If, on the other hand, a serious social conflict can be defused by the extension of a welfare program, thereby reducing a threat to the system itself, it has a good chance of passing. Profit making is what capitalism is all about, and this fundamental drive should be brought out into the open rather than kept hidden behind ideological facades such as "full employment" and "growth."

Nor does this viewpoint imply an absence of conflicts within the capitalist class. There are policies, for example, that will increase the profits of multinational corporations and at the same time decrease profits of strictly domestic firms. But the approach does assume that there are many basic policies, including, for instance, that of moderating wage demands, which are in the general interest of the business class, and that it is this general interest that is paramount.

In the domestic area, postwar Administrations have promoted corporate profits through high employment and growth policies. These have consisted mainly of monetary and fiscal policies designed to achieve a growing aggregate demand for goods and services, which, however, has been kept within bounds so as not to generate "excessive" or "unreasonable" wage demands. On the average, this policy has called for an unemployment rate of about 5 per cent — probably, in fact, 7 or 8 per cent when underemployment and labor force dropouts are accounted for. Thus, a considerable reserve of unemployed has been kept in the wings during much of the postwar period to moderate wage demands and to strengthen work discipline. This employment policy has been consistent with Congress's charge to the government, in the Employment Act of 1946, "to promote maximum employment . . . in a manner calculated to foster and promote free competitive enterprise and the general welfare." "Free competitive enterprise" is best promoted by growth policies that, at the same time, keep labor in its place; and there has been little difficulty in selling the whole thing as a general welfare program.[2]

During the postwar period, United States trade and especially foreign investments grew enormously throughout the capitalist world and became increasingly important as sources of profits for United States corporations. Successive national Administrations protected and promoted these increasingly profitable international activities by the general policy of keeping as much of the world as possible open for trade, investment, and raw materials acquisition by the giant corporations. This aim was pursued by economic aid to "friendly" governments (i.e., those receptive to United States direct investment and trade or those in strategic positions to further the global aims of the United States), partly to strengthen them economically, partly to provide supporting overhead capital for United States private enterprise, and partly to increase export markets of United States corporations. Postwar Administrations have also extended military aid to "friendly" governments for the purposes of fostering the weapons and aircraft output of United States corporations and of protecting these client governments from the militant opposition of some of their own people. The United States has, moreover, conducted counterinsurgency operations throughout the underdeveloped capitalist world, and, when all else has failed, it has used military force in pursuit of its basic aim — the maximization of the area of the world that is open for profitable corporate activities.

Considering both domestic and international aspects, the overriding aim of postwar Administrations has been to widen and strengthen private profit-making activities based on the ownership and control of domestic and world resources; and the means employed have ranged all the way from monetary policy to armed invasion.

It is within this context that monetary and fiscal policies should be judged — not within the context of so-called "national," "public interest," or "pluralistic consensus" goals such as full employment and price stability, all of which are subsidiary goals to the main one and serve to hide the dominant-class interests of our society. If we wish to get to the heart of the matter, we should not inquire into the success of monetary and fiscal policies in achieving "growth," but into their success in raising corporate profits.

II

Now, the fact is that corporate profits, throughout the postwar period, have been increasingly threatened by both international and domestic forces, and in the past five years they have suffered badly, declining in real terms, after taxes, by about 25 per cent. This is the crucial fact in gauging the failure of monetary and fiscal policies and in understanding the pressing need for new economic policies.

The overwhelming superiority of United States capitalism of the early postwar years has been greatly eroded in the past few decades by two international forces. The first is the expansion of the Communist world and the strengthening of its economic and military capabilities, the combination of which has reduced the area of profitable capitalist activity and at the same time has increased the cost to the U.S. of preventing militant nationalist and Communist movements from gaining other vital pieces of global capitalism. The other major force against the U.S. has been the spectacular growth of its main capitalist competitors — in particular, Japan, West Germany, and the Common Market. These two forces together have made international profit making by U.S. corporations increasingly expensive, difficult, and harzardous; and they have weakened the international financial position of the U.S.

In the domestic sphere, the main threat against United States corporate profits has been the growing ability of labor to obtain wage increases in excess of productivity gains. These wage increases have required corporations repeatedly to raise commodity prices in attempts to restore their profits. But this has become more and more difficult for them to do, and in the last few years virtually impossible, in the face of both a deteriorating international situation and deflationary policies at home which have been intended, but have not been able, to curb the growing power of labor.

The fact is that the large Vietnam war expenditures pushed the economy to levels of employment that greatly increased labor's bargaining power and that created deeply held expectations throughout the economy of continuing inflation. When Nixon took office, he attempted at first to stem this adverse tide by deflationary monetary and fiscal policies, which in time almost doubled the unemployment rate.

However, these policies proved a failure: they not only failed to reduce wage demands, but they came very close to toppling a large part of the financial structure of Wall Street, when stock prices fell sharply because of a declining ability of corporations to raise their prices, as aggregate demand weakened, to counter the continuing large wage increases.

Nixon was then forced to retreat to moderately expansionary monetary and fiscal policies. But these, while bolstering the financial structure, gave added power to labor and reinforced the already deeply embedded expectations of future inflation, which threatened to hit corporate profits hard both from the side of U.S. labor and from the side of foreign capitalist competition. Nixon at this point was squeezed between two unworkable policies, and his only alternatives were to stay put or to jump clear.

Thus, these adverse domestic and international trends against United States capitalism have compelled new economic policies and diplomatic moves by the Nixon Administration. The new actions are intended to shift income from labor to capital in the United States, and to shift income from Japanese and German capitalists (and no doubt ultimately from their working classes) to United States capitalists. The first shift of income is being attempted through wage and price controls at home, which it is hoped will permit profits to rise with the growth of the economy while "unreasonable" wage demands are curbed, and by further net subsidies to the capitalist class. The second shift is being implemented by a new international policy that is intended to change relative prices, relative trade and investment barriers, and relative defense burdens in favor of the United States capitalist class, and by new diplomatic overtures to China that are meant to establish a less costly and a more profitable area in Asia for trade, investment, and natural resource exploitation by U.S. corporations.

III

This brief outline indicates that monetary and fiscal policies have had during the postwar period, an increasingly unfavorable environment within which they could be used for their major aim of enhancing the profitability of United States private enterprise in both its domestic and international operations. In view of the strong forces that have been accumulating against the United States business class, it is not too surprising that monetary and fiscal policies by themselves have become decreasingly effective in stemming this tide.

The really pressing need for the drastic new domestic programs of the Nixon Administration can hardly be appreciated if that need is measured by the gaps between potential and actual output, by the excess of actual over acceptable inflation, or by shortfalls in real growth or employment rates.   None of these measures signals acute danger. But if one concentrates on what businessmen are most concerned about, and considers the growing threat of labor to those profits, set against a deteriorating international background, then the reason for pressing the panic button can be better appreciated.

ENDNOTES

[1] Every ruling class describes its self-serving purposes in public-interest terms. Everything done is advertised as being in the national interest or even in the interest of the very class that is being hurt.   Thus, wage controls are for the purpose of protecting the country's export markets; a deflationary policy that leads to high unemployment is promoted as in the interest of national price stability; an investment tax credit program can be billed as a jobs development program; and "growth" can be chosen over "equity" as in the long-run interest of everyone.   It must also be said that many economists, in their official positions, have been very accommodating to these self-serving policies of the capitalist class. See Richard B. Du Boff and Edward S. Herman, "The New Economics: Handmaiden of Inspired Truth."   Mimeograph, 1971.

[2] Businessmen are more likely to get right to the heart of the matter, disdaining the use of the cover-up terms that politicians and economists generally employ, but nevertheless expressing their self-serving actions as in the public interest.   Witness this from a *Business Week* editorial of Sept. 18, 1971:

If the United States is to get the gains in output that will create jobs and raise standards of living, business will have to get bigger profits as the recovery proceeds.   And if business is to make the huge investments necessary to increase productivity and meet foreign competition on even terms, it must have not only profits but the additional stimulation of the investment credit.

Labor's real interests do not lie in putting a ceiling on corporate earnings. They lie in promoting a vigorous expansion of production, jobs — and profits.

David M. Gordon was born in Washington, D.C., and received both his undergraduate degree and his Ph.D. in economics from Harvard. He served as editor of the Harvard Crimson, *co-editor of the* Harvard Review, *and was one of the co-founders of* The Southern Courier. *He is the editor of* Problems in Political Economy: An Urban Perspective.

When asked to describe his position within the economics profession, he sent this statement.

My position within the economics profession is that I want to get out of it. As a radical, I find much of the orthodox tradition not only irrelevant but unbearably lifeless; the continuing ambition of orthodox economists appears to be that they hope to show that we all act just like machines. I also find the academy itself rather stifling. Though undeniably smart, many academics seem to me self-indulgent, hypocritical and complacent about the world. When I taught at Yale last year, I kept bumping up against those qualities. I loved the students but found the faculty somewhat grating. So, I'm going off on my own for a while. I bowed out of the academic job market this year and plan to spend at least next year doing my own independent work, a combination of academic research and writing on the one hand and popular free-lance writing — economic and noneconomic — on the other. If I can keep myself alive that way, I'll keep trying to find people and to found institutions on the Lower East Side that can provide a way for as many as possible to live decently, constructively, in communities together.

16 Class and the Economics of Crime

David M. Gordon

Then in his second semester at Eastern District High School, he gave up working in school altogether. "I don't really know why, and I don't want to rationalize about it, but it may have been that I had been systematically de-educated. With all the emphasis on discipline, all the fire gets damped down. I knew I had a given role in society, and you wonder what do you need to know about Plato to fix the engine of an automobile. Anyhow, I flew apart, I began cutting classes, gambling in the bathroom, the whole bit. . . . I picked pockets. I was a little crook."

[Nine months in a reformatory intervened.] When he came out, Franklin K. Lane High School never jelled, and eventually he began to hustle. "I took a bunch of nothing jobs — they lasted a month on the average, and then I'd go to the movies instead. I bounced

around, I'd hustle when it was necessary — gambling, numbers, a little petty larceny.   And when I was 19 I committed a burglary and that was the end of the ball game."
— From the story of a thirty-year-old black ex-con[1]

Like a brush fire, crime in the United States has seemed recently to be raging out of control.   The public, the government and the experts have all raced to cool the blaze.   In one way or another, we have all been drawn into the fight.   With slogans and occasional compassion, with weapons, courts, prisons, and patrols, especially with perplexity and confusion, we have probably served in the end to frustrate our own good intentions, to fan the flames rather than douse them.   We seem to have as much trouble understanding the problem of crime as we do effecting its solution.

Meanwhile, amidst the confusion, orthodox economists have been striding elegantly to our rescue.   Cool, fearless, the perfect picture of professionalism, they have been promising to guide us toward "optimal" crime prevention and control.   Off with our silliness!   Off with our psychological muddle-headedness!   Gary Becker, a sort of guru among them, explains how easily we can understand it all [3, p. 170]: ". . . a useful theory of criminal behavior can dispense with special theories of anomie, psychological inadequacies, or inheritance of special traits and simply extend the economist's usual analysis of choice."   Come let us maximize together!

As I have read and thought recently about the problem of crime in the United States, I've found myself returning over and over to the same conclusions — that our public understanding of the problem is mistaken, that the government's policy responses are misguided, and that the recent orthodox economic analyses have been misleading.   In this short paper, I want very briefly to try to amplify those impressions. I have not tried to present a detailed brief against the conventional wisdom and the orthodox economic view.   Instead, I have tried to articulate my differences with those positions by formulating an alternative, radical analysis of criminal behavior and by evoking an alternative normative view of an appropriate social response to crime.

The paper has five sections.   The first offers a brief descriptive summary of the nature and extent of crime in the United States.   The second surveys some conventional public perspectives on the problems of crime, while the third outlines recent orthodox economic approaches to the problem.   In the fourth section, I sketch the framework of a radical economic analysis of crime in the United States.   In the final section, I amplify an alternative normative view of the appropriate social response to criminal behavior.[2]

A. CRIME IN AMERICA

In order to compare some alternative analytic approaches to the problem of crime, one must first try to clarify its empirical dimensions. Several useful summaries of the nature and extent of American crime are easily available, especially in the summary report of the President's Commission on Law Enforcement and the Administration of Justice [32] and Ramsey Clark's recent book, *Crime in America* [8].[3] Relying primarily on the basic facts documented in those sources, I have tried in the following paragraphs to outline the most important questions about the problem of crime which any analysis must try to resolve.

It seems important to emphasize, first of all, that crime is ubiquitous in the United States. Our laws are so pervasive that one must virtually retire to hermitage in order to avoid committing a crime. According to a national survey conducted in 1965 by the President's Crime Commission [32, p.v], 91 per cent of all adult Americans "admitted that they had committed acts for which they might have received jail or prison sentences." The Crime Commission also found that in 1965 "more than two million Americans were received in prisons or juvenile training schools, or placed on probation" — well over 2 per cent of the labor force. Criminal behavior, it appears, is clearly a norm and not an aberration.[4]

Given that ubiquity, it seems equally important to emphasize our extraordinary selectivity in our attention to the problem of crime. We focus all our nearly paranoid fears about "law 'n' order" and "safe streets" on a limited number of crimes while we altogether ignore many other kinds of crime, equally serious and of much greater economic importance.

One can sketch the dimensions of this selectivity quite easily. The crimes on which the public *does* concentrate its fears and cannons are often lumped together as "urban" or "violent" crimes. These crimes can be usefully summarized by those for which the FBI accumulates a general statistical index. Seven "Index Crimes" are traced in the Bureau's periodic Crime Report: willful homicide, forcible rape, aggravated assault, robbery, burglary, larceny (of more than $50), and motor vehicle theft. Together, these seven crimes encompass the raging fire in fear of which we hide inside our homes.

Some basic facts about these seven fearsome crimes are well-known. The measured incidence of the Index Crimes has been increasing rapidly in the United States in the past ten to fifteen years.[5] The Index Crimes occur twice as frequently in large cities as they do on average throughout the country. Within large cities, they occur most frequently in ghetto areas. The threat and tragedy of violent crime notwithstanding, almost all of these crimes are economically motivated; as Clark notes quite simply [8, p. 38], "their main purpose is to obtain money or property." Seven-eighths of them are crimes against property and only one-eighth are crimes against person. Moreover, many of the relatively few "violent" crimes against person actually occur inadvertently in the process of committing crimes against property.

A large part of the crime against property is committed by youth. Clark concludes from the scattered statistics [8, p. 54] that half of all property crime is committed by people under twenty-one.[6] Certainly more important in considering the evolution of public attitudes, blacks commit disproportionate numbers of these seven Index Crimes (and are also disproportionately the victims of the same crimes). Although arrest rates bear an obviously spurious relationship to the actual incidence of crime, some of the figures seem quite astonishing.[7] In 1968, for instance, official statistics indicate that 61 per cent of those arrested for robbery were black and nearly half of those arrested for aggravated assault were black, despite the fact that blacks represent only twelve per cent of the population. As astonishing as those figures sometimes seem, however, the public exaggerates them further; public attitudes often appear to presume that *all* of the Index Crimes are committed by blacks and that every black male is on the verge of committing a crime.[8]

The crimes our society chooses consistently to *ignore* seem just as obvious. Many kinds of relatively hidden crimes, most of them called "white-collar" crimes, occur with startling frequency and profitability. Tax evasion, price fixing, embezzlement, swindling, and consumer fraud capture billions of dollars every years. Clark provides some simple examples of the magnitudes of these kinds of crimes [8, p.38]:

Illicit gains from white-collar crime far exceed those of all other crime combined. . . . One corporate price-fixing conspiracy criminally converted more money each year it continued than all of the hundreds of thousands of burglaries, larcenies, or thefts in the entire nation during those same years. Reported bank embezzlements cost ten times more than bank robberies each year.

As Clark also notes, the public and the media choose to pay almost no attention to either the existence or the causes of those kinds of crime.

The selectivity of public opinion is matched, moreover, by the biases of our governmental system of the enforcement and administration of justice. The system prosecutes and punishes some crimes and criminals heavily while leaving others alone. One might assume that the system concentrated most heavily on those crimes of greatest magnitude, but this does not appear to be the case; the Index Crimes on which it focuses account for rather small proportions of the total personal harm and property loss resulting from crime in the United States. Deaths resulting from "willful homicide" are one-fifth as frequent as deaths from motor vehicle accidents, for instance; although many experts ascribe nearly half of motor vehicle accidents to mechanical failure, the system rarely pays attention to those liable for that failure. The economic loss attributable to Index Crimes against property — robbery, burglary, and so on — are one-fifth the losses attributable to embezzlement, fraud, and unreported commercial theft, and yet the system concentrates almost exclusively on the former.

Rather than to the relative magnitude of crimes, the selectivity of our police, courts and prisons seems more closely to correspond to the relative class status of those who perpetrate different crimes. We seem to have in this country, as both the Crime Commission [32] and Goldfarb [13] have most clearly shown, a dual system of justice. The public system concentrates on crimes committed by the poor, while crimes by the more affluent are left to private auspices. Our prisons function, as Goldfarb notes, like a "national poorhouse," swallowing the poor, chewing them up and occasionally spitting them back at the larger society. Goldfarb concludes [13, p. 312]:

When upper- or middle-class people or their children get in trouble — drunk in public; paternity charges; fights; mischief in the school, neighborhood, country club, resort, downtown; even homicide — ordinarily private action is quickly taken. The person's problem is analyzed sympathetically, the best treatment sought. Restitution, medical or psychiatric assistance, special educational steps, legal advice are enlisted from the family and community. . . . The point is: in the classes of offenses committed by rich and poor *equally,* it is rarely the rich who end up behind bars.

It is one thing to cite this "duality" as a fact, of course, and quite another thing to explain it. I shall cite it now as a phenomenon requiring explanation and try to explain it later.

It seems necessary to add, finally, that none of the system's selectivity works in the ways we pretend that we intend it to work. One gets the impression that the public thinks that concentration on a few crimes will at least improve the effectiveness of the system in controlling those few crimes — leading to greater prevention and deterrence and perhaps equally to greater rehabilitation. Buoyed by that hope, the various governments in the United States spent roughly $4.2 billion on police, prisons and the courts in 1965, while private individuals and corporations spent an additional $1.9 billion on prevention and insurance. And yet, despite those billions, our systems of enforcement and administration of justice appear considerably to *exacerbate* the criminality they seek selectively to control.   The prisons in particular, as Clark notes [8, p. 212], are veritable "factories of crime": "Jails and prisons in the United States today are more often than not manufacturers of crime. Of those who come to jail undecided, capable either of criminal conduct or of lives free of crime, most are turned to crime." As both the Crime Commission Report and Clark document, very few of those who get started in crime ever actually leave it as a result of the system's deterrent or rehabilitative effect.   Clark adds [8, p. 55]:

The most important statistic of all in the field of criminal justice is the one which tells us that probably four out of five of all felonies are committed by repeaters — that 80 per cent of all serious crime is committed by people convicted of crime before.   The first crime was nearly always committed as a teenager.   Approximately half of all the persons released from prisons return to prison, many again and again.

These very brief observations on the dimensions of crime and our responses to it are sufficient to suggest the rather obvious and critical questions we must seek to answer about the problem.   Why is there so much crime?   Why do the public and the government concentrate so selectively on such a small part of the criminal activity in this country? And why do all our billions of dollars fail so miserably in curbing even that small part of the total problem?

B. CONVENTIONAL PUBLIC ANALYSES

I would argue, as many others have also suggested, that conventional public analyses of crime divide roughly into two views — "conservative" and "liberal" — the specific features of which correspond to more general "conservative" and "liberal" perspectives on social problems. The two perspectives begin from some relatively common general views of society and its governments, diverging more and more widely as they debate the specifics of crime prevention and control.[9]

The conservative perspective on crime has an appealing simplicity.[10]   Since conservatives believe that the social "order" is ultimately rational and is adequately reflected in the laws of our governments, they also believe that those who violate it can be regarded as irrational citizens and social misfits.   As such, criminals should be punished regardless of the social forces which may well have produced their criminality.   They represent a threat to the safety and property of those who act with civility and reason, and should be isolated until society can be sure of their good behavior.   The more violent the crimes, the more seriously we must regard their consequences.

Since criminals (and especially violent ones) act irrationally, we can deter and prevent their actions only by responding to them with comparably irrational actions — principally by the threat or application of raw force. Toward that end, conservatives engage in two kinds of policy calculations. First, they discuss the potential deterrence of a variety of crime-prevention techniques. If only enough deterrent force could be mustered, they assume, crime could be stopped. Typically, they urge more police and more equipment to prevent crime. Second, they tend to favor preventive detention as a necessary means of protecting the social order from the threat of probable criminality; they make their argument, normally, on relatively pragmatic grounds.[11]

Liberals tend to agree with conservatives, ultimately, that the social order tends toward rationality. They are more likely to pay attention to imperfections in the social order, however, and are therefore more likely to lean toward government action to correct those imperfections. As a justification for government action, they usually rely on what has been called the "pluralistic" view of democratic governments — that those governments generally act in everyone's interests because they are constantly checked and balanced by the competition of many different interest groups for the favors of government action.[12]

Given those general predilections, liberals tend to regard the problem of criminal activity as a much more complicated dilemma than do their conservative counterparts.[13] Since the social order can be viewed as an ultimately rational state, those who violate it can indeed be regarded as "irrational." At the same time, however, liberals regard the interactions of individuals with society as extremely complex processes, fraught with imperfections in the allocation and distribution of social rewards. Through those imperfections, some individuals are much more likely than others to be *pushed* toward the irrationality of criminal behavior. Criminality should be regarded as irrationality, but we should nonetheless try to avoid *blaming* criminals for their irrational acts. And since different individuals are pushed in very different ways by different social circumstances, there is a wide variety of behavior among criminals. As the Crime Commission concludes [32, p. v], "No single formula, no single theory, no single generalization can explain the vast range of behavior called crime."

Some of these heterogeneous crimes are more serious than others, liberals continue, because they are more violent and therefore more threatening. Liberals tend to agree with conservatives and the FBI that the FBI Crime Index adequately encompasses the potentially most violent crimes. But liberals tend to disagree with conservatives in arguing that these kinds of relatively violent crimes cannot simply be prevented by force, that they cannot ultimately be curbed until the social imperfections which underlie them are eliminated. The prevalence of "violent" crime among youth, blacks and ghetto residents derives from the diseases of poverty and racism in American society, most liberals have finally concluded. Given those basic social imperfections, as the Crime Commission argues [32, p. 5], ". . . it is probable that crime will continue to increase . . . unless there are drastic changes in general social and economic conditions."

Can we do nothing about crime until we eliminate the sores of poverty and racism? Liberals respond on two different levels. On the one hand, they argue that we can marginally improve our prevention of crime and our treatment of criminals if we can at least marginally rationalize our system of enforcement and administration of justice. We need more research, more analysis, more technology, more money, better administration, and more numerous and professional personnel.[14] And since liberals place considerable faith in the disapassionate beneficence of the government, they expect that the government's responses to crime can be improved simply by urging the government to make those improvements.

On another level, liberals argue strongly — and in relatively sharp opposition to many conservatives — that we should not tolerate abridgements of civil liberties while we wait for our ultimate solutions to the problems of crime. Though a bit confused and rarely articulated with any real coherence, the liberals' defense of civil liberties appears to derive from the high priorities they conventionally place on social equality and justice, while conservatives seem to be more swayed by their own concern for social order and the preservation of the integrity of private property. However confused its sources, this debate between liberals and conservatives cannot easily be ignored. Fred Graham has written [17, p. 68], "A coincidence of events has heightened the traditional tensions between the forces of enforcement and of justice, and has greatly increased the likelihood of a constitutional crisis somewhere down the line."[15]

In short, the conventional liberal and conservative analyses of crime pose fairly simple answers to the most important questions about crime. They argue that criminals are essentially irrational, with liberals adding that such irrationality sometimes seems, in one sense or another, partially justified. They agree that we should concentrate most heavily on trying to prevent the most violent crimes, and they both conclude that the admitted selectivity of public opinion and of governmental response roughly corresponds to the degree of violence latent or manifest in different kinds of crime. Conservatives suspect that we have failed to curb those especially violent kinds of crimes because we have not been willing to apply enough force to deter and punish those kinds of criminals. Liberals suspect that we have failed because poverty and racism are so deeply rooted in our society, but that we can at least marginally improve our enforcement and administration of justice in the short run through more rational public policies, and that we can ultimately curb crime through public action to eliminate the basic social causes of crime.

C. ORTHODOX ECONOMIC ANALYSIS

In the past few years, several orthodox economists have tried to clarify our analysis of criminal behavior and our evaluation of alternative public policies to combat it.[16]   Although a few nineteenth-century classical economists like Jeremy Bentham had originally applied economics to the analysis of the problem of crime, as Becker [3] and Tullock [49] note, economists since then have generally left the problem to sociologists and psychologists.   Recent advances in neoclassical microeconomic theory permit us, we are now told, to "extend the economist's usual analysis of choice" to an analysis of criminal behavior and its "optimal" prevention and punishment.   Since each of the recent applications of orthodox economics outlines the mode of analysis rather clearly, since the approach so directly reflects the more general predispositions of orthodox microeconomics, and since Gordon Tullock has illustrated the approach in his adjoining article in this volume, I need only make a few very brief observations about its underlying assumptions in this short section.

The central and most important thrust of the orthodox analysis is that criminal behavior, like any other economic activity, is eminently rational; in this important respect, the economists differ fundamentally with conventional liberal and conservative public analyses.   As Becker formulates this central contention quite simply [3, p. 176],

. . . a person commits an offense if the expected utility to him exceeds the utility he could get by using his time and other resources at other activities.   Some persons become "criminals," therefore, not because their basic motivation differs from that of other persons, but because their benefits and costs differ.

More specifically, individuals are assumed to calculate the returns to and the risks of "legitimate" employment and "criminal" activity and base their choices between those two modes of activity on their cost/benefit calculations.   Stigler adds [42, p. 530], "The details of occupational choice in illegal activity are not different from those encountered in the legitimate occupations."

Given those assumptions of rationality, orthodox economists argue that we can construct some "optimal" social policies to combat crime.

They assume, first of all, that there is a social calculus through which the costs and benefits of criminal offenses to each member of society can be translated into a common metric — the calculus is conveniently expressed in terms of a "social welfare function." Society (through its several governments) should then try to minimize the "social loss" from criminal offenses as measured by the social welfare function. In their formulation of the parameters of these calculations, they hypothesize that criminals respond quite sensitively in their own decision-making to variations in the level and probability of punishment. They also assume, as Becker puts it [3, p. 174], that "the more that is spent on policemen, court personnel, and specialized equipment, the easier it is to discover offenses and convict offenders." They then proceed to the final argument: we can choose (through our governments) some combination of punishment levels and social expenditures — with expenditures determining the probability of capture and conviction — which will minimize our social losses from crime subject to the revenue constraints in our public and private budgets.

Behind the orthodox economic analysis lie two fundamental assumptions. First, although the assumption is rarely made explicit, the economists obviously assume that governments behave in democratic societies in such a way that everyone's preferences have an equal chance of influencing the final outcome, that public policy formulations can adequately reflect the costs and benefits of criminal offenses to all individuals in society. Without that assumption, the basis for minimization of social "losses" through a social welfare function is undercut.[17]

Second, the orthodox economists assume some simple and identifiable relationships between the amount of money we actually spend on prevention and enforcement, the amount of prevention and enforcement we would *like to achieve,* and the amount of prevention and enforcement we can *actually achieve.* This involves the assumption, noted above, that larger expenditures automatically increase the probability of apprehension and conviction. It also involves another, related assumption — that the level of government expenditures on prevention and punishment accurately reflects society's desired level of prevention and enforcement instead of, for example, the influence of vested interests in maximizing expenditures. If a state or locality spends more on its police, courts, and prisons, *ceteris paribus,* orthodox economists assume that they do so because they seek to deter crime more effectively through the (expected) increase in the probability of arrest and punishment.

D. A RADICAL ANALYSIS

Much too briefly, I want to outline in this section the structure of a radical analysis of crime in the United States. Many points in the argument will seem quite obvious, simple elaborations of common sense. Other points will bear some important similarities to one or another of the views described in the preceding sections. Taken all together, however, the arguments in the following analysis seem to me to provide a more useful, coherent, and realistic interpretation than the models discussed above. In the analysis, I have tried as simply as possible to apply some general hypotheses of radical economic analysis to a discussion of the specific problem of crime in this country. My intention, quite clearly, is to argue that we cannot realistically expect to "solve" the problem of crime in the United States without first effecting a fundamental redistribution of power in our society.

I have divided the analysis into five separate parts. The first sketches the major hypotheses of the general radical framework through which I have tried to view the problem of crime. The second tries to explain a basic behavioral *similarity* among all the major kinds of crime in the United States. Given that fundamental similarity, the third part seeks to explain the most important dimensions of *difference* among various crimes in this country. Given a delineation of the sources of difference among crimes, the fourth part attempts an historical explanation of the sources of those sources of difference — an analysis, as it were, of the underlying causes of some immediate causes of difference. The fifth part argues that we cannot easily reverse history, that we cannot easily alter the fundamental social structures and trends that have produced the problem of crime today. A final paragraph provides a brief summary of the central hypotheses of the entire argument.

SOME GENERAL ASSUMPTIONS

The radical analysis of crime outlined in this section applies several basic radical assumptions or hypotheses.[18] It presumes, first of all, that the basic structure of social and economic institutions in any society fundamentally shapes the behavior of individuals in that society, and therefore that one cannot in fact understand the behavior of individuals in a capitalist society like the United States without first understanding the structures and biases of the basic "system-defining" institutions in this country. It argues, furthermore, that the "social relations of production" in capitalist societies help define an economic class structure and that one cannot therefore adequately understand the behavior of individuals unless one first examines the structure of institutionally determined opportunities to which members of the respective economic classes are more or less confined.[19] The analysis depends, at another level, on the radical theory of the state, according to which radicals hypothesize that the activities of the state in capitalist societies serve primarily to benefit members of the capitalist class — either directly, by bestowing disproportionate benefits upon them, or indirectly, by helping preserve and solidify the structure of class inequalities upon which capitalists so thoroughly depend.[20] The radical analysis expects, finally, that various social problems in capitalist societies, although they may not have been created by capitalists, cannot easily be solved within the context of capitalist institutions because their solution would tend to disrupt the functioning of the capitalist machine. If the disruptive potential of solutions to such problems therefore inclines the state to postpone solution, one can expect to solve those problems only by changing the power relationships in society so that the state is forced to serve other interests than those of the capitalist class.[21]

Each of these general hypotheses underlies all of the more specific hypotheses about crime which follow.

COMPETITIVE CAPITALISM AND RATIONAL CRIME

Capitalist societies depend, as radicals often argue, on basically competitive forms of social and economic interaction and upon substantial inequalities in the allocation of social resources. Without inequalities, it would be much more difficult to induce workers to work in alienating environments. Without competition and a competitive ideology, workers might not be inclined to struggle to improve their relative income and status in society by working harder. Finally, although rights of property are protected, capitalist societies do not guarantee economic security to most of its individual members. Individuals must fend for themselves, finding the best available opportunities to provide for themselves and their families. At the same time, history bequeaths a corpus of laws and statutes to any social epoch which may or may not correspond to the social morality of that epoch. Inevitably, at any point in time, many of the "best" opportunities for economic survival open to different citizens will violate some of those historically determined laws. Driven by the fear of economic insecurity and by a competitive desire to gain some of the goods unequally distributed throughout the society, many individuals will eventually become "criminals." As Adam Smith himself admitted in *The Wealth of Nations* [41, p. 670], "Where there is no property . . . civil government is not so necessary."

In that respect, therefore, radicals argue that nearly all crimes in capitalist societies represent perfectly *rational* responses to the structure of institutions upon which capitalist societies are based. Crimes of many different varieties constitute functionally similar responses to the organization of capitalist institutions, for those crimes help provide a means of survival in a society within which survival is never assured. Three different kinds of crime in the United States provide the most important examples of this functionally similar rationality among different kinds of crime: ghetto crime, organized crime, and corporate (or "white-collar") crime.[22]

It seems especially clear, first of all, that ghetto crime is committed by people responding quite reasonably to the structure of economic opportunities available to them. Only rarely, it appears, can ghetto criminals be regarded as raving, irrational, antisocial lunatics.[23] The "legitimate" jobs open to many ghetto residents, especially to young black males, typically pay low wages, offer relatively demeaning assignments and carry the constant risk of layoff. In contrast, many kinds of crime "available" in the ghetto often bring higher monetary return, even higher social status, and — at least in some cases like numbers running — sometimes carry relatively low risk of arrest and punishment.[24] Given those alternative opportunities, the choice between "legitimate" and "illegitimate" activities is often quite simple. As Arthur Dunmeyer, a black hustler from Harlem has put it [5, p. 292],

In some cases this is the way you get your drug dealers and prostitutes and your numbers runners. . . . They see that these things are the only way that they can compete in the society, to get some sort of status. They realize that there aren't any real doors open to them, and so, to commit crime was the only thing to do, they can't go back.

The fact that these activities are often "illegal" sometimes doesn't really matter; since life out of jail often seems as bad as life inside prison, the deterrent effect of punishment is negligible. Dunmeyer expresses this point clearly as well [5, p. 293]:

It is not a matter of a guy saying, "I want to go to jail [or] I am afraid of jail." Jail is on the street just like it is on the inside. The same as, like when you are in jail, they tell you, "Look, if you do something wrong you are going to be put in the hole." You are still in jail, in the hole or out of the hole. You are in jail in the street or behind bars. It is the same thing. . . .[25]

In much the same way, organized crime represents a perfectly rational kind of economic activity.[26]   Activities like gambling and prostitution are illegal for varieties of historical reasons, but there is a demand for those activities nonetheless. As Donald Cressey writes [10, p. 294], "The American confederation of criminals thrives because a large minority of citizens demands the illicit goods and services it has for sale." Clark makes the same point [8, p. 68], arguing that organized crimes are essentially "consensual crimes . . . , desired by the consuming public." The simple fact that they are both illegal and in such demand provides a simple explanation for the secrecy, relative efficiency and occasional violence of those who provide them. In nearly every sense, for example, the organization of the heroin industry bears as rational and reasonable a relationship to the nature of the product as the structures of the tobacco and alcoholic beverages industries bear to the nature of their own products.[27]

Finally, briefly to amplify the third example, corporate crime also represents a quite rational response to life in capitalist societies. Corporations exist to protect and augment the capital of their owners. If it becomes difficult to perform that function one way, corporate officials will quite inevitably try to do it another. When Westinghouse and General Electric conspired to fix prices, for instance, they were resorting to one of many possible devices for limiting the potential threat of competition to their price structures. Similarly, when Ford and General Motors proliferate new car model after new car model, each differing only slightly from its siblings, they are choosing to protect their price structures by what economists call "product differentiation." In one case, the corporations were using oligopolistic power quite directly. In the other, they rely on the power of advertising to generate demand for the differentiated products. In the context of the perpetual and highly competitive race among corporations for profits and capital accumulation, each response seems quite reasonable. In his pioneering studies of corporate crime, the eminent criminologist Edwin H. Sutherland made the same points about corporate crime and linked their behavior to lower-class criminality [44, p. 310]:

I have attempted to demonstrate that businessmen violate the law with great frequency. . . . If these conclusions are correct, it is very clear that the criminal behavior of businessmen cannot be explained by poverty, in the usual sense, or by bad housing or lack of recreational facilities or feeblemindedness or emotional instability. Business leaders are capable, emotionally-balanced, and in no sense pathological. . . . The assumption that an offender must have some such pathological distortion of the intellect or the emotions seems to me absurd, and if it is absurd regarding the crimes of businessmen, it is equally absurd regarding the crimes of persons in the lower economic class.

CLASS INSTITUTIONS AND DIFFERENCES AMONG CRIMES

If most crime in the United States in one way or another reflects the same kind of rational response to the insecurity and inequality of capitalist institutions, what explains the manifold differences among different kinds of crimes? Some crimes are much more violent than others, some are much more heavily prosecuted, and some are much more profitable. Why?

As a first step in explaining differences among crimes, I would apply the general radical perspective in a relatively straightforward manner and argue quite simply that many of the most important differences among different kinds of crime in this country are determined by the *structure of class institutions* in our society and by the *class biases* of the state. That argument has two separate components.

First, I would argue that many of the important differences among crimes in this society derive quite directly from the different socioeconomic classes to which individuals belong. Relatively affluent citizens have access to jobs in large corporations, to institutions involved in complicated paper transactions involving lots of money, and to avenues of relatively unobtrusive communication. Members of those classes who decide to break the law, as Clark puts it [8, p. 38], have "an easier, less offensive, less visible way of doing wrong." Those raised in poverty, on the other hand, do not have such easy access to money. If they are to obtain it criminally, they must impinge on those who already have it or direct its flow. Robert Morgenthau, a former United States attorney, has written [25, p. 20] that those growing up in the ghetto "will probably never have the opportunity to embezzle funds from a bank or to promote a multimillion dollar stock fraud scheme. The criminal ways which we encourage [them] to choose will be those closest at hand — from vandalism to mugging to armed robbery."

Second, I would argue that the biases of our police, courts, and prisons *explain* the relative violence of many crimes — that many of the differences in the degree of violence among different kinds of crime do not cause the selectivity of public concern about those crimes but *are in fact caused by that selectivity*. For a variety of historical reasons, as I noted in the first section of this article, we have a dual system of justice in this country; the police, courts, and prisons pay careful attention to only a few crimes. It is only natural, as a result, that those who run the highest risks of arrest and conviction may have to rely on the threat or commission of violence in order to protect themselves. Many kinds of ghetto crimes generate violence, for instance, because the participants are severely prosecuted for their crimes and must try to protect themselves however they can. Other kinds of ghetto crimes are openly tolerated by the police, like the numbers racket, and those crimes rarely involve violence. It may be true, as Clark argues [8, p. 39], that "violent crime springs from a violent environment," but violent environments like the ghetto do not always produce violent crimes. Those crimes to which the police pay attention usually involve violence, while those which the police tend to ignore quite normally do not. In similar ways, organized crime has become violent historically, as Cressey especially argues [10], principally because its participants are often prosecuted. As long as that remains true, the suppliers of illegal goods require secrecy, organization, and a bit of violence to protect their livelihood. Completely in contrast, corporate crime does not require violence because it is ignored by the police; corporate criminals can safely assume they do not face the threat of jail and do not therefore have to cover their tracks with the threat of harming those who betray them. When Lockheed Aircraft accountants and executives falsified their public reports in order to disguise cost overruns on the C–5A airplane in 1967 and 1968, for instance, they did not have to force Defense Department officials at knife-point to play along with their falsifications. As Robert Sherrill reports in his investigation of the Lockheed affair [40, p. 43], the Defense Department officials were entirely willing to cooperate. "This sympathy," Sherrill writes, "was reflected in orders from top Air Force officials to withhold information regarding Lockheed's dilemma from all reports that would be widely circulated." If only local police were equally sympathetic to the "dilemmas" of street-corner junkies, the violent patterns of drug-related crimes might be considerably transformed.[28]

In short, it seems important to view some of the most important differences among crimes — differences in their violence, their style, and their impact — as fundamental outgrowths of the class structure of society and the class biases of our major institutions, including the state and its system of enforcement and administration of justice. Given that argument, it places a special burden on attempts to explain the historical sources of the duality of the public system of justice in this country, for that duality, coupled with the class biases of other institutions, plays such an important role in determining the patterns of American crime.

THE SOURCES OF DUALITY

One can explain the duality of our public system of justice quite easily, it seems to me, if one is willing to view the state through the radical perspective. The analysis involves answers to two separate questions. First, one must ask why the state *ignores* certain kinds of crimes, especially white-collar crimes and corporate crimes. Second, given that most crimes among the poor claim the poor as their victims, one must ask why the state bothers to worry so incessantly about those crimes.

The answer to the first question draws directly from the radical theory of the state. According to the radical theory, the government in a capitalist society like the United States exists primarily to preserve the stability of the system which provides, preserves and protects returns to the owners of capital. As long as crimes among the corporate class tend in general to harm members of other classes, like those in the "consuming" class, the state will not spontaneously move to prevent those crimes from taking place. On the other hand, as Paul Sweezy has especially argued [45], the state may be pressured either nominally or effectively to prosecute the wealthy if their criminal practices become so egregiously offensive that their victims may move to overthrow the system itself. In those cases, the state may punish individual members of the class in order to protect the interests of the entire class. Latent opposition to the practices of corporations may be forestalled, to pick several examples, by token public efforts to enact and enforce antitrust, truth-in-lending, antipollution, industrial safety, and auto-safety legislation. As James Ridgeway has most clearly shown in the case of pollution [37], however, the gap between the enactment of the statutes and their effective enforcement seems quite cavernous.[29]

The answer to the second question seems slightly more complicated historically. Public responses to crime among the poor have changed periodically throughout American history, responding both to changes in the patterns of the crimes themselves and to changes in public morality. The subtlety of that historical process would be difficult to trace in this kind of discussion. But some patterns do seem clear.

Earlier in American history, as Clark has pointed out [8, pp. 55–56], we tended to ignore many crimes among the poor because those crimes rarely impinged upon the lives of the more affluent. Gambling, prostitution, dope, and robbery seemed to flourish in the slums of the early twentieth century, and the police rarely moved to intervene. More recently, however, some of the traditional patterns of crime have changed. Two dimensions of change seem most important. On the one hand, much of the crime has moved out of the slums. As Clark explains [8, p. 55], "Our concern arose when social dynamics and population movements brought crime and addiction out of the slums and inflicted it on or threatened the powerful and well-to-do." On the other hand, the styles in which ghetto criminals have fulfilled their criminal intent may have grown more hostile since World War II, flowing through what I have elsewhere called the "promised land effect" (in [15]) , after the title of the book by Claude Brown [4]. As Brown points out, second-generation Northern blacks — the sons and daughters of Southern migrants born in Northern slums — have relatively little reason to hope that their lives will improve. Their parents migrated in search of better times, but some of those born in the North probably believe that their avenues for escape from poverty have disappeared. Brown puts it well [4, p. 8]:

The children of these disillusioned colored pioneers inherited the total lot of their parents — the disappointments, the anger. To add to their misery, they had little hope of deliverance. For where does one run to when he's already in the promised land?

Out of frustration, some of the crime among younger ghetto-born blacks may be more vengeful now, more concerned with sticking it to whitey. Coupled with the spread of ghetto crime into other parts of the city, this symbolic expression of vengefulness undoubtedly heightens the fear that many affluent citizens feel about ghetto crime. Given their influence with the government, they quite naturally have moved toward increasing public attention to the prevention and punishment of crimes among the poor.

Once the patterns of public duality have been established, of course, they acquire a momentum and dynamic all their own. To begin with, vested interests develop, deriving their livelihood and status from the system. The prison system, like the defense industry, becomes a power of its own, with access to public bureaucracies, with workers to support and with power to defend. Eldridge Cleaver has made special note of this feature of our public system [9, p. 185]:

The only conclusion one can draw is that the parole system is a procedure devised primarily for the purpose of running people in and out of jail — most of them black — in order to create and maintain a lot of jobs for the white prison system. In California, which I know best — and I'm sure it's the same in other states — there are thousands and thousands of people who draw their living directly or indirectly from the prison system; all the clerks, all the guards, all the bailiffs, all the people who sell goods to the prisons. They regard the inmates as a sort of product from which they all draw their livelihood, and the part of the crop they keep exploiting most are the black inmates.

In much the same way, the police become an interest and a power of their own.[30] They are used and manipulated by the larger society to enforce the law selectively; as Clark writes [8, p. 137], "We send police to maintain order, to arrest, to jail — and to ignore vital laws also intended to protect life and to prevent death. . . ." As agents of selective social control, the police also inevitably become the focus of increasing animosity among those they are asked selectively to control. Manipulated by the larger society, hated by those at the bottom, the police tend to develop the mentality, as Westley [50] has called it, of a "garrison." They eventually seek to serve neither the interests of the larger society nor the interests of the law but the interests of the garrison. One reaches the point, finally, where police interests interject an intermediate membrane screening the priorities of the state and society on the one hand and the interests of their victims on the other. Westley concludes [50]: "When enforcement of the law conflicts with the ends of the police, the law is not enforced. When it supports the ends of the police, they are fully behind it. When it bears no relation to the ends of the police, they enforce it as a matter of routine."

THE IMPLAUSIBILITY OF REFORM

One needs to ask, finally, whether these patterns can be changed and the trends reversed. Can we simultaneously eradicate the causes of crime and reform our dual system of justice? At the heart of that question lies the question posed at the beginning of this essay, for it simultaneously raises the necessity of explaining the failures of our present system to prevent the crime it seeks most systematically to control.

I would argue, quite simply, that reform is implausible unless we change the basic institutions upon which capitalism in the United States depends. We cannot legitimately expect to eradicate the initial causes of crime for two reasons. First, capitalism depends quite substantially on the preservation of the conditions of competition and inequality. Those conditions, as I argued above, will tend to lead quite inevitably to relatively pervasive criminal behavior; without those conditions, the capitalist system would scarcely work at all. Second, as many have argued, the general presence of racism in this country, though capitalists may not in fact have created it, tends to support and maintain the power of the capitalists as a class by providing cheap labor and dividing the working class. Given the substantial control of capitalists over the policies and priorities of the state, we cannot easily expect to prod the state to eliminate the fundamental causes of racism in this country. In that respect, it seems likely that the particular inequalities facing blacks and their consequent attraction to the opportunities available in crime seem likely to continue.

Given expectations that crime will continue, it seems equally unlikely that we shall be able to reform our systems of prosecution and punishment in order to mitigate their harmful effects on criminals and to equalize their treatment of different kinds of crime. First and superficially, as I noted above, several important and powerful vested interests have acquired a stake in the current system and seem likely to resist efforts to change it.   Second and more fundamentally, the cumulative effect of the patterns of crime, violence, prosecution, and punishment in this country play an important role in helping legitimize and stabilize the capitalist system.   Although capitalists as a class may not have created the current patterns of crime and punishment, those patterns currently serve their interests in several different ways.   We should expect that the capitalists as a class will hardly be eager to push reform of the system.   Given their relative reluctance to reform the system, we should expect to be able to push reform only in the event that we can substantially change the structure of power to which the state responds.

The current patterns of crime and punishment support the capitalist system in three different ways.

First, the pervasive patterns of selective enforcement seem to reinforce a prevalent ideology in this society that individuals, rather than institutions, are to blame for social problems.   Individuals are criminally prosecuted for motor accidents because of negligent or drunken driving, for instance, but auto manufacturers are never criminally prosecuted for the negligent construction of unsafe cars or for their roles in increasing the likelihood of death through air pollution.   Individual citizens are often prosecuted and punished for violence and for resisting arrest, equally, but those agents of institutions, like police and prison guards, or institutions themselves, like Dow Chemical, are never prosecuted for inflicting unwarranted violence on others.   These patterns of selectivity reinforce our pervasive preconceptions of the invulnerability of institutions, leading us to blame ourselves for social failure; this pattern of individual blame, as Edwards and MacEwan have especially argued [11], plays an important role in legitimizing the basic institutions of this kind of capitalist society.

Second, and critically important, the patterns of crime and punishment manage "legitimately" to neutralize the potential opposition to the system of many of our most oppressed citizens.   In particular, the system serves ultimately to keep thousands of men out of the job market or trapped in the secondary labor market by perpetuating a set of institutions which serves functionally to feed large numbers of blacks (and poor whites) through the cycle of crime, imprisonment, parole and recidivism.   The system has this same ultimate effect in many different ways.   It locks up many for life, first of all, guaranteeing that those potentially disaffected souls keep "out of trouble."   For those whom it occasionally releases, it tends to drive them deeper into criminality, intensifying their criminal and violent behavior, filling their heads with paranoia and hatred, keeping them perpetually on the run and unable, ultimately, to organize with others to change the institutions which pursue them.   Finally, it blots their records with the stigma of criminality, effectively precluding the reform of even those who vow to escape the system and to go "straight" by denying them many decent employment opportunities.[31]

The importance of this neutralization should not be underestimated. If all young black men in this country do not eventually become criminals, most of them are conscious of the trap into which they might fall. George Jackson has written from prison [20], "Blackmen born in the U.S. and fortunate enough to live past the age of eighteen are conditioned to accept the inevitability of prison. For most of us, it simply looms as the next phase in a sequence of humiliations." And once they are trapped, the cycle continues almost regardless of the will of those involved. Prison, parole and the eventual return to prison become standard points on the itinerary. Cleaver has written [9, pp. 154–155]:

I noticed that every time I went back to jail, the same guys who were in Juvenile Hall with me were also there again. They arrived there soon after I got there, or a little bit before I left. They always seemed to make the scene. In the California prison system, they carry you from Juvenile Hall to the old folks' colony, down in San Luis Opisbo, and wait for you to die. Then they bury you there. . . I noticed these waves, these generations . . . graduating classes moving up from Juvenile Hall, all the way up.

And those who succeed finally in understanding the trap and in pulling themselves out of it, like Malcolm X, Claude Brown, Eldridge Cleaver, and George Jackson, seem to succeed precisely because they understand how debilitating the cycle becomes, how totally dehumanizing it will remain. Another black ex-con has perfectly expressed the sudden insight that allowed him to pull out of the trap [6]:

It didn't take me any time to decide I wasn't going back to commit crimes. Because it's stupid, it's a trap, it only makes it easier for them to neutralize you. It's hard to explain, because you can't say it's a question of right and wrong, but of being free or [being] trapped.

If the system did not effect this neutralization, if so many of the poor were not trapped in the debilitating system of crime and punishment, then they might otherwise gather the strength to oppose the system that reinforces their misery. Like many other institutions in this country, the system of crime and punishment serves an important function for the capitalist class by dividing and weakening those who might potentially seek to overthrow the capitalist system. Although the capitalists have not created the system, in any direct sense, they would doubtlessly hate to have to do without it.[32]

The third and perhaps most important functionally supportive role of the current patterns of crime and punishment is that those patterns allow us to ignore some basic issues about the relationships in our society between institutions and individuals. By treating criminals as animals and misfits, as enemies of the state, we are permitted to continue avoiding some basic questions about the dehumanizing effects of our social institutions. We keep our criminals out of sight, so we are never forced to recognize and deal with the psychic punishment we inflict on them. Like the schools and the welfare system, the legal system turns out, upon close inspection, to rob most of its "clients" of the last vestiges of their personal dignity. Each of those institutions, in its own way, helps us forget about the responsibilities we might alternatively assume for providing the best possible environment within which all of us could grow and develop as individuals. Cleaver sees this "role" of the system quite clearly [9, pp. 179, 182]:

Those who are now in prisons could be put through a process of real rehabilitation before their release. . . . By rehabilitation I mean they would be trained for jobs that would not be an insult to their dignity, that would give them some sense of security, that would allow them to achieve some brotherly connection with their fellow man. But for this kind of rehabilitation to happen on a large scale would entail the complete reorganization of society not to mention the prison system. It would call for the teaching of a new set of ethics, based on the principle of cooperation, as opposed to the presently dominating principle of competition. It would require the transformation of the entire moral fabric of this country. . . .

By keeping its victims so thoroughly hidden and rendering them so apparently inhuman, our system of crime and punishment allows us to forget how sweeping a "transformation" of our social ideology we would require in order to begin solving the problem of crime. The more we forget, the more protected the capitalists remain from a thorough reexamination of the ideological basis of the institutions upon which they depend.

A LITTLE SUMMARY

It seems useful briefly to summarize the analysis outlined in this section, in order both to emphasize the connections among its arguments and to clarify its differences with other "models" of crime and punishment. Most crimes in this country share a single important similarity — they represent rational responses to the competitiveness and inequality of life in capitalist societies. (In this emphasis on the rationality of crime, the analysis differs with the "conventional public analyses" of crime and resembles the orthodox economic approach.)   Many crimes seem very different at the same time, but many of their differences — in character and degree of violence — can usefully be explained by the structure of class institutions in this country and the duality of the public system of the enforcement and administration of justice.   (In this central deployment of the radical concepts of class and the class-biased state, the analysis differs fundamentally with both the "public" and the orthodox economic perspectives.)   That duality, in turn, can fruitfully be explained by a dynamic view of the class-biased role of public institutions and the vested interests which evolve out of the state's activities.   For many reasons, finally, it seems unlikely that we can change the patterns of crime and punishment, for the kinds of changes we would need would appear substantially to threaten the stability of the capitalist system.   If we managed somehow to eliminate ghetto crime, for instance, the competitiveness, inequalities and racism of our institutions would tend to reproduce it.   And if, by chance, the pattern of ghetto crime was not reproduced, the capitalists might simply have to invent some other way of neutralizing the potential opposition of so many black men, against which they might once again be forced to rebel with "criminal acts."   It is in that sense of fundamental causality that we must somehow change the entire structure of institutions in this country in order to eliminate the causes of crime.

E. A NORMATIVE VIEW OF CRIME

Strangely enough, I find it easiest to evoke an alternative normative view of crime and to compare it with our current social responses to the problem by drawing on a recent exchange in the legal literature.

In a widely-heralded article written in 1964 [30], Herbert Packer a leading American legal expert on criminal process, argued that most legal discussion of criminal procedure involves a conflict between (or dialogue between) two different models of the criminal process.   Packer called one of these models the "Crime Control Model" and the other the "Due Process Model."   The emphases embodied in each model closely resemble the difference in emphasis between the general conservative and liberal views of crime, respectively, as described in the second section of this article.   The Crime Control Model, according to Packer, "is based on the proposition that the repression of criminal conduct is by far the most important function to be performed by the criminal process."   The Due Process Model, on the other hand, derive from the "concept of the primacy of the individual and the complementary concept of limitation on official power."

In reply to Packer's article, John Griffiths argued [18] that Packer's two models represent qualitatively similar views of the relationship between the criminal and society, deriving from some common ideological assumptions about the law. Griffiths calls this set of shared assumptions the "Battle Model of the Criminal Process." He argues that both the "conservative" and "liberal" views derive from a common vision of conflict and hostility between the aberrant, deviant individual on the one hand and the social "order" on the other. To illustrate the communality of the two models proposed by Packer, Griffiths suggests a third "model" that closely resembles what I presume to be the radical vision of how society should respond to its "criminals." Griffiths calls this the "Family Model of the Criminal Process." He suggests that society's treatment of criminals could easily be patterned after the treatment by families of those family members who betray the family trust. The Family Model begins from an assumption, Griffiths writes [18, p. 371], "of reconcilable — even mutually supportive — interests, a state of love." In contrast to the Battle Model, the Family Model would propose that "we can make plain that while the criminal has transgressed, we do not therefore cut him off from us; our concern and dedication to his well-being continue. We have punished him and drawn him back in among us; we have not cast him out to fend for himself against our systematic enmity." As in the best families, society would work actively, supportively, and lovingly to restore the state of trust and mutual respect upon which the family and society should both be based. Rather than forcing the criminal to admit his failure and reform himself, we would all admit our mutual failures and seek to reform the total community — in which effort the criminal would play an important, constructive and educative role.

The Battle Model, as Griffiths describes it, obviously reflects not only "liberal" and "conservative" views of crime but the manifest reality of our social treatment of criminals in this country. A psychiatrist's recent description of the ideology underlying the California prisons exactly reflects this Model of crime and punishment:[33]

The people who run these places . . . believe that the way to get a man's behavior to change is to impose very strict controls and take away everything he values and make him work to get it back. But that doesn't make him change. It just generates more and more rage and hostility.

The Family Model, in contrast, illustrates the fundamentally different priorities that might motivate institutional responses to criminal behavior in a radically different kind of society, one in which human needs were served and developed by social institutions rather than sacrificed to the interests of a single dominant class.   That vision of social response may seem like a very distant dream in this country, but it seems like a dream worthy of all our most determined pursuit.

ENDNOTES

[1] From a fascinating article by Bell Gale Chevigny about three ex-cons who had pulled themselves up and out of the world of crime. See [6].

[2] I am not an expert on crime and I have not pursued extensive research about the problem.   The thoughts in this paper draw mainly on some limited elementary reading and, as a sort of layman in the field, I offer these thoughts with considerable hesitation.   That hesitation has especially affected my style of argument.   Since I do not speak with authority, I have tried wherever possible to include quotes from respected and respectable "authorities" to support my arguments.   Sometimes it seems to me that the essay is overburdened with quotation as a result.

I should also add that this paper is based largely on my introduction to the chapter on crime in the book of readings about urban problems I recently edited (see [15], pp. 273–280).   I have lifted an occasional paragraph from that introduction almost word-for-word, and have done so with the additional permission of the publisher, D. C. Heath and Company.

[3] For some useful summaries of the basic data, see the first two reading selections in the chapter on crime in [15].   Another useful summary of information about "urban crime" can be found in Wolfgang [55].   For much more detailed information, see the appendices to the Crime Commission Report [33], [34], [35].   For some interesting comments on the Crime Commission Report, see Wilson [51].

[4] One should add, of course, that these figures refer only to those harmful acts which actually violate some law.   Many other tangibly harmful acts have not yet been declared illegal, like faulty manufacture of automobiles or certain kinds of pollution.

[5] Clark also notes [8] that the increase may be misleading, simply because many kinds of crime are much more likely to be reported these days than comparable crimes, say, thirty years ago.

[6] Violent crimes, on the other hand, are more frequently committed by adults. As Clark explains it [8, p. 55], "It takes longer to harden the young to violence."

[7] The reason that the arrest rates may be spurious is that, as Clark [8] and Goldfarb [13] have especially noted, blacks are much more likely than whites to be arrested whether they have committed a crime or not.   Despite that immeasurable bias in the arrest statistics, it is nonetheless assumed that blacks commit a larger percentage of most crimes than their share of urban populations.

[8] Fred P. Graham has written a particularly interesting article about the prevalence and exaggeration of public fears about black crime.   He writes [17, p. 64] "Every nation has its equivalent of the mythical emperor who wore no clothes In the fable, nobody could bring himself to believe what he saw until a child

blurted out the truth, and then everyone had a laugh at the emperor's expense. In the United States, the naked emperor was for years the high Negro crime rate; the boy who broke the spell was George Wallace, and nobody laughed. . . ."

9 For an easy reference to the differences between the general "liberal" and "conservative" views, see Chapter 1 on "General Perspectives — Radical, Liberal, Conservative" in my book of readings [15]. For a good example of traditional discussion of the problem, see Sutherland [43].

10 For the clearest exposition of the conservative view on crime, see the chapter on crime in Banfield [2].

11 Banfield has clearly formulated the conservative equation [2, p. 184] "In any event, if abridging the freedom of persons who have not committed crimes is incompatible with the principles of free society, so, also, is the presence in such society of persons who, if their freedom is not abridged, would use it to inflict serious injuries on others. There is, therefore, a painful dilemma. If some people's freedom is not abridged by law-enforcement agencies, that of others will be abridged by law breakers. The question, therefore, is not whether abridging the freedom of those who may commit serious crimes is an evil — it is — but whether it is a lesser or a greater one than the alternative."

For the increasing tendency of the Nixon Administration to apply the conservative perspective in its policies toward crime, see Harris [19]. For a superb analysis of the legal aspects of the major Nixon crime legislation, see Packer [31].

12 For a summary of the general liberal perspective, once again, see Chapter 1 in Gordon, ed. [15]. For a good statement of the pluralist argument, see Rose [38].

13 The clearest expressions of the liberal view on crime are contained in three reports of Presidential commissions published in the late 1960s, the Presidential Commission on Law Enforcement and the Administration of Justice [32], the National Advisory Commission on Civil Disorders [27] and the National Commission on Violence [28].

14 Wolfgang writes [55, p. 275], "Urban crime might be reduced by significant proportions if more talent, time, and funds were put into public use to produce the kind of research findings necessary to make more rational informed decisions." The Commission on Violence concluded [28, p. 40], "We reiterate our previous recommendations that we double our national investment in the criminal justice process. . . ."

15 This debate, indeed, has some fascinating historical roots, for both the liberal and conservative positions have borrowed in very different ways from classic nineteenth-century liberalism, especially from the work of John Stuart Mill. For one of the clearest comparisons of the two perspectives and their common legacies, see Wolff [53].

16 For the most notable pieces of the recent literature, see Becker [3], Stigler [42], Thurow [46], and Tullock [48, 49]. Some attempts have been made to apply the orthodox analysis empirically; for one such attempt, still unpublished at the time of writing, see Landes [22].

17 Becker admits [3, p. 209] that the analysis is hampered by "the absence of a reliable theory of political decision-making." Tullock is the only one who makes the underlying political assumption precise and explicit. He writes [48, II-2]: "My first general assumption, then, is that the reader is not in a

position to assure himself of special treatment in any legal system. That is, if I argue that the reader should favor a law against theft, one of the basic assumptions will be that he does not have a real opportunity to get a law enacted which prohibits theft by everyone else but leaves him free to steal himself." He adds that this assumption ". . . will . . . underlie all of the specific proposals" he makes in his manuscript.

[18] For a summary of those basic perspectives in richer detail, see my introduction to Chapter 1 in [15], and the selection by Edwards and MacEwan [11].

[19] For an amplification of these contentions, see [15] and especially [11]. There is some confusion, admittedly, about the proper definition of the concept of class in the radical literature, in part because Marx himself deployed several different meanings of the term. For a useful discussion of the different kinds of meaning of the concept, see Ossowski [29]. For a clear description, however short, of the analytic link in the Marxist analysis between the "social relations of production" and the definition and determination of "economic class" see Tucker [47].

[20] For a useful discussion of the radical theory of the state, see Sweezy [45], and Milliband [24].

[21] The argument is best illustrated by the "problems" of racism and sexism in capitalist societies. Capitalists did not create the problems but the phenomena of racism and sexism serve useful functions in the United States through their pervasiveness. They help forge large pools of cheap labor and help divide the labor force into highly stratified groups of workers, thrust into competition, among whom united worker opposition to capitalists becomes relatively more difficult to develop. If one somehow erased the phenomena of racism and sexism by creating a perfect equality of opportunities among the races and sexes, the processes through which capitalists are able to accrue their profits and keep the working class divided would be substantially threatened. In that respect, one can hardly expect capitalists to favor the eradication of racism and sexism spontaneously, although they might be forced to move toward their eradication if the costs of not doing so became too high. For more on this kind of reasoning, see the chapters on Employment, Education and Poverty in Gordon, ed. [15].

[22] This is not meant to imply, obviously, that there would be no crime in a communist society in which perfectly secure equal support was provided for all. It suggests, quite simply, that one would have to analyze crime in such a society with reference to a different set of ideas and a different set of institutions.

[23] Our knowledge of ghetto crime draws primarily from the testimony of several ex-ghetto criminals, as in Brown [4], Cleaver [9], Jackson [20], and Malcolm X [23]. For other more analytic studies, see Shaw and McKay [39], and Wolfgang and Ferracuti [54]. For interesting evidence on the different attitudes toward crime of poor and middle-class youth, see Goodwin [14]. For a bit of "analytic" evidence on the critical interaction between job prospects and rates of recidivism, see Evans [12].

[24] For more on the structure of jobs available, see Chapter 2 in Gordon, ed. [15]. One often finds informal support for such contentions. A Manhattan prostitute once said, about her crimes, "What is there to say? We've got a living to earn. There wouldn't be any prostitution if there weren't a demand for it." Quoted in the *New York Times,* May 29, 1970. A black high school graduate discussed the problem at greater length with an interviewer in a recent book

(quoted in Goro [16], p. 146) : "That's why a lot of brothers are out on the street now, stinging, robbing people, mugging, 'cause when they get a job, man, they be doing their best, and the white man get jealous 'cause he feel this man could do better than he doing. 'I got to get rid of him!' So they fire him, so a man, he lose his pride. . . . They give you something, and then they take it away from you. . . . And people tell you jobs are open for everybody on the street. There's no reason for you to be stealing. That's a lie! If you're a thief, I'd advise you to be a good thief. 'Cause you working, Jim, you ain't going to succeed unless you got some kind of influence."

25 A friend of Claude Brown's made a similar point about the ineffectiveness of the threat of jail [4, p. 412]: "When I go to jail now, Sonny, I live, man. I'm right at home . . . When I go back to the joint, anywhere I go, I know some people. If I go to any of the jails in New York, or if I go to a slam in Jersey, even, I still run into a lot of cats I know. It's almost like a family."

26 For two of the best available analyses of organized crime, see Cressey [10] and Morris and Hawkins [26].

27 As Cressey points out [10], for instance, it makes a great deal of sense in the heroin industry for the supplier to seek a monopoly on the source of the heroin but to permit many individual sellers of heroin at its final destination, usually without organization backing, because the risks occur primarily at the consumers' end.

28 It is possible to argue, as this point suggests, that heroin addicts would not be prone either to violence or to crime if heroin were legal and free. The fact that it is illegal and that the police go after its consumers means that a cycle of crime and violence is established from which it becomes increasingly difficult to escape.

29 This rests on an assumption, of course, that one learns much more about the priorities of the state by looking at its patterns of enforcement than by the nature of its statutes. This seems quite reasonable. The statutory process is often cumbersome, whereas the patterns of enforcement can sometimes be changed quite easily. (Stigler [42] makes the same point.) Furthermore, as many radicals would argue, the State in democratic societies can often support the capitalist class most effectively by selective enforcement of the laws, rather than by selective legislation. For varieties of relatively complicated historical reasons, selective enforcement of the law seems to arouse less fear for the erosion of democratic tradition than selective legislation itself. As long as we have statutes which nominally outlaw racial inequality, for instance, inadequate enforcement of those laws seems to cause relatively little furor; before we had such laws in this country, protests against the selective statutes could ultimately be mounted.

30 For some useful references on the police, see P. Chevigny [7], Westley [50], and Wilson [52]. For a review of that literature, with some very interesting comments about the police, see Kempton [21]. For one discussion of the first hints of evidence that there may not, in fact, be any kind of identifiable relationship between the number of police we have and their effectiveness, see Reeves [36].

31 For the most devastating story about how the neutralization occurs to even the most innocent of ghetto blacks, see Asinof [1].

32 One should not underestimate the importance of this effect, equally, for quantitative as well as qualitative reasons. In July 1968, for instance, an esti-

mated 140,000 blacks were serving time in penal institutions at federal, state, and local levels. If the percentage of black males in prison had been as low as the proportions of white men (by age groups), there would have been only 25,000 blacks in jail. If those extra 115,000 black men were not in prison, they would likely be unemployed or intermittently employed. In addition, official labor force figures radically undercount the number of blacks in the census because many black males are simply missed by the census-taker. In July 1968, almost one million black males were "missed" in that way. On the conservative assumption that one fifth of those "missing males" were in one way or another evading the law, involved in hustling, or otherwise trapped in the legal system, then a total of 315,000 black men who might be unemployed were it not for the effects of the law were not counted in "measured" unemployment statistics. Total "measured" black male unemployment in July 1968 was 317,000, so that the total black unemployment problem might be nearly twice as large as we "think" it is were it not for the selective efforts of our police, courts, and prisons on black men.

[33] Quoted in *The New York Times*, February 7, 1971, p. 64.

REFERENCES

[1] Eliot Asinof, *People vs. Blutcher*. New York: Viking, 1970.

[2] Edward C. Banfield, *The Unheavenly City*. Boston: Little, Brown, 1970.

[3] Gary Becker, "Crime and Punishment: An Economic Approach," *Journal of Political Economy*, March–April 1968.

[4] Claude Brown, *Manchild in the Promised Land*. New York: Macmillan, 1965.

[5] Claude Brown and Arthur Dunmeyer, "A Way of Life in the Ghetto," in Gordon, ed. [15].

[6] Bell Gale Chevigny, "After the Death of Jail," *The Village Voice*, July 10, 1969. Partially reprinted in Gordon, ed. [15].

[7] Paul Chevigny, *Police Power*. New York: Pantheon, 1969.

[8] Ramsey Clark, *Crime in America*. New York: Simon and Schuster, 1970.

[9] Eldridge Cleaver, *Post-Prison Writings and Speeches*. New York: A Ramparts Book by Random House, 1969.

[10] Donald Cressey, *Theft of the Nation: The Structure and Operations of Organized Crime*. New York: Harper & Row, 1969.

[11] Richard Edwards, Arthur MacEwan, *et al.*, "A Radical Approach to Economics," *American Economic Review*, May 1970. Reprinted in Gordon, ed. [15].

[12] Robert Evans, Jr., "The Labor Market and Parole Success," *Journal of Human Resources*, Spring 1968.

[13] Ronald Goldfarb, "Prison: The National Poorhouse," *The New Republic*, November 1969. Reprinted in Gordon, ed. [15].

[14] Leonard Goodwin, "Work Orientations of the Underemployed Poor," *Journal of Human Resources*, Fall 1969.

[15] David M. Gordon, ed., *Problems in Political Economy: An Urban Perspective*. Lexington, Mass.: D. C. Heath and Company, 1971.

[16] Herb Goro, *The Block*. New York: Random House, 1970.

[17] Fred P. Graham, "Black Crime: The Lawless Image," *Harper's*, September 1970.

[18] John Griffiths, "Ideology in Criminal Procedure, or a Third 'Model' of the Criminal Process," *Yale Law Journal*, January 1970.

[19] Richard Harris, *Justice*. New York: Dutton, 1970.

[20] George Jackson, *Soledad Brother*. New York: Bantam Books, 1970.

[21] Murray Kempton, "Cops," *The New York Review of Books*, November 5, 1970.

[22] William Landes, "An Economic Analysis of the Courts," National Bureau of Economic Research, 1970, unpublished mansucript.

[23] Malcolm X, *Autobiography*. New York: Grove Press, 1964.

[24] Ralph Milliband, *The State in Capitalist Society*. New York: Basic Books, 1969.

[25] Robert Morgenthau, "Equal Justice and the Problem of White Collar Crime," *The Conference Board Record*, August 1969.

[26] Norval Morris and Gordon Hawkins, *The Honest Politician's Guide to Crime Control*. Chicago: University of Chicago Press, 1969.

[27] National Advisory Commission on Civil Disorders, *Report*. New York: Bantam Books, 1968.

[28] National Commission on the Causes and Prevention of Violence, *To Establish Justice, To Insure Domestic Tranquility*. New York: Bantam Books, 1970.

[29] Stanislaw Ossowski, *Class Structure in the Social Consciousness*. New York: Free Press, 1963, trans. by Sheila Patterson.

[30] Herbert Packer, "Two Models of the Criminal Process," *University of Pennsylvania Law Review*, 1964.

[31] ———, "Nixon's Crime Program and What It Means," *New York Review of Books*, October 22, 1970.

[32] President's Commission on Law Enforcement and Administration of Justice, *The Challenge of Crime in a Free Society*. Washington, D.C.: U.S. Government Printing Office, 1967.

[33] ———, *Corrections*. Washington, D.C.: U.S. Government Printing Office, 1967.

[34] ———, *The Courts*. Washington, D.C.: U.S. Government Printing Office, 1967.

[35] ———, *Crime and Its Impact — An Assessment*. Washington, D.C.: U.S. Government Printing Office, 1967.

[36] Richard Reeves, "Police: Maybe They Should Be Doing Something Different," *The New York Times*, January 24, 1971.

[37] James Ridgeway, *The Politics of Ecology*. New York: Dutton, 1970.

[38] Arnold Rose, *The Power Structure: Political Process in America*. New York: Oxford University Press, 1968.

[39] Clifford Shaw and Henry McKay, *Juvenile Delinquency and Urban Areas*. Chicago: University of Chicago Press, 1969.

[40] Robert Sherrill, "The Convenience of Being Lockheed," *Scanlan's Monthly*, August 1970.

[41] Adam Smith, *The Wealth of Nations*. New York: Modern Library, 1937.

[42] George Stigler, "The Optimum Enforcement of Laws," *Journal of Political Economy*, May–June 1970.

[43] Edmund H. Sutherland, *Principles of Criminology*, 6th ed.   Philadelphia: Lippincott, 1960.

[44] ———, "The Crime of Corporations," in Gordon, ed. [15].

[45] Paul Sweezy, "The State," Chapter XIII of *The Theory of Capitalist Development*.   New York: Monthly Review Press, 1968.   Partially reprinted in Gordon, ed. [15].

[46] Lester C. Thurow, "Equity and Efficiency in Justice," *Public Policy*, Summer 1970.

[47] Robert Tucker, *The Marxian Revolutionary Idea*.   New York: W. W. Norton, 1969.

[48] Gordon Tullock, *General Standards: The Logic of Law and Ethics*, Virginia Polytechnic Institute, 1968, unpublished manuscript.

[49] ———, "An Economic Approach to Crime," *Social Science Quarterly*, June 1969.

[50] William Westley, *Violence and Police*.   Cambridge, Mass.: M.I.T. Press, 1970.

[51] James Q. Wilson, "Crime in the Streets," *The Public Interest*, No. 5, Fall 1966.

[52] ———, *Varieties of Police Behavior*.   New York: Basic Books, 1969.

[53] Robert Paul Wolff, *The Poverty of Liberalism*.   Boston: Beacon Press, 1968.

[54] Marvin E. Wolfgang and Franco Ferracuti, *The Subculture of Violence*. New York: Barnes and Noble, 1967.

[55] Marvin E. Wolfgang, "Urban Crime," in James Q. Wilson, ed., *The Metropolitan Enigma*.   Cambridge, Mass.: Harvard University Press, 1968.

Gordon Tullock was born in Rockford, Illinois, studied at the University of Chicago, and earned a law degree there in 1947. He served in World War II and was a China specialist for the State Department. He is a prolific author of articles and books, the latter including The Calculus of Consent *(with James M. Buchanan),* Toward a Mathematics of Politics, *and* The Logic of Law.

Tullock describes himself as a libertarian. He sees the social scientist's role as obtaining information, partly to satisfy curiosity and partly to provide a base upon which we can improve our lives. He feels that many of our existing public institutions are suboptimal — including our system of justice.

17 Economics of Crime

Gordon Tullock

Although this meeting is billed as a debate between the conservative, liberal, and radical positions, the existing conventional wisdom is apparently not going to be represented here. From preliminary conversation with Dr. Gordon, I gather that he does not support it and I certainly do not. In fact, his position is rather closer to that of the average member of the Establishment than is mine. For this reason, it seems reasonable to begin my statement with a very brief, and perhaps prejudiced, discussion of the point of view held by most students of problems of crime, which you can then contrast with the views of Dr. Gordon and myself. Historically, there have been three basic "explanations" for the criminal justice procedure. Perhaps the oldest is simply that the criminals are wicked and should be punished. We may call this the retribution explanation. Second, more modern, is the deterrence theory. We punish criminals in order to put a price on crime; hence, we hope to reduce the amount of it people consume. This is the point of view which I hold and which, in a somewhat modified form, is held by Dr. Gordon. We have distinguished predecessors, since Bentham and John Stuart Mill and a number of other nineteenth-century writers held this view, but so far as I can tell, it has never been the dominant motive in the minds of the people actually running systems of justice.

The third explanation is what I may call the rehabilitation theory. The slogan, "the criminal is a sick person who should be treated, rather than a wicked person who should be punished," well summarizes this basic position. At the moment, this third position is the dominant view of members of the Establishment. Although it is dominant, it is intriguing that so far as I have been able to discover in quite an extensive bit of research, there is absolutely no empirical evidence for it. Indeed, I would like to improve my research on this point a little bit by asking all of you members of this large audience if you know of or can find *any* empirical evidence indicating that the average criminal is in any sense sick. If so, I would appreciate your giving me the citation. Note I said the average criminal; there are, undeniably, a small minority of criminals who are very seriously mentally disturbed. They are to be found primarily among the serious sex offenders.

The present situation is, in a way, quite remarkable, since most people operating our criminal justice system will discuss what they are doing in terms of the current conventional wisdom, but as a matter of fact, their activity is not at all in accord with what they say. For example, the American prison system does very little in the way of rehabilitating prisoners. There is almost no "treatment." It would appear that we confront here a particularly clear case of double-think on the part of a large collection of people. I am rather unhappy that we do not have a defender of the Establishment here today, partly because it does seem to me that the dominant point of view should be represented, and partly because, putting it frankly, I think we could get a good deal of amusement by having him explain what actually goes on at Lorton under the rubric of "rehabilitation." So much, however, for the traditional view; let me now turn to my explanation of my position, which is more or less the position held by Bentham, John Stuart Mill, Gary Becker, and, in a modified form, by Dr. Gordon. In order to explain it, I should like to turn to a discussion of the commonest single law violation: overtime parking. I feel fairly confident that there is no one in this room who has not had personal experience with this particular crime. This experience may take the form of not being able to find a parking space because somebody else *is* overtime parking or of overtime parking yourself. In fact, I feel confident, once again, that all of you have both violated this law and been inconvenienced by other people violating it. There are obviously great advantages when you are discussing some social institution to choosing an aspect of it with which all of us have had personal experience.

Considering, then, the problem of overtime parking, in general the laws against overtime parking have two purposes: 1) to ration out the limited number of parking spaces available and 2) to derive revenue for some governmental unit. The latter objective is, of course, not inconsistent with the former and, in fact, I shall assume for the purpose of the rest of this discussion that the sole motive in the minds of the people designing the laws in this area is simply maximization of the revenue derived from parking. This is a simplification of the real world, but I think not a bad simplification. Particularly for a brief presentation such as this, we must leave out some of the complications of the real world. In the event any of you are hired to assist in the planning of a parking system, you would be well-advised to take a more complex view than I am taking today and use a more complex set of equations than I will use today. Nevertheless, I think you would find that these more complex equations were members of the same family as the simple (even simple-minded) equations that I am going to use.

$$P = R + F - P_C - C - M \qquad (1)$$

In equation (1), I show, on the left, the payoff from the system, and, on the right, four items. The first of these is simply the revenue, i.e., what the meter maids find in the parking meter. The second is the fines charged on people whose cars are found parked with an expired meter. These are the two sources of income and the costs are shown by subtracting, first the cost of the police force insofar as it is devoted to control of the meters, second the cost of the courts, and finally, the physical maintenance of the meters themselves. It not infrequently turns out that the sum of the last three will be higher than the first two in light density areas. Hence, rational municipal administrations do not put meters in areas where parking is expected to be fairly light. This, however, is a very easy problem and we will pay no more attention to it.

The policy of the municipal administration, then, is to maximize the value of P. Obviously, we do not have enough information in (1) to permit anything in the way of such maximization and, in fact, rather difficult empirical investigations would probably be necessary in order to get any clear idea of these values.

$$R + T + PF_E < PF \qquad (2)$$

Let us, however, continue. Inequality (2) shows the decision calculus for an individual deciding whether or not to violate the law against parking his car where there is a red flag showing on the meter.

Once again, the individual will be attempting to maximize his net receipts which, in this case, means minimizing his expenditures. If the quantity on the left is less than the quantity on the right, he should feed the meter. The first item, of course, is the money that he might decide to put in the meter. I have used the same symbol as was used for revenue in equation (1). In addition, there is a T showing the trouble involved in putting the coin in the meter. When you park, there is very little trouble, provided you have the correct change. But frequently people fail to put coins in the meter because they do not want to return to their car at about the time that they know the meter will expire.

In estimating the final cost of compliance with the law, I include the probability (which in most cases is very slight) that you will be erroneously fined. These three positive costs of compliance are then contrasted — by way of the negative sign — with the probability that you will be fined if you are so injudicious as to leave your car parked without a coin in the meter, multiplied by the size of the fine. Note that F has changed its meaning slightly between equations (1) and (2). An individual would either put his coin in the meter or not, depending on the specific circumstances in any given case.

Note that the individual has only a simple decision as to whether or not to comply with the law requiring that he put a coin in the meter. The general parameters of the system are designed by the municipal government. It will, of course, take (2) into account in designing the system, because it is attempting to maximize the payoff. Needless to say, this would require a good deal of empirical information as to the shape of the various functions; but we can make a few very general statements about the government's problem by examining the remaining three equations.

$$R = f\,(PF - PF_E) \tag{3}$$

$$P\,(F_E) = -\,f\,(P_C C) \tag{4}$$

$$P\,(F) = f\,(P_C) \tag{5}$$

First, the revenue is a positive function of the difference between the probability of being fined if you overtime park and the probability of being fined if you do not. The incentive to put a coin in the slot is not only affected by the frequency with which you will be caught and fined if you *do not* put the coin in the slot, but also, negatively, by the likelihood that you will be fined anyway. The probability of an erroneous fine is a negative function of your investment of resources in the police system and in the courts as shown in equation (4) and the probability that you will be fined correctly if you do not put the coin in is largely a function of the investment in police resources. The difference between equations (4) and (5) simply reflects the fact that, in our society, the police are largely responsible for detecting criminals, and the courts are responsible for, let us say, restraining the enthusiasm of the police by sorting out those cases where the police have grabbed the wrong man. Needless to say, none of these agencies work perfectly.

Maximizing the government's payoff from parking is a fairly simple procedure and our method involves putting a cost on the violation of this particular law. We believe that people will consume less of something or other if you raise the cost, and this is true of the crimes and misdemeanors as well as other things. I should say that, although the evidence so far collected on this point with specific respect to crime is scanty, the evidence that people buy more of things that are cheap is overwhelmingly strong in other areas.

There is one final point that should be discussed in specific reference to parking before I turn to other crimes. It is widely believed, although I am not sure that this is more than simple tradition, that the court process should be biased in favor of the accused. The arguments for this procedure are actually quite weak when examined with care; however, I do not wish to spend much time on this subject today. It is rather complicated and if you are curious about it, you will find it discussed in a book that I am bringing out in February called *The Logic of the Law*. My point today, however, is simply that it is probable that in the particular case of parking violations, we would be relatively uninterested in this matter, even if we happened to believe in the tradition with respect to more serious crimes such as murder. For most of us, the prospect of very occasionally getting an unjust ten-dollar fine for parking is of considerably less importance than the cost of improving the court and police systems handling parking in such a way that such errors would be rarer. Indeed, for minor traffic offenses, most people prefer to simply pay the fine rather than going through the necessary court procedures even in cases where they are quite convinced they are innocent. Presumably, a general policy of improving the court procedures with the increase in resource commitment (including the need for the defendant to spend a good deal of time in court) would be regarded by most people as a net detriment to their well-being.

So much for parking. As I said, I have chosen this crime because most of you have had fairly direct personal experience with it, both as a criminal and as a person inconvenienced by the crime. I take it that there will be relatively few among you who will have any significant objection to my analysis. Although you surely do not go through the computations formally, you do act this way. What I think many of you may say, however, is that, although this is okay with respect to parking, other crimes are different. There are undeniably some other crimes that are different because there is a small collection of crimes that are committed by certifiable lunatics and that are very hard to prevent. You may have read a short time ago about a man who walked into a police station and said that he couldn't remember anything. The police drove him to a hospital for psychiatric examination. As he was getting out of the car at the hospital, he pulled one of the policemen's guns from his holster, shot and killed one policeman, and injured the other. It seems likely that it would be difficult if not impossible to design a set of legal institutions to prevent this particular type of crime.

As we turn to more normal crimes, however, the evidence seems to be fairly strong that they are, in general, much like parking. Most of you have probably been behaving in more or less accord with the equations I have put on the board for parking. Most of you, on the other hand, probably have not consciously gone through this calculation. The same phenomenon would appear to be true of more serious crimes. Insofar as we can tell, raising the price of a crime will always reduce the frequency with which it is committed. A standard example of this phenomenon, of course, is the different crime rates found in Europe and in the United States. European countries, in general, have much larger police forces than the United States, and a court system which is much more likely to convict a man who is arrested than is the American system. We should not, therefore, be particularly surprised that they have a markedly lower crime rate.

We might go even further by comparing Washington, D.C., and Blacksburg, Virginia, where I live. For a variety of reasons, the costs of committing crimes are rather low in Washington and rather high in Blacksburg. As a consequence of this, I can wander around at night without the slightest concern for my well-being in Blacksburg, whereas in Washington, I am told that this is not so. People seem to believe that this difference between large and small cities is somehow a magic effect of size; but there *are* large cities in the world in which one is perfectly safe at any time — day or night. I was in Paris this fall and also in London. In both of these cities, I walked through poor districts late at night without the slightest risk and no one that I knew in the area regarded this as in any way an unusual activity on my part. The small size of Blacksburg is relevant to this problem only in that the police know most of the people in town and find it particularly easy to pick up criminals. This raises the price of crime.

It will be noted that the recent efforts to reduce the Washington crime rate take the form, almost entirely, of raising the cost of crime. This is true whether we regard the efforts which are "liberal" or "conservative." The liberals seemed to be delighted with the proposal to sharply increase the size of the police force that surely increases the likelihood that a person committing a crime will be caught and, hence, drive up the cost. The "conservatives," on the other hand, seem mainly concerned with a desire to change the organizations and institutions in such a way as to increase the conviction rate. Needless to say, they are not opposed to the increase in the police force.

It should be noted in this case that we have a clear example of the difficulty of getting any meaning out of such terms as "liberal" or "conservative." The "liberals" are absolutely devoted to our traditional way of doing things and are willing only to change it in the sense of spending more money for the same thing. The alleged "conservatives," on the other hand, are quite willing — even eager — to depart from our sacred traditions. From simply examining the words, one would normally assume that it would be the conservatives who are unwilling to make any change in procedure and the liberals who would be seeking improvements.

So far my discussion has been entirely theoretical. This is partly because the empirical work which has been done in the field of crime is, generally speaking, extremely poor. Further, the question of whether or not criminals respond to changes in the price of their crimes has been subject to very little testing. There are, however, a few bits of empirical evidence on this subject. First, studies of murder — the crime for which our data is best — indicate that driving up the cost of crime, either by lengthening the imprisonment or by making the imprisonment more probable or, better, by both, will in fact reduce the number of murders. There has been some work in attempting to apply the same line of research to other crimes. Unfortunately, the data problems are extremely bad in the field of criminology. As I mentioned before, the data are better for murder than for anything else; hence, there is the possibility of running tests with much less difficulty there. Nevertheless, studies have been run on the statistics, using cross-sectional analysis, for many other crimes — partly on California data and partly by one of Gary Becker's students using national data — and they do show that the crime rate can be reduced by making crime more expensive to the criminal. To put the same thing in other terms, increasing the length of the sentence and/or making the probability greater that a person will be sent to prison after he commits a crime will reduce the number of crimes committed. As an economist, I find this is a fairly elementary thought since I am convinced that people normally buy more of things that are cheaper than of things that are expensive.

I have been supervising some research done under the auspices of the National Science Foundation in which we attempt to find out whether or not crime pays for the people now participating in it. In general, our investigation so far would seem to indicate that it does. In other words, there is no evidence of irrationality in the behavior of the burglars who are the people we happen to be studying.

The widespread public attitude that crime is a matter of mental disease rather than a matter of mental calculation I think can be explained by two factors. First, most of the intellectuals — upper-class people like you and me — would not be well-advised to take up a criminal career, except perhaps embezzlement. My cost-benefit studies show very decidedly that burglary may well be a suitable trade for someone whose alternatives are fairly low-quality labor jobs, but is not a sensible trade for people who have better opportunities. Thus, since everybody in this room has natural talents which will put his income well above that of burglars, it is very hard to imagine such a decision. It is hard to put oneself in the shoes of someone whose opportunities are so much more restricted than those available to us. It is unfortunately true, however, that there will always be a bottom 20 per cent of our population and it seems reasonable to believe that such people will always be well-advised to consider supplementing their income by burglary, unless the punishment for burglary is fairly severe.

The second reason, I believe, for the widespread popularity of the "criminals are sick" hypothesis is simply that it is nicer. Most people don't like to think of themselves as living in a world in which there are nasty people who go about doing crimes, and in which the only way of stopping it is to do something nasty to the criminal. We would much prefer to accentuate the positive, rather than use negative incentives. This is, I think one of the dominant characteristics of American culture. Clearly, it is not international since the communist countries not only make very extensive use of negative incentives for all sorts of things, but they seem proud of it. They periodically announce in the Russian newspapers that they have shot somebody for "economic" crimes, which normally means for something that we would regard as either a minor crime or perhaps, in many cases, no crime at all. You will all recall Castro's threats of instant execution for those who interfered with the sugar crop.

Americans, I think, do not like to use punishments in dealing with problems, and, if you do not wish to use punishments, you may be able to convince yourself that you are not doing so. How anyone can visit a modern American penitentiary and believe that it is engaged in rehabilitation, rather than simply locking people up in a not-too-pleasant place as a way of imposing costs on them, I do not know. Nevertheless, it is an observed fact that many students in this area have succeeded in carrying off the trick.

Those who notice that rehabilitation is a modest portion of the activities of the prison normally become very indignant about this and insist that rehabilitation should be undertaken. The fact that our experience with efforts to rehabilitate has so far been extremely poor is normally ignored. Further, if the view that I have been presenting in this lecture is correct, rehabilitation is in essence impossible. The person who commits a crime does not commit a crime because he is in any sense sick or different from the rest of us, he commits it because it is in his best interest to do so. As long as it is possible to benefit oneself by taking someone else's property (or the state property in communist countries) — and I do not see how institutions could be set up in which it would not be possible to benefit oneself in this way — then we must control such activities by putting a cost on theft.

To take an extreme example, suppose we had a completely egalitarian state in the sense that everyone was given the same amount of whatever material happened to be produced in the society. Under these circumstances, the only way in which one could better one's living standard would be to steal from one's neighbor. Obviously preventing this from occurring would require the use of negative sanctions. The simplicity of this line of reasoning escapes many people, not because it is logically difficult but because of emotional and cultural problems. Most Americans would rather not think of the less pleasant aspects of the world, and what we have been talking about today is one of those unpleasant aspects.

QUESTIONS

Crime
Gordon / Tullock

1. Will putting a high cost on crime eliminate it (as argued by Tullock) or just make it more violent (according to Gordon)?
2. What has been the historical impact of negative sanctions on crime in the United States?
3. Is man a rational calculator, criminal or otherwise?
4. How does corporate crime reflect "economic insecurity and a desire to gain some of the goods unequally distributed throughout society"?
5. What are the implications of the Family Model for governmental policy?
6. Is the only way to prevent socially undesirable behavior through the use of negative sanctions?
7. Who benefits from crime?
8. Is crime productive?
9. Is crime profitable for business enterprise?
10. Doesn't Gordon ignore those people who can never adjust to living in society?
11. If so many people are at odds with the institutions of our society, is it possible that our institutions need altering to fit the people's needs?

SECTION V

Economic Aspects of Some Unresolved Problems of American Capitalism

A. Is There a Relationship Between Capitalism and Racism?
B. Is There a Relationship Between Capitalism and Sexism?

A conflict arises over the basis for economic discrimination against blacks and women. Radicals argue that although racism and sexism antedate capitalism, that the institutions of capitalism perpetuate these injustices. How? By virtue of the inequalities and alienation created by the system. Workers realize their status is inferior to those who own capital and to those who manage industry. They feel angry and need scapegoats. Blacks and women play these roles of scapegoats.

Orthodox economists argue that capitalism is inherently antithetical to economic discrimination based on race or sex. Capitalists are profit maximizers and will employ anyone and sell to anyone, if it is profitable. In so far as capitalists discriminate, it is a carryover from previous economic systems.

Writing from a radical perspective, Michael Reich argues that racism is supportive of the capitalist system. We can contrast Reich's argument with that of orthodox economists (represented here by Professor Bergmann), who argue that racism hurts those capitalists who have to pay whites higher wages because they exclude blacks. Racism limits the supply of labor and pushes white wages up — thus damaging capitalist's interests and helping white workers. Reich argues just the opposite.

He presents data that tend to show that where racism is most evident — as measured by the ratio of black/white income — white workers are worse off. Racism keeps white workers' incomes low and capitalists' incomes high. By keeping a pool of reserve black labor available, capitalists can keep white workers' wages down, keep white workers from unionizing, and can keep spending on public schools (and therefore taxes) at a minimum.

Reich argues that the capitalist system requires inequality. Therefore, some people are going to be at the bottom of the heap. They need scapegoats. Blacks play this role in America. Racism, thus, has a crucial role in preserving the stability of American capitalism.

Barbara Bergmann presents the orthodox economist's analysis of racial discrimination. This analysis starts from the premise that everyone in a capitalist society is motivated to make as much money as possible. In order to make money, one wants to buy cheap and sell dear, and it doesn't matter whether those one deals with are black, white, red, or green.

The capitalist who refuses to hire blacks (even if they are the most qualified) reduces his supply of labor and thus raises the wage that must be paid white workers. This cuts into the capitalist's profit and is thus inconsistent with the capitalist ethic. A similar analysis is presented for landlords and others who discriminate. Thus, capitalism and racism are essentially antithetical, and racism exists in capitalist countries for noneconomic reasons. Professor Bergmann presents data to show that the economic position of blacks improved markedly during the 1960s, thus giving the lie to the argument that racism cannot be eliminated under capitalism.

Nancy Barrett argues that capitalism and discrimination against women are not compatible. Capitalists desire to hire those workers who are most efficient and pay them the lowest possible wage. To discriminate against women reduces the supply of labor available to capitalists and thus tends to raise the wage. Capitalists do discriminate against women, because women are not seen to be as efficient workers as men, i.e., women put their careers second to their roles as wives and mothers — their rate of absenteeism is higher because they stay home to take care of sick children, for instance. The fact that employers perceive women employees in this way is not a product of capitalism. It is instead a result of the institution of the family and the necessity for a parent to stay home with young children. If men come to share this role with women, they will also be discriminated against.

Professor Barbette Blackington of American University appeared with Dr. Barrett to discuss the relationship between the economic system and the alienation of women. However, she did not submit a paper for inclusion in this volume. In her oral presentation, she made the following points:

In all economic systems, women have been subordinate. Thus, to argue that women are better off in capitalist then in feudal societies is irrelevant. After more than half a century of socialism in the Soviet Union, the status of women there contradicts all the theoretical principles of socialist thought.

We know of no human society in which women have not been subordinate to men. There are many theoretical explanations of how this condition of subordination came about. Women are naturally and numerically superior to men. More women are born, they survive the vicissitudes of childhood better, they are able to withstand all sorts of hardships better — pain, cold, concentration camps, etc., they are immune to many illnesses to which men are subject, they mature intellectually and physically earlier than men, and they live longer than men. Men are superior in only one attribute and that is physical strength, and this may explain male domination of women. But it is an attribute that has become obsolete. In a technologically sophisticated society, income and status do not derive from brute strength. Income, wealth, power, and status come as the result of intellectual and social skills that are unrelated to physical strength. Thus, the basis for male domination has disappeared, and some men are now suffering trauma in our society as a result. We are now moving toward new definitions of sexual roles and relationships, and this is an extraordinarily difficult and painful process.

Michael Reich was born in Poland in 1945, attended public schools in New York City, received his B.A. from Swarthmore and his Ph.D. from Harvard. *He is a member of the Union for Radical Political Economics, an Assistant Professor at Boston University, and co-editor of* The Capitalist System: A Radical Analysis of Contemporary American Society.

18 The Economics of Racism

Michael Reich

In the early 1960s it seemed to many that the elimination of racism in the United States was proceeding without requiring a radical restructuring of the entire society. There was a growing civil rights movement, and hundreds of thousands of blacks were moving to Northern cities where discrimination was supposedly less severe than in the South. Government reports pointed to the rapid improvement in the quantity of black schooling as blacks moved out of the South: in 1966 the gap between the median years of schooling of black males aged twenty-five to twenty-nine and white males in the same age group had shrunk to one-quarter the size of the gap that had existed in 1960.[1]

But by 1970 the optimism of earlier decades had vanished. Despite new civil rights laws, elaborate White House conferences, special ghetto manpower programs, the War on Poverty, and stepped-up tokenist hiring, racism, and the economic exploitation of blacks has not lessened.

Copyright © 1970 by Michael Reich. This essay is based on my Ph.D. thesis. I am indebted to Samuel Bowles for critical guidance at every stage. A somewhat different version of this paper appeared in David M. Gordon, ed., *The Political Economy of Urban Problems*, D. C. Heath, 1971.

During the past twenty-five years there has been virtually no permanent improvement in the relative economic position of blacks in America. Median black incomes have been fluctuating at a level between 47 per cent and 62 per cent of median white incomes, the ratio rising during economic expansions and falling to previous low levels during recessions.[2] Segregation in schools and neighborhoods has been steadily increasing in almost all cities, and the atmosphere of distrust between blacks and whites has been intensifying. Racism, instead of disappearing, seems to be on the increase.

Racism has been as persistent in the United States in the twentieth century as it was in previous centuries. The industrialization of the economy led to the transformation of the black worker's economic role from one of agricultural sharecropper and household servant to one of urban industrial operative and service worker, but it did not result in substantial relative improvement for blacks. Quantitative comparisons using Census data of occupational distributions by race show that the economic status of black males is virtually the same today as it was in 1910 (the earliest year for which racial data are available).[3]

Besides systematically subjugating blacks so that their median income is 55 per cent that of whites, racism is of profound importance for the distribution of income among white landowners, capitalists, and workers. For example, racism clearly benefits owners of housing in the ghetto, where blacks have no choice but to pay higher rents than for comparable housing elsewhere in the city. But more important, racism is a key mechanism for the stabilization of capitalism and the legitimization of inequality. We shall return to the question of who benefits from racism later, but first we shall review some of the economic means used to subjugate blacks.

Beginning in the first grade blacks go to schools of inferior quality and obtain little of the basic training and skills needed in the labor market. Finding schools of little relevance, more in need of immediate income, and less able anyway to finance their way through school, the average black student still drops out at a lower grade. In 1965 only 7.4 per cent of black males aged 25 to 34 were college graduates, compared to 17.9 per cent of whites in the same age bracket.

But exploitation really begins in earnest when the black youth enters the labor market. A black worker with the same number of years of schooling and the same scores on achievement tests as a white worker receives much less income. The black worker cannot get as good a job because the better-paying jobs are located too far from the ghetto, or because he was turned down by racist personnel agencies and employers, or because a union denied admittance, or maybe because of an arrest record. Going to school after a certain point doesn't seem to increase a black person's job possibilities very much. The more educated a black person is, the greater is the disparity between his income and that of a white with the same schooling. The result: *in 1966 black college graduates earned less than white high school dropouts.* And the higher the average wage or salary of an occupation, the lower the percentage of workers in that occupation who are black.

The rate of unemployment among blacks is twice as high as among whites. Layoffs and recessions hit blacks with twice the impact they hit whites, since blacks are the "last hired, first fired." The ratio of average black to white incomes follows the business cycle closely, buffering white workers from some of the impact of the recession.

Blacks pay higher rents for inferior housing, higher prices in ghetto stores, higher insurance premiums, higher interest rates in banks and lending companies, travel longer distances at greater expense to their jobs, suffer from inferior garbage collection and less access to public recreational facilities, and are assessed at higher property tax rates when they own housing. Beyond this, blacks are further harassed by police, the courts, and the prisons.

When conventional economists attempt to analyze racism they usually begin by trying to separate various forms of racial discrimination. For example they define "pure wage discrimination" as the racial differential in wages paid to workers of identical marginal productivity, that is with years and quality of schooling, skill training, previous employment experience and seniority, age, health, job attitudes, and a host of other factors held constant. They presume that they can analyze the sources of "pure wage discrimination" without simultaneously analyzing the extent to which discrimination also affects the factors they hold constant.

But such a technique distorts reality. The various forms of discrimination are not separable in real life. Employers' hiring and promotion practices, resource allocation in city schools, the structure of transportation systems, residential segregation and housing quality, availability of decent health care, behavior of policemen and judges, foremen's prejudices, images of blacks presented in the media and the schools, price gouging in ghetto stores — these and the other forms of social and economic discrimination interact strongly with each other in determining the occupational status and annual income, and welfare, of black people. The processes are not simply additive, but are mutually reinforcing. Often, a decrease in one narrow form of discrimination is accompanied by an increase in another form. Since all aspects of racism interact, an analysis of racism should incorporate all of its aspects in a unified manner.

No single quantitative index could adequately measure racism in all its social, cultural, psychological and economic dimensions. But, while racism is far more than a narrow economic phenomenon, it does have very definite economic consequences: blacks have far lower incomes than whites. The ratio of median black to median white incomes thus provides a rough, but useful, quantitative index of the economic consequences of racism for blacks. We shall use this index statistically to analyze the causes of racism's persistence in the United States. While this approach perhaps overemphasizes the economic aspects of racism, it is nevertheless an improvement over the narrower approach taken by conventional economists.

How is the historical persistence of racism in the United States to be explained? The most prominent view among economists was formulated in 1957 by Gary Becker in his book, *The Economics of Discrimination*.[4] Racism, according to Becker, is fundamentally a problem of tastes and attitudes. Whites are defined to have a "taste for discrimination" if they are willing to forfeit income in order to be associated with other whites instead of blacks. Since white employers and employees prefer not to associate with blacks, they require a monetary compensation for the psychic cost of such association. In Becker's principal model white employers have a taste for discrimination; marginal productivity analysis is invoked to show that white employers lose (in monetary term) while white workers gain, from discrimination against blacks.

Becker does not try to explain the source of white tastes for discrimination. For him, these attitudes are determined outside of the economic system. (Racism could presumably be ended simply by changing these attitudes, perhaps by appeal to whites on moral grounds.) According to Becker's analysis, employers would find the ending of racism to be in their economic self-interest, but white workers would not. The persistence of racism is thus implicitly laid at the door of white workers. Becker argues that long run market forces will lead to the end of discrimination anyway: less discriminatory employers, with no "psychic costs" to enter in their accounts, will be able to operate at lower costs, thus driving the more discriminatory employers out of business.[5]

The approach to racism argued here is entirely different. Racism is rooted in the economic system and not in "exogenously determined" attitudes. Historically, the American Empire was founded on the racist extermination of American Indians, was financed by profits from slavery, and was extended by a string of interventions, beginning with the Mexican War of the 1840s, which have been at least partly justified by white supremacist ideology.

Today, by transferring white resentment toward blacks and away from capitalism, racism continues to serve the needs of the capitalist system. Although an individual employer might gain by refusing to discriminate and agreeing to hire blacks at above the going black wage rate, it is not true that the capitalist class as a whole would profit if racism were eliminated and labor was more efficiently allocated without regard to skin color.   The divisiveness of racism weakens workers' strength when bargaining with employers; the economic consequences of racism are not only lower incomes for blacks, but also higher incomes for the capitalist class coupled with lower incomes for white workers. Although capitalists may not have conspired to consciously create racism, and although capitalists may not be its principal perpetuators, nevertheless racism does help in the perpetuation of capitalism.

We have, then, two alternative approaches to the analysis of racism. The first suggests that capitalists lose and white workers gain from racism.   The second predicts the opposite — capitalists gain while workers lose.   The first says that racist "tastes for discrimination" are formed independently of the economic system; the second argues that racism is symbiotic with capitalistic economic institutions.   The first suggests that racism can be easily uprooted; the second suggests that ending racism will require the destruction of capitalism.

The two approaches reflect the theoretical paradigms of society from which each was developed.   Becker follows the paradigm of neo-classical economics in taking "tastes" as exogenously determined and fixed, and then letting the market mechanism determine outcomes. The radical approach follows the Marxian paradigm in arguing that racial attitudes and racist institutions must be seen as part of a larger social system, in placing emphasis on conflict between classes and the use of power to determine the outcomes of such conflicts.   The test as to which explanation of racism is superior is, in some ways, an interesting test of the relative explanatory power of these competing social paradigms.

The very persistence of racism in the United States lends support to the radical approach.   So do repeated instances of employers using blacks as strikebreakers, as in the massive steel strike of 1919, and employer-instigated exacerbation of racial antagonisms during that strike and many others.[6]   However, the particular virulence of racism among many blue- and white-collar workers and their families seems to refute the radical approach and support Becker.

Which of the two models better explains reality?   We have already mentioned that the radical approach predicts that capitalists gain and workers lose from racism, while the conventional Beckerian approach predicts precisely the opposite.   In the latter approach racism has an equalizing effect on white income distribution, while in the former racism has an unequalizing effect.   The statistical relationship between the extent of racism and the degree of inequality among whites provides a simple, yet clear test of the two approaches.

The appendix contains a fuller explanation of the statistical test.

However, in brief the test shows that where racism is greatest (where the ratio of black median family income to white median family income is lowest) that income inequality among whites is also greatest. This result is consistent with the radical model and inconsistent with the predictions of Becker's model.

Two factors that might help explain this statistical relationship are examined. First, it is hypothesized that total wages of white labor are reduced by racial antagonisms — in part because union growth and labor militancy are inhibited. Second, it is hypothesized that the supply of public services — particularly education — available to low-income whites is reduced as a result of racial antagonisms. The results of statistical tests (elaborated on in the appendix) confirm the above two hypotheses. Where racism is greater, union members are a smaller percentage of the working force. Where racism is greater, we also find greater inequality of schooling among whites. The results of these tests suggest that racism is in the economic interest of rich whites and against the economic interests of poor whites and white workers.

A full assessment of the importance of racism for capitalism would probably conclude that the primary significance of racism is not strictly economic. The simple economics of racism does not explain why many workers seem to be so vehemently racist, when racism is not in their economic self-interest. In extra-economic ways, racism helps to legitimize inequality, alienation, and powerlessness — legitimization that is necessary for the stability of the capitalist system as a whole. For example, many whites believe that welfare payments to blacks are a far more important factor in their taxes than is military spending. Through racism, poor whites come to believe that their poverty is caused by blacks who are willing to take away their jobs, and at lower wages, thus concealing the fact that a substantial amount of income inequality is inevitable in a capitalist society. Racism thus transfers the locus of whites' resentment towards blacks and away from capitalism.

Racism also provides some psychological benefits to poor and working-class whites. For example, the opportunity to participate in another's oppression compensates for one's own misery. The parallel here is to the subjugation of women in the family: after a day of alienating labor, the tired husband can compensate by oppressing his wife. Furthermore, not being at the bottom of the heap is some solace for an unsatisfying life; this argument was successfully used by the Southern oligarchy against poor whites allied with blacks in the interracial Populist movement of the late nineteenth century.

Thus, racism is likely to take firm root in a society which breeds an individualistic and competitive ethos. In general, blacks provide a convenient and visible scapegoat for problems that actually derive from the institutions of capitalism. As long as building a real alternative to capitalism does not seem feasible to most whites, we can expect that identifiable and vulnerable scapegoats will prove functional to the status quo. These extra-economic factors thus neatly dovetail with the economic aspects of racism discussed earlier in their mutual service to the perpetuation of capitalism.

APPENDIX

First we shall need a measure of racism. The index we use is the ratio of black median family income to white median family income (abbreviated as B/W). A low numerical value for this ratio indicates a high degree of racism. We have calculated values of this racism index, using data from the 1960 census, for each of the largest forty-eight standard metropolitan statistical areas (SMSAs). It turns out there is a great deal of variation from SMSA to SMSA in the B/W index of racism, even within the North; Southern SMSAs generally demonstrated a greater degree of racism. The statistical techniques used exploit this variation.

We shall also need measures of inequality among whites. Two convenient measures are: 1) the percentage share of all white income that is received by the top 1 per cent of white families, and 2) the Gini coefficient of white incomes, a measure that captures inequality within as well as between social classes.[7]

Both of these inequality measures vary considerably among the SMSAs; there is also a substantial amount of variation in these within the subsample of Northern SMSAs. Therefore, it is very interesting to examine whether the pattern of variation of the inequality and racism variables can be explained by causal hypotheses. This is our first source of empirical evidence.

A systematic relationship across SMSAs between racism and white inequality does exist and is highly significant: the correlation coefficient is $-.47$ (the negative sign indicates that where racism is greater, income inequality *among whites* is also greater).[8] This result is consistent with the radical model and is inconsistent with the predictions of Becker's model.

This evidence, however, should not be accepted too quickly. The correlations reported may not reflect actual causality, since other independent forces may be simultaneously influencing both variables in the same way. As is the case with many other statistical analyses, the model must be expanded to control for such other factors. We know from previous inter-SMSA income distribution studies that the most important additional factors that should be introduced into our model are:

1. the industrial and occupational structure of the SMSAs,
2. the region in which the SMSAs are located,
3. the average income of the SMSAs, and
4. the proportion of the SMSA population that is black.

These factors were introduced into the model by the technique of multiple regression analysis. Separate equations were estimated with the Gini index and the top 1 per cent share as measures of white inequality.

All the equations showed strikingly uniform statistical results: racism was a significantly unequalizing force on the white income distribution, even when other factors were held constant. A 1 per cent increase in the ratio of black to white median incomes (that is, a 1 per cent decrease in racism) was associated with a .2 per cent decrease in white inequality, as measured by the Gini coefficient. The corresponding effect on top 1 per cent share of white income was two and a half times as large, indicating that most of the inequality among whites generated by racism was associated with increased income for the richest 1 per cent of white families. Further statistical investigation reveals that increases in racism had an insignificant effect on the share received by the poorest whites, and resulted in a decrease in the income share of the whites in the middling income brackets.[9] This is true even when the Southern SMSAs are excluded.

Within the radical model, we can specify a number of mechanisms that further explain the statistical finding that racism increases inequality among whites. We shall consider two mechanisms here: 1. total wages of white labor are reduced by racial antagonisms, in part because union growth and labor militancy are inhibited, and 2. the supply of public services, especially in education, available to low- and middle-income whites is reduced as a result of racial antagonisms.

Wages of white labor are lessened by racism because the fear of a cheaper and underemployed black labor supply in the area is invoked by employers when labor presents its wage demands. Racial antagonisms on the shop floor deflect attention from labor grievances related to working conditions, permitting employers to cut costs. Racial divisions among labor prevent the development of united worker organizations both within the workplace and in the labor movement as a whole. As a result, union strength and union militancy will be less, the greater the extent of racism. A historical example of this process is the already mentioned use of racial and ethnic divisions to destroy the solidarity of the 1919 steel strikers. By contrast, during the 1890s, black-white class solidarity greatly aided mineworkers in building militant unions among workers in Alabama, West Virginia, and other coalfield areas.[10]

The above argument and examples contradict the common belief that an exclusionary racial policy will strengthen, rather than weaken the bargaining power of unions. Racial exclusion increases bargaining power only when entry into an occupation or industry can be effectively limited. Industrial-type unions are much less able to restrict entry than craft unions or organizations such as the American Medical Association. This is not to deny that much of organized labor is egregiously racist.[11] But it is important to distinguish actual discrimination practice from the objective economic self-interest of union members.

The second mechanism we shall consider concerns the allocation of expenditures for public services. The most important of these services is education. Racial antagonisms dilute both the desire and the ability of poor white parents to improve educational opportunities for their children. Antagonisms between blacks and poor whites drives wedges between the two groups and reduces their ability to join in a united political movement pressing for improved and more equal education. Moreover, many poor whites recognize that however inferior their own schools, black schools are even worse. This provides some degree of satisfaction and identification with the status quo, reducing the desire of poor whites to press politically for better schools in their neighborhoods. Ghettos tend to be located near poor white neighborhoods more often than near rich white neighborhoods; racism thus reduces the potential tax base of school districts containing poor whites. Also, pressures by teachers' groups to improve all poor schools is reduced by racial antagonisms between predominantly white teaching staffs and black children and parents.[12]

The statistical validity of the above mechanisms can be tested in a causal model. The effect of racism on unionism is tested by estimating an equation in which the percentage of the SMSA labor force which is unionized is the dependent variable, with racism and the structural variables (such as the SMSA industrial structure) as the independent variables. The schooling mechanism is tested by estimating a similar equation in which the dependent variable is inequality in years of schooling completed among white males aged twenty-five to twenty-nine years old.[13]

Once again, the results of this statistical test strongly confirm the hypothesis of the radical model. The racism variable is statistically significant in all the equations and has the predicted sign: a greater degree of racism results in lower unionization rates and greater amounts of schooling inequality among whites. This empirical evidence again suggests that racism is in the economic interests of capitalists and other rich whites, and against the economic interests of poor whites and white workers.

ENDNOTES

[1] "The Social and Economic Status of Negroes in the United States, 1969," Bureau of Labor Statistics Report No. 375, p. 50.

[2] The data refer to male incomes, and is published annually by the U.S. Census Bureau in its P-60 Series, "Income of Families and Persons . . ." Using data for the years 1948 to 1964, Rasmussen found that, after controlling for the effects of the business cycle, the average increase in the racial ratio of median incomes was only .3 per cent per year, or 5 per cent over the sixteen years. See David Rasmussen, "A Note on the Relative Income of Nonwhite Men, 1948–64," *Quarterly Journal of Economics,* February 1970. Thurow, using a slightly different technique, estimated that no relative increase in black incomes would occur after unemployment was reduced to 3 per cent. See L. Thurow, *Poverty and Discrimination* (Washington, D.C.: Brookings Institution, 1969), pp. 58–61. Batchelder found stability in the ratio over time despite migration from the South to the North; within regions in the North, the ratio declined. Alan Batchelder, "Decline in the Relative Income of Negro Men," *Quarterly Journal of Economics,* November 1964.

[3] Since income data by race are not available before 1940, a relative index must be based on racial occupational data. Hiestand has computed such an index: he finds at most a 5 per cent increase in blacks' status between 1910 and 1960; most of this improvement occurred during the labor shortages of the 1940s. See D. Hiestand, *Economic Growth and Employment Opportunities for Minorities* (New York, Columbia University Press, 1964), p. 53.

[4] University of Chicago Press.

[5] Some economists writing on discrimination reject Becker's "tastes" approach, but use the marginal productivity method of analysis. See, for example, L. Thurow, *op. cit.* The main substantive difference in their conclusions is that Thurow expects racism will be a little harder to uproot. See also A. Krueger, "The Economics of Discrimination," *Journal of Political Economy,* October 1963.

[6] See, for example, David Brody, *Steelworkers in America: the Nonunion Era* (Cambridge: Harvard University Press, 1966) ; Herbert Gutman, "The Negro and the United Mineworkers," in J. Jacobson, ed., *The Negro and the American Labor Movement* (New York: Anchor, 1968) ; S. Spero and H. Harris, *The Black Worker* (New York: Atheneum, 1968), *passim.*

[7] The Gini coefficient varies between 0 and 1, with 0 indicating perfect equality and 1 indicating perfect inequality. For a more complete exposition, see H. Miller, *Income Distribution in the United States* (Washington, D.C. G.P.O., 1966). Data for the computation of G_w and S_1 for 48 SMSAs were taken from the 1960 census. A full description of the computational technique used is available in my dissertation.

[8] The correlation coefficient reported in the text is between G_w and B/W. The equivalent correlation between S_1 and B/W is r = −.55. A similar calculation by S. Bowles, across states instead of SMSAs, resulted in an r = −.58.

[9] A more rigorous presentation of these variables and the statistical results is available in my dissertation.

[10] See endnote 6.

[11] See, for example, H. Hill, "The Racial Practices of Organized Labor: the Contemporary Record," in J. Jacobson, ed., *The Negro and the American Labor Movement* (New York: Anchor Books, 1968) .

[12] In a similar fashion, racial antagonisms reduce the political pressure on governmental agencies to provide other public services which would have a pro-poor distributional impact. The two principal items in this category are public health services and welfare payments in the Aid to Families with Dependent Children program.

[13] These dependent variables do not perfectly represent the phenomena described, but serve as reasonable proxy variables for these purposes.

Barbara R. Bergmann studied economics at Harvard in the 1950s and taught there until 1961. She then became a member of the staff of President Kennedy's Council of Economic Advisors, subsequently did research at the Brookings Institution, taught at Brandeis and the University of Maryland, where she is now Professor of Economics. The primary focus of her current research is on employment discrimination against women. She does not describe herself as a radical: "However, it is no secret that there is a great deal of room for improvement in our economy and in our society, and I would like to see more rapid progress."

19 Can We End Racial Discrimination Under Capitalism?

Barbara R. Bergmann

The affliction of American society by the evils of discrimination, poverty, crime, wars, pollution, and alienation have led an indeterminate number of people to a belief that "the system" that is responsible for such evils must be radically altered. Since a chief feature in almost anybody's view of "the system" is our capitalist economy, there is a tendency to declare the capitalist nature of our economic setup to be the chief culprit in creating these evils and perpetuating them. While it is tempting to reason in this way, particularly if one enjoys believing that all evils arise out of a single source, I believe such reasoning to be mistaken. In particular, *I believe that racial discrimination can be reduced drastically in the absence of a revolution or even an evolution that would overthrow capitalism.* I must confess that this belief is far from certitude. No really serious student of racial affairs pretends to a clear view of the future of racial discrimination in the United States; anyone who does is a propagandist. Only tendencies can be discerned and these only dimly.

Our first task is to explore the connection between racial discrimination and capitalism. Is the nature of capitalism such that racial discrimination is natural to it? Is racial discrimination beneficial to the continued existence of capitalism and to the prosperity of the capitalists? Or is racial discrimination inimical to capitalism and capitalism inimical to racial discrimination? To put the matter succinctly, is racial discrimination meat and drink to capitalism, or is it poison?

I shall argue that the essential nature of capitalism is such as to discourage rather than encourage discrimination, which I believe persists among us for noneconomic reasons. Arguing that capitalism and racial discrimination are inimical to each other is not sufficient, however, to establish that racism can be cured without a revolution. If capitalism *is* inimical to racism, then its persistence in the United States for so long and in so virulent a form would argue that the underlying disposition toward it in our society is a strong one. Thus it might be true that to get rid of it a cataclysmic event such as the overthrow of capitalism might be necessary. However, there is evidence that after decades of no progress, we are now moving ahead and that even more rapid progress is possible and probable. This part of the argument is on somewhat slighter ground than the argument about the capitalism-racism connection, and the reader will have to draw his or her own conclusions as to whether the degree of progress on this problem (and others) will be such as to justify maintaining an economic system which in major outline is like the present one.

DISCRIMINATION AND CAPITALISM

Marx tells us that the emergence of capitalism meant that the "cash nexus" became the relationship *par excellence* between man and man. In precapitalist societies the right to buy or sell was often restricted according to the social class or location one was born into; much property was inalienable, elaborate restrictions hedged each transaction. Under pure capitalism, all that is necessary for transactions to take place is the desire of the parties and the wherewithal on the part of the buyer. For example, the notion that certain people should be debarred from certain types of work unless they are members of certain families, while a commonplace in village India, is completely alien to the ideology of capitalism. The questions "How is this man related to me socially?" "Do I like him?" "Is his face black or white?" are not the questions *homo oeconomicus* of capitalism is supposed to ask himself when he is contemplating a sale or a purchase.

The economy of the United States is not, of course, pure *laissez-*

faire capitalism, and Americans do sometimes give jobs to their dumb nephews, give discounts to their friends, and refuse to buy from and sell to black people when it might be in their financial interest to do otherwise. The point to understand here is that such behavior is anomalous from the point of view of the capitalist ideology, and is a deviation from normal capitalist practice. The normal practice is that each man buys as cheap as he can and sells as dear as he can, without regard to the identity of those he trades with.

Let us look more closely at the effects of racial discrimination on the financial welfare of those private citizens who practice it. Practicing racial discrimination usually means excluding blacks from the possibility of making certain transactions. "I won't hire you for this job because you are black," "I will not rent this apartment to you or sell you this house because you are black," "You cannot eat a sandwich at my soda fountain because you are black." This kind of behavior undoubtedly injures the black people against whom it is directed. *But it also causes financial losses to the discriminator.* The reason is that the discriminator is trifling with the law of supply and demand, the most sacred law in the capitalist canon. When he refuses to hire blacks he artificially reduces the supply of labor to himself, raising the price he must pay to the white labor he does hire, and therefore hurting himself financially. When he refuses to sell his product or his house to blacks he artificially reduces the demand for them, thus reducing the price he extracts from the white customers he does deal with.

I do not want to give the impression that the losses to the discriminator are large and unmixed with gains. Certainly, the losses to the discriminator must be very small as compared to the losses of the discriminated-against. Moreover, when the discriminator refuses to hire blacks he may be forcing them to overcrowd those occupations considered "fitting" for blacks, and thus his actions may have the effect of lowering the wage in those occupations. Thus what the discriminator loses by refusing to hire blacks as machine operatives he may make up to some degree by the low wage for which he can hire a janitor. Nevertheless, the proper conclusion seems to be that no important financial gains accrue to discrimination; in all probability discriminators suffer losses because of their discriminatory conduct.

Of course, some people do gain from discrimination. First and foremost are those who have no qualms about buying or selling to blacks. These include employers in industries (such as laundries) that have lots of jobs considered "fit" for blacks. They include slumlords who rent apartments to the blacks who are excluded by discriminator from other apartments. They also include those few black businessmen who can monopolize a segregated black clientele. And, of course, they include those white workers who are protected in some occupation from the competition of black workers. I have elsewhere made estimates of the wage rate gains accruing to white workers from this source. I found them to be on the order of 10 per cent for white workers with less than an elementary education and trivial for all other white workers.[1]

One interesting thing about this list of the financial beneficiaries of discrimination is that the beneficiaries of discrimination are in general different people from the actual discriminators. While there is some overlap (the slumlord may own some property on the white side of the tracks), it is probably correct to say that the discriminators and the beneficiaries of discrimination are for the most part different. Undoubtedly, some of the beneficiaries cheer on the discriminators from the sidelines, but the cheerleaders are not part of the playing team in this game, for the most part.

The second interesting thing is that the financial gains we have been able to discover from discrimination are not large. Few if any businessmen are making a very lucrative business out of discrimination, least of all the ones who are most guilty of conducting the exclusionary policy on which our whole racial system is based. Some radicals claim that the real economic benefit from discrimination is that it gives discriminatory bosses the power to threaten their white workers with the hungry blacks who will be glad to take their jobs unless the white workers continue to knuckle under at low wages. While such a threat may be effective in isolated instances, it can hardly be considered as an important factor in labor relations in the United States of today.

WHY RACIAL DISCRIMINATION?

If economic incentives on discriminators under capitalism discourage discrimination rather than encourage it, how can it persist? The answer, of course, is that economic forces are far from the whole story in racial matters and are probably a minor part of the story. Human beings seem to have the tendency to set up hierarchical relationships, and to live in social systems in which A is treated with more respect than B for reasons X, Y, and Z. The reasons for looking down on a person can be the presence of calluses on the hands, the absence of a penis, the presence or absence of a cross around the neck, the presence of a pigment in the skin. This tendency has displayed itself in the United States under capitalism, but it has also displayed itself under other flags,

"The Effect on White Incomes of Discrimination in Employment," *Journal of Political Economy*, March–April 1971.

under other economic systems, and in other eras.   The division of labor, so lauded by economists since the time of Adam Smith, seems to be a powerful force in pushing one part of the population to think itself as superior to the other part.   The division of labor is hardly a fault attributable to capitalism, although noncapitalist economies may be better able to reduce it if they desire to do so.

I would expect a given degree of racial prejudice in the population to express itself in economic terms more virulently under a socialist system such as that of the Soviet Union than under a capitalist system. Under capitalism, the desire to hold down people of the wrong race (or sex, or religion) may be moderated by the incentive to make money out of buying from them and selling to them.   In a socialist economy such a moderating force may be entirely absent, since individual managers are typically given little or no personal financial incentive to make any purchase or sale.   One might believe that a noncapitalist government would be more willing and more able to reduce the degree of racial prejudice in the country's population; unfortunately, we have the counterexample of the government of the Soviet Union in fanning the anti-Semitic feelings of the population.

IS RACIAL DISCRIMINATION LESSENING IN THE U.S.?

In the post-World War II period we have annual data on nonwhite and white median incomes.   Between 1947 and 1965 the ratio of nonwhite to white median incomes fluctuated between .51 and .57. During this nineteen-year period, its fluctuations seem random; they have little connection with fluctuations in the unemployment rate or any other likely variable.   In 1965, the ratio was .55.   Then in 1966 it climbed to an unprecedented .60 and it climbed again in 1967 and 1968 to .62 and .63, a 15 per cent increase in four years.[2]   Now it is certainly possible to make too much out of a three-year rise in this ratio, and we will certainly want to watch it closely during the current recession.   Nevertheless, I would like cautiously to suggest that this movement in the ratio represents the first fruit of the agitation of the 1960s in favor of a better deal for black citizens.

Some evidence that is to me even more persuasive is the improvement over the period 1960–1969 in the occupational distribution of black men.   In that period, black men over twenty-five increased their participation in professional and technical occupation by 107 per cent In 1960 black men had 72 per cent of the jobs in such fields that one

[2] *Consumer Income: Income in 1968 of Families and Persons in the United State* (Washington, D.C.: U.S. Bureau of the Census, 1969) .

might have expected them to hold judging from their educational achievement. In 1969, this percentage had risen to 82 per cent. In managerial occupations, participation of black men increased by 117 per cent over this period, with the ratio of actual jobs to expected jobs rising from 27 per cent in 1960 to 36 per cent. Jobs as craftsmen for black men increased 52 per cent over the period and sales jobs by 42 per cent.

An interesting event of the 1960s from our point of view was the desegregation of public accommodations under federal law with remarkably little fuss, showing everyone that changes staunchly resisted in advance can be quite calmly accepted if the force is there to push them. These days even the most hardened racists probably think nothing about sharing restaurants with Negroes. On a much more limited scale, white workers are more or less cheerfully sharing work places with Negroes, although most of those who now do so would have abhorred the idea ten years ago.

Only continued agitation for fair-employment practices and improved enforcement of laws against discrimination will insure the continuance of this trend. However, I think there is good reason to hope that it may accelerate. That hope is based on the nature of the capitalist system. It is good business to sell to blacks and good business to hire them. As time goes on, it will become more and more *respectable* to hire and sell to them with fewer and fewer restrictions. As this happens, good business sense will insure that these opportunities are taken advantage of. Those black men and women modeling clothes in the recent Sears catalogs may have been put there because of threats of boycott. They will probably stay there because it is good business to keep them there.

Finally, capitalists are vitally concerned with the preservation of the system in something like its present form and will give ground if they think they have to. If capitalists are convinced that racial injustice is helping to create resentments which endanger the system, they are sufficiently flexible to do their part to end it. It is up to all of us to keep the pressure on them to see that they do.

QUESTIONS

Racism
Reich / Bergman

1. What accounts for the differences between Reich and Bergmann?
2. Does the exclusion of blacks from certain jobs and from consuming certain items really affect prices?

3. If we include social and psychological benefits along with profit, what effect does this have on Bergmann's idea that rational businessmen wouldn't be racists?

4. Does the methodology of either Bergmann or Reich allow them to ask only certain questions and not others, and to deal with the problem of racism in certain limited ways only?

5. Do "human beings have a tendency to set up hierarchical relationships," or is this merely an outgrowth of particular institutional arrangements?

6. If blacks were not discriminated against, then what group of people would take their place at the bottom of society? Isn't it just a game of musical chairs?

7. Are statistics reliable indicators of the economic status of blacks?

8. Can we end racism in a capitalist society?

9. Doesn't Bergmann assume perfectly competitive markets? Is this a valid assumption in the United States today?

10. What is the gain to a merchant who refuses to sell to certain groups or individuals? What is the gain to landlords who refuse to rent or sell to certain groups or individuals? What is the gain to employers who refuse to employ certain groups of people?

11. How would Reich explain the success of those capitalist countries that are not racist, e.g., Sweden, Norway, Japan, Iceland?

12. Is there any incentive for businessmen to end racism?

Nancy S. Barrett is a graduate of Goucher College and holds an M.A. and Ph.D. degree in economics from Harvard University. She is currently Associate Professor of Economics at The American University and author of The Theory of Macroeconomic Policy.

20 Economics and the Alienation of Women: A Feminine Critique

Nancy S. Barrett

Let us agree at the outset that women are treated differently from men in the American economic system. The median income of women employed full-time in the labor force is substantially below that of men doing similar work and they generally occupy lower-status occupations when equivalent educational and socioeconomic backgrounds are taken into account.

Despite the fact that over one third of working-age women participate in the labor force, the American educational system socializes girls to perform the wife-and-mother role and any job they might decide to perform is to be considered ancillary thereto. However, in a society in which status is largely related to income, the housewife has no status apart from her husband's. Since housewifely activities receive no monetary compensation, they have no status-worth in a society in which value is measured in dollars and cents. This places the woman in a subservient position.

THE ECONOMICS OF DISCRIMINATION AGAINST WOMEN

The idea that "a woman's place is in the home" is at the heart of the differential treatment of women in the economic system. I hesitate to use the word "discrimination" because of its implication that a woman's lot is necessarily inferior to that of her male counterpart in American society. Whether or not women are worse off than men implies a value judgment which I am not prepared to make. Yet it is clear that the belief that a woman should not enter the labor force unless the family is in dire need of supplementary income or until she has reached that point in life that should be (if the system were rational) the pinnacle of her "career" — that point at which her children have left the nest, having been successfully prepared for life under her tutelage — this belief is the essential basis for discrimination against women.

Various agents are at work in our society to imbue in women a sense of guilt if she abandons her family for the labor force. These same agents serve to convince the male (and reinforce his inherent male-chauvinistic attitudes) that a woman has no place in the labor force, at least in jobs that require responsibility, long hours, and a commitment to stability and longevity in service.

Modern theories of child development, epitomized by the work of Dr. Spock, emphasize the necessity of maternal care in the so-called "formative years" of childhood.

In addition, in many high-status occupations, there is paid great lip service to the role of the wife in aiding her husband's career. In many cases, a working wife is viewed as a distinct disadvantage to the husband's ability to succeed in these occupations, although the role of the wife as a participant in the job is limited at best. One has the impression that in such fields as the upper-echelon military establishment, wives' activities are primarily a means of keeping the women occupied while the men pursue their masculine endeavors. Yet the belief is widely held in military circles, that an attractive, home-loving wife is a prime requisite for success in this field.

In view of the conventional ideology that the moral and occupational fiber of American society would indeed collapse if women gave up child-rearing and activities supportive of their husbands' career, it is easy to see how discrimination against women in American industry can be justified. "Discrimination" here is used in a strict economic sense. Suppose a man and a woman both apply for a single job. If the woman is better qualified and the employer selects the man, this is discrimination. From an economic point of view, discrimination must be costly, since an inferior worker was selected. Discrimination also occurs when equally qualified men and women receive different rates of pay for the same work. It is costly to hire men at a higher wage — why not staff the entire operation with lower paid but equally productive women?

Milton Friedman points out that there is an economic incentive in capitalism to separate economic efficiency, or productivity, from other characteristics of an individual.[1] Since an employer must "pay" to discriminate, there must be some perceived benefit to him in doing it.

A principal reason cited for undergoing the cost of discrimination is the idea that a woman's career is necessarily secondary to her duties as wife and mother. If the woman is unmarried, the employer assumes she will quit work when she does marry or at least when she has children. Given the structure of the American social system, this is probably quite true, particularly in the middle- and high-income brackets. Jobs that require long or costly training or familiarization periods are generally given to men. Men acquire seniority and with it, higher income and more status and responsibility. Women who enter the labor force after their children are grown are penalized for lack of experience or, in academic circles, for being "out-of-date." Aspiring young men are always preferred to middle-aged women who are "over the hill." Thus, because of the perceived instability of women as employees, employers view the long-run costs of hiring women to be greater than for men, especially in jobs that require training and experience for proficiency.

In periods of slack economic activity, the unemployment rate for women always rises much faster than the jobless rate for men. This is largely due to the practice of discrimination against women in the belief that women "don't need" jobs as much as men. The same sort of reasoning accounts for lower pay scales for women and slower rates of pay increase. A woman's job is viewed as ancillary to the husband's — anything she makes is icing on the cake. If she is single, her financial needs are also limited. Quite clearly, however, in a society in which status is associated with income, such a practice demeans the position of women in the economic system.

Finally, there is the belief (or contention) held in some quarters that women are actually inferior to men. This is probably the least important of all the bases for discrimination. It is unimportant because it is easily shown to be invalid if equal educational opportunities are taken into account (as was the case with a similar attitude toward blacks and other minority groups) . Furthermore, it is unimportant because it is unnecessary, given the systemic bases for discrimination

[1] Milton Friedman, *Capitalism and Freedom* (Chicago: University of Chicago Press, 1962) , p. 109.

described above. Racial discrimination, based on such a weak reed as a hypothesized "inferiority," can — and to a large degree has been — overcome by an integrated educational system with special opportunities for minority groups to obtain quality university education free of charge. But discrimination against women cannot be eliminated in such a way since it is based on the institution of the family and the peculiar cultural phenomena associated with it in American society.

Occupations which are largely staffed by women reflect the stereotypical view of the feminine role — man's helper and the nurturer of small children. Women are secretaries, nurses, and elementary school teachers. These jobs also reflect the need of women to be able to take on part-time work. Wages in these fields can be lower than those for men because of discrimination in other, male-dominated areas. Because of this discrimination, women view themselves as inferior in the economic system and are willing to work for less pay.

CAN DISCRIMINATION BE ELIMINATED?

Two questions come immediately to mind. First, is there any conceivable way to eliminate discrimination against women in the American economic system? Second, does such discrimination as now exists necessarily place women in an inferior position?

If we accept the proposition that discrimination against women is systemic, then clearly the only way to achieve complete equality for women is either to eliminate the family system as we now know it or to alter radically the role of the woman within the family. The Swedish experiment with shared family responsibilities and shared income — earning responsibilities is a step in the latter direction. To achieve equality, however, such changes cannot be voluntary, that is, a woman must not be allowed to *choose* the traditional role for herself as a wife and mother. If she were to do so, her husband would take on a full-time job in the economic system. And if full-time workers were available, they would receive preferential treatment, more pay and responsibility, and a higher status than part-time workers, male or female. Discrimination would continue in most occupations, although it would be extended to those males who voluntarily assume household duties and offer themselves for part-time employment only.

Furthermore, if she is to be given the option of choosing the traditional role for herself, she must receive some preparation for her role as wife and mother. If the process of sex identification and role socialization is effective it is unlikely that she would avoid the frustration experienced by many women today — the conflict between her desire for intellectual stimulation and her feelings of responsibility to her family — a responsibility that is perceived as nurturant, not economic. A similar conflict, incidentally, is experienced by the traditionally socialized male who attempts to share in the care and upbringing of children — a conflict between his desire for the humanistic ties of the family experience and his feelings of responsibility to his family — a responsibility which is economic, not nurturant.

THE FRUITS OF EQUALITY

This brings us to the second question. What do women want equality for? There is a curious orientation in the growing literature of the women's liberation movement toward *work*. The "liberated" woman enters the labor force and does as much work as her male counterpart. In some cases, women's liberation advocates propose that women should pay alimony and should be obliged to perform military service. It appears that the Protestant Ethic is still one of the most important influences on American intellectual thought. When Nietzsche wrote, "Man is made for war and woman for the recreation of the warrior — all else is folly," male chauvinism was not directly linked to the economic system. Man is a warrior; woman a lover — the roles defined independent of economic production.

When participation in the economic system meant physical drudgery — work in the coal mines and sweatshops that characterized the Industrial Revolution, women's rights movements fought to wrest women from the economic system and to return them to the home.[2] Much of the discriminatory legislation existing today is the result of such efforts.

However, in the modern technological society, participation in the labor force is not backbreaking. Many jobs require a college education. Furthermore, modern household conveniences have given the great majority of American women a good deal of free time, so that once the children are out of diapers, they become bored with suburban living and decide it might be nice to follow a "career" in the economic system.

But what of the economic system? Modern technology has replaced the need for physical exertion with the requirements of participation in huge, faceless bureaucracies. Highly educated bureaucrats sit in identical offices, writing reports and memoranda to each other.

[2] In the Soviet Union today, which is in some respects still in the "heavy industry" stage of its Industrial Revolution, women are purported to have equal status with men. In many cases this condition requires women to perform arduous physical labor.

Competition consists of vying for the privilege of writing these same reports and memoranda to someone of slightly higher status. The scenario need not be described at length here, but the total lack of the humanistic experience, the lack of outlets for creative expression among individuals who purportedly have engaged in the liberalizing experience of university life and, perhaps most important, the lack of any outlet at all for the male to achieve that dominance through aggression for which he has been socialized — all of these things add up to a totally castrating experience for the American male. No wonder he is intolerant of women in his profession — perhaps it is merely a fear that his castration will be exposed to the opposite sex.[3]

Given the economic system in which we operate, is the engineer, physicist, or financial tycoon any less alienated than the suburban housewife? Perhaps the alienation is of a different sort. At least, however, the housewife has one humanistic experience — her relationship to her children. Perhaps this is why the typical American woman takes so much pride in superloving and superdependent children and worries so much about her husband's "need" for her. This, most certainly is a reflection of her alienation just as a certain degree of male-chauvinism may be a reflection of the psychological castration experienced by men in today's supertechnocratic economic environment. To say that a woman's position in today's society is different from a man's is indisputable. To say that it is inferior, however, becomes a normative judgment.

STEPS IN THE RIGHT DIRECTION

Although women are trained for different roles from men in American society, a woman should be able to overcome her socialization and enter the economic system. Women's liberation should strive for changes in the social order that will facilitate this endeavor.

A first step in this direction is to reduce the extent to which the educational system socializes females in the role of nurturant mother and to reduce sex identification associated with certain occupations. If sex-role-identification is less severe, it will be easier to overcome. However, in all fairness, girls should be offered the wife-mother role as the alternative that it is.

To facilitate her entry into the labor force and concomitant exit from the home, low-cost day-care centers should be available and, for

---

[3] It is interesting to observe that many men take pride in their wife's professional career, but are quite intolerant of women in their own field.

the family who believes in Dr. Spock, an income tax deduction for the cost of private child care.   Liberalized abortion and divorce laws would loosen a woman's obligations to in-family service, although such laws should be carefully designed so as not to interfere with a woman's right to economic security or her right to bear children.   Furthermore, more careful scientific studies should be made of the role of the mother in the early psychological development of children.   More opportunities for intellectually stimulating, part-time work should also be made available.

There are still some unanswered questions.   Suppose the society which the "liberated woman" seeks is attained.   Day-care centers are provided, husbands share in the responsibilities of the home, laws prohibiting discrimination against women are passed.   Women join the faceless bureaucracy — undoubtedly in lower-status jobs despite policies of nondiscrimination.   How many of these women could truly free themselves from a culturally imbued belief in feminine responsibility for family nurturance and the frustrations associated with the attempts to succeed in two oft-conflicting roles?   And, when the society of female equality is attained, will a male liberation movement demand equality of opportunity not-to-work?   If so, will the male find himself handicapped as a nurturant — handicapped by the anxiety associated with *his* culturally imbued sense of responsibility for the economic welfare and security of his family?   These are the questions which cannot be answered until the experiment has been undertaken.

QUESTIONS

Women
Barrett / Blackington

1. Are people really alienated from their work?   How can we account for retired workers desiring to continue to work, or for steelworkers who were given sabbaticals and then found a second job?
2. Are most men really worried about the threat of women taking over positions previously only held by men?
3. Are men really insecure because they can no longer justify their dominant role?
4. In what ways has the male been socialized to be aggressive?
5. Has the male been totally "castrated" by his work experience?
6. What does it mean to say that women have inferior status in our society?
7. Were there ever any societies in which women were dominant?
8. Are males dominant in our society?

9. What does it mean to be masculine or feminine?

10. Can we end sexism in a capitalist society?

11. Blackington has argued that men are more alienated than women in the U.S. today. What is going to happen when women achieve equality with men? Will they be as alienated as men are now?

12. Should women be subject to the draft and have to pay alimony?

13. What would happen to productivity in the economy if jobs were divided so that men worked twenty hours a week and their wives worked twenty hours a week and they shared child-rearing responsibilities equally?

14. Is the Women's Liberation Movement devoted to the Protestant Ethic and the idea that to be liberated, women must have employment outside the home?

15. Is economic discrimination against women based on the division of labor?

16. Why is it that some women believe that the roles played by men are more desirable than their own?

SECTION VI

Economic Aspects of United States Foreign Policy

A. Is the United States an Imperialistic Nation?
B. Is the Vietnam War an Outgrowth of the Political-Economic System in the United States?

What is the impact of United States foreign policy on underdeveloped countries? What are the economic aspects of the Vietnam war?

Harry Magdoff asks two questions. What is United States foreign policy? What are the major restraints on modernization of underdeveloped countries? He answers the questions by arguing that United States foreign policy contains two components. The first is the drive to maintain the globe free for private enterprise. The second is the promotion of counterrevolution. Magdoff argues, however, that it is precisely socialist revolutions that are the order of the day in poor countries.

He argues that the capitalist road has led to two results: one, successful capitalist countries where continuous growth has been the rule and secondly, unsuccessful countries that are left with dualistic economies (one part of which is backward and the other part of which is modern) but in which stagnation, illiteracy, and poverty are predominant.

How did the successful capitalist countries develop? They acquired part of their wealth through the slave trade, through piracy, and through pillage. They were able to expand their external and internal markets and bring off agricultural and industrial revolutions in their countries.

The unsuccessful capitalist countries were colonies. The economies in these countries were used to meet the needs of the advanced capitalist countries, i.e., military, trading, and raw material needs. In these unsuccessful countries, there was a weak ruling class, no capitalist class to speak of, and the ruling class allied itself with the ruling class in the colonial countries. Successful capitalism, however, requires independence from the colonial country and the ascendance of a capitalist class. The inability of today's unsuccessful capitalist countries to develop leads them to choose socialism. However, United States foreign policy works (despite our good will and foreign aid) to keep the underdeveloped countries within the existing social framework. The United States is afraid of revolutions. We tolerate military coups but are anxious to prevent sweeping social revolutions. It is thus Magdoff's contention that United States foreign policy is inimical to economic development of today's poor countries.

Benjamin Cohen argues that there are other bases for United States foreign policy than economic considerations. Every nation wants to maximize its power. In a world of anarchy and independent nation-states, it is inevitable for nations to try to achieve maximum power for themselves.

Cohen uses orthodox economics as a framework for studying international economic problems. He defines imperialism as domination of one nation over another. According to that definition, the United States is imperialistic because it does dominate other countries. However, he denies that this domination of other countries leads to exploitation.

In the original discussion, Tom Riddell argued that the war in Vietnam is a natural outgrowth of the political-economic system in the United States. The people who run the country have an intense desire to insure the continuance and the development of capitalism throughout the world. This desire explains our opposition to the expansion of communism and our interference in wars of national liberation.

Riddell's main points can be summarized briefly: the primary effect of the Vietnam war has been inflation. In order to fight this war-induced inflation, our national government has instituted economic policies which have had severe side-effects: unemployment, recession, tight money, high interest rates, and declining housing starts. Although the war has had adverse effects on the economy as a whole, it has been very helpful to some companies.

Leon Keyserling's reply (included in this volume) is a blunt statement of the traditional, liberal view of the national economy's relationship to war and military spending. He argues that inflation, unemployment, and high interest rates are due to unwise economic policies that existed prior to Vietnam. He also argues that slum housing, racism, inadequate schools, etc., are problems that existed long before the war began. In fact, he argues that unemployment would have been even higher today were it not for Vietnam.

Keyserling argues that inflation and unemployment have come about because of the slow rate of economic growth. He proposes full employment and rapid growth policies and calls for a rational debate on the role the United States should play in the world in order to bring about world peace.

The traditional liberal view rides on the assumption that the prosperity of capitalist economies in no way depends on military spending as opposed to other forms of public expenditures. The important point of modern Keynesian macroeconomics is that national prosperity depends on the ability of government to insure a steadily rising level of total spending. Whether expenditures come from private sources or government, military, public works or space programs, makes little difference. Public spending on domestic projects is acceptable and private domestic spending is even better, but increased military spending is, as a last alternative, better than a recession that might result from inadequate spending.

The traditional liberal theory takes into account the spurts in economic growth in the United States which coincided with World War II, the Korean War, and the war in Vietnam. Increases in military spending probably explain the coincidence of war and economic growth. However these wars and the "Cold War" are political accidents, and the world now would be better off if international conditions would have permitted the United States to spend an equal amount on domestic priorities.

Michael Reich presents a radical view of the relationship between the prosperity of capitalist economies and military spending. He argues that inadequate private demand (or "effective demand" in Keynesian terminology) forces capitalist governments to supplement private demand with public expenditures, that military spending is a politically attractive means for capitalist governments to insure rising levels of total annual expenditures, and that increases in public spending on domestic priorities are both more difficult to sell to the voting public and are a potentially damaging intrusion of government into the profit-making interests of capitalists. Thus, given the alternatives of (1) public expenditures for domestic priorities, or (2) military spending, capitalist economic systems are more likely to turn toward military spending.

Harry Magdoff is co-editor, with Paul Sweezy, of the leading American journal of Marxist thought, **Monthly Review.** *He has been a government employee, financial consultant, stockbroker, insurance consultant, publisher, and Professor of Economics at the New School for Social Research. His book* **The Age of Imperialism** *is a basic text for radical analysis of U.S. economic policy toward underdeveloped countries.*

21 The Impact of United States Foreign Policy on Underdeveloped Countries

Harry Magdoff

Compressing an analysis of the impact of United States foreign policy on underdeveloped countries into a twenty-minute presentation must necessarily result in what may appear to be a recitation of dogmatic assertions. This will seem especially so when the position taken flies in the face of conventional wisdom and the common currency of academic discourse. Yet even though such compression involves omission of supporting evidence, steps in the reasoning process, and necessary qualifications, a digest of the main argument may nevertheless help clarify the essential differences between the radical and customary views on the subject.

The crux of my position is that there exists a fundamental clash between United States foreign policy and the interests of the people in the underdeveloped world. To examine the roots of this clash — of what in effect is a conflict of interest — we need first to be clear about the answers to two questions: (1) What is U.S. foreign policy? and (2) What are the major restraints on the modernization of underdeveloped nations?

The stumbling block to answering the first question is that United States foreign policy may at first blush seem to be but a jumble of diverse, bumbling, and contradictory actions and programs. In fact, learned journals specializing in international affairs will at times publish lengthy articles complaining about the absence of a clear-cut foreign policy consistent with avowed principles. But these yearners for consistency overlook, on the one hand, the variety of pressures that contribute to day-to-day policy decisions, and, on the other hand, the inevitable contrast between the ideology and ideals of foreign policy around which public opinion is mobilized and the underlying reality.

Even though the day-to-day policy decisions are the product of numerous, and not necessarily consistent, political, military, and economic variables, and even though these decisions are made by diverse human beings, some competent and some incompetent, a clearly discernible major trend of foreign policy nevertheless does exist. We know from physics and chemistry that elements and compounds will, under certain conditions of volume, pressure, and temperature, assume different phases. But we also know that while water, for example, may under certain conditions appear as steam and, under other conditions, as ice, its inherent nature remains H_2O. A similar essential nature of United States foreign policy can be detected throughout the various phases of hot war, cold war, strident militancy, and moments of hesitation. This major drift of United States foreign policy has two closely related components:

1. A drive to maintain as much of this globe as possible free for private trade and private enterprise. Subsumed under this are such considerations as (a) the prevention of competitive empires from acquiring privileged trading and investment preserves to the disadvantage of United States business interests, and (b) wherever feasible, the attainment of a preferred trading and investment position for United States business.

2. The promotion of counterrevolution. This too is composed of several elements: (a) abortion of incipient social revolutions, (b) suppression of social revolutions in process, and (c) counterrevolution against established socialist societies — through war, economic pressure, or corruption of leaders and nations in the socialist fold.

Such a basic foreign policy is not peculiar to the United States, nor is it a policy peculiar to the post-Second World War period. The conflict of interest among the advanced capitalist nations for the division and redivision of the world has been an integral part of what the textbooks call "modern history," hammered into the annals by two world wars. Nor is the nervous, military reaction to social revolutions merely a current policy aberration. It is now one hundred years since the conquering German army joined forces with the conquered French army to throttle the Paris Commune. Long before the atom bomb was developed and long before the Soviet Union could be considered an effective expansionist power, the Allied Powers at the Versailles Treaty table were plotting the destruction of the infant Bolshevik Revolution. In fact, the United States along with other Allied Powers sent armed forces to join the counterrevolution against the Bolsheviks. It is within this historic context, and the even longer record of expansionism in the growth of our republic, that the consistency of United States foreign policy can be traced.

A foreign policy of this sort has special relevance for the underdeveloped nations because it is precisely social revolution — the nemesis of United States policy — that is the order of the day in the Third World. To appreciate this clash of interests we need to examine the second question raised above: what holds back modernization of the underdeveloped nations?

The usual textbook approach to the industrial backwardness of the Third World is to list a host of twenty, thirty, and more common characteristics of underdevelopment. The trouble with such an approach is that little distinction is made between symptoms and causes. More often than not, in this seemingly hopeless amassing of difficulties, a way out is sought by focusing on a panacea such as population control — and even that panacea is examined as a technical problem, independent of the social and economic environment which contributes to the pressure of population and remains an obstacle to "gimmicky" solutions.

If these long, eclectic arrays of symptoms of underdevelopment have any virtue, it is to illustrate that the problem has deeper roots than, for example, the popularly held notion that lack of natural resources is a major cause of a nation's poverty and stagnation. In fact, there are advanced countries with poor resources and underdeveloped countries with rich natural resources. More important, the very extensiveness of the number of characteristic features of underdevelopment suggests the potential inadequacy of mere tinkering with reforms of existing social structures, and introduces the issue of a need for wholesale restructuring and redirection of these societies.

The main direction of United States academic thought and United States foreign policy, however, is to shrink from the dangerous implications of restructuring social and economic systems. Instead, the focus is on simpler, more comfortable, and safer ways out: population control and the spread of modern technology through foreign investment and foreign aid. The more thoughtful advocates of the population-control remedy recognize that it is far from a cure-all. At best, it is a stop-gap measure (assuming it can work under the existing socioeconomic conditions) to hold the line against a mounting danger of mass starvation in face of the slight progress made in increasing food production.

The more basic remedy is usually identified as the transfer of capital and technology from the rich to the poor nations: a consequence of the conventional diagnosis that the underlying causes of backwardness are the lack of modern technology and the shortage of domestic capital. Such a prescription is clearly consistent with the diagnosis; it is also consistent with the ideology under which United States foreign policy parades. The trouble is that the diagnosis is wrong.

To many in the advanced nations, and especially to those in the United States, technology looms as a talisman, a type of magic art: just let it loose in foreign lands and all the wonders of prosperity will follow. One needs only to reflect a bit on the United States condition to realize how shallow this faith is. Thus, despite the availability of the most advanced technology and despite the large transfers of funds, the Appalachian region remains a major pocket of poverty and underdevelopment. And how far has technology and a surplus of domestic capital gone in solving the poverty of the ghettos?

The dimensions of the poverty problem are much greater, of course, in the underdeveloped nations. But to understand the question of inadequate technology in those regions we have to recognize that technology does not stand alone — it needs people to use it. And it is on the latter we have to concentrate for an answer: the willingness and ability of the people inside the country to apply improved technology that will put the unemployed to work and which will raise the output of the people at work. To take advantage of technology, it is necessary, among other things, to have a literate population, a high social evaluation of science and scientific method, and receptivity on a mass scale to technological innovation. This is especially so because the technology most needed is not arcane computers and complex electronic systems in a few key cities, but an extensive spread of technology throughout the agricultural sector — that sector in which the largest part of the population of the underdeveloped countries is to be found.

This does not mean that more advanced technology could not be used to good advantage. We need to understand though that there is no instant magic, no basic solution to the problems of development, in the wonders of modern science and technology. The requirements in the Third World — where an agricultural as well as an industrial revolution is needed — extend to steel plows, wheel barrows, small pumps, and irrigation systems. The need is not only for equipment, but for selection of seeds and plants and improved techniques in the use of the land. For this, the mass of farmers who till the soil have to be involved. And for this the mass of people have to change.

The crucial obstacles to the changes needed are not to be found in the innate nature of the people, or in special features of their culture, or in their religion. The obstacles, instead, are located in the social institutions under which the people live, in the type of landowning, in the vested interests of the large landowners and businessmen, and in the social priorities imposed by the ruling classes. Let me cite a simple illustration. One of the puzzling aspects of India's economic trials has been the seeming indifference of small farmers to undertake simple work needed to irrigate the land they worked. The Indian government has spent large sums of money to dig broad canals in order to make more water available for farming. But the farmers failed to take advantage of this potential boost to their output; they did not dig the ditches needed to bring the water from the rivers and canals to their small plots. I once asked a leading United States agricultural specialist who had spent a great deal of time in India: what went wrong? was it laziness? stupidity? ignorance? The conservative agronomist laughed at my naive questions. The simplest and most ignorant farmer, he explained patiently, knows the importance of water. But the irrigation ditches had to pass over land owned by big landowners who exacted a tax for the use of the ditches — a tax the farmers could not possibly pay.

Furthermore, given a profit-directed economy along with extensive poverty, there is no percentage in the mass production of improved farm tools, equipment, and chemicals needed for upping farm output. The technology for most of these essential products is not complex, nor are the domestic businessmen stupid. The entrepreneurs do not do what is needed for economic development because there is not enough potential profit in such undertakings, or because they can make more profit in other ventures.

For these reasons, and others, social revolutions are the order of the day for most of the underdeveloped world: social revolutions that remove the power of those classes whose interests are in the status quo; social revolutions that change the social priorities, open the floodgates of education, arouse the enthusiasm of large masses of the people, and change the production structure to produce what is needed for the advancement of the people and not for that which brings the most profit to the property owners.

Once the issue of social revolution is introduced, the capital-shortage factor — a primary canon of economic orthodoxy — assumes a new significance. First, the revolution can quite quickly halt two major sources of waste of capital: a. by severely reducing the consumption of the rich and the better-heeled middle classes, and b. by confiscating foreign-owned investments. Such steps are useful in two ways: a. the profits of agriculture, manufacturing, mining, and commerce can be fully utilized for the most important development projects, and b.

scarce foreign exchange can be more effectively applied to purchase of raw materials and equipment, instead of being drained off for the import of luxuries and for payment of profits, interest, royalties, and management fees to foreign investors.

The second contribution a social revolution makes to the tackling of the capital-shortage obstacle is through mobilization of labor to be used to some degree as a substitute for capital. A great deal of necessary construction, for example, can be obtained this way. Naturally, it would be better to use machinery. But if there is no machinery, and the need is great, the idle and under utilized labor can be used, for example, for road-building, flood control, irrigation works, and housing construction — as was done in the centuries before there were bull-dozers, trucks, cranes, etc. This is not the ideal solution, but it is a solution that faces up to the reality that God helps those who help themselves.

A third contribution to overcoming the capital-shortage problem is the revolution's concentration on education and health for the masses. Aside from humanitarian considerations, improved nutrition and medical care contribute to raising the productivity of labor. Education quite obviously adds to human capital. For many of these countries, the issue is not only the achievement of universal literacy but redirection of the educational priorities from one of training an elite ruling group (schooled in the humanities, law, and medicine) to one that builds on a. science and mathematics needed for mastery of technology and greater self-reliance, and b. politics and economics needed for resourceful and effective economic and social planning. Again, the need is not only for the seemingly esoteric and complex. To advance in scientific farming, farmers who can confidently keep books and do arithmetic are needed. The question we need to ask ourselves is: why in the twentieth century it has taken social revolutions to make the most dramatic leaps in health and education for the vast majority of the population?

From whichever angle we approach the problem of development, we hit against the limits imposed by the established social institutions and the priorities (or values, if you wish) protected by the existing ruling classes. And these are the very ruling classes that are protected and nurtured by the advanced capitalist nations — most particularly in these days, by the military and foreign policy of the United States. The social systems of the underdeveloped countries have a long history, one that is dominated by the colonial and semicolonial arrangements imposed under the *force majeure* of the successful and rich capitalist nations. Primarily by force, but perpetuated by resulting economic relations, the Third World was converted into becoming primarily a supplier of raw materials and food for the metropolitan centers, and a buyer, to the extent its resources permitted, of the manufactured goods produced in the industrialized nations. The resulting economic structure created at one and the same time a. an economy whose resources are bent to supply the needs of the industrialized nations, and b. ruling classes whose prosperity, whether they like it or not, stems from a perpetuation of this dependency: in short, a subservient component of the imperialist network of trade and investment.

A new departure toward development, instead of underdevelopment, entails a restructuring of these industrially backward economies to obtain greater flexibility and a more effective use of their own resources, a redirection of their societies to meet the needs of the people rather than to foster the prosperity of the wealthy at home and abroad. Necessarily contained in this new departure is, in addition, a release from the psychological dependence on the culture and "superiority" of the advanced nations, along with the blossoming in the population as a whole of self-confidence, self-reliance, and independence in thought and action. By exerting its efforts to contain the revolutionary impulse that seeks to free itself from the material and psychological bonds of imperialism, United States foreign policy (including its military posture and action), in effect, is the primary obstacle to the development of the underdeveloped nations.

Benjamin J. Cohen received his
A.B. and Ph.D. degrees from Co-
lumbia University and is currently
an Associate Professor of Economics
at the Fletcher School of Law and
Diplomacy at Tufts University.
He is the author of several books
and articles focusing on the inter-
national monetary system, including
The Future of Sterling as an In-
ternational Currency.

22 On United States "Imperialism"

Benjamin J. Cohen

I.

Our subject is: "The impact of United States foreign policy on under-developed countries." I shall take as my principal texts *The Age of Imperialism* by Harry Magdoff and *Monopoly Capital* by Baran and Sweezy. Together, these two sources comprise an unusually coherent expression of the modern Marxist view of American policy in the Third World.

According to this view, American policy in the Third World is distinctly "imperialistic." This results from the nature of the modern capitalist system, of which the United States happens to be the arche-typical example. The line of argument goes like this. Modern capitalism is monopoly capitalism. Monopoly capitalism tends to generate an ever-increasing economic surplus. The central problem of modern capitalism, therefore, is to find ways to absorb or utilize its economic surplus. Absorption of the surplus via capitalist consumption or investment, however, is ruled out as unlikely; and absorption via government spending of a nonmilitary nature is ruled out as impossible. That leaves government spending of a military nature — which is really quite convenient, because a vast military establishment also just happens to coincide with the perceived class interest of the oligarchy. The class interest of the oligarchy, the monopoly capitalists, is to grow and expand — to continually search for new sources of supply, for new markets, for new investment outlets. Monopoly capital's goal, eventually, is to dominate and control the world market and raw material sources — and what could be more useful for this purpose than a large military establishment dedicated to the preservation of what is conventionally called "the free-enterprise system"?

In short, United States policy is imperialistic because it has to be. It is imperialistic because the economic surplus has to be absorbed, and because the monopolistic position of United States business abroad had to be protected. In Harry Magdoff's words (slightly rephrased):

The tap-root of United States foreign policy is to be found in modern imperialism, in capitalism as an expansionist system. . . . Imperialism is not a matter of choice for capitalist society; it is the way of life of such a society.

This is what Mr. Magdoff calls the "imperialism hypothesis."

Now, the imperialism hypothesis is by no means as solidly founded, either in fact or in logic, as one might infer from reading *The Age of Imperialism* or *Monopoly Capital*. It is, in fact, suspect at a number of points. The notion of economic surplus, for instance, is never adequately spelled out in these sources, nor is the argument why the economic surplus must continually grow both absolutely and relatively (as a share of total output) as the capitalist system develops. Nor are the sources very convincing in arguing why military spending, and military spending alone, can be relied upon to absorb the economic surplus; or why government policy can be relied upon always to act in support of business interests abroad. I remain unconvinced on all these points, although I shall not discuss them in detail here. That is not what this debate is about.

What *is* solidly founded in fact is that the United States is extensively involved in the Third World; one need only read Mr. Magdoff's heavily documented book to be convinced on that score. Moreover, it *is* solidly founded in fact that many describe United States policy in the Third World as "imperialistic"; one need only read Mr. Magdoff's book to be convinced on that score also. But the problem is whether that is a fair description. Is the impact of United States policy in the Third World really "imperialistic"? *That* is what this paper is about.

II.

To answer the question, we must first ask what is meant by imperialism. Unfortunately, imperialism is one of those words, like liberal or conservative or communist (or hippie), whose precise meaning has long since been lost sight of. Once it was used to describe a specific historical phenomenon; at present it means virtually all things to all men. As a technical tool of analysis it no longer has any use at all. "Imperialism is no word for scholars," wrote one scholar. The word has become too emotive, too value-laden, too much tied up with political battles and propaganda, too much of a slogan. Indeed, for some it has actually become a swearword, a term of opprobrium exceeded in obloquy only by some of the very choicest among the famous four-letter words of the English language.

Originally, the term imperialism was connected with the Latin word *imperator* and was usually associated with the ideas of dictatorial power, highly centralized government, and arbitrary methods of administration. In modern times the term was first employed by a group of British writers and administrators in the late 1870s — men who were advocates of the strengthening and expansion of the British colonial empire; imperialism was the name they gave to the policy they were urging on the British public. Likewise, imperialism was the name given to the policy of colonial expansion being advocated elsewhere in Europe as well. Toward the end of the century the meaning of the term was clear; it was equivalent to "colonialism" — the establishment and extension of the political sovereignty of one nation over alien peoples and territories.

But then along came the critics of capitalism — Marxists like Kautsky, Rosa Luxemburg, Hilferding, and Lenin; and liberals like the Englishman John Hobson. Emphasis soon shifted from straightforward political relationships to more subtle economic forces and motivations — from simple colonialism to more complex forms of economic penetration and domination of markets, sources of supply, and investment outlets. The shift of emphasis was further stimulated in the post-World War II period by the gradual disappearance of most colonial empires of the more traditional political kind. Today it is impossible to speak of imperialism at all without at least some reference to the economics of the matter. Certainly it would be impossible to speak of the Baran-Sweezy-Magdoff imperialism hypothesis without some reference to the economics of the matter.

To my mind, the irreducible core of meaning in the word imperialism is *domination* — the domination of one nation over another. The form of domination may be direct or indirect, its object may be political or economic. However, whatever its form or object, its essence is plain. It is *power* — the power to influence and ultimately to control.

According to the imperialism hypothesis, the form of domination by the United States in the Third World is principally indirect and principally economic. The object is exploitation. That is, the United States has an empire, but the empire exists informally rather than formally; and it exists because of the nature of the American economic system rather than because of the character of the international political system. The object of the empire is to exploit markets and sources of supply to the advantage of American business. Underdeveloped countries are forced into a position of dependence for the sake of monpoly capital.

In short, American imperialism expresses itself as a simple equation: imperialism equals dependence plus exploitation. That, according to the modern Marxist view, describes the impact of United States policy on underdeveloped countries. The question before us is whether that is an accurate description of the impact of United State policy. *Is* the Third World uniquely dependent on the United States? *Is* the Third World exploited by the United States? Let us take these questions one at a time.

III.

Consider, first, the question of dependence. To begin with, it should be emphasized that there is no connotation of shame in this notion. Dependence is simply the price one pays for the benefit of a division of labor. Independence is possible only in isolation. Dependence follows automatically from participation in any system of interrelationships. This is as true of the individual family as it is of the family of nations. All participants are dependent to a greater or lesser extent.

But there is the catch: "to a greater or lesser extent." Like Orwell's equals, in any system of interrelationships some participants are more dependent than others. This is also as true of the individual family as it is of the family of nations. It is even more important at the international than at the personal level because of the nature of the world system, which is basically one of anarchy and competing sovereignties. Unlike the individual family member, the individual nation-state cannot typically take survival for granted. Each state's sovereignty and security, its territorial integrity and political independence, are by definition perpetually being threatened. Each state's response is to seek to enhance its security by broadening its range of foreign-policy options to the maximum degree feasible — in other words, to maximize its international power position, since power sets the limits to its range of choice among policies and strategies. Power takes the form of the ability to control, or at least to influence, the behavior of other states. The source of power is the mutual dependence inherent in the international system itself.

The dependence of one state on another gives the latter influence through its control over that for which the former depends on it. That is, if country A depends on country B for, say, oil, B can influence A thought its ability to control — and *in extremis* to halt — the flow of oil to A. True, B may do itself harm in the process. But if in greater measure A requires oil and cannot locate alternative sources of supply, B's influence over A is effective. Here is the essential source of power which states acquire in the international system: the capacity to interrupt vital relationships, particularly relationships of a commercial or financial character.

Now, no one would deny that many countries of the Third World, and especially most countries of Latin America, are dependent on the United States. They depend on us as a market for their goods, as a source of industrial imports, as a supplier of vital capital. But dependence is, as I have indicated, a two-way street: the United States is dependent on the Third World as well. Indeed, if the imperialism hypothesis is correct, the United States may be even more dependent on the underdeveloped countries than they are on us. For if the modern Marxists are correct, the American system as we know it could not survive without the markets, the raw materials, and the investment outlets provided by the Third World. If these relationships were to be interrupted or halted in any manner, we would presumably be in a very bad way indeed. My example of oil was not chosen lightly.

To be sure, the United States also benefits from the divisions of the Third World. We are able to play one country off against another, according to the time-honored principle of divide and rule. Vis-à-vis single underdeveloped countries, therefore, the United States is generally able to maintain a position of dominance rather than dependence. But the point is, this has little or nothing to do with economics per se. It is, as I have argued, simply a function of the international political system in which we live — an anarchic system of competing sovereignties in which power politics must predominate. All nations behave the way the United States behaves — even socialist nations. All nations seek to minimize their own dependence on others, and where possible to maximize their own dominance abroad. The Soviet Union seeks to exert dominance over dependent countries, just as we do — and for similar reasons. What real difference was there, after all, between our intervention in the Dominican Republic and Soviet intervention in Czechoslovakia? What real difference was there between Vietnam and Hungary? All were examples of dominance being enforced by a Great Power within its own roughly defined sphere of influence.

In short, my argument is this: yes, much of the Third World, at least as it is in its presently divided condition, is dependent on the United States; but no, this dependence is not unique. One of the most useful laws of science is the so-called Law of Parsimony, or Occam's Razor. This dictates that one cannot explain a behavioral phenomenon by a higher, more complex process if a lower or simpler one will do. What I am arguing here is that the subtle and complex reasoning of the imperialism hypothesis is unncessary to explain the enforcement of Third-World dependence by the United States. A less complex explanation will do — namely, an explanation based simply on the obvious nature of the international political system in which we live.

IV.

What, then, about exploitation? Writers like Mr. Magdoff, I suspect, would not necessarily disagree with my argument that dominance and dependence are a way of life in our contemporary international system. Nevertheless, they would undoubtedly argue that there is still something unique about the dependence forced on underdeveloped countries by the United States and other capitalist countries — something that cannot be explained or understood *except* by reference to the subtle and complex reasoning of the imperialism hypothesis; the Law of Parsimony simply will not suffice in this case. That special "something," of course, is the perceived *object* of United States dominance — namely, economic exploitation. That, supposedly, is what makes the impact of American policy on the Third World so painfully distinctive. Hence the question remains to be answered: is the Third World exploited by the United States?

Certainly the *opportunity* for exploitation by the United States does exist. The opportunity for exploitation always exists in any situation of asymmetrical dependence. And I have already admitted that America's position in relation to the Third World is decidedly one of dominance rather than dependence. But does this mean that this country *uses* its opportunity for exploitation? That is another matter entirely. Basically, it depends on what one means by exploitation.

According to some writers, exploitation simply means "utilization for one's own advantage or profit." But if that is the meaning we choose, then we must conclude that exploitation is one of the most ubiquitous of all human conditions, for only saints and fools ever enter into interrelationships with absolutely no thought at all of some sort of personal aggrandizement.   Ordinary mortals — and states — naturally expect something of value, some advantage or profit, to result from social intercourse.   Otherwise, they would be hermits.

A more reasonable definition of exploitation would add the adjective "unfair"; exploitation means *"unfair* utilization for one's own advantage or profit."   This means, of course, that there can be no such thing as an objective definition of exploitation.   The word "unfair" obviously implies an ethical or value judgment.   It follows that only a *normative* definition of exploitation is possible.   It also follows that there can be no agreement at all regarding whether exploitation even exists unless there first is prior agreement or consensus on the relevant normative beliefs.

We have now arrived at a crucial juncture — and it is at precisely this point that I and Mr. Magdoff begin to part company.   For between Marxist writers such as Mr. Magdoff on the one hand, and non-Marxists such as myself on the other, there is no common agreement on the relevant normative beliefs.   Marxists tend to believe in the inevitability of conflict of interests, at least under capitalist conditions: someone — some individual, some group, some nation — is thought always to gain, someone else is thought always to lose, within the context of a free-enterprise system.   This follows directly from the Marxist theory of value, which insists that the labor power of workers produces more in value than it receives in wage payments, the resulting surplus being appropriated by the owners of the means of production.   In the words of one writer: "Capitalist relations in all cases result in exploitation."

Non-Marxists, by contrast, unimpressed by this outlook, tend to deny that the interests of individuals or groups or nations are so much in conflict.   Interests may not exactly be harmonious, but at least they are thought to be reconcilable.   Not all parties may gain from capitalist relations, but certainly no one is presumed to lose *by definition*. Whether exploitation exists is assumed to be an empirical question, not a foregone conclusion.

How do non-Marxists identify exploitation?   If the concept is to have any meaning at all, it must be defined in terms of opportunity cost.   A relationship may be considered exploitative if the rate of return to one of the parties — its wage or price, in other words its income — falls below what the party could obtain in the absence of that relationship.   Exploitation exists, in other words, whenever the terms of trade are inadequate — inadequacy being determined by reference to alternative opportunities.

By reference to this standard, are undeveloped countries being exploited by the United States? Obviously, this is not an easy question to answer: it is like asking what history would have been like if things had been different. Still, there is a strong presumption that, by this standard, the answer to this question must, in the majority of cases, be no. Most underdeveloped countries are probably better rather than worse off — that is, more highly developed in economic terms — than they would have been had they never entered into economic intercourse with the United States (and other capitalist countries) in the first place. True, many of them have developed in a very lopsided fashion; true, many of them still get unsatisfactory prices for their raw material exports or find market access difficult for their manufactured goods. But are we really to believe that these countries would have grown more rapidly in isolation from the capitalist world — without capitalist markets or investment goods, without capitalist technology or money? I rather doubt it.

Marxists, by contrast, do not doubt it for a minute. It is precisely Mr. Magdoff's point, for instance, in *The Age of Imperialism,* that capitalist relations *do* prevent the underdeveloped countries from growing more rapidly:

> The integration of less developed capitalisms into the market as reliable and continuous suppliers of their natural resources results, with rare exceptions, in a continuous dependency on the centers of monopoly control that is sanctified and cemented by the market structure which evolves from this very dependency. Integration into world capitalist markets has almost uniform effects on the supplying countries: 1. they depart from, or never enter, the paths of development that require independence and self-reliance; 2. they lose their economic self-sufficiency and become dependent on exports for their economic viability; 3. their industrial structure becomes adapted to the needs of supplying specialized exports at prices acceptable to the buyers, reducing thereby such flexibility of productive resources as is needed for a diversified and growing economic productivity (197) .

The fallacy of Mr. Magdoff's reasoning is not difficult to find. It is that integration into the world economy is always a bad thing, self-sufficiency always a good thing: external dependence inhibits development, self-reliance promotes it. But this just is not so in most cases. It may have been so for the Soviet Union, which covers one sixth of the world's surface and is uniquely endowed to develop by autarkic methods; it may turn out to be so for China as well. But as Cuba and the countries of Eastern Europe have learned the hard way, it is not so for less well endowed nations. In fact, integration into the world economy can promote rather than inhibit rapid economic development. Otherwise, how can we explain the dramatic success over the last century and a half of the countries of northwestern Europe, North America, Japan, and Australia?   All of these areas were still underdeveloped when Britain, having begun the Industrial Revolution, was already considered an imperial power.   All were themselves able to initiate takeoff into economic development only because of the stimulus provided by foreign markets and foreign capital (in particular, of course, British markets and British capital) — in other words, precisely *because* they became integrated into the world economy.   Likewise, many other countries elsewhere in the world — such as Mexico, Venezuela, Brazil, Chile, Turkey, Israel, Pakistan, Taiwan, Hong Kong, Korea — are currently experiencing a takeoff into economic development precisely because of their integration into the world economy.   Dependence, as I have already suggested, is not necessarily shameful.   It is, to repeat, simply the price one pays for the benefits of division of labor.   And in cases such as those cited, the benefits in terms of economic development have far exceeded any costs involved.

This is not to deny that in other cases benefits may have fallen short of costs.   In fact, there are a number of countries, especially in Africa but also elsewhere, which have little to show but stagnation for their part in the world economy.   Exploitation in these cases does not seem an inappropriate description.   But it is hardly appropriate to generalize from these experiences to the experience of the Third World as a whole.   Nothing could be more seriously misleading.

Basically, the problem with Marxist writers such as Mr. Magdoff is that they assume, in effect, that dependence and exploitation are identical.   It is not the latter they are objecting to: it is the former.   They see that most underdeveloped countries are in a dependent relationship vis-à-vis the United States.   Being Marxists, they therefore conclude that these countries must also be exploited by the United States.   Their argument, in other words, is tautological, and my point is that the tautology is fallacious.   Dependence creates the *opportunity* for exploitation, it does not create the *necessity* of exploitation; and in fact many underdeveloped countries are clearly *not* being exploited by the United States in any meaningful sense, even though they are dependent on us.

Conversely, some countries dependent on the Soviet Union are clearly being exploited to the advantage of the Russian economy, even though these are not capitalist societies.   It is well known that higher prices are charged for exports to the countries of Eastern Europe, and lower prices are paid for imports, than would obtain if these nations could trade freely with the West.   That is not to say that a socialist society necessarily generates exploitation, any more than a capitalist society necessarily does.   It is only to say, once again, that dependence generates an opportunity for exploitation — and in the case of her Eastern European dependencies, Russia has seized the opportunity.

In short, what I am arguing is that there is nothing unique about the dependence forced on underdeveloped countries by the United States and other capitalist countries; there is nothing unique about the object of this dominance.   Yes, the United States and some other capitalist countries are imperialistic, but so too are other nations, the Soviet Union not excluded.   The reasons for all these imperialisms are everywhere the same — namely, the competition of sovereignties inherent in the international political system.   The Law of Parsimony does suffice in this case after all.   The Baran-Sweezy-Magdoff imperialism hypothesis adds no additional insight.

QUESTIONS

Imperialism
Magdoff / Cohen

1. Why is that Magdoff and Cohen come to such different conclusions?

2. Cohen states that the United States has the power to be imperialistic, to exploit the underdeveloped countries, but that it doesn't exploit them.   If this is so, then why doesn't the United States use its power?

3. Are the underdeveloped countries really better off now than they were before contact with the West as Cohen argues?

4. Is foreign policy mainly motivated by rational economic self-interest as Magdoff claims?   Doesn't the belief that ours is the best system play some role in this process, i.e., what is the role of ideology?

5. Does it make any economic difference to poor countries whether United States foreign policy is based on rational economic calculation or on ideological bases?

6. Who receives the benefits of United States foreign economic policy — the country as a whole or specific business interests?

7. Why do nations seek power or seek to control and influence other nations?

8. What is the basis of a nation's power in the world?   With what economic system did we see the development of nation states?

9. Isn't there a connection between dependence and dominance? Isn't it true that the more dependent you are the more likely you are to be dominated?

10. Isn't it misleading to talk in terms of benefits to nation-states, when policy and decision making is carried out by certain class or group interests both in the United States and in the underdeveloped nations?   The United States may be exploiting an underdeveloped

country as a whole, but may not this still be beneficial to certain interests within the underdeveloped countries?

11. Is the present world division of labor a "natural" one based on comparative advantage or an artificial one created by the dominant industrial nations?

12. What is the economic impact of United States foreign policy?

13. Is the United States really counterrevolutionary?

14. How does Magdoff explain the economic growth of those countries tied into the international capitalist economy, e.g., Mexico, Taiwan, Korea, Brazil, etc.?

15. Is the United States really dependent on underdeveloped countries?

16. Is the United States dependent upon Third World countries for their markets and raw materials?

17. Cohen argues that the rich countries are also dependent on the poor ones. Isn't there a difference between the slave's dependence upon the master and the master's dependence on the slave?

18. Is the United States an imperialistic nation?

19. Is it not the nature of exchange that both parties gain in an exchange?

20. Are there alternatives for underdeveloped countries today?

21. How would Magdoff explain the imperialism of precapitalist societies?

22. Is the Soviet Union an imperialist power?

23. What mechanism is there in the present situation which will redress the present inequality between the nations of the world?

Leon H. Keyserling served as Chairman of the Council of Economic Advisors during the administration of President Truman. He came to this position after serving as Legislative Assistant to Senator Robert Wagner, as Deputy Administrator of the United States Housing Authority, and as General Counsel of the National Housing Agency. He grew up in South Carolina and received his A.B. from Columbia and his law degree from Harvard. He is presently a consulting economist and attorney and President of the Conference on Economic Progress.

23 Economics and the War in Vietnam

Leon H. Keyserling

I hope that at no stage in the proceedings this afternoon will I be engaged in a debate of any kind with my friendly participant in the program, because I do not regard him as a perpetrator of any evil of any kind whatsoever. He is merely the victim of what has happened to our thinking since the commencement of the war in Vietnam. Perhaps I might tell a little story about how I feel when I consider what has happened.

There was a not very distinguished college which had a football team that won the national championship and then they won the Rose Bowl game. But of the eleven varsity players on the team, seven of them were seniors, and when they came to the final exams, all seven of the seniors flunked. So the President of the college called the leading members of the faculty and said, "Say, we've got a bad situation here. Nobody has ever heard of our college, but everybody's heard of our football team. What are we going to do? Besides, the football team brings in most of the money for the college." So the faculty said,

"What can we do?" The President said, "I have an idea. We will call these seniors into my office. We will ask them a few simple questions which they will undoubtedly be able to answer, and then we will be able to give them their degrees." So the meeting was held, and at first, the quarterback was called. He was really dazzling, he was world famous. The question was put to him, "Mr. Struttlemeyer, what is ten and five?" Struttlemeyer answered just like that, "Nineteen." The faculty was nonplused. But the President of the college said, "Well, now, Struttlemeyer was under a little pressure. Let him go out in the hall and think about this a little bit and we will bring him in again." So they called the fullback, Mr. Rupplemeyer. They said, "Mr. Rupplemeyer, what is ten and five?" He said, "Eighteen." So, the faculty was more and more worried. They sent Mr. Rupplemeyer out. They brought Struttlemeyer back in. They said, "Now you've had a chance to think it over. What is ten and five?" Struttlemeyer answered just like that, "Eighteen." So they sent him out again, and the faculty said to the college President, "You see, there is nothing that can be done about this." The college President said, "Oh, I think you are too hard on the chap. After all, the second time, he only missed it by one." I feel that way when I hear some of the current discussions about national policies. And here's why.

Now for two equally important observations about the American economy. First — and I am not going to attempt to document this — we have within my adult lifetime, although not within yours, made far more economic progress, far more social progress, far more civil progress, far more progress in the equitable distribution of income, than any country has made in the history of the world. And this is based on data that I am not going to attempt to review, although I will be glad to do so during the question period. This is one side of the coin. It is important because, unless we recognize this, we lose hope for a positive, affirmative future program because we would have no basis for believing that progress can be made if progress had not been made.

But second, on the other side of the coin, and I don't need to document this either, because I don't know anybody who has said more about it than I have, we are far behind most industrial nations in meeting our economic responsibilities, our human responsibilities, our social responsibilities, relative to our resources, relative to the progress we have made, relative to our knowledge, and relative to what we can do. We have to bear these two sides of the coin equally in mind.

Now, I come to the war in Vietnam, and I would not dream for a moment of discussing here the merits or demerits of that war. Let us assume, for the purposes of our discussion here today, that I agree with the clear majority sentiment within this room about the war in Vietnam. Let us just assume that and get that off the subject of debate.

But it really has nothing to do with what I am here to discuss today. For my concern here today is that the debate which has surrounded the war in Vietnam has so deteriorated on all sides, that everyone, in his desire to support his side, introduces arguments that are irrelevant, immaterial, and probably untrue. And the most extreme of these errors is the argument that either economically, socially, morally, or politically, the reason why we have inflation, or the reason why we are neglecting our great domestic priorities is because of the war in Vietnam.

This has two dangers. The first danger is that, if we ascribe the wrong cause, we are not going to think constructively about the right remedy. In fact, the acceptance by liberals and progressives of all ages that the war in Vietnam is the reason why we are not doing what we should now be doing at home translates itself almost automatically into a tacit, or implicit, or subconscious agreement on the part of these very people to join hands with the most profound reactionaries in the country in accepting the proposition that we should not or cannot be doing more about these things now because we are in the war in Vietnam. This is the first evil result of this approach.

The second evil result of this approach is in international affairs. It is my firm conviction that the greatest single problem in the world confronting the American people is in the area of international affairs. You know, we are a very volatile people. For a few years, we swing along in one direction and view the important issues in one way, and then we swing along in another way and say the all important issue is an opposite way. I would be perfectly willing to be moderately complacent that the American people and American economy will work out their domestic affairs, although as I said, I am not satisfied with the way they are going now. But I am most concerned about everybody being blown up. When I see the great powers of the world, including the United States, including the Soviet Union, including China, including many others, engaged in an ever-accelerating arms race, I am primarily concerned about the international situation.

Therefore, any debate about the international situation, any debate about whether we should be in Vietnam or whether we should not be in Vietnam, should not be conducted on the false grounds that this is why we are not serving our domestic needs. It should be debated on the ground of what is a sound and intelligent and peace-promoting policy for the United States. A peace-promoting policy does not consist merely of saying we want peace. A peace-promoting policy does not consist solely of saying, let's get out of Vietnam as rapidly as possible. It does not even consist of saying, let us unilaterally resolve to end the war as rapidly as possible, whatever anybody else may do.

A practical peace-pursuing policy consists of saying, here's the kind of world we live in, and what kind of international policy is likely to work in this difficult world? This might involve sometime, some resistance at some places to aggressors, or it might not. It may involve a large or a small military establishment. It may or not may involve new types of weapons, or the abandonment of new types of weapons. It may involve intercontinental ballistic weaponry, or it may not. All these subjects need to be discussed and weighed by the intelligent citizenry. But such meaningful debate has been set aside largely, such debate has been forgotten largely, and we are caught up in a massive movement which says, let's forget about these things, and let's not really discuss these things on their merits. Let's talk instead about the effect of the war in Vietnam upon our domestic situation.

This is bound to divide the nation, because there will always be some people who think the problem of peace and international security is a real problem. And when they are confronted by those who say, "You have to abandon that interest in order to remove the slums in Harlem," they won't agree. There is no use telling the slumdwellers, the whites as well as well as the blacks, you've got to wait to have the slums attended to until the war in Vietnam is over. They are two separate issues.

Why are they two separate issues? Let's take the economic aspects. Everything that has been said here today, to the effect that the war in Vietnam has caused the vast inflation is, in my view at least, quite incorrect. What causes inflation? At least according to the thesis advanced by the previous speaker, inflation is caused by an added demand upon the economy which brings spending power above normal productive capabilities. Then there are too many dollars chasing too few goods. That this is the cause of inflation is the general thesis. It is conventional economics.

A good example of this was World War II. In World War II, we had a real economic growth of 9 per cent a year. In World War II, we brought unemployment down to less than 1 per cent. In World War II we had a $50 billion annual increase in the federal budget. In World War II, we were burning up more than half of our goods for noncivilian use. This produced a classic inflation, although I must say, after a short time in World War II, by equitable, sound, and vigorous policies, we controlled inflation. That's the kind of inflation people are talking about when they talk about the inflation caused by Vietnam.

Thus, we are told that the increased war expenditures for Vietnam in 1966 were imposed upon an overheated economy, and overstrained economy, and that this is what caused the inflation. But the economic facts do not bear this out. What's happened from 1966 to the third quarter of 1970? The economic growth rate, which was 5 per cent a year for several years just previously, has averaged only 2½ per cent annually since 1966. It sunk to 2 per cent from 1968 to now. It sunk to −0.5 per cent during the most recent year. We were in an absolute economic recession during the past year. During the past year, unemployment, instead of being reduced to 1 per cent as during World War II, has increased by 66 per cent. Plants are operating at 77 per cent of capacity, when 92 per cent would be normal. So how has the inflation been caused by excessive demand, in turn caused by the increased spending for the war in Vietnam?

As a matter of fact, if you go back to the history of four years ago, it was perfectly clear in 1966 that we were just around the corner from another economic recession because of the bad economics of the "New Economics." The only way we were saved from that recession at that time was because of the increased spending for the war in Vietnam. Now, I am not saying that increased spending for war is the right way to straighten out the economy, if, on the grounds of sound international policy, we should not have gone to war.

But the fact remains that, from 1966 forward, we had four years of stagnation. We have had economic recession. We have had vastly rising unemployment despite the increased spending in Vietnam, and, other things being equal, we would have had more unemployment and still sooner but for the war in Vietnam. This is a sad commentary on how our national policies operate, but that is the case. There is no merit whatsoever for the proposition that we have unusual inflation because of the war in Vietnam.

I could also discuss what we mean by inflation, and what its effects are. Take the statement that inflation is an evil and that everybody bears the burden of it. Well, we have had inflation since the time of George Washington, and if inflation *per se* were just a burden, I could easily prove that the American people have borne a burden that runs to trillions of dollars since the time of George Washington. How then did we build our uniquely productive economy and uniquely high living standards? The really crucial issue is not simply whether or not prices are rising. The crucial issue is whether they are rising in consequence of programs of value to the people, or rising in consequence of the kind of erroneous monetary and fiscal policies we have had since 1966 and earlier. The real problem is actually distribution of income, and almost nobody wants to talk about that.

I come to the final point really, which is: Has the war in Vietnam had anything much to do with the neglect of our great domestic priorities? This is the argument advanced by those who say that, *because* of this war, we have been neglectful of the domestic scene. But let's look at it realistically. From the economic point of view, a war forces us to be neglectful of the domestic scene only if the war is preempting such a large part of our resources that we don't have enough left over to do the domestic job. This was true in World War II. We had to stop housing during World War II. But how can a war be preempting enough of our resources to prevent us from doing the domestic job, when the unused productive resources of the United States are enough to cover several times the cost of the job we are not doing, and when the economy since the beginning of the war in Vietnam (even with the stagnation) has grown far more than the cost of that war so we have more to work with domestically now than we had at the beginning of that war?

What is the real reason we are neglecting the domestic job? Let's take the programs one by one.

We are not neglecting housing because of the war in Vietnam. I helped write, in 1949, the great Housing Act that promised a decent home to every American family in twenty years. You know the highest we ever got in housing for low-income people before the war in Vietnam? Less than 75,000 units a year, when we admitted that we needed 200,000 a year in 1949. And adjusting for growing population and wealth, we now need 400,000 a year. The neglect was just about as great before the Vietnam war as since the war started. After a twenty-year neglect, during which the slums have grown as fast as they have been cleared, how can you blame slums on the war in Vietnam?

Take the matter of tax policy. In 1964, we were really not in the war in Vietnam yet. And yet, we enacted a tax bill, which I opposed at the time, which reduced taxes by $20,000,000,000 annual rate, and gave most of the benefits to those who needed it least, and the least to those who needed it most, whether we consider tax policy on social grounds or consider what kind of tax policy is good for the economy. And everything that has happened since has borne out my opposition to that tax reduction.

This immense error was not because of the war in Vietnam. We should, at that time, if we were really concerned about our domestic priorities, have stimulated the economy by spending money for schools, to reduce poverty, to provide health services, and for all the other things we so seriously need, instead of handing out bonanzas to people who had tremendous incomes, or handing it out to corporations who were overinvesting already. So that was not due to the war in Vietnam.

Take the tight money and rising interest rate policies. The rising interest rates are not due to the war in Vietnam. You can go back to 1964, which was really before the war in Vietnam, and the book I published then told about the rising interest rates. You can go back to John F. Kennedy's campaign in 1960 — one of the two big issues in his domestic campaign was tight money and rising interest rates. I started fighting that issue in 1952 when the Treasury and the Federal Reserve reached their so-called accord, whereby we started a policy of tight money and rising interest rates which we had not had before, and which we did not have during World War II. With all the demand for money and all the capital investment and the 9 per cent rate of economic growth during World War II, we held interest rates stable and low, because it was the national policy and the national conscience to do so. The rising interest rates since 1952, which accelerated in 1969 and 1970, but actually fell slightly in the fall of 1970, despite the war in Vietnam, had nothing to do with the war in Vietnam.

This money policy has been a complete turning back of the clock on the low interest rate, liberal money policy that was one of the greatest single reforms of the New Deal. This has nothing to do with the war in Vietnam. The banks who have benefited most by the high interest rates are hardly a part of the military-industrial complex. The Federal Reserve Board is not part of that complex.

The unemployment certainly is not due to the war in Vietnam. But for Vietnam, there would be more unemployment, other things being equal.

Let's go back a little further and recall the whole area of civil rights and equality of treatment. I happened to grow up in South Carolina. I lived there. I remember back fifty-eight years. I remember when I used to go to the courthouse there, because I was interested in the murder trials, and always it was a white man who had killed a Negro, and the judge would charge the jury, saying, "Remember, a white man has never been convicted of killing a Negro in South Carolina." As young as I was, I wondered whether the judge was directing the acquittal or whether the judge was asking the jury at long last to do its duty.

The Negroes could not walk on the same side of the sidewalk as the white people. We built a Carnegie library, then imposed a local tax, and the Negroes could not draw the books but had to pay the tax. And the living conditions were indescribable. None of that was due to war in Vietnam.

I used to say, as a liberal Southerner, you wait until you get a pinch in the north, in Los Angeles, New York, and Boston, where the white man is actually confronted by the Negro encroaching on his job or encroaching on his housing, and you will find that racial hatred and bitterness and prejudice and indecency are not limited to any one section of the country. And that too has come to pass. It started before the war in Vietnam. It has nothing to do with the war in Vietnam. And it is not going to be cured by getting out of Vietnam.

So let's get down to brass tacks. The greatest evil and the greatest damage of this whole confusion has been done to the young people, because they are well meaning and they are earnest. But they have become so inebriated with one issue, one single issue, that they have had extracted from them any constructive, affirmative, positive program on the domestic front, which really might be the best way of getting out of Vietnam, and the best way of beating our swords into plowshares. Because you can't fill a vacuum with nothing. If the world really became concerned with programs for helping people, that might well be the best way of getting disarmament and peace. You hardly hear much talk about this anymore.

What ought we to do? What we ought to do is very simple. The inflation has not been caused by the war in Vietnam, and the inflation has not been caused by an overheated economy but rather by a stagnant economy. In other words, contrary to conventional economics, the prices really rise fastest when the economy is sluggish. The best way to fight against price inflation is to employ the unemployed. We ought to reactivate immediately a vigorous expansionary program. We ought to legislate lower interest rates. We ought to require the Federal Reserve Board to expand the money supply, at a rate of 6 to 7 per cent a year. We ought to enact, instead of vetoing, programs to make the federal government the agent of last resort for employing unemployed people. And actually, this is not just an employment program. We need people in the public sector. We ought to be thinking of ways of getting some people out of working at luxury hotels at Miami Beach and at gas filling stations, and putting them to work on air pollution and things of that kind. This requires the investment of vast sums of federal money.

In other words, we have a continuing liberal, social, political, and economic battle in the United States. It has always been thus. There was a time when the Supreme Court said the progressive income tax was unconstitutional. There was a time when Congress would not enact it, even after the Supreme Court said it was constitutional. There was a time when hearings were held on the original Social Security Act. I was there. I was one of the managers of the hearings. You could only get one businessman in the whole country to testify for the act. A few years before that, the AFL was opposed to unemployment insurance.

We need a continuing crusade for positive programs. And I think there would be nothing more useful than for the young people and older people to devote themselves concretely, specifically, and positively, toward the great things that need to be done in this country. This would be entirely consistent with maintaining their vital interest in our international policy, and in how fast we should get out of Vietnam. They should do both. They are both equally important. And, above all, they should not remain confused in ways that make it impossible for them to be effective on either front.

Michael Reich was born in Poland in 1945, attended public schools in New York City, received his B.A. from Swarthmore and his Ph.D. from Harvard. He is a member of the Union for Radical Political Economics, an Assistant Professor at Boston University, and co-editor of The Capitalist System: A Radical Analysis of Contemporary American Society.

24 Does the United States Economy Require Military Spending?

Michael Reich

> It is, it seems, politically impossible for a capitalistic democracy to organize expenditure on the scale necessary to make the grand experiment which would prove my case — except in war conditions.
>
> J. M. Keynes

Since 1950 the United States government has spent well over a trillion dollars on the military, or about one-tenth of total economic output; in recent years $30 billion has been spent annually on destruction in Southeast Asia alone. Why does this murderous and seemingly irrational allocation of resources occur? Why give the Pentagon $80 billion

Michael Reich is Assistant Professor of Economics, Boston University, and National Bureau of Economic Research. For many of the ideas in the present paper, I am indebted to the Harvard collective of the Union for Radical Political Economics, and to Paul Baran and Paul Sweezy. Parts of the present paper are based on an earlier paper by Michael Reich and David Finkelhor, 1970. Additional footnotes and references are available from the author.

per year in spending money when so many basic social needs go unmet both in the United States and in the rest of the world? What sorts of changes in our political-economic system are needed to reorder fundamentally the militaristic priorities of the United States?

I shall argue in this paper that a major shift in social and economic priorities would require a fundamental transformation of the United States capitalist economy. The growth and persistence of a high level of military spending is a natural outcome in an advanced capitalist society that both suffers from the problem of inadequate private aggregate demand and plays a leading role in the preservation and expansion of the international capitalist system.[1] In my view, barring a revolutionary change, militarism and military spending priorities are likely to persist for the foreseeable future.

In what follows, I shall present three principal propositions on the role of military spending in the United States economy. 1. In the period beginning in 1950, if not earlier, the United States economy was not sufficiently sustained by private aggregate demand; some form of government expenditure was needed to maintain expansion. Without such stimulus, the growth rate of the United States as well as the international capitalist economy would have been substantially lower. 2. The United States government turned to military spending as the outlet for needed government expenditures precisely because it provides the most convenient such outlet; in a capitalist context, spending on the military is easily expandable and highly attractive to corporations. Military spending supplements rather than competes with private demand, more is always "needed" for adequate "defense," it is highly profitable to the firms that receive weapons contracts, and no interest group is explicitly against it. 3. Federal expenditures on socially useful needs on a scale comparable to the military budget are not a feasible substitute. Massive social expenditures would tend to undermine profitability in many sectors of the private economy, remove potential areas of profitmaking, interfere with work incentives in the labor market, and weaken the basic ideological premise of capitalism that social welfare is maximized by giving primary responsibility for the production of goods and services to profit-motivated private enterprises. In short, military spending is much more consistent than is social services spending with the maintenance and reproduction of the basic social relations of capitalism.

These propositions contrast sharply with the conventional wisdom. The dominant view among economists is that military spending is not necessary for the prosperity of the United States economy and should not be blamed on capitalism per se. To stimulate the economy any form of government spending is about as good as any other; the *aggregate* amount of demand is what matters and not its compositon. Expenditures on social needs could easily replace military spending, provided demand is maintained by a proper mix of monetary and fiscal policies.   The implication is that, apart from the difficulties of converting a few large military contractors and the retraining of specialized engineers and scientists, the problem of "conversion" is political rather than economic.   Many economists have also argued from analogy with other capitalist nations: advanced capitalist economies in Europe and Japan have experienced fairly high rates of economic growth with considerably lower proportions of their *GNP* allocated to military expenditures.   Finally, many economists point to the changing composition of government spending in the United States in recent years: while military spending has declined slightly as a percentage of *GNP,* the total of Federal, state and local nonmilitary expenditures has been increasing as a percentage of *GNP.*   Thus, the United States seems to be moving away from dependence on military spending.   None of these points is convincing, and in what follows I will try to answer each of them.

I. THE INADEQUACY OF PRIVATE DEMAND

Let me turn now to my first proposition.   Private investment and consumption demand have by themselves been insufficient to maintain low unemployment and an adequate rate of growth; some form of government expenditure has been necessary since at least the late 1940s to stimulate the United States economy and maintain expansion.   This proposition has been amply verified by historical evidence and needs little substantiation here.   For example, Hickman's elaborate econometric analysis of postwar investment demand showed that sluggish growth in the period 1948–63 was caused by a *downward* trend in business fixed investment as well as a full employment surplus in the government budget.   Without the stimulus that was provided by government spending, economic growth in this period would have been substantially lower.   In other words, autonomous investment demand has not been constrained by the claims on economic resources induced by government expenditures.

The government stimulation that is necessary must include increased government expenditures as well as tax cuts.   While the economy can be stimulated for a time without increased government expenditures by reducing taxes and running larger deficits, such tax cuts cannot be used indefinitely.   As the tax rate approaches zero, a further decrease in taxes has very little leverage effect on the economy, and further stimulus will necessarily involve increasing government expenditures; a large budget with a small deficit can have as stimulating an effect on the economy as a small budget with a large deficit (see Musgrave, 429–43). So expenditures can and must play a role in stimulating the economy. Since 1950, military expenditures, averaging about 10 per cent of *GNP,* have played this stimulative role. And within the strategic capital goods-producing industry, the sector of the economy that is most subject to cyclical fluctuations and is most affected by secular declines in business fixed investment, military spending plays a stimulative role that is twice as great as in the economy as a whole (see Reich and Finkelhor).

Note that I am not asserting here that every capitalist economy must at all times be suffering from inadequate aggregate demand. Nor am I offering an explanation of *why* the private sector has been inadequate.[2] I am asserting *only* that the U.S. economy has been sick in this regard for the last several decades.

It may also be the case that the international capitalist system as a whole has been suffering the disease of inadequate demand in recent decades. By seeing each capitalist nation as part of a larger international system, we can explain the apparent ability of some developed capitalist countries within that system to prosper without leaning so heavily on military spending. Although I have not engaged in any quantitative calculations, it seems plausible to hypothesize that military spending by the United States in the postwar period has been not only a direct prop for the American economy but also an indirect prop for the economies of Europe and Japan as well. Certainly, the export performance of these economies would have been substantially less conducive to growth had the major U.S. market for imports been much softer. The prosperity of these capitalist economics is thus related to the growth of the United States market partially caused by United States military expenditures.

II. THE ATTRACTIONS OF MILITARY SPENDING

My second proposition is that, given the necessity of some form of government expenditures, military spending provides the most convient outlet for such expenditures. Military contracts are both easily expandable in the economy without confronting any corporate opposition and are highly attractive to the firms that receive them.

Military spending is easily expandable basically because it adds to rather than competes with private demand. The amenability of military spending to expand to fill the need can be outlined with desperate brevity as follows.

First, a convenient rationalization of the need for massive armaments expenditures exists. The ideology of anticommunism and the Cold War has been drummed into politicians and public alike for over twenty years. This is a powerful force behind military spending as well as a general legitimizer of capitalism. The United States government's role as global policeman for capitalism has reinforced this rationale for military expenditures.

Second, armaments are rapidly consumed or become obsolete very quickly. Bombers are shot down in Southeast Asia, ammunition is used up or captured, etc. The technology of advanced weapons systems becomes obsolete as fast as defense experts can think of "improvements" over existing weapons systems (or as soon as Soviet experts do). So the demand for weaponry is a bottomless pit. Moreover, the kind of machinery required for armament production is highly specific to particular armaments. So each time a new weapon is needed or a new process is needed or a new process created, much existing production machinery must be scrapped. Extensive retooling at very great new outlays is required. Since the technologies involved tend to be highly complex and exotic, much gold-plating (or rather titanium-plating) can occur; only specialists know how superfluous a particular frill is, and whether a $1 billion missile would work as well as a $2 billion missile.

Third, there is no generally agreed upon yardstick for measuring how much defense we have. The public can't recognize waste here as it would in, say, education or public housing. How do we know when an adequate level of military security is achieved? National security managers can always claim that by some criteria what we have is not enough. Terms like missile gaps and nuclear parity and superiority are easily juggled. Military men always have access to new "secret intelligence reports" not available to the general public. Since few people are willing to gamble with national defense, the expertise of the managers is readily accepted. Politicians and the general public have little way of adequately questioning their judgment.

Fourth, military contracts are highly advantageous to the firms that receive them. Boondoggling and profiteering are endemic in the nature of the "product" and of the buyer-seller relationship in the military "market." While the structure and performance of the military "industry" has been analyzed in detail elsewhere (see Adams and Kaufman 1970), a few summary comments here will indicate the inherent structural reasons for waste and profiteering.

Briefly, it has always been presumed that as much as possible and ideally all armaments production should be carried on by private profit-seeking corporations. Theoretically, the government, as sole buyer, would purchase from the most efficient, least-cost firms. But given the long lead times and the inherent cost and technological uncertainties in developing and producing complicated weapons systems, the government would find it difficult, to say the least, to identify in advance and reward the most efficient military contractors. In fact, of course, the Pentagon has rarely shown any interest in holding down costs or identifying efficient firms, since until recently, it has not faced a real budget constraint of its own. The reality is that contractors and Pentagon both follow the maxim of socialized risk, but private profits — in C. Wright Mills' words, "socialism for the rich."

The profit incentives in the military contracts reward boondoggling and waste.[3] The Pentagon provides without charge much of the fixed and working capital for major military contracts, underwrites and subsidizes the costs of technological research and development for firms that engage in civilian as well as military production, and negotiates (and when necessary, renegotiates) cost-plus contracts that virtually guarantee the contractors against any losses. It is thus not surprising that careful and objective studies of profit rates on investment in military contracts have found that such profits are significantly and substantially higher in military work than in comparable civilian work.

Nor is it surprising to find that most of the major corporations in the United States have become involved in military contracts. One hundred corporations receive two-thirds of the prime contract dollars, but among these top one hundred are twenty of the top twenty-five industrial firms in the United States.[4] The attraction of military spending to the major corporations is also apparent when one examines the impact of military contracts on sectoral growth and on the concentration of economic power. First, the rapidly growing industries of the postwar economy — aerospace, electronics, communications — owe a great deal to military dollars for research and development and final production. Second, in a typical year fifty firms get about 60 per cent of the military procurement contract dollar, whereas in the economy as a whole, the top one hundred firms usually account for only 35 per cent of manufacturing sales (see Reich and Finkelhor). So military procurement is much more concentrated than is the economy as a whole. Certainly, an expenditure program that benefits twenty of the top twenty-five corporations and contributes to the concentration of economic power among the corporate giants is going to enjoy a political power base that lies deep in the heart of the United States economy.

So military spending is easily expandable, is highly profitable and amenable to boondoggling, and benefits the major corporations in the economy. These factors combine so that military expenditures can be enormous and expandable almost without limit and not incur major corporate opposition. But the same cannot be said for the nonmilitary sector.

III. THE OPPOSITION TO SOCIAL SERVICE EXPENDITURES

The last of my three major propositions was that federal spending on socially useful needs on a scale comparable to the military budget is not a feasible substitute.   The contrast between government spending on the military and government spending on social services indicates how post-Keynesian macroeconomic theory has artificially separated economics from politics, i.e., from power relationships.   Social services spending is unlikely to be as profitable and expandable as is military spending.   Social expenditures have never had the blank check that the military until recently have enjoyed.

Investments in social facilities are usually durable — they do not become obsolete very quickly and are not rapidly consumed.   Right now, of course, there are plenty of unmet needs in these areas.   But once taxes have been increased and everyone is provided with a decent house, once there are new schools and health clinics stocked with materials, then what?   They cannot be immediately torn down and built all over again.

The technology of social welfare facilities is not particularly exotic. Very conventional standards exist to tell us how much a house or a hospital should cost.   The possibility for enormous padding to absorb funds is much less, since there are readily accessible yardsticks to ascertain how well social needs have been met.   The public knows when adequate and convenient public transportation is available.   No one would want to extend it out to a suburb that did not exist.

In general, social spending beyond a certain point cannot be rapidly and wastefully expanded.   The difference here is that investment in social services deals with people, not remote objects like weapons.   People are resistant to allowing their lives to be dominated and their tax dollars used up by the priorities of waste — even if it does help to keep the economy running.   For example, what would happen if a housing project or a school were built in the same way as a new missile?   If a missile doesn't work, the company is excused and the planners go back to their drawing boards armed with another huge contract.   Since it already has the expertise, the same company is more than likely to get a new missile contract.   Imagine the political repercussions of an inadequate, but expensive, school or housing project? The community complains, a public scandal is declared, and all contracts with the offending company are cancelled.   The school or housing bill has a rougher going the next time it comes up in the legislature.[5]

So social spending cannot provide the opportunities for waste that are provided by military spending. But more important, massive social spending inevitably interferes with the existence and reproduction of the social relations of production under capitalism.[6]

First, many kinds of social spending put the government in direct competition with particular industries and with the private sector as a whole (see Baran and Sweezy, Chap. 6). This goes against the logic of a capitalist economy. For example, government production of low-cost housing in large amounts would substantially reduce profits of private builders and landlords who own the existing housing stock. The supply of housing would be increased and land would be taken away from private developers who want to use it for commercial gain. Similarly, building *effective* mass public transportation would compete with the automobile interests.

Any one of these interests taken by itself might not be sufficient to put insurmountable obstacles in the way of social spending. Most social service programs affect only one particular set of interests in the private economy. But there are so many forms of potential interference. All of the vested interests are aware of this problem explicitly or through their ideology and so work to help one another out. They adopt a general social ideology that says that too much social spending is dangerous and that governmental noninterference is good.

Furthermore, the capitalist system as a whole is threatened by massive governmental social spending because the very necessity of private ownership and control over production is thereby called into question. The basic assumption in any capitalist society, that goods and services should be produced by private enterprise according to criteria of market profitability, thus also fuels the general ideology limiting social spending. This limits the satisfaction of collective needs such as clean air and water, esthetic city planning, etc., that cannot be expressed in market terms as demand for individually saleable commodities.[7]

Massive social spending also tends to upset the labor market, one of the essential institutions of a capitalist economy. Public expenditures on an adequate welfare program would make it difficult for employers to get workers. If the government provided adequate nonwage income without social stigma to recipients, many workers would drop out of the labor force rather than take low-paying and unpleasant jobs. Those who stayed at jobs would be less likely to put up with demeaning working conditions. The whole basis of the capitalist labor market is that workers have no legitimate income source other than the sale of their labor power, and capitalist ideology has long made a cardinal rule that government should not interfere with this incentive to work. Powerful political forces thus operate to insure that direct income subsidization at adequate levels does not come into being.

Social service spending is also opposed because it threatens the class structure. Education, for example, is a crucial stratification mechanism, determining who gets to the top and legitimizing their position there (see Bowles 1971). Good free universal education, extending through college, would undermine the transmission of inequality from one generation to the next. A truly open admissions system of higher education would undermine the labor market as well: workers would not settle so willingly for miserable, low-paying jobs (see Bowles 1972). In general, many social service expenditures, because of their public good character, are consumed equally and so the distribution of their benefits is more equal than the overall distribution of income. For this reason, such expenditures are often opposed by the rich.

Finally, good social services, since they have given people some security, comfort, and satisfaction, i.e., fulfill real needs, interfere with the market in consumer goods. Corporations can only sell people goods by playing on their unsatisfied needs and yearnings. New needs are constantly being artificially created: the need for status, security, sex appeal, etc. These needs are based on fears, anxieties, and dissatisfaction that people have and that are continually pandered to by the commercial world. But if people's needs were being more adequately fulfilled by the public sector, that is, if they had access to adequate housing, effective transportation, good schools, and good health care, they would be much less prey to the appeals of the commercial hucksters. These forms of collective consumption would have interfered with the demand for consumer products in the private market.

Military spending is acceptable to all corporate interests. It does not interfere with existing areas for profit making, it does not undermine the labor market, it does not challenge the class structure, and it does not produce income redistribution. Social spending does all these things, and thus faces obstacles for its own expansion.

I do not mean to imply by the above analysis that a capitalist economy has not and will not provide any basic social services through government expenditures. Some social overhead investment is obviously important and necessary for the smooth functioning of any economy, and the provision of local and national public goods has always been considered a proper activity for capitalist governments. For example, expenditures on education, highways, and transportation are obviously necessary for the production of workers and for getting them to the point of production; such expenditures are motivated by the needs of production, and only incidentally to fill human needs (see Gorz and O'Connor). In fact, most state and local government expenditures have been directed to these basic infrastructural needs.

In recent decades production has become, as Marx put it, more social in character: the economy has become much more complex, more interdependent, more urbanized, more in need of highly schooled labor. The recent increase in state and local expenditures can be explained by these increases in the social costs of production. Expenditures for such needs would be consistent with and are often necessary for private profitability.[8]

Moreover, state and local expenditures are not motivated by the need to stimulate aggregate demand, for only the federal government is concerned with maintaining aggregate demand.[9] But nonmilitary Federal purchases have increased barely, if at all, as a percentage of *GNP* since the 1930s. Nonmilitary federal purchases of goods and services were only 2.3 per cent in 1970. By contrast, nonmilitary federal purchases as a per cent of *GNP* were 4.6 per cent in 1938 and 1.9 per cent in 1954.[10] It thus cannot be said that the Federal government has significantly turned to social services expenditures and away from military expenditures to meet the problem of inadequate aggregate demand.

This brings me to a final point regarding the meaning of the question, is military spending really necessary to capitalism? I have tried to frame the answer to this question in the following way. A capitalist economy with inadequate aggregate demand is much more *likely* to turn to military than to social spending because the former is more consistent with private profit and the social relations of production under capitalism. If this military outlet were cut off, say by massive public opposition, it is possible that a capitalist economy might accommodate and transform itself rather than commit suicide. But such reasoning misses the point. Military spending is favored by capitalists and is likely to be defended with considerable vigor, as recent years have shown. Perhaps a parallel with imperialism will clarify this point. It is not essential to a capitalist economy that it be imperialist, for growth can be domestically based. But so long as there are lands to be conquered and markets to be penetrated, it is natural to expect that capitalism will have an imperialist character. Similarly, so long as there is profit to be made in military spending, capitalists will turn to it.

ENDNOTES

[1] An important factor in the development of military spending has been the assumption by the United States since World War II of the role of global policeman for capitalism. I shall not focus on this issue here because the importance of international operations to U.S. capitalism has been well sketched by others. See for example Harry Magdoff 1969, 1970, and Arthur MacEwan.

[2] For a recent ambitious, though inadequate, attempt to explain theoretically the insufficiency of investment demand in the United States since 1929, see Baran and Sweezy.

[3] For references see Reich and Finkelhor, Kaufman, 1970, Chap. 4, and 1972.

[4] Of the remaining five, one is the principal Atomic Energy Commission contractor, two are oil companies indirectly affected by military sales, and one is a steel company also indirectly affected. For a detailed analysis of the wide range of corporations and industries involved in military contracts, see Reich and Finkelhor.

[5] This is not to deny that there is considerable waste and profiteering in civilian government contracts, for example in housing programs. But the potential magnitudes are much smaller.

[6] Recall that capitalist relations of production are characterized by private ownership and control of production, with a hierarchical social division of labor between those who control, the capitalists and managers, and those who are controlled, the wage and salary workers.

[7] For a discussion of the subordination of collective needs to private profit as well as a general Marxist analysis of civilian government expenditures under capitalism, see Andre Gorz.

[8] Nonetheless, a relative impoverishment of living standards has taken place, as the destruction of the city and the environment has far outrun government provision of social goods. See Gorz and O'Connor.

[9] Variations in state and local expenditures usually run counter to the stabilization needs of the aggregate economy.

[10] Data from *The Statistical Abstract of the United States,* 1971.

REFERENCES

W. Adams, "The Military-Industrial Complex and the New Industrial State," *American Economic Review,* May 1968, 58, 652–65.

P. Baran and P. Sweezy, *Monopoly Capital.* New York: Monthly Review Press, 1965.

S. Bowles, "Unequal Education and the Reproduction of the Social Division of Labor," *Review of Radical Political Economics,* Winter 1971, 3, no. 4, reprinted in Edwards, Reich and Weisskopf, 218–29.

———, "Contradictions in Higher Education in the United States," in Edwards, Reich and Weisskopf, 491–503.

R. Edwards, M. Reich, and T. Weisskopf, eds., *The Capitalist System.* Englewood Cliffs, N.J.: Prentice-Hall, Inc., 1972.

A. Gorz, *A Strategy for Labor.* Boston: Beacon Press, 1967.

B. Hickman, *Investment Demand and United States Economic Growth.* Washington, D.C.: Brookings, 1965.

R. Kaufman, "MIRVing the Boondoggle," *American Economic Review,* May 1972.

———, *The War Profiteers,* Indianapolis, 1970.

J. M. Keynes, *New Republic,* July 29, 1940.

A. MacEwan, "Capitalist Expansion, Ideology and Intervention," in Edwards, Reich and Weisskopf, 409–20.

H. Magdoff, *The Age of Imperialism.* New York: Monthly Review Press, 1969.

————, "Is Imperialism Really Necessary?", *Monthly Review,* Oct. and Nov. 1970, 22, Nos. 5 and 6.

R. Musgrave, *The Theory of Public Finance.* New York: McGraw-Hill, 1959.

J. O'Connor, "The Fiscal Crisis of the State," *Socialist Revolution,* Spring 1970, 1, Nos. 1 and 2.

M. Reich and D. Finkelhor, "Capitalism and the Military-Industrial Complex: The Obstacles to Conversion," *Review of Radical Political Economics,* Fall 1970, 2, No. 4, 1–25; reprinted in Edwards, Reich and Weisskopf, 392–406.

QUESTIONS

Vietnam
Keyserling / Reich

1. How can we account for continued inflation after 1969 despite deflationary policies and a recession?

2. Was the war in Vietnam a normal outgrowth of the political-economic system in the United States?

3. Can the United States have full employment and prosperity without war?

4. Was the war in Vietnam the primary reason the United States did not deal with its social and economic problems in the 1960s?

5. What was the economic impact of the Vietnam war?

6. Is the war in Vietnam a symptom of weakness in the capitalist system? Does the system need to be changed entirely in order to prevent new Vietnams?

7. Does the United States go around the world forcing capitalism on other countries?

SECTION VII

Economic Organization for the Future

What will future economic systems be like? What will the future be as history? What is the future of capitalism? What is the future of socialism? These are the issues addressed in this section.

Robert L. Heilbroner defines socialism as a philosophy of society based on planning and on an ideology of egalitarianism, cooperation, and confraternity. There are in the world two distinct types of socialist societies — the revolutionary socialism found in underdeveloped countries such as China and Cuba and the socialism found in developed socialist countries such as the USSR. Heilbroner concentrates on the problems faced by developed socialist states.

One such problem is the role to be played by markets. Heilbroner argues that socialist countries are going to use markets to a much greater degree in the future. There is among socialists, however, a curious fear about market relationships that is colored by the inequalities of power existing in present-day market economies.

In today's socialist states there are great pressures to conform. Thus, a second problem to be faced by socialist societies is how to deal with the problem of individuation — how to encourage different lifestyles, attitudes, and behaviors.

The third problem that has not been solved by socialist states is the problem of politics — the question of who governs. An important unsolved problem is: how is democracy to work? This problem takes on acute importance as technology proceeds and makes affluence possible.

Paul M. Sweezy sees capitalism — not as a social system in individual countries — but as the social system of the whole earth for the past 400 years. It started in Europe after the European invention of firearms that enabled Europeans to conquer, subjugate, and exploit the rest of the world. This activity was the basis for the economic takeoff that occurred in Western Europe. The loot from the colonies provided for capital accumulation. The peasants were uprooted from the soil and became the proletariat — the propertyless workers.

This development was the beginning of the split between the rich, exploiting countries on the one hand and the multitude of poor, exploited countries on the other. This split has continued and widened down to the present day. This world system (split between rich and poor) is the way capitalism works, and it cannot be remedied within capitalism. The only way out is the rejection of capitalism through socialist revolution. But the rich exploiters want to keep the underdeveloped countries in the capitalist compound. Thus the prospect is for global civil war.

Will socialism triumph? Sweezy is not at all sure. He does argue, however, that there is no prospect for humanity to go forward under capitalism. If humanity is to survive, we must develop nonexploitative, nondivisive society, i.e., socialist society.

Robert T. Averitt contends that there is a difference between classical or developmental capitalism and the newer exchange capitalism. The most fundamental rule of developmental capitalism is that participants must always try to minimize their losses and/or maximize their profits. Acceptance of this attitude implies that the urge toward economic gain is the most important urge. A new capitalist ethic had to be developed that changed greed from a vice into a virtue.

Averitt argues that our Founding Fathers disagreed fundamentally on the question of the role of government. Hamilton desired rapid economic development and was willing to sacrifice democratic participation. Jefferson, on the other hand, advocated a policy of laissez faire, an agrarian society, and opposed forced industrialization. However, a developmental capitalistic system without democracy was eventually adopted, essentially for military reasons. Developmental capitalism ended in this country during the early part of the twentieth century. The Great Depression ushered in a major crisis, which was solved by letting the direction of government spending be changed. The government budget assumed a very large role in the economy. The country then went to a system of competitive-interest capitalism. Those groups in the government that based their appeal on fear (the military) naturally won this contest and gained the dominant role in the government. Averitt is unsure as to whether capitalism can continue, primarily because it seems to sustain such vices as fear and greed. It does not seem to bring out the best in human nature.

Murray N. Rothbard also argues that there are two different conceptions of capitalism. He argues that there is a fundamental difference between free market and state capitalism. The former employs peaceful, voluntary exchange wherein both parties are better off as a result of the exchange. The latter is synonymous with violent expropriation. Rothbard argues that government intervention involves prohibiting or partially prohibiting voluntary economic exchange between people. This is done through taxation, seizure, or legal codes. Rothbard sees nothing wrong with greed. He distinguishes between productive greed and exploitative greed. He feels that excess greed has been a result of the tradition of despotism that preceded the advent of capitalism.

Rothbard is very optimistic about the future of market capitalism. He feels that we are now reverting to conditions similar to those that existed during the period when capitalism was just emerging. Even socialist countries, realizing that socialism will not work in rich countries, are shifting to markets. He also points to the fact that the New Left has espoused such formerly Right-Wing positions as decentralization, community control, and the abolition of the draft.

Rothbard is not optimistic about the future of state capitalism. He sees the failure of income redistribution to the poor, the decay of the welfare state, and the hypocrisy of farm subsidy programs as evidence of its doom. He argues that the Depression was not a result of the failure of the free market, but of attempts at governmental intervention. He argues that present-day attempts at government manipulation of the economy might produce similar results.

Herbert Gintis argues that the most important problem faced by residents of capitalist countries is the problem of alienation. This alienation takes many forms and Gintis gives several examples. However, the source of the various forms of alienation is the same — the core institutions of capitalist society, i.e., markets in labor and land and profit-maximizing corporations.

Men do not control the kind of work they do — labor is allocated to its most efficient employment by impersonal market mechanisms. This is an inherently alienating process, i.e., it does not reflect the conscious desires of people but the impersonal "needs" of the market system.

Gintis argues that hierarchical organizations give workers a feeling of powerlessness. Specialization and division of labor causes workers to feel that their work is meaningless. Competition with other workers causes the workers to feel isolated and makes solidarity and community difficult. The result of all these forces is that workers come to feel themselves to be mere instruments — to be means to an end. Thus, they come to feel alienated.

Gintis argues that capitalist organization of work — hierarchy, specialization of labor, competition between workers, etc., is not dictated by technology nor in the interest of efficiency. Instead these institutions were created and are maintained in order to insure capitalist domination. He argues further that experiments have demonstrated that decentralized decision-making and job enlargement result in greater worker satisfaction, lower absenteeism, and greater output. If true, this is indeed a profound indictment of capitalist economic institutions and on capitalism's own terms. Capitalism's great claim to fame has always been that it was an efficient system of production. Gintis presents evidence that this is not true and that alternative institutions would be more efficient.

Gintis argues that markets in land mean that nature comes to be viewed as a privately owned profitable commodity and thus is used for that purpose which returns the greatest private profit to the owner. This means that cities are designed and built with little concern for people's needs. The resulting cities make community difficult.

The operations of these capitalist institutions leave people powerless, without meaningful work, without a feeling of community and solidarity with fellow workers and neighbors — alienated as workers and citizens. In only one area are people able to do as they wish, and that is in the area of consumption. Capitalist economies provide people vast quantities of goods and services to consume. However, Gintis argues that this is no longer enough for growing numbers of young Americans. They recognize that people are more than just consumers, but that capitalist institutions make it difficult to be fulfilled in their roles as workers and citizens. This consciousness of capitalism's inherent weaknesses is spreading and will, in Gintis' view, lead to the rejection and replacement of capitalist institutions.

This section presents two different Utopian visions. Rothbard sees Utopia in much the same way as Adam Smith. Utopia is a society in which everybody goes out to seek maximum gain. By producing the most possible goods and services, the individual benefits all of society. The forces of competition and the working of the market will prevent exploitation of fellowmen and women and will prevent monopolies. The invisible hand will work to insure that as everybody works to achieve their own maximum advantage they will be led to achieve the maximum gain for the whole society. The greatest good for the greatest number emerges when people are left absolutely free of government intervention. Consumption of goods and services is the route to happiness. The ultimate Utopia, of course, would be anarchy, in which there would be no government at all. However, realizing the practical limitations of anarchy, Rothbard is willing to concede the need for government to carry out such functions as national defense.

The Utopia espoused by socialists downgrades materialism. They argue that maximizing consumption of goods and services is not the way to a good life. People need approval, love, social acceptance, rewarding and fulfilling work, the respect of one's fellows, feelings of fraternity and community with one's family and fellows, good relationships with the environment, etc. This type of Utopia is very different from that held out by the capitalists. Capitalists assume that man is basically greedy. Socialists accept the notion that man is greedy today, but they argue that this is a result of capitalist institutions. Capitalist institutions build on and inculcate greedy values as the norm. Anthropologists tell us about societies in which people are not motivated primarily by greed. It is possible to construct modern societies in which other values are important. Socialist man can be created.

Socialists concede that the efforts to build a better society in the Soviet Union and elsewhere in Eastern Europe have been largely failures. Those societies would be called state capitalism by many socialists today. They have all the trappings of capitalist society, bureaucracy, hierarchies, social classes, alienation, inequality, and so forth. Socialists are quite hopeful of the opportunities and alternatives being developed in China. They are trying a different path to the creation of a good society, and many socialists think that they are having far more success than the American press has reported.

Robert L. Heilbroner is the author of the books that introduced many Americans to economics — The Worldly Philosophers *and* The Making of Economic Society. *His recent books are* Between Capitalism and Socialism *and* The Limits of American Capitalism. *His articles and reviews appear frequently in* Commentary, New Republic, *and the* New York Review of Books. *He received his B.A. from Harvard College and his Ph.D. from the New School for Social Research, where he is currently Chairman of the Department of Economics.*

25 Socialism and the Future

Robert L. Heilbroner

I.

Some years ago, writing on the prospects for American capitalism, I began by asserting that the capitalist system, whatever the strains and stresses to which it would be subject, bade fair to remain the dominant system in America and Western Europe during our lifetimes, and that any serious attempt to project large-scale social trends should begin from that premise.[1] Now I should like to undertake a similar speculative examination of the prospects for socialism, for I also take it as a datum that some form of socialism will be the predominant economic system in most of the rest of the world during our lifetimes, and that even in Europe and America it will constitute the image of a society against which capitalism will be measured by its critics.

But no sooner do we raise the question of the prospect for socialism than we encounter a difficult problem. It is the problem of deciding

Reprinted from *Commentary,* Vol. 48, No. 6, December 1969, by permission of the author and the American Jewish Committee. © Copyright 1969 by the American Jewish Committee.

what we mean by socialism. How is one to speak of the prospects of a "system" that presumably embraces Norway as well as Russia, or that is expressed by the ideas of Bernard Shaw as well as of Mao Tse-tung? If there is a single identificatory mark of socialism, it is certainly not visible on the surface.

Yet, at second look, perhaps we can find a way of penetrating the surface variety of socialist institutions and thought to reach a common core. For it is not socialism alone that presents us with a confusing heterogeneity of systems, but capitalism as well; and yet we feel perfectly assured in applying the common term "capitalist" to worlds as far apart as those depicted by Sinclair Lewis and Thomas Mann, or Faulkner and Proust. And there is a very good reason for our generalizing approach to the societies of capitalism. This is the presence within all of them of a common set of institutions and ideas — the institution of the basically uncontrolled market system and the ideas of the legitimacy of the private ownership of the means of production. In a word, we find a *business system* at the core of all capitalist societies, no matter how diverse their other characteristics. Whatever their incompatibilities in culture or life-styles, Buddenbrooks and Babbitt were both businessmen, and as such they understood and shared important common activities and values and goals.

Hence the obvious question is whether there is not, within the variety of socialist nations, a similar systemic core that might play the same identificatory role as does business within the many forms of capitalism. The question has an obvious answer: one element of the socialist system must certainly be the structural element that we find within all socialist societies, corresponding to the market system in capitalism. This is the predominance of some form of *planning*.

But this structural element is by no means enough in itself to provide an infallible identification for socialism — after all, one can find some degree of planning in all capitalist nations and some evidences of the market in all socialist societies. Hence we must add a critical second attribute by which socialism can be identified. This is the common presence of a guiding socialist *ideology*, corresponding to the business ideology in capitalism.

What is the content of this socialist ideology? It will help if we begin by differentiating it from that of capitalism. I think it is fair to say that the beliefs of the business system mainly concern themselves with the justification of the prevailing economic order, especially the institution of private property and of the relatively free market. To put it differently, no capitalist nation or philosopher or economist has any grand designs for the fundamental reshaping of society through capitalism. Certainly capitalism aims at the material well-being of its constituents, but equally certainly it entertains no thought that the pursuit of well-being will alter the basic class character of the system or modify the competitive or acquisitive drives from which the system derives its momentum. That is what it means to say that capitalist thought is essentially conservative.

By way of contrast, socialist thought is primarily concerned with bringing into existence a social order very different from that which it finds in the world. Thus its use of planning — or, for that matter, of the market mechanism — is guided by purposes wholly at variance with those of capitalism. Capitalism uses the market or planning to service and support a social system in which the prosperity of the capital-owning class is a central aim of economic policy. Socialism not only denies the legitimacy of this underlying conception, but it intends the instrumentalities of plan and market to create an egalitarian society in which no class may gain the strategic position conferred by the ownership of society's productive assets. Further, far from ignoring the effects of economic progress on classes and motives, as does capitalism, socialism intends progress to lead to the creation of a wholly new kind of society, free of invidious striving and built on new motives of cooperation and confraternity.

Now, it need hardly be said that there is a long step between socialist declaration and reality. In addition, let us reiterate the point with which we began — that the variation among socialist nations is very great. Clearly, the mere presence of similar institutions and ideologies no more produces a common existential quality to socialism than it does under capitalism — indeed, life in "socialist" Yugoslavia may well resemble life in "capitalist" Italy more than it does that in "socialist" China.

What, then, is the usefulness of emphasizing the common features of planning and ideology? The answer is that these features make it possible to talk about the future of socialism. For the central presence of planning and its ideology has as important a consequence for socialism as the presence of the business system for capitalism. It is that within each type of society *these common elements give rise to common kinds of problems.*

Thus, in reflecting on the prospects for, say, capitalism in Japan and America, it is necessary to bear in mind that for all the dissimilarity of their social and cultural environments, both are societies that must contend with the peculiar problems of a business structure and a business ideology. And in the same way, when we attempt to reason prospectively with regard to the outlook for the socialist nations, we must recognize that underlying their varied internal and external challenges, all of them must cope with problems characteristic of the institution of planning and endemic to the ideological goal in whose service the activity of planning is carried on.

II.

Our aim, in the following pages, will be mainly to explore the nature of these problems of socialism.   But we must begin by bringing to the fore an aspect of the problem of socialism that complicates any discussion of its future trajectory.   It is that socialism in our day must be considered with reference to two very different kinds of societies in two very different settings.   On the one hand, socialism appears as a powerful force for change in the most backward and underdeveloped countries in the world; on the other hand, it also exists as an agency or as an ideal for social change in the most advanced and wealthy nations.

It is hardly surprising that the problems associated with planning or with the realization of the socialist vision are not at all alike in these two radically contrasting environments; the analogy is with the striking contrast between the problems of primitive capitalism, with its grim struggle between the classes, and those of advanced capitalism, with its vast middle class obedient to an advertising culture.   The difference, however, is that whereas the problems associated with nascent capitalism are now largely relegated to the history books, those of "early" socialism exist side by side with those of "late" socialism.   Thus we cannot discuss the problems of socialism without distinguishing between the forms these problems take in each of its two contemporary manifestations.

Of the two, it is easier to describe the problems of socialism in the underdeveloped nations.   I have written elsewhere on this, so here I shall be very brief.   The situation in most of the backward nations today can only be described as desperate.   Present standards of living exceed subsistence requirements by so little that the least misfortune threatens catastrophe on a giant scale.   Strongholds of foreign capital inhibit the redirection of the energies of the people.   Incompetent or indifferent regimes seem unable or unwilling to galvanize their moribund societies.   And above this nightmarish landscape, in which everything moves in slow motion, towers an oncoming tidal wave of population advancing with horrendous speed: within the next ten years the number of women in the most fertile age brackets will double.

In these circumstances, the task of those socialist governments that have come to power, or of those that will, is clearly marked.   It is to place their nations on a war footing against existing conditions, to mobilize whole populations for production, to attack the psychological as well as the physical deficiencies of the backward areas with all the zeal and ardor of a military campaign.

Moreover, there is little doubt that revolutionary socialism, utilizing all-out planning, can accomplish these objectives.   The prodigies of the Russian advance, the extraordinary achievements in the modernization of China, the remarkable arousal of the Cuban people[2] all testify beyond possibility of doubt that "war planning" can realize its giant, but essentially simple, aims.   That this kind of massive planning is likely to be accompanied by enormously costly errors, or that it may, from time to time, imperil the success of the whole development effort through an excess of mindless zeal, is also to be expected.   Yet the most serious and deeply rooted problems of planning in the backward world are not likely to be these perhaps inevitable mistakes of planning. Rather, as the examples of Russia and China and Cuba all show, *the endemic problem of planning in the underdeveloped nations resides in the noneconomic measures required to bring about the economic changes that revolutionary socialism so imperatively seeks.*

For the objectives of economic development do not lie, like a military citadel, exposed to the thrust of a single daring campaign.   On the contrary, the development assault is better likened to a long grueling march through a hostile hinterland.   The real resistance to development comes not from the old regimes, which can be quickly overcome, but from the masses of the population who must be wrenched from their established ways, pushed, prodded, cajoled, or threatened into heroic efforts, and then systematically denied an increase in well-being so that capital can be amassed for future growth.   This painful reorientation of a whole culture, judging by past experience, will be difficult or impossible to attain without measures of severity; and when we add the need to maintain a fervor of participation long beyond the first flush of spontaneous enthusiasm, the necessity for stringent limitations on political opposition and for forcible means of assuring economic cooperation seems virtually unavoidable.

To be sure, one must not overgeneralize as to this grim prospect. As with the not unrelated distortions of life imposed under the aegis of early capitalism, the extent of the deforming pressures of early socialism will vary from one milieu or regime to another.   Some nations, unfortunate in their resource endowments or in their political connections with the industrialized nations, may be forced to undergo a more or less thoroughgoing totalitarian transition.   Others, better endowed or better connected, may pass through the thirty or fifty years of the modernizing transformation with a minimum of repression.

In general, however, when we seek to project the problems of socialism in the underdeveloped areas, we cannot sidestep the probability that intellectual stiflement, political repression, and enforced social conformity will figure prominently among them.   Let me be quite explicit that when the alternatives to such a disciplined existence are degradation, misery, and premature death, the exercise of sternness and indoctrination appears in a very different light from that of an arbitrary and capricious tyranny. Nonetheless, the exercise of these measures, however necessary to assure the success of the development effort, is likely to affect the future of the nations who must suffer them no less severely than the hated influence of imperialism affected their past. Thus, when we inquire as to the outlook for socialism in the backward lands, it is necessary to recognize that it is likely to emerge both as the salvation of its otherwise doomed people, and also as the source of a moral and intellectual infection from which it may take generations to recover.

III.

However uncertain its outcome, it is at least clear what the general objectives of revolutionary socialist planning must be in the underdeveloped areas. But the matter gets much more complicated when we now begin to look into the problems of socialist planning at the other end of the spectrum — in the advanced nations where the modernization process is already complete.

Here it may help if we quickly review the history of the problem before examining its present-day characteristics. It is interesting to note that the very identification of planning as an intrinsic aspect of socialism is a relatively modern development. Before the Russian Revolution, the main concern of the leaders and theoreticians of socialism was largely historical — namely, how a new social order would emerge from the conflicts within an old one. Not until an actual socialist society had come into existence did the question of planning, only glancingly referred to by Marx and airily dismissed by Lenin, assume the central position of importance that it occupies today.[3] And not surprisingly, shortly thereafter came an attack on planning as the Achilles heel of a socialist system. Indeed, the most intellectually respectable criticism of socialism in the mid-thirties was the effort of Ludwig von Mises and Friedrich Hayek to destroy the credibility of socialism as a desirable social order, not by inveighing against its ideals or its excesses, but by demonstrating that the economic system on which it was based would not work.

In brief, the criticism of Hayek and von Mises was based on the contention that socialism was intrinsically unable to achieve a *rational* economic order — that is, a system in which all the factors of production were employed as efficiently as possible — because it lacked one critical mechanism: a market in which capital could be valued by the free offers of owners of capital and by the free bids of would-be hirers of capital. Since by definition there could be no private ownership of capital, no free market price for it could ever be ascertained. As a result, the only way of deciding which enterprises were to have capital, and which were not, was perforce the essentially arbitrary decision of some Central Planning Board. Such a system, it was presumed, could not long endure.

This line of attack against socialism did not fare very well. In the mid-thirties it was effectively demolished by Oscar Lange, a Polish economist then at Harvard. What Lange demonstrated in two brilliant articles was that Mises had failed to see that a Central Planning Board could indeed plan rationally, for the simple reason that it would receive exactly the same information from a socialized economic system as did entrepreneurs under a market system.[4] The only difference would be that the Board would not learn about the condition of relative scarcity or plenty of capital goods or other commodites by price changes, as under capitalism, but by the building-up or running-down of inventories. That is, when a good was underpriced, instead of its price going up, as in a free market, the planners would discover that supplies of the good were being depleted faster than they were being replaced. All the Board would then have to do would be to raise the price until the level of inventories was again constant. As a result, it could allocate its resources quite as efficiently as any capitalist system. In fact, the allocation of capital (or other factors) arrived at in this way by a socialist state would not only be rational, but would be in many ways the *same* as that of a market system. The main difference would lie in the ability of the Board to supply articles of public consumption (such as education or parks or welfare services) on a more generous scale than in a laissez-faire system, and in its ability to set a higher rate of saving-and-investment than might be forthcoming under an uncontrolled system. But since a major criticism against laissez faire was precisely its failure to provide adequate public services or to generate a sufficiently high rate of growth, these departures from the market idea seemed certain to enhance rather than to diminish social well-being.

Indeed, Lange quickly shifted from the defensive to the offensive. Not only would a planned economy meet the criteria for rationality, but its superior performance would soon reveal the outmoded inadequacy of a free enterprise economy. *"The real issue,"* Lange wrote in italics, *"is whether the further maintenance of the capitalist system is compatible with economic progress."*[5] Or, as Benjamin Lippincott wrote in 1938 in the introduction to the little book in which Lange's articles appeared, "Where many under a capitalist economy must choose between a coat and a pair of shoes, under a socialist, many could choose between a radio and a telephone."[6]

More than a generation has now elapsed since the Lange articles appeared, and it should be possible to pass some sort of judgment on the debate. And the first judgment seems to be the irrelevance of the problem itself.[7] It is true, of course, that the absence of a market for capital can distort planning efforts — the Soviet predilection for huge and uneconomical dams and factories during their first Five Year Plans reflected their failure for many years to include a charge for capital in their projected industrial enterprises. But the obvious irrationality of this neglect of capital was eventually recognized, and a charge for capital was thereafter instituted.

But the whole question has an air of unreality. For what is the value of "rationality" as a criterion of economic performance? Are we to judge the Russian planning effort irrational because it has sacrificed present consumption for future growth to a far greater degree than the sacrificing generation might have voted for, had it been given the opportunity, but not, in all likelihood, to a greater degree than future generations would have voted for, if they could have? Per contra, are we to deem the American economy rational because it obediently provides its consumer markets with often trivial goods while it starves its housing market, or its central cities?

Clearly, the trouble with rationality is that it has two meanings. On the one hand it implies "reasonableness" — an attribute that is often glaringly absent under the market disposition of things as well as under a planned disposition. On the other hand, rationality also means that we will conserve the scarce resources of society by applying them where the need is greatest. That might seem to be a definition identical with "reasonableness," except for one thing: in a market society, "need" is determined by the existing distribution of income and wealth. An economy that produces lavishly for the rich and meanly for the poor is therefore "rational" in the sense that it is devoting its resources to those uses for which the greatest market demand exists, but it is hardly rational in the sense of being reasonable or of being just.[8]

Lange himself sensed that the basic problem was not really that of rationality at all. *"The real danger of socialism,"* he wrote (again in italics), *"is that of a bureaucratization of economic life."*[9] It is true that he raised the problem almost to dismiss it — bureaucratization would happen in any event, he thought, and there would actually be a better chance of controlling it under socialism because "officials subject to democratic control seem preferable to private corporation executives who are practically responsible to nobody"[10] — but at least he saw that the test of socialist planning would be provided by criteria very different from those of a textbook on microeconomic perfection.

It need hardly be said that the experience of socialist planning, especially in the Soviet Union and Eastern Europe, has amply confirmed Lange's fears. For decades Lange's plan for a market-based socialism was ignored or dismissed as heresy, while the bureaucracies he warned against proved themselves increasingly incapable of handling their enormous ministries.   Retrospectively, it now seems clear that corporation executives "who are practically responsible to nobody" are under far greater necessity to combat the stagnation of bureaucracy than socialist factory managers who find themselves personally responsible to a bureaucrat.   The lesson of the postwar socialist experience is that the mechanism of planning is much more effective in laying in the foundations for an industrial society than in administering such a society after it has been brought into being.   The more tightly linked the industrial activities of an economy, the more numerous its nodes of interdependence, the more problems does the planning apparatus encounter — not necessarily in the strictly economic form of irrational allocations of goods, but in the guise of low morale and productivity, frequent bottlenecks and partial breakdowns, poor quality of output, etc.   As Paul Sweezy has commented with regard to the Soviet sphere in 1968, "Mass apathy, faltering productivity, economic stagnation — these and other symptoms of impending crisis were visible throughout the region."[11]

Thus the debate on socialist planning has come to a curious conclusion.   If the theoretical dispute has been settled in favor of socialism, the practical question seems to have gone the other way.   The giant corporations of capitalism have outperformed the lumbering ministries of production at every hand.   This does not mean, however, that socialism has met an impassable barrier in the form of an inherent limit imposed by its planning capabilities.   On the contrary, it has only brought about a belated move in every advanced socialist nation in the direction urged by Lange — away from centralized toward decentralized planning, and in particular away from the directives of a monolithic Central Planning Board toward the autonomy and flexibility of a market-based system.   In the Soviet Union we have the much publicized reforms of Liberman, in Czechoslovakia those of Ota Sik (at least until the Russian invasion), in Yugoslavia the adoption of a virtual "laissez-faire" market system in which the individual firm is run as a profit-making enterprise that vanishes via bankruptcy if it fails to meet the test of market viability, and in which the reach of central planning has been steadily reduced in scope.

Thus, ironically enough, socialist planning has been able to survive the difficulties inherent in the supervision of a complex industrial state only by reverting to the very market system whose shortcomings it was originally intended to redress.   And yet, socialism has passed one test only to face another.   The use of the market mechanism has unquestionably rescued socialism from a severe functional crisis.   The question must now be faced as to whether it has done so by ceasing to be socialist.

IV.

Does the market mechanism constitute a threat to socialism? The question is not an easy one to answer. On the one hand, there seems no more reason why the market cannot be used for socialist ends under a socialist state than why planning cannot be used for capitalist ends under a capitalist state. On the other hand, just as the mere presence of planning poses a sharp challenge, both structurally and ideologically, to capitalism, so the introduction of the market poses its inescapable problems for socialism.

Essentially the difficulty lies in the fact that in a market-run society, as we have seen, it is the distribution of purchasing power that sets the effective demands to which social effort will cater. But this raises a deep-seated problem for a socialist order. For if dollar votes are to shape the purposes for which social activity is carried on, it is important that these votes be distributed in accord with some principle of socialist equity. Nor is it difficult to discern what that principle should be. By every tenet of socialist belief in the inherent equality of men as human beings, there is a strong inherent bias toward a distribution of dollar voting power that will minimize the difference between one man's power to influence the outcome of the economic process and another's. To put it differently, there is a deep socialist belief in the propriety of income equality, perhaps tempered by social allowances for age, family size, etc.[12]

But the trouble with this solution is that incomes serve another purpose, even in a socialist society, beside that of constituting the source of the demand for goods and services. Incomes also constitute the rewards for labor: and insofar as labor has different degrees of difficulty, danger or unpleasantness, skill, and so on, it must be expected to command different rewards. Were this not the case, it would be exceedingly difficult for any economy that depended on the market to organize its production effectively. If skilled labor were paid no more than common labor, there would neither be any incentive for factory managers to economize on the former, nor much incentive for workers to undertake training that would ordinarily lead to a higher income.

Hence there are powerful reasons why a market society, socialist or other, must use a hierarchy of remunerations. But whereas this solves the problem of efficiency, it raises awkward questions of ideology. Is a society that permits or deliberately encourages differentials in income truly "socialist"? Is not the moral basis of socialism impaired when one man, who happens to be more adept or intelligent, is allowed to enjoy a higher standard of living than one who is not, although the latter may be more loving, or loyal, or more dedicated to the ideals of socialism?

If these questions should be brushed aside as smacking of impractical idealism, there is another reason to fear the inequality of rewards — to wit, that in allowing income differences to exist, a socialist society will be reintroducing, wittingly or otherwise, the very institution of class privilege against which it presumably struggles. At least in the eyes of some socialist critics, the emergence of a genuinely autonomous market sector (as in Yugoslavia) signals nothing less than a "peaceful transition from socialism to capitalism." The fear of these theoreticians is that the recrudescence of the profit motive as the driving force of society will lead inexorably to the reconstitution of the factory manager as capitalist and to the reenslavement of the worker to the wage system.[13] And beyond these particular institutional threats lurks the still more profound fear that the very existence of market relationships constitutes in itself a source of "corruption" for a socialist society. "Market relationships," writes Paul Sweezy, a leading socialist critic of market socialism, "are *inevitable* under socialism for a long time, but they constitute a standing danger to the system, and unless strictly hedged in and controlled will lead to degeneration and retrogression."[14]

To these charges not all socialists would agree. The Yugoslavs, for example, point out that in their system the factory manager is legally subservient to Workers Councils elected from the factory floor and empowered with full directors' rights over the manager, including the right to fix his salary or to fire him. Other socialists would argue that a certain amount of economic inequality is compatible with socialism, provided that it does not bring with it political or social inequality. As for the matter of corruption, that is a question we shall look into ourselves later on.

Thus it is difficult, perhaps impossible, to decide the merits of this controversy now. On the one hand, it is clear that socialism is being steadily forced to retreat from the centralized planning that was its original idea: "It is plain at the present day," writes the Canadian sociologist and socialist, T. B. Bottomore, "that the public ownership of industry is not by itself sufficient to establish a socialist society, and that it may in fact produce conditions which are directly inimical to the creation or functioning of such a society."[15] At the same time there seems as well to be a rise of a "capitalist spirit" in Yugoslavia, and the probable consequences of Russian decentralization in giving new power to the class of Soviet industrial managers have been frequently commented on.[16]

All this suggests that socialism has yet to make its peace either with the market system or with centralized control. Perhaps one had better use the Marxian terminology and point out that there are "contradictions" as deeply rooted in the institutions and ideology of socialist planning as those lodged in the operations of a capitalist market system — contradictions that will not be resolved as long as socialism must be concerned both with the workaday problems of production and distribution in a world of scarcity on the one hand, and with its pursuit of the ideals of human equality and confraternity, on the other.

V.

But will not this contradiction be resolved by the "abolition" of scarcity? It has become a commonplace to point out that science and technology constitute the truly revolutionary force of our day. Is not the *social* aspect of that revolution the impending end of the age of scarcity through the immense abundance that a completely technologized society will enjoy?[17]

That scientific technology has the capability of vastly raising the level of productivity and thereby ushering in an era of material abundance is beyond doubt. But just as this very abundance, with its scientific and technological preconditions, poses deep-seated challenges for the maintenance of the traditional structure of capitalism,[18] so I also believe that it holds equally profound difficulties for the prevailing realities or conceptions of socialism.

The challenges to socialism as well as to capitalism are of two kinds: psychological and organizational. With capitalism, the psychological problem lies in the likelihood that affluence will weaken the condition of economic dependency on which the market system is tacitly based, opening the prospect that normal differentials of income payments will no longer suffice to attract men to less desirable jobs, and thereby requiring that capitalism resort more and more to planning and coercion. Much the same motivational problem is likely also to affect the operation of a socialist market economy, pushing it, however unwillingly, in the direction of coercive planning, with all the difficulties of efficiency and morale that such measures must bring.

These psychological problems are apt to be less important, however, than the organizational necessities imposed on socialism by the domination of science and technology. There is a romantic tendency on the part of some socialists to picture the age of science as inherently favorable to the egalitarian aims of the socialist ideology. But this is not in fact what the hegemony of science promises. For both the production and the maintenance of the scientific mastery of the New Society will require the presence of a highly trained research elite supported by a large technical service staff. This necessary organizational core, with its collective expertise so essential for the maintenance of the general society, has all the attributes of a potential ruling class. "There is nothing to be gained," writes Radovan Richta, head of a Czech interdisciplinary team for research into the social implications of the scientific revolution, "by shutting our eyes to the fact that an acute problem of our age will be to close the profound cleavage in industrial society that, as Einstein realized with such alarm, places the fate of the defenseless mass in the hands of an educated elite, who wield the power of science and technology. Possibly this will be among the most complex undertakings facing socialism."[19]

Is elitism inherent in a society dominated by scientific technology? Certainly the underlying conditions for a highly stratified social system are implicit in the pyramidal educational requirements and the vastly differing social powers of the technologized society in which many will tend automated machines and a few will carry on the critical activity of discovery. "Ultimately," writes Richta, "the only solution will be to make professionals of us all" — a solution that reminds us of pious suggestions in our society that everyone should become a capitalist.

But even if the tendency toward elitism is successfully curbed, there remains one final challenge for socialism posed by technology. It is that the hastening pace of technical change has begun to pose a wholly new problem for all mankind — the problem of maintaining the ecological balance, the very viability, of the earth itself.

For the other side of the coin of affluence has been a steady deterioration in the quality of the environment — a deterioration brought about by enormously enhanced demands for resources, by gigantic scales of physical and chemical transformation of materials, and by the need to dispose of gargantuan quantities of end products, including the peculiarly lethal ones of radioactive wastes. Meanwhile, as the proliferation of production spoils the environment, it also makes possible the support of larger and larger concentrations of humanity, which in turn exacerbates the pollution process.

This spectacle of a steadily worsening environment coupled with an unsustainable rate of population increase gives rise to the uncomfortable feeling that the technological process is "running wild." And so it is. For at bottom, the ecological disequilibrium only reflects a still more profound unbalance between the technological and scientific capabilities of society and its social and self-governing capacities. The problem is that the first are cumulative and the second are not: each generation of scientists and technicians stands on the shoulders of preceding generations, bringing to the control over nature successively larger powers, whereas each generation of statesmen or administrators begins, for all intents and purposes, from scratch, in no way enhanced by the activities of its predecessors in understanding or controlling social processes. In its paradigm, of course, we have the spectacle of the unbelievable magnification of the capabilities of mass weaponry which is placed in the charge of men who are in no way whatsoever enlarged in their capability to govern, or even to understand, the world.

In this unequal race, which is visible in the socialist nations quite as much as in the capitalist ones, inevitably the technical capacities of a society come to exceed by an enormous margin its capabilities for exercising effective social control. The result is a technology that continuously escapes confinement, that develops in unforeseen directions, and that disturbs social systems by exerting its influences in unanticipated and unwelcome ways, such as the poisoning of the environment. It may well be that socialism will cope with this looming problem more effectively than capitalism, for assuredly planning lies at the very center of an effort to reestablish a workable balance between man and nature. The point is, however, that the technological imperative will present socialist planning with a range of problems requiring extensive and penetrative social intervention, rather than with a condition of general affluence in which a "liberated" community will spontaneously establish itself.

It is difficult at this juncture to foresee exactly what programs of control will be required to bring about a balanced ecology. All that can be said is that stringent limitations will have to be imposed, not alone on the productive apparatus of society, but very possibly on its consumptive patterns and certainly on its reproductive freedom. This will pose enormous problems for all social systems, but in the case of socialism the problem takes on a special significance. For the fact is that the known techniques of social planning do not today enable us to assert a mastery over the behavior of large communities — at least not if this mastery is to be made compatible with a high degree of civil liberty. Nor, for that matter, can we as yet even design a reliable program for the guidance of the advanced countries that carries the compelling logic of a socialist program for the underdeveloped countries. The sobering conclusion is that socialism will find its task made not easier but more difficult by the demands and consequences of the technological revolution on which it pins so many of its hopes.

VI.

We have dealt at some length with the particular problems that seem likely to trouble the future of socialism by virtue of the inherent "contradictions" of socialist planning. Now we must examine a second group of problems more closely associated with the content of the socialist ideology.

Here it will be useful if we once again begin with a comparison of socialism and capitalism. We have already noted at the very beginning of this essay the essentially conservative purpose of the ideology of capitalism. By defining and articulating a consensus of business beliefs, a capitalist ideology serves to mark out the boundaries of "what can be done" within a system whose fundamental commitment is to leaving things alone. The result is twofold. On the one hand, the business ideology acts to limit the interventory reach of the state as an agency for social change. On the other, by buttressing the nature of things as they are, it risks leaving society without any feeling of forward motion, of collective purpose, of high destination. Except perhaps in late nineteenth- and early twentieth-century America — certainly not in America today — the capitalist ideology has always had a practical, not an inspirational, appeal.

A totally different quality strikes us when we examine the ideology of the socialist world. Here the commitment to equality and to fraternal solidarity serves not to inhibit but to encourage the exercise of social intervention. And beyond that, the socialist vision of a transcendent society has shown itself to be second only to religion (if indeed second it be) as a source of inspiration, solace, and conviction.

Moreover, the nature of that extraordinary power of socialist ideas is not difficult to discover. Again in sharp contrast with the indifference of capitalist thought with regard to the matter, socialism has always affirmed its unshakable faith in the perfectibility of man. That is, socialism has always maintained that man is the product of his environment, so that the ugliness of society today or yesterday becomes an indictment, not of mankind, but of its past or prevailing institutions. Furthermore — and this is the crux of the charismatic power of socialist thought — it follows that in a society in which the deforming institutions of the past and present were removed, man would be "shaped" or "released" to discover his long-delayed fulfillment.

Thus, whereas capitalist thought has little to say about the future, other than to promise a general affluence, socialist thought envisages the transformation, indeed the liberation, of man:

By abolishing commodity production and opening the age of plenty, socialist society will give the signal for an extraordinary flowering of the human personality. Among hundreds of millions of individuals who today are indistinguishable in one gray mass, this personality will awaken, develop and flower in a thousand different directions, as yet unknown and unsuspected. Released from the wretched servitude of having to struggle for daily bread, human energy will be concentrated in art and science, in education and in physical and mental well-being. The place of competition between individuals for material existence will be taken by emulation in the pursuit of aims of research, of beauty and truth. Aggressiveness will be sublimated into creative purposes.[20]

That such a vision should have the power to motivate mankind is understandable enough. And yet we can see at the same time the problems inherent in such a view.   One of them, which we have already examined, is a failure to confront with unflinching honesty the social constraints and organizational requirements of the society of abundance.   The second, to which we now turn, is the failure to examine with equal fearlessness how man would actually behave in his "liberated" state.

There is no doubt as to how socialists would like him to behave. "What exactly is to be considered by *liberated man?*" asks one socialist writer.   She describes him as follows:

One might say that the liberated man is the generous and disinterested man; he is also a creative man, who can express his personality and talents in a creative action without constraint, whether in manual, intellectual, or artistic work, or in his relations and friendship with other men.   The free man is one who feels himself at the same time fully himself and in accord with other men.   He is an individual without idols, dogmas, prejudices or *a priori* ideas.   He is tolerant, inspired by a profound sense of justice and equality, and aware of himself as being at the same time an *individual* and a *universal* man.[21]

The difficulty with such a description is obvious enough.   As the critics of socialism have maintained since the day of the Utopian Socialists, this vision of man, however appealing, lacks a sense of toughness, of realism.   In the language of the nineteenth century it was faulted because it was based on an inadequate appreciation of "human nature," and whereas we are more chary of such phrases nowadays, we also sense a certain wishfulness in this delineation of what man could be.   The point, let me emphasize, is not to counter the socialist vision with mutterings that man is vile.   It is rather to insist that the deepest weakness of its vision has been its failure to formulate a conception of human behavior in all its historical, sociological, sexual, and ideational complexity, a conception that would present "man" as being at once biologic as well as social, tragic as well as heroic, limited as well as plastic.

To this criticism, socialism has always returned two rejoinders. The first is that it is unfair to expect it to rest its philosophy on such a "theory" of human behavior without requiring at least as much of other social systems of belief.   But this answer misses the point.   In the first place, capitalism actually has such a theory, for it believes implicitly in the ubiquitous acquisitive and competitive nature of man.   Second, capitalism does not require such a theory, for as with all social systems that rest content with the status quo, it takes "human nature" as it is — which is to say, it accepts the manifestations of the culture in which it finds itself, adapting its institutions to the prevailing character traits and behavioral characteristics of men rather than attempting to design a set of institutions that will nurture the essence of Man out of his imperfect prevailing self. And finally, in encouraging or acquiescing in these existing traits, capitalism does not claim that it is being more than expedient. "While minds are coarse they require coarse stimuli and let them have them," wrote J. S. Mill in his *Principles of Economics.* Only socialism, by virtue of its belief in the possibility of creating a liberating environment, requires an understanding of the ultimate nature of the human being whose innate capabilities must now be allowed to unfold.

To this critique, the socialist will offer his second rejoinder. It is that socialism does not try to discover or to nurture a "given," although heretofore stunted, germ of human character. Rather, it is a prime belief of socialism that man makes himself. Thus socialism can dispense with the need to formulate a conception of "human nature" by concentrating instead on the institutions by which that nature will be formed. In a word, human nature will be in the end what we want it to be.

But this rejoinder too misses the mark. For it ignores the very thing we wish to find out—that is, the extent to which man *can* make himself. So far as I know, only Herbert Marcuse has squarely faced the question of the ultimate limits of adaptability of man's psychobiologic makeup. In *Eros and Civilization* he has boldly argued that man's instinctual nature is capable of dramatic change in an environment of genuine abundance. In such a setting, Marcuse claims, where the historic pressures of material scarcity were finally lifted, the social need for the repression of man's narcissistic and erotic nature would no longer prevail, and Eros and the Nirvana principle could at long last take their places as the organizing elements of both the individual and the society.

Such a statement is indeed a theory of human nature, and if verified would place socialist ideology on a wholly new and much firmer footing. But I do not believe that there is any evidence, either theoretical or empirical, to support Marcuse's view of the instincts as creatures of the environment. As Sidney Axelrad has commented in the *Journal of the American Psychoanalytic Association:* "[I]nstincts are for Marcuse forces capable of being influenced by consciousness, rather than borderline somapsyche phenomena which are always unconscious and which can never lose their homeostatic functions and tendencies. [Marcuse's] prescription for a utopia of the future is not within the confines of psychoanalytic theory. It is a hope, an illusion. . . ."[22]

VII.

The absence of a satisfactory foundation of knowledge beneath the socialist conception of human nature is important not only because it blurs the long-term goals of socialism, but also because it carries short-term practical consequences of considerable importance.

The first of these is the failure of socialism to frame a coherent and cogent attitude toward the problem of motivation. Inherent in the distinction between "socialism" and "communism," for example — that is to say, between the society that a socialist government might inherit and one that it might make — is the deep-seated Marxist belief that man at a low level of culture and well-being will still require the motivation of invidious striving for monetary rewards, whereas once the high plateaus of a truly affluent society have been reached, it will be possible to discard these "bourgeois" traits and to move people by the famous principle of "from each according to his ability, to each according to his needs."

Yet in actuality we perceive exactly the opposite state of affairs. In the poorest and lowliest of societies — China, Cuba, the first years of the Russian Revolution — we find the power of nonmaterial, noninvidious incentives to be greatest, whereas in the richer and more advanced socialist societies — Yugoslavia, Czechoslovakia, present-day Russia — we discover an increasing need to rely on incentives of monetary inequality, managerial preferment, and competitive vying.

Much of this inability to form a reliable theory of motivation harkens back to an ancient ambivalence toward wealth and its effect on the human personality that socialism has inherited from Western religious and philosophic thought. Socialism continually talks of affluence for society, but it recoils at the contagions that affluence will bring to the individual. An instance in point is the justification of the expropriation of 55,000 small businesses in Cuba in March 1968. As the Havana newspaper *Granma* explained, this action was needed to remove "nests of parasites, hotbeds of corruption, illegal trading and counter-revolutionary conspiracy":

To get a good idea of the degree of corruption spawned by these activities, we need only cite the results of the investigation made by the Party of private businesses in Metropolitan Havana. According to this report, twenty-seven per cent of the proprietors were workers before setting themselves up in business (and the great majority of these sprang up after the triumph of the Revolution) . . . . It is intolerable that a worker, whose labor may benefit the whole people, should become a potential bourgeois, a self-centered money-grubber and exploiter of his countrymen.[23]

Such sentiments speak volumes as to the consequences of the psychological views which socialism expounds.   If the rise of a worker to the precarious status of a small shopkeeper is enough to endanger the sentiments and institutions on which socialism is based, then socialism must constantly live in fear of betrayal from the secret corruptibility of the people.   The parallel with the paranoid purity of extreme religious sects is all too apparent, and in one case as in the other, the vehemence with which evidences of corruption are denounced leads to the suspicions that both movements fear these "corruptions" are deeply embedded in the human psyche.

No less important as a consequence of the uncertain socialist conception of human behavior is its failure to examine the nature and consequences of alternative motivations to those of material incentives. If socialism seeks to perfect man in an environment in which the cash nexus will no longer provide the cohesive force for social organization, it must offer other motivations that will secure the necessary cooperation of a complex society.   Such nonmaterial incentives certainly exist — monastic orders, for instance, maintain their internal discipline by relying on wholly different motives of personal enlistment from those of a money-oriented society, as do military establishments and some kinds of professional groups.

What remains unasked, however, is whether a society knit together by such ties — a society in which a strict internalization of discipline has supplanted the external sanctions of the marketplace — would constitute a favorable environment for the perfection of man.   In this regard, the famous quotation of John Stuart Mill bears repetition:

The question is whether there would be any asylum left for individuality of character; whether public opinion would not be a tyrannical yoke; whether the absolute dependence of each on all, and the surveillance of each by all, would not grind all down into a tame uniformity of thoughts, feeling, and actions.[24]

In a word, socialist thought, in its avoidance of a study of human behavior, has not directly faced the problem of how the individual is to be integrated into the community, or the degree to which individual behavior must be governed by social norms, or the appropriate boundaries between social and private spheres of existence.   A fervent commitment to "participatory democracy" is today much voiced among Western socialist writers, but little or no consideration has been given to the means by which this participation can avoid what one commentator has called "the merciless masochism of community-minded and self-regulating men and women."[25]   (Oscar Wilde once remarked that socialism would take too many evenings, and the quip deserves to be taken seriously.)

Finally, the inadequacy of the socialist grasp of behavior reveals itself in the ferocious impatience with which socialism demands that "human nature" must change. The relinquishment of market incentives, for example, is not regarded as a goal to be achieved over several decades but one that must be sought within a single generation; motives of socialist cooperation are not viewed as behavioral patterns to be patiently inculcated over a number of generations, but attitudes that must be evidenced almost overnight. What lacks so fatally in this view is any appreciation of the depth of behavioral characteristics formed by social experience and of the power of family cultures to transmit these learned patterns of attitude and behavior despite the counterinfluences of organized social pressure. Hence, the repeatedly demonstrated unpreparedness of socialist thought before such behavioral realities as the persistence of "Russian" traits of government or "Chinese" xenophobia.

Here the dangers are twofold. On the one hand, the forces of nationalism — surely the single most powerful molding influence on social behavior in our time — are ignored, or worse, incorporated into socialist thought: as Paul Henri Spaak has observed, "The thing that socialists have learned to nationalize best is socialism."[29] On the other, there is the grave risk that the innocent inertia of ordinary behavior will be interpreted as a deliberate betrayal of socialist ideals. The Cuban incident above is a case in point.

VIII.

These reflections must now be placed in some final perspective. That socialism faces inherent problems springing from the difficulties of planning and from both the reach and the limitations of its ideology is, I think, undeniable. What is necessary is to confront these problems without a sense of either defeat or satisfaction. To examine the future of socialism, in the underdeveloped areas or in the advanced nations, without taking into account these, or perhaps other, challenges it must face is simply not to take socialism seriously — that is, as a political movement which must struggle with the intransigent realities of history and which, like all such movements, is likely to be bested by some of them.

In this struggle, two main resistances can be discerned. One of these is the rampant force of technology with its new networks of interdependence, its new frontiers of physical and chemical potentiality, its new dangers. In our day, at least, technology will not make its peace with socialism; socialism will have to make its peace with technology. The other is the stubborn inertia of the social personality, no doubt capable of great change, but only slowly and painfully, exerting meanwhile a continuous counterpressure against the radical alterations in actions and attitudes that socialism seeks to bring.

As we have suggested, it is likely that these resistances will establish the "limits" of socialism over the foreseeable future, much as similar forces set the boundaries of possible capitalist adaptation. But it would be wrong to end this essay on such a note. For unlike capitalism, which exists largely for its own sake in the present, socialism exists largely for the sake of the future. Inherent in the indistinct but bright vision of perfectible man is the source of an evolutionary momentum that carries a precious freight of human aspiration. Thus, unlike capitalism, socialism contains a core of belief that should be capable of maintaining its power to move human beings despite the obstacles that will hamper its performance.

Socialism is, at its root, the effort to find a remedy in social terms for the affront to reason and morality in the status quo. As such it is not limited to any particular place or time in history, but adapts its programs and its objectives to the indignities against which it fights. Thus, if socialism today in the United States derives its impetus from the spectacle of concentrated wealth, the commercial manipulation of human beings, or the indifference of the established power structure to the plight of the poor or the Negro, in the Soviet Union a genuinely socialist movement would (and some day will) take its organizing impulse from the concentration of political power and from the imprisonment of mind and spirit by Communist authorities and doctrines alike. In each and every nation the presence of power and privilege thus establishes the fortresses against which socialism presses its attack.

It may well be that each attack succeeds only to fail; that new walls of power and privilege are built as rapidly as old ones are torn down; that the ultimate goal of a transformed — indeed, transfigured — man is only a chimera. Yet the vitality of socialism seems unlikely to be daunted by that possibility. For taking socialism seriously means more than acknowledging its difficulties as a political movement. It means understanding as well that socialism is the expression of a collective hope for mankind, its idealization of what it conceives itself to be capable of. When the fires of socialism no longer burn, it will mean that mankind has extinguished that hope and abandoned that ideal.

ENDNOTES

[1] See *The Limits of American Capitalism*, I, pp. 3–4.

[2] Let me cite the three most objective sources I know to buttress these assertions. On Russian growth: Richard Moorsteen and Raymond Powell, *The*

Soviet Capital Stock, 1929–1962 (also Charles K: Wilbur, *The Soviet Model and the Underdeveloped Countries*) ; on Chinese modernization: Barry Richman, *Industrial Society in Communist China;* on the Cuban effort: Wassily Leontieff, *New York Review of Books,* August 21, 1969.

[3] In a famous passage in *State and Revolution* (Chapter V, 4) , Lenin described the activities of administering a socialist state as having been *"simplified by* capitalism to the utmost, till they have become the extraordinarily simple operations of watching, recording, and issuing receipts, within the reach of anybody who can read and write and knows the first four rules of arithmetic."

[4] *Review of Economic Studies,* October 1936 and February 1937; subsequently published in *On the Economic Theory of Socialism,* 1938.

[5] *ibid.,* p. 110.

[6] *ibid.,* p. 32.

[7] It is interesting to note that in an article written toward the end of his life, Lange declared that were he to compose his famous articles on the possibility of rational planning again, he would give the problem much shorter shrift. For the computer, Lange believed, would give the Planning Board even *better* information than the market was capable of, especially with regard to long-term planning. "The market process with its cumbersome tâtonnements appears old-fashioned. Indeed, it may be considered as a computing device of the pre-electronic age." "The Computer and the Market," in *Socialism, Capitalism and Economic Growth,* C. H. Feinstein, ed., p. 158.

[8] Economists will recognize as well that whereas it is easy to specify what a rational distribution means in a static economy, it is impossible to do so when we deal with an economy growing over time.

[9] Lange, *On the Economic Theory of Socialism,* p. 109.

[10] *ibid.,* p. 110.

[11] *Monthly Review,* October 1968, p. 11.

[12] See A. P. Lerner, *The Economics of Control,* Chapter 3.

[13] Not the least interesting aspect of this controversy is the abandonment of the traditional Marxist belief that the movement from capitalism to socialism was a "one-way street." The admission that the trend toward socialism is reversible, even if only for a while, constitutes a profound challenge to the classical Marxian analysis of historical evolution.

[14] *Monthly Review,* March 1969, p. 12, author's italics. See also "Peaceful Transition from Socialism to Capitalism?," *Monthly Review,* March 1964, and the exchange between Bettelheim and Sweezy, *ibid.,* March 1969. Also Ernest Mandel, *Marxist Economic Theory,* p. 655.

[15] "Industry, Work and Socialism" in *Socialist Humanism,* Erich Fromm, ed., p. 362.

[16] See, for example, the essays in *Planning and the Market in U.S.S.R. in the 1960s* by Balinky, Bergson, Hazard and Wiles.

[17] For a recent (pre-invasion) Czech statement of this prospect, see Radovan Richta, *Civilization at the Crossroads, Social and Human Implications of the Scientific and Technological Revolution,* Prague, 1969. Cf. also Mandel, *op. cit.,* Chapters 16–17.

[18] See *The Limits of American Capitalism,* Part III.

[19] Richta, *op. cit.,* p. 250.

[20] Mandel, *op. cit.*, p. 672.

[21] Mathilde Niel, "The Phenomenon of Technology," Fromm, *op. cit.*, p. 306.

[22] *Supra cit.*, January 1960, pp. 182, 184.

[23] Paul Sweezy and Leo Huberman, *Socialism in Cuba*, p. 137.

[24] *Principles of Economics*, Book II, Chapter I, 3.

[25] The phrase is Melvin Tumin's, quoted in "A Day in the Life of a Socialist Citizen," by Michael Walzer, *Dissent*, May/June 1968.   The remark by Wilde is quoted in the same article.

[26] Quoted in "Humanistic Socialism and the Future" by Norman Thomas, in Fromm, *op. cit.*, p. 327.

Paul M. Sweezy is co-editor, with Harry Magdoff, of the leading American journal of Marxist thought, Monthly Review. *Prior to establishing this journal he taught at Harvard, from which university he received his A.B. and Ph.D. His books include* Monopoly Capitalism (*with Paul Baran*) *and* The Theory of Capitalist Development.

26 The Future of Socialism

Paul M. Sweezy

The last thing I want to do is enter into a formal debate with Professor Heilbroner. With much of what he says on the subject before us,[1] I am in agreement; and even where I am not in agreement, I find most of what he has to say interesting and worthwhile. It would, I think, be largely a waste of time for all of us if I were to single out and elaborate on differences of this kind.

There are, however, differences of another sort that are not mentioned or even alluded to in his presentation that I think are important and that I want to make explicit. These are what you might call differences of approach and emphasis that, taken together, I suppose define my view of the future of socialism as not only different from his but also in a way incommensurate with his.

Professor Heilbroner sees capitalism and socialism as two coexisting, alternative, and at least to some degree competing social systems. He believes that both will be in existence during our lifetime (and I presume he means yours as well as his and mine), and he presents no reason for thinking that the same situation will not prevail during the lifetimes of our children and children's children. The two systems are there for everyone to see and evaluate: you pays your money and take your choice.

I'm afraid I can't quite see it that way. Capitalism is not a matter of individual countries and still less of free choice. It is a matter of the history of the whole globe — or, as the ecologists like to say nowadays, of the spaceship earth — for the last four hundred years, i.e., for the whole of what is commonly called modern history. In my view you cannot understand capitalism or socialism, hence the future prospects of either system, except as the product of that historical experience.

Capitalism had its birth in a small corner of the globe in Mediterranean and Northwestern Europe. But it did not become a decisive historical force until the European capitalist societies mastered firearms and the art of long-distance navigation. Armed with these technological achievements, they broke out of their small corner and roamed the seven seas — conquering, subjugating, looting, and trading. It was these proceedings that gave the impetus to the famous economic takeoff. At home the peasantry was uprooted from the land to form the basis for that *sine qua non* of any capitalist system, a free wage-working proletariat — free of feudal ties, free of property, and with no way to earn a livelihood save through the sale of its labor power. The other side of the capitalist coin was the amassing of liquid capital, much of which was provided from the loot and profits derived from the subjugated countries of the periphery. This whole process — the formation of a proletariat and the amassing of capital — was given a name by Marx: the original accumulation of capital.[2] It was the beginning of the split of the globe between a handful of rich exploiting countries and a multitude of poor exploited ones.

What must be understood is a. that the split has continued in existence ever since, despite all changes in forms and techniques of dominance; b. that it has grown relatively wider and wider; and c. that the situation of the poor exploited countries has deteriorated not only relatively but in many respects absolutely as well. This contrast between development of a few countries on the one hand and continuous underdevelopment of many on the other is the key to all modern history.

The split and its aggravation are aspects and consequences of the global capitalist system: *they are the way the system works.* To talk about remedying the situation within the framework of the capitalist system is a contradiction in terms. It is a reflection either of ignorance or of a will to deceive.

The only way out of this bind is through rejection of the capitalist system, i.e., through socialist revolution. And more and more countries have been taking it since Russia pioneered the way in 1917. The obverse, inevitable under the circumstances, has been that the increasingly dominant concern of the rich exploiters has been to keep the remaining ones inside the capitalist compound. Leadersip in this task naturally falls to the lot of the dominant capitalist power, which explains why the United States since the Second World War has assumed in the eyes of the world the role of global gendarme and prison warden.

So we have now, as the result of four centuries of history, two overriding processes in the capitalist world: deepening underdevelopment in its dependent part, and global civil war (overt or latent as the case may be) between the dominant metropolis and the dominated periphery.

There are enough reasons, I think, for believing that this system has no *historical* future: by this I mean that it may last my lifetime or yours or our children's but that it offers no prospect for humanity to go forward and is therefore historically doomed. As it happens, however, there are other reasons of a different order that are equally compelling, and any speculation about the future which omits them from consideration can no longer be considered adequate. I refer of course to the threat of ecological disaster that has always been inherent in capitalism's inexorable drive to expansion and that now, in the second half of the twentieth century, has moved from the wings to the center of the historical stage. Here I can do no better than quote the words of Professor Heilbroner himself:

Ultimately, the ecological crisis represents our belated awakening to the fact that we live on . . . our Spaceship Earth. As in all spaceships, sustained life requires that a meticulous balance be maintained between the life-support capability of the vehicle and the demands made by the inhabitants of the craft. Until quite recently, those demands have been well within the capability of the ship, both in terms of its ability to supply the physical and chemical requirements for continued existence and to absorb the waste products of the voyagers. This is not to say that the earth has been generous — short rations have been the lot of mankind for most of its history — nor is it to deny the recurrent advent of local ecological crises: witness the destruction of whole areas like the erstwhile granaries of North Africa. But famines have passed and there have always been new areas to move to. The idea that the earth as a whole was overtaxed is new to our time.

For it is only in our time that we are reaching the ceiling of earthly carrying capacity, not on a local but on a global basis. Indeed, as will soon become clear, we are well past that capacity, provided that the level of resource intake and waste output represented by the average American or European is taken as a standard to be achieved by all humanity. To put it bluntly, if we take as the price of a first-class ticket the resource requirements of those passengers who travel in the Northern Hemisphere of the Spaceship, we have now reached a point at which the steerage is condemned to live forever — or at least within the horizon of the technology presently visible — at a second-class level; or at which a considerable change in living habits must be imposed on first class if the ship is ever to be converted to a one-class cruise.[3]

Commenting on this analysis, Professor Gurley of Stanford adds:

This analysis has many implications for both the rich and the poor. . . . In attempting to achieve economic development, today's poor around the world have a few advantages over their predecessors of a few hundred years ago — the advantages of increased knowledge and of better technologies. But they are at a disadvantage in several crucial ways. First, they do not have the opportunities which the early Europeans and Americans had of gaining huge flows of economic resources through plunder, slavery, and fraud. Second, I have argued that they are burdened by a powerful alliance within the world capitalist system which works for ends that are often opposed to their basic needs. And finally, to the extent that the above "ecological argument" is correct, the present poor are further condemned by the fact that the rich states are hell-bent on a growth path of demanding and producing ever more GNP, and in the process using up exhaustible resources that the poor must have if they are ever going to raise their own living standards to half-way decent levels.[4]

For the purpose of my present argument, all I need to add is that both the "powerful alliance within the world capitalist system" and the condition of being "hell-bent on a growth path of demanding and producing ever more GNP" are absolutely basic aspects of capitalism itself. We are rapidly approaching a time when the continued existence of capitalism will no longer be compatible with the continued existence of the human race.

Is socialism the inevitable alternative and answer? This, it seems to me, is the way the problem of the future of socialism should be posed. And the answer, I think, is that if the human race survives, it can *only* be through socialism, i.e., through developing a nonexploitative, collective society which has been able to learn the lessons of four centuries of capitalism and has come to understand that a radically different course is a *sine qua non* if mankind is to have any historical future at all.

The first half century of socialism hardly provides conclusive evidence as to whether or not mankind has actually found the key to survival. Soviet Russia has great achievements to its credit, not least the defeat of Nazi Germany in the Second World War. But I do not believe it can be said that the USSR has created, or even shown the way to, a radically new society; and as time goes on it seems to revert more and more to the condition of a class society with values and goals increasingly difficult to distinguish from those of developed capitalist societies. In this connection, allow me to quote what Leo Huberman and I wrote about Soviet experience on the occasion of the fiftieth anniversary of the Russian Revolution:

The facts indicate that relative to most other countries in the world today, the Soviet Union is a stable society with an enormously powerful state apparatus and an economy capable of reasonably rapid growth for the foreseeable future.   It is also a stratified society, with a deep chasm between the ruling stratum of political bureaucrats and economic managers on the one side and the mass of working people on the other, and an impressive spectrum of income and status differentials on both sides of the chasm.   The society appears to be effectively depoliticized at all levels, hence *a fortiori* non-revolutionary.   In these circumstances the concerns and motivations of individuals and families are naturally focused on private affairs and in particular on individual careers and family consumption levels.   Moreover since the economy is able to provide both an abundance of career openings and a steadily expanding supply of consumer goods, these private motivations are effective in shaping the quantity, quality, allocation, and discipline of the labor force.   There is probably no capitalist country in the world today, with the possible exception of Japan, in which classical bourgeois mechanisms operate as efficiently to secure the kinds and amounts of work needed to propel the economy forward.

But the prevalence of these mechanisms, and indeed their very success, cannot but have a profound influence on the quality of the society and the "human nature" of its members.   This is part of the ABC of socialist thought and need not be elaborated upon here: suffice it to say that the privatization of economic life leads necessarily to the privatization of social life and the evisceration of political life.   Bourgeois values, bourgeois criteria of success, bourgeois modes of behavior are fostered. Politics becomes a specialty, a branch of the division of labor, like any other career.   And of course the other side of the coin is the perpetuation and deepening of that alienation of man from his fellows which many socialists have felt to be the ultimate evil of bourgeois society."[5]

Unfortunately, nothing that has happened in the years since this was written has led me to revise this negative view of trends in Soviet society.   Rather the contrary: I am more and more inclined to accept Charles Bettelheim's contention that Soviet society today is a form of state capitalism ruled by a new state bourgeoisie.[6]   If this is true, it means that the world's first attempt to build a socialist society was abortive.

Similar things have happened in history before.   For example, there can be little doubt that genuine capitalist societies arose in a number of Italian city states during the Middle Ages, only to wither away or be destroyed from outside.   Apparently capitalism needs to attain a certain critical size in terms of population and territory before it can be assured of survival, and this did not occur until the (European) Age of Discovery in the fifteenth and sixteenth centuries.   Capitalism, in other words, put in a few abortive appearances before it finally "made it" on the stage of history.   Perhaps we are witnessing an analogous process now as China and North Korea and North Vietnam struggle to build socialist societies independently of, and partly in opposition to, the Soviet Union.

The crucial question, it seems to me, is whether these new attempts to build socialism are doomed to follow the Soviet Union on the road back to class-dominated societies, or whether they have succeeded in creating genuinely new social structures which have a reasonable prospect of moving forward toward the historic goals of socialism (and ultimately communism). If only because of its size and population, I suppose it would be generally admitted that China is the country most likely to provide a conclusive answer. And it is precisely in China that we find what I think are the most interesting and encouraging developments. There is unfortunately no possibility, within the limited scope of this paper, to explore this subject in any detail, but I would not want to end without at least indicating the respects in which I believe China to be pioneering a course radically different from that which has led the Soviet Union to its present condition. And for this purpose I can do no better than quote at some length from a remarkable study by Professor Gurley of Stanford University who has been cited above in a different context. Gurley's subject is "Capitalist and Maoist Economic Development,"[7] but what he says about capitalist development could be applied, with only minor modifications, to Soviet development as well.

The Maoists' disagreement with the capitalist view of economic development is profound. Their emphases, values, and aspirations are quite different from those of capitalist economists. To begin with, Maoist economic development occurs within the context of central planning, public ownership of industries, and agricultural cooperatives or communes. . . . The profit motive is officially discouraged from assuming an important role in the allocation of resources, and material incentives, while still prevalent, are downgraded.

But perhaps the most striking difference between the capitalist and Maoist views is in regard to goals. Maoists believe that, while a principal aim of nations should be to raise the level of material welfare of the population, this should be done only within the context of the development of human beings and of encouraging them to realize fully their manifold creative powers. And it should be done only on an egalitarian basis — that is, on the basis that development is not worth much unless everyone rises together; no one is to be left behind — either economically or culturally. Indeed, Maoists believe that rapid economic development is not likely to occur *unless* everyone rises together. Development as a trickle-down process is therefore rejected by Maoists, and so they reject any strong emphasis on profit motives and efficiency criteria that lead to lopsided growth. Their emphasis, in short, is on man rather than on "things" (pp. 37–38).

The failure of many economic experts on China to tell the story of her economic development accurately and fully is bad enough. But even worse, I think, has been the general failure to deal with China on her own terms, within the framework of her own goals and methods for attaining those goals, or even to recognize the validity of those goals. Communist China is certainly not a paradise, but it is now engaged in perhaps the most interesting economic and social experiment ever attempted, in which tremendous efforts are being made to achieve an egalitarian development, an industrial development without dehumanization, one that involves everyone and affects everyone.   But all those efforts seem not to have affected Western economists. . . . Apparently it does not matter that 775 million people are involved in a gigantic endeavor to change their environment, their economic and social institutions, their standards of living, and themselves . . . (pp. 45–46) .

To which I would add only that this "most interesting economic and social experiment ever attempted" is precisely a fully conscious effort to realize the historic goals of socialism.   I believe that much in the future not only of socialism but of mankind in general depends on its success or failure.

ENDNOTES

[1] In the essay "Reflections on the Future of Socialism" in his book *Between Capitalism and Socialism,* New York, 1970.

[2] The usual English translation is "primitive accumulation."   This, however, is both inaccurate and misleading.   The German word is *ursprünglich,* which literally means "original" and is exactly what Marx meant to convey.

[3] Robert L. Heilbroner, "Ecological Armageddon," in *Between Capitalism and Socialism, op. cit.,* pp. 270–71.

[4] John G. Gurley, "The State of Political Economics," paper prepared for delivery at the 1970 annual meeting of the American Economic Association.

[5] Leo Huberman and Paul M. Sweezy, "Lessons of Soviet Experience," *Monthly Review,* November 1967, pp. 11–12.

[6] See, for example, Charles Bettelheim, "On the Transition Between Capitalism and Socialism," *Monthly Review,* March 1969.

[7] *Bulletin of Concerned Asian Scholars,* April–July 1970.

QUESTIONS

Socialism
Heilbroner / Sweezy

1.   Are there really any differences between Heilbroner and Sweezy?
2.   Is capitalism as inflexible as Sweezy implies?
3.   Is capitalism really doomed?

4. Is socialism *inherently* anti-imperialist?

5. Is capitalism inherently imperialistic?

6. Can *world* progress take place for all under a capitalist system?

7. Do the people of the underdeveloped countries really need to be "pushed, prodded, cajoled, or threatened into heroic efforts" to develop? Is the only alternative massive deprivation?

8. Is socialism the only alternative to capitalism?

9. Is socialism relevant to problems now faced in the United States?

10. What is the future of socialism?

11. What are the real differences between the *economic* systems in the United States and the USSR?

12. Is there an alternative to the way the United States and USSR developed?

13. Is China a viable alternative to the paths followed by the United States and USSR?

14. Aren't there inherent contradictions in socialist development that will inevitably lead to a Soviet-type system?

15. Is it possible to create "socialist man" i.e., man interested in human betterment, fraternity, and cooperation?

16. What is the role of markets in a socialist economy?

17. Who governs in a socialist economy and how are these persons chosen?

18. Is it possible to eliminate classes in a socialist economy?

19. Can one be sure that individuality will survive in a socialist country?

20. Why did classes emerge in the Soviet Union?

21. Some observers argue that China is the most bureaucratic country in the world. Is bureaucracy consistent with the ideas of a good society advanced by the socialist thinkers?

22. Socialist countries have pollution problems and will create more in the process of development. Is socialism inherently any less polluting than capitalism? Is it an easier system in which to control pollution than capitalism?

23. Are the basic institutions of socialism any less likely to lead to imperialism than those of capitalism?

24. Socialist countries have been established by violent revolutions and the suppression of certain people. Can systems established on such a basis ever be humane?

*Robert T. Averitt is Professor of
Economics and Chairman of the
Department of Economics at Smith
College. He received his B.A. degree from North Texas State College and his Ph.D. from the University of Texas. He is the author
of* The Dual Economy.

*In response to a question con-
cerning his position within economics, he made the following
statement:*

"*My primary professional interest is in structural dynamics, the
economics of the long run. I am
currently exploring the possibility
of applying general systems theory
to economic problems, including a
modern version of a time theory
of value. I am convinced that
teaching undergraduates is one of
the most important things that economists do. My quarrel with economics
as presented to undergraduates is that both micro and macro theories are informed by an essentially short-run perspective. Since undergraduates have a
life expectancy of about half a century, it is the long run consequences of current economic activity that will most forcefully condition their life-style.
The pace of life is now so rapid in America that today's college students will
not, as Keynes prophesied, be dead in the long run; they will instead live
through several long run economic cycles.*"

27 The Future of American Capitalism

Robert T. Averitt

Let me begin with a general comment on the nature of social systems.
Every social system can be seen as a set of behavioral activities sanctioned by an ideological construct. Capitalism, for example, can be
visualized as a set of households and business firms engaged in exchange
relationships through a complex of markets. Households, or families,
sell labor-time, or some other production component, to business firms,
who in turn use this labor-time to produce commodities for sale to
households. Seen on this level, the economic system is composed of
human actions that can be summarized as exchange, production, and
consumption.

TWO CONCEPTS OF CAPITALISM

But an economic system is more than a network of patterned, antlike behavior. A human social system must make sense to its participants. Thus the activity level of an economy must always be reinforced by an appropriate sanctifying fiction which imparts meaning to daily life. Football fosters good sportsmanship and a sense of teamwork. War keeps the world safe for democracy. Playing with dolls gives little girls a strong sense of motherhood. So it is with economic activity. Capitalism is an economic system sustained by a dual ideology, developed at different times in the Anglo-American past. The first justification of capitalism was articulated by John Locke, Adam Smith, and a procession of economists extending roughly through John Stuart Mill. Their doctrine was preeminent in the English-speaking world from about 1776 to 1870, and they are referred to as the classical economists. Let us call their defense of capitalism *development capitalism*.

The second ideological underpinning for a capitalist economy arrived in England during the 1870s with the writings of William Stanley Jevons and was fully articulated by Alfred Marshall by 1890. This second group of economists extending from Jevons through Marshall and continuing until the present is conventionally referred to as neoclassical economists. Their wisdom is now codified in that branch of our subject called price theory. Neoclassical economics, unlike classical economics, is still taught in every undergraduate economics curriculum. Let us call the neoclassical explication of a market economy *exchange capitalism*.

CAPITALISM'S INSTITUTIONAL RULES

In a capitalist economy, the vast majority of all productive activity must be performed by organizations who purchase their inputs (land, labor, capital, and management) in an input or factor market, who sell their output in an output or commodity market, and who are subject to the rule of commercial survival: thou shalt take in more money than thou payest out. Any violation of this cardinal capitalist rule even for a short time must immediately occasion an agonizing reappraisal by management of the organization's life expectancy. No capitalist enterprise can ignore the imperatives of financial integrity over long periods without ceasing to be either capitalist, or an independent enterprise, or both.

Having satisfied the requirement of commercial survival, a vigorous capitalist firm is free to pursue the complementary rule of commercial success: thou shalt arrange the organization's operations so that the difference between money inflow and money outflow cannot be increased. Taken together, the rule of survival and the rule of success decree that capitalist enterprises shall at all times seek to minimize their losses and/or maximize their profits. To the extent that business firms do not conform to these dual strictures of commercial behavior, they are not behaving as capitalists in the full sense of that term.

The rules for prudent household behavior resemble those of the business firm. The household sells its assets, usually its labor-time, in the market to a business firm on the best terms available. The revenue thus acquired is used to cover the household's consumption costs. If the household is to survive in the financial sense, income must equal or exceed outgo. The wise household will spend its income so that it receives in return a maximum of consumer satisfaction. As the business firm maximizes profit, so the household optimizes satisfaction.

Under capitalism, the urge toward economic gain must be a major motivating factor underlying much of the community's social intercourse. Here we have an ethical dilemma. Throughout the history of ethical and moral thought in Western civilization, material greed has been considered a vice, not a virtue. One man's untoward accumulation of this world's goods has traditionally been assumed to take place at another man's expense. My economic gain was seen as the source of your deprivation. A major prerequisite for the acceptance and promulgation of the capitalist ethic was the creation of a new social fiction converting human greed, an ancient vice, into a modern virtue.

THE EMERGENCE OF DEVELOPMENT CAPITALISM

During the seventeeth and eighteenth centuries just such a sanctifying fiction emerged. Its fundamental propostions can be summarized as follows. Men operate with the maximum energy and for the longest time in economic matters when they are motivated by personal greed. Man's material desires are subject to infinite expansion, but nature yields her treasures reluctantly. Thus the means for material satisfaction are scarce and must always remain so. The transformation of a hostile natural environment into a humanly gratifying one demands that egoistic men be allowed to accumulate private property subject only to the restraint of competition. So long as no man, or small group of men, is allowed to monopolize a significant segment of the economy's productive assets for an appreciable length of time, greed, while a personal vice, can be converted into a public virtue.

John Locke stated the fundamentals of the developmental capitalist paradigm in 1690: ". . . he who appropriates land to himself by his labor does not lessen but increases the common stock of mankind. For the provisions serving to the support of human life produced by one acre of enclosed and cultivated land are ten times more than those which are yielded by an acre of land of an equal richness lying in common. And therefore he that encloses land, and has a greater of the conveniences of life from ten acres than he could have from a hundred left to nature, may truly be said to give ninety acres to mankind." Notice Locke's assumptions. Nature is available in plenitude, but is of small use in its natural state. Men have the *ability* to greatly enlarge nature's productivity, but they have the *will* to do so only when granted the legal protection of private property.

John Locke, Adam Smith, John Stuart Mill, and their fellow creators of the ideology of development capitalism made it clear that capitalism's justification rested firmly upon its ability to sustain what we now call economic development, the expansion of the nation's capacity to produce. The right of private ownership and the license for commercial markets is conditional, not absolute; their continuation is contingent on the conversion of private possessions into public assets. While transferring ownership from the public domain to private appropriation seemingly reduces the public wealth, it will not in fact do so when the same material is put to a more productive use and the result sold to the public at competitive prices.

The social ethic of development capitalism is legitimized by capitalism's ability to foster economic development, and economic development is synonymous with industrialization. Economic development demands a more productive use of labor-time, the introduction of production, distribution, and communication techniques that yield a larger output for each representative hour of human toil. In agriculture, for example, human time can be more productive if the land is fertilized and planting and harvesting accomplished with the aid of power-driven machinery. In industry, labor-intensive, handicraft production can be replaced with mass production; if the product can be standardized, and if a large market can be created, assembly lines can be introduced to speed the productive flow. The common denominator of all these developmental production techniques is that they progressively diminish the raw human content per unit of output.

The mechanization of production, substituting inanimate energy for animate, machine work for manual work, is a prerequisite for saving large quantities of labor-time. Development demands a shift from labor-intensive production to an emphasis on capital goods, a reliance on machine-power rather than manpower. The possibilities for increasing the work-speed of men are severely circumscribed. Humans have a narrow range of effective working rhythm. A healthy man can work faster and longer than a sickly one, but only a little faster and longer. But once the major burden of supplying energy, processing raw materials, transferring materials, and regulating the quality of output is assigned to mechanical devices, the quickening of output per human man-hour can begin in earnest. Machinery does not tire easily, and it can be continually reorganized to give a higher yield per hour.

CAPITALIST AMERICA

In the United States, the first major industrializing surge began in the 1840s. Pushed forward in spurts by the spread of the great new industries, typified by the railroads, iron and steel, electricity, and the automobile, the American industrial momentum continued, with sporadic interruptions, until the decade of the 1930s. An industrial economy does not develop painlessly, not even in a nation rich in nature's materials. But with the single, major exception of the American Civil War, the dislocating process of creating an industrial structure served to unify a new nation that otherwise threatened to fall into factional disarray.

Pose for yourself the difficult question of nation-building faced by our founding fathers. Your aim is to establish a nation based upon the principles of democratic capitalism. You have defined democracy in the Declaration of Independence as a system wherein all men are created free and *equal*. Thus a democratic government is egalitarian, giving every man the same vote. Yet capitalism is hierarchical, allowing all men to compete in the marketplace where some will become rich, others remain relatively poor. Furthermore, a free market system will base its output on the volume of dollar votes, assuring that the poor will have little say in economic matters. Would you, like Jefferson, stress the *democratic* side of democratic capitalism, forgoing industrialization for self-sufficient yeoman agriculture wherein every man is his own employer? Or would you, like Hamilton, emphasize the *capitalist* component of the American tradition, restricting the egalitarian, democratic principles to the choosing of politicians?

The argument for stressing capitalism is a strong one. When developmental capitalism is working well, an economic issue can be settled by making *all* parties to a dispute better off through compromise and cooperation. In matters economic, all may win, even if many are but small winners. Economics is not a zero-sum game, where total gains must equal total losses. But religious, moral, and social issues cannot so easily be settled by allowing all to emerge as gainers. The realization of this profound truth, that only the economic product is infinitely divisible and subject to prodigious expansion, tempted the new American nation to deemphasize democratic politics, where my growth in political power necessarily decreases your influence. The new nation, with its irreconcilable ethnic and ideological diversities, was nudged into a primarily economic province. Even Jefferson gave in when, as President, he realized that an agrarian nation could not hope to defend itself in an industrial world. As ever, the needs of the military ended the debate. Between the 1840s and the early 1930s, the United States became the most capitalistic nation the world has known. Not until the thirties did the collapse of the American economy suggest a major compromise between the inherent inequality of capitalist expansion and the political promise of democracy.

THE DECLINE OF CAPITALIST DEVELOPMENT

All known growth curves, economic and noneconomic, resemble an elongated letter "S." In the beginning growth is slow, perhaps barely evident. Then a surge takes place, inaugurating a phase of rapid expansion. But in time the easy gains are realized, the environment becomes more resistant, the growth rate slows awaiting a new impetus for its resumption. By the 1930s the key industries forming the base of American development had reached a relatively mature state. No longer could their expansion fuel the economy and employ its labor force at the late-nineteenth-century pace. The basic sectors would continue to expand, and they would be joined by a few new industries of economic importance. But the standard pattern of rapid development based on a filling out of the modern industrial complex, the articulation of a complete, interlocking system of production, distribution, transportation, and communication would not longer provide sufficient dynamism to make the fiction of a vigorous, unattended capitalist development fully convincing.

What was becoming evident in the 1930s was that the capitalist motivation grounded on competitive greed was convincing only when most who sought gainful employment could find it. And the industrialization of the continent, while a process consuming an enormous quantity of man-hours for several decades, had a proximate beginning and a proximate end. In the labor-scarce American economy, employers were under constant pressure to cut labor costs with labor-saving machinery. Yet during the period when the nation's usable social overhead capital was being installed, labor-saving machinery could not reduce the total secular demand for labor. They merely allowed more work to be done. Yet eventually, as the population continued to grow at a rapid pace through natural increase and immigration, the ability of new investment to absorb the energies of our ever-growing labor force declined. The money panic of the 1930s proved to be more than just another money panic. It signaled the opening of a new economic era in America.

The new source of economic expansion was accumulating in the residue of the old. Rapid industrial development inevitably creates a condition of social imbalance, one in which the provisions of public services — education, health, public welfare — are slighted relative to more marketable products. When nature is abundant, labor scarce, and technical advance rapid, we have seen that a market system facilitates economic development. It does so by factoring consumer demand into innumerable fragments. Every individual is free, at least in theory, to satisfy his personal desires as he sees them. Consumption is largely a private affair. With small exception, no particular good or service is compulsory. When, as in the case of electricity, modern life does demand a particular service, the production and price of that item is commonly removed from market forces and regulated by an arm of government. Public goods, those items like literacy, health, and defense that must be consumed in common if their use is to have the maximum effect, tend to be provided in a minimal fashion.

ECONOMIC EXPANSION THROUGH COMPETITIVE POLITICS

During the New Deal years of the 1930s the principles for restoring America's economic dynamism seemed clear even if the techniques for doing so were obscure. The vast reservoir of public needs left poorly attended during the long industrialization drive must now be tackled. The poor and downtrodden must be raised from economic oblivion. Competition, the catalyst that had proven so successful in converting greed into abundance, would be pressed into the public service. Economic self-interest could remain a cardinal virtue in American life, even though it must now be organized into interest groups expressing their demands in a public, rather than a private, market. The new era of economic advance would be fueled by expanding government expenditure to meet competing social demands under a system of competitive democracy.

The economic theory of the New Deal is clear, at least in retrospect. The problem was to recreate full employment. John Maynard Keynes, the most prominent English economist of the twentieth century, was in the process of demonstrating that full employment of the labor force results from a high level of expenditures, public and/or private. It is spending that creates jobs, and any kind of spending will do so long as it can be given ideological justification. To quote Keynes, "Ancient Egypt was doubly fortunate, and doubtless owed to this its fabled wealth, in that it possessed two activities, namely, pyramid-building as well as the search for the precious metals, the fruits of which, since they could not serve the needs of man by being consumed, did not stale with abundance. The Middle Ages built cathedrals and sang dirges. Two pyramids, two masses for the dead, are twice as good as one; but not so two railroads from London to York."

That government had to fill the spending gap so suddenly left vacant by the private sector was evident. But true to our long-standing capitalist tradition, the *direction* of government spending would still be determined by demand. Social demand would simply replace private demand. The strength of a particular type of social demand would be measured by the size, cohesiveness, and persistence of that demand's issue-public. An issue-public is a group of citizens formed around their mutual interest in a specific problem, for example, low farm incomes, the protection of labor's rights, or the need for good roads. The political process of competitive elections is used to further these interests. Under the system of liberal politics dominating American government since the thirties, various issue-publics demand the financing of those aspects of social development that they deem most useful to themselves. The importance of the individual under this system is closely related to the importance of his group, and to his importance within this group.

To a large segment of the last generation of Americans, the liberal solution of competitive democracy seemed ideal. The competitive attitude is one of long standing. The marketplace of private goods had proven reasonably successful; why not a political marketplace for public demands? But the critical difference between government and a business firm, between social and private needs, began to assert itself through the years. Unlike development under a market orientation, there is no social mechanism relating price to quantity demanded, and no profit incentive linking the supply of social services to reduced unit costs. The financing of liberal social development is factored among all citizens through the levying of income and excise taxes or by allowing inflation to erode the currency's purchasing power. In either case the individual taxpayer cannot keep a tight control over public costs.

In brief, economic expansion based upon social demands and financed by general taxation or inflation does not provide a mechanism for relating the worth of a specific program to the value of some alternative resource use. Converted into the language of economics I am saying that opportunity cost, the loss of those things that are not produced because resources are used in a particular way, is not taken into account. When government attempts to fulfill its social demands without weighing their opportunity costs, the final result is likely to be a total program substantially larger than available resources at full employment will permit. The adoption of Keynesian economic attitudes, with their attack on the usefulness of a balanced national budget, removes the last remaining barrier to governmental inflation. Whatever its other faults, the concept of a public budget in balance at least represented an attempt to relate *total* revenue to *total* expenditures, even if the value of particular programs cannot be closely compared with their cost.

There are imminent signs that in America our system of liberal politics has lost much of its conviction. In the short run the strength of politically directed spending emanates from its separation of cost and price from demand. Tax costs are dispersed throughout the citizenry, so that each taxpayer's support of any specific program, even when he deems the activity useless, does not easily move him to action. Or at least so it was until that collection of interests known as the military-industrial complex seized such a large portion of our tax revenue. The intensity of the farmer's demand for agricultural price supports is strong and heavily concentrated, while the intensity of the urban taxpayer's revolt against agricultural subsidies is widely scattered and weakened by tax dispersion. The benefits of social programs are usually concentrated and socially visible to the recipients, while the specific cost is fragmented and socially hidden.

Once the principle of government by social demand is fully established, every vested interest is impelled to seek government support. And once a multitude of groups, including the poor who received much of the New Deal's rhetoric but little of its cash, organize to avoid taxes and increase their subsidies, the *localized* advantages of the system begin to disappear. Liberal politics benefits the farmer, for example, only so long as his subsidy exceeds his tax contribution in support of other issue-publics. When the whole society becomes politically effective, much of the advantage attached to any particular interest group is lost. And the poor, the last to organize, are likely to be the most deserving, and the least polite, in asserting their demands. In politics as in business, a monopoly position established by innovators is first diluted, then eliminated when imitators are free to enter the field. In short, liberal politics *is* a zero sum game. Your subsidy does increase my taxes, while reducing the money available to subsidize me.

IS EXCHANGE CAPITALISM AN ALTERNATIVE?

But if the liberal attempt to retain at least the competitive element in capitalism while shifting from industrial development to social development is failing, what of the conservative alternative? Can we not now shift to capitalism's second ideological justification, exchange capitalism? Several prominent neoclassical economists, including Milton Friedman, suggest that we can. They tell us that we can retain most of the advantages of a traditional capitalist market system even when government expenditure is a major portion of total expenditure if we separate the *financing* of public goods from their *supply*. Surely government must finance a major portion of health care, education, defense, and similar goods demanding a high degree of joint community consumption, but much of the supply of these goods can remain private and market oriented by funding individuals, not organizations. We can allow the parents of each child to spend his publicly financed education allotment with any school, public or private, meeting minimum educational standards. And we can have a volunteer army of virtually any size by simply raising military pay to a level sufficient to induce the required number of participants. In both examples the activity is publicly financed, but the individual retains a range of choice not available under the prevailing procedures.

This argument is appealing, particularly at a time when the zero-sum quality of liberal politics is becoming evident. It seems to preserve a high degree of economic choice, the ultimate value of exchange capitalism as a system of belief. Pose for yourself the ultimate value question in economics. What should the consumer consume? What constitutes the good life? Is the consumption of Beethoven records better than the purchase of Beatles records? Economists have dealt with such classic philosophical questions in an ingenious way. We assume that the ultimate value in matters of taste is freedom of choice. For you, Beethoven may be better; for me, the Beatles. We can share the good society when you are free to choose Beethoven while I select the Beatles.

Notice that this elevation of consumer choice to the position of ultimate good assumes that my welfare is a function of my own consumption, and that I have reliable information about the consequences of my choices. Both of these assumptions are increasingly violated under the conditions of contemporary capitalism. Most of my current consumption is composed of technically complex goods sold to me by impersonal organizations. Although I may know that I like the looks and performance of a Chevrolet, and the taste of Fresca, I cannot know that my car is unsafe at any speed, and that the additives to my bottled and canned diet are cumulatively, silently and finally reducing my life expectancy. Even if, unaffected by mass advertising, I independently perfect my personal tastes, without expert knowledge I cannot know the second order consequences of my consumption pattern. Even if such information is known and potentially available to me, I do not have time to learn about food chemistry and mechanical engineering principles necessary to protect myself. To do so would make consumer sovereignty more than a full-time job for all consumers.

Furthermore, my welfare is strongly affected by my neighbor's consumption in a crowded, technologically complex society. His exhaust fumes pollute my air, his detergents spoil my fishing. Thus contrary to the assumptions of exchange capitalism, my welfare is significantly conditioned by your consumption. Population growth is an outstanding case in point. Population expansion and freedom of individual action are closely intertwined. Your individual decision to have five children crowds my social universe and restricts my freedom. Just as we cannot allow the freedom to shout "fire" in a crowded theater, so we cannot provide the behavioral latitude of a Montana cowboy to the residents of Manhattan. As the nation's resources, including the scarce resources of land and air, are subjected to increasing competitive demands, we must impose more laws and regulations restricting the individual's actions. For Americans, having inherited a frontier psychology, less freedom is likely to mean more tension.

DOES CAPITALISM HAVE A FUTURE IN AMERICA?

I can summarize my position on the future of capitalism in America as follows. Our Founding Fathers chose development by stressing the hierarchical capitalist ethic rather than the more egalitarian democratic ethos because development capitalism was not a zero-sum game and it promised military might. The vision of America as a land of economic opportunity carried enough conviction to sustain itself until the 1930s, when the growing point of the economy was shifted to government, with the rules of public expenditure based upon competitive issue-publics. A system of competitive issue-publics is satisfactory only so long as most citizens are outside the game, but help finance it, and so long as a single issue-public does not emerge victorious by capturing the bulk of the public funds. The game begins to lose its appeal if one group of players monopolizes and manipulates the rewards of the system, as the military-industrial group now does. The winners cannot be faulted for unsportsmanlike conduct, since they merely pursued their own interests according to the rules. And they cannot be faulted economically, since 2000 nuclear missiles aimed at the Soviet Union which we dare not fire are twice as good as 1000 missiles so established. Like ancient Egypt, we have found our pyramids.

The expansion of government spending since the 1930s to ensure full employment was unquestionably prudent. The loss of its citizens' productive time is, for society, an irretrievable one. But basing the allocation of these funds on a system of competitive politics was a tragedy of major proportions. In the zero-sum game of competitive issue-publics, one group is certain in time to capture most of the prize. What qualities might we expect in a winner of the game of government grab, American style? Since the first instinct of a politician is to spend public funds so that everyone gains something, the winner must promise a payoff that all citizens can share. Predictably the strongest player will be the one whose gains are rationalized as public gains and whose rhetoric appeals to the largest base of felt-needs. Once again a negative human trait becomes the organizing sanction for expansion of the military-industrial coalition. How easily the human need for security becomes an obsession when fear is exploited and sanctioned. The rapid growth of the defense industry should not have been unexpected as it promises to defend every American's way of life, lowly as it may be, and the amount of defense necessary is incalculable where fear reigns.

Thomas Jefferson was right in reasoning that the tragic flaw in relying on competitive greed as the major social cement for America is that sanctions, negative as well as positive, are self-reinforcing and cumulative in their impact. Negative virtues drive out positive ones, just as bad money drives out good. By stressing avarice as the cardinal cohesive force in the American community we built a social system that destroyed community. In a dog-eat-dog world, it is self-evident that puppies do not thrive. Hamilton's solution did not, as he thought, merely take men as they are, but it created a system that made them less than they might be.

As greed was to an earlier America, so fear is in our time. During our industrialization drive, competitive greed was the business of America. Now collective fear of the other nations in the world motivates most federal spending. Yet between greed and fear there is one critical difference. Institutionalized avarice may indeed yield material benefits when the major barrier to human survival and comfort is a hostile natural environment. We allowed greed to infuse our collective conscience, creating a nation of men who cannot live easily together. But in the process we generated the social energy to challenge the elements with muscle and wit, and we won. Our natural world lies prostrate, everywhere potentially subject to our collective will. Even if pollution is seen as nature's way of fighting back, this, too, can be overcome. Having conquered nature, we must now face ourselves.

We are the recipients, in America, of a dual mythic heritage. Those generations preceding us chose to emphasize the capitalist portion of democratic capitalism for reasons they thought sound in their day. But we have been shifting away from development capitalism and its struggle with nature toward government and the relations among men for over a generation. And yet we have retained the negative sanctions of greed and fear, creating the absurdity of self-serving individuals in a service economy. A government rewarding the alienating vices cannot create and sustain a nation of free and equal men. We must now set upon the democratic task of informing our citizens about the full range of life's potential choices. Could we but launch this system of political economy, we may yet achieve enough distance from our personal and domestic obsessions to consider seriously the contagious maladies afflicting our fellow passengers on the spaceship earth.

Capitalism is failing us now because it sustains our vices, not our virtues. Business thrives on greed, the military needs our collective fear. Greed and fear cohabit in the human psyche, providing a compatible underpinning for the dominant military-industrial complex. Both live on the dark side of human nature. But free men must have an expansive faith in themselves and a society rationalized in that faith. We must begin at once to build that society.

*Murray N. Rothbard was born in
New York City, has a Ph.D. in
economics from Columbia, and is
now a Professor of Economics at
the Polytechnic Institute of Brooklyn.* He is the author of four books,
Man, Economy, and State, The
Panic of 1819, America's Great
Depression, *and* Power and Market,
*several articles, pamphlets, and nu-
merous contributions to books and
symposia. Forthcoming are a co-
authored book, with Ronald Radosh,
of essays on twentieth-century
American history and a book on
the American Right. He is the
editor of a monthly periodical,*
The Libertarian Forum *and formerly co-editor of* Left and Right.

*He comments on his philosophy
as follows:*

*"As for my values and biases, I am in basic philosophy an Aristotelian
and a rationalist, in social philosophy a believer in natural law and natural
rights, in economics a "neo-Austrian" follower of the Austrian tradition from
Bohm-Bawerk through von Mises, and in political philosophy an adherent
of* laissez-faire *and libertarianism, i.e., a believer in the absolute liberty of
each individual from the force and violence of government or anyone else.
In sum, in political economy, I am an "anarcho-capitalist," a believer in that
free-market variant of anarchism that believes that every good and service,
including legal defense and justice, is most efficiently and most morally supplied by the free market rather than by coercive government."*

28 The Future of Capitalism

Murray N. Rothbard

In order to discuss the "future of capitalism," we must first decide what
the meaning of the term "capitalism" really is. Unfortunately, the
term "capitalism" was coined by its greatest and most famous enemy,
Karl Marx. We really can't rely upon him for correct and subtle usage.
And, in fact, what Marx and later writers have done is to lump together two extremely different and even contradictory concepts and
actions under the same portmanteau term. These two contradictory
concepts are what I would call "free-market capitalism" on the one
hand, and "state capitalism" on the other.

The difference between free-market capitalism and state capitalism is precisely the difference between, on the one hand, peaceful, voluntary exchange, and on the other, violent expropriation. An example of a free-market exchange is my purchase of a newspaper on the corner for a dime; here is a peaceful, voluntary exchange beneficial to both parties. I buy the newspaper because I value the newspaper more highly than the dime that I give up in exchange; and the newsdealer sells me the paper because, he, in turn, values the dime more highly than the newspaper. Both parties to the exchange benefit. And what we are both doing in the exchange is the swapping of *titles of ownership:* I relinquish the ownership of my dime in exchange for the paper, and the newsdealer performs the exact opposite change of title. This simple exchange of a dime for a newspaper is an example of a unit free-market act; it is the market at work.

In contrast to this peaceful act, there is the method of violent expropriation. Violent expropriation occurs when I go to the newsdealer and seize his newspapers or his money at the point of a gun. In this case, of course, there is no *mutual* benefit; I gain *at the expense of* the victimized newsdealer. Yet the difference between these two transactions — between voluntary mutual exchange, and the holdup at gunpoint — is precisely the difference between free market capitalism and state capitalism. In both cases we obtain something — whether it be money or newspapers — but we obtain them in completely different ways, ways with completely different moral attributes and social consequences.

Here I can't resist the temptation of pointing out that I have an entirely different interpretation of Jefferson and Hamilton from that of Professor Averitt. I don't regard Jefferson as some sort of early Franz Boas–type, an early Left-Wing anthropologist. He wasn't. My reading of Jefferson is completely different; on my reading, Jefferson was very precisely in favor of *laissez-faire,* or free-market, capitalism. And that was the real argument between them. It wasn't really that Jefferson was against factories or industries *per se;* what he was against was *coerced* development, that is, taxing the farmers through tariffs and subsidies to build up industry artificially, which was essentially the Hamilton program.

Jefferson, incidentally, along with other statesmen of his time, was a very learned person. He read Adam Smith, he read Ricardo, he was very familiar with *laissez-faire* classical economics. And so his economic program, far from being the expression of bucolic agrarian nostalgia, was a very sophisticated application of classical economics to the American scene. We must not forget that *laissez-faire* classicists were *also* against tariffs, subsidies, and coerced economic development.

Furthermore, the term "equality," as used by Jefferson and Jeffersonians, was employed in the same sense as Jefferson's friend and colleague George Mason used when he framed the Virginia Declaration of Rights shortly before Jefferson wrote the Declaration of Independence: "that all men are by nature equally free and independent." In other words, "equality" did not then mean what we often mean by equality now: equality of condition or uniformity. "Equality" meant that each person has the right to be equally free and independent, to enjoy the right to "equal liberty," as Herbert Spencer would phrase it a century later. In other words, again what I am saying is that the *Jeffersonian* wing of the Founding Fathers was essentially free-market, *laissez-faire* capitalists.

To return to the market: the free-market is really a vast network, a latticework, of these little, unit exchanges which I mentioned before: such as exchanging a dime for a newspaper. At each step of the way, there are two people, or two groups of people, and these two people or groups exchange two commodities, usually money and another commodity; at each step, each benefits by the exchange, otherwise they wouldn't be making it in the first place. If it turns out that they were mistaken in thinking that the exchange would benefit them then they quickly stop, and they don't make the exchange again.

Another common example of a free market is the universal practice of children swapping baseball cards — the sort of thing where you swap "two Hank Aaron" for "one Willie Mays." The "prices" of the various cards, and the exchanges that took place, were based on the relative importance that the kids attached to each baseball player. As one way of annoying liberals we might put the case this way: liberals are supposed to be in favor of any voluntary actions performed, as the famous cliché goes, by "two consenting adults." Yet it is peculiar that while liberals are in favor of any sexual activity engaged in by two consenting adults, when these consenting adults engage in trade or exchange, the liberals step in to harass, cripple, restrict, or prohibit that trade. And yet both the consenting sexual activity and the trade are similar expressions of liberty in action. Both should be favored by any consistent libertarian. But the government, especially a liberal government, habitually steps in to regulate and restrict such trade.

It is very much as I were about to exchange two Hank Aarons for one Willie Mays, and the government, or some other third party, should step in and say: "No, you can't do that; that's evil; it's against the common good. We hereby outlaw this proposed exchange; any exchange of such baseball cards must be one for one, or three for two" — or whatever other terms the government, in its wisdom and greatness, arbitrarily wishes to impose. By what right do they do this? The libertarian claims by no right whatsoever.

In general, government intervention can be classified in two ways:

either as prohibiting or partially prohibiting an exchange between two people — between two consenting adults, an exchange beneficial to both parties; *or* forcing someone to make an "exchange" with the government unilaterally, in which the person yields something up to the government under the threat of coercion. The first may include outright prohibition of an exchange, regulating the terms — the price — of the exchange, or preventing certain people from making the exchange. As an example of the last intervention, in order to be a photographer in most states, one must be a duly licensed photographer — proving that one is of "good moral character" and paying a certain amount of moolah to the state apparatus. This in order to have the right to take somebody's picture! The second kind of intervention is a forced "exchange" between us and the government, an "exchange" that benefits only the government and not ourselves. Of course, taxation is the obvious and evident example of that. In contrast to voluntary exchange, taxation is a matter of leaping in and coercively seizing people's property *without* their consent.

It is true that many people seem to believe that taxation is *not* imposed without our consent. They believe, as the great economist Joseph Schumpeter once said, that taxes are something like club dues, where each person voluntarily pays his share of the expenses of the club. But if you really think that, try not paying your taxes sometime and see what happens. No "club" that I know of has the power to come and seize your assets or jail you if you don't pay its dues. In my view, then, taxes are exploitation — taxes are a "zero-sum" game. If there's anything in the world that's a zero-sum game, it's taxation. The government seizes money from one set of people, gives it to another set of people, and in the meanwhile of course lops off a large chunk for its own "handling expenses." Taxation, then, is purely and pristinely robbery. Period.

As a matter of fact, I challenge any of you to sit down and work out a definition of taxation that would not also be applicable to robbery. As the great libertarian writer H. L. Mencken once pointed out, among the public, even if they are not dedicated libertarians, robbing the government is never considered on the same moral plane as robbing another person. Robbing another person is generally deplored; but if the *government* is robbed all that happens, as Mencken put it, "is that certain rogues and loafers have less money to play with than they had before."

The great German sociologist Franz Oppenheimer, who wrote a magnificent little book called *The State,* put the case brilliantly. In essence, he said, there are only two ways for men to acquire wealth. The first method is by producing a good or a service and voluntarily exchanging that good for the product of somebody else. This is the method of exchange, the method of the free market; it's creative and expands production; it is *not* a zero-sum game because production expands and both parties to the exchange benefit. Oppenheimer called this method the "economic means" for the acquisition of wealth. The second method is seizing another person's property without his consent, i.e., by robbery, exploitation, looting. When you seize someone's property without his consent, then you are benefiting *at his expense,* at the expense of the producer; here is truly a zero-sum "game" — not much of a "game," by the way, from the point of view of the victim. Instead of expanding production, this method of robbery clearly hobbles and restricts production. So in addition to being immoral while peaceful exchange is moral, the method of robbery hobbles production because it is parasitic upon the effort of the producers. With brilliant astuteness, Oppenheimer called this method of obtaining wealth "the political means." And then he went on to define the state, or government, as "the organization of the political means," i.e., the regularization, legitimation, and permanent establishment of the political means for the acquisition of wealth.

In other words, the state is organized theft, organized robbery, organized exploitation. And this essential nature of the state is highlighted by the fact that the state ever rests upon the crucial instrument of taxation.

I must here again comment on Professor Averitt's statement about "greed." It's true: greed has had a very bad press. I frankly don't see anything wrong with greed. I think that the people who are always attacking greed would be more consistent with their position if they refused their next salary increase. I don't see even the most Left-Wing scholar in this country scornfully burning his salary check. In other words, "greed" simply means that you are trying to relieve the nature given scarcity that man was born with. Greed will continue until the Garden of Eden arrives, when everything is superabundant, and we don't have to worry about economics at all. We haven't of course reached that point yet; we haven't reached the point where everybody is burning his salary increases, or salary checks in general. So the question then becomes: what *kind* of greed are we going to have, "productive greed," where people produce and voluntarily exchange their products with others? Or exploitative greed, organized robbery and predation, where you achieve your wealth at the expense of others? These are the two real alternatives.

Returning to the state and taxation, I would point out incidentally that Saint Augustine, who is not famous for being a libertarian, did however set forth an excellent libertarian parable. He wrote that Alexander the Great had seized some pirate, and asked the pirate what he meant by seizing possession of the sea. And the pirate boldly replied: "What you mean by seizing the whole earth; but because I do it with a little ship, I am called a robber, while you, because you do it with a great fleet, are called an emperor." Here Augustine highlights the fact that the state is simply robbery writ large, on an enormous scale, but robbery legitimated by intellectual opinion.

Take, for another example, the Mafia, which also suffers from a bad press. What the Mafia does on a local scale, the state does on an enormous scale, but the state of course has a much better press.

In contrast to the age-old institution of statism, of the political means, free-market capitalism arrived as a great revolutionary movement in the history of man. For it came into a world previously marked by despotism, by tyranny, by totalitarian control. Emerging first in the Italian city-states, free market capitalism arrived full-scale with the Industrial Revolution in Western Europe, a revolution that brought about a remarkable release of creative energy and productive ability, an enormous increase of production. You can call that "greed" if you wish; you can attack as "greed" the desire of someone on a poverty level who wishes to better his lot.

This reminds me of an interesting point on "greed" that cuts across the usual "Left-Right" continuum. I remember when Russell Kirk first launched the contemporary conservative movement in this country, in the mid-1950s. One of the leading young conservatives of that era addressed a rally, and opined that the whole trouble with the world, and the reason for the growth of the Left, is that everyone is "greedy," the masses of Asia are "greedy," and so on. Here was a person who owned half of Montana, attacking the mass of the world population, who were trying to rise above the subsistence level, to better their lot a bit. And yet they were "greedy."

At any rate, free-market capitalism, the Industrial Revolution, saw an enormous outpouring of productive energies, an outpouring that constituted a revolution against the mercantilist system of the seventeenth and eighteenth centuries. In fact, the mercantilist system is essentially what we've got right now. There is very little difference between state monopoly capitalism, or corporate state capitalism, whatever you want to call it, in the United States and Western Europe today, and the mercantilist system of the pre–Industrial Revolution era. There are only two differences; one is that their major activity was commerce and ours is industry. But the essential modus operandi of the two systems is exactly the same: monopoly privilege, a complete meshing in what is now called the "partnership of government and industry," a pervasive system of militarism and war contracts, a drive toward war and imperialism; the whole shebang characterized the seventeenth and eighteenth centuries. The really *key* difference is that they didn't have a gigantic P.R. apparatus; they didn't have a fleet of intellectuals trumpeting to all and sundry the wonders of the system: how it promotes the common good and the general welfare, how this is Liberalism In Action. *They* said, "We're out to shaft the public and we're doing it!" They were very honest in those days. It's really refreshing, by the way, to go back and read the material before 1914 and bask in the honesty of the period.

One of the concepts important in this connection is that of Albert Jay Nock, a great libertarian thinker and follower of Franz Oppenheimer. Nock coined two concepts: what he called "social power" on the one hand, and "state power" on the other. Social power is essentially what I have been talking about: the productive energies released by the free market, by voluntary exchanges, people interacting voluntarily and peacefully. "State power" is parasitism, exploitation, and the state apparatus in general — organized taxes, regulation, etc. And Nock saw history as essentially a race between social power and state power. In the Industrial Revolution period, for example, from various circumstances state power was minimal, and this allowed social power to take a tremendous burst upward. And what has happened in the twentieth century is essentially that state power has caught up; they've moved in on society and started crippling it once again.

What, then, is my view of the "future of capitalism" — our topic for today? My view of the future is highly optimistic. I really think that free-market capitalism, even though it is supposed to be a reactionary, Neanderthal institution, is the wave of the future. For one thing, it *was* the wave of the future a hundred and two hundred years ago, and what we have now is only a reactionary reversion to the previous system. The present system is not really "progressive" at all. Second, it was discovered by Ludwig von Mises back in 1920 that socialism — the other polar alternative to our present neo-mercantilism — cannot run an industrial system. An agricultural system can be run indefinitely by almost anyone, as long as you leave the peasants alive. You can have almost any kind of tyrannical system over the peasants. But in an industrial system you need much more than that: you need a market, you need profit-and-loss tests, you can't run the system haphazardly. And Mises proved that a socialist system cannot calculate economically, because it doesn't have a price system for capital goods, and therefore socialism will not be able to run an industrial system. All the textbooks say that Mises was quickly refuted by Oskar Lange and others, but he really wasn't refuted.[1] I haven't got time to go into the theoretical argument. But *in practice* what has happened is that, in response to industrialization, there has been a tremendous shift in the last fifteen years in the socialist countries of Eastern Europe away from

[1] Editor's note: see the article in this volume by Robert Heilbroner.

socialism and towards a free market. For a believer in freedom and the free-market, this shift is one of the most exciting developments of the past two decades. Now there are only two interpretations of this development: *either* you have to say, as the Chinese do, that the Yugoslavs, the Poles, the Czechs, the Slovaks, the Hungarians have all sold out to capitalism — they've gone in secret to the American Embassy and received their pay. *Or* you have to say that something deeper is happening, that what is essentially happening is that they tried socialism and it didn't work, especially as the economies began to industrialize. They found in practice, pragmatically, without reading Mises (though there's evidence that they've read Mises by this time) and Hayek and others, that socialism can't calculate, they came to that conclusion themselves. Lenin, indeed, came to that conclusion very early, when "War Communism" was scrapped in 1921. "War Communism" was an attempt, shortly after the Bolshevik Revolution, to leap into full communism, into an economy without money and without prices, in which everyone was supposed to — and in practice was forced to — present his goods to the common heap, and withdraw from that heap to satisfy his needs. The system of War Communism proved to be a total disaster — not because of the Civil War (that rationalization only came much later) , but because of the communist system itself.[2] Lenin soon realized what was happening, and quickly instituted the New Economic Policy, which was essentially a return to a quasi-free market system. And now the Eastern European countries, especially Yugoslavia, have been moving very rapidly since the 1950s away from socialism and central planning and toward a free-market system. In Yogoslavia, for example, agriculture, still the main industry, is almost completely private; a flourishing private sector exists in trade and small manufacturing; and the "public sector" has been turned over in fact as well as in law by the state to the ownership of the workers in the various plants — essentially functioning as producers' cooperatives. Furthermore, there is substantially a free market between these producers' co-ops, with a flourishing price system, stern profit and loss tests (when a firm loses enough money, it goes bankrupt) . Moreover, the most recent Yugoslav economic reform which began in 1967 and is still underway, saw a tremendous drop in the rate of taxation of their co-ops — a drop from the previous approximately 70 per cent income tax rate to about 20 per cent. This means that the central Yugoslav government no longer exercises complete control over investment: investment, too, has been decentralized *and* destatized. As a matter of fact, if one reads the Communist economists in Yugoslavia — especially in the relatively in-

2 On War Communism, see the important article by Paul Craig Roberts, "War Communism: A Re-examination," *Slavic Review* (June 1970) , pp. 237–61.

dustrialized areas of Croatia and Slovenia — they sound very much like Barry Goldwater or Ronald Reagan. "Why should we productive Croats or Slovenes," they ask, "be taxed in order to subsidize those lazy slobs down in Montenegro?" And: "why should we build uneconomic ("political") factories? Everyone should stand on their own feet", etc. The next step in Yugoslavia is that the banks — which, incidentally, are largely competitive private co-ops owned by their business clients — are agitating for a stock market in a Communist country, which would have been considered incredible ten or twenty years ago. And what they are proposing to call this system — literally — is "socialist people's capitalism."

On this point, a few years ago I was teaching a course in Comparative Economic Systems. Naturally, I spent the term praising the free market, and attacking socialism and central planning. Finally, I invited an exchange professor from Hungary — an eminent Communist economist — to give a guest lecture, and the kids felt: "Ah, at least we're going to get the other side of the picture." And what did the Hungarian economist do? He spent the entire lecture praising the free market and attacking central planning. He said almost exactly what I had been saying up till then.

In Eastern Europe, then, I think that the prospects for the free market are excellent — I think we're getting free-market capitalism and that its triumph there is almost inevitable. In the United States, the prospects are a little more cloudy, but here too we see the "New Left" picking up a lot of the positions that we "extreme Right-Wingers" used to have. Much of the position that used to be called "extreme Right-Wing" twenty years ago is now considered quite leftish. As a result, I, with the same position I had then, have been shifted bodily from extreme right to left without any effort on my part at all. Decentralization; community control; attack on Leviathan government, on bureaucracy, on government interference with each person's life; attack on the state-ridden educational system; criticism of unionism, which is tied up with the state; opposition to militarism, war, imperialism, and conscription; all these things that the Left is now beginning to see, is precisely what we "extreme Right-Wingers" have been saying all along. And, as far as "decentralization" goes, there is nothing that is so decentralized as the free market, and perhaps this too will come to the attention of the public.

And so, I'm very optimistic about the future of free-market capitalism. I'm *not* optimistic about the future of state capitalism — or rather, I *am* optimistic, because I think it will eventually come to an end. State capitalism inevitably creates all sorts of problems which become insoluble; as Mises again has pointed out, one intervention into the system to try to solve problems only creates other problems, which then demand further interventions, etc., and so the whole process keeps snowballing until you have a completely collectivist, totalitarian system. It's very much like the escalation in Vietnam, by the way; the principle, as we all know by this time, is that government intervention in Vietnam creates problems which demand further escalation, etc.   The same thing happens in domestic intervention, the farm program being a splendid example of this process.   Both in Vietnam and in domestic government intervention, each escalating step only creates more problems which confront the public with the choice: either press on further with more interventions, or repeal them — in Vietnam, withdraw from the country.   Now in Yugoslavia and the rest of Eastern Europe, they have taken the opposite path: of progressive deescalation, of continuing repeal of one intervention after another, and on toward the free market.   In the United States we have so far taken the path of accelerating interventions, of ever greater hobbling of the free market.   But it is beginning to become evident that the mixed system is breaking down, that it doesn't work.   It's beginning to be seen, for example, that the Welfare State does *not* tax the rich and give to the poor; it taxes the poorer to give to the richer, and the poor in essence pay for the Welfare State.   It is beginning to be seen that foreign intervention is essentially a method of subsidizing favored American corporations instead of helping out the poor in the undeveloped countries.   And it is now becoming evident that the Keynesian policies only succeeded in bringing us to the present impasse of inflation-*cum*-recession, and that our Olympian economists have no way of getting out of the present mess at all, except to cross their fingers and their econometric models and pray.   And, of course, we can look forward to another balance-of-payments crisis in a couple of years, another episode of inflationary crisis in a couple of years, another episode of gold-outflow hysteria.

Thus, we have a lot of crises looming in America, some on their way, others imminent or already here.   All of these crises are the products of intervention, and none of them can really be solved by more intervention.   Again, I believe that we will eventually reverse our present course — perhaps taking Yugoslavia as our paradigm.   Incidentally, Professor Averitt mentioned the Great Depression.   The Great Depression has always been considered as the product of free-market capitalism of the 1920s.   It was the result of very heavy government intervention in the 1920s, an intervention, by the way, that is very similar to the current intervention.   In the 1920s, we had the newly imposed Federal Reserve System, which all the Establishment economists of the day assured us would eliminate all future depressions; the Federal Reserve System would henceforth manipulate prices and the money supply and iron out business cycles forever.   Nineteen twenty-nine and the Great Depression were the results of that manipulation guided by the wise hands of Establishment economics — they were not the results of anything like free-market capitalism.

In short, the advent of industrialism and the Industrial Revolution has irreversibly changed the prognosis for freedom and statism. In the pre-industrial era, statism and despotism could peg along indefinitely, content to keep the peasantry at subsistence levels and to live off their surplus. But industrialism has broken the old tables; for it has become evident that socialism cannot run an industrial system, and it is gradually becoming evident that neomercantilism, interventionism, in the long run cannot run an industrial system either. Free-market capitalism, the victory of social power and the economic means, is not only the only moral and by far the most productive system; it has become the only viable system for mankind in the industrial era. Its eventual triumph is therefore virtually inevitable.

QUESTIONS

Capitalism
Averitt / Rothbard

1. Are there any essential differences between Averitt and Rothbard?
2. How do we decide what should and what should not be exchanged in markets?
3. What kind of ethical values are consistent with a market society?
4. Does the use of a market in socialist countries mean they are capitalist? What are the key institutions that differentiate capitalism from socialism?
5. Has Rothbard shown how laissez-faire capitalism could or would have eliminated the problems that state intervention has not been able to solve or correct? Has he shown why the state failed?
6. Is man inherently greedy?
7. Does greed mean to want more or to want more than one needs?
8. Is capitalism productive greed or do capitalists achieve wealth at the expense of others?
9. Are all exchanges in a market free and voluntary? What alternative does a worker have to selling his labor?
10. What alternative is there to purchasing socially determined goods and services?
11. How can one buy pure air, clean water, and quiet in the market?
12. Are our economic institutions democratic?
13. Are political decisions made by interest groups?

14. Do we have a market system in politics and competition between unequals (groups and/or individuals) as Averitt argues?
15. Are democracy and industrialism compatible goals?
16. What is the future of capitalism?
17. Does the goal of industrialization justify the use of undemocratic means? Do the means determine the end?
18. Once industrialization has been achieved by use of undemocratic institutions, can the society change and become democratic?
19. What is the justification for inheritance?
20. Does Rothbard equate the giant corporation with the single individual engaging in an act of exchange?
21. Isn't the essence of capitalism private ownership of the means of production? If so, are Eastern European countries adopting private property?
22. Does the profit motive in capitalist countries lead to more pollution and more difficulty in controlling pollution than occurs in socialist countries?
23. Can capitalism exist without being expansionist?
24. Can capitalist countries overcome their fundamental problems?
25. Are the goals of the Old Right and the New Left merging?
26. Are monopolies a natural outgrowth of capitalism, the free market, and competition between unequals?
27. What is the moral basis for a capitalist economy?
28. How would Rothbard deal with the problems of urban sprawl, air pollution, and noise pollution?
29. In the society proposed by Rothbard what would happen to inequality?
30. Does Rothbard have any concern at all about the degree of inequality in society?
31. Isn't there a degree of coercion in an exchange in which the person's only alternative to the exchange is starvation?
32. Are taxes theft?

Herbert Gintis was born in Philadelphia and received a B.S. in Mathematics at the University of Pennsylvania. He received his Ph.D. in Economics from Harvard in 1969. His Ph.D. dissertation Alienation and Power: Towards a Radical Welfare Economics *must be one of the most widely quoted unpublished dissertations in history. Gintis rewrote his dissertation in free verse form and the Union for Radical Political Economics published it in that form as an occasional paper in 1970. Gintis is currently doing research on the relationship between educational and economic systems at the Graduate School of Education at Harvard University.*

29 Alienation and Power

Herbert Gintis

I. INTRODUCTION

Ever since the Industrial Revolution hit Europe and America in the eighteenth and nineteenth centuries, capitalism has had major critics. Except for a very few (isolated intellectuals and Utopian reformers), the critics' basic thrust has been that capitalism, rather than bettering the welfare of all equally, has set the relative misery of masses of individuals against the affluence of a select minority. In short, the historical demand for socialism (the shift of control of the means of production from the minority of nonworkers to the majority of workers) has centered almost exclusively on the desire for an equitable distribution of material goods and services among workers, and between workers and nonworkers in society.

This paper is truly the product of a group effort. It has passed through some ten revisions, through the hands of the Harvard URPE collective, the twenty-odd members of the staff of our radical economics course Social Sciences 125, and personal friends. Special thanks for integral contributions are due to Sam Bowles, Jim Campen, Rick Edwards, Jay Mandle, Steve Marglin, Ralph Pochoda, Stephan Michelson, Mike Reich, Art MacEwan, Frank Roosevelt, and Jim Weaver.

Much of the social and political ferment in the advanced capitalist countries today can indeed be traced to demands for material equality. But many modern problems point to a future where a search for an alternative to capitalism will hinge not only on distributional equity, but a host of issues of broader scope. Some of these issues involve the quality of life in capitalist society: the meaningfulness of work, the integrity of community, and the quality of our natural environment. Other issues concern the ability of capitalism to promote the psychic, social, and cultural development of individuals themselves. Capitalist society teaches men and women to be competitive, materialistic, subordinate to authority, status-minded, uncreative, and unspiritual. Indeed, the astronomic rise in drug and alcohol use, mental instability, as well as the counter-cultural and radical movements in the past decade attest to an underlying malaise that will likely motivate the burning political issues of the future. As capitalist countries become more and more affluent and individuals find themselves none the happier for it, these issues of quality of life and culture can be expected to dominate the political arena.

The catchword of disillusionment with the capitalist "good life" of so-called middle-class America (ostensibly the future of all Americans) is *alienation*. Young people, blacks, women, and others who are trying to reorganize their lives, their work, their communities, and their culture are thought of as "alienated" from society, and their actions are attributed to subjective, psychological aberration.

We shall argue that alienation is *not* an aberration. Indeed, we shall see that alienation is not the private disease of the dissident minorities. In fact, even the most timid and conformist capitalist man and capitalist woman is alienated from his/her society. It is the basic underlying alienation of *all* workers and citizens that gives rise to the modern malaise of advanced capitalist society, the dissidents being that (for the time being) minority who have attained consciousness of their oppression and sought to attack its sources. Others, equally alienated and equally suffering, bear with it, either unaware of the social nature of our condition, or unwilling to take arms against it.

But alienation has not been universally taken as an individual aberration. In the "Silent Decades" after World War II, before the rise of the New Left and the counterculture movements, alienation was proposed as a part of the "Human Condition" by noted French philosophers, among whom Sartre, Camus, and Beckett are the most widely read in the United States. We personally encounter the phenomenon on this subjective level, and we respond most immediately to its manifestations in our own lives, in the Beatles' "Nowhere Man," Nichols's *The Graduate,* and Philip Roth's *Portnoy's Complaint.* Yet we shall see that while alienation is nearly universal in modern society, its sources are not found in the Nature of Man in the abstract. I shall argue that alienation comprises quite objective elements, and its sources inhere in the social system itself. Alienation as we know it coincides with the rise of capitalism.

The treatment of alienation as an element of human nature is merely symptomatic of the "Silent Decades" political quiescence. Indeed, the very *appearance* of the concept of "alienation" coincides with *the rise of industrial capitalism,* in the philosophical works of Hegel and Marx, and the literary works of Kafka and Dostoevski.

Yet the growing awareness of the social basis of alienation — an awareness of quite recent vintage — still fails to achieve the proper analytical depth. This is due in part to the particular *form* in which this awareness is couched: alienation is seen to arise directly from the nature of technology in "modern industrial society," and hence to remain independent of any particular set of economic institutions. This view is reinforced through our understanding of the historical development of capitalism's main "competitor," state socialism in the Soviet Union and Eastern Europe. So-called "socialist man" seems to differ little from his capitalist counterpart, and so-called "socialist society" seems little better equipped to avoid the problems of Alienated Man than its avowed adversary.

We shall try to show in this paper not only that alienation is a social rather than a psychological problem at its root, but that it results from the structure of technology only in the most immediate and superficial sense, in that the form that technological development takes is itself strongly influenced by the structure of economic institutions and their day-to-day operations. If capitalist and so-called socialist economies experience these same problems, it is due to the essential similarity of their basic economic institutions, a similarity only minimally affected by differences in the legal patterns of ownership of capital. Similarly, we shall see that differences in the structure of political power — democratic or not, Left or Right — are of little import in affecting the alienated character of social life, given basic economic organization. Democracy in the political sphere is an ineffective antidote to totalitarian organization of economic life.

Following a brief description of the psychological manifestations of alienation (Section II), we shall locate its sources in the pattern of *power* in capitalist society: the way in which the constellation of political and institutional forces determine the quality of social roles available to the individual (Section III). We shall then trace the social implications of this pattern of power on essential areas of social life: the distribution of income, the nature of work, the structure of community and political life (Sections IV–VII). In that who we are is in large part determined by the quality of our social relations, and since major social roles are alienated, it is fair to say that in capitalist society men and women are alienated from themselves. We shall treat this question of self-development and culture in Section VIII, where the particular role of the education system will be emphasized. In the conclusion (Section IX), we shall analyze some of the implications for social change in America.

II. THE EXPERIENCE OF ALIENATION

Before analyzing the social sources of alienation, a short description of its various tangible implications is in order. I shall treat alienation from work in some detail, and give other types of alienation (community, environment, political process, body, psyche) only in the form of anecdotal "snapshots" the reader might relate to his or her own life and experience.

The worker experiences alienation in the form of powerlessness, meaninglessness, isolation, and self-estrangement. He is *powerless* because work is bureaucratically organized, ruled from the top, through lines of hierarchical authority treating the worker as just another piece of machinery, more or less delicate and subject to breakdown, to be directed and dominated. His work seems *meaningless* because it is divided into numberless fragmented tasks, over only one of which he has some expertise, and whose contribution to the final product is minimal, impersonal, and standardized. His work seems meaningless equally because workers realize only too well how little his activities contribute to social welfare. If he produces steel, his factory pollutes atmosphere and streams. If he makes automobiles, his product congests, smogs, kills, and finally, after three-score months of "service" falls apart. If he sells insurance, he knows his success depends only on his relative cunning and talent in conning his customer.

Moreover, the worker is supremely and uniquely *isolated* in work. Fragmentation of tasks precludes true solidarity and cooperation. Hierarchical authority lines effectively pit workers on different "levels" against one another, and since workers do not determine through their social interaction the important decisions governing producion, no true work community develops. Last, the powerless, meaningless, and isolated position of the worker leads him to treat work merely as an *instrument,* as a *means* toward the end of material security, rather than an end in itself. But work is so important to a man's self-definition and self-concept, that he then comes to view *himself* as an instrument, as a means, to some ulterior end. Hence his *self-estrangement.*

That a man may be self-estranged — alienated from himself, his essence, and his psyche — has been characterized as the focal point of the industrial worker's self-concept — be he blue collar or white collar. As Erich Fromm notes in *The Sane Society*, "(A man) does not experience himself as an active agent, as the bearer of human powers. He is alienated from these powers, his aim is to sell himself successfully on the market. His sense of self does not stem from his activity as a loving and thinking individual, but from his socio-economic role . . . he experiences himself not as a man, with love, fear, convictions, doubts, but as that abstraction, alienated from his real nature, which fulfills a certain function in the social system. His sense of value depends on his success: on whether he can make more of himself than he started out with, whether he is a success. His body, his mind, and his soul are his capital, and his task in life is to invest it favorably, to make a profit of himself. Human qualities like friendliness, courtesy, kindness, are transformed into commodities, into assets of the 'personality package' conducive to a higher price on the personality market."

Snapshot: A young ex-marine perched atop a twenty-story University of Texas building with rifle and rangefinder, topples several unknown passers-by. He is alienated — alienated from his fellow men and women in the strongest sense of the word.

Snapshot: A car salesman spends his waking hours foisting on families automobiles more expensive than they can afford, less useful than he leads them to believe, and so constructed that the customer must return two-and-a-half years later for another go-round. The salesman is alienated from his fellow men and women in that less dramatic manner familiar to us all.

Snapshot: A clot of people on a crowded rush-hour street see a man stagger and fall to the ground unconscious. They walk on by, nonplused, not wanting "to get involved." Again, a young woman is threatened, then stabbed to death in full view of her Queens, N.Y., neighbors. They do not intervene and notify neither police nor ambulance. They are similarly alienated from their fellow men and women.

Snapshot: A girl shows her engagement ring to a friend: "You know what did it? I prepared a home-cooked meal for him — in a bikini." As an aspect of the "division of labor" between women and men, and discrimination against the former, she is alienated from her body, and the course of her life may consist in substituting her physical attributes for her true self — exchanging her body for affluence and security.

Snapshot: A man arrives home from a brutalizing day's work, sits before the television set watching football, hockey, boxing, baseball; drinks beer and smokes cigarettes; never engages in sports or physical activity himself. He experiences the "humanity of his own body" only vicariously through a Hank Aaron, Joe Namath, or an Arnold Palmer, while he slowly kills himself. He is alienated from his body.

Snapshot: A teen-ager retreats to his room, liquefies twenty of his mother's diet pills, inserts the solution into a syringe, and finds a vein. He will be dead in three years. He is alienated from his body.

Snapshot: A junior sales and promotion executive has three martinis for lunch at work (his wife does the same at her bridge club at home), and three more before dinner. Their common nonworking life is diffused with Scotch and experienced in an alcoholic haze. They succeed in muting their anxieties and in staving off the brute realization of their personal loneliness and isolation at the cost of destroying themselves. They are also alienated from their bodies.

Snapshot: A throng of furious blacks in Watts (or Harlem, or Detroit, or Baltimore, or Washington, D.C., or . . .) riot, loot, and burn, destroying square blocks of ghetto "property." They realize their lack of control over their communities and lives. They are alienated from their community in a most overt form.

Snapshot: An old couple sits in a dingy room, yellowed papers and magazines collecting in ragged and dusty piles, visited only at Christmas by their children living in other cities; unconscious of, unaided by, and cut off from their neighbors, waiting to die. They are alienated from their community.

Snapshot: A ghetto resident does not bother to vote in the municipal elections because, as he correctly perceives, "the people don't have any say anyway."

Snapshot: A suburbanite commutes thirty miles to work each day, does not know even his next-door neighbors beyond their daily opinions on the weather prospects, joins forces with them only in the face of such "external threats" as higher property taxes, a teachers' strike for better schools and working conditions, the threat of teaching sex education in the schools, or the imminent entrance of a black family down the street. This suburbanite is alienated from his community.

III. ALIENATION AND THE STRUCTURE OF DECISION-MECHANISMS

In this section I shall lay the basis for a social theory of alienation. I shall argue that the major decisions that affect people's daily lives in capitalist society lie essentially outside their control, however democratic a political process they enjoy. This will require a rather elaborate set of conceptual tools that will be used throughout the rest of the paper. First, we shall view the individual as "plugging into" society through the concrete socially-defined *role-position* open to him or her. The individual's alienation will be seen to depend on the extent to which the structure and character of these roles are tailored to the satisfaction of his or her needs and conducive to his or her personal development.   Second, we shall discuss the concrete *social decision-mechanisms* (political, private-administrative, and institutional) that determine the structure of important roles.   Third, we shall analyse the relations among these various decision-mechanisms, concluding that the impersonal "institutional decision-mechanisms" of capitalism are basic, and set strict limits on the latitude of both state and private administrative decision-making.   Fourth, we enumerate these basic economic institutions in some detail.   Future sections will argue that these decision-mechanisms are alienated in that, not only are they not *controlled* by individuals whom they affect, but the implicit criteria according to which they "make decisions" (i.e., produce outcomes) are independent from individual needs.   Thus the final purpose of this section is to give a definition of alienation compatible both with daily observation and our later analytical needs of the paper.   In short, I shall argue that individuals are alienated in capitalist society because the way they are permitted to "plug into" society is determined independent from their needs and personal welfare.

The root meaning of the verb "to alienate" is "to render alien" or more concretely, "to separate from" (e.g., "She alienated my husband's affections from me"), and we can use this root meaning to motivate a social definition of alienation: when your pocket is picked, you are "alienated" from your wallet; similarly, when the structure of society denies you access to life-giving and personally rewarding activities and relationships, you are alienated from society.   Alienation, on the subjective level, means that elements of personal and social life that should be meaningful and integral, become meaningless, fragmented, out of reach, and if one has an existentialist bent — absurd.   The alienated individual is powerless to control central aspects of his life, just as he cannot "control" the wallet snatched from him.

Alienation appears on many levels.   Most of these can be explained in terms of *social roles*.   A social role is a "slot" that people fit into, carrying with it characteristic duties and obligations, defined by institutionalized expectations as to the behavior of the role-occupant. "Butcher," "baker," "worker," "soldier," "capitalist," "lover," "husband," "community member" — all these are social roles.   The nature of these roles and their availability to the individual are quite as important as the distribution of material goods and power in assessing the value of a social system.   Alienation occurs because the roles open to individuals do not satisfy their immediate needs in terms of their interpersonal activities in family, community, and work, and their requirements for healthy personal psychic development.   Thus, we center on the role-concept to emphasize the inherently *social* nature of alienation.   To be alienated is to be separated in concrete and specific ways from "things" important to well-being, but these "things" are not physical objects or natural resources, but types of collaboration with others, with society, and with nature. These "things" are social roles.

The structure of roles at a point in time, and the way they change and develop over time, depend on criteria and priorities required by basic social and economic institutions. This is not an obvious assertion, and its truth can only be ascertained through specific examples to be presented below. But its truth allows us a particularly simple *causal* explanation of alienation under capitalism: alienation arises when the institutionally patterned social criteria determining the structure and development of an important social role are *essentially independent of individual needs.*

Our discussion of social roles takes us some distance in understanding alienation as a social rather than purely psychological phenomenon. An individual's welfare depends on the constellation of social roles available to him as worker, community member, and citizen, as well as the material goods and services that enable him to act to the limit of his capacities in these roles. Thus, for instance, an individual's alienation from his work is due to the fact that the social criteria explicitly or implicitly used to determine the value of his work do not take into consideration his personal needs. Yet the source of the "gap" between individual needs and social roles remains to be analyzed. This depends in turn on who has *power* to determine social roles.

How are social roles determined? What is the relative *power* of various social forces in choosing from the set of potential social roles those that will actually be available? We can think of two broad types of power: *institutional* and *political.*

Institutional decisions are those where outcomes are determined by impersonal forces outside the control of any group of individuals. All the decision-mechanisms of this type that we shall treat are market-mechanisms, where the price of a commodity or factor of production (land, labor, capital) is determined by the "impersonal" forces of supply and demand. Very few outcomes in modern society are the result of purely institutional decision-mechanisms. An example would be the price of a perfectly homogeneous commodity supplied by a large number of small producers and demanded by a large number of individual consumers. The prices of most goods and services are determined on a market over which individual producers and consumers have only limited control. Hence our analysis of power and alienation will emphasize the overriding power of institutional decision-mechanisms. For, as we shall see, they provide the structured environment within which political decision-mechanisms operate, and they strongly affect — if not essentially determine — the actual decisions reached concerning the pattern and distribution of essential social roles and resources.

By a *political* decision-mechanism we mean one in which the outcome is determined by the direct, consciously applied power of a group of individuals. There are two types of political power that are important for our analysis of alienation. On the one hand there is *state* power — legislative and state-administrative. Examples of social outcomes determined by legislative decision mechanisms are tax schedules, minimum wage laws, zoning regulations, and the size of the military budget. Examples in the domain of state-administrative decisions are the setting of postage rates and the choice of military technology.

On the other hand, there are important decisions that are definitely political in the sense of being consciously made by either one or several individuals, but are not state decisions. For example, the owners and managers of a firm *decide* what is to be produced and with what technologies and work-roles, although their decisions are powerfully circumscribed by the firm's institutional environment. Similarly, the wage structure in General Motors is determined by collective bargaining, again a political decision-mechanism, however constrained by its institutional context. We shall call this form of "political" power *private-administrative*. Thus private-administrative decision-mechanisms determine, although only in the most immediate sense, the structure of work-roles, the direction of technological development, the use of natural resources, and the pattern of community land-use and development. All are effected and implemented by those who own capital, land, and have some control over production.

The shape of society at a point in time, and the way it changes over time depends on institutional power, state power, private-administrative power and how they interrelate. We shall see that available social roles and the forms of social interaction in the most important areas of life are determined *outside* the area of state decision-making.

The distribution of income, the prices of factors of production, the historical development of technology, the organization of work-activities, the structure and development of communities are all basically directed through the impersonal operation of market institutions and private-administrative control. In fact, we shall argue that, given the backdrop of economic institutions (markets and private-administrative decision-mechanisms), the *latitude* of state power for autonomous effective decision-making is severely limited.

What about the relative power of institutional and private-administrative decision-mechanisms? We should note that *both* forms are involved in most private economic decisions. For instance, while wages are determined basically by the supply and demand for different types of labor (institutional decision), they are also affected by union-management negotiations, as well as racial and sexual discrimination (private-administrative decision). Similarly, while capitalists can decide the technologies to be used and the work-roles used to apply them, their decision will be closely affected by the prices of capital goods and various types of labor — all determined by essentially institutional decision-mechanisms.

Thus the real question is not *which* decisions are primarily institutional and *which* are basically private-administrative. Rather, we must ask: What is the *latitude* of private-administrative power in the determination of any particular outcome? Here, we shall see that for the most important decisions that affect our daily lives, this latitude is rather minimal. The small capitalist in a perfect market for a homogeneous commodity in fact has no latitude at all. The prices of his factors of production, as well as the price of his product and its quality are determined by the market (institutional power). The work-roles he chooses must be those that minimize his costs, or else he will lose money and go out of business. Such producers merely *ratify* and *implement* decisions really made in the sphere of institutional power. Oligopolistic producers do indeed have some independent latitude — they can control both price and quality of output to some extent, and to some degree the demand for their product through advertizing and political lobbying (e.g., the so-called "defense" industries). Nevertheless, even here the latitude of their administrative power is highly circumscribed. For they must grow and maximize profits to satisfy their owners and stockholders. This is most strikingly seen in collective bargaining, which is a private-administrative decision-mechanism having quite limited power to alter the market-determined wage rate. Workers can only bargain over "excess" profit — what is left over *after* interest, dividends, taxes, management wages, and raw materials cost are deducted from total revenue. Moreover, since the corporation requires these "excess" profits for the expansion without which its position on the stock market would seriously deteriorate, wage increases must be followed either by unemployment in the industry, or price increases which hurt consumers. The latitude corporate directors have does not include the ability to permit a rise in the share of labor significantly above that determined by the market in labor (an institutional decision-mechanism). We shall see that the latitude of private-administrative power is in other social spheres equally limited.

Thus institutional power lies at the base of all of social life and social development. It is the context within which both state power and private-administrative power must be analyzed. The importance cannot be overemphasized, because it cuts counter to our most immediate political experience. We *experience* the war in Vietnam — an inherently political decision — while the most important aspects of the capitalist domination of poor countries are effected through the normal operation of international commodity, factor and financial markets.

We *observe* the political battle over tax rates, minimum wage legislation, income redistribution, and welfare programs — all determined by political decision-mechanisms — while the fact that the income distribution is basically determined by supply and demand of privately owned factors of production is so immediate it remains unnoticed. We *observe* collective bargaining — again a political decision mechanism — when in fact the level of wages is determined largely by market mechanisms, and the institutional context within which the wage bargain is fought sets the determining limits of its outcome. And so on.

This observation sheds light on the problem of alienation. We have already argued that alienation is not merely a psychological problem, and hence cannot be cured by purely individual means (drugs or psychiatrists). We now see that alienation is an *institutional* problem, not merely political. In this sense it is a *problem of everyday life,* not of political struggle divorced from the immediate day-to-day concerns of individuals. Nor could it be otherwise, for as I shall sketch below, the application of political power — however "progressively realigned" — is severely delimited by the institutional contexts within which it works. To change the course of historical development requires a change in economic institutions at their base — in everyday life.

The liberal theory of the state, in contrast, views state decision-making as the guiding force in social development, insofar as technology itself does not determine outcomes. Thus such economic problems as inequality, poverty, ecological destruction, alienation, and the like are either seen as inevitable or due to *political mismanagement* and can be cured by a turnover of political representatives. Whether this mismanagement is due to the "backward ideas" of political leaders, or that they have "vested interests" in the status quo, or that they are controlled by large corporations and congressional lobbies, or that government is simply an unwieldy and unresponsive bureaucracy, the solution is the same: elect "progressives" who will respond to the people's needs. We shall see, however, that since the real guiding force in social development is the set of economic institutions, the political power to cure social problems is quite limited, unless the state (i.e., political activity) attacks, destroys, and replaces basic capitalist economic institutions at their root. Thus even if perfect democracy were achieved in the state sphere, the major contours of people's lives would be determined by processes beyond their control.

The state is really a dependent force, whose main function is to preserve, in as pure a form as is feasible, the basic capitalist institutions that determine social development. The growth of the state is due to several conditions: (a) basic economic institutions have functioned less perfectly over time, so increasing intervention to "shore them up" has been necessary; (b) conflicts between various groups of capitalists have become increasingly severe, requiring more and more legislative mediation; (c) more and more state palliatives have been necessary to avoid the "politicization" of workers and citizens over intolerable social conditions; and (d) certain services necessary to the expansion of capital (e.g., roads, education, the military) can only be supplied by the state. In all cases, state power is a dependent and conditionally applied power.

But if the operation of the state depends on capitalist economic institutions, then the study of institutional decision-making becomes central. This is in turn captured in the theory of alienation. *A decision-mechanism will be termed "alienated" when the criteria — implicit or explicit — according to which it determines outcomes are substantially independent from the needs of individuals whom the outcome affects.* Hence the consequences of decisions made according to these criteria will only by accident serve the needs of affected individuals.[1] Insofar as this is true we shall say that the individuals are alienated from the social object (be it a physical object, a social role, another individual, an element of culture, the natural environment, or their own personalities) that is the outcome of the decision-mechanism.

I shall argue that the basic institutional decision-mechanisms of capitalism are alienated. Since political decision-mechanisms — even within their rigidly circumscribed sphere of effective action — must conform to the dictates of the capitalist institutional environment, they are alienated as well. Hence the course of history within capitalism is itself a series of alienated outcomes.

Thus the study of capitalist societies and their evolution must start with an understanding of their basic institutions. I shall begin by enumerating the most important of these institutions. These are: 1. *Private ownership* of factors of production (land, labor, and capital), according to which the legal owner has full control over their disposition and development; 2. a *market in labor,* according to which a. the worker is by and large divorced from ownership of nonhuman factors of production (land and capital), b. the worker relinquishes control over the disposition of his labor during the stipulated work day, by exchanging it for money, and c. the price of a particular type of labor (skilled or unskilled, white collar or blue collar, physical, mental, managerial or technical) is determined essentially by supply and demand; 3. a *market in land,* according to which the price of each parcel of land is determined by supply and demand, and the use of such parcels is individually determined by the highest bidder; 4. income determination on the basis of the *market-dictated returns to owned factors* of production; 5. *markets in essential commodities* — food, shelter, social insurance, medical care; and 6. *control of the productive process by owners of capital* or their managerial representatives.

According to this enumeration, the United States, Canada, England, and most of Western Europe are capitalist — among others.

In the following sections I shall argue that the major characteristics of social life under capitalism — specifically its alienation from work, inequality, fragmentation of community, repressive education and stunted self-development — all stem from the normal operation of these institutions.

IV. ALIENATION FROM WORK-PROCESS AND -PRODUCT

Work is of utmost importance for one's personal life. Work directly engages nearly half of one's waking daily activity and is potentially the single major outlet for initiative, creativity, and craft. Moreover, work-roles are basic and formative in individual personality development. But are these considerations reflected in the actual social decisions determining the structure of work-roles? For instance, is the factory worker's welfare considered when the capitalist decides to produce automobiles by routine and monotonous assembly line operations? Are the secretary's needs considered when she (or he?) is reduced to the full-time subservient role of typing, stenography, and stamp-licking? NO! The structure of work-roles is essentially determined by a set of basic economic institutions which operate on quite different criteria. The most important of these is the market in labor, which, by depriving the worker of control over his services, leaves the determination of work-roles to those who control capital and technology.

In rudimentary and small-scale capitalist production, the control proceeds directly from capitalist to the mass of workers, with perhaps a few foremen as middlemen. But in firms of greater complexity, the requirements of secure control for the top dictates an increasing number of levels in the hierarchical ladder of authority. Thus the modern form of *bureaucratic order in production* is born. Bureaucratic order protects the firm against decentralized, participatory, and "bottom-up" decision-making, all of which threaten the determination of technologies and work-roles according to profit criteria. Because of its flexibility in promoting control from the top, this form of work organization has been taken over intact by most of the state-socialist countries (in the Soviet Union and Eastern Europe).

The fact that the institutions controlling work are alienated has both subjective and objective implications. Subjectively, workers for the most part experience their work-activities as "alien" — as opposing rather than contributing to their personal well-being and psychic growth. This is understandable in that their own needs were peripheral in the decision-process determining the nature of work-roles — their work-activities have been snatched from them.

Defenders of capitalist production have argued that it is *not* an alienated decision-process because, although the worker has no control once he accepts a working position, he does have choice over which position to accept. Thus the desirability of various jobs are reflected in the supply-price of labor, and capitalists have an incentive to organize work as relevant to the worker as possible, in order to lower his labor costs. Indeed, this aspect of the market in labor is operative to some extent. An individual can decide to be a postman rather than an assembly-line worker, because the former position allows him or her more control over his or her activities. Since the greater desirability of the job leads to an increased supply of postman-labor, its wage-level may be lower than that of assembly-line work. The individual then chooses between more pay and a little more control. Similarly an electrician can work in unionized construction with higher pay, or in independent contracting, with more individual control at lower pay. The university professor is in a similar position.

Indeed all of us, in deciding our life's work make some tradeoffs between income and job desirability. The capitalist does have some incentive to make work attractive, hence lowering his labor costs. That this aspect of the market in labor is not operating to any major extent should be clear, however, from the fact that wages and salaries are in general *higher* for more desirable jobs, not lower. This is because the labor force is *stratified,* so that only a restricted number of alternatives are open to a given individual. An assembly-line worker does not have the choice to become an electrician, a salesman, or a university professor because of his or her social class background, and level of education (contrary to common opinion, intelligence is *not* an important factor in determining job-status and income). Hence capitalists have no incentive to improve working conditions beyond the few real alternatives available to the workers in a given occupational stratum. This is one reason why there is no tendency for all jobs to approach the most unalienated work-roles in desirability.

But there are other reasons as well. First, the cultural ideology of alienated labor is involved. This ideology tells us that work is *inherently* bad, and that all we can expect from our jobs is income and status. So long as workers value their jobs mainly in terms of relative wage and status, the capitalist has free reign to organize production along lines of profit-rationality, job fragmentation, and secure control from the top. Second, in the sphere of corporate production and state administration, secure control from the top is a *precondition* to profit-making and so-called "decision-making flexibility." Beyond a certain minimal point, no lowering of labor costs through providing less alienated work-roles is warranted, as any extensive worker control threatens the very basis of bureaucratic order.

Work is what it is because of the alienated decision-mechanisms that govern the structure of work-roles. In the early stages of the Industrial Revolution, this took the form of brutalizing, unhealthy, boring, and repetitive tasks, and long hours. In recent times, in bureaucratic organization, individual work-roles are so fragmented and formalized that the worker finds his initiative and autonomy totally muffled by and subordinated to a mass of regulations and "operating procedures." Also, hierarchical stratification of workers along lines of status and authority subjugates some workers to the control of managers and capitalists and precludes cooperation and equality as a condition of production. Hence bureaucratic organization and hierarchical control are the concrete modern manifestations of the worker's alienation from his work-activities.

But in capitalist society the worker is not only alienated from the *process* of his work. He is also alienated from its *product* — the good or service he produces. When the good or service the worker helps produce neither reflects his personal contribution through its properties and attributes, nor contributes to his welfare either personally or through those with whom he has bonds of community, the *goal* of his work-activities becomes meaningless and absurd. He is alienated from his product. In an integrated society, workers control their activities, and hence the attributes of their product, as skilled craftsmen. The worker's attachment to his product results not only from his pride in the object of his labor, but also in the personal regard he holds for the community it serves. But in capitalist society, both disappear. Since the market in labor and capitalist control of production eliminate worker's control of resources, fragment and impersonalize community, his product becomes impersonal and external. Moreover, since the attributes of products are determined on the basis of profit, in a decision-process out of workers' hands, intrinsic craft is sacrificed to superficial saleability, enforced obsolescence, stylistic frills, shoddiness, and irrational waste foisted upon the consumer either unwilling, or ignorant of the craft involved.

Of course, there is a standard objection to the above analysis. Whereas we have attributed alienation from work-activities to the set of economic institutions — free markets in labor and capital, hierarchical control over production decisions — some argue that bureaucratic organization and hierarchical control are simply immutable aspects of "industrial technology," that, in effect, any "advanced" society must experience alienated labor. This view is essentially incorrect. It is not true that bureaucratic organization is chosen by capitalists only because it is "efficient" and "modern." It is chosen because it is the only means of maintaining and stabilizing control over the profit generated in production, and of avoiding workers' gaining enough general expertise and initiative to embark on cooperative production on their own, or to challenge the hegemony of capitalists in the factory or office. Technologies that potentially increase the breadth of collective and individual control of workers, however productive and efficient, must be avoided if the "stability" of the corporate enterprise is to be secured. The loss of control, even in minor areas, might get out of hand: workers collectives might voice "wild" and "unrealistic" demands in a sort of free-for-all; union and management alike might lose control over workers.

Proof that task fragmentation, job specialization, and hierarchical control in the modern factory system are not technologically determined is not immediate. Both the social relations of modern production and their underlying material technologies in fact developed concurrently, making causal arguments quite difficult. The arguments presented above are only *logical*, urging that we not embrace technological determinism by superficial appearance. The fact that modern science is applied to production in an alienated manner does not mean that technology is *itself* inherently alienating. For other applications of science may be available but undeveloped because they conflict with the bureaucratic order of production that the capitalist deems desirable in itself. Modern communications instruments like two-way television and tape records, the information systems of computer technology, and cybernetic automation could all lead to the abolition of the most alienating jobs and an extensive decentralization of production, although such applications are scarcely compatible with present social relations of production just as programmed and computerized learning could free classroom time for democratic participation by all, if this were not incompatible with the present social relations of education (see Section VIII).

I have also presented the *logical* argument that from the fact that capitalists both maximize profits and choose hierarchical and job-fragmented work-roles, it does not follow that bureaucratic order in production is itself technically efficient. A system of worker control, job rotation, equal participation, decentralization, and job enlargement cannot be ruled out as impractical and inefficient merely because they are not embraced by bosses.

But I should like to present some *empirical* evidence supporting this view. First I shall argue that in the first Industrial Revolution, which occurred in England late in the eighteenth century, the minute division of labor of the putting-out and factory systems, as well as the centralized control of the factory system, derived not from their technical efficiency — from more output per unit of factor inputs. Rather, capitalists saw both as necessary to preserve their lucrative position between the actual producers and the consumers of his product, to enforce a longer work-week and more strenuous pace of work, and to tap a low-wage labor market of women and children.

Thus the factory system was not even *historically* a product of new technologies.   Independent peasant and guild production used much the same technologies as the early capitalist organization.   This situation maintained, with rapid growth of the factory sector and vast capital accumulation, until a firmly ensconced factory system began to utilize modern sources of power.

In addition to historical material, I shall argue that recent experiments in worker control and investigations in industrial social psychology show fairly conclusively that bureaucratic order is *not* efficient from the point of view of cost-minimization, worker performance, or job satisfaction.   Thus the social relations of production under capitalism are far from technologically determined.

Let us begin with the division of labor.[2]   Before the Industrial Revolution in England, fragmentation of work was not a major problem.   Most families were rural, practiced farming on individual plots of land, and supervised agricultural production from beginning to end. What little nonagricultural production there was took place either in the family or in the system of craft-guilds.   The apprentice in a particular trade could expect to become competent in all aspects of his trade, and pass to the level of journeyman and eventually, with some luck, of a master craftsman in his own right.

The Industrial Revolution changed all that.   Small individual farms were appropriated by large capitalist landowners, and the rural population was freed for fragmented farm labor, or upon emigrating to the larger uban areas, for equivalent factory jobs.   The craft-guilds were destroyed and replaced by fragmented capitalist production.

It is generally acknowledged that the triumph of capitalist over guild production was due to the lower production costs of the former. Just as today many attribute the success of the giant corporation to its bureaucratic order, so many attribute the success of the early capitalist entrepreneur to his implementation of a minute division of labor. Adam Smith, the first of the great proponents of capitalism among economists, gave three reasons for the increased technical superiority of job fragmentation.   First, said Smith, specialization in a narrow task increases the dexterity and speed of operation of each worker.   Second, the minute division of labor saves time otherwise lost in passing from one task to another.   Third, job specialization allows the introduction of machinery rigidly engineered to specific operations.

While Smith's reasoning is appealing, it is probably incorrect.   The argument concerning time-saving in passage from task to task is correct, but implies only that the worker must process a large amount of material at each stage.   Instead of spinning a few yards of thread, then weaving it, then fulling and dyeing, spinning more yarn, etc., the efficient worker will spin a great deal, thus minimizing time loss. In continuous process industries, where excessive standing time between stages is impossible (e.g., in steel production, where the product must be treated while it is still at the proper temperature), Smith's argument implies a work-group of equals — each performing all operations at different times. But this is exactly how a group of guild-journeymen operated! This argument cannot explain the hegemony of capitalist production.

For similar reasons, Smith's third argument is not relevant. The use of specialized machinery will increase the number of separate steps in the production process and perhaps require a larger work-group in a continuous process industry, but requires neither hierarchy, inequality, or job specialization. Also, the early putting-out and factory system did *not* use technologies very different from direct peasant and guild production![3]

Thus we are left with Smith's first argument: job fragmentation leads to increasing dexterity on the part of each worker. However, Marglin's evidence suggests that all the various skills in early factory and putting-out production were quickly learned even by children. For instance, it required only six weeks for an average fourteen year old boy to learn the art of weaving cotton. When the Napoleonic Wars erupted, enlisting all able-bodied men, women quickly learned wool weaving and took their place.[4] Much the same occurred in the United States during World War II. Moreover, workers seem to perform more satisfactorily when they rotate jobs. Even today it is likely that most jobs can be rotated — within blue-collar and white-collar jobs and between the two. The exceptions are mainly in areas of specialized technical expertise (e.g., computer, chemical, and electronic technologies).

Why then the historical emergence of capitalist production? The answer seems to be that it was an efficacious means of social control. First, if all workers could perform all tasks, their knowledge of the production process would allow them to band together and go into production for themselves. In the guild system this was prevented by legal restrictions — the guild-masters had control over the number of new masters admitted, and all production had to be under the direction of a legal guild-approved master. In "free enterprise" this form of control was interdicted.

Second, even within the capitalist firm, the boss's control depended on the *lack* of control of each worker. To allow all workers the capacity to deal knowledgeably and powerfully with all parts of the production process both increases their sense of control and autonomy, and undercuts the boss's legitimacy as the coordinator of production. Yet it is this legitimacy that maintains his position of financial control and intermediary between direct producers and consumers. Job rotation and job enlargement would soon threaten the political stability of the firm. That this policy of "divide and conquer" through task-fragmentation was central in the minds of bosses is amply illustrated in Marglin's cited essay.

But if early factories used pretty much the same technologies as the contemporary worker-controlled operations, and if the division of labor did not increase efficiency, why were the former able to undersell and eventually displace their more traditional competitors? To what was the increase in per-capita productivity in the early Industrial Revolution due? The answer seems to lie in the system of hierarchical control. Having all workers under one roof allowed the capitalist to increase drastically the length of the work week. Instead of making his or her own work-leisure choice, the capitalist worker is forced to accept a fifteen- or eighteen-hour work-day, or have no work at all. Since all workers were paid more or less subsistence wages *independent* of length of work-day, the factory system drastically reduced labor costs. Moreover the system of direct supervision in the factory allowed the capitalist to increase the pace of work and the exertion of the worker. Lastly, the factory system used pools of pauper, female and child labor at much lower cost than able-bodied men.

As a result, the capitalist was able to pay generally higher weekly wages to the male labor force, while reducing the cost of output and accruing huge profits. But this was due to increased exertion of labor, not the technical efficiency of the factory system. This situation forced the independent producers to increase their own work-day to meet falling prices of their product, but these producers maintained their position alongside the factory for over a quarter century.

Eventually, however, the factory system did win out on technical grounds. The reasons are interesting in light of our discussion of technological determinism. First, because only the capitalist producer had the financial resources to invest heavily in new machinery, inventors geared their innovations to types compatible with the social relations of factory production. Second, because of the large number of independent producers, it would have been impossible to protect patent rights, whereas the large size of the capitalist firm provided a stable and conspicuous market for the inventor. Third, most inventors aimed at allying with a capitalist partner and going into production for himself.

All these reasons led the direction of innovation toward the hierarchical, fragmented capitalist firm. Rather than technology dictating the social form of production, the reverse was preponderantly the case. The same is likely true today. Some modern empirical proof of this possibility follows.

First, bureaucratized and routinized tasks do not flow from the nature of "technology" but from the needs of centralized control. As Vroom notes in his masterful survey of experimental literature in industrial social psychology:[5]

[the evidence indicates that] decentralized structures have an advantage for tasks which are difficult, complex, or unusual, while centralized structures are more effective for those which are simple and routinized.

That is, given that the corporate unit is based on centralized control, the most efficient technologies will be those involving routinized, dull, and repetitive tasks. In a decentralized environment, the exact reverse would be true.

Second, workers do not like fragmented jobs. The experimental literature shows that job enlargement and decision-making control on the part of workers increases their satisfaction, while lowering absenteeism and turnover (Vroom, pp. 199–201). Nevertheless, managers have organized the normal bureaucratic division of tasks so that actual worker performance is *substantially independent of the worker's attitudes and satisfactions.* This startling, counterintuitive fact is one of the major results of fifty years of investigation by industrial psychologists (Vroom, p. 199).

Third, bureaucratic organization of production, while insuring managerial control and corporate security against the vagaries of workers' morale, is by no means efficient in the wider sense. For even *moderate* worker participation in decisions and goal-setting increases productivity (Vroom, p. 228). The mean quality of decisions made by a group is, moreover, greater than the mean quality of individual decisions (Vroom, p. 230), and the best results are obtained when individuals *think up* solutions individually, and *evaluate and choose* among them as solidary team (Vroom, p. 232–33).

Let us give some examples. The MIT-generated Scanlon Plan of "participatory management" has been tried in some ten United States plants. This plan gives workers unlimited power to organize and improve the work process and working conditions, guaranteeing them a share in the proceeds of cost-reduction. In these ten plants the average yearly increase in productivity amounted to 23.1 per cent, and in one company 408 out of the 513 innovative ideas were successfully implemented because they led to real improvements in the productive process. Clearly a stable dialogue between workers, technicians, and planners would even increase this fertile activity.

These results are reproduced in many other individual studies: when workers are given control over decisions and goal-setting, productivity rises dramatically (Vroom, pp. 234–36). As Blumberg concludes:[6]

There is scarcely a study in the entire literature which fails to demonstrate that satisfaction in work is enhanced or . . . productivity increases accrue from a genuine increase in worker's decision-making power. Findings of such consistency, I submit, are rare in social research . . . the participative worker is an involved worker, for his job becomes an extension of himself and by his decisions he is creating his work, modifying and regulating it.

But such instances of even moderate worker control are instituted only in marginal areas and in isolated firms fighting for survival. When the crisis is over, there is a return to "normal operating procedure." The threat of workers escalating their demand for control is simply too great, and the usurpation of the prerogatives of hierarchical authority is quickly quashed. Hence, efficiency in the broader sense is subordinated to the needs of bureaucratic control.

Moreover, it is wrong to think of "technology" as a single unidimensional force of which an economy can only have "more" or "less," but whose substance and form are essentially independent of social decision. What "technology" is at a point in time is the sum-total of the past decisions made as to what *forms of research* are undertaken, and which *results of research* are embodied in actual production in factory and office. Technology is "alienating" in capitalist society (and its state-socialist imitators) in the first instance because it is developed and diffused on the sole criterion of profit, and it is "locked into" bureaucratic organization only because capitalist and managerial representatives will introduce no new technology which is incompatible with their maintenance of power. Thus liberated, integrated, and antihierarchical technologies can develop only when we replace capitalist economic institutions by a system of direct worker and community control. Workers are alienated from their work-activities because they are powerless to determine, or even significantly affect, the nature of work-roles that hold sway over their lives. Even when workers are organized into unions, they are able to affect only the wage scale and the grossest aspects of work-process — health conditions, coffee breaks, line speeds, etc. The white-collar unions are no exception to this rule.

Work is for the most part "meaningless" not because of the nature of technology and the division of labor, but because the institutions determining them are alienated — the criteria according to which they make decisions (i.e., produce outcomes) are independent from workers' needs.

V. ALIENATION AND INEQUALITY

In our introductory remarks, we noted that the major issues treated would *not* concern material inequality, but rather the quality of life and culture. However, we quickly found that these latter issues depend on the basic constellation of power in capitalist society. This same analysis applies to the decision mechanisms determining the distribution of income.

I shall argue that the distribution of income is not determined in the sphere of state decision-making. While the government can ameliorate the worst aspects of income inequality — destitution and biological insecurity — through taxes, transfers, and public services, it can do little to change its overall character. Moreover, the income distribution is not determined in *any* sphere over which individuals have control. Collective bargaining and other processes that directly involve individual participation have necessarily minor impact on the overall distribution of income. In fact, I shall argue that the income distribution is basically determined by institutional decision-mechanisms according to criteria essentially independent from individual and social need.

Certainly in the first instance the distribution of income derives from institutional power: legitimate claims to income derive from ownership of factors of production (land, labor, and capital), and the economic return to these factors (rent, wages, and salaries, interest and profit) is determined by supply of and demand for their services. But the institutions of private ownership and market determination of factor rewards do not merely serve to distribute income. In addition they perform the essential economic function of allocating factors to productive uses. This is, of course, elementary economic theory. Demand curves for various types of land, labor, and capital are determined as the aggregation of private-administrative decisions by firms as to factor needs. These needs are themselves determined on the basis of profitability and compatibility with secure hierarchical control. Supply curves for factors of production, on the other hand, are determined by the pattern of ownership and the willingness of owners to provide differential factor outlays at different prices.

Thus factor markets insure the allocation of the proper amount of each factor to its proper place in the production system. As a *by-product* of this allocation process, a particular initial distribution of income arises.

Clearly this institutional decision mechanism is not controlled by the individuals it affects. People cannot get together to decide the market distribution of income in any sense. Also, it is in and of itself an *alienated* decision-mechanism. For the criteria according to which it apportions income are *allocational,* not distributional at all. Markets in factors of production, as allocative mechanisms, provide the capitalist firm maximum flexibility to maximize profits and growth, and the actual constellation of factor prices leads to the greatest efficiency in the production of marketable goods and services compatible with bureaucratic organization.

Where does state power fit into this decision process?   It is often held that whatever the initial distribution of income determined in the private-sphere, the state can correct to any desired pattern by redistribution in the form of progressive taxation, guaranteed incomes, minimum wages, welfare, and the like.   However, it is easy to see that given the economic context of private ownership of factors of production, the market in labor, and hierarchical stratification of labor in production, extensive attempts to redistribute income threatens the allocational function of factor markets.

First, the state could reduce the share of profits somewhat through taxation and confiscation of wealth at death.   But beyond a certain point, these procedures would curb profit incentives and elicit the organized opposition of those few who own the bulk of the wealth and are responsible for the control of the several hundred large corporations that are the life-line of our economy.   The private-administrative power of the owners of capital insures that a serious attack on their wealth position would lead to economic chaos.

Second, on the lower end of the income distribution, the state can insure basic biological security (adequate food and health care).   But it cannot insure even a minimally adequate standard of living for all families without completely stemming the supply of unskilled and semi-skilled labor.   For those who hold these jobs — the most undesirable of work-roles — would surely prefer a secure guaranteed income to even a somewhat higher income from degrading work.   The market mechanism in labor would then operate to raise the wage of unskilled and semiskilled labor significantly *higher* than even skilled labor.   Because the legitimacy of the hierarchical stratification of production requires that wage differentials across levels of skill and status be maintained, this would lead to a strong rise in the wages of skilled labor and so on up the line.   The result would be either a massive inflation (eliminating the guaranteed income) or lower profits, hence economic stagnation and unemployment.   A similar analysis applies to schemes of negative income taxation, minimum wage legislation, and the like.

In an earlier section I argued that collective bargaining does not significantly alter the market distribution of income.   We now see that, due to the institutional decision-mechanism's allocational function in capitalist society, state power is incapable of effecting basic changes in the market distribution of income.   Since the latter is an alienated outcome, we conclude that the overall process of income determination is alienated as well.

VI. COMMUNITY AND THE STRUCTURE OF POWER

The institutional basis for alienation from work-activities has counterparts in other social spheres. For instance, individuals are alienated from their community in capitalist society. The roles open to the individual allowing him to relate to his social community are among the most central to his welfare and personal development. They define his contact with social life. Aside from his work and his basic living and consumption unit — be it nuclear family or more extended commune — social community is the most important potential contribution to his well-being. Yet when his community is ugly, vast, and impersonal, and through its fragmented and impotent role-structure, fails to provide adequate personal outlets, the individual becomes alienated from his community.

The community in capitalist society is molded by its economic institutions. Because land is controlled individually rather than communally its use conforms to private as opposed to social interests. If this individual control were distributed equally throughout the population, possibly commonness of interest would lead owners to cooperate in the interests of all. But land and property are highly unequally apportioned.

How do powerful owners of land and capital decide its use? Clearly through maximizing their own benefit — i.e., their profit Here a basic economic institution enters in, the market in land, whereby each parcel of community property is allocated to the highest bidder for its most remunerative personal use. Traditional economic theory shows that markets in factors of production and commodities insures, through Adam Smith's famous "invisible hand," the amassing of labor and the allocation of land according to their most "efficient" use in individual commodity production. Thus maximal remuneration leads to gargantuan agglomerations of individuals, in "urban environments" and "sleeping suburbs" whose only purpose is to supply the labor needs of monolithic bureaucratic enterprise. Commercial land-use conforms to profit criteria independent of community needs.

Since the community as an autonomous entity, aside from minor zoning and tax regulations, has no control over economic activity and patterns of land use, the basis of stable and solidary community relations withers and disappears. An architecturally and socially integrated community cannot thrive when the only power the community holds over the autonomous activities of profit-maximizing capitalists takes the form of crude constraints on their creative, synthesizing enterprises and activities.

Rather, a true community must be *itself* a creative, initiating, and synthesizing agent, with the power to determine the architectural unity of its living and working spaces and their coordination, the power to allocate community property to social uses such as participatory child-care and community recreation centers, and the power to insure the preservation and development of its natural ecological environment.

Nor is this all an idle Utopian dream. I have personally visited many living-working communities exhibiting architectural, ecological, aesthetic, and social integrity: the New England town, the Dutch village, the moderate-sized cities of Mali in sub-Saharan Africa, and the desert communities of Djerba in Tunisia. These communities are, however, fairly static and untouched by modern technology. We normally think of technology as destroying the structure of community. But the potential in a technologically advanced country for decent community is truly staggering, given the proper pattern of community decision mechanisms.

We are not surprised that capitalist "communities" evince so little and such apathetic support from their members. The individual estranged from his community is realistic in understanding his lack of control over major community decisions. Clearly, alienation from community corresponds to our general propostion: the institutions determining the role-structure, the power-structure, and the physical structure of community operate apart from the needs of individuals.

VII. ALIENATION FROM POLITICS AND THE STATE

As we have seen, the state plays an essential, but an essentially auxiliary role in social development. That is, the primary decisions that govern social development are made in the economic sphere, through the integrated institutional decision mechanisms embodied in basic economic institutions. The state has no essential control over income distribution, work-activities, the development of community or technology. This is not to say, however, that the state as an active agent is superfluous. In fact, the state apparatus must enforce the legal relations which preserve the operation of basic capitalist institutions, in the face of sporadic onslaughts on the part of a predominantly noncapitalist electorate. In recent years, in addition, the state apparatus has extended its sphere of influence ever more directly into the economic realm, both as a direct employer, and as a dominant regulator of industrial activity. Here again, however, the state has no choice but to act as an *appendage* to the economic system. The basic institutions simply do not operate properly in their "pure form," and it is the function of the state to correct malfunctions through regulation in the economic sphere, to *increase* the effectiveness of their operation, e.g., child labor laws and factory safety legislation were important to the generation of an adequate labor force in the early stages of the Industrial Revolution, and hence for the operation of the market in labor.   Similarly in modern times we can analyze zoning regulations, highway programs, welfare programs, etc., as *perfecting* and *stabilizing* rather than *undermining* the operation of core economic institutions.   Since the state must follow the dictates of alienated economic institutions, politics is itself *alienated* in the strict sense of the word.

Thus the state is alienated not only because it is not controlled by the people, but because it is divorced from effective power over everyday life, whatever its size.   For while politics is at least formally democratic, our everyday economic life is the most advanced form of totalitarianism ever devised by man.   Owners of capital and their managerial representatives control our work, our communities, and our environment.

Just as the state has not *caused* the problems of modern capitalism, so it cannot cure them.   We do not lack "good leadership" or "progressive government"; nor do we need merely a "dictatorship of the proletariat" instead of a capitalist ruling class.   What we lack is democratic institutions that regulate our daily lives in schooling, the communications media, work, and community.   Hence a true revolution is *social,* not merely political.

Marx once said that under capitalism, "all social relations are reduced to exchange relations."   In other words, major social roles are tailored to the needs of efficiency, profitability, and control in commodity production.   Markets in factors of production and corporate profit-maximization imply that the structure of community, work, and even natural environment, conform to the criteria of profit-maximization.   This is indeed the source of alienation and the divergence of role-determination criteria from human need.

The "virtue" of capitalism is its level of economic growth in individual — as opposed to social — commodities, and the system accomplishes this at the expense of destruction in other social realms.   Capitalism "delivers the goods" at the expense of destroying society, and this cannot be cured by merely altering the forms of political control.

VIII. ALIENATION FROM SELF AND CULTURE

Alienation from work-activities and community are the basis of the individual's estrangement from all aspects of social life.

According to this explanation, alienation is a form of deprivation — deprivation from important social roles. But this deprivation holds deep personal implications because *individual psychic development is controlled by social experience.* Just as "individuals develop through their social relations of production" and hence become incomplete individuals when alienated from their work-activities, so individuals develop through their roles relating to community, product, and other individuals. When deprived of these formative influences in healthy forms, they become "self-alienated." To continue a metaphor, society may alienate a man's psyche as much as a pickpocket his wallet. We are alienated from ourselves when we are not what we really could be — when we cannot love, play, run, work, spiritualize, relate, create, empathize, aid as much as our potential allows.

Self-alienation in this sense is often seen as a personal rather than social problem, and the "afflicted" troop to counselors and psychiatrists (and drugs) in search of themselves. But the social base of even this most intimate form of alienation lies in the deprivation of growth-conducive social environments and relationships, and its cure is accordingly *social.* When one grows up alienated from others, he cannot love or relate; alienated from work, he cannot create; from community, he cannot mature as a social being. Dominant economic institutions, especially markets in labor, land, and capital, and their control by individuals making decisions on the basis of profit rather than human need, provide unrewarding social roles. Hence psychic growth is thwarted, much as vitamin deprivation inhibits physical development.

Individuals become alienated from themselves for yet another reason. To produce workers with the proper ideologies, values, and personalities to participate effectively in alienated social roles requires special attention on the part of those institutions which regulate the development of youth. Thus communications media, especially advertising, instill materialist values which hold meaningful work and community of no importance in comparison with individual consumption. They depersonalize and objectivize interpersonal, intersexual, interracial, and international relations, reducing them to brute power, competition, and ruse, by equating the individual's success as lover, worker, or community member with what he possesses in the form of goods or status.

Similarly schools, by mirroring the impersonal and competitive relations of community and the bureaucratic-authoritarian aspects of alienated work, thwart the development of true initiative, independence, and creativity in their charges. Thus they attempt to produce docile, unimaginative workers fitting the needs of hierarchical commodity production. The media and the schools are alienating, but are not the true culprits — they merely serve an economic mechanism that shapes community and work in patterns alien to human needs.

Nevertheless, the educational system warrants special attention in any analysis of alienation. For it is the educational system that is turning out cultural and political revolutionaries, as well as disaffected and unhappy workers. Why are schools beginning to fail in producing properly alienated workers? There are many reasons for this, and we shall discuss only several of the most important.

First, there has been an important qualitative shift in the composition of the work in modern corporate, bureaucratic capitalism. Most important, the middle class and the capitalist class no longer coincide as in the days of early entrepreneurial capitalism. Indeed they scarcely overlap. The vast majority of middle-class people today are workers, in the sense that they sell their labor in a market and have no control over production. The social technology of corporate capitalism has reduced the bourgeoisie to the middle strata of the labor force. Students, who are by and large of middle-class background, are thus *future members of the working class,* and their political actions must be viewed in this light. Moreover, long-term trends in occupational structure exhibit a shift away from the traditional blue-collar manufacturing stratum, toward the white-collar corporate-bureaucratic (clerical, secretarial, sales, administration, and technical) and service (teacher, government worker, postman, policeman, soldier) strata. Hence the political views of students will be increasingly transferable to the working class as time goes on.

But the student movement is especially important because of the *special position* of education in relation to the modern capitalist economy. Bureaucratic order in production requires *an increasing period of socialization of labor* for the occupational roles the worker must assume. Educational institutions — high schools, junior colleges, and universities — are among the instruments of this socialization process. The schooling process — a basic formative influence on individual personality — is progressively reduced to its functional role in instilling the psychological requisites of an adequate alienated labor force. Men become "alienated from themselves" in the sense that their personal development is geared to the requirements of an economic system whose needs are based on criteria independent of human values.

It is assumed by liberal and radical alike that the purpose of schooling is primarily intellectual. Schools produce "good workers" by supplying individuals with the cognitive and psychomotor skills to operate in an increasingly "technological" work-environment. This is in large part false. In fact, *one cannot account for the contribution of schooling to worker earnings in terms of the concrete cognitive attainments of students.* Given the number of years of schooling an individual has attained, additional information as to his IQ or actual cognitive achievement (reading and math facility, logical reasoning, etc.) have virtually no value in prediction of eventual income or position in the status-hierarchy of production. Cognitive development is associated with occupational status only through their common association with level of educational attainment. There is little direct causal connection.[7]

In fact, schooling contributes to the generation of an adequate labor force through the *inculcation of a "bureaucratic mentality" in students.*[8] This enables them to function properly in alienated work-environments; i.e., by directing the *emotional development* of the future worker. Since an increasing proportion — nowadays a large majority — of workers pass through this process of "psychic bureaucratization," *the development of a counterculture negating the bureaucratic mentality is a necessary instrument in the emergence of working class consciousness.*

The Marxist principle that socialism can result only from the political activity of a working class conscious of itself as an oppressed class remains essentially correct today. However, psychic conditioning as student is an essential and increasingly time and energy-consuming segment of every worker's life. Education serves the production of alienated labor. Contradictions in the educational system are quickly transformed to factories and offices themselves.[9] A breakdown in the educational system produces "imperfectly socialized" workers — workers who enter the labor force in unalienated form, and hence are incapable of and unwilling to submit to the meaninglessness and oppressiveness of bureaucratic order and hierarchical control. These are the revolutionary labor organizers of the future.

However, there have developed important contradictions within the educational system. First, schools perform their function *only in so far as they operate as objectively repressive institutions.* The "liberated" school cannot produce adequate workers, and education is *productive* only in so far as it is *repressive.* The otherwise astute analyses of Paul Goodman, George Leonard, Charles Silberman, John Holt, and Edgar Z. Friedenberg, falter precisely on this point. The seeming "irrationalities" of formal education are in fact highly functional to the operation of capitalism. First, the *social relations* of education mirror the social relations of hierarchical control in alienated production. Firm authority lines (administration, teacher, student), emphasis on precise rule-conformity in punctuality, interpersonal relations and teacher-dominance, and the treatment of fellow students as competitors rather than cooperators ("cooperation in task performance," as Robert Dreeben notes, "is known in school circles as cheating") are of course obvious examples. More important, perhaps, is that the motivation and reward structure of schooling mirror that of alienated labor. Just as the worker on the job is not motivated by the subjective value of his work or the goal of that process — the object or service produced — so the student must learn to be motivated by external reward in the form of grades. Second, the *content of grading* is in itself repressive and conducive only to the development of alienated and bureaucratic mentality. Discipline, subordination to authority, and suppression of affective and creative modes of personality response are required of all strata in the labor force under bureaucratic conditions. Empirical investigation shows these traits are in themselves rewarded in terms of higher grades — in both high school and college — independent of their actual contribution to cognitive achievement.[10] Schooling impedes the development of the liberated individual by direct penalization of the liberated act, and not irrationally, but in the service of the economic system.

Thus education exhibits the basic contradiction of capitalist alienation at its source — in the generation of alienated labor. This is the fertile backdrop for radical student activity and must be an ultimate source of socialist consciousness. For in order to operate, *the student must submit to his own alienation.* The political failure to submit on the part of one student, when linked to a social movement, equals the creation of one politically conscious worker, and the rendering inoperative of one school as a bureaucratic socializing instrument equals the creation of a mass of potentially revolutionary workers. This is what we now observe in admittedly chaotic and politically undeveloped form in the student movement today. This disintegration of capitalist society is the social backdrop within which the student can evaluate this decision to submit.

Thus history is on the side of the radical organizer. I have emphasized that basic capitalist institutions naturally operate (a) to progressively fragment and destroy major aspects of social life — community, work, leisure, environment, consumption, justice, and (b) in favor of the secure control over production and, within this constraint, the maximization of the volume of marketable goods and services. This progressive deterioration is a process reaching critical proportions observable to all, especially to the incompletely socialized youth. On the other hand, growth in material product is itself subject to a self-negating dialectic. The "virtue" of capitalism lies in its productivity, but this productivity becomes, as incomes rise progressively the production of the superfluous over the necessary, to use a phrase of Andre Gorz. This economic growth, by liberating the young individual from biological needs, renders it unnecessary that he submit to his own alienation — e.g., through schooling — and to realize the extent of his current needs. This is the historical dialectic within which latter day radicals are privileged to operate. It is the privilege to opt for equality, justice, community, worker control, spiritual transcendence, and the sacrifice of irrational production to the needs of a rational society.

Indeed, it is in the objective interests of the working class — and the student as a future member of this class — to do so. In this way capitalism offers up its own negation, and economic growth becomes a tool against itself.

The second abiding contradiction in education results from the fact that, due to the increasing bureaucratization and stratification of labor, *higher education no longer confers elite status.* Rather it serves to staff the middle and upper-middle strata of the labor force. American education has always consisted of two school systems. *The two are now beginning to clash where they overlap,* causing severe social dislocation.

The one system derives from the Olympian heights of "critical enlightenment culture" and the free flow of ideas. This system, as embodied in the elite colleges and universities, has traditionally served only those few destined to staff the ranks of the corporate, political, theological, and professional ruling class. The "critical spirit" has never been a threat to capitalism when restricted to its chosen elite. Indeed, it can be seen as an essential symbol of "good breeding" in the more sophisticated circles of the ruling class.

The other school system arose in the United States "from the bottom up." Elementary and later secondary schooling intersected not at all with the values of the liberal enlightenment. Rather, they responded to the needs of the burgeoning industrial order for a disciplined, submissive, and Godfearing blue-collar proletariat. *The extension of bureaucratic technology has led this "second school system" to filter up even to the college level, where it now clashes with the first.* The *content* of higher education is indeed one of "critical enlightenment" (however biased and insufficient it may seem to the student radical). But the *form* has become, as we have seen, the mirror of the alienated structure of production. This contradiction is seen most clearly in the state and junior colleges which sincerely transmit the cultural facade of liberality to the content of education, yet equally sincerely impose the structural limitations required by capitalist bureaucratic organization. This contradiction, in post-high school education (and increasingly even in high schools), takes the form of administrators and teachers *consciously* having to sully the principles of free inquiry to the reality of repressive organization and economic need, and to weaken the repressive structure in conformance with the (even minimal) dictates of liberal education. Out of this clash has come student activism and skepticism, in a dialectical movement that might have made Marx himself proud. Changing economic conditions — developed through the endogenous "progress" of technology — has pitted formerly functional and stabilizing institutions — in this case the two school systems — against one another. The outcome, given the proper political environment, can contribute to revolutionary consciousness.

In short, the educational system is part of a pervasive culture of *commodity fetishism,* whereby individuals are driven to shunt all their personal aspirations in the direction of status in work and material consumption. Capitalism's "virtue" in "delivering the goods" would be acceptable to workers and community members only under one condition: that the "goods" the system delivers be valued as the ultimate source of individual welfare. The submission of the individual to his personal alienation is thus based on the ideological belief that material goods are the path to personal salvation, and this belief is instilled and reinforced through media and schools. Yet it is doubtless false.

We must define the individual not by what he *has* — in the form of individual commodities — but by what he *is* and what he *does* — by his ability to undertake self-fulfilling *activities*. Commodities cannot do for you what you cannot do for yourself; they can act only as *instruments,* used in the process of human activity. The possibility of self-realizing activity depends as much on the *social contexts* open to the individual as on the means available to their performance. Thus the quality of community, work, and environment appear alongside of individual commodities as sources of individual welfare. An increase in the mass of goods available to the individual will enhance his well-being only in so far as they *expand the sphere of his activities* and hence only if the social roles involved in individual activity — roles defined by community, work, and environment — are themselves maintained or expanded. Economic growth cannot overcome the individual's alienation from these social spheres.

Moreover, the individual's ability to undertake self-fulfilling activities depend on his own *level of personal psychic development,* in terms of physical, emotional, cognitive, aesthetic, and spiritual capacities. The individual alienated from himself, being alienated from growth-conducive social roles — through his forced reduction to a purely efficient worker or child-raiser — is incapable of true fulfillment, and for him or her, commodities become a substitute for, rather than a complement to, personal activities. Instead of devoloping a beautiful body, he or she buys clothes. Instead of engaging in sports, he or she watches them on TV. Instead of being a beautiful person, he or she buys a beautiful car or motorcycle. The individual discovers his or her alienation only by realizing this basic fact.

IX. CONCLUSION

But the consciousness of alienation occurs not through the moralist ministrations of the "converted," but the day-to-day experiences of workers themselves, and a major force in this realization is the *process of economic growth.* Capitalist ideology holds that increasing personal income is the main path to happiness, that all that we are not, our money and status can be for us. Yet even taking account of inflation, GNP doubles every twenty-five or thirty years in the United States, and we are not happier — on the contrary, social life continues to disintegrate and fragment. Economic growth itself gives the lie to the consumerist ethic. We cannot buy decent environment with increased income — the total supply of "ecological balance" is limited and declines through the normal operation of economic institutions, and the rich bid away this dwindling supply. We cannot buy decent community and decent work-activities when their very destruction is the basis of capitalist growth.

While economic growth renders us each decade more aware of our alienation, and while we may identify alienation as a social problem rooted in the structure of economies, and their supporting social and cultural institutions, its cure is not easy. Clearly integrated work-activities require the destruction of the market in labor, and introduction of worker control of production. Clearly attachment to product and integration of community requires decentralized community control of land and capital and the concomitant destruction of markets in the "factors of production." Clearly the elimination of bureaucratic organization requires the development of technologies according to the intrinsic needs of workers rather than the dictates of profit or party control. And clearly the destruction of hierarchy in production and conspicuous consumption requires income equality.

The precise form of these alternative institutions will appear only as their need is realized by masses of citizens. But these changes, however necessary, are by no means sufficient to insure an active, functioning, and humane society. In fact, a new society is perforce burdened by two basic legacies of the social order it has struggled to replace. First, we are stuck with a technology geared specifically to alienated production, many parts of which cannot be tranferred to a really participatory community. Even the most vigorous, flexible, and creative democratic society must face an extended transitional phase, in which alienating jobs are shared by all while technologies are developed leading to their abolition. Second, socialist institutions, however well engineered, cannot operate within the cultural and psychological patterns of Capitalist Man. Yet we are who we are, and to expect communal, creative, and generally Socialist Man to arise full-blown and spontaneously from a mere institutional shift is clearly absurd. Proper operation of institutions in the new society will require the development of socialist culture *within the womb of capitalist society.* Therefore, the role of counterculture in the movement for revolutionary change acquires an importance perhaps hitherto unknown in the history of social change.

In this huge task to create a humane society, it is the brute *productivity* of capitalist technology that is our helping hand. The creation of decentralized socialism may involve a sacrifice of efficiency in production in the interests of a full social development. This sacrifice need entail no loss in the qualitative satisfaction of even our material needs. Most of the military-industrial complex, advertising, financial, sales, and insurance effort can simply be eliminated, and these sectors account for the activities of one worker in four. A rational transport system — both public transport and reasonable, unfrilled, and durable private transport — can free another worker in eight. Rational agriculture can vastly increase the output of foods, and especially the supply of meat and luxury food stuffs. Worker's control can increase efficiency. And this is only the start.

Similarly, a reasonable socialism would see an increase in the *size of the productive labor force.* Elimination of profit would require (former) capitalists to work for the social good, instead of simply collecting interest and dividends. Reduction in the size of the military would free a million men for work. Elimination of racism and sexism would free blacks and women to perform socially necessary — as well as personally rewarding — labor in far greater numbers than today, increasing the labor force by some 25 per cent. The elderly could be allowed to continue the rewarding aspects of production — craft and skill — far beyond the capitalist "mandatory retirement age," which is a benefit to the elderly only when work is by nature alienating.

All this and more are within the realm of the possible — indeed as well within reach. It requires only our dedication to a vibrant and healthy movement for social change.

ENDNOTES

[1] The reader who has thought a good deal about this problem will notice a basic ambiguity in this definition. What do we mean by "needs?" Do we mean immediate, experienced, felt needs? Or do we mean "real" needs as determined by the scientist, moralist, or who have you, whether or not the individual realizes them? In fact, we mean neither of these. Rather, we mean the needs which capitalist society is *in the process of developing in individuals,* whether it means to or not. These needs are neither presently manifest in everyone, nor are they abstractly determined. We can discover them only by analyzing historical trends and contradictions in modern society. We may call these needs "dialectically generated."

[2] The following material draws heavily on an unpublished report of a friend and colleague Steve Marglin, *What Do Bosses Do?,* Harvard University, February 1971. Mimeograph.

[3] See Marglin, *op. cit.,* for a detailed argument of this proposition.

4 See Marglin, *op. cit.*

5 Victor H. Vroom, "Industrial Social Psychology," *The Handbook of Social Psychology,* Vol. V, 2nd ed., Gardner Lindzey and Elliot Aronsen, eds., Addison-Wesley, Reading, Massachusetts, 1969.

6 Paul Blumberg, *Industrial Democracy,* Constable, 1969.

7 For empirical support, see Herbert Gintis, "Education, Technology, and the Characteristics of Worker Productivity," *American Economic Review,* May 1971.

8 *Ibid.*

9 A "contradiction" is a process wherein the normal operation of a social system produces a condition which tends to undermine normal operation itself. Dialectical social analysis holds that social change takes place because a social system creates through its internal contradictions, the conditions for its own breakdown. Hence the study of history becomes the study of developing contradictions in a society.

10 See Gintis, *op. cit.*

INDEX

Index

Blumberg, Paul, 450–451
Boas, Franz, 420
Boulding, Kenneth, 22, 63
Bowles, Samuel, 7, 81, 82–83, 165–200,
212, 365
Budget for family of four, 141–143
Burns, Arthur, 136–137, 139

Capital:
free movement of, 177
human, 213
and occupation, 213
market for, 382
Capitalism, 37, 43, 73
and business system, 376
contemporary, 415–416
critics of, 431
defined, 407–408
development vs. exchange, 370
development of, 34, 407, 410, 416
and discrimination, 313–315
vs. environment and community, 40
exchange, 407–410, 415, 416
expansion of and ecology, 400
free market vs. state, 371, 419–426
future of, 427
future of, 370, 419–430
American, 406–418
history of, 370, 399, 402, 408–411, 424
vs. human development, 63
ideology, 407
industrial, and corporate state, 98
and influence on underdeveloped
countries, 345
institutional rules of, 407
liberals and competitive, 414–415
and market system, 377, 386
mature, 411
monopoly, 338, 341
and economic surplus, 338–339
nature of American, 75–200
as oppressor, 17, 58
poverty, and mature, 135–136
and institutions of, 207
rational crime and competitive,
267–269
vs. socialism, 398–399
and society, 376–377
socialist people's, 427
as social system, 406–407
state, of USSR, 7
unresolved problems of, 297–326
Capitalist countries, 327, 432
successful, 327–328
unsuccessful, 327–328
as colonies, 328
and socialism, 328

Capitalist institutions, 441–442
and individual welfare, 44
and primitive economies, 47
and social alienation, 457
Capitalists, 17, 41–42
social power of, 72
and workers, 18
Capitalist society:
alienation and power, 433, 452
and alienation from community, 454
quality of life in, 432, 452
Capitalist system:
and government spending, 364
international, 358–360
and state-socialist system, 46
state, of USSR, 15–16, 46
world, 399
United States dominance in, 73
Caplovitz, David, 142
Carlyle, Thomas, 93, 103
Chenery, Hollis, 58–60
Chesterton, G. K., 157
China:
communist, 404
and egalitarian development, 403
and socialism, 403
Cities:
bad design of, 372
housing problems, 110
increase in crime, 110
noise, 111
pollution, 110
pollution-free, 115
suggestions for livability, 116
transportation in, 110, 114
uglification of, 110
Civil rights, 355
failure of legislation, 222
Clark, Ramsey, 258, 259, 261, 269, 270,
271, 272, 273
Class:
capitalist, 61, 238
conflict, 153–156
conflicts of interest, 59
lower, 154
ruling vs. peasants, 59
status and income, 209
upper, 159
Classical economists, 21, 22, 407
Ricardian, 34
Class structure, 48–49, 79
and division of labor, 166
and government spending, 365
hierarchical in United States, 16
and higher education, 171, 193
inequalities, 193
perpetuation of, 185
and technology, 386
in USSR, 402

Okun, Arthur, 204, 239–248
Old people (*see also* Efficiency, Poverty) :
  alienation of, 436
  and future, 114
Olson, Jr., Mancur, 3, 12, 15, 19–32
Oppenheimer, Franz, 422–423, 425
Optimal growth theory, 26
Optimality, 25
Orthodox economics, 1–4, 6, 8–12
  definition of, 57
  materialist bias of, 5
  and radical political economy, 328
Orthodox economists, 1–12, 16, 17, 76,
  81, 133, 203, 257
Orwell, George, 109, 341

Pacifism, 20
Packer, Herbert, 278–279
Palme, Olaf, 162–163
Pareto-optimality, 23–26, 29
  in allocation of resources, 29
  frontiers of, 38
Parker, Richard, 11, 80, 133–152
Parsonian School of Sociology, 26–32
Peace Corps, 190, 192
Peasants, 59, 105
  as proletariat, 370, 399
Pechman, Joseph, 132, 139, 149
Pentagon, 357, 362
Pericles, funeral oration of, 10
Permanent-trade-off, 71
Physiocracy, emergence of, 34
Planning (*see also* Socialist system) :
  social, 388
Pochoda, Ralph, 15, 33–54
Political Economics, 61, 73, 213
  state of, 55–74
Political economic theory, 213
  and poverty, 214
Political economists, 17
  radical, 2, 3
Political economy, 42, 50
  of imperialism, 127
  radical, 15–74
Political stability, and economic growth,
  30
Politics, liberal, 413–415
Pollution, 16, 127, 312
  air in cities, 125
  environmental, 108–111
  and growth, 79, 125–126, 418
  poor as victims, 78
  solution for, 115
Poor, 11, 17, 20, 215–216
  as deprived, 146
  handicapped, 211
  number of, 148–149
  rural, 217

and state, 217
  today's, 401
  as victimized minorities, 145–146
  working, 161, 202, 210
Population growth:
  control, 333–334
  limitation of, 115
  and limitation of freedom, 416
  and resources, 63
  stopping, 126
  threat to environment, 387
Poverty, 16, 201–205, 208–209, 220,
  223–224, 228–229, 334
  case poor, 136
  and crime, 204, 263
  definition of, 141, 229–230
  insular poor, 136
  and minorities, 209
  and myth of New Affluence, 135–137
  and old age, 218–220
  programs, 7, 217, 223, 234, 235
  radical perspective of, 207–227
  theories of, 209, 214–215
  War on, 221, 222, 233, 301
Power, 58, 97, 98, 99
  community and structure of, 354
  differential in society, 17, 28
  economic and political, 228
  Galbraith's conception of, 96–101
  imperialism as, 341–342
  institutional, 438, 440
  political, 21, 23, 202–203, 438
  private-administrative, 439, 453
  social vs. state, 425
  state, 98, 439, 453
  of workers, 72
Prebisch Thesis, 128
Prison:
  as crime factory, 260–261
  life in, 268
  system, 273, 288
Private ownership, 61–62
Product (*see also* Commodity) :
  marginal, 62
Production:
  bureaucratic order in, 443, 446, 447,
    450, 458
  community control of, 115
  of education, 183
  of goods and services, 38
  minorities and, 18
  socially useful, 44
  social relations of, 166–167, 169, 185,
    187, 190, 267, 364, 366, 446, 447
    hierarchy in, 169
    vs. growth, 183
Productivity, 17, 29
  economic, 37
  and humane society, 464

Productivity (*cont.*)
  maximum, 6
  under system of constraints, 12
Professional workers, 165–166 (*see also* Middle Class)
Professions:
  ethics, 28
  goals of organizations, 194–195
  radical organizations, 192–193
Profits, 45–46, 108
  and alienation, 456, 457
  corporate, 252–253
    threats to, 253
  vs. inflation, 73
  undeserved, 17
Proletariat, rise of industrial, 34
Prosperity, 241
  and military spending, 329
  myth of, 137
  and recession, 329
  and spending, 329
Proust, Marcel, 376

Racism, 16, 193, 305–309, 355
  and capitalism, 297–311, 312–317
  and crime, 263
  economics of, 301–311
  and education, 309
  and poverty, 222
  and workers, 298, 304
Radical, 1–12, 100
  economists, 18, 35, 36, 58, 71–72, 76, 80, 81
    analysis of crime problem, 257, 266
    intentions of, 43–50
    and Middle America, 133–134
  political economist, 12
  student movement, 165
Radical economics, 40, 48
Radicalism, white collar, 165–166
Recession, 135
  of 1970's, 81, 352–353
  and New Economics, 353
Rehabilitation:
  cooperation vs. competition, 277
  theory of, 288
Reich, Charles, 9, 75, 159
Reich, Michael, 297, 298, 301–311, 329, 357–368
Republican party, 155, 156, 158, 159
Research:
  curbing of, 115
  fragmentation of, 177–178
  universities and, 176
Resources, 23, 25
  allocation of, 26
    and war, 354, 357
  reallocation of, 29–30

Revenue and Expenditure Control Act, 245
  and fiscal policy, 245
Revolution:
  agricultural and industrial, 328
  Bolshevik, 333, 426
  economic and political, 228
  French, motto of, 7
  scientific, 387
  social, 333, 334, 335–336
  socialist, 327, 337, 370, 399
  United States suppression of social, 332
  history of, 332–333
Ricardo, David, 20, 34, 420
Rich, power bases of, 61
Richta, Radovan, 386, 387
Riddell, Tom, 328
Robinson, Joan, 62
Role-performance, sociology of, 47
Role:
  social, 438
    and alienation, 437, 457
    and education, 462
    structure of, 438
  work, 439
    and alienation, 443–445
    and economic institutions, 443
    fragmentation of jobs, 445–449
      worker's dislike of, 450
    and small capitalist, 440
Roosevelt, President Franklin D., 80, 154
Rothbard, Murray, 4, 6, 9, 371–372, 419–430
Rousseau, Jean Jacques, 122
Ruskin, John, 93, 103
Russia (*see* USSR)

Saint Augustine, 423–424
Samuelson, Paul, 136–137
Saving, effect of on rich and poor, 62
Scanlon Plan, 450
Scarcity, 2, 3, 5, 9, 104, 391
  and economic theory, 15, 23
  and greed, 423
  of jobs, 241
  and resources, 24, 31
School (*see also* Education):
  and alienation, 457
  one-room vs. consolidated, 111
Schooling (*see also* Education):
  functions in capitalist society, 167
  and labor force, 459
  motivation and reward structure, 459
  purpose of, 458
Schultze, Charles, 70–71
Schumpeter, Joseph, 26, 422
Science (*see* Technology)

Ascent To Affluence:
A History of American Economic Development
Charles H. Hession
Hyman Sardy

Comparative Economic Systems:
A Decision-Making Approach
Egon Neuberger
William J. Duffy

Allyn and Bacon, Inc.
470 Atlantic Avenue
Boston, Massachusetts
02210

09373